Third Edition

MANAGEMENT SKILLS FOR EVERYDAY LIFE

THE PRACTICAL COACH

Paula J. Caproni, Ph.D.

Management and Organizations Department
Stephen M. Ross School of Business
University of Michigan
Ann Arbor, Michigan

Prentice Hall

Boston   Columbus   Indianapolis   New York   San Francisco   Upper Saddle River
Amsterdam   Cape Town   Dubai   London   Madrid   Milan   Munich   Paris   Montreal   Toronto
Delhi   Mexico City   Sao Paulo   Sydney   Hong Kong   Seoul   Singapore   Taipei   Tokyo

Editorial Director: Sally Yagan
Editor in Chief: Eric Svendsen
Senior Acquisitions Editor: Kim Norbuta
Editorial Project Manager: Claudia Fernandes
Editorial Assistant: Carter Anderson
Director of Marketing: Patrice Lumumba Jones
Senior Marketing Manager: Nikki Ayana Jones
Marketing Assistant: Ian Gold
Production Manager: Meghan DeMaio
Cover Designer: Jodi Notowitz
Full-Service Project Management/Composition: Niraj Bhatt/Aptara®, Inc.
Printer/Binder/Cover Printer: Courier Companies
Text Font: Times

Credits and acknowledgments borrowed from other sources and reproduced, with permission, in this textbook appear on appropriate page within text.

Prentice Hall
is an imprint of

ISBN 10:   0-13-247907-9
ISBN 13: 978-0-13-247907-3

To Julia and Leah, with love

BRIEF CONTENTS

CONTENTS

PREFACE

This book, now in its third edition, is designed to translate the science of success (what researchers know about success) into the practice of success (what you should know about success). My goal in this book is to provide ideas, techniques, and best practices that will help you achieve the success that you desire—*however you define success*. For some people, success is climbing the ladder to the top of their organization or profession. For others, success is becoming an entrepreneur or finding a job that they love, continuing to learn in that job, and making a significant contribution without feeling the need to move up the organizational ladder. And for others, success is having the flexibility to take time off from work to invest more in other parts of life and then being able to get back to work when the time feels right (if they choose to do so).

Specifically, this book will help you get better results at work, enhance your career (marketability, promotions, salary increases, job satisfaction, and job flexibility), and improve your general well-being (happiness, health, and the ability to spend time with the people you love). Let me say this up front: If you are effective at your job but your family and friends cannot remember the last time you paid attention to them, if you never take a vacation without worrying about your work, if you do not have a moment to spare to contribute to your community, if you feel you can succeed only if you give into unethical temptations, and if you are headed for poor health or a premature death because of the stress of your job, these are not strategies for success that will serve you, others, society, or your organizations well.

This book is based on the assumption that the most successful people achieve their goals by working *smarter*, and not always harder, than less successful people. People who achieve the success that they desire do not necessarily have the highest IQs, stellar college entrance exam scores, degrees from top-rated universities, well-connected families, or the full support of devoted bosses and mentors. Rather, successful people earn their success by achieving goals and expertise that are meaningful to them and others, learning the perspectives and skills that help them reach these goals, understanding themselves (their styles, strengths, and weaknesses, as well as how they are perceived by others), developing a broad and diverse network of high-quality and mutually supportive relationships, and—if they are managers—creating a work context that brings out the best in others.

This book assumes that you are—or want to be—a manager. So what is management? Management textbooks say it is about getting things done through others, but it is more than that, much more. For many of us, being a manager is an important part of our identity. It is how we spend our days, it is what we do with and to others, it is how we express (or suppress) our competence, it can bring out our best selves and worst selves, and it offers us the opportunity to make the world a better place through our everyday decisions and actions. Notably, you will find this book very useful even if you do not plan on becoming a manager, as long as your work requires that you get results by working with others – and if others depend on you to achieve their goals as well.

NEW INFORMATION IN THIS THIRD EDITION

Although many of the characteristics that predict success in work and life are no different today than they were when the first two editions of this book were published, the context in which we live and work continues to change. Undoubtedly, throughout your career, there will be economic booms and busts. New technologies will continue to transform the way we work and live, and older technologies will become obsolete. New generations of employees will bring new lifestyles, perspectives, needs, and skills that will change the way work get done. Natural disasters and those created intentionally or ignorantly by human beings will continue to affect lives around the world. The spirit of innovation and the collaboration of hardworking people will continue to bring us products and services that enhance the quality of our lives. Acts of kindness and generosity will continue to renew our faith in the human spirit.

Although none of us can predict the future, it's clear that history tends to repeat itself. So, it's not surprising that most of the lessons from the first and second editions of the book remain useful today—even more so because the benefits of success and the costs of failure are higher due to the increased complexity and global interconnectedness of today's opportunities and problems. I have made several revisions to this third addition to update the themes from the earlier editions, as well as to better reflect the many social and economic changes that have occurred since the previous editions.

Specifically, I have integrated useful ideas from the most recent research into each chapter. For example, you'll be able to find new research in the upcoming chapters that helps you answer the following questions:

- How long does it take to become an expert, what steps can you take to systematically develop expertise, and what are some of the downsides of expertise (Chapter 1)?
- How does spending more time on the screen—e.g., Internet and video games—affect learning (Chapter 2)?
- Does openly admitting medical errors increase or decrease hospitals' litigation costs—and why does admitting errors have this result (Chapter 3)?
- How can a simple checklist save 1,500 lives and $1.5 million in one year, why do people resist using checklists despite their usefulness, and how can you use checklists to enhance results and reduce error (Chapter 4)?
- In a recent study, what percentage of analysts (who are supposed to provide unbiased industry information) received favors from company executives, and what percentage of those who received these favors failed to downgrade that company's stock after receiving reports of poor company earnings—and why (Chapter 5)?
- How can an organization create a culture of compassion (Chapter 6)?
- What kinds of people work most successfully in diverse teams (Chapter 7)?
- What are the best practices for coaching teams, including the best times to intervene in a team's work and the best times to stay out of the team's way (Chapter 8)?
- Why does psychological safety increase the effectiveness of virtual teams, and how can you create it in your teams (Chapter 9)?
- Based on a recent study, how many hours of overtime work predicted an increase risk of heart disease (Chapter 10)?

These are just a few of the interesting and relevant questions this new edition addresses that weren't included in the previous editions. In addition to including new research in this edition, I also included several new cases throughout the book. For example, you will learn why many smart and successful people (including one professor whose research focuses on gullibility) invested in corrupt financier Bernie Madoff's ponzi scheme, which collectively cost investors over $50 billion. Through this case, you will learn how you can protect yourself from engaging in the same kinds of irrational, yet common, human biases that made naïve victims out of Madoff's investors. Another new case in this edition focuses on how ordinary people in one organization showed extraordinary compassion during a crisis. Through this case, you will learn strategies for creating organizations that inspire compassion in times of need.

I added new leadership examples throughout this edition that will provide you with insights into how people become extraordinary leaders. Among these examples are President Barak Obama, PepsiCo CEO Indra Nooyi, and U.S. Airways pilot Chesley "Sully" Sullenberger who orchestrated a particularly skillful emergency landing of a disabled plane into the Hudson River in 2009, saving the lives of 115 people. I removed examples that were becoming out-of-date. To help you stay current with global trends, I added new data to this third edition, including statistics related to the global use of the Internet. I also introduced new self-assessments and end-of-chapter questions.

For instructors, I revised the comprehensive instructor manual to include more supporting materials, as well as new recommendations for useful resources such as Web sites, online videos, simulations, short exercises, and additional readings that will help bring the materials to life and make teaching these materials a pleasure. The sample syllabi, chapter outlines, test item files, and slides have also been revised to reflect the changes that I made for this third edition.

Clearly, much effort went into revising the book for this third edition. My goal with each edition is to ensure that this book continues to reflect the challenges and opportunities that you are likely to face on a daily basis so that you can achieve the short and long-term goals that are important to you.

ASSUMPTIONS OF THIS BOOK

Several themes are woven throughout this book. The first is that managing in an increasingly diverse, global, fast-changing, technologically driven, and environmentally challenged economic environment requires a more complex set of skills than those needed by managers in the past. Unfortunately, even though we are well into the twenty-first century, many management books are implicitly (if not explicitly) being written for the organizational man in a gray flannel suit (except on casual Fridays, when he wears khaki) who works in a brick-and-mortar organization and who can focus without distraction on his work because someone else is managing the caretaking at home. However, today's manager is just as likely to be a man or woman in a dual (or triple) career relationship who works in a organization that is largely dependent on communication technologies and that advocates work-life balance while simultaneously expecting a 24/7 commitment to work. Like it or not, it is commonplace to hear people conducting business on their smartphone while they are having lunch with friends, strolling their baby down their local neighborhood street, or getting dressed in their gym's locker room. This book is designed to reflect this changing landscape and help you navigate the opportunities and hurdles of today's and tomorrow's social, organizational, and economic environment.

The second theme is that one of the biggest mistakes managers can make is to assume that their technical skills and book smarts will ensure their professional effectiveness and career success. Professor John Tropman, my colleague at the University of Michigan, says that when people become managers, they tend to think of their new job as being "the same as their old job only bigger." In other words, they try to use the skills that worked for them in the past as individual contributors even though their current responsibility as managers is to create a context in which *others* can do their best work. This book is designed to help you move from an individual contributor mindset to a managerial mindset.

The third theme is that the ability to develop mutually supportive relationships at all levels inside and outside one's department and organization is one of the most important skills that managers can have. Indeed, substantial research suggests that people with a broad and diverse network of relationships tend to be significantly more effective at their jobs, have more successful careers, and lead happier, healthier, and longer lives than those who do not. Not surprisingly, the ability to manage professional relationships becomes increasingly important as people move through their careers. Yet even though building effective relationships is critical to managerial and organizational success, many managers mistakenly categorize relationship-building skills as "nice to have" rather than "need to have." Consequently, they miss out on daily opportunities to build the trust, respect, support, and influence that enable them to get better results in less time using fewer resources, with less stress, and more enjoyment. This book is designed to help you develop relationship-building skills that will benefit you, others, and your organizations regardless of your professional and personal goals.

The fourth theme is that today's managers are becoming increasingly saturated with information and are being exposed to a seemingly endless deluge of management theories, fads, and gurus. Consequently, they need to become more critical consumers of managerial knowledge and advice. To help you navigate through the never-ending information that comes your way, I present what I believe are some of the most insightful and useful theories and research studies available to managers today. Some are from classic studies that have stood the test of time. Others are based on cutting-edge research that are not yet well known but that can transform the way you think about work and life. My purpose is to provide you with food for thought, trigger your imagination, and offer useful frameworks and techniques that help you do your best work and live your best life. As social psychologist Kurt Lewin once said, "There is nothing so practical as a good theory."

Keep in mind that few, if any, theories work for all people and all situations all of the time. Too often, management gurus, theorists, and educators present their ideas as universally applicable, even when these ideas are culturally biased and when their effectiveness is limited to particular situations. Applying theories as though they are universally useful can lead you astray and cause more harm than good. This is particularly important to keep in mind when a theory promotes one way of seeing or acting as *universally* normal, effective, or moral. When presenting theories and research studies in this book, I often use phrases such as "research suggests that" and "researchers have concluded that" to avoid falling into the "theory is truth" trap and to leave room for alternative views. When I have forgotten to do so, I hope that you continue to keep the theories and best practices offered here in their place—as useful conceptual tools that broaden your conceptual and behavioral toolkit that can help you respond wisely and quickly to the routine and complex situations that you face in everyday work life. The words of Maya Lin, architect and designer of the Vietnam memorial in Washington, DC, best express the spirit of this book: "I create places in which to think, without trying to dictate what to think."

CourseSmart eTextbook

CourseSmart eTextbooks were developed for students looking to save on required or recommended textbooks. Students simply select their eText by title or author and purchase immediate access to the content for the duration of the course using any major credit card. With a CourseSmart eText, students can search for specific keywords or page numbers, take notes online, print out reading assignments that incorporate lecture notes, and bookmark important passages for later review. For more information or to purchase a CourseSmart eTextbook, visit www.coursesmart.com.

ACKNOWLEDGMENTS

In addition to the many researchers and theorists cited throughout this book, I am indebted to many people at Prentice Hall. David Shafer, former management editor, and Leslie Oliver, former sales associate, who enthusiastically and persistently encouraged me to write the first edition of the book. For this edition, I thank Kim Norbuta, Acquisitions Editor; Claudia Fernandes,

Senior Project Manager; Meghan DeMaio, Production Manager; and Niraj Bhatt, Project Manager who expertly and patiently helped me craft this latest edition.

I offer a special thanks to my friend and colleague Maria Eugenia Arias who I had initially hoped would be a coauthor of this book. Unfortunately for me, she decided that her heart is in consulting. However, she continues to offer me valuable advice and encouragement. I am also thankful to Clayton Alderfer, Ella Bell, David Berg, and Linda Smircich, my early mentors at Yale University and the University of Massachusetts who inspired me to think critically about managerial knowledge and practice, and to encourage others to think critically as well.

I owe sincere thanks to the many people who stimulated and clarified my thinking, recommended books and articles, read and edited chapters, and provided technical and emotional support. Although there are too many to specifically mention in this preface, I want to acknowledge the ongoing support of my colleagues at the Ross School of Business at the University of Michigan, especially the encouragement from my colleagues in the Management and Organizations Department over the years. They have provided me with an incredibly supportive and intellectually stimulating work environment. I also want to thank the members of the Organizational Behavior Teaching Society and the Academy of Management Learning and Education Division, and the many reviewers of the previous editions. I owe special thanks to Bill O'Connor who provided me with new ideas, enthusiastic support and, when needed, a quiet place to work on the book when there seemed to be no other place that was free of distraction.

I am also grateful to the students and executives who have attended my courses in many countries, including Brazil, China, Finland, Germany, Manila, Nigeria, Poland, Sweden, South Korea, Thailand, Vietnam, and the United States. Their wisdom, warmth, and good humor have made teaching and learning from them a joy and a privilege.

In my previous editions of this book, I offered many thanks to the staff at Community Day Care and in particular to Trudi Hagen, the director, and Tara Sturgeon, who was Julia and Leah's babysitter when they were younger. I was able to focus on writing the first edition of this book only because I knew that my daughters were safe and happy in their loving and competent care. Although my children are now older and will soon be heading off to face the world on their own, I will always be indebted to the day care providers and teachers who contributed so much to my daughters' lives and helped them grow into the happy and wise young adults that they are today.

I am deeply thankful for the support that my family has given me throughout the years. I am appreciative of the many sacrifices that my parents and grandparents made so that their children and grandchildren could have a better life (I have a great life). My sister, Sandi Buckhout, responded to my many panicked and frustrated e-mails with unconditional patience, understanding, and support. I remain in awe of my wonderful daughters, Julia and Leah. They are the light of my life. They are also a constant reminder that the work that each one of us does is important because it shapes the world for all children and for future generations. Finally, I must note that Julia, when she was eight years old, suggested that I call this book *Management Skills for Smarty Pants*. I only wish I had been courageous enough to use her clever title.

Paula J. Caproni
Ann Arbor, Michigan
February 2011

ABOUT THE AUTHOR

Paula J. Caproni is on the faculty of the Management and Organizations Department at the Stephen M. Ross School of Business at the University of Michigan. Professor Caproni received her MBA from the University of Massachusetts and her Ph.D. in Organizational Behavior from Yale University.

Professor Caproni is the Director of the Day MBA Program and is the Professional Development Coach for the Executive MBA Program. In addition, she teaches in the day and part-time MBA Programs, as well as for the Ford School of Public Policy. She has taught Executive Education courses in the United States, China, Malaysia, Manila, Thailand, and Vietnam, as well as Global MBA programs in Brazil and South Korea. She has also taught courses for the Helsinki School of Economics (Finland, Sweden, Poland, and Germany) and for Management Sciences for Health in Nigeria. In 2008, Caproni received the Victor L. Bernard Teaching Leadership Award for "outstanding contributions in the areas of leadership, interpersonal skills, and team development" at the Ross School of Business. Her book, *Management Skills for Everyday Life: The Practical Coach*, now in its third edition, is designed to help executives become better value creators, attain the career success they desire, and enhance their general well-being. She is currently writing a new book called *What Predicts Success: What Researchers Know That You Don't Know*.

In addition to teaching courses in leadership, interpersonal skills, and team development, she teaches and consults with organizations in both the public and private sector, including Ascension Health, Avon, Chrysler (MOPAR), Exxon, Ford Motor Company, Ford Medical Group, Internal Revenue Service, Mead-Johnson, National Arts Strategies, Philips, Phelps-Dodge, and Management Sciences for Health.

She has presented her research at several conferences in the United States and abroad, including the Academy of Management Meetings, the Organizational Behavior Teaching Conference, the Academy of International Business, the European Standing Conference on Organizational Symbolism, and the European Group for Organizational Studies. Her article "Work Life Balance: You Can't Get There From Here" received the McGregor Award from the *Journal of Applied Behavioral Science*.

Professor Caproni has been a reviewer for several academic journals, including the *Academy of Management Review, Human Resource Management Journal, the Journal of Management Inquiry, Journal of Management Education,* and *the Journal of Business Ethics*. She has served on the Editorial Board of *the Journal of Applied Behavioral Science* and *the Academy of Management Journal of Learning and Education*. She has also served on the Teaching Committee of the Academy of Management Organizational Behavior Division and the Board of Directors of the Organizational Behavior Teaching Society.

Contact Information
Stephen M. Ross School of Business
University of Michigan
Ann Arbor, Michigan 48109-1234
Phone: (734) 763-1010
E-mail: pcaproni@umich.edu

1

■ ■ ■

What Predicts Success?

This chapter will help you:

■ Understand the changes that are affecting managerial work today.

■ Learn why many high-potential managers derail.

■ Learn why IQ (performance on intelligence tests) is, by itself, not a strong predictor of success.

■ Learn what other characteristics and skills predict success.

■ Develop strategies for ongoing personal learning and change.

It's not the strongest of the species that survive, nor the most intelligent, but the one most responsive to change.

—CHARLES DARWIN

For people who thrive on challenge and making a difference in organizations, the managerial profession is one of the most fulfilling avenues to personal growth, organizational change, and social contribution. After studying managers for decades, management researcher Henry Mintzberg wisely states: "No job is more vital to our society than that of the manager. It is the managers who determine whether our social institutions serve us well or whether they squander our talents and resources."[1] Certainly there are other professions that are equally vital to any society, but the fact remains that managers in private, public, and nonprofit organizations significantly influence whether our organizations' and societies' resources are well used or wasted.[2]

More than ever, today's managers must see themselves as value creators whose primary responsibility is to turn the resources they manage into measurable results that matter to the people, organizations, and societies they serve. Yet, despite the central role managers play in turning organizational resources into results, many talented people are promoted to managerial positions with little more than a congratulatory pat on the back, a salary increase, and a set of new responsibilities. They must now think more strategically, solve more complex problems, create a work environment in which *others* can do their best work, turn diverse individuals into high-performing teams, regularly connect to people outside their own departments, and influence people over whom they have no direct control. Too often, newly promoted managers are left to figure out for themselves how to move from their role as individual contributors to their new roles as managers. Even experienced managers often hit a wall when promoted to the next managerial level, especially when many of the skills that made them successful in their previous jobs are insufficient for the demands of their new jobs.

This book is designed to help you avoid common pitfalls associated with promotions to management. It's also designed to help you achieve three goals, regardless of whether you are a new manager, experienced manager, or professional who is not currently managing others yet is responsible for turning organizational resources into results. First, this book provides you with a well-rounded set of skills that will help you achieve results through others at work in both stable and challenging times. Second, this book helps you achieve the career success that you desire, however you define success. Third, it helps you enhance your well-being because many of the skills that contribute to your professional success also help you lead a happier, healthier, and longer life.

These are lofty goals but not impossible ones. Although there are few guarantees in life, the advice given in this book is based on decades of practical research about what predicts success. One of the most important lessons that you learn from this book is that the most effective people—those who bring significant value to their organizations and who obtain the professional and personal success that they desire—don't necessarily have higher IQs, bigger budgets, or higher-status educations than others. They do not necessarily work more hours than those who are less effective, although they do tend to work harder in a more disciplined way toward meaningful goals that provide measurable value to organizations. They do not follow the same path to success (e.g., they do not necessarily climb the organizational or professional ladder in predictable stages), nor do they define success in the same way. They do not necessarily have the best bosses, nor are they all blessed with perfect mentors who are selflessly devoted to their success. Successful people are not born leaders or heroic figures, nor are they flawless. They do not share the same personality style. Some are big-picture oriented, whereas others are detail oriented. Some are extroverts and others are introverts. Some are fast on their feet, whereas others are slow and steady. Some are overtly charismatic, and others prefer to avoid the spotlight. But successful people do tend to share several characteristics (all of which can be learned), and you will read about these characteristics later in this chapter.

> I've got my faults, but living in the past isn't one of them. There's no future in it.
> —SPARKY ANDERSON,
> *Former Manager of the Detroit Tigers*

Another important lesson that you learn from this book is that significant social and economic trends such as increased diversity, globalization, and technological advances will continue to fundamentally change the nature of managerial work. Consequently, many managerial behaviors that were used in the past—and are still firmly entrenched in many organizations today—are no longer adding value (and some didn't add much value in the past either). Therefore, all managers must constantly pay attention to the larger social, cultural, political, economic, environmental, and technological context in which they live and work—what *Wall Street Journal* columnist Hal Lancaster calls the "defining issues of their time"[3]—and determine how these issues affect their clients, employees, organizations, and the communities they serve.

Despite the changes that will continue to affect individuals, organizations, and societies, managerial work will always have some common themes across time, place, and culture. Managers will always be human and, thus, imperfect. Consequently, self-awareness—understanding one's values, styles, strengths, weaknesses, and biases, as well as how one is perceived by others—will always be a hallmark of successful managers. Managers will always work with others, so the ability to build trust and respect with a broad and diverse group of people will always be the foundation on which effective and enduring work relationships are built. Managers will always need the support of others, so the ability to communicate effectively, motivate others, influence people, and manage organizational politics will always be critical to success.

Teams will always be a building block of most organizations, so the ability to design a work context that enables people working within and across teams to achieve their collective goals will always be in demand. There will always be opportunities to cheat and take advantage of people, so a personal commitment to being ethical despite the many temptations to do otherwise will always be essential. Social, cultural, political, economic, environmental, and technological forces will continue to transform the nature of work, so the willingness to engage in ongoing learning and change will always be a competitive advantage. And because there is more to life than work, the ability to integrate the dual themes of love and work, intimacy and mastery, will always be at the heart of our humanity.

> **If you can't stop the waves, you may as well learn how to surf.**
> —JON KABOT-ZINN,
> *Founding Director of the Stress Reduction Clinic at the University of Massachusetts Medical School*

IS THERE A DIFFERENCE BETWEEN MANAGING AND LEADING?

In my teaching and consulting, I am often asked, "What is the difference between managing and leading?" Frankly, this is a false distinction. Management tends to be associated with ensuring effectiveness and efficiency through planning, organizing, controlling, budgeting, and motivating. Leadership tends to be associated with thinking strategically, setting a clear and meaningful direction, aligning stakeholders, inspiring others, and guiding change. However, it's difficult to imagine how a manager can achieve results without setting a team's direction, inspiring the team to move in that direction, and enabling the team to adapt to change. And no one wants to work for a leader who creates an inspiring vision yet is completely out of touch with the details involved in implementing this vision. You may have heard the phrase: "Managers do things right; leaders do the right thing." It's a seductive and clever phrase, but anyone who is responsible for turning organizational resources into results—regardless of whether they call themselves managers, leaders, or individual contributors—have the responsibility to both do things right and do the right thing.

Professors Kim Cameron and Robert Quinn at the University of Michigan explain that the people who add the most value to organizations have a long-term vision and a short-term plan, inspire change and promote stability, empower employees and hold them accountable, and think creatively and focus on the bottom line. In other words, successful people do what's right for the situation.[4] For simplicity and consistency throughout this book, I most often use the label "manager" rather than "leader" because people are expected to show leadership qualities within the managerial role. What if you don't have an official managerial or executive role? Is it still important to learn the perspectives and skills described in this book? Regardless of your official job title, the answer is "yes" if you work with others, make and implement decisions, and are responsible for turning organizational resources into results.

Before we turn to the characteristics that predict success, we take a sobering look at the hurdles people face that hold them back from achieving the success that they desire. For most people, the first hurdle to overcome is oneself.

MANAGERIAL DERAILMENT

Most managers come to an organization with a strong intellect, solid education, substantial technical skills, desire to be competent, motivation to work hard, and the aspiration to succeed. Yet according to research conducted by the Center for Creative Leadership, almost half never reach their full potential, shortchanging themselves and their organizations.[5] This phenomenon is called derailment.

Derailment occurs when a high-potential manager expects to advance in an organization and initially was judged as having the ability to do so, yet is fired, demoted, or plateaued below anticipated levels of achievement. Derailment does not refer to individuals who, by their own choosing, change jobs, decline promotions, or quit their jobs to pursue other careers or life goals. Rather, derailment is involuntary and frequently preventable.[6]

Derailment is costly to individuals, organizations, and society. Derailed managers and their families suffer emotionally and financially. Organizations lose their financial and intellectual investment in derailed managers and must invest substantial recruitment and development costs to replace them. And if an organization has a reputation for having high levels of derailment, talented people may avoid joining the organization or leave the organization prematurely (and go to the competitors) because they fear that they too will face the same fate.

Why Managers Derail

Derailment often comes as a surprise to unsuspecting managers who see themselves as intelligent, well educated, and technically competent. They learn too late that these assets are necessary but insufficient characteristics for long-term effectiveness and success, especially when their success depends not only on their individual performance but also on their ability to think more strategically and design a work context that brings out the best in others.

After decades of research on managerial derailment, researchers have concluded that managers who derail often share similar characteristics. They tend to have limited self-awareness. In particular, they are less likely than successful managers to be aware of their styles, strengths, weaknesses, and biases. Equally important, they tend to be unaware of how they are perceived by others.[7] Furthermore, managers who derail often overestimate their abilities and over-rely on strengths that served them well in the past. Consequently, they tend to use a one-size-fits-all approach to solving problems. Sydney Finklestein, professor at Dartmouth's Tuck School of Business and author of the book *Why Smart Executives Fail*, explains that many of the highly successful executives he studied eventually failed "not because they couldn't learn, but because they had learned one lesson all too well."[8] By relying too much on a narrow skill set, they missed opportunities to learn different skills and limited their ability to adapt when the environment changed.

In contrast to derailed managers, successful managers tend to have a more accurate understanding of their abilities (or may slightly underestimate their abilities), seek more feedback on their performance, and invest more in continuous learning and self-improvement. Consequently, they develop a broader skill set that enables them to grow into their new jobs and serves them well in a variety of situations.[9]

Derailed managers, if they reflect on their experience, learn three important lessons. First, intelligence isn't enough for long-term success. Second, the same talents that once brought them early success can later lead to failure. Third, flaws and blind spots that seemed insignificant earlier in their careers suddenly matter.[10]

Intelligence Isn't Enough

Researchers who study managerial success and failure have concluded that cognitive intelligence—commonly referred to as "book smarts" (the kind of knowledge that is typically taught in school and evaluated on intelligence tests)—is at best only a moderate predictor of professional success. For example, in a 20-year study of 115 members of the Harvard Business School's Class of 1974, researcher John Kotter found "no positive correlation between their GMAT (Graduate Management Admissions Test) score and how well they're doing on the job in terms of income and responsibility." Similarly, in their study of MBA graduates, Stanford researchers Charles O'Reilly and Jennifer Chatman concluded that high GMAT scores were an insufficient predictor of success. They found that the MBAs who had a personality characteristic called "conscientiousness"—a combination of how ambitious, efficient, hard-working, and dependable one is—in addition to their high GMAT scores were more likely than other MBA graduates to achieve higher salaries and promotions early in their careers.[11]

> I never let my schooling interfere with my education.
> —MARK TWAIN

Robert Sternberg, one of the world's most renowned experts on the link between IQ (intelligence quotient as assessed through standardized intelligence tests) and success, agrees that successful people do not tend to have the highest IQ scores or most impressive grades in school. After reviewing decades of research designed to understand how well performance on IQ tests predicts success on the job, he concluded that performance on these types of intelligence tests predicts only between 4% and 25% of the variation among people in their job performance. "Scarcely something to write home about," says Sternberg.[12]

Sternberg argues that many people assume that "being smart is the same thing as being intelligent, and they define intelligence as how well people do on standardized tests and grades in school." Yet, the kind of intelligence that predicts how well you handle your job and your life in general is based, in large part, on many characteristics that are not assessed on standardized intelligence tests. After all, real-life problems are ambiguous, have multiple solutions (each with assets and liabilities), and must be solved and implemented in large part through talents that are not assessed on tests of analytical intelligence. These talents include the flexibility to deal with ambiguity, the ability to think creatively, the willingness to take calculated risks, the desire to learn and adapt, the ability to use good judgment in routine and stressful times, the willingness to cooperate and coordinate with others, the ability to make collective (rather than individual) decisions, the ability to influence others, and the resilience needed to bounce back from failure and cope with inevitable challenges of everyday life.[13]

Box 1.1, for example, illustrates how IQ and career success don't necessarily lead to effective decision-making when it comes to building wealth. Another problem with linking success too closely to scores on intelligence tests is that performance on IQ tests, rather than being stable over time, can change. Specifically, providing an intellectually stimulating and supportive environment can make a 12–18 point difference in the IQ scores for some people. This difference in scores can affect whether someone is categorized as one with low or average intelligence or one with an average or above-average intelligence. Not surprisingly, environments that are lacking in intellectual stimulation and support can significantly reduce IQ scores. Indeed, each year of school that a child misses results, on average, in a 6-point drop in IQ scores.[14]

That said, there's no doubt that it's important to invest in developing your analytical intelligence because it is *one* of the many important factors that helps you make better decisions at work and in life. And there's no denying that investing in your formal education can provide a significant pay off throughout your lifetime. According to recent U.S. census data, the median earnings for full-time workers in the United States were as follows:[15]

- Without a high school degree, $24,964
- With a high school degree, $32,862

BOX 1-1   The Limits of Analytical Intelligence on Financial Success

To understand the limits of analytical intelligence, it's useful to look at two examples of situations in which intelligence doesn't predict wise personal financial management: the ability to acquire wealth and the ability to avoid being duped by financial scams.

Does IQ Predict Wealth?

In an interesting study of more than 7,000 people in their mid-40s, Ohio State research scientist Jay Zagorsky found that while IQ predicts an increase in income, it is not a strong predictor of wealth. He found that each point increase in IQ test scores can lead to $202 to $616 more income each year. Based solely on this income advantage, a person who scores at the high end of the IQ range would earn between $6,000 and $18,500 more per year than someone who scores 100, the average IQ score. However, it turns out that people with the highest IQ scores don't necessarily turn that income advantage into greater wealth. In fact, people with a slightly higher than average IQ score of 105 had an average net worth that was higher than those with a score of 110. They were also less likely than those with higher IQ scores to have financial difficulties such as low savings, bankruptcy, and late payments on bills and credit cards.

Zagorsky doesn't speculate why people at the high end of the IQ scale are not stellar savers or wealth-builders. I'll leave to the readers of this book to speculate why. But, this study illustrates that being book smart does not necessarily lead to wealth and that the rules of basic money management are not rocket science.

Do Smart, Successful People Fall for Financial Scams?

In 2009, corrupt financier Bernard Madoff was sentenced to 150 years in prison after being found guilty of developing a multi billion dollar Ponzi scheme that Judge Denny Chin called an "extraordinary evil" fraud that took "a staggering human toll." Among his victims were the award-winning director Stephen Spielberg, Nobel Prize winner and holocaust survivor Elie Wiesel, and scholar Stephen Greenspan, who, of all things, studies gullibility. Greenspan describes a Ponzi scheme as follows: "A Ponzi scheme is a fraud in which invested money is pocketed by the schemer, and investors who wish to redeem their money are actually paid out of proceeds from new investors. As long as new investments are expanding at a healthy rate, the schemer is able to keep the fraud going. Once investments begin to contract as through a run on a company, the house of cards quickly collapses." Madoff's Ponzi scheme was exposed in 2008 when too many people who put their money into his fraudulent investments tried to redeem their funds in response to the turmoil in the U.S. financial markets and found that their money was no longer there.

In his *Wall Street Journal* article, "How Bernie Madoff Made Smart Folks Look Dumb," personal finance columnist Jason Zweig argues that many of the people who were lured into Madoff's scam fell for common psychological traps for which one's book smarts and professional success don't provide protection. They assumed Madoff was ethical because he was the former chairman of the NASDAQ stock exchange and was well known for supporting charities. They felt safe putting their money into Madoff's investments because other people in their social circle were doing so. They believed Madoff's funds were exclusive, and this exclusivity led them to desire these funds even more. Researcher Robert Cialdini, a leading expert on influence strategies, called these very human cognitive biases—trust in authority, social proof, and believing that things that are scarce are more valuable—a "triple threat" in the Madoff case. These biases (that we all share) led many smart people to invest in Madoff's funds based on faith rather than due diligence and to ignore the suspiciously consistent gains in Madoff's funds for two decades despite multiple market downturns during this period.

An important lesson from the Madoff scandal is that our intelligence and success do not protect us from normal and predictable limitations in human decision-making. Regardless of our intelligence, we are often lazy decision makers who use "cognitive shortcuts" (e.g., authority, social proof, and scarcity) rather than thoughtful analysis to make everyday decisions, even critically important ones. As Greenspan humbly noted after being duped in the Madoff scandal despite his status as a college professor and his own research on gullibility, "Anyone can have a high IQ and still prove gullible."

Source: Zweig, Jason. 2008. "How Bernie Madoff Made Smart Folks Look Dumb." *Wall Street Journal,* December 13–14: B1; Greenspan, Stephen. 2009. "Why We Keep Falling for Financial Scams." *Wall Street Journal,* January 30: W1-W2; Zagorsky, Jay. 2007. "Do You Have to Be Smart to Be Rich? The Impact of of IQ on Wealth, Income, and Financial Distress." *Intelligence*, 35(5): 489–501.

- With some college or associate's degree, $40,769
- With a bachelor's degree, $56,118
- With an advanced degree, $75,140

The important points to remember about the link between scores on intelligence tests and professional success are these: analytical intelligence, though important, is only one predictor of success; performance on intelligence tests can change to some extent on the basis of effort and environment; and over-relying on analytical intelligence can prevent you from developing other talents that will help you achieve the work results, career satisfaction, and general well-being that you desire and deserve. In short, if you don't complement your analytical intelligence with additional characteristics and skills that predict success, you are likely to perform significantly below your potential.

Early Success Can Lead to Failure

Those who invest in the stock market are repeatedly warned that past performance is no guarantee of future performance. The same warning is true for people. Managers who derail learn the hard way that the skills that led to their previous success may not bring them future success, particularly when the current and future environment no longer look like the past. Employee development consultant and executive coach Lois Frankel, Ph.D., explains:[16]

> The common thread for people who derail is that they exhibit superior skill in a particular area to the exclusion of developing complementary ones. Even when a change in a job assignment requires them to apply a different skill set, or when they see people around them develop in diverse areas, they fail to notice that they're limiting themselves and turn up the volume on those behaviors that they already do well, hoping that doing more of the same will save them.

Robert Sternberg and psychologist Peter Frensch illustrated how being an expert can be detrimental under certain circumstances, particularly under conditions of fundamental change. In a clever experiment, they had experts and novices play bridge against a computer. When the rules of the game were the same as standard bridge, the experts played better than the novices. However, when the rules of the game were fundamentally altered, the experts were hurt by the "deep changes" more so than were the novices because the experts' "expertise got in the way of their adapting to the new rules."[17] The novices, not entrenched in a particular way of thinking, were able to learn and adapt to the new rules more quickly.

> I skate where the puck is going to be, not where it has been.
> —WAYNE GRETZKY, *Hockey Champion*

BOX 1-2   Intelligence versus Common Sense

A few years ago, researcher Richard Wiseman, together with the British Association for the Advancement of Science, conducted a study designed to identify the world's funniest jokes. People were asked to post their best joke on Wiseman's Web site. After the jokes were posted, viewers were asked to vote for their favorite joke. Out of 40,000 jokes and 1.5 million votes for the best joke, the following joke was among the worldwide winners. After you read the joke, consider why people think this joke is so funny. What does it tell you about intelligence versus common sense? You can learn about the study and see some of the other winning jokes at http:// www.laughlab.co.uk.

Sherlock Holmes and Dr. Watson go on a camping trip. After a good dinner, they retire for the night, and go to sleep. Some hours later, Holmes wakes up and nudges his faithful friend. "Watson, look up at the sky and tell me what you see."

"I see millions and millions of stars, Holmes," replies Watson.

"And what do you deduce from that?" asks Holmes.

Watson ponders for a moment. "Well, astronomically, it tells me that there are millions of galaxies and potentially billions of planets. Astrologically, I observe that Saturn is in Leo. Horologically, I deduce that the time is approximately a quarter past three. Meteorologically, I suspect that we will have a beautiful day tomorrow. Theologically, I can see that God is all powerful and that we are a small and insignificant part of the universe. What does it tell you, Holmes?"

Holmes is silent for a moment. "Watson, you idiot!" he says. "Someone has stolen our tent!"

Source: Arrow, 2002. *Laughlab: The Scientific Search for the World's Funniest Joke.* Used with permission.

Like Frensch and Sternberg's expert bridge players, when the rules change, managers often don't notice changes in the environment until it's too late, or they become paralyzed and unable to adapt because they lack the broad perspective and flexibility that can help them respond quickly and effectively to the new rules. Instead, they do what they've done successfully in the past with even more intensity, often escalating rather than resolving the problems that they currently face.

The point being made here is this: Doing more of the same things you've done in the past only better and faster will not necessarily help you get to where you want to go in the future. Rather, you need to be able to anticipate, develop, and use new skills that will help you survive, even thrive, especially if the environment or your job responsibilities differ in significant ways from the past.

A Flaw Now Matters

Many derailed managers learn that flaws and blind spots that once seemed insignificant or were masked by their strengths suddenly matter.[18] Indeed, many executives today are learning that behaviors that were once encouraged, tolerated, ignored, or seen as acceptable misdemeanors by organizations and societies are now viewed as newsworthy events that can derail one's career, an organization's reputation, and shareholders' assets.[19]

We'll never fully understand the motivations of highly successful people who tarnish their own reputations, damage the reputations of their organizations, and harm the people they are supposed to serve. But their actions are certainly proof that intelligence and a track record of success do not protect smart people from personal flaws that lead them to make bad choices.

Success is a lousy teacher. It seduces smart people into thinking they can't lose.
—BILL GATES,
Cofounder of Microsoft

Why do smart executives derail themselves by engaging in unethical, irresponsible, and illegal activities? Researchers have found common themes.[20] For many highly successful people, their weaknesses tend to be the flip side of their strengths. Exceptionally successful people often have extraordinary talent and stellar track records, yet these strengths may lead them to lack humility and feel invulnerable to failure. Extremely successful people are likely to be great risk takers, yet they may underestimate challenges and find themselves unprepared when these challenges exceed their abilities. They may become overconfident in their judgment and may continue to support failing programs in which they are personally invested despite compelling evidence that these programs may not be working.[21]

In addition, very successful people often achieve success partly by bending and breaking rules, but they can begin to mistakenly believe that all rules are meant to be broken and that they are above the law. They may become blinded by their own power and develop a sense of entitlement as well as an unbridled appetite for extravagant lifestyles. This may explain why executives at the insurance company AIG spent over $440,000 on a corporate retreat at an upscale resort in 2008, shortly after receiving an $85 billion government bailout that was designed to help save the company from bankruptcy. The cost of the retreat included hotel rooms that cost over $350, spa services, food, cocktails, and golf. Said one congressman, "They're getting their pedicures and their manicures and the American people are paying for that." Stanford professor Rod Kramer explains that although extremely successful people have a solid understanding of business, they may have "an impoverished sense of self," may be unaware of what drives them, and may use organizations to fulfill their own needs.[22]

Many highly successful people surround themselves with people who won't confront them or give them bad news, so they are unlikely to be warned when they are deluded or when their ideas or actions are leading them down an ineffective or unethical path. Rarely does an executive make unethical or inappropriate decisions in isolation. For example, a *New Yorker* magazine article published after Martha Stewart, founder of Martha Stewart Living Omnimedia, was convicted of conspiracy, obstruction of justice, and two counts of making false statements, stated that the situation was "in many ways a story of her support system in action. At every stage—from the transaction to the investigation by the Securities and Exchange Commission and the FBI to, finally, her criminal trial—people mobilized to help her: assistants, brokers, lawyers, even other celebrities. Yet the more they tried to help, the more excruciating Stewart's problems became. With the guidance of her entourage, she invariably made the wrong decisions, and the result was humiliation and conviction."[23]

> Learn from the mistakes of others. You can't live long enough to make them all yourself.
> —ELEANOR ROOSEVELT

The point to remember is this: Intelligence and a track record of success will not buffer you from engaging in unethical and ineffective behavior that can derail your career, damage your organization's reputation, and harm the people you are supposed to serve. Indeed, intelligence and a history of success—when combined with hubris and a support system that protects successful people from the consequences of their behaviors when they go astray—can be a recipe for stunning failure. In short, the lessons to be learned from derailed executives are clear:

- Your intelligence alone will not predict your long-term success.
- Doing more of the same things you've done in the past better and faster will not necessarily help you get to where you want to go in the future.
- Inattention to personal flaws and limitations, especially when combined with hubris, can backfire on you, others, and the organizations to which you belong.

WHAT PREDICTS SUCCESS?

Just as researchers have identified characteristics that lead to professional derailment, they have also identified several characteristics that lead to professional success. Figure 1.1 summarizes these characteristics, and each is discussed in more detail in the subsequent sections.

Believing Intelligence Is Fluid Not Fixed

Researcher Carol Dweck and her colleagues have found that our *beliefs* about intelligence and personality influence our ability to be successful. In her article, "Beliefs That Make Smart People Dumb," Dweck explains that people tend to think about intelligence in either one of two ways. People who believe intelligence is *fixed* assume that it is an innate trait of a person and is consistent across time and place. In other words, they are likely to say things like "I'm smart" or "I'm not good at math." People who believe intelligence is *fluid* assume that it is, in large part, malleable and can change depending on how much effort a person is willing to apply to succeed at that task. In other words, they are likely to say things like "I'm smarter when I'm prepared" or "I do better at math when I study longer and get a tutor." Dweck and her colleagues estimate that approximately 85% of people believe in either fixed or fluid intelligence, and the other 15% tends to be undecided.[24]

Dweck and her colleagues found that people who believe intelligence is fluid are more likely to be successful than people who believe it is fixed. People who believe intelligence is fixed tend to tie their self-worth (and possibly the worth of others) too closely to what they perceive to be innate intelligence. In short, they can become "too invested in being smart" and in proving their intelligence. Consequently, they become vulnerable to several negative outcomes.

Overly concerned about looking smart (rather than being effective), they are less likely to take risks; more likely to lose confidence when faced with a task beyond their current ability; less likely to engage in learning new skills beyond their area of expertise; more likely to give up when faced with failure; and more likely to underestimate the power of learning, effort, and persistence. Of course, the same can be said for people who are invested in believing they are not too smart. They, too, can tie their identity and self-worth to their beliefs about their intelligence, cutting off opportunities to learn, grow, and succeed in areas in which they believe they don't have "natural" abilities. As Dweck explains, "One of the dumbest things people with the fixed view of intelligence do is to sacrifice important learning opportunities when those opportunities contain a risk of revealing ignorance or making errors."

> It's not necessary to change. Survival isn't necessary.
> —W. EDWARDS DEMING

In contrast, people who believe that intelligence is fluid are less likely to tie their self-worth (or the worth of others) to scores on intelligence tests or tests of academic achievement. They believe that failure is a consequence of a lack of effort rather than an innate lack of ability. Thus, they are more likely to believe that putting more time and effort into learning new skills will pay off. They are also more willing to ask seemingly "dumb" questions, seek out feedback, take risks, cope well with failure, and persist when faced with obstacles. In short, they are more likely to see negative outcomes as "information about ways to improve the learning process, rather than as indicators of stable low ability." Not surprisingly, people who believe that intelligence is fluid are more likely to achieve higher performance (including higher grades in school), navigate school transitions better, succeed at demanding business tasks, bounce back from failure, and manage conflict and difficult relationships successfully.[25]

Fortunately, people can learn the fluid theory of intelligence and personality and thus reap the rewards.[26] For example, in one study, college students were shown a movie that showed how people's brains make new connections throughout life in response to intellectual challenges. The same group of students were then asked to write a letter to "a struggling younger student" explaining how intellectual stimulation and hard work can rewire the brain, making it smarter. Compared to two control groups who did not learn that the brain can be rewired to be "smarter", the students who learned the fluid theory of intelligence (and explained it to the younger students) were more likely to have higher grades and express greater enjoyment of school after learning and teaching the fluid theory of intelligence.[27]

Researcher Yin-Yi Hong and colleagues found similar results in a study of college students at a university in Hong Kong. They gave students purported "academic" articles that promoted either a fixed or a fluid view of intelligence. In other words, one group of students was taught that intelligence is a fixed trait, and the other was taught that intelligence is fluid and often can be changed if one persists and puts in more effort. The researchers then gave students from each group a challenging task. The students who read the articles that proposed that intelligence is fluid persisted more at the challenging task and were more likely to succeed at the task.[28]

No doubt, researchers will continue to enthusiastically debate the degree to which intelligence and personality characteristics are fixed versus fluid. But it's wise to remember that you will be better off if you believe that intelligence and personality are more fluid than fixed because doing so is more likely to help you achieve the success you desire.

Developing Expertise through Mindful, Deliberate Practice

Regardless of profession, it pays to be an expert at something that matters to others. What does it mean to be an expert? Experts are people who have achieved the highest level of performance in their fields and who have a reputation for having achieved this level of expertise. They are in demand because they see situations within their area of expertise in more complex and accurate ways than do nonexperts. Consequently, they are better able to select appropriate strategies, respond faster, and adjust their actions more quickly when situations change. In addition, experts are more likely to notice their own errors (rather than ignore or deny them), adapt based on what they learn from their errors, and rebound from failure. Indeed, rather than see failure as a weaknesses, experts tend to see failure as a normal part of the learning process.

How do you become an expert? Researchers who study the development of expertise agree that "natural" talent is highly overrated.[29] For example, many people are born with an innate ability that helps them identify and imitate pitch in music, but few of these people become world-class musicians by turning that raw talent into outstanding performance. Researchers have found that what looks like exceptional innate ability is usually the result of at least 10 years of commitment, concentrated effort, and deliberate practice. For example, Tiger Woods, one of the most successful golfers of all time and among the highest paid professional athletes, intensively practiced golf since he was two years old. Many people consider Winston Churchill, British Prime Minister during World War II, to have been one of the greatest orators of the twentieth century. Churchill also had a speech impediment that he worked to overcome for years by practicing his speeches compulsively.

Researcher K. Anders Ericsson and his colleagues found that people who achieve outstanding performance have much in common. They have a strong desire to become among the very best at what they do. Consequently, they engage in highly disciplined practice for years to achieve their goals. While most people stop practicing once the practice gets too difficult or is no longer enjoyable, experts-in-training continue to practice because they are determined to succeed at something that is meaningful to them, not because the practice is easy or enjoyable.

Simply having years of experience and attending training programs won't lead to world-class performance. While experience, training, and practice can certainly enhance one's skills, people who become *outstanding* in a particular area of expertise engage in these activities in a much more focused, rigorous, and organized way than others do. For example, experts-in-training break down their larger goal into small and specific techniques. They repeatedly practice each of these techniques in a context that stretches their abilities and provides them with immediate feedback so that they can continually assess and adapt their performance. Steve Kerr, former leadership development chief at Goldman Sachs, says that immediate feedback is critical for skill development. "Without it, two things happen: One, you don't get any better, and two, you stop caring," says Kerr.[30]

People who are determined to become experts also build stretch goals and failure into their practice. Challenges help them expand their abilities and get accustomed to learning from failure as well as success. Experts know that while it may feel good to experience repeated success and avoid failure, it doesn't build expertise. In a study of leadership development, University of Michigan researchers Scott DeRue and Ned Wellman focused on how people learn leadership skills in the context of their everyday work. They found that people develop leadership expertise through *optimal* levels of challenge. If their work is too easy, they don't get the challenges they need to develop new skills. If their work is too difficult, they can become overwhelmed by the "cognitive demands" of the challenges they face, which can result in excess anxiety and uncertainty that may "divert cognitive resources from learning." They also found that ongoing feedback and reflection on performance are some of the most important contributors to the development of expertise, especially in challenging situations, because feedback and systematic reflection can reduce ambiguity and help leaders-in-training identify what's working and what isn't so that they can adapt their strategy accordingly.[31]

In addition to intensive practice, expert performers are more likely than others to seek out additional resources (e.g., books, Web sites, training) that help them develop their judgment and skills. Many experts-in-training also have a coach, especially early in their careers. Structured coaching provides a planned learning experience that is tailored to individual needs, as well as ongoing feedback in a challenging yet supportive environment. Although having a coach is useful, much of the practice is self-motivated and done alone. Eventually experts-in-training become more independent in developing their own challenging development plan and building in feedback. And, here's good news for some readers of this book (and for the author): Afternoon naps in between practice sessions may increase performance.[32]

The lesson here is this: If you want to become an exceptional manager or professional, it's wise to keep in mind that the skills associated with success in organizations can be developed to high levels of expertise through mindful, deliberate practice. In addition to the technical and analytical competencies associated with your job, these skills include building trust, communicating effectively, delegating, motivating, networking, decision making, influencing others, managing conflict, and leading teams. Every day, your job presents many opportunities to practice specific techniques associated with these skills and to seek out mentors and others who can provide you with advice, support, and feedback. And, there is no lack of books (such as the one you are now reading), Internet resources, and formal training programs that can help you develop skills that add value to organizations and enhance your career. See Case 1.1 about Pilot Chesley B. "Sully" Sullenberger at the end of this chapter for an excellent example of how the development of expertise can pay off, especially during a crisis.

Being Conscientious

One of the most powerful moments at the August 9, 2008, Opening Ceremony at the Beijing Olympics occurred when nine-year-old Lin Hao, together with basketball star Yao Ming, led the Chinese team through Birds' Nest Stadium. Just three months earlier, Lin survived the devastating Sichuan earthquake that took the lives of 69,000 people. Two-thirds of Lin's classmates perished in the earthquake. After he escaped the collapsed school building, he went back through the rubble and rescued some of his classmates from the fallen building. Lin then led the group of surviving students in singing songs because he felt it would keep their spirits up while they awaited help. When asked why he put himself in danger to save his classmates, he explained that he did this because he was a hall monitor and he believed that taking care of the other students was his personal responsibility. Even as his world crumbled around him, young Lin Hao fulfilled his responsibilities as hall monitor. For his exceptional commitment to his responsibilities, Lin was granted the honor of leading the Chinese team at the opening ceremony.

Through his actions, young Lin Hao displayed a characteristic called conscientiousness, one of the most significant predictors of success. Conscientiousness refers to being achievement-oriented, goal-directed, dependable, hardworking, self-disciplined, planful, organized, and persistent. In short, people who are conscientious are committed to coming through for others and completing the jobs for which they are accountable. They are internally motivated to fulfill their responsibilities to the best of their abilities and do not need constant supervision to stay motivated or on track. Researchers have found that people who are conscientiousness are more likely to have greater academic achievement, better work performance, more promotions, and higher salaries.[33]

Although generally linked to success, conscientiousness can backfire when it is not complemented with adaptability, risk-taking, and a characteristic that researchers call "agreeableness". People who are conscientious are known to be good rule followers, and this serves them and their organizations well in most situations. However, when the environment changes and the rules don't work as well as they did in the past or in a different environment, people who are high on conscientiousness may need to be particularly attuned to these changes and the need to challenge inappropriate rules so that they can adapt and be successful in the new environment.[34]

> I developed the idea very early that if there were rules that didn't make sense, you had to think carefully about how you broke them. If you got caught, well, OK, you got caught, but that was not a reason to stop thinking.
> —MARY CATHERINE BATESON quoting *Alice d'Entremont in Composing a Life*

Some researchers have found that people who are high on conscientiousness yet low on agreeableness tend to receive *lower* performance ratings by their supervisors. People who are agreeable are viewed by their colleagues as helpful, cooperative, tolerant, flexible, generous, courteous, and socially competent. When highly conscientious people lack social skills and empathy for others, their commitment to achieving results may lead them to become unreasonably demanding, critical, uncooperative, and inflexible. Consequently, these managers may not achieve the results or success that they desire from their hard work, especially when their performance depends in large part on achieving results through others.[35]

Researchers have found that people who are conscientious are more likely to be healthier and live longer and are more likely to engage in behaviors that promote good health, including having stable jobs, living in healthy environments, getting physical exams, wearing seatbelts, checking fire alarms in the home, and avoiding risky behaviors such as speeding and smoking.[36]

Being Proactive

People who are proactive have a "can do" attitude that helps them succeed in both good and bad times. They see opportunities that others don't see, believe in possibilities that others may not believe exist, anticipate the future, create plans to try to shape the future, and take actions to turn these plans into reality.[37] They are doers as well as thinkers. They are more likely than others to seek out information and feedback, build networks, use innovative strategies, show political savvy, persist when faced with obstacles, engage in organizational change efforts, and actively manage their careers. Consequently, they are more likely to perform better at work, earn more promotions, get paid more, be perceived as leaders, become more involved in their communities, and be more satisfied with their jobs and careers. Researcher Lillian Eby and colleagues explain:

> Successful people proactively manage their career rather than expect that someone will manage it for them [or] that their life will follow an expected trajectory . . . [They manage their careers by] joining professional organizations, subscribing to industry trade journals to stay on top of trends and engaging in both self and environmental exploration on a continual basis, taking advantage of learning opportunities and stretch assignments within one's organization, attending seminars and training, or going back to school to diversify one's portfolio of skills.[38]

People who are less proactive are more "passive and reactive." They tend to adapt to circumstances rather than anticipate situations and try to influence them. Note that proactive people don't simply express their ideas and criticize the ways things are. Rather, they *do* something about their concerns. Indeed, researchers have found that people who complain about the way things are without offering reasonable solutions and taking actions to remedy situations tend to receive fewer promotions and lower salaries.[39]

BOX 1-3   Proactive Personality Scale

Please respond based on a scale ranging from 1 (strongly disagree) to 7 (strongly agree). The higher your score, the more proactive you perceive yourself to be.

I am constantly on the lookout for new ways to improve my life.	1	2	3	4	5	6	7
Wherever I have been, I have been a powerful force for constructive change.	1	2	3	4	5	6	7
Nothing is more exciting than seeing my ideas turn into reality.	1	2	3	4	5	6	7
If I see something I don't like, I fix it.	1	2	3	4	5	6	7
No matter what the odds, if I believe in something I will make it happen.	1	2	3	4	5	6	7
I love being a champion for my ideas, even against others' opposition.	1	2	3	4	5	6	7
I excel at identifying opportunities.	1	2	3	4	5	6	7
I am always looking for better ways to do things.	1	2	3	4	5	6	7
If I believe in an idea, no obstacle will prevent me from making it happen.	1	2	3	4	5	6	7
I can spot a good opportunity long before others can.	1	2	3	4	5	6	7

Source: Bateman, Thomas, and J. Michael Grant. 1993. "The Proactive Component of Organizational Behavior." *Journal of Organizational Behavior,* 14: 103–118. Copyright 1993 by John Wiley & Sons Limited. Reproduced by permission.

Some research suggests that proactive people tend to manage stress better be- **The best way to predict the** cause they are more likely to anticipate future stressful events, prepare for these **future is to create it.** events, and continue to gather information about stressful events as they unfold. They **—PETER DRUCKER** are also more likely to seek out support and develop personal coping mechanisms that help get them through difficult periods.[40] See Box 1-3 to assess your own proactivity.[41]

Having a Learning Goal Orientation

In his article, "Goal Orientation: Why Wanting to Look Successful Doesn't Always Lead to Success," researcher Don VandeWalle explains that there are at least three types of goal orientations. Some people have a "*performance goal orientation*," which means that they focus primarily on achieving a successful result and looking successful in the eyes of others. This sounds good at first, except that there's a catch. People with a performance goal orientation believe that it's critically important to always look good to others and to have successful outcomes from their efforts. Consequently, they often stay with the tried-and-true strategies, take fewer risks, avoid negative feedback, and forego opportunities to learn new skills. In their efforts to look good, they may also try to outperform rather than help their colleagues—a strategy that can get in the way of building mutually rewarding work relationships.

Other people have an "*avoidance goal orientation*," which means that they focus primarily on finding ways to avoid looking bad to others. Although their goal appears to be different from that of people with a performance goal orientation, they share the fundamental focus on maintaining a successful image rather than achieving results that benefit the organization. As a result, they also tend to stay with the tried-and-true strategies, take fewer risks, avoid negative feedback, and forego opportunities to learn new skills.

In contrast, people with a "*learning goal orientation*" are less preoccupied with **Nothing is a waste of time if** their self-image and more focused on learning new skills that serve their organiza- **you use the experience** tions' needs. Consequently, they are more likely to take on challenging assignments **wisely.** in which they may make mistakes while learning new skills, use more effective cop- **—RODIN** ing strategies when faced with problems, and persist in the face of difficulty—and thus are more likely to achieve success not only for themselves, but for their organizations as well. You can take an assessment to assess your goal orientation in Box 1-4.[42]

Using Creative and Practical Intelligence

Most of us know people who did very well in school, yet didn't achieve expected levels of success. Researcher Robert Sternberg argues that both creative intelligence (generating ideas) and practical intelligence (street smarts, common sense) are needed to turn analytical intelligence (e.g., the ability to think critically, analyze information, and solve complex problems) into results. People with creative intelligence often have the same information that other people have, but they are more likely to tinker with that information, see beyond the obvious, and explore multiple options that enable them to use that information in unique and innovative ways.

However, having analytical and creative intelligence isn't enough to have an impact. People with practical intelligence have a knack for turning the knowledge they gain from their analytical and creative intelligence into results that *matter* to others. Practical intelligence is based primarily on "tacit knowledge," which most people think of as common sense. Practical intelligence is most useful when solving real everyday problems that are not well defined, have not been faced before, and do not have one right answer. People with highly developed practical intelligence excel at reading situations, using effective short-cuts to achieve results, leveraging

---

BOX 1-4 Learning Goal Assessment

Instructions: Individuals have different views about how they approach work. Please read each statement below and select the response that reflects how much you agree or disagree with the statement.

1	2	3	4	5	6	7
Strongly disagree	Disagree	Sort of disagree	Neither	Sort of agree	Agree	Strongly agree

1. I am willing to select a challenging work assignment that I can learn a lot from.
2. I often look for opportunities to develop new skills and knowledge.
3. I enjoy challenging and difficult tasks at work where I'll learn new skills.
4. For me, further development of my work ability is important enough to take risks.
5. I like to show that I can perform better than my coworkers.
6. I try to figure out what it takes to prove my ability to others at work.
7. I enjoy it when others at work are aware of how well I am doing.
8. I prefer to work on projects where I can prove my ability to others.
9. I would avoid taking on a new task if there was a chance that I would appear rather incompetent to others.
10. Avoiding a show of low ability is more important to me than learning a new skill.
11. I'm concerned about taking on a task at work if my performance would reveal that I had low ability.
12. I prefer to avoid situations at work where I might perform poorly.

To identify your strongest goal orientation profile, sum and average your responses to questions 1 through 4 for the learning goal orientation, questions 5 through 8 for the proving dimension of a performance goal orientation, and questions 9 through 12 for the avoiding dimension of a performance goal orientation.[*]

Source: Adapted from VandeWalle, Don. November 2001. "Goal Orientation: Why Wanting to Look Successful Doesn't Always Lead to Success." *Organization Dynamics*, 30(2): 162–171. Used with permission of VandeWalle.

[*]The category with the highest score suggests your preferred goal orientation. Although it sometimes makes sense to want to "look good" or avoid "looking bad," having a higher score in "learning goal orientation" is more likely to predict success.

---

their strengths, compensating for their weaknesses, gaining support for their ideas, influencing their environments, and knowing when it makes sense to persist and when to let go.[43]

Sternberg and his colleagues explain that practical intelligence involves "knowing what to say to whom, knowing when to say it, and knowing how to say it for maximum effect.[44] Tacit knowledge is a hard-to-copy competitive advantage because it isn't written down in formulas or guidelines, is rarely taught or tested in school, and can be difficult to explain to others.

Developing Self Awareness

Studies of managerial development have consistently concluded that an ongoing commitment to self-awareness is a core managerial competency for several reasons.[45] First, managers who know their goals, values, styles, strengths, and weaknesses are more likely to find and thrive in jobs that are meaningful to them. Second, managers who understand their biases—and we all have biases—are more likely to manage their biases by seeking out information from people with different perspectives. Consequently, they're more likely develop a broader perspective, make better decisions, and gain the support they need to implement these decisions.

Third, managers who understand that others may not perceive them as they see themselves are more likely to seek out feedback to get a better understanding of how other people see them and the consequences of these perceptions. In contrast, people who are unaware of how they are perceived by others quickly become a liability. In studies that compared managers' self-evaluations with their direct reports' evaluations of them, researchers found that the managers who overestimated their abilities performed worse than those whose self-ratings were consistent with those of their followers or who underestimated their abilities. Managers who overestimate their abilities may be more likely to minimize the importance of their weaknesses, ignore criticism, and avoid taking personal responsibility for failure.[46]

Finally—and equally important—effective managers understand that *context* significantly affects their own and others' behavior. Most people attribute their own and others' behavior to innate personality characteristics. For example, they say that someone is a sociable person, an analytical person, an ethical person, or a compassionate person. Researchers call this tendency to attribute behavior primarily to personality the "fundamental attribution error."[47] However, the reality is that many of our behaviors are significantly influenced by the contexts in which we find ourselves. While some contexts bring out the best in us, other contexts bring out the worst in us.

Princeton University psychologists John Darley and Daniel Batson conducted a now-famous experiment at the Princeton Theological Seminary to explore the power of context on behavior.[48] It is called the "Good Samaritan" study because it is based on the biblical story from the New Testament in which two men of pious callings (a priest and a Levite) and a Samaritan (a man from a tribal group that was less respected at the time) were traveling and came across a man who had been beaten, robbed, and left for dead on the side of the road. Upon seeing the man, the priest and Levite crossed to the other side of the road and continued on their journey without stopping to help him. The Samaritan, however, stopped to take care of the man's wounds, brought him to an inn to get additional care, and paid the innkeeper to take care of him.

With this parable as inspiration, Darley and Bateson met with a group of seminarians and gave them an assignment. They asked the seminarians to prepare a short talk and then walk to a nearby building and present the talk. The researchers varied the conditions presented to each of the seminarians. Some were asked to talk about seminary work, and others were asked to talk about the story of the Good Samaritan. The researchers also varied the amount of "hurry" they presented to each seminarian. One-by-one, they told the seminarians to leave to go to another building to give their talk. Some were told that they were already late (high hurry), some were told that they had a few minutes before their presentation but they should head over anyway (moderate hurry), and others were told they had plenty of time to get to their presentation site (low hurry).

The experiment was set up so that each of the seminarians would have to go through an alley where they would inevitably see a man slumped over, coughing, and moaning. The psychologists' goal was to identify how many seminarians would stop and help the man and how many would pass by without helping. They also wanted to know if differences in the conditions of the type of talk seminarians were asked to give (e.g., seminary work or the Good Samaritan) or the hurry for which they were primed might affect their decision to stop and help the man.

The results? Whether they were asked to prepare a talk about seminary jobs or the parable of the Good Samaritan made no significant difference in whether they stopped to help the man or walked by. However, the amount of hurry the seminarians were in had a significant effect. Overall, only 40% of the seminarians offered some help to the victim. Sixty-three percent of those in the "low hurry" situation helped, 45% in the "medium hurry" situation helped, and only 10 % of those in the "high hurry" situation helped. Some seminarians even stepped over the man to get to their presentation on time.

The message here is that we should not assume that our beliefs, values, and behaviors are consistent across time and place. To be self-aware means to understand how context affects our own and others' behavior. Understanding the power of context helps us in at least two ways. If we want to be consistent with a particular set of values and behaviors, we have to overlearn them so that we can try to overcome the powerful influence of context. And if we want to others to exhibit particular behaviors (e.g., motivation, risk-taking, ethical behavior), we must create contexts that encourage them and enable them to do so.

> We shape our dwellings, and afterwards our dwellings shape us.
> —WINSTON CHURCHILL

Having Social Skills

Successful people understand that managing relationships at work is at least as important as managing the technical aspects of their work. Consequently, they proactively manage their relationships with their bosses, direct reports, peers, customers, suppliers, distributors, community leaders, and others.[49] They invest in building a broad and diverse set of relationships because they realize that their social capital—the resources they give and get through their social networks—enables them and others to get better results and enhances their career prospects. Researchers Wayne Baker and Jane Dutton explain that people who develop high-quality relationships have resources available to them that are less available to others, including trust, good-will, information, advice, and support.[50] Managers with high-quality connections are better able to make contacts when needed, manage conflict, leverage diversity, motivate others, solve problems quickly, influence others, obtain emotional support, bring out the best in teams, span organizational boundaries, and coordinate fluidly with others.

The importance senior executives place on social skills is reflected in what has become known in business circles as "The Waiter Rule." Many CEOs and senior executives use the waiter rule as an informal way of assessing a person's social skills and career potential because they believe, "You can tell a lot about a person by the way he or she treats the waiter."[51] Decades before he became CEO of Office Depot, Steve Odland was a busboy. Recalling his experience in an interview, he said, "Some people treated me wonderfully and other people treated me like dirt. . . . Your value system and ethics need to be constant at all times regardless of who you're dealing with." When considering candidates for executive positions, Panera Bread CEO Ron Shaich asks his assistant how they treated her because some applicants are "pushy, self-absorbed and rude" to her before she transfers their calls to him, which gives him insight into how these candidates may treat others as well. The point of the waiter rule is clear: People who don't treat others well (or who are selective about who they treat well and who they treat poorly) are seen as liabilities because they are unwilling to collaborate well with others and bring out the best in others—two skills that are critical for organizational success. By the way, it's not only CEOs who use the waiter rule. "It's Just Lunch", a dating service for professionals, conducted a survey designed to understand which behaviors offend lunch dates the most. Being rude to waiters was ranked as the number one turn-off in dining etiquette.[52]

> The most important single ingredient in the formula of success is knowing how to get along with people.
> —THEODORE ROOSEVELT, *Former U.S. President*

The quality of your relationships also has a significant impact on your well-being. Positive social relationships increase your happiness, enhance your mental health, and help you live longer. In contrast, negative relationships and feelings of isolation are damaging to your mental and physical health. Researchers have found these effects hold for both men and women and in both collectivist (e.g., Japan) and individualistic (e.g., United States) societies.[53] Notably, in a study of more than 10,000 people, researcher Ross Andel and his colleagues found that jobs that require complex interpersonal relationships (e.g. managing people, negotiating, and dealing with customers) may provide some protection from Alzheimer's disease later in life. Although jobs that require complex analytical skills may also provide some protection from Alzheimer's disease, the researchers found that complex social skills may be even more protective.[54]

Managing Emotions: Emotional Intelligence, Positive Emotions, and Hardiness

EMOTIONAL INTELLIGENCE   The link between emotional intelligence and success was virtually unknown by most managers and professionals before psychologist and journalist Daniel Goleman wrote his best-selling book, *Emotional Intelligence*, in 1994. Today, there are over 1,200 books about emotional intelligence listed on Amazon.com (some more credible than others). Researchers who study emotional intelligence agree that the ability to identify, understand, and manage one's emotions, particularly in stressful times, significantly predicts success in life.[55] Emotionally intelligent managers understand their own feelings, manage their moods when distressed, and control their own impulses. They are able to read others' emotions and respond appropriately. They use their understanding of their own and others' emotions to make sense of situations, build relationships, and give themselves and others the support they need to manage the ups and downs and everyday life. Consequently, they are better able to communicate appropriately, motivate others, build employee commitment, manage conflict, make decisions that meet the needs of multiple constituents, tolerate uncertainty, and reduce employees' anxiety.[56]

POSITIVE EMOTIONS   People who experience and express positive emotions are more likely than others to bring out the best in themselves, others, and organizations.[57] Positive feelings such as joy, hope, love, compassion, generosity, gratitude, optimism, pride, serenity, and forgiveness serve many purposes. When we feel positive emotions, we tend to think more broadly and creatively, seek out new information and experiences, behave more flexibly, have more confidence in our own abilities and the abilities of others, build trust and respect, persist more, get over bad experiences and emotions more quickly, and give and get more social support. In contrast, negative emotions such as anger, defensiveness, fear, resentment, frustration, guilt, and shame tend to narrow our focus and flexibility, often limiting our perspective and clouding our judgment just when we need them most. For example, anger can lead to the desire to attack, fear can lead to the desire for escape or to hoard resources, and guilt and shame can result in the desire to withdraw.

In a *Fortune Magazine* article, "The Best Advice I Ever Got," PepsiCo CEO Indra Nooyi describes the advice she received from her father:[58] "From him I learned to always assume positive intent. Whatever anybody says or does, assume positive intent. You will be amazed at how your whole approach to a person or problem becomes very different." Nooyi goes on to explain that when you assume negative intent from another person, you react defensively. Consequently, you're not likely to listen to what the other person is saying and your decisions become impulsive and clouded with negative emotions. However, when you assume positive intent, you are more likely to try to see the situation from the other person's point of view, and this enables you to be more open-minded and to make more thoughtful decisions.

As Nooyi's example illustrates, while negative emotions narrow our ability to think and act in complex ways, positive emotions broaden these abilities and enhance our ability to get results.[59] This is not to say that there's no place for appropriately placed negative emotions. Regret, for example, helps you reflect on the consequences of your behavior, apologize to people you may have hurt, learn from the experience, and not repeat the same behaviors for which you have regret.

Not surprisingly, researchers agree that positive emotions, in general, are good for your mental and physical health. For example, positive emotions are related to stronger immune systems, more effective coping strategies, and increased social support. Negative emotions have been related to negative health outcomes, including heart disease.[60] Interestingly, researcher Becca Levy and her colleagues studied the mortality rates of more than 650 seniors and found that those who had positive attitudes about old age when they were 20 years younger tended to live an average of 7.5 years longer than those who didn't have a positive view of aging.[61]

HARDINESS   Successful people do not "win" all the time, nor do they always get what they want. At work, they face the same stress-inducing experiences as others—looming deadlines, difficult colleagues, tense meetings, reorganizations, reduced budgets, mistakes in judgment, failed decisions, and competing demands for their time. Despite the challenges inherent in life and at work, they maintain their composure under stress, recover more quickly from failure, and keep going, becoming wiser and stronger with each experience. This ability to cope with the inevitable challenges of everyday life is called hardiness. In an eight-year study of business executives, psychologist Suzanne Kobasa found that some executives managed stress much better than did others. She found that the executives who coped well tended to have three characteristics that served them well in stressful times: challenge, commitment, and control. The executives who managed stress most successfully viewed problems not as threats but as normal parts of life and worthy challenges that helped them stretch their abilities. Furthermore, these executives tended to be committed to something meaningful at their work, home, or community. This sense of meaning helped buffer them from becoming alienated in response to organizational stresses. Rather than feeling helpless, the hardy executives took control of the situation by proactively making decisions and taking actions that were likely to influence the outcomes. This mix of challenge, commitment, and control enabled the executives to survive, even thrive, in situations in which other executives crumbled.[62]

ONE MORE TIME: IQ IS ONLY A MODERATE PREDICTOR OF SUCCESS

By now, it should be abundantly clear that successful people don't rely primarily on book smarts, innate talent, or luck to achieve their goals. Instead, they systematically build an expertise that matters to others. They believe that intelligence is fluid rather than fixed. They are less concerned with appearances and more concerned about learning and growing in ways that are of value to their organizations and the people they serve. Rather than being reactive, they proactively seek out opportunities to influence their environments. They are hardworking and organized, and they conscientiously deliver on the results they promise. They understand their styles, strengths, and weaknesses, as well as how they are perceived by others. They manage their biases by developing a diverse network and listening to other people's perspectives. They build mutually supportive relationships that help them get better results in less time using fewer resources. They seek to understand their own and others' emotions, and they use their knowledge of emotions to make better decisions. They find meaning in their work and life, so the challenges they face feel like worthy challenges and opportunities for personal growth. And they understand that context matters, so they find environments that bring out the best in them.

Although successful people are persistent in pursuing their goals, they also know that it's sometimes wise to quit a course of action that isn't working and divert their resources elsewhere. Researchers Gregory Miller and Carsten Wrosch explain that people who are unable to disengage from goals that are unattainable, not worth the effort, or that block them from achieving more meaningful goals not only miss the opportunity to put themselves in situations in which they are more likely to succeed, but they may even be putting themselves at risk for health problems.[63]

I'm sure that some readers are thinking about people they know who have succeeded—at least for a while—while being arrogant, inflexible, undependable, unethical, and socially inept. However, these people are not worth emulating because their professional success tends to be self-serving (and often damaging to others), their victories short-lived, and their health and well-being at greater risk. Before leaving this discussion of the characteristics that predict success, I want to pass on some words of wisdom from organizational scholar Karl Weick. Drawing on the work of Fritz Roethlisberger, Weick explains that "people who are preoccupied with success ask the wrong question. They ask, 'What is the secret of success?' when they should be asking, 'What prevents me from learning here and now?' To be overly preoccupied with the future is to be inattentive toward the present where learning and growth take place. To walk around asking, 'Am I a success or a failure?' is a silly question in the sense that the closest you can come to answer is to say, 'Everyone is both a success and a failure.'"[64] Wise words indeed.

In the following sections, I first draw on Weick's research about what prevents us from learning in the here and now. I then describe some of the changes and challenges that managers face today. Finally, I provide best practices for ongoing learning and personal change and describe how the chapters in this book will help you in your ongoing quest for learning and growth.

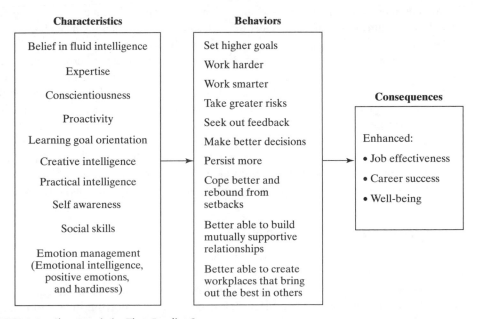

FIGURE 1-1 Characteristics That Predict Success

WHY WE HOLD ONTO PAST BEHAVIORS THAT NO LONGER SERVE US WELL

One reason we don't learn in the here and now is that tend to cling to outdated ways of thinking and acting even when these ways of thinking and acting are no longer useful, and may instead be quite costly. To better understand this phenomenon, Weick has spent decades studying human thought processes in crisis situations. He makes the case that our behavior tends to be amplified in extremely stressful situations, and this provides insight into how we think and act in non-crisis situations as well. He has concluded that "cognitive rigidity," the tendency to get stuck in established routines and ways of thinking, significantly contributes to many crises. For example, he investigated why 13 men died fighting a forest fire in Montana in 1949 and 12 men and women died under similar circumstances fighting a forest fire in Colorado in 1993. In these two cases, the fires involved were different from the ones that the firefighters had been trained for, yet the firefighters did not adapt their thinking and behavior to the new situation. One of the biggest mistakes the firefighters made was that they didn't drop their heavy backpacks filled with tools even when the tools were no longer useful and weighed them down. Weick argues that the failure of these "wildland firefighters to follow orders to drop their heavy tools so they could move faster and outrun an exploding fire led to their death within sight of safe areas."[65] He cites the U.S. Forest Service analysis of the 1993 fire that concluded that the firefighters would have increased their chances of survival if they had "perceived the threat from the start" and "dropped their packs and tools" because doing so may have enabled them to "move quicker exerting the same amount of energy."[66]

My strength is seeing through the smoke into chaos, and operating where everything is exploding.
—Darla Moore,
CEO of Rainwater Inc.

Weick explains that his research on firefighters is relevant for managers as well. One of his key insights is that "dropping one's tools is a proxy for unlearning, for adaptation, for flexibility." He argues that, similar to the firefighters, managers and management educators fail to see approaching threats and opportunities and hold onto their heavy tools (e.g., assumptions, knowledge, styles, and skills), even when dropping them might enable them to be more effective and survive in fast-changing environments.

We don't drop our tools for a variety of reasons. Sometimes we don't hear a clear message from anyone that the environment is changing and that we must adapt our ways of thinking and behaving in response. We may keep our old tools because it appears that others around us are keeping their tools. Sometimes we keep our taken-for-granted tools because we don't know how to drop them. And we get our identities from our tools. For example, many managers are reluctant to create an environment in which people can do their best work without direct supervision because these managers tie their identities to feeling needed by their employees. It is not surprising that these managers are more likely to design work environments that create dependence rather than independence and spend their time micromanaging employees rather than thinking more strategically about how they can add more value to their organizations. Box 1-5 summarizes Weick's conclusions about why we tend to cling to taken-for-granted routines, are unwilling to unlearn old behaviors, and are unable to improvise new behaviors that could help us respond to threats and opportunities more quickly and effectively.

STEPS TOWARD PERSONAL CHANGE

Ursula Burns, who became CEO of Xerox in 2009, recently provided the graduates of the Rochester Institute of Technology with this advice: "I can't pretend to know how your world will change, but I know it will and at a pace that will continue to increase exponentially. You can't stop it. Learn to love it. And make it your friend." Engaging in the following steps will help you

BOX 1-5   Reasons Why We Don't Drop Our Tools Even When Doing So Will Enhance Our Survival

1. **Listening.** Sometimes we don't hear the clear message from anyone that it is important to drop our tools.
2. **Justification.** We persist when we are given no clear reasons to change.
3. **Trust.** We persist when we don't trust the person who tells us to change.
4. **Control.** Professional training provides us with assumptions about cause-and-effect relationships for survival; changing these assumptions means giving up a sense of security and control.
5. **Skill at dropping.** We may keep our tools because we don't know how to drop them.
6. **Skill with replacement activity.** We may keep our familiar tools in a frightening situation because an unfamiliar alternative is even more frightening.
7. **Failure.** To drop our tools may be to admit failure. To retain our tools is to postpone this admission and to feel that we are still winning.
8. **Social dynamics.** We may keep our tools because everyone else around us is keeping their tools. Each person may be fearful but mistakenly concludes that everyone else is calm. Thus, the situation appears to be safe, except that no one actually believes that it is.
9. **Consequences.** We won't drop our tools if we don't believe that doing so will make a difference. Small changes seem like trivial changes, so nothing changes.
10. **Identity.** We get our identities from our tools. Certain tools are distinguishing trademarks of our profession and, thus, central to our identity.

Source: Quoted and adapted from Weick, Karl E. 1996. "Drop Your Tools: An Allegory for Organizational Studies." *Administrative Science Quarterly,* 41: 301–313.

make the most of the opportunities you have for learning, unlearning, and adapting to whatever opportunities and challenges you face at work and in life:[67]

- *Believe that you can change and remember* that you are more likely to put in the effort to learn new skills if you believe your abilities are fluid rather than fixed.
- *Learn* the beliefs, characteristics, and skills that are likely to lead to success in your current and future environment. You're taking an important step in this direction by reading this book.
- *Think critically* and keep in mind when reading this book or any book about managerial skills that it is important to engage in critical reflection when you are learning new skills. Blindly following advice in any article, book, or Web site is a recipe for mediocrity because claims to one-right-way and one-size-fits-all answers, although comforting, are naïve and misleading. At times, you will need to adapt the knowledge and skill you learn in this book and other resources to better reflect your specific context—your personal and professional goals, your organizational culture, your national culture, and the complexities of the situation you're facing.
- *Assess* your personal styles, strengths, and weaknesses through self-assessment and feedback from others. There are several self-assessments throughout this book that will help you better understand your styles, how others may perceive you, and the consequences of these styles on your potential for success.

- *Practice new skills with the goal of achieving small wins,* not only in the classroom but also in your natural environment at work and at home. This requires a willingness to take risks and tolerate the discomfort, imperfection, and mistakes that often accompany skill development, particularly in the early stages of skill development. After all, children don't learn how to walk or ride a bike without falling down several times along the way, and adult learning is no different. It's advisable to reach for small wins rather than try to change too much at one time. If you take a small-wins approach, you are more likely to see tangible positive results more quickly, build on these successes, learn from your experience, and stay motivated to engage in additional change.[68]
- *Obtain feedback* on your progress, especially from the people who are affected by the changes you are making.
- *Overlearn new behaviors* that are working well for you so that you don't fall back on your old habits, particularly during stressful times.

The above steps for personal change provide a framework for ongoing change rather than a one-time fix. They will help you stay nimble enough to react quickly and mindfully to the present and be ready for whatever changes the future will present to you.

THE NEW RULES

Undoubtedly, the world is changing and, in response, so is the work of the manager. What do we expect of managers today? Managers must be able to manage a diverse workforce in a de-centralized, global, and boundaryless organization. Managers must be able to manage virtual teams in which team members rarely or never meet face to face. To achieve and maintain competitive advantage, managers must be able to decrease product cycle time without compromising quality or costs. They must understand and lever-age new technologies that are changing the way people create their professional identities, build their networks, communicate inside and outside the organization, gather and store information, and manage complex organizational processes.

> If you're not confused, you don't know what's going on.
> —WARREN BENNIS

Managers must be able to establish credibility with their employees, many of whom are empowered knowledge workers who, because of their specialized training and experience, may know more than their managers about the organization's products, technologies, and customers. Empowered knowledge workers may not be easily impressed by hierarchy, so managers must be able to influence them without depending solely on the power of their position in the hierarchy.

Because of downsizing, managers must be able to accomplish more with fewer employees. They must be able to motivate and inspire commitment from employees without being able to promise promotions or long-term employment in return. Furthermore, managers must be fully invested in adding value to their current organizations while increasing their marketability else-where. They must do all of this while they and others may be balancing two or more careers in their household, taking care of children, helping aging parents, and trying to take care of their own health and well-being as well.

So, what skills does the ideal manager need? *Fortune Magazine*, in an article called "Reengineering the MBA," described the managerial ideal as follows:

> Every B-school dean knows what to confidently promise: The ideal executive of the future . . . Global in outlook, facile with information systems and technology. Able to capitalize on diversity. A visionary. A master of teamwork and a coach. Walks on water, too.[69]

TABLE 1-1	Trends Changing Managerial Work

Old	New	Consequences for Managers
Stable, predictable environment	Changing, unpredictable environment	From routinization to improvisation, adaptability, and flexibility
Stable and homogeneous workforce (or at least the workforce was treated as such)	Mobile and diverse workforce	From one-size-fits-all styles to multiple management styles
Capital and labor-intensive firms	Knowledge- and service-intensive firms	From machine and industrial relations models of organizations to learning models of organizations
Brick-and-mortar organizations	Brick-and-click (or just click) organizations (e-commerce)	From managing relationships face-to-face to managing relationships through communication technologies as well
Knowledge and product stability	Knowledge and product obsolescence; mass customization	From emphasis on routinization to emphasis on innovation
Knowledge in the hands of a few	Knowledge in the hands of many (in large part due to advances in information and communication technologies)	From manager as expert and information broker to manager as a creator of a context that enhances collective learning
Stability of managerial knowledge and practices	Escalation of new managerial knowledge and practices	From a focus on learning to a focus on learning and unlearning; from uncritical acceptance of managerial knowledge to becoming wise consumers of managerial knowledge
Technology as a tool for routine tasks (data processing era)	Escalating information and communication technologies (knowledge and relationship era)	From using technology primarily for routine tasks to using technology as a key leadership resource for wide-scale personal, organizational, and societal changes
Relationship building face-to-face	Relationship building face-to-face and through communication technologies	From online relationship-building as a complement to face-to-face relationship-building to online social networking as increasingly central to relationship-building
Local focus	Local and global focus	From one-size-fits-all styles and standards to multiple styles and standards
Bureaucracy	Networks	From command and control to relationship building; from autonomy to interdependence; from clear to permeable boundaries inside and outside the organization
Managers as fixed cost	Managers as variable cost	From security to pay for performance
Predictable, trajectory careers	Multiple careers	From employment to employability
One-breadwinner families	Dual and triple career families	From an emphasis on traditional family and work roles to an emphasis on fluid family roles, flexible work schedules, and work/life integration

Although walking on water is beyond the scope of this book, I believe that being able to understand and respond to fundamental organizational and societal changes is the most pressing challenge for managers today.

The trends influencing management today are summarized in Table 1-1. These trends do not imply that managers must completely shift their thinking from one model to another. Rather, they imply that managers must simultaneously manage stability and change; see the big picture and the details; attend to the present and focus on the future, create routines, and inspire improvisation; operate in hierarchies and fluid networks; control the workplace and liberate employees' potential; create a collective identity and encourage diversity; engage in slow, deliberate long-term planning and act quickly. In other words, managers must develop a broad repertoire of seemingly contradictory skills and shift quickly from one skill set to another as appropriate.[70]

> The test of a first-rate intelligence is the ability to hold two opposing ideas in mind at the same time and still retain the ability to function.
> —F. Scott Fitzgerald

HOW THIS BOOK IS ORGANIZED

The following nine chapters in this book provide you with the perspective and skills that will prepare you to achieve the success you desire in your current and future environments, in good times and in challenging times: "Developing Self-Awareness"; "Building Trust"; "Communicating Effectively"; "Developing Sustainable, Ethical Power and Influence"; "Managing Relationships with Your Direct Reports, Bosses, and Peers"; "Managing Cultural Diversity"; "Creating High-Performing Teams"; "Diverse Teams and Virtual Teams: Managing Differences and Distances"; and "Crafting a Life." Each chapter provides practical research-based advice that will help you increase your immediate and long-term effectiveness, career potential, and general well-being. Each chapter also includes self-assessments that will help you increase your self-knowledge, end-of-chapter questions that will help you reflect on what you learn, and guided activities for applying what you learn to your everyday life.

> Never mistake motion for action.
> —Ernest Hemingway

As the author of this book, I see myself as a provocateur. Throughout this book, I encourage you to hold on to the timeless lessons of the past, unlearn those that are no longer useful, and learn new lessons that will help you make the most of whatever the future brings. At times, I intentionally push the boundaries of what traditionally has been considered normal, desirable, and effective managerial thinking and behaving. I encourage you to use common sense and think critically about what you learn in each chapter and how it applies—and doesn't apply—to your own life. I encourage you to look for the explicit and implicit assumptions in each chapter and consider whether you agree with them or not. Which materials are and are not relevant to your cultures, work environments, and personal goals? Under what conditions is the knowledge useful and when might it be problematic? Are any perspectives excluded, misrepresented, or disadvantaged in any way by any of the theories, ideas, and recommendations presented in this book? Are there alternative ways of thinking that are not presented in the book that could enrich individuals, organizations, and society? In short, I want you to think of this book as a conversation rather than a monologue and a work in progress rather than the final word on immutable and universal truths.

> Learn as if you were going to live forever. Live as if you were going to die tomorrow.
> —Mahatma Gandhi

Ultimately, my goal in writing this book is to help you make a contribution to your organizations and the people you serve, achieve the career success that you desire, have time to spend with the people that you care about, and lead a long, happy, and healthy life.

Chapter Summary

This is an exciting time to be a manager—full of challenges and opportunities. Today's organizations are increasingly complex, unpredictable, and fast-paced. Significant social and economic trends such as diversity, globalization, and technological advances have fundamentally changed the nature of managerial work. In such an environment, the ability to have a learning orientation, to think broadly from a wide variety of perspectives, and the willingness to learn new skills are some of the most important skills a manager can have.

Derailment occurs when a high-potential manager expects to advance in an organization, and was judged initially to have the ability to do so, yet is fired, demoted, or plateaued below anticipated levels of achievement. Derailment does not refer to individuals who, by their own choosing, change jobs, decline promotions, or quit their jobs to pursue other careers or life interests. Rather, derailment is involuntary and frequently preventable.

When derailed managers reflect on their experience, they learn three important lessons. First, intelligence isn't enough for long-term success. Second, the same talents that once brought them early success can later lead to failure. Third, flaws and blind spots that seemed insignificant earlier in their careers suddenly matter.

Research suggests that successful people share several characteristics: a belief that intelligence is fluid rather than fixed; an expertise developed through mindful and deliberate practice; conscientiousness (being achievement-oriented, hardworking, planful, organized, and dependable); proactivity; a learning goal orientation; creative intelligence; practical intelligence; self-awareness; social skills; attention to their own and other's emotional life (emotional intelligence, positive emotions, and hardiness); and the ability to learn new perspectives and skills that serve them well and unlearn those that hold them back.

Steps to behavioral change include believing that you can change; understanding the beliefs, characteristics, and skills that lead to success; thinking critically about what you're learning rather than accepting everything you hear as appropriate for your particular situation; assessing your personal strengths and weaknesses through self-assessment and feedback from others; practicing new skills by taking the small-wins approach; obtaining feedback on your progress from people who are affected by the changes you are making; and overlearning new behaviors so that you don't fall back on old habits, especially when under stress.

CASE 1.1

The Development of Expertise:

Pilot Chesley B. "Sully" Sullenberger

On January 15, 2009, a flock of birds flew into the jet engines of U.S. Airways Flight 1549, causing both engines to fail only one minute after takeoff from LaGuardia National Airport in New York. On realizing that the plane encountered a devastating "bird strike," pilot Chesley B. "Sully" Sullenberger, 57 years old, determined that that the plane would not make it safely back to LaGuardia, and he told air traffic controllers, "We're gonna be in the Hudson." With 115 people onboard, Sullenberger orchestrated an extraordinarily skillful emergency landing into the frigid waters of the Hudson River after calmly but firmly telling passengers to "brace for impact." Passenger Joe Hart described Sullenberg's controlled landing by saying that the "impact wasn't a whole lot more than a rear end (collision). It threw you into the seat ahead of you." The passengers and crew quickly exited the plane and waited in the icy water until they were taken to safety by rescue teams. After everyone exited the plane, Sullenberger walked the aisles of the plane twice to ensure that no one was left on the plane, and then he took the last raft to safety. All 115 people on board survived what has been called one of the most impressive emergency landings in the history of commercial aviation.

Lauded as a hero, Sullenberger told people that he was just doing his job, and he gave credit to his copilot, the flight attendant crew, the first responders, and the cooperative passengers for their seamless coordination during the emergency. Regarding the flight attendants, he said, "Even though we were intensely focused and very busy, I remember thinking that as soon as I made the public address announcement in the cabin, within a second or two, I heard even through the hardened cockpit door the flight attendants in unison shouting their commands. 'Heads down. Stay down.' And it was comforting to me to know that they were on the same page, that we were all acting in concert. It made me feel that my hope and my confidence in completing this plan was reasonable and that they knew what needed to be done and were doing their part." Notably, the flight attendants—Sheila Dail, Doreen Welsh, and Donna Dent, each had over 25 years of in-flight experience.

Sullenberger's copilot, 49-year-old Jeffrey Skiles, had been flying since he was 15, had over 26 years of flying experience with U.S. Airways, and had experience as a captain. However, this was Skiles' first trip on an Airbus 320, and he had only recently completed training for flying this type of aircraft. Consequently, Sullenberger decided to take the lead on all key decisions during this flight. However, Sullenberger realized that he himself hadn't been through the required annual pilot training in nearly one year, although Skiles had just completed it. Therefore, Sullenberger decided that Skiles would be better at managing the critical emergency checklists. Sullenberger explained, "So I felt it was like the best of both worlds. I could use my experience, I could look out the window and make a decision about where we were going to go, while he was continuing his effort to restart the engines and hoping that we wouldn't have to land some place other than a runway. He was valiantly trying until the last moment to get the engines started again." This "textbook ditching" has become the gold standard "how to" case for understanding not only what went right at the moment of the crisis, but also for understanding the kind of experience, training, and coordination that help pilots and crews successfully respond to emergencies.

Referring to Sullenberger's professionalism throughout the crisis, Alfus Rothman, a business psychologist and career management expert at The Wenroth Group in New York, explained, "Staying composed in the face of disaster seems to be an ageless—and essential—skill, whether landing a plane or navigating a tumultuous economy fraught with job insecurity and professional uncertainty." In an interview shortly after the successful ditching of the plane, Sullenberger said, "The way I describe this whole experience—and I haven't had time to reflect on it sufficiently— is that everything I had done in my career had in some way been a preparation for that moment."

How did Sullenberger develop a world-class expertise that would provide him with the quick judgment, exceptional skill, and calm demeanor that he needed during the crisis? He earned his pilot's license when he was a teenager. At the Air Force Academy, he was named best aviator in his class. From 1973 to 1980, he served in the Air Force and flew fighter planes and served as a flight leader. He studied the psychology of cockpit crews, including the psychology of crews during emergencies, and he received two degrees in psychology from the Air Force Academy and Purdue University. In 1980, he became a commercial pilot. He participated as a volunteer on National Transportation Safety Board teams that investigated aviation accidents. In 2006, Sullenberger started a consulting firm Safety Reliability Methods, which is designed to offer companies expertise in the latest safety advances in commercial aviation. In short,

Sullenberger became a world-class expert because, as one of his colleagues said, he "has not just spent his life flying airplanes but actually has dug very deeply into what makes things work."

When asked who he admired early in his career, Sullenberger mentioned his first flight instructor, L.T. Cook Jr., who had been a Civilian Pilot Training Program instructor during World War II. He said, "Among the thousands of cards I received [after the ditching], I discovered one from his widow. She wrote, 'L.T. wouldn't be surprised, but he certainly would be pleased and proud.'"

References

"Air and Space Interview: Sully's Tale." February 18, 2009. Air Space Smithsonian, http://www.air-spacemag.com/flight-today/Sullys-Tale.html; McClain, Erin. January 17, 2009. "A Lifetime of Training Prepared Hero Pilot." http://www.azcentral.com/news/articles/2009/01/17/20090117planepilot0117; "Maturity Touted in Hudson River Landing." January 19, 2009. http://www.upi.com/Health_News/2009/01/19/Maturity-touted-in-Hudson-River-landing/UPI-96981232388007/.

Food for Thought

1. What is the one most useful thing you learned in this chapter, and why?

2. Based on what you learned in this chapter, what is the one most important thing about yourself that you want to change or unlearn? What would the benefits be to you, others, and/or your organizations if you succeeded in making this change? In the spirit of small wins, practice making this change this week, beginning today if possible. Then reflect on what you learned and gained (and perhaps lost) by doing so.

3. In *FastCompany* magazine, well-known executive coach, Marshall Goldsmith, wrote a column titled, "Making a Resolution That Matters." In this column, he asked readers the following question: "I want you to imagine that you're 95 years old. Before taking your last breath, however, you're given a great gift: the ability to travel back in time—the ability to talk to the person who is reading this column, the ability to help this person be a better professional and lead a better life. The 95-year-old understands what was really important and what wasn't, what mattered and what didn't, what counted and what really didn't count. What advice would this wise 'old you' have for the 'you' who is reading this page?" Answer Goldsmith's question, focusing on the personal and professional advice you would give yourself, as well as how you would define success.

4. Based on this chapter, what are the characteristics that predict success? Of these, which are your strengths? Which of these do you still need to develop to enhance your job effectiveness, career potential, and general well-being—and to achieve the success you described in question 3 above.

5. Read the case of Pilot Chesley B. "Sully" Sullenberger in this chapter. What did you learn from this case about how "Sully" developed this expertise and how he displayed it during the crisis? What did you learn that is useful to you personally about the development of expertise in your own life?

6. Research the case of Pilot Chesley B. "Sully" Sullenberger online. What did you learn about the event beyond what is described in the case? If you had to add another paragraph to the case, what would this paragraph say and what would be your key point?

7. What characteristics predict derailment? Do you have any of these characteristics? If so, what do you need to do to avoid derailment in your professional and personal life?

8. What are the three most critical changes that are transforming the environment in which you work? What new perspectives and skills do you need to develop to succeed in this environment?

9. What did you learn about yourself based on taking the assessments in this chapter? Specifically, describe your

styles, strengths, and weaknesses. How do you think you are perceived by others, for better and worse?

10. Describe three changes you made in your life since you were in high school. What motivated these changes? What were the consequences? What "heavy tools" did you drop? What have you learned about what motivates you to change and your strategies for personal change?

11. Imagine that you work for a magazine called *The Smart Manager's Guide to Management Theory*. The purpose of this magazine is to help managers wade through the escalating number of management theories that come off the press every day and judge their usefulness. Similar to *Consumer Reports, The Smart Manager's Guide to Management Theory* has developed a set of criteria against which it judges each theory. What criteria would you use to assess the usefulness of a management theory, and why?

12. Imagine that you could have three people throughout history, living or dead, to be your management consultants for a day. Who would these people be, and why? What kinds of lessons would you want to learn from them?

Endnotes

1. Mintzberg, Henry. 1975. "The Manager's Job: Folklore and Fact." *Harvard Business Review*, 1990 republished, March–April: 163–176.

2. Thakor, Anjan. 2008. *Becoming a Better Value Creator: How to Improve the Company's Bottom Line—And Your Own*. San Francisco: Jossey-Bass.

3. Lancaster, Hal. 1997. *The Wall Street Journal*. May 6: B1.

4. Cameron, Kim, and Robert Quinn. 2005. *Diagnosing and Changing Organizational Culture: Based on the Competing Values Framework*. San Francisco: Jossey-Bass.

5. Lombardo, Michael, and Robert Eichinger. 1991. *Preventing Derailment Before It's Too Late*. Greensboro, NC: Center for Creative Leadership.

6. Ibid., p. 1.

7. Church, Allan. 1997. "Managerial Self-Awareness in High-Performing Individuals in Organizations." *Journal of Applied Psychology*, 82(2): 281–292.

8. Finklestein, Sydney. 2003. *Why Smart Executives Fail: And What You Can Learn from Their Mistakes*. New York: Portfolio, 237.

9. Shipper, Frank, and John Dillard Jr. 2000. "A Study of Impending Derailment and Recovery of Middle Managers Across Career Stages." *Human Resource Management*, 39(4): 331–345; Atwater, L.E., and F. J. Yamminanno. 1992. "Does Self-Other Agreement on Leadership Perceptions Moderate the Validity of Leadership and Performance Predictions?" *Personnel Psychology*, 45: 141–164; Hogan, Robert, Gordon Curphy, and Joyce Hogan. 1994. "What We Know About Leadership: Effectiveness and Personality." *American Psychologist*, June: 493–504; Bass, Bernard and Francis Yamminarino. 1991. "Congruence of Self and Others' Leadership Ratings of Naval Officers for Understanding Successful Performance." *Applied Psychology: An International Review*, 40(4): 437–454; Vancouver, Jeffrey B., Charles M. Thompson, Casey Tischner, and Dan Putka. 2002. "Two Studies Examining the Negative Effects of Self-Efficacy on Performance." *Journal of Applied Psychology*, 83(3): 506–516.

10. Lombardo, Michael, and Robert Eichinger. 1991. *Preventing Derailment Before It's Too Late*. Greensboro, NC: Center for Creative Leadership.

11. Ibid. O'Reilly, Charles, and Jennifer Chatman. 1994. "Working Smarter and Harder: A Longitudinal Study of Managerial Success." *Administrative Science Quarterly*, 39(4): 603–628; Kotter, John. 1995. *The New Rules: Eight Business Breakthroughs to Career Success in the 21st Century*. New York: Free Press.

12. Sternberg, Robert J. 1996. *Successful Intelligence: How Practical and Creative Intelligence Determine Success in Life*. New York: Simon and Schuster, 224.

13. Sternberg, Robert. 1997. *Successful Intelligence: How Creative and Practical Intelligence De-termine Success in Life*. New York: Penguin Group.

14. Nisbett, Richard. 2009. *Intelligence and How to Get It: Why Schools and Cultures Count*. New York: W.W. Norton.

15. U.S. Census Bureau. 2007. Educational Attainment in the United States: 2007. http://www.census.gov/prod/2009pubs/p20-560.pdf

16. Frankel, Lois P. 1997. *Overcoming Your Strengths*. New York: Harmony Books, 3–4.

17. Sternberg, Robert J. 1996. *Successful Intelligence: How Practical and Creative Intelligence Determine Success in Life*. New York: Penguin Group. 216–217.

18. Lombardo, Michael, and Robert Eichinger. 1991. *Preventing Derailment: What to Do Before It's Too Late*. Greensboro, NC: Center for Creative Leadership.

19. Caproni, Paula, and Joycelyn Finley. 1997. "When Organizations Do Harm: Two Cautionary Tales. In Pushkala Prasad, Albert J. Mills, Michael Elms, and Anshuman Prasad (eds.). *Managing the Organizational Melting Pot: Dilemmas of Workplace Diversity*. Sage Publications, 255–284.

20. Finklestein, Sydney. 2003. *Why Smart Executives Fail and What You Can Learn from Their Mistakes*. Portfolio; Kramer, Roderick. 2003. "The Harder They Fall." *Harvard Business Review*, 81(10): 58.

21. Staw, Barry, and Jerry Ross. 1987. "Knowing When to Pull the Plug." *Harvard Business Review*, March–April: 68–74; Whyte, Glen, Alan Sakes, and Sterling Hook, 1997. "When Success Breeds Failure: The Role of Self-Efficacy in Escalating Commitment to a Losing Course of Action." *Journal of Organizational Behavior*, 18: 415–432.

22. Kramer, Roderick. 2003. "The Harder They Fall." *Harvard Business Review*, 81(10): 58.

23. Toobin, Jeffrey. 2004. "A Bad Thing: Why Did Martha Stewart Lose?" *The New Yorker*, March 22: 60–72.

24. Dweck, Carol S. 2002. "Beliefs That Make Smart People Dumb." In Robert Sternberg (ed.). *Why Smart People Can Be So Stupid*. New Haven: Yale University Press, 24–41.

25. Blackwell, Lisa, Kali Trzesniewski, and Carol Dweck. 2007. "Implicit Theories of Intelligence Predict Achievement Across an Adolescent Transition: A Longitudinal Study and an Intervention." *Child Development,* 78: 246–263; Grant, Heidi, and Carol S. Dweck. 2003. "Clarifying Achievement Goals and Their Impact." *Journal of Personality and Social Psychology*, 85(3): 541–553.

26. Dweck, Carol. 2008. "Can Personality Be Changed? The Role of Beliefs in Personality and Change." *Current Directions in Psychological Science*, 17(6): 391–394.

27. Aronson, J. 1998. "The Effects of Conceiving Ability as Fixed or Improvable on Responses to Stereotype Threat." Unpublished manuscript, University of Texas; Dweck, Carol, and L. Sorich. 1999. "Mastery Oriented Thinking." In C. R. Snyder (ed.). *Coping*. New York: Oxford University Press.

28. Hong, Yin-Yi, C. Chiu, Carol S. Dweck, D. Lin, and W. Wan. 1999. "A Test of Implicit Theories and Self-Confidence as Predictors of Responses to Achievement Challenges." *Journal of Personality and Social Psychology,* 77: 588–599.

29. Ericsson, K. Anders. 2006. "The Influence of Experience and Deliberate Practice on the Development of Superior Expert Performance." In K. Anders Ericsson, N. Charness, P. Feltovich, and R. R. Hoffman (eds.). *Cambridge Handbook of Expertise and Expert Performance*. Cambridge, UK: Cambridge University Press, 685–706.

30. Colvin, Geoffrey. 2006. "What It Takes to Be Great." *Fortune Magazine*, 154(9). http://money.cnn.com/magazines/fortune/fortune_archive/2006/10/30/toc.html.

31. DeRue, Scott, and Ned Wellman. 2009. "Developing Leaders via Experience: The Role of Developmental Challenge, Learning Orientation, and Feedback Availability." *Journal of Applied Psychology*, 94(4): 859–875.

32. Ericsson, K. Anders, Ralph Krampe, and Clemens Tesch-Romer, 1993. "The Role of Deliberate Practice in the Acquisition of Expert Performance." *Psychological Review*, 100(3): 363–406.

33. Robertson, Ivan T., Helen Baron, Patrick Gibbons, Rab MacIvcr, and Gill Nyfield. 2000. "Conscientiousness and Managerial Performance." *Journal of Occupational and Organizational Psychology*, 73:171; Smithikrai, Chuchai. 2007. "Personality Traits and Job Success: An Investigation in a Thai Sample." *International Journal of Selection and Assessment,* 15(1): 134–138.

34. Griffin, Barbara, and Beryl Hesketh. 2005. "Are Conscientious Workers Adaptable?" *Australian Journal of Management*, 30(2): 245–260.

35. Judge, Timothy, Joyce Bono, Remus L. Lies, and Megan Gerhardt. 2002. "Personality and Leadership: A Qualitative and Quantitative Review." *Journal of Applied Psychology*, 87: 765–780.

36. Roberts, Brent W., Kate E. Wilson, and Tim Bogg. 2005. "Conscientiousness and Health Across the Life Course." *Review of General Psychology,* 5(2): 156–168; Kern, Margaret, Howard Friedman, Leslie Martin, Chandra A. Reynolds, and Gloria Luong. 2009. "Conscientiousness, Career Success, and Longevity: A Lifespan Analysis." *Annals of Behavioral Medicine*, 37(2): 154–163; Kern, Margaret L., and Howard Friedman. 2008. "Do Conscientious Individuals Live Longer? A Quantitative Review." *Health Psychology*, 27(5): 505–512.

37. Crant, Michael J. 2000. "Proactive Behavior in Organizations." *Journal of Management*, 26: 435–462; Grant, Adam, and Susan Ashford. 2008. "The Dynamics of Proactivity at Work," *Research in Organizational Behavior*, 28: 3–34; Seibert, Scott E., Maria L. Kraimer, and Michael J. Crant. 2001.

"What Do Proactive People Do? A Longitudinal Model Linking Proactive personality and Career Success." *Personnel Psychology*, 54(4): 845–874.

38. Eby, Lillian, Marcus Butts, and Angie Lockwood. 2003. "Predictors of Success in the Era of a Boundaryless Career." *Journal of Organizational Behavior,* 24: 689–708.

39. Schibert, Scott, Maria Kraimer, and Michael Crant. 2001. "What Do Proactive People Do: A Longitudinal Model Linking Proactive Personality and Career Success." *Personnel Psychology,* 54(4): 845–874.

40. Aspinwall, Lisa, and Shelly. 1997. "A Stitch in Time: Self-Regulation and Proactive Coping." *Psychological Bulletin*, 121: 417–436.

41. Seibert, Scott, Michael Crant, and Maria Kraimer. 1999. "Proactive Personality and Career Success." *Journal of Applied Psychology,* 84: 416–427.

42. VandeWalle, Don. 2001. "Goal Orientation: Why Wanting to Look Successful Doesn't Always Lead to Success." *Organization Dynamics*, 30(2): 162–171; Grant, Heidi. 2003. "Clarifying Achievement Goals and Their Impact." *Journal of Personality and Social Psychology*, 85(3): 541–553.

43. Sternberg, R. J., G. B. Forsythe, J. Hedlund, J. A. Horvath, R. K. Wagner, W. M. Williams, S. A. Snook, and E. L. Grigorenko. 2000. *Practical Intelligence in Everyday Life*. New York: Cambridge University Press.

44. Ibid., 11.

45. Church, Allan. 1997. "Managerial Self-Awareness in High-Performing Individuals in Organizations." *Journal of Applied Psychology*, 82(2): 281–292.

46. Tekleab, Amanuel, Henry Sims, Seokhwa Yun, Paul Tesluk, and Jonathan Cox. 2008. "Are We on the Same Page? Effects of Self-Awareness of Empowering and Transformational Leadership." *Journal of Leadership & Organizational Studies*, 14(3); Atwater, L. E., D. A. Waldman, and J. F. Brett. 2002. "Understanding and Optimizing Multisource Feedback." *Human Resource Management*, 41: 193–208; Ashford, Susan, and Ann Tsui. 1991. "Self-Regulation for Managerial Effectiveness: The Role of Active Feedback Seeking." *Academy of Management Journal*, 34: 251–280.

47. Ross, Lee. 1977. "The Intuitive Psychologist and His Shortcomings: Distortions in the Attribution Process." In L. Berkowitz (ed.). *Advances in Experimental Social Psychology*. New York: Academic Press, 10: 173–220; Jones, Edward, and Victor Harris. 1967. "The Attribution of Attitudes." *Journal of Experimental Social Psychology*, 3: 1–24.

48. Darley, John, and Daniel Batson. 1973. "From Jerusalem to Jericho: A Study of Situational and Dispositional Variables in Helping Behavior." *Journal of Personality and Social Psychology*, 27: 100–119.

49. Baker, Wayne E. 2000. *Achieving Success through Social Capital: Tapping the Hidden Resources in Your Personal and Business Networks*. San Francisco, CA: Jossey-Bass.

50. Baker, Wayne, and Jane Dutton. 2007. "Enabling Positive Social Capital in Organizations." In Dutton, Jane, and Belle Rose Ragins (eds.). *Exploring Positive Connections at Work*. Mahway, NJ: Lawrence Erlbaum Associates, 325–345.

51. Jones, Del. 2006. "CEOs Say How You Treat a Waiter Can Predict a Lot about Character." *USA Today*. April 17. http://www.usatoday.com/money/companies/management/2006-04-14-ceos-waiter-rule_x.htm

52. Ibid.

53. Umberson, Debra, Meichu Chen, James House, Kristine Hopkins, and Elle Slaten. 1996. "The Effect of Social Relationships on Psychological Well-Being: Are Men and Women Really So Different?" *American Sociological Review*, 61(5): 837–857; Lansford, Jennifer, Toni Antonucci, Hiroko Akiyama, and Keiko Takahashi. 2005. "A Quantitative and Qualitative Approach to Well-Being in the United States and Japan." *Journal of Comparative Family Studies*, 36(1): 1–22.

54. Andel, Ross, Michael Crowe, Nancy Pedersen, James Mortimer, Eileen Crimmins, Boo Johansson, and Margaret Gatz. 2005. "Complexity of Work and Risk of Alzheimer's Disease: A Population-Based Study of Swedish Twins." *Journal of Gerontology: Psychological Sciences*, 60B(5): 251–258.

55. Bar-On, Reuven. 1997. *Bar-On Emotional Quotient Inventory: Technical Manual*. Toronto: Multi-Health Systems. Goleman, Daniel, Richard Boyatzis, and Annie McKee. 2001. "Primal Leadership." *Harvard Business Review*, December: 43–51; Goleman, Daniel. 1998. *Working with Emotional Intelligence*. New York: Bantam; Mayer, J. D., P. Salovey, and D. Caruso. 2000. "Models of Emotional Intelligence." In Robert J. Sternberg (ed.). *The Handbook of Emotional Intelligence* 2nd ed. New York: Cambridge University Press, 396–420.

56. Goleman, Daniel, Richard Boyatzis, and Annie McKee. 2004. *Learning to Lead with Emotional Intelligence*. Cambridge, MA: Harvard Business Press; Shipper, Frank, Denise Rotondo, and Richard C. Hoffman. 2003. "A Cross Cultural Study of Linkage Between Emotional Intelligence and

Managerial Effectiveness." Presented at the Academy of Management Meeting, Seattle, Washington, August 1–6, 2003; Hogan, Robert, Gordon Curphy, and Joyce Hogan. 1994. "What We Know About Leadership Effectiveness and Personality." *American Psychologist*, 49(6): 493–503.

57. Frederickson, Barbara. 2002. "Positive Emotions." In C. R. Snyder and Shane J. Lopez (eds.). *Handbook of Positive Psychology*. Oxford University Press: Oxford, 120–134.

58. The Best Advice I Ever Got: Indra Nooyi, http://money.cnn.com/galleries/2008/fortune/0804/gallery.bestadvice.fortune/7.html

59. Fredrickson, Barbara L. 1998. "What Good Are Positive Emotions?" *Review of General Psychology,* 2: 300–319.

60. Folkman, Susan, and Judith Moskowitz. 2000. "Positive Affect and the Other Side of Coping." *American Psychologist*, 55: 647–654; Stone, A., J. M. Neale, D. S. Cox, A. Napoli, H. Valdimarsdottir, and E. Kennedy-Moore. 1994. "Daily Events Are Associated with a Secretory Immune Response to an Oral Antigen in Men." *Health Psychology*, 13: 440–446; Gallo, Linda, Shiva Ghaed, and Wendy Bracken. 2004. "Emotions and Cognitions in Coronary Heart Disease: Risk, Resilience, and Social Context." *Cognitive Therapy and Research*, 28(5): 660–694.

61. Levy, Becca, Martin Slade, Stanislav Kasl, and Suzanne Kunkl. 2002. "Longevity Increased by Positive Perceptions of Aging." *Journal of Personality and Social Psychology*, 83(2): 261–270.

62. Kobasa, Suzanne, 1979. "Stressful Life Events, Personality, and Health: An Inquiry into Hardiness." *Journal of Personality and Social Psychology*, 37:1–11; Maddi, Salvatore, and Deborah Khoshaba. 2005. *Resilience at Work: How to Succeed No Matter What Life Throws at You*. New York: Amacom.

63. Miller, Gregory, and Carsten Wrosch. 2007. "Goal Disengagement and Systematic Inflammation in Adolescence." *Psychological Science*, 18(9): 773–777.

64. Weick, Karl E. 2004. "How Projects Lose Meaning: The Dynamics of Renewal." In R. Stablein and P. Frost (eds.), *Renewing Research Practice*. Stanford, CA: Stanford.

65. Weick, Karl E. 1996. "Drop Your Tools: An Allegory for Organizational Studies." *Administrative Science Quarterly*, 41: 301.

66. U.S. Forest Service. 1994. *1994 Report of the South Canyon Fire Accident Investigation Team,* August 17, 1994, pp. A3–5. Washington, DC: U.S. Forest Service.

67. Brookfield, Stephen. 1986. *Understanding and Facilitating Adult Learning*. San Francisco: Jossey-Bass; Whetton, David, and Kim Cameron. 2005. *Developing Managerial Skills*. New Jersey: Prentice Hall; Dweck, Carol S. 2002. "Beliefs That Make Smart People Dumb." In Sternberg, Robert J. (ed.). 2002. *Why Smart People Can Be So Stupid*. New Haven: Yale University Press, 24–41; Kolb, David. 1984. *Experiential Learning: Experience the Source of Learning and Development*. Upper Saddle River, NJ: Prentice Hall.

68. Weick, Karl. 1984. "Small Wins." *American Psychologist,* 39: 40–49.

69. O'Reilly, Brian. 1994. "Reengineering the MBA." *Fortune*, January 24: 39.

70. Denison, Daniel. 1984. "Bringing Corporate Culture to the Bottom Line." *Organizational Dynamics* 5–22; Cameron, Kim, and Robert E. Quinn. 1999. *Diagnosing and Changing Organizational Culture*. Reading, MA: Addison Wesley.

2

■ ■ ■

Developing
Self-Awareness

This chapter will help you:

- Understand why self-awareness is important to your professional effectiveness and well-being.
- Learn about your self-concept and how it is constructed through everyday life at home, at work, and in society.
- Develop a personal brand that is consistent with how you want to be perceived by others.
- Understand how having high self-esteem can backfire.
- Understand how diversity, globalization, and new technologies are changing the ways we think about ourselves, others, and relationships.
- Understand the postmodern manager and implications for the managerial self-concept.
- Learn why it may be helpful to develop multiple selves rather have a solid, stable sense of self.

I've always wanted to be somebody.
Now I realize I should have been a little more specific.

—PLAYWRIGHT JANE WAGNER

The Search for Signs of Intelligent Life in the Universe

Self-awareness is a hallmark of effective managers. Successful managers know what they want, understand why they want it, and have a plan of action for getting it. They know how their styles, strengths, and weaknesses influence their ability to achieve their goals. They understand how they are perceived by others and how these perceptions affect their ability to gain support.[1] Also, they have a special combination of self-confidence, humility, and adaptability that enables them to appreciate the views and styles of others and to thrive in the ambiguous, imperfect, and often stressful world of management.

Walter Kiechel, columnist for *Fortune*, contrasts effective managers with what he calls "empty suits." He describes empty suits as having "much form, style and dress-for-success dash; little substance, skill or managerial accomplishment."[2] Although such managers emphasize form over substance and self-promotion over self-understanding, they are not necessarily without competence. Researcher David Campbell of the Center for Creative Leadership explains that some of these managers "might be bright and effective, but in a very predictable, very cubbyholed way,"[3] hardly a formula for success in today's complex and fast-changing environment. But it is not only empty suits who lack self-awareness.

Researchers Robert Kaplan, Wilfred Drath, and Joan Kofodimos studied "expansive executives" who, like empty suits, don't place self-awareness high on their list of leadership skills.[4] Unlike empty suits who look out for themselves, expansive executives are genuinely committed to the success of their organizations. They set high standards for their work and the work of others. They make heroic efforts to meet their own high standards, typically working longer and faster than others. Expansive executives tend to be very competent, ambitious, and successful in conventional terms—high salaries, high-level positions, and substantial organizational power. Yet, beneath their success lie serious problems.

According to Kaplan and his colleagues, expansive executives gain their sense of self-worth primarily through their unconscious needs for control, mastery, and professional success. They pursue these goals at all costs, often sacrificing their health and personal relationships. Despite these sacrifices, their goals are always beyond their reach. After all, total control is an illusion in today's complex and unpredictable environment, and mastery is fleeting in an era of rapid change. Consequently, expansive executives are always performing below the impossible standards they set for themselves, faithfully (and desperately) running a race that never ends and that they cannot win.

On the surface, it would seem that executives who set such high standards and endure such sacrifices would be beneficial to their organizations, but that is often not the case. Expansive executives are driven primarily by their unconscious needs for control, perfection, and status rather than the needs of the organization.[5] Despite their commitment to the success of the organization, their lack of self-awareness prevents them from seeing the consequences of their behavior. For example, they may become overly critical micromanagers who resist delegating to others, or they may avoid taking risks because it involves giving up the feelings of control that are so important to them.

> Mastery of others is strength; mastery of yourself is true power.
> —Lao-Tzu

Although empty suits and expansive executives are common in organizations, most managers are less extreme in their behaviors. Yet both empty suits and expansive executives hold important lessons for us all. Like empty suits and expansive executives, we are all, to some degree, unaware of how our ways of thinking, feeling, and behaving affect our decisions, actions, and relationships—and ultimately our personal well-being, professional effectiveness, and the success of our organizations. But the simple fact is that we can't manage others effectively unless we learn how to manage ourselves first.

BARRIERS TO SELF-AWARENESS

Unfortunately, lack of self-awareness may be an occupational hazard of managerial work. Long work hours and the fast pace of work make it difficult for managers to take time out for thoughtful self-reflection. Managers routinely face the pressures of tight deadlines, workflow interruptions, unexpected crises, and the threat of being "dejobbed". Although the ability to learn new ways of seeing, thinking, and behaving is most valuable during stressful periods, most managers' "ability to learn shuts down precisely at the moment they need it most."[6] Indeed, during times of stress, most people fall back on their habitual ways of thinking and acting, even though these probably contributed to their predicament in the first place.

In addition to job pressures, there are many other obstacles to managerial self-awareness. People typically get promoted to managerial positions because of their past achievements. Thus, a "leading reason for resisting attempts at inner-directed change is the fear of losing effectiveness by tampering with a 'winning formula.'"[7] Because of the status differences between managers and those who report to them, many managers do not make themselves accessible to the people who work for them. Even when they ask their direct reports for feedback, their direct reports may be hesitant to provide honest feedback, especially when that feedback is negative. Consequently, they are unlikely to receive useful advice and feedback from the people who are most affected by their behavior. Furthermore, managers "hire people in their own image" and are thus more likely to receive reinforcement for their decisions and actions rather than useful constructive criticism from those they hire.[8]

Managers' busy personal lives also leave little time for self-reflection. Although home life traditionally has been viewed as a retreat from job pressures, many managers today take their work home with them to keep up with the escalating work responsibilities. Many managers are also balancing the demanding schedules of dual (or triple) career couples, often while caring for dependent children and aging parents. Indeed, given the multiple pressures of coordinating and caretaking in the home, as well as the lack of immediate feedback (one doesn't know how well one is raising children until the children grow up), many managers find the workplace to be a welcome escape from the emotional and physical demands of home life.[9] As a colleague recently told me on a Monday morning, "I've had a very busy weekend at home and it's time for a work break."

Despite these hurdles to managerial self-awareness, many managers make good-faith efforts to increase their self-knowledge. Although some people are "developmental couch potatoes" who avoid the challenges of personal growth,[10] the proliferation of self-help books and professional development workshops suggest that many managers actively invest their time and money in their quest for self-understanding and personal growth. Steven Covey's book *The Seven Habits of Highly Effective People*, for example, has sold more than 15 million copies in 70 countries and is translated into 38 languages. The executive coaching business—designed to help managers better understand how their attitudes, thinking patterns, and interpersonal styles affect their well-being and professional effectiveness—is thriving. The International Coaching Federation has more than 10,000 members who offer coaching services, up from 1,500 in 1999. Annual worldwide revenue for the coaching industry exceeds $1 billion.[11]

THE BRAND CALLED YOU

Recently, management gurus have been advising professionals to think of themselves as a one-person enterprise for which they are their own CEOs.[12] Popular management author and consultant Tom Peters, in his classic and controversial Fast Company article called "The Brand Called You," boldly advises managers and professionals to know themselves, understand their customers, develop unique and marketable competencies that help them stand out from the crowd, reinvent themselves if necessary, and then package and sell their personal brand. "To be in business today," says Peters, "your most important job is to be head marketer for the brand called You. . . . You're every bit as much a brand as Nike, Coke, Pepsi, or the Body Shop."[13]

Seeing oneself as a unique, marketable, and portable product may be a reasonable survival strategy in an era in which the psychological contract between individuals and organizations no longer promises the security of lifetime employment. But seeing oneself as a product to be bought and sold may come with a price. It can leave one feeling alienated from one's self, estranged from others, and of questionable loyalty to one's current organization. In cultures that are based on an ideology of collectivism and loyalty to one's group and organization, promoting oneself can be a lonely, difficult, and ultimately unrewarding enterprise.

Whether you want to consider yourself a brand is, of course, your own decision, depending on whether you find this a compelling or distasteful idea. But one thing is certain. You should not assume that people will simply notice your hard work and contributions without some assistance from you. Frankly, if you have something of value to offer, you don't want to be the best-kept secret in your organization or profession. As a professional, it is your responsibility to help others place you where you can make your best contributions, and proactively letting others know where you can best add value is one way that you can do that. Says communications coach Peggy Klaus, "It's stunning to me how many people think that if they keep their heads down and work hard, their boss 'will just know' what they're contributing and how valuable they are, as if there were some kind of psychic connection there. . . . You have to let the people above you know what you're doing, what skills you're developing, which goals you're achieving. . . . Don't make them guess." And if you want to be noticed, be sure you notice others. Klaus also advises, "Listen [to others]. . . . Showing a genuine interest in other people's goals really floors them. . . . They're just not used to it."[14] Tom Peters suggests that you build your brand around the following questions:

- What do I do that I'm most proud of?
- What do I do that adds remarkable, measurable, distinguished, distinctive value?
- What do my colleagues and customers say is my greatest and clearest strength . . . [and] most noteworthy personal characteristic?
- What have I done lately—this week—that added value to the organization (and that was noticed by others)?
- In what ways is what I do difficult to imitate?

Peters also recommends that you become "a broad-gauged visionary" who understands the bigger issues, challenges, and opportunities that face your organization; anticipate problems before they become crises; become an expert in an area that is not easy to copy and that adds real value to the organization; be a dependable and supportive colleague and team member; think of your job as a compilation of distinct projects, each of which adds measurable value to the organization; consistently deliver high-quality work on time; and complete projects within or under budget. In short, your brand must have substance.[15]

The Internet has made it possible—even advantageous—to build your brand online as well. Increasingly, recruiters and college admissions personnel are going online to conduct background checks on potential employees and students. They search Google, Yahoo, Facebook, LinkedIn, Friendster, and other online sites to look for additional information about candidates, including "red flags" (e.g., inappropriate language or photos) that may suggest poor judgment, a lack of professionalism, or a lack of fit with the values of the organization. This "shadow resume," the information that recruiters and admissions personnel find online, can quickly override whatever you say on your resume and at your interview. The lesson here: Google yourself to see what others may see about you online and then build your online brand to be consistent with the image you want to project.[16]

As every manager who seeks self-awareness and professional development sooner or later realizes, there are no shortcuts. It takes commitment, time, and effort to identify your styles, strengths, and weaknesses and to build a reputation that will serve you, others, and the organization well. It's not easy to understand how you are perceived by others, nor is it easy to understand how these perceptions affect your ability to be effective and to bring out the best in others. There are many long and winding paths to personal and professional growth, and each comes with its own possibilities, limitations, and trade-offs.

What's a Well-Intentioned Manager to Do?

It's hard to imagine that our self-improvement efforts will be successful without considering what is this "self" that we want to develop. Most of us couldn't imagine trying to fix a car without understanding how it works, yet many of us routinely engage in self-development efforts without understanding how marvelously complex we are as human beings and how we got to be who we are. In the following sections, I define the self-concept, explore the many different ways that we develop our self-concept, and consider the kind of self-concepts that are most likely to enhance our professional effectiveness and personal well-being in today's diverse, global, fast-changing, and technologically driven organizational environment.

BOX 2-1   The Costs of High Self-Esteem

"Self-esteem" refers to one's general feelings about his or her self-worth. Many parents and teachers, particularly in the United States, have become preoccupied with the development and benefits of high self-esteem. They assume that the payoffs of high self-esteem include greater happiness, personal success, and contributions to one's organizations and communities. Many researchers, however, are challenging the widely held assumption that high self-esteem is inevitably a positive characteristic. People who have high self-esteem do tend to be happier, have more self-confidence, and expect to have a good future, in part because they have self-enhancing biases (e.g., they think they have more positive characteristics than have many others). But their high self-esteem doesn't necessarily translate into higher grades, more kindness toward others, better job performance, greater leadership ability, or positive citizenship behavior. Indeed, gang members often have high self-esteem, and they often pursue that self-esteem through destructive behaviors. Furthermore, compared with people with high self-esteem, people with low self-esteem are not more prone to behaviors that are destructive to oneself or others.

Researcher Jennifer Crocker and her colleagues argue that it's how one *pursues* self-esteem, rather than whether one has high or low self-esteem, that determines whether high self-esteem will benefit oneself, others, organizations, and one's communities. For example, if one overly attaches his or her self-worth to high academic achievement, looking good to others, or having abundant material success, these goals can backfire by creating excessive stress, physical problems, and even increased drug and alcohol use. People with these goals may use unethical or destructive means to achieve these goals. People may cheat on exams to do well at school, take drugs to maintain the high energy it may take to work excessive hours, get into extreme debt to obtain material possessions that are beyond their financial means, or sunbathe because they believe the tan will make them look good, despite ample medical evidence that doing so increases one's chances of getting cancer.

Notably, Crocker and her colleagues found that students who base their self-esteem on grades do not necessarily get better grades than those who do not, but they do tend to feel worse when they receive poor grades and show "greater drops in self-esteem, positive emotions, and more detachment from their majors when they received poor grades." Furthermore, researchers Harry Wallace and Roy Baumeister argue that high self-esteem can turn into narcissism, and some research suggests that narcissists are more likely to put considerable effort into highly visible projects in which their efforts will be admired by others, yet are more likely to reduce their effort when the spotlight isn't on them.

The lesson here is that if we want to achieve greater benefits and fewer costs associated with high self-esteem, we should focus not only on whether one has high or low self-esteem but also on how one pursues feelings of self-worth. Strategies based on achieving external standards, such as how one appears to others (grades, physical appearance, or material possessions), are less likely to bring benefits than are strategies based on contributing to others, living in accordance with personal values, and being able to control one's behaviors when these behaviors may be harmful to oneself or others.

Crocker and her colleague Lora Park remind well-intentioned parents and teachers that "attempts to raise children's self-esteem by teaching them that they are 'special,' 'fabulous,' or 'unique' may be teaching narcissism rather than self-worth and self-respect." Instead, achieving healthy self-esteem "requires the strong motivation that results from having goals that are larger than the self."

Sources: Bushman, Brad J., Roy Baumeister, Sander Thomaes, and Ehri Ryu. 2009. "Looking Again, and Harder, for a Link Between Low Self-Esteem and Aggression." *Journal of Personality*, 77(2): 427; Crocker, Jennifer, Amara Brook, Yu Niiya, and Mark Villacorta. 2006. "The Pursuit of Self-Esteem: Contingencies of Self Worth and Self-Regulation." *Journal of Personality*, 74(6): 1749; Crocker, Jennifer, Diane Quinn, Andrew Karpinski, and Sara Chase. 2003. "When Grades Determine Self-Worth: Consequences of Contingent Self-Worth for Male and Female Engineering and Psychology Majors." *Journal of Personality and Social Psychology*, 85(3): 507–516; Park, Lora, Jennifer Crocker, and Amy K. Keifer. 2007. "Contingencies of Self-Worth, Academic Failure, and Goal Pursuit." *Personality and Social Psychology Bulletin*, 33(11): 1503; Zhang, Liqing and Roy Baumeister. 2006. "Your Money or Your Self-Esteem: Threatened Egotism Promotes Costly Entrapment in Losing Endeavors." *Personality and Social Psychology Bulletin*, 32(7): 881. Wallace, Harry and Roy Baumeister. 2002. "The Performance of Narcissists Rises and Falls with Perceived Opportunity for Glory," *Journal of Personality and Social Psychology*, 82(5): 810–834

THE SELF-CONCEPT: I THINK, THEREFORE I THINK I AM

Researchers agree that individuals differ from each other in many ways, including (but not limited to) worldview, values, skills, abilities, learning styles, problem-solving styles, and interpersonal styles. Researchers disagree, however, about the degree to which these personality differences are created by nature or nurture. There is compelling and controversial evidence that certain characteristics, such as tendencies toward introversion and extroversion, conscientiousness, sociability, challenge seeking and risk aversion, optimism and pessimism, desire for dominance, resilience, and vulnerability to anxiety, may be influenced, in part, by our genetic programming. Yet despite considerable evidence that some tendencies may be partly inherited, researchers agree that our genes are not our destiny.[17] Whether genes account for 5% or 50% of our personality, that still leaves a large percentage of who we are and how we behave to be shaped by our experiences in our environments, how we make sense of our experiences (e.g., "Was my reluctance to network with others at the conference due to innate shyness or was it due to my lack of specific networking skills that I could learn if I tried?"), and our willingness to proactively create opportunities to learn new ways of thinking and behaving.[18]

In one study, for example, researchers taught a group of students that intelligence is influenced by the environment and that the brain develops new connections throughout life especially when faced with intellectual challenges. The students who were taught that intelligence can change with effort became significantly more conscientiousness (a characteristic that is thought to be influenced by genes) than did students who weren't taught that intelligence can change with effort. Researchers have also found that people can become more optimistic (another characteristic that is thought to be influenced by genes) by learning how to manage their beliefs and developing behaviors that enhance their optimism and happiness.[19]

Journalist Jason Zweig, writer of the Intelligent Investor column for the *Wall Street Journal,* wisely describes the link between nature and nurture in his article, "Is Your Investing

Personality in Your DNA?" Using DNA testing and brain scans, Zweig worked with a medical researcher to identify some of his genetic profile. Through these tests, he found he had genes that "dampened" his "fear circuitry," intensified his "reaction to the prospect of making money" and response to gambling," and increased his craving for "the immediate gratification of a quick profit" suggesting that he "may get an even more visceral rush out of making money than other investors do." However, his DNA and brain tests also showed that he was more fearful of loss than the average person and had, according to the doctor who did the testing, "Zen-like patience." Zweig explains how he developed his thoughtful and measured investing style:

> The contrast between the raw material of my genes and the final output of my behavior isn't usual. Perhaps about 20% of the variation in risk-taking among individuals is genetically determined; the rest comes from our upbringing, experience, education, and training. So, while my genes bias my brain toward spooking easily and trying to make a quick buck, that isn't how I actually behave. I hold investments for years, even decades. I don't panic in bear markets and bull markets make me uncomfortable. Those habits, I now understand, don't come naturally to me. I have been fighting my genes for years. . . . Growing up on a farm, with warm parents who knew a great deal about history, may have trained me to evaluate momentary changes in a longer-term context and to think twice before acting on gut feelings. From studying the writings and careers of Benjamin Graham and Warren Buffett, I learned to distrust the crowd and to remember that future returns depend on today's prices.[20]

An important lesson for you, of course, is to believe that genes are only one potential influence on a person's abilities and behaviors. You can develop deep changes in your fundamental belief systems and behavioral styles if you believe that such changes are possible, invest in developing new perspectives and skills, and put yourself in environments that help you learn new perspectives and behaviors that bring out the best in you and help you achieve your goals.

What Is the Self-Concept?

The self-concept is an internalized set of perceptions that each of us has about ourselves that are relatively stable over time, consistent across situations, resistant to change, and of central importance to us.[21] Our self-concept is made up of our beliefs about our personalities, values, interests, skills, strengths, weaknesses, what makes us similar to others, and what makes us unique. Our self-concept influences our everyday thoughts and actions, including how we see the world, what we perceive to be threats and opportunities, how we make decisions, how we cope with stress, how we define success, and how we behave toward others. Perhaps most important, our self-concept influences our fundamental beliefs about who we are, who we should be, who we can be, who we can never be, and who we are afraid of becoming.[22]

People seldom improve when they have no other model but themselves to copy themselves after.
—OLIVER GOLDSMITH,
Cited in www. greenleafenterprises. com/quotes/s.html

Our self-concept is, in large part, socially constructed throughout our lives in our families, schools, workplaces, communities, and other social institutions. These institutions socialize us into ways of thinking, feeling, and acting that enable us to function in ways that are considered natural, appropriate, and effective within our cultural contexts.[23]

In short, we develop our beliefs about who we are, who we should be, who we can be, and who we can never be through taken-for-granted social practices such as the media, language, norms, rituals, and reward and punishment systems (which may include formal means such as laws or informal means such as peer pressure).

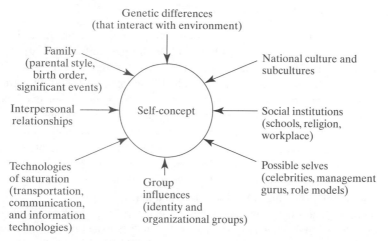

FIGURE 2-1 Influences on the Self-Concept

In the following sections, I discuss how our cultures, families, interpersonal relationships, and groups influence our self-concept and how our self-concept, in turn, influences our day-to-day feelings, thoughts, and actions. See Figure 2-1 for a summary of these influences on the self-concept.

CULTURAL INFLUENCES ON THE SELF-CONCEPT: THE INDEPENDENT AND INTERDEPENDENT SELF

If our self-concept is, in large part, socially and culturally determined, then it follows that our beliefs about the ideal self—and ideal manager—vary across cultures.[24] From the moment we are born and first reach out to other human beings, we begin the lifelong process of trying to make sense of ourselves, others, and our relationships. One of the most fundamental lifelong challenges we face is to reconcile our basic needs to be both connected to and separate from others, to be both "a part" of others and "apart" from others.[25] We learn how to reconcile these basic needs for separateness and connectedness through our informal cultural norms and formal cultural institutions. Different cultures provide their members with different ways to reconcile these needs. Some cultures (often labeled individualistic) emphasize independence from others, and other cultures (often labeled collectivist) emphasize interdependence with others. Each is described below.

> The most simple but powerful understanding of all is the understanding that every successful and happy "me" is dependent upon the establishment of an operationally sound, effective, and successful "us."
> —JAMES MUSGRAVE AND MICHAEL ANNISS, *Authors of Relationship Dynamics*

As you read the following sections, keep the following in mind: (1) The descriptions of independent and interdependent conceptions of the self do not imply that either one is better or worse than the other—simply different with different implications for how people think, feel, act, and interpret the behavior of others; (2) any references to national cultures are generalizations and not all people in a particular culture will reflect that culture's tendencies, in part because each nation has many subcultures; (3) descriptions of the independent and interdependent self are described as extremes on a continuum, although all individuals and nations have a blend of the characteristics of independent and interdependent self-concepts;[26] and (4) culture is one of many influences on the self-concept. Despite these caveats, the following descriptions are useful for understanding many subtle, yet significant, differences among people.

The Independent Self-Concept

You are what you think.
—Buddha

Cultures that promote an independent self-concept encourage individuals to see themselves as separate from others and be unique, self-sufficient, self-promoting, and, ideally, free from social constraints.[27] Cultures that favor an independent view of the self tend to value self-actualization and individual freedom over social obligations, personal rights over mutual obligations, and the pursuit of personal happiness over personal sacrifice.[28] An ideal life in these cultures is one in which one is able to be true to oneself, express oneself honestly to others, follow one's dream, aspire to be the best one can be, and achieve personal success and self-fulfillment. In individualistic cultures, people who fail to separate from others, who are easily influenced by others, who prefer to go unnoticed, and who don't stand out from the crowd are often encouraged to be more independent, think more for themselves, make themselves heard, and identify (and promote) their unique qualities.

In such cultures, one's behavior is assumed to be largely independent of outside influences such as the social and cultural context, driven instead by one's personality, internal motivations, and personal skills and abilities. Consequently, the "private self" ("Who am I and what do I need and want?") tends to be more developed and more complex than the "public self" ("What do other people think of me?") and the "collective self" ("I am a member of this community.").[29] People who emphasize the private self try to differentiate themselves from others in many ways, including through their clothing, material possessions, communication patterns, and other personal styles.[30]

Researchers Sheena S. Iyengar and Mark R. Lepper found in their studies of Anglo American and Asian American children that the Anglo American children (who tend to be influenced by independent cultures) were more likely to be motivated and perform better when they were able to make choices for themselves because, for them, "making a personal choice offers not only an opportunity to express and receive one's personal preference, but also a chance to establish one's unique self-identity." In contrast, the Asian American children (who tend to be influenced by interdependent cultures) were more likely to be motivated and perform better when they were given specific instructions (rather than personal choice) by "valued in-group members" (e.g., mother or peers) because, for them, following instructions from a trusted in-group member provided "a greater opportunity to provide harmony and to fulfill the goal of belonging to the group."[31]

In independent cultures, feelings of self-worth come from being able to express oneself and confirm that one has positive characteristics.[32] People from such cultures tend to have what is called a "uniqueness bias."[33] They tend to see their strengths as unique talents ("I received a top grade on the exam because I'm smart.") and their weaknesses as common limitations that are shared by others or as caused by external factors such as poor training, problematic team members, or ineffective management ("I did poorly on the exam because the professor is a poor teacher."). People from cultures that promote an independent sense of self also tend to have what is called a "self-enhancement bias" in which they tend to see themselves as better than the average person on important positive characteristics such as intelligence, motivation, or interpersonal skills. In one study, for example, more than 50% of a sample of North American college undergraduates reported that they were in the top 10% in "intergroup sensitivity."[34] It should come as no surprise that many management development programs in the United States refer to personal "weaknesses" as "developmental opportunities," which is a more palatable phrase in a culture that promotes self-enhancement.

Recent research suggests that people from independent cultures are more likely to believe that talking out loud is a positive act because it is a form of individual expression. They also are more likely to believe that talking out loud is associated with thinking and learning. In contrast, people from interdependent cultures are more likely to believe that one may think and learn better while staying silent. For example, in one study, researcher Heejung S. Kim found that thinking out loud while trying to solve reasoning problems hampered Asian Americans' performance but did not affect the performance of European Americans. This difference in perceptions is important because a person who believes that talking is related to thinking may misinterpret silence as a lack of interest or motivation rather than a problem-solving strategy that can enhance a person's performance. And someone who believes that one can solve problems better when one is concentrating silently may think that people who talk while they are solving problems may be immature, distracting, and unfocused.[35]

Why are some cultures more individualistic than others? Research suggests that cultures that have significant affluence, diversity, and mobility are more likely than others to promote an independent self-concept. Affluence decreases one's dependence on others. Acceptance of diversity enables one to belong to multiple groups and reduces one's dependence on any one group. And mobility (such as moving geographically away from family and friends to take new jobs) requires self-reliance and the willingness to psychologically and physically join and leave groups quickly.[36]

The Interdependent Self-Concept

Cultures that promote an interdependent self-concept encourage individuals to fit in with others, to attend to the needs of others, and to create and fulfill mutual obligations. People with an interdependent self-concept tend to be motivated by a desire to be connected to others and a willingness to sacrifice their own needs, wants, and opportunities for the welfare of the groups to which they belong. In such cultures, fundamental values are belonging, reciprocity, empathy, dependence on others, group cohesion, interpersonal harmony, and occupying one's proper place. In Japan, for example, where connectedness to the group is central to one's identity and sense of self-worth, the word for "self" is "jibun," which refers to "one's share of the shared life space."[37]

People with an interdependent self-concept are likely to be uncomfortable when they feel disconnected from others, stand out from the group, are inattentive to the needs of others, act in ways that are inappropriate for their social role, and fail to fulfill their social obligations. Maturity in these cultures is seen as the ability to voluntarily control one's personal emotions, needs, and goals to advance significant relationships and the community as a whole. It is viewed as immature and irresponsible to express oneself freely without considering the needs of others or the social context. Thus, in these cultures, the public self ("What do other people think of me?") and collective self ("I am a member of this community.") tend to be more developed and complex than the private self ("Who am I, and what do I need and want?").[38] Consequently, people from collectivist cultures are likely to develop a wide range of skills that enable them to fit in with others and focus on the overall success of the groups to which they belong. These skills include the willingness to pay attention to others, the perceptual acuity to notice subtle patterns and changes in behaviors and social contexts, and the insight to interpret and respond to these subtle cues in socially appropriate ways.

People from interdependent cultures tend to derive feelings of self-worth from their ability to control themselves in social situations, maintain harmony, and adjust and contribute to the group.[39] Research suggests that although people from individualistic cultures tend to have uniqueness and self-enhancement biases, people from

You don't want to be the fattest pig in the pen. You will be the first to be slaughtered.

—INDIAN PROVERB

collectivist cultures are more likely to have self-critical and self-improvement biases. In other words, they are more likely to attribute their success to luck or the effort of the group as a whole ("I received a high grade because I had a great study group.") and to attribute their weaknesses to a lack of personal ability or talent ("I received a poor grade because I didn't study hard enough.").[40] In collectivist cultures, this self-critical bias serves several purposes. By focusing on fixing their personal shortcomings, group members work toward improving the overall capability of the group.[41] In addition, by taking personal responsibility for errors, they enable other group members to save face, and by doing so, show loyalty to the group and enhance their relationship to the group.

Certainly, people from all cultures recognize that individual and collective survival depends on both independence and interdependence. We all know that there are times when we must do things ourselves and times when we must depend on the group. However, cultures differ in the degree to which they emphasize one over the other. For example, people from Western nations are more likely to emphasize an independent self-concept. People from Eastern societies are more likely to emphasize an interdependent self-concept. Researchers Hazel Markus and Shinobu Kitayama describe this difference as follows: "In America, the squeaky wheel gets the grease" and in Japan, "The nail that sticks out gets pounded down."[42]

Table 2-1 summarizes differences between independent and interdependent self-concept. You can take the "Twenty Questions: I Am" assessment in Box 2-5 at the end of this chapter to better understand your own orientation toward independence or interdependence.

TABLE 2-1	**Differences Between the Independent and Interdependent Self-Concept**	
Feature Compared	**Independent**	**Interdependent**
Relationship to others	Separate	Connected
Focus	Internal, private self (e.g., own thoughts, feelings, and behavior)	External, public self (e.g., status in group, roles, relationships)
Personal goals	To be unique, express oneself, promote own needs	To belong, conform, occupy one's place, promote others' needs
Basis of self-esteem	Ability to understand, express, and validate one's self	Ability to understand and adjust to others, control oneself, maintain harmony
Types of emotions	Self-focused emotions (e.g., pride, anger, frustration)	Other-focused emotions (e.g., shame, sympathy, interpersonal connectedness)
How emotions are expressed	Publicly expressed	Emotions that may negatively affect relationships are kept private
Credit for success and blame for failure	Self-serving bias: takes the credit for success and blames others or the situation for failure	Other-serving bias: gives the group credit for one's success and takes personal responsibility for failure
Self-expression	Confidently display and express one's own strengths (e.g., self-enhancement and self-promotion)	Show humility and modesty (e.g., self-critical and self-improvement)

Source: Adapted from Markus, Hazel, and Shinobu Kitayama. 1991. "Culture and the Self: Implications for Cognition, Emotion, and Motivation." *Psychological Review,* 98(2): 224–253.

Advantages of a Cultural View of the Self-Concept

In today's diverse and global economic environment, a cultural perspective on the self-concept has many advantages for managerial effectiveness. A cultural perspective:

- encourages us to look outward to our cultures in order to better understand who we are and how we got to be that way, which gives us a more complex understanding of ourselves and others;
- makes us more inclined to try to understand and respond to others on their terms rather than as variations of or deviations from ourselves, which makes us better able to create relationships based on mutual understanding and respect;
- broadens our ways of thinking about what constitutes normal and effective behavior, which expands our ways of seeing the world and our repertoire of behaviors;
- enables us to be wise consumers of managerial knowledge because we become more skeptical of "one-size-fits-all" theories and best practices;
- enables us to implement management practices that are respectful of the ways of thinking, feeling, and acting that are considered normal and effective in the particular culture in which we are working at any given time, thus increasing our individual and organizational effectiveness.

For example, individual empowerment programs that are highly acclaimed in the United States may not work in all cultures (and don't always work in the United States, either).[43] Empowerment may be more desirable in cultures that promote an independent self-concept that emphasizes individual choice, personal control, and equality over hierarchy. Yet empowerment programs based on individualism may be less desirable in cultures that promote a collectivist orientation, which emphasizes adherence to the established order and dependence on authority figures (the boss) rather than equality. Certainly, empowerment programs may work in collectivist cultures, but the success of these programs depends on the degree to which managers consider the cultural context and integrate cultural values, beliefs, and norms when designing, implementing, and evaluating these programs.

Remember that cultures are constantly changing. As people from one culture are exposed to other cultures, they inevitably compare their own perceptions of the world and cultural norms with those of others. People from younger generations typically grow up more exposed to outside cultures than did their parents and are more likely to be influenced by cultures outside their own. It's important to remember that you cannot predict anyone's behavior simply based on their culture because there are many influences that shape a person's worldview and behavior. The main value of a cultural view of the self is that it expands our assumptions about what is normal human behavior, helps us accept and learn from other whose norms are different from our own, and enables us to be wiser and more effective world citizens.

SOCIAL INFLUENCES ON THE SELF-CONCEPT: SEEING OURSELVES AS OTHERS SEE US

Our self-concept is developed, sustained, and changed through our day-to-day interactions with others.[44] Each time we interact with people who are significant to us—parents, children, friends, partners, spouses, teachers, students, colleagues, bosses, direct reports—they send us signals about how they perceive us. These signals may be descriptive ("You completed the task on time and under budget.") or evaluative ("You have the skills to be an excellent manager."). Consciously and unconsciously, we interpret their words, tone of voice, gestures, and body language to make inferences about whether they see us as interesting ("Is that a yawn I see?"), competent ("Why did she ignore my last comment?"), worthy ("Why didn't the boss return my phone call?"), and influential ("Why wasn't I invited to the meeting?"). The signals we receive from others, as well as our interpretations of these signals, affect our perceptions of ourselves. As organizational scholar Karl Weick explains: "How can I know who I am until I see what they do?"[45]

Family Influences on the Self-Concept

Our early relationships within our families significantly influence our self-concept. Childhood experiences within our families—particularly parental style, pleasurable family experiences, early losses and tragedies, birth order, and sibling relationships—influence many aspects of our self-concept, including our sense of competence, feelings of belonging, and willingness to trust ourselves and others. For example, through our early social interactions within our families, we determine whether we can depend on others or must be self-reliant, whether emotional attachments are fulfilling or threatening, and whether the authority figures in our lives will be benevolent or harsh. The degree to which parents show love and affection (whether they are accessible or distant, whether love is unconditional or conditional), how they discipline their children (whether they are authoritarian, democratic, or hands-off), and the moral lessons they pass on to their children through words and deeds (whether they treat all people as equals or treat some people better than others) powerfully influence the development of their children's self-concept and their behavior as adults.

Parental Style

Jack Welch, former CEO of General Electric, attributes much of his success to his late mother:

> Like I've said many times, my mother was the greatest leadership teacher I ever had, even though she was never in a formal leadership position herself. (The truth was, she did 'run' the neighborhood). My mother taught me about unconditional love and, at the same time, set very tough standards for achievement. That combination . . . brought out the best in me, and I used it myself to bring out the best in others.[46]

Rajat Gupta, current special advisor on management reforms to the secretary general of the United Nations and former worldwide managing director of McKinsey & Co, discussed the importance of his father's teachings about Hinduism's karma yoga:

> "You have a right only to work, never to the results of that work." To me that means that not only must you do the right thing, but you must do it with the right motives. And you must always do your very best. It was my father who first taught me this idea. He never worried about what the results would be but always did the right thing. If I was disappointed about something, he would ask only: " Did you do your best?"[47]

Carol Bartz, CEO of Yahoo, described how her grandmother's teachings about self-reliance influenced her current leadership style:

> I grew up in the Midwest. My mom died when I was 8, so my grandmother raised my brother and me. She had a great sense of humor, and she never really let things get to her. My favorite story is when we were on a farm in Wisconsin; I would have probably been 13. There was a snake up in the rafter of the machine shed. And we ran and said, "Grandma, there's a snake." And she came out and she knocked it down with a

shovel, chopped its head off and said, "You could have done that." And, you know, that's the tone she set. Just get it done. Just do it. Pick yourself up. Move on.[48]

Ann Fudge, former CEO of advertising giant Young & Rubicam, attributes her stellar success as an African American woman, in part, to having had strong parental role models (her mother worked as a manager at the National Security Agency and her father worked with the U.S. Postal Service) and a tight and supportive community when she was growing up that outweighed the societal messages of racism.[49]

Early Losses

For some people, the early loss of a parent or other family tragedy can create a drive to succeed. People who lose a parent at a young age may believe that their life, too, may be cut short and may strive to achieve as much as they can early in life. Their sense of security may be shaken and they may want to achieve financial success for the security it can offer. They may want to live up to their perceptions of the lost parent's expectations or they may want to "right a wrong" by making a mark on the world in memory of the people who can no longer do so themselves. And they may develop characteristics such as compassion, resiliency, and risk taking that help them persist in the face of personal hardship.

In an interview, U.S. President Barack Obama acknowledged the influence of his mother, whom he believed was the "dominant influence in his life," by saying "the values she taught me continue to be my touchstone when it comes to how I go about the world of politics." His father left the family when Obama was two years old and died when Obama was 21 years old. Obama described how the loss of his father influenced him:

> I think that maybe having an absent father meant also that . . . you have to grow up faster, you feel . . . that you need to take responsibility and make sure that you're able to solve problems and step into the breach because there's nobody other than you who's going to solve them.[50]

Investing wholeheartedly in work can help some people cope with loss. At age 13, Morrison and Foerster Law Firm partner Linda Shostake lost her mother to cancer. Says Shostake, "I just immersed myself in my work so I didn't have to think about it . . . On the one side I developed an incredible work ethic, but I also compartmentalized my emotions. Yet I know I am not alone. When I went to Harvard Law, only a handful of women were graduates, and the majority had only one parent. I never believed that was a coincidence."[51]

Birth Order

Researchers debate whether birth order has a significant influence on personality. Those who support the view that birth order influences personality believe that the order in which one is born into a family (e.g., first born, second born, last born) influences the investments parents make in each child. These investments include affection, financial resources, and time to spend with each child. After the first child is born, each additional child stretches the parents' resources, and each child adopts different strategies to compete for these resources. Consequently, each child carves out a unique place for themselves in the family dynamics and develops personality characteristics that support their place in the family. The role each child takes in the family in their younger years influences their outlook and behaviors throughout their lives.[52]

For example, science historian and former MacArthur Fellow Frank Sulloway makes the controversial argument that birth order (whether we are born first, second, third, etc.) significantly influences our personalities, particularly with regard to whether we are likely to become conservative or radical, leaders or innovators. He contends that firstborns try to earn their parents' attention by following the rules and, thus, are more likely to become rule followers (conservative) when they grow up. Laterborns try to earn their parents' attention (which is now more scarce because it is divided among more than one child) by rebelling against these rules and, thus, are more likely to become more rebellious when they grow up.[53] Says Sulloway:

> [M]ost individual differences in personality, including those that underlie the propensity to rebel, arise within the family. . . . Siblings raised together are almost as different in their personalities as people from different families. . . . It is natural for firstborns to identify more strongly with power and authority. They arrive first within the family and employ their superior size and strength to defend their special status. Relative to their younger siblings, firstborns are more assertive, socially dominant, ambitious, jealous of their status, and defensive. As underdogs within the family system, younger siblings are inclined to question the status quo and in some cases to develop a "revolutionary personality." In the name of revolution, laterborns have repeatedly challenged the time-honored assumptions of their day.[54]

Of course, Sulloway's theory is much more complex and controversial than is represented here. Other researchers have found little or no influence of birth order on personality and behavior. They argue that it is too difficult to separate the effects of birth order from other factors that influence the dynamics of family life, including parental income, age of parents at a child's birth, parental education, spacing between births, and the role of adoptions.[55]

The useful point to take away from this section is that family dynamics and the early lessons we learn about our place in the world may continue to get unconsciously played out throughout our lives in our personal and professional roles as friends, partners, spouses, colleagues, bosses, and direct reports. If you understand how your family dynamics may have influenced your beliefs, values, and behaviors, then you can leverage those that are serving you well and work to change those that may be holding you back.

Other People's Expectations of Our Self-Concept

People's expectations of us can powerfully influence our self-concept. For example, our sense of competence tends to rise or fall in accordance with other people's expectations, a phenomenon that is referred to as the self-fulfilling prophecy. In the 1960s, researchers Robert Rosenthal and Lenore Jacobson conducted one of the most well-known studies of the self-fulfilling prophecy. They wanted to determine whether a teacher's expectations of students could influence the students' performance on cognitive tests. They randomly selected 20% of the children in the teachers' classes and told the teachers that these children showed "unusual potential for intellectual growth." At the end of the school year, these randomly chosen students showed greater improvement on cognitive test scores than did the other children.

The teachers did not know that these students were randomly chosen. Furthermore, they were told not to say anything to the students or the students' parents about their perceived superior intellectual potential. What, then, made the difference in the students' performance? The researchers concluded that "the change in the teachers' expectations regarding the intellectual performance of these allegedly 'special' children had led to an actual change in the intellectual performance of these randomly selected children."[56] Because the teachers had high expectations of the "high-potential" students, they gave them subtle but powerful cues that enhanced the students' actual performance, including more positive responses, more challenging work, and more feedback.

This study powerfully illustrates how people's expectations for another person's behavior can result in a self-fulfilling prophecy in which the person begins to act as expected, for better or worse. It is not surprising that managers, through their expectations and the subtle (and not-so-subtle) assumptions about and behaviors toward others, may influence the effectiveness of others.

Group Influences on the Self-Concept

Our group memberships also shape our developing self-concept. We all belong to many identity groups (e.g., gender, race, nationality, and religion) and organizational groups (e.g., profession, organization, and hierarchical level).[57] Through socialization within our groups, we come to believe that our groups are distinctive and meaningful, become emotionally attached to our groups, and learn to take on many of the values, perspectives, and behaviors that we believe are characteristic of our groups.[58]

Our group memberships affect us in several ways. We tend to see ourselves as having more in common with people from our identity and organizational groups than with other people. We also tend to see people from our own groups as more competent and trustworthy. Consequently, we may be more cooperative, empathic, and trusting toward them. Depending on the degree to which we feel emotionally connected to our groups, we may actively advocate on their behalf, as women and African Americans did so passionately (together with many men and non-African Americans) during the women's and civil rights movements in the United States in the 1960s.[59] Indeed, our identity and organizational group members may expect us to act on behalf of the group and may be disappointed with us when we do not do so.

Even if we do not have a sense of connection to a particular social or organizational group, we may be seen by others as having more in common with people from our identity and organizational groups than with people from other groups. For example, we may expect people from North America to be assertive, people from Japan to be team oriented, and engineers to be logical. Consequently, even if we don't feel attached to a particular group, other people may see us as members of that group and encourage us to behave in ways that reinforce their perceptions and stereotypes of those groups.

In short, our group memberships influence our self-concept by (1) our personal regard for and loyalty to our groups, (2) internal group pressure to conform, and (3) external pressures to conform to what are perceived by others as our group memberships.

WHY THE SELF-CONCEPT IS IMPORTANT

Our self-concept is important because it is one of the factors that influence how we think, feel, and act in everyday organizational life. Understanding the self-concept is particularly important for managers because self-knowledge helps managers understand why they do the things they do and how their beliefs, decisions, and behaviors affect themselves, others, and the organization—for better and worse.[60] Specifically, the self-concept influences the following:

> Not only do we see different things, but we see the same things differently.
> —MIHNEA MOLDOVEANU AND ELLEN LANGER, *Social Pychologists*

- *Attention.* Our self-concept acts like a filter that lets some information in and keeps other information out. We tend to notice things that are important to our self-concept, things that are novel, and things that challenge our self-concept.[61] In addition, we are more likely to "see and find sensible those things [we believe we] can do something about."[62]

- *Memory and speed of attention.* We tend to remember and process information that is consistent with our self-concept more quickly. For example, in one study, individuals were asked to read a story that was congruent with high Machiavellianism (a tendency to be "opportunistic, manipulative, and motivated by a need for power"). People who rated themselves high on a Machiavellianism scale read the story more quickly than did people who rated themselves low on the Machiavellianism scale.[63]

- *Interpretations and decision making.* Our self-concept provides us with a frame of reference for making sense of what we notice. It affects whether we interpret who and what we see as relevant or irrelevant, interesting or boring, and threatening or opportune. It provides us with the logic we use to understand our world, particularly the categories we use to organize our world and the connections we make among these categories. Researcher Celia Harquail explains: "For example, to a Muslim diplomat choosing a menu for a state dinner, a categorization system that distinguishes among Jews, Christians, and Muslims and thus distinguishes among religious dietary restrictions will be more appropriate for her situation than a system which categorizes diplomats, politicians, and journalists."[64]

- *Social relations.* Our self-concept significantly influences who we view as similar to and different from us, who we judge as trustworthy and competent, and who we seek out and who we avoid. Consequently, it affects the breadth, diversity, and quality of our network of relationships. It also affects our assumptions about how we should relate to others and how we handle important interpersonal challenges of the managerial job such as cooperation and competition, power and influence, and authority and delegation.

- *Moral decision making.* Our self-concept influences our assumptions about what is right and wrong, what is ethical and unethical, and how we should resolve moral dilemmas. The research of psychologist Carol Gilligan and her colleagues suggests that people who emphasize an independent self-concept are more likely to make moral decisions on the basis of a universal set of standards of right and wrong. In other words, they are likely to believe that the same set of rules should apply to all people, regardless of the circumstances. For example, someone with an independent self-concept may feel that all people who come to work late, regardless of the reasons, should be subject to the same penalty. In contrast, people who emphasize an interdependent self-concept are more likely to make moral decisions in response to the particular person and circumstances involved.[65] From this perspective, whether one is penalized for coming in late depends on the reason for being late. Someone who overslept may be penalized, whereas someone who was caring for a sick parent may be given an opportunity to make up for the lost time rather than be penalized.

- *Ability to cope with stress.* Our self-concept helps us deal with the challenges of managerial work. A healthy self-concept gives us the psychological resources we need to find meaning among the chaos, complexity, and contradictions of contemporary organizational life; a sense of identity in a vast and largely anonymous world; confidence during times of change; integrity during periods of moral ambiguity and ethical temptation; and effective coping strategies, including a sense of personal control that enables us to take proactive and organized action during stressful times.[66]

In short, our self-concept is important because it significantly influences our effectiveness in our managerial and professional roles. It shapes what we notice and ignore, how we interpret what we notice, how we make decisions, how we manage our work relationships, how we make moral decisions, and how we cope with the ambiguity and complexity of organizational life.

THE SELF IN CONTEMPORARY ORGANIZATIONS

Regardless of our culture or the defining issues of our time, we all share five fundamental needs: the need to find meaning in our lives, the need to belong, the need to feel competent, the need for control, and the need for consistency.

Meaning

We all need to make sense of ourselves, the world, and our place in it. We all strive to answer the questions "Who am I?", "What is true and real?", "What are my values?", "What is worth doing?", and "What are my goals?" The need to find meaning in our life is particularly important during difficult times of disruption, change, and loss.[67]

Belonging

We all need to be appreciated not only for what we do but for who we are. As social beings, we want to create and maintain "lasting, positive, and significant interpersonal relationships" that are characterized by mutual caring, emotional connection, and frequent interaction.[68] Our effectiveness and well-being depend on our ability to form what the late psychiatrist John Bowlby called "a secure base," unconditional emotional attachments to others, which enable us to go out into the world knowing that we will be welcomed home again, where we will be "nourished physically and emotionally, comforted if distressed, reassured if frightened." Paradoxically, our ability to become independent and self-reliant in a healthy way depends, in part, on whether or not we have developed a secure base of attachment that enables us to trust both ourselves and others. Consequently, a sense of belonging may be particularly critical in an age in which one must take personal responsibility for proactively managing his or her career.[69]

Competence

We all need to feel competent at something that we value. This need to believe that we are capable of successfully performing the tasks that are important to achieving our goals and influencing our environments is called the "self-efficacy" motive. Our work and achievements are important to us because they help us define our identity, build our self-confidence, and develop a skill-set that matters to ourselves and others.[70]

Control

We all need to believe that we have some control over our lives. Research suggests that having a sense of control over our work gives us a sense of ownership of our work, inspires us to be more problem focused and proactive in solving work problems, and enhances our work satisfaction and our health.[71]

Consistency

We all need to believe that the world is coherent, orderly, and bounded and that tomorrow will be somewhat similar to today. A consistent and predictable environment helps us have an impact on our environment by enabling us to learn from our experiences, understand cause-and-effect relationships, identify deviations from the norm, anticipate situations, process information efficiently, make decisions quickly, develop shared understandings, and build connections with others that enhance coordination.[72]

BOX 2-2   Clean Homes, Organization, and Success

Does a sense of order early in life predict success later in life? A study of 3,395 young adults conducted by researchers at the Institute for Social Research at the University of Michigan suggests that it does. The researchers found that young adults who grew up in orderly households tended to stay in school longer and earn more money than did those who grew up in less orderly households. After controlling for parental education, income, socioeconomic background, cognitive ability, and other factors, the researchers found that the children who grew up in homes that were rated "clean" to "very clean" completed an average of 13.6 years of school and earned an average of $14.17 as young adults, compared with 12 years of school and $12.60 an hour for those whose childhood homes were rated as "not very clean" to "dirty." Why this difference? Researcher Rachel Dunifon explains, "Parents who keep their homes clean may be more organized and efficient than others and these characteristics may carry over to other aspects of their lives such as parenting. . . . Keeping a clean and organized home reflects an overall ability and desire to maintain a sense of order in a wide range of life activities. . . . These are qualities that also seem to be important in predicting intergenerational success."

Source: Dunifon, Rachel, Greg. J. Duncan, and Jeanne Brooks-Gun.2004. "The Long-Term Impact of Parental Organization and Efficiency." In Kalil, A., and T. DeLaire (eds.). *Family Investments in Children: Resources and Behaviors That Promote Success.* Mahway, NJ: Lawrence Erlbaum, 85–118.

In short, when our basic needs for meaning, belonging, competence, control, and consistency are fulfilled, we believe that what we do matters and that we can proactively influence our environments. We have the confidence that helps us achieve the competence that enables us to do what we do well, and we are able to build trust in ourselves and others that enables us to work both independently and collectively, as appropriate, to achieve important goals in life and work.

Managers who understand these fundamental human needs will be better able to create relationships and work environments that support these needs. By doing so, they will be more likely to create a workplace that brings out the best in themselves, others, and their organizations.

The Challenges for Managers Today

Profound societal changes—including new technologies, globalization, and the increasingly diverse workforce—are challenging our feelings of belonging, competence, control, and consistency as well as our ability to make sense of ourselves, the world, and our place in it. These changes are also fundamentally shifting the means by which we construct our self-concept. As mentioned earlier in this chapter, we develop our beliefs about who we are and who we should be in large part through our families, neighborhoods, group memberships, and stable cultural institutions such as our schools, religious institutions, and work organizations. However, today's families come in many forms, our neighborhood is a global village that often connects through cyberspace, and many of us identify with an increasing number of groups. Furthermore, our cultural institutions are mired in heated debates about who does and doesn't belong, the standards for excellence, and the truths and moral foundations upon which social institutions should be built.

These changes in the social context in which we construct our identities are due, in large part, to the rapid development of new technologies throughout the past century. Psychologist Kenneth Gergen,[73] in his book, *The Saturated Self: Dilemmas of Identity in Everyday Life*, explains:

> As a result of advances in radio, telephone, transportation, television, satellite transmission, computers, and more, we are exposed to an enormous barrage of social stimulation. Small and enduring communities, with a limited cast of significant oth-

ers, are being replaced by a vast and ever-expanding array of relationships. . . . [T]his massive increment in social stimulation—moving toward a state of saturation—sets the stage for both radical changes in our daily experiences of self and others. . . . Beliefs in the true and good depend on a reliable and homogeneous group of supporters who define what is the reliable "there," plain and simple. With social saturation, the coherent circles of accord are demolished, and all beliefs thrown into question by one's exposure to multiple points of view.[74]

Cars, trains, airplanes, telephones, smart phones, radio, television, movies, commercial publishing, the Internet, and other technologies are bringing us all closer to each other, faster and more often, and exposing us to new perspectives, choices, and ways of acting. These communication, information, and transportation technologies result in what Gergen calls "social saturation"—personal feelings of overload and confusion as well as excitement and opportunity. Of course, everyone is not equally affected by technologies of saturation. Some of us are affected more, some less, yet few of us can escape the effects of social saturation though technology altogether. Consequently, we all need to consider how information, communication, transportation, and other technologies influence our sense of ourselves, as well as the means by which we construct our identities. We also need to consider what kind of self-concept can enhance our managerial effectiveness and psychological well-being in a global, diverse, and technologically driven social and economic environment. To arrive at some answers to these questions, let us focus on two technological forces that are profoundly affecting our identities: the Internet and the mass media.

Identity in the Age of the Internet

In her compelling book *Life on the Screen: Identity in the Age of the Internet*, Massachusetts Institute of Technology sociologist Sherry Turkle argues that the Internet has become a "gateway of communication" through which we are redefining human identity and relationships. Through the Internet, we can converse with people we may never meet face-to-face, take on multiple identities, participate in virtual communities, and "form on-line relationships that can be more intense than real ones."[75]

Ego surfing: Scanning the Internet to find references to one's own name.

Turkle argues further that increasingly we are using the computer as a flexible toy to experiment, play, and learn with, not as a rigid machine that requires sophisticated technical expertise. Indeed, most of us don't try to decipher the detailed and complex technical manuals that come with our computers. Rather, we are more likely to solve our computing problems by talking to friends and colleagues, experimenting, and improvising solutions as we go along.

Turkle uses the term "bricolage" to characterize online tinkering with the computer and Internet environment. People who engage in bricolage challenge the belief that there is one true way to think about problems and that step-by-step logic is the quickest and most effective way to solve them. Bricoleurs play with the different conceptual and material resources they have, combining them in different ways—often by trial and error—to see what happens. Bricoleurs are sophisticated, experienced "problem-solvers who do not proceed from top–down design but by arranging and rearranging a set of well-known materials."[76]

Through video games, we can create new identities for ourselves, connect to others who have created online identities, enact everyday actions and life events, and design the spaces in which we can live out these actions and events. Some researchers suggest that playing such video games may enhance children's information processing and problem-solving capabilities. Playing video games like "The Sims" encourages children to plan ahead and make thoughtful decisions by anticipating the many possible outcomes of their decisions, tinker with the online characters and environment, evaluate the outcomes (as well as unintended consequences) of their choices, and design their next steps in response to what they have learned.[77] To illustrate the use of bricolage in cyberspace, Turkle describes multiuser domains (MUDs) in which people jointly create virtual spaces with virtual characters whose virtual lives are entwined in virtual ongoing sagas that engage the mind with real problems and evoke real emotions. She explains:

> MUDs are a new kind of virtual parlor game and a new form of community. In addition, text-based MUDs are a new form of collaboratively written literature. MUD players are MUD authors, the creators as well as consumers of media content. In this, participating in a MUD has much in common with script writing, performance art, street theater, improvisational theater—or even commedia dell'arte. But MUDs are something else as well.
>
> As players participate, they become authors not only of text but of themselves, constructing new selves through social iteration. . . . The anonymity of MUDs—one is known on the MUD only by the name of one's character or characters—gives people the chance to express multiple and often unexplored aspects of the self, to play with their identity and to try out new ones.[78]

One does not have to participate in MUDs to experience how cyberspace is influencing everyday life. E-mail, Facebook, LinkedIn, and Twitter enable us to create and sustain relationships with a broader and more diverse range of people than ever before possible, and to do so faster, from any place, in real or delayed time. As our personal networks change, our self-concept may change as well.

Self-knowledge comes too late and by the time I've known myself I am no longer what I was.
—ADEMOLA REFLECTIONS: NIGERIAN PROSE AND VERSE

When we tinker with life on the screen, we also tinker with our selves, our relationships, and the actual worlds in which we live and work. As we pretend to be someone else on the screen, we may get a better view of who we are and who we could be. As we reach out to others around the world, we expose ourselves to different worldviews and ways of acting in the world and often change ourselves in the process. As we create and participate in virtual communities, we consider how we can use what we learn from our virtual communities to create new kinds of relationships, organizations, and societies.

As we make information and communication available to more people in more places, we challenge traditional bases of power in organizations and societies. Computer-savvy 12-year-olds often have faster access to more people and information than seasoned 50-year-old executives. Someone who is silenced in one's home, workplace, or country can send a message to thousands of people in seconds and be heard around the world. And people learn that they can do the impossible, as a father in China learned when his son, Shao-Shao, was born with a congenital heart defect. Doctors in China told him that his son's heart condition was incurable and that the child would die. The father posted a message on a Web page created in Sweden by a human rights activist, asking for assistance, saying, "To all the kind people of the world, please help me save my son." A woman in the United States responded and enlisted others on the Web to find a physician to donate surgery for the child; raised $100,000 in donations to help the family with expenses; and found a family to host Shao-Shao and his parents during the successful surgery and recuperation period.

Certainly, life on the screen has both risks as well as rewards. After analyzing over 50 studies about the impact of television, computers, the Internet, and video games on learning, UCLA researcher Patricia Greenfield concluded that time spent on the screen has both positive and negative consequences. She found that the increase in the use of these technologies appears to have improved visual skills and the ability to multitask. For example, Greenfield described one study in which surgeons' "video game skill predicted laparoscopic surgery skills . . . . The best video game players made 47 percent fewer errors and performed 39 percent faster in laparoscopic tasks than the worst video game players."

Greenfield also found that as the use of these technologies have increased, skills associated with critical thinking, analysis, and retaining knowledge have decreased. In one study, students who were allowed to use the Internet in class performed worse when tested on the class lectures than did students who did not have access to the Interent during class. Greenfield noted that the use of print media (e.g., reading books for pleasure), which has been on the decline, improves imagination, critical thinking, and vocabulary. She also cited research that concluded that video games that contain violence can increase aggressive behavior and decrease sensitivity to real violence.

Greenfield concluded that "No one medium is good for everything. . . . If we want to develop a variety of skills, we need a balanced media diet. Each medium has costs and benefits in terms of what skills each develops."[79] As we continue to use various technologies for communication, learning, and entertainment throughout our lives, we'll undoubtedly continue to change ourselves, relationships, organizations, and societies in the process.

Identity in the Age of Mass Media and Celebrities

Futurists Jim Taylor and Watts Wacker argue that we live in an age of celebrity perpetuated by our broad exposure to mass media.[80] Television, motion pictures, and commercial publishing are exposing us to a growing number of superstars, management gurus, and life style role models who are shaping our beliefs about who we are, who we should be (a highly effective person), who we can be (a millionaire), who we can never be (Mark Zuckerberg, founder of Facebook), and who we are afraid of becoming (you fill this in). This exposure to celebrities, management gurus, and role models is important to our self-concept because we develop our self-concept, in part, by comparing ourselves to others.[81] This tendency to compare ourselves with others is known as the "looking glass self."[82] Social psychologists Penelope Lockwood and Ziva Kunda explain:

> The superstar illustrates the wonderful heights of accomplishment one can hope to achieve, encourages and motivates one to strive for this now all the more palpable success, indicates particular goals to aim for along the way, points to the road one should follow to achieve them, and makes one feel more competent and capable of such achievement. On the other hand, if the superstar's success seems unattainable, one will be discouraged and demoralized. The superstar's success highlights one's own failures and shortcomings. One realizes that one can no longer hope for comparable stardom, one's own lesser achievement seems paltry by comparison, and one feels disheartened and inferior.[83]

In addition to inflating and deflating our egos, superstars increase our "pool of possible selves,"[84] both those we strive to become and those we don't want to become. Hazel Markus and Paula Nurius make a compelling case that our awareness of possible future selves may be more important to our well-being and effectiveness than our current self-concept for several reasons. First, possible selves can influence our satisfaction with our current self and guide our aspirations for our future self. Second, possible selves can be liberating because exposure to a possible self helps us believe that we can change and that there is always a different and potentially better future self.[85] Third, possible selves can inspire us to create new identities for which our society has no previous models, such as Madeleine Albright did when she became the first woman Secretary of State in the United States during the Clinton and Gore administration. When Henry Kissinger, former U.S. Secretary of State during the Nixon and Ford administration, congratulated Albright by saying, "You're number 64 [U.S. Secretary of State]. Welcome to the fraternity,"

Albright replied, "Henry, it's no longer a fraternity."[86] Each time someone pursues and achieves a possible self that is not the norm for their organization and society, they change not only themselves but also their organizations and societies in the process.

MANAGEMENT GURUS AND THE MANAGERIAL SELF-CONCEPT   Management gurus play a critical role in the development of the managerial self-concept. Over the past few decades, particularly in the United States, we have seen an increasing number of management gurus writing books, appearing on television, conducting seminars, appearing as keynote speakers at conferences, and consulting to organizations. These gurus have achieved celebrity status within the managerial and professional community and are able to charge up to $50,000 a day for their advice.

The popularity of management gurus cannot be explained solely by their ability to solve managerial problems. Most of us are well aware that it's risky business to put too much faith in the newest management consultants, theories, or trends.[87] Yet we continue to buy their books, download their lectures, watch their videos, go to their seminars, search online for their advice, and hire them to help us fix our organizations. Researcher Bradley Jackson explains that we do so, in large part, because management consultants help managers "make sense of their own lives and their place in the scheme of things."[88]

Management gurus help us feel important and proud of our managerial work by giving us a sense of purpose and emphasizing the moral imperative of managerial work (e.g., "Managers must solve organizational problems or people will lose their jobs."). In addition, management gurus respond to our "need for a measure of predictability in an increasingly uncertain world" and "reduce the feeling of insecurity that is an inevitable fact of managerial life."[89] They offer us simple and straightforward ways of framing and solving complex problems, give us an opportunity to "stand back from [our] everyday pressures and encourage [us] to reflect on what [we] are doing,"[90] and provide us with hope for a better future. Finally, management gurus motivate us with their enthusiastic can-do delivery (often called edutainment) and engage us in ways that our day-to-day jobs often don't. Although management gurus may not solve all of our business problems, they help us fulfill our fundamental needs to be somebody, to feel competent at our work, to feel like we have control over our increasingly complex environment, to find meaning in our everyday lives as managers, and to enjoy the pleasure that comes from watching or listening to an engaging presentation.

In short, celebrities and management gurus give us alternative ways to construct our selves and enact our managerial, professional, and personal roles. We can be happy slackers with time on our hands or fast-trackers with money in our pockets. We can choose upward mobility or downward nobility.[91] We can work for large organizations or become entrepreneurs. We can be working parents, stay-at-home parents, or work-from-home parents. We can manage by walking around (as recommended by Tom Peters) or clowning around (as recommended by Herb Kelleher, founder and former CEO of Southwest Airlines). Each choice has its own costs and benefits. Although our increased awareness of possibilities offers us more opportunities than ever before, it also opens the door to self-doubt (Did I make the right decision?), regret (I could have been a contender.), and a paralyzing lack of focus given all the perceived opportunities before us.

THE PROMISE, PERILS, AND SELF-CONCEPT OF THE POSTMODERN MANAGER

Technology—from the Internet to the mass media—can broaden our perspective; increase our speed and capacity for certain types of learning; help us develop a broader and more diverse network of relationships; and expand our intellectual, emotional, and behavioral repertoire—all of which enable us to become more effective and responsible managers, professionals, and world citizens. But living in such a stimulating and information-rich world can also increase our concerns about the gaps "between what we understand and what we think we should understand"[92] and who we think we are and who we think we should be. These are just a few of the dilemmas of today's manager, whom we shall refer to as the postmodern manager.

The postmodern manager must try to make sense of a world that is increasingly difficult to understand, make decisions even though many of today's problems are too complex to anticipate all the consequences, and feel a sense of control in a world that is in continuous flux. Today's manager is expected to be both high tech and high touch; manage both global and local interests; create unity while promoting diversity; reach across organizational and social boundaries that have traditionally divided people, organizations, and nations; and help people find meaning among the chaos and confusion that are the hallmark of our time. This world of the postmodern manager is both exciting and nerve-racking. Psychologist Robert Doan explains:

> Being part of the postmodern age can have its advantages. It offers the potential of less restrictions and intolerance than preceding years. It promises flexibility, diversity, and the space to author a story that is primarily informed by one's own perceptions, memories, and meanings. It challenges the weight of undisputed authority and is, perhaps, the inevitable result of trusting a single informing metaphor for too many years, that is, assuming the world can be best understood as a machine that can be reduced to its various parts.

It has, of course, an equal potential for the opposite. The same aspects that make the aforementioned claims possible can also be experienced as a state of psychological free fall, with no parachute or net. One can be left without a foundation on which to base life's decisions and a gnawing sense of being lost with no map within reach.[93]

Doan's words remind us that despite all the changes that we face today, some things stay the same. Our fundamental needs to make sense of our world and to find our place in it haven't changed, nor have our basic needs for belonging, competence, control, and consistency. However, for many of us, fulfilling these needs today requires a more fluid and sophisticated way of understanding ourselves and our roles as managers and professionals.

The Updated Managerial Self-Concept

Today's managers are being asked to sail into the future without a map. To be effective, it's less likely that they will be able to fall back on conventional theories and practices that advocate "the one best way," "that's the way it should be," or "that's the way it has always been done" to solve problems. Having a rock-solid identity and one-size-fits-all approach to solving problems may be more constraining, less effective, and more frustrating than ever before. To be effective, managers' identities and sense-making abilities must be at least as complex as their environment, and they must increasingly see themselves as being:

- bricoleurs who are able to combine taken-for-granted resources in novel ways to address novel situations;
- managers of meaning who can unite diverse employees toward common goals by helping employees make sense of the organization and their role in it;
- rich in self-complexity, which may mean developing multiple selves that serve different needs rather than holding on to a stable, unified self-concept; and
- thoughtful about when to stay true to valued personal beliefs and when to adapt to others as a means to achieve important goals.

TABLE 2-2   Contrasting the Managerial Self-Concept in the Industrial and Postmodern Ages

	Self in Industrial Age "I think, therefore I am"	Self in Post-Modern Age "I think, therefore I think I am"
Work environment	Concrete, stable, homogeneous, predictable	Virtual, fluid, heterogeneous, Unpredictable
Characteristics of identity	One fixed identity	Multiple selves
Alignment	Well-integrated, bounded, and aligned identity	Shifting, less bounded, and sometimes contradictory identities
Consistency	Stable self across time and place "To thy own self be true"	Adaptable, flexible self "To thy own selves be true"
Problem solving	Fact-finders and planners	Meaning makers and bricoleurs
Purpose of self-development	Self-discovery: finding one's "true self"	Self-expansion: developing, making sense of, and leveraging multiple identities

Of course, there are times when there will be one right answer and one best way to accomplish a task. And there are some parts of our identities that will always be precious to us and that we will hold onto regardless of how our world changes. But the need for consistency in managerial identity and behavior has been overstated in most management books, and research suggests that broadening our view of the managerial self-concept can enhance our professional effectiveness and personal well-being. Table 2-2 contrasts the traditional and postmodern view of the manager.

Managers as Bricoleurs

To be someone . . . is one of the deep urges of the human heart. . . . [It] is a need that becomes more intensely felt—and also more difficult to satisfy—as the course of history carries us all further away from the old realities that structured our identities and life experiences for us.
—POLITICAL SCIENTIST WALTER TRUETT ANDERSON, *Reality Isn't What It Used to Be*

Political scientist Walter Truett Anderson argues that an organism's survival depends on its conformity to "the 'law of requisite variety,' meaning that an organism, if it is to survive, must be at least as complex as its environment."[94] In an age in which exceptions increasingly are becoming the norm, today's managers must become comfortable tinkering with ideas about themselves, others, and their environment and improvising new ways of thinking and behaving on the spot. Effective tinkering involves changing habitual routines, breaking traditional boundaries, and using taken-for-granted resources (ideas, materials, and people) in new ways.[95] In short, today's managers must think of themselves as bricoleurs.

Sherry Turkle explains that bricoleurs "tend to try one thing, step back, reconsider, and try another. For planners, mistakes are steps in the wrong direction; bricoleurs navigate through midcourse corrections."[96] Organizational Scholar Karl Weick echos this view, saying that bricoleurs "remain creative under pressure, precisely because they routinely act in chaotic conditions and pull order out of them. Thus, when situations unravel, this is simply normal natural trouble for bricoleurs, and they proceed with whatever materials are at hand. Knowing these materials intimately, they then are able, usually in the company of other similar skilled people, to form the materials or insights into novel combinations."[97]

Managers as Meaning Makers

In a world with shifting meanings, multiple realities, and conflicting yet often equally reasonable ideas, managers must not only try harder to make sense of themselves, the world, and their place in it, but they must help others to do the same. Consequently, say organizational scholars Linda Smircich and Gareth Morgan, managers must see themselves as "managers of meaning" whose primary task is "framing experience in a way that provides a viable basis for action, e.g., by mobilizing meaning, articulating and defining what has previously remained implicit or unsaid, by inventing images and meanings that provide a focus for new attention, and by consolidating, confronting or changing prevailing wisdom."[98] Smircich and Morgan explain:

> The person that is most easily recognized as an organizational leader is one who rises above and beyond the specification of formal structure to provide members of the organization with a sense that they are organized, even amidst an everyday feeling that at a detailed level everything runs the danger of falling apart.[99]

To be credible and effective managers of meaning, managers must learn to think of themselves as "homo narratus"[100] and become storytellers who can focus and energize their constituents. Good stories are important to individual and organizational well-being and effectiveness because they help people make sense of who they are by enabling them to find their place in the story. Good stories hold the organization together by pulling seemingly disparate parts of the organization together, articulating both a shared past and future, and sometimes creating common enemies. Good stories are engaging to listen to, creating heroes and hurdles that challenge people to stretch their goals and skills. And, many good stories have moral lessons that help people identify and resolve moral dilemmas that are a part of everyday organizational life.

Managers of meaning do not deny that the world consists of immutable facts, concrete realities (bodies, buildings, and natural resources), and real events (people get hired, promoted, demoted, and fired). However, they also realize that human beings interpret these facts, concrete realities, and events through the filters of their cultures, organizations, and self-concept. Consider the following example. Financial data may show that an organization's profits have decreased in the last quarter by 10%, but whether this is viewed as a threat or an opportunity (or both) depends on how we interpret the situation (e.g., "Well, it could be worse because the average decrease in our competitors' profits has been about 25%." "The challenges in this tough economy give us a chance to think more creatively about how we run our business.").

In short, managers of meaning take seriously the critical role they play in helping others interpret facts and events and use these interpretations to motivate organized action that adds value to the organization. Managers of meaning also recognize the importance of creating enabling stories not only for others, but for themselves as well. A manager and part-time MBA student eloquently explained the link between stories and personal success: "I think success can be defined as being able to put yourself in a position to live a life where multiple success stories can be written with respect to family, social commitments, religious beliefs, spiritual beliefs, financial goals, and career goals."

Managers of meaning realize that some of the most important human concepts—love, morality, effectiveness, happiness, and success—are always ambiguous and open to interpretation. Perhaps most important, managers of meaning pay attention to what psychoanalysts M. Knight and Robert Doan refer to as "stories that have gone awry or outlived their usefulness and stories [that] are in collision,"[101] as well as "the inherent danger of the one story that has no room for alternative accounts."[102]

Managers as Multiple Selves

Twentieth-century management literature promoted the image of an effective manager as someone with a unified, stable, and predictable self-concept. From this perspective, the goal of self-awareness and professional development is to know one's true self, to be centered, to be well integrated, and to be consistent across a variety of situations. This view of the self fits with the Latin root of the word identity—*idem*—which means "the same." But as the late author Adolf Huxley once said, "The only completely consistent people are the dead."

> No sooner do we think we have assembled a comfortable life than we find a piece of ourselves that has no place in it.
> —GAIL SHEEHY,
> *Passages*

It's not a stretch to imagine that the twenty-first century's managerial self-concept must be more complex than that of the past. In the industrial age, organizations were often described as machines in which well-tuned, solid, and stable parts fit precisely together and worked together through predictable routines to create a consistent product. In such a context, a well-defined, clearly bounded, stable, and predictable managerial self-concept was considered to be the hallmark of professional effectiveness and psychological well-being. However, this solid, stable, and consistent self-concept may be out of date and ineffective for many people in today's fast-changing, multicultural, and technologically driven social and economic environment in which we are routinely exposed to new people and ideas, novel situations, and increasingly complex problems with no clear solutions.

Today, many managers are likely to find it more difficult to be centered, well integrated, and consistent. In contrast to the model of the "rock solid" ideal manager of the industrial age, many managers today must develop a self-concept that is more complex, more open to experience, more fluid, more dependent on others, more comfortable with change, and less sure of oneself but more certain that what one does matters. In short, many managers are likely to find it more effective and psychologically fulfilling to see themselves as having fluid, often fragmented multiple selves. Although the notion of multiple selves is relatively new to the management literature, it is not a new concept. More than 50 years ago, sociologist Erving Goffman argued that the self is a collection of roles that a person turns on and off depending on the characteristics of the situation.[103]

For many people—particularly those who routinely interact across multiple cultures, cross-organizational boundaries, or manage complex personal and professional lives (e.g., working parents who engage fully in both their parental and professional roles)—the ability to develop multiple selves and shift among these selves as appropriate is a necessary and effective survival skill. Historian W. E. B. Dubois, the first African American to receive a Ph.D. from Harvard University and cofounder of the National Association for the Advancement of Colored People in 1910, coined the term "double consciousness" to refer to the need and ability to live in multiple worlds simultaneously. Scholar Aida Hurtado, describing the experience of women of color, uses the phrase "shifting consciousness" to refer to the ability "to shift from one group's perception of social reality to another, and, at times, to be able simultaneously to perceive multiple social realities without losing their sense of self-coherence."[104] In the management literature, organizational researchers Ella Bell and Mary Yoko Brannen use the term "biculturalism" to refer to individuals who are members of, and accountable to, at least two significant identity groups simultaneously, each with its own worldviews, values, norms, and expectations.[105]

Yet having multiple selves is most often framed as a problem to be fixed rather than a skill to be developed. Hurtado argues that "nonconflictual and monocultural social identities are [considered] superior and desirable" and that the "dominant paradigm emphasized in mainstream scholarship for understanding 'biculturality' is the pain and stress of transitioning from one 'cultural world' to another . . . marginality, alienation, acculturation stress, and so on."[106] She notes that when having multiple selves is viewed as a problem, people are encouraged to integrate these selves, a strategy that requires diluting or disowning one or more treasured selves. Similarly, terms such as "role overload" (the stress placed on a person when one has to manage too many roles) and "role conflict" (when the demands of one role prevents one from meeting the demands of other roles) are well-known concepts in the psychology and management literature,[107] whereas the healthy functions of multiple roles are less known.

Many researchers are focusing on how people can develop and use multiple roles to get better results at work, achieve their career goals, and enhance their well-being. When having multiple selves is viewed as a normal, desirable, and effective adaptive mechanism, people are encouraged to actively cultivate different selves, learn to shift among these selves, and become more comfortable leaving one self aside for a while, only to pick it up later when the situation is more appropriate. Researchers call this ability to develop and shift among multiple "selves" "high self-complexity," and they've found that people differ in the degree to which they cultivate self-complexity.[108]

Although living in multiple worlds and having multiple selves can be frustrating, even painful at times, there are advantages for many people. Hurtado explains that people with multiple selves reap the rewards of the "unique knowledge" that is gained by membership in multiple groups, the freedom that is gained by being able to "rise above the restrictions defined by these memberships," and the value of being able to bring both an insider's and outsider's perspective and knowledge to one's multiple groups. People who cultivate multiple selves may be better able to resist categorization and "avoid polarization," accept their own and others' "inconsistent personae,"[109] and adapt more fluidly to diversity in general.

Speaking from his own experience, a Japanese MBA student explained: "The benefits of having multiple selves are the quick assimilation into different environments, the ability to influence a group from inside instead of outside, and the satisfaction of being effective in different settings. With multiple selves between home and work, I can easily separate the two worlds, so that the frustration and stress that I might experience in one tend not to be carried over to the other."

Research studies support the view that for some people, "high self complexity" can reap many personal and professional rewards, including greater job effectiveness, as well as greater psychological and physical well-being.[110] Specifically, researchers have found the following:

- People with highly complex selves may have more diverse resources such as skills, knowledge, experience, and relationships on which to draw to enhance their performance, especially when facing complex problems.
- People who sometimes keep their roles separate may be better able to turn off the demands of one role while focusing on another, which can lead to better performance. In contrast, when people are unable to separate and turn off some of their different roles when appropriate, they may find themselves constantly multitasking and unable to concentrate on the responsibilities of one role because of their simultaneous attention to the other.
- People who are willing to try on new possible selves may be better able to find a greater variety of jobs, as well as succeed in the jobs they obtain because they may be better able to see themselves in different roles (and thus think more broadly about job possibilities), test out new ways of behaving that may be inconsistent with prior selves, and adopt new characteristics and skills that can make them more effective in new roles.
- People who have multiple selves may have greater feelings of happiness when things are going well because they can experience well-being on many fronts.

- People with multiple selves may find this self-complexity to be a particularly effective coping mechanism. The pleasure people experience through one role may balance the pain experienced in another role. When one is having problems in one role, one may still derive pleasure from other selves, thus sustaining well-being despite life's challenges. And if one loses an important part of his/her identity (e.g., being a manager), one still has other identities from which to draw fulfillment (e.g., being a parent).

In short, having multiple identities can be replenishing rather than draining, clarifying rather than confusing, and opportunity enhancing rather than constraining.[111] The following studies and examples illustrate these benefits.

I'm the kind of woman who wants to enjoy herselves in peace.
—ALICE WALKER,
The Temple of My Familiar

In a study of experienced engineers and other professionals, researchers Janice Beyer and David Hannah found that people with more complex identities were better able to adjust when they took on new jobs because they had more "cognitive materials and personal resources" from which to draw.[112] In a different study of 61 women between the ages of 26 and 57 who were managers and executives, researcher Marian Ruderman and colleagues found that women who managed multiple roles tended to be rated more highly by their managers and peers on interpersonal skills and task performance. They explain:[113]

> [The] roles women play in their personal lives provide psychological benefits, emotional advice and support, practice at multitasking, relevant background, opportunities to enrich interpersonal skills and leadership practice that enhances effectiveness in the management role. Multiple role commitment positively relates to life satisfaction, self-esteem, and self-acceptance. Commitment to multiple roles was also related to interpersonal and task-related managerial skills. . . . Work-family conflict may be overstated for some women . . . because as one accumulates additional roles in life, they also accumulate additional skills and mechanisms (e.g., support systems) for travelling between and integrating roles.

Researcher Nancy Rothbard explains that women such as these are not portraying the superwoman syndrome, but rather have learned a more sophisticated way of taking advantage of the benefits of having multiple roles.[114]

On the basis of her research on job transitions, Insead professor Herminia Ibarra argues that having "provisional selves" can help us find and adapt to new work roles. In one study, she asked men and women who were consultants and investment bankers about their career development (e.g., she asked, "What does it take to be successful and effective in your current job?" "Tell me a bit about your career to date. What are the key events of your years at the firm?"). Many of these consultants and investment bankers told stories about how they transitioned to new roles, such as when one moved from being an individual contributor to a boss by trying on new practice or trial selves to see if these new identities fit or if they could grow into them. Ibarra says, "By rehearsing these clumsy, often ineffective, sometimes inauthentic selves, they learned about the limitations and potential of their repertoires and thus began to make decisions about what elements to keep, refine, reject, or continue to search for."[115] To illustrate, she quotes the words of a participant in Harvard professor Linda Hill's study on new managers' career development:

> I even dressed like him [a favorite boss], to look like an authority figure. . . . [He] always kept people up. You enjoyed coming to the office, because he always had fun up his sleeve. I wanted to create that kind of atmosphere. But guess what I found out? I don't have much of a sense of humor and I'm not spontaneous like him. If you have to work at making something funny, it falls flat. I had to come up with another

way that fit who I am to create the right office atmosphere. I could keep his concepts but I had to put my own words and form around them.[116]

In another study, Ibarra interviewed managers and professionals during career transitions. She found that many people did not find new jobs by undertaking a systematic process of identifying their "true calling" ("Who am I and what's the perfect job for me?"). Rather, Ibarra found that many successful job searches began with a broader question: "Among the many possible selves that I might become, which is most intriguing to me now?" She concluded that many successful job searchers succeed through a "process of tinkering with a whole set of possibilities: imagining new ones, trying them on for size, elaborating on some, dropping others, getting rid of outdated images, coming to grips with the fact that some might languish."[117]

> When stuck on a hard problem (MIT-educated invester) Levy tries a mental trick he invented in the third grade. He asks himself, "How would I answer this if I were a smart person?"
> —Fortune

In their book, *Dealing with People You Can't Stand*, authors Rick Brinkman and Rick Kirschner provided a clever example of a woman using a different "self" to deal with her problem boss. Brinkman and Kirschner describe the discussion they had with Marge about her difficult boss:[118]

> We asked Marge what she needed to deal effectively with her boss. She said she needed to be more assertive. We asked if there was anywhere in her life she was assertive. She couldn't think of one. So we asked if she knew of anyone who could handle her boss. She said, "Katherine Hepburn! She wouldn't take any guff from my boss!" We then asked Marge to imagine Katherine Hepburn sitting at her desk at the office, as the boss walks in. Not surprisingly, Katherine Hepburn had the right stuff. Marge watched, listened, and learned, and then walked herself through the same scene as if she were Katherine Hepburn.

Marketers have also recognized the importance of acknowledging multiple selves when marketing their products. Melinda Davis is the founder of the Next Group marketing firm, which helps companies such as AT&T, Corning, and Merck anticipate the future. She explains:[119]

> What's going on inside our heads keeps getting more complicated. There's a new fascination with the Sybil syndrome—not as a psychiatric disorder, but as an aspirational value. People are dividing themselves into multiple, virtual identities as a way to handle an increasingly complex, chaotic world. Consumers are enthusiastic about products that allow them to switch identities at will . . . The implications for marketers: Each of your customers is actually many customers fitting into multiple segmentation models.

In short, many people today are finding that having multiple selves (rather than an integrated self) helps them be more effective at their jobs, more successful in their careers, and happier and healthier as well. Indeed, for many people, having multiple selves is a creative adaptive mechanism that can open up new opportunities that would be closed if they clung to a solid, stable sense of self. Of course, even for people with high levels of self-complexity, the different parts of one's selves are integrated in part by some deeply held common beliefs and values that are consistent over time and place. Furthermore, having multiple selves is likely to have greater benefits when one chooses one's identities (e.g., choosing to be both a working professional and a parent) and sees them as a desirable part of oneself rather than a burden or a façade.

> Be careful of what you pretend to be because you may become what you pretend to be.
> —Kurt Vonnegut, Jr.
> *Author*

Managers as Self-Monitors

Self-monitoring refers to a person's willingness and ability to be attentive to "social and interpersonal situational cues" and to adapt one's behavior to these cues.[120] High self-monitors are highly sensitive to social and interpersonal cues in their environment and are willing and able to modify their behavior in response. Low self-monitors are less sensitive to social and interpersonal cues and less willing and able to adapt their behaviors in response.[121] "In a social situation, high self-monitors ask the following: 'Who does this situation want me to be and how can I be that person?' By contrast, low self-monitors ask, 'Who am I and how can I be me in this situation?'"[122]

As you read the following paragraphs, keep in mind that neither high or low self-monitoring is inherently better or worse than the other—it depends on the situation and what you want to accomplish. Furthermore, remember that each of us has characteristics that are associated with both high and low self-monitoring, although we tend to use one style more often than the other. Whether you should be more or less self-monitoring depends on what you want to achieve in your professional and personal life. To enhance your effectiveness, it makes sense to understand your self-monitoring style and the impact it has on your behavior, how others perceive you, and the ways in which it is helping and hindering you from achieving your professional and personal goals.

How do high and low self-monitors differ?[123] Researchers have concluded that high self-monitors are more likely to engage in impression management; seek out status and prestigious work; rely more on their social networks to make career decisions; experience higher levels of job involvement; have lower commitment to their organizations; rationalize their actions and manage impressions when their projects fail; change employers and geographic locations; get rated more highly in managerial performance evaluations; achieve more promotions; emerge as leaders of work groups; take on boundary spanning roles in organizations; have more central positions in organizational networks and more instrumental relationships; be less committed to current relationships; and be more open to the possibility of forming new relationships in different settings.[124]

Low self-monitors tend to be more predictable in their behavior; be more committed to current employers, organizations, friends, and geographic locations; be more likely to invest emotionally in particular relationships so that they can be themselves; be more comfortable with ambiguity, perhaps because high self-monitors may look more to others for clues about what to do, whereas low-self monitors may use their own values and beliefs to make decisions; seek out jobs that are compatible with their interests rather than jobs that are prestigious; and have greater self-knowledge about their career preferences so that they may not feel the need to gather a lot of information about various career options. Notably, researchers David Day and Deirdre Schleicher conducted a meta-analysis of the research on self-monitoring, and found that "men had higher average self-monitoring scores than women. Although care must be taken when interpreting this finding given the relatively small, (albeit robust) effect—and that there are likely to be larger within-sex than between sex differences in self-monitoring—it does raise the spector of harmful effects on the career progress of women when considered across all organizational levels."[125]

> Adaptable as human beings are and have to be, I sometimes sympathize with the chameleon who had a nervous breakdown on a patchwork quilt.
> —JOHN STEPHEN STRANGE

The late Akio Morita, who was a co-founder and CEO of Sony, may have been a high self-monitor. In his book, *Sony: The Private Life*, author John Nathan says: "What accounted for Akio Morita's unique ability as a Japanese businessman to establish and sustain beneficial relationships with the most important Western business and political leaders? There is striking agreement among those who knew him over time that he was special because he was someone who seemed to understand them, and, as important, whom they could understand." Morita's self-monitoring may not have come without effort and some personal costs, however. Says Nathan:

> But was he really as effortlessly at ease in the company of his foreign friends as he appeared, as familiar and at home with their way of perceiving the world and acting in it? . . . [T]here is evidence to suggest that Morita had to labor hard to achieve

what may have been the illusion of familiarity. . . . There is even room for speculation that Morita's lifelong, tireless campaign to install Sony in the West required a painful personal struggle to reconcile a foreign sensibility with his own . . . and he was never able to resolve that tension satisfactorily.[126]

Research on the influence of self-monitoring behavior on managerial careers and performance is relatively new, and there is still much to be learned. For example, we don't know if certain jobs lend themselves better to high or low self-monitoring. Nor do we know if the flexible and status-seeking orientation of the high self-monitor or the more consistent orientation of the low self-monitor is more desirable at senior organizational levels in which providing clear direction, "steering the ship," adapting to the environment as needed, and putting the organization's needs first are central obligations.[127]

We also don't know how high or low self-monitoring behavior affects a manager's mental health; for example, who tends to be happier, high or low self-monitors? So far, researchers have found no relationship between self-monitoring style and job satisfaction. However, some research suggests that high self-monitors may feel added stress because they are more likely to be in boundary spanning roles at work, which sometimes require that they manage conflicting demands from different people in the organization.[128]

As new research on self-monitoring behavior emerges, we will gain additional insights into how particular characteristics of both high and low self-monitoring can enhance and inhibit our effectiveness, careers, and well-being. It may also provide insights into how both high and low self-monitoring behaviors can complement each other in ways that add value to organizations (e.g., helping organizations manage the delicate balance between the need for both stability and flexibility). For now, it's worth thinking about your self-monitoring behavior and whether it's helping you achieve important goals. For example, in what ways does your self-monitoring style help and hinder you from earning others' trust, getting along well with people who are different from you in significant ways, engaging in work that is meaningful to you, achieving important results at work, and attaining the promotions and salary that you desire. You can assess your self-monitoring style by completing the self-monitoring assessment in Box 2-6.

> Everybody must learn this lesson somewhere—that it costs something to be what you are.
> —SHIRLY ABBOT,
> *Womenfolks: Growing Up Down South*

Authenticity Is a Work-In-Progress

At this point, you may be asking yourself about how authenticity fits into this discussion of the self-concept. Can someone who shifts "selves" and presents oneself in multiple ways depending on the context be authentic and trustworthy? Can someone who tenaciously holds onto his or her "true self" in an increasingly diverse and complex world respond empathetically and effectively to others' needs?

Philosophers have been struggling with questions related to the self and authenticity for centuries (and will continue to do so), so we won't be able to fully answer those questions here. But, perhaps it's useful to view authenticity as a work-in-progress rather than a static end state. Viewing authenticity as a work-in-progress assumes that we are always learning about ourselves, the world around us, and what others need from us. It assumes that responding ethically and effectively to others and our environments challenges us to be thoughtful about when to fully express ourselves and when to hold back and consider others' feelings and needs; when to stick to our position and when to find common ground so that we can connect to others; when to hold on to parts of ourselves that are precious and when to let go of parts of ourselves so that we can grow.

In short, it may be most useful to view the concepts of the "true self" and "multiple selves" not as opposites, but as options, both of which can help us achieve the authenticity that we desire and that others deserve from us.

MANAGERIAL GROWTH AND DEVELOPMENT

Undoubtedly, developing self-awareness is essential to our long-term work effectiveness, career development, and personal well-being. Many of us are drawn to go beyond who we currently are toward who we are capable of becoming. Yet leadership researcher and consultant Wilfred Drath explains that personal growth can be disconcerting as well as exhilarating because "to grow personally, [we] must give up a deeply personal meaning, a fundamental way of understanding the self and relating the self to the world," that gives our lives coherence and predictability.

You've got to do your own growing, no matter how tall your grandfather was.
—IRISH PROVERB

Growth does not simply mean moving in logical, concrete steps toward a particular direction, nor does it imply constant change. We grow and develop, not steadily, but by advancing a little and then plateauing or even retreating. What looks like regression may actually be a necessary retreat or plateau that gives us the time we need to assimilate important changes. Sometimes growth occurs in spurts and sometimes very slowly. Sometimes we are aware that we are learning something new and at other times our learning is unconscious—all we feel is the tension that often accompanies personal growth.[129]

We can promote personal growth by taking time out for self-reflection, putting ourselves in challenging situations that require us to go beyond our current ways of thinking and behaving, developing relationships with a diverse range of people who can provide us with alternative ways of being, and asking others for feedback on how we are perceived and how our behavior affects other people and organizations. Remember that our self-concept and the authenticity that we desire will always be a work in progress, and our personal growth will always be, in part, under our control.

Chapter Summary

Our self-awareness contributes to our managerial success. The more we know about ourselves and how we are perceived by others, the better we can understand how our ways of seeing, thinking, feeling, and acting affect our work effectiveness and psychological well-being.

It may be useful to consider developing "the brand called you" because it is naïve to assume that others will see, understand, and reward our contributions. It's important to proactively identify, develop, and "market" our strengths and contributions.

The online environment enables us to create and market our brand in a way that reaches more people than ever before, and we need to be aware of what people read about us online to ensure that what they see is the image we want to project.

The self-concept refers to an internalized set of perceptions that each of us has of ourselves that are relatively stable over time, consistent across situations, resistant to change, and of central importance. Although the self-concept is relatively stable, it can change over time if one puts himself or herself in experiences and environments that inspire and enable change.

The self-concept is, in large part, socially and culturally constructed through our families, interpersonal relationships, identity and organizational group memberships, and social institutions.

Understanding our self-concept is important because it influences what we pay attention to, how we interpret what we see, how we make decisions, who we interact with and how we interact with them, how we make moral choices, and how we cope with the stress and complexity of work and life in general.

One of the most important lifelong challenges we face is to reconcile our basic needs to be both connected to and separate from others. We learn how to reconcile these basic needs for separateness and connectedness through our culture. Different cultures provide their members with different ways to reconcile these needs. Some cultures (often labeled individualistic) emphasize independence from others, and other cultures (often labeled collectivist) emphasize interdependence with others. These different conceptions of the self have implications for how we see the world, make sense of what we see, interpret the behavior of others, and behave in our everyday life.

Despite cultural differences in the construction of the self-concept, people the world over share universal human needs: meaning, belonging competence, control, and consistency. These needs become more relevant in times of change or adversity.

Today's managers live and work in a multicultural, technology-driven, fast-paced, fast-changing, and unpredictable environment. This environment exposes us to an increasing number of possible selves, which expand our assumptions about who we are, who we should be, who we can be, and who we can never be.

Today's manager can be described as a postmodern manager. Postmodern managers have a self-concept that is more complex, more culturally aware and responsive, more open to experience, more relational, more comfortable with change, more fragmented, and less sure of oneself, but more certain that what one does matters.

In today's complex work environment, effective managers see themselves as

- bricoleurs who are able to combine taken-forgranted resources in novel ways to address novel situations;

- managers of meaning who can bring a community together by helping people make sense of the organization and their role in it; and
- rich in self-complexity, which may mean developing multiple selves that serve different needs rather than holding on to a stable, unified self-concept.

Self-monitoring refers to one's willingness and ability to be attentive to interpersonal and contextual cues and to adapt one's behavior in response. High self-monitors ask themselves, "What does this situation want me to be and how can I be that person?" Low self-monitors ask themselves, "How can I be myself in this situation?" Although each of us has characteristics associated with high and low self-monitoring, we tend to prefer one style of self-monitoring over the other and use it more often. These styles have implications for how we choose jobs, behave in those jobs, whether we are drawn to status, whether we prefer to have deep personal relationships or many relationships that may be more superficial, and many other behaviors associated with organizational life.

Authenticity may be best viewed as a work-in-progress rather than an end state because responding successfully to changing environments and the needs of others who depend on us constantly challenges us to strategically decide which parts of ourselves to express, when (and how) to express each part of ourselves, when to hold on to our personal point of view and when to find common ground so that we can connect with others, what we want to offer the world and what others need from us, what parts of ourselves are precious and unchanging and which parts of ourselves are open to change, and when to fully express ourselves and when to consider the feelings of others.

Personal growth is not always a logical, linear process. We learn some things quickly, some things slowly, and sometimes we're not even aware that we're learning at all. However, we can control our growth to some degree by creating a context that promotes our personal and professional development.

Food for Thought

1. What is the one most useful thing you learned in this chapter, and why?

2. Based on what you learned in this chapter, select one behavior to do differently this week. Practice this behavior, and note any benefits and progress you make.

3. Do you agree with the idea that you should develop "Me, Inc" or "The Brand Called You" as described in the beginning of this chapter? Why or why not?

4. Answer the five questions posed by Tom Peters in his article, "The Brand Called You," and summarized at the beginning of this chapter. These include: What do I do that I'm most proud of? What do I do that adds remarkable, measurable, distinguished, distinctive value? What do my colleagues and customers say is my greatest and clearest strength . . . [and] most noteworthy personal characteristic? What have I done lately—this week—that added value to the organization (and that was noticed by others)? In what ways is what I do difficult to imitate? What do your answers tell you about your brand as it stands now? What do you need to do to enhance and market your brand?

5. Complete the "I am" assessment at the end of this chapter. Does your self-concept emphasize independence or interdependence? Under what conditions is this self-concept (independence or interdependence) useful and under what conditions is it a problem?

6. What forces (e.g., family, group membership, social institutions) most shaped your self-concept to date, and in what ways? How does your current self-concept affect your work style, work effectiveness, career potential, and psychological well-being?

7. Draw a "lifeline" that includes critical periods of your life, influential events and people, and discuss the effects that they had on your worldview and behavior today.

8. Think about the heuristics, or rules-of-thumb, that you learned when you were younger. Heuristics include statements such as "save for a rainy day," "if you want a job done right, you have to do it yourself," or "a stitch in time saves nine." Identify three heuristics that you learned when you were younger that still serve you well today, and describe how they help your effectiveness and/or well-being. Identify three heuristics that you learned when you were younger that you still use today, but hinder your ability to be effective, successful, and happy. What can you do to stop using these heuristics that don't serve you well anymore?

9. Research suggests that we often underestimate the degree to which we change over time. List five things that have changed about yourself since you were in high school. Why did these changes occur, and what benefits and/or costs have they created?

10. How have technology, globalization, and diversity changed your personal and professional life? What have you gained from these changes, and what have you lost?

11. Think of a time when you solved a problem in a novel way. What were you trying to accomplish, and how did you do it? What lessons from this experience can you (or do you) use to solve problems today?

12. Do you have multiple selves? If not, why not? If so, why and in what ways are they helpful and in what ways are they problematic? How do you manage your multiple selves?

13. Are you a low or high self-monitor? What are the consequences of your self-monitoring style on your effectiveness, career, and well-being? Remember that both high and low self-monitoring styles bring advantages and disadvantages. Based on what you learned about your self-monitoring style, which behaviors would you want to change and which would you want to keep the same? Why?

14. Visit someone's office and look around. What assumptions do you make about the person based on their office? Ask the person what the office says about him or her. What did you learn about that person's sense of self or selves?

15. Complete the personality assessment in Box 2-4 included in this chapter. What did you learn from it? How might your styles influence how you solve problems and how you are perceived by others? Under what conditions might you be more or less effective? Do you agree with the way this assessment categorizes you? Why or why not?

BOX 2-3   A Note on Personality Assessments

Self-assessments traditionally have been an important cornerstone of managerial development. The use of self-assessments is based on the reasonable assumptions that (1) people have habitual ways of seeing and acting in the world, (2) different people have different ways of seeing and acting in the world, (3) these different ways of seeing and acting have consequences on our effectiveness and well-being, (4) these differences can be identified through self-assessment instruments, and (5) personal change is possible and desirable. Furthermore, personality assessments assume that if we understand the different ways people see and behave—and their reasons for doing so—we can better understand the world from multiple perspectives, appreciate the value that these perspectives bring, understand our strengths and weaknesses, and learn to be more flexible. There are hundreds of instruments designed to assess a variety of personality characteristics, including learning style, problem-solving style, interpersonal style, self-monitoring tendencies, locus of control, moral development, creativity, multicultural competence, emotional intelligence, and stress management, to name just a few. Some assessments, including one similar to the popular Myers-Briggs Assessment (Box 2-4), are included at the end of this chapter. There are other self-assessments throughout this book as well. Many self-assessments are also available through the Internet (although some are more credible and research-based than others).

Developing self-awareness through personality instruments has several advantages, including encouraging personal and professional growth; increasing our self-awareness and our understanding of how we are perceived by others; helping us make career choices; enhancing our decision making; and helping us improve our interpersonal relationships through better communication, conflict management, and increasing our acceptance of people who differ from us in thinking and behavioral styles.

Although personality assessments can enhance individual and organizational performance, they have limitations as well. Although many personality assessments are often (though not always) based on well-developed theories of human behavior and are often (though not always) well researched, they are often (some would argue always) biased. Assessments are often presented as universally applicable, yet many tend to reflect the cultural biases of the researcher(s) who created the assessments and the segments of the population that the researcher studied. In addition to these limitations, people who put too much emphasis on personality assessments may compartmentalize people into rigid categories, may underestimate the degree to which people's "styles" change over time and place, and may overemphasize the impact of personality characteristics and underemphasize the impact of situational variables on our behavior. Individuals can manipulate their answers to assessments to obtain results that they want or that they believe others (e.g., hiring organizations, dating services) prefer to see. Of course, as one executive recruiter warns, "If you lie or try to manipulate your answers to land a job that doesn't fit you or your personality, you're more likely to be miserable at work."[130]

Despite these limitations, self-assessments can significantly contribute to individual and organizational effectiveness when used wisely. Thoughtful use of personality assessments can help you learn more about your styles, strengths, weaknesses, and how you are perceived by others. Self-assessments can also help you identify the kinds of tasks and jobs that are likely to be most enjoyable to you (job fit), and provide you with insights into how you can adapt tasks and jobs to fit better with your interests and strengths. To enhance the usefulness of assessments, take a variety of self-assessments and look for patterns across them. Have other people assess you and compare your self-assessment with their perception of you. When interpreting results, carefully consider how the assessment may reflect cultural biases. This is especially important when the assessment claims universal applicability or when certain "styles" are claimed to be generally more normal, moral, or effective than others. In addition, although people's ways of perceiving and acting tend to be somewhat consistent over time, people do change as a consequence of training, effort, significant emotional experiences (e.g., births, deaths, illness, travel, or job termination), or socialization into a profession or culture. Finally, remember that personality assessments can give you pieces of data about yourself, and only you can make sense of this data based on your knowledge of your life history, cultural group memberships, and future career and life goals.

BOX 2-4   Self-Assessment Personality Inventory

What Is My Personality Type?

For each item, select either a or b. If you feel both a and b are true, decide which one is more like you, even if it is only slightly more true.

1. I would rather
   a. Solve a new and complicated problem.
   b. Work on something I have done before.
2. I like to
   a. Work alone in a quiet place.
   b. Be where the action is.
3. I want a boss who
   a. Establishes and applies criteria in decisions.
   b. Considers individual needs and makes exceptions.
4. When I work on a project, I
   a. Like to finish it and get some closure.
   b. Often leave it open for possible changes.
5. When making a decision, the most important considerations are
   a. Rational thoughts, ideas, and data.
   b. People's feelings and values.
6. On a project, I tend to
   a. Think it over and over before deciding how to proceed.
   b. Start working on it right away, thinking about it as I go along.
7. When working on a project, I
   a. Maintain as much control as possible.
   b. Explore various options.
8. In my work, I prefer to
   a. Work on several projects at a time, and learn as much as possible about each one.
   b. Have one project that is challenging and keeps me busy.
9. I often
   a. Make lists and plans whenever I start something and may hate to seriously alter my plans.
   b. Avoid plans and just let things progress as I work on them.
10. When discussing a problem with colleagues, it is easy for me to
    a. See "the big picture."
    b. Grasp the specifics of the situation.
11. When the phone rings in my office or at home, I usually
    a. Consider it an interruption.
    b. Do not mind answering it.
12. Which word describes you better?
    a. Analytical.
    b. Empathetic.
13. When I am working on an assignment, I tend to
    a. Work steadily and consistently.
    b. Work in bursts of energy with "down time" in between.
14. When I listen to someone talk on a subject, I usually try to
    a. Relate it to my own experience and see if it fits.
    b. Assess and analyze the message.
15. When I come up with new ideas, I generally
    a. "Go for it."
    b. Like to contemplate the ideas some more.

16. When working on a project, I prefer to
    a. Narrow the scope so that it is clearly defined.
    b. Broaden the scope to include related aspects.
17. When I read something, I usually
    a. Confine my thoughts to what is written there.
    b. Read between the lines and relate the words to other ideas.
18. When I have to make a decision in a hurry, I often
    a. Feel uncomfortable and wish I had more information.
    b. Am able to do so with available data.
19. In a meeting, I tend to
    a. Continue formulating my ideas as I talk about them.
    b. Only speak out after I have carefully thought the issue through.
20. In work, I prefer spending a great deal of time on issues of
    a. Ideas.
    b. People.
21. In meetings, I am most often annoyed with people who
    a. Come up with many sketchy ideas.
    b. Lengthen meetings with many practical details.
22. I am a
    a. Morning person.
    b. Night owl.
23. What is your style in preparing for a meeting?
    a. I am willing to go in and be responsive.
    b. I like to be fully prepared and usually sketch an outline of the meeting.
24. In a meeting, I would prefer for people to
    a. Display a fuller range of emotions.
    b. Be more task oriented.
25. I would rather work for an organization where
    a. My job was intellectually stimulating.
    b. I was committed to its goals and mission.
26. On weekends, I tend to
    a. Plan what I will do.
    b. Just see what happens and decide as I go along.
27. I am more
    a. Outgoing.
    b. Contemplative.
28. I would rather work for a boss who is
    a. Full of new ideas.
    b. Practical.

In the following, choose the word in each pair that appeals to you more:

29. **a.** Social.
    b. Theoretical.
30. **a.** Ingenuity.
    b. Practicality.
31. **a.** Organized.
    b. Adaptable.
32. **a.** Active.
    b. Concentration.

(continued)

Scoring

Score your responses as follows: Count one point for each item listed below that you have marked in the inventory.

Scoring Key

Score for I	Score for E	Score for S	Score for N
2a	2b	1b	1a
6a	6b	10b	10a
11a	11b	13a	13b
15b	15a	16a	16b
19b	19a	17a	17b
22a	22b	21a	21b
27b	27a	28b	28a
32b	32a	30b	30a

Total
Identify the one with the more points— I or E.

Identify the one with the more points— S or N.

Score for T	Score for F	Score for J	Score for P
3a	3b	4a	4b
5a	5b	7a	7b
12a	12b	8b	8a
14b	14a	9a	9b
20a	20b	18b	18a
24b	24a	23b	23a
25a	25b	26a	26b
29b	29a	31a	31b

Total
Identify the one with the more — T or F.

Identify the one with the more points— J or P.

Analysis

This assessment is similar to the popular Myers-Briggs Type Indicator and Keirsey Bates personality assessments. It classifies people as extroverted or introverted (E or I), sensing or intuitive (S or N), thinking or feeling (T or F), and perceiving or judging (P or J). These classifications can then be combined into 16 personality types (e.g., INTJ, ENTP).

This assessment is based on the assumption that different people have different ways of seeing the world and solving problems. It is designed to assess your tendencies toward:

- Introversion or extroversion: The tendency to get energized by focusing inward (introversion) or to the outer world (extroversion)
- Sensing or intuition: The tendency to see the world and acquire information by focusing on details (sensing) or by focusing on the big picture (intuition)

- Thinking or feeling: The tendency to make decisions based on systematic logic (thinking) versus values (feeling)
- Judging or perceiving. The tendency to take a planned, orderly approach to the world, and come to closure quickly (judging) or a flexible spontaneous approach and a tendency to leave decisions open as long as possible (perceiving)

No one preference is better than the others. Rather, your effectiveness depends on your ability to be aware of the impact of your preferences on your behavior, being able to use the most appropriate way of thinking and acting for each particular situation, and respecting and leveraging different styles when they are expressed by others.

Knowing your preferred ways of interacting with the world and solving problems is useful for several reasons. It helps you be aware of the different ways that people make sense of and interact with their environment. This awareness can make you more accepting, even encouraging, of these differences. Being able to understand and respect differences in styles can also help you become a more effective communicator, negotiator, conflict manager, and team leader because you can learn to leverage your strengths and minimize or compensate for your weaknesses.

Source: D. Marcic and P. Nutt. 1989. "Personality Inventory." In D. Marcic, (ed.). *Organizational Behavior: Experiences and Cases.* St. Paul, MN: West. Reprinted with permission.

BOX 2-5   Self-Assessment 20 Questions: "I Am"

Complete the following sentences, all of which begin with "I am . . . ," to describe yourself. You do not have to show your answers or discuss your results with anyone. This is for your use only. Do not turn the page until you have completed the sentences.

1. I am _____
2. I am _____
3. I am _____
4. I am _____
5. I am _____
6. I am _____
7. I am _____
8. I am _____
9. I am _____
10. I am _____
11. I am _____
12. I am _____
13. I am _____
14. I am _____
15. I am _____
16. I am _____
17. I am _____
18. I am _____
19. I am _____
20. I am _____

Please see next page for a discussion of your responses.

"I Am" Interpretation of Responses: The Private, Public, and Collective Self-Concept

How you completed these sentences gives you some insights into your self-concept. Your responses reflect your tendencies to emphasize a private, public, or collective self-concept.

- *Private self-concept.* Responses that emphasize your personal traits, states, or behaviors (e.g., I am creative, I am a big thinker, I am introverted, I am kind, I am competitive, I am conscientious) and do not make reference to connections to others, perceptions of others or your membership in specific groups. These responses are more aligned with an independent self-concept than with an interdependent self-concept.
- *Public.* Responses that emphasize your relationships, connection to others, or perceptions of others (e.g., I am respected by others, I am trusted, I am loved). These are associated with a tendency to emphasize your public self and a concern with how others view and experience their relationship with you. These responses are more associated with an interdependent self-concept than with an independent self-concept.
- *Collective.* Responses that mention specific social groups or cultural institutions (e.g., I am Asian American, or I am an MBA) or your role in the group (I am a parent, I am a manager, or I am an engineer). These are associated with a tendency to emphasize group memberships that have value and emotional significance to you. These responses are more associated with an interdependent self-concept than with an independent self-concept.

Analysis: Count your responses for each of the categories. Your responses will probably include private, public, and collective responses, but you may have emphasized some over others. Do your responses suggest that you emphasize a private, public, or collective self? Do you agree? Why or why not? What implications does this have for your effectiveness in different types of situations?

Source: Adapted from Triandis, H. C. 1989. "The Self and Social Behavior in Different Cultural Contexts." *Psychological Review,* 96: 506–520. Copyright ©1989 by the American Psychological Association. Reprinted with permission.

BOX 2-6   Self-Monitoring Assessment

The statements on this page concern your personal reactions to a number of different situations. If a statement is TRUE or MOSTLY TRUE as applied to you, circle "T". If a statement is FALSE or NOT USUALLY TRUE as applied to you, circle "F". Answer honestly.

T   F   1. I find it hard to imitate the behavior of other people.

T   F   2. At parties and social gatherings, I do not attempt to do or say things that others will like.

T   F   3. I can only argue for ideas that I already believe.

T   F   4. I can make impromptu speeches even on topics about which I have almost no information.

T   F   5. I guess I put on a show to impress or entertain others.

T   F   6. I would probably make a good actor.

T   F   7. In a group of people, I am rarely the center of attention.

T   F   8. In different situations and with different people, I often act like very different persons.

T   F   9. I am not particularly good at making other people like me.

T   F   10. I am not always the person I appear to be.

T   F   11. I would not change my opinions (or the way I do things) in order to please someone.

T   F   12. I have considered being an entertainer.

T   F   13. I have never been good at games like charades or improvisational acting.

T   F   14. I have trouble changing my behavior to suit different people and different situations.

T   F   15. At a party, I let others keep the jokes and stories going.

T   F   16. I feel a bit awkward in public and do not show up quite as well as I should.

T   F   17. I can look anyone in the eye and tell a lie with a straight face (if for a right end).

T   F   18. I may deceive people by being friendly when I really dislike them.

Please see next page to determine your self-monitoring style.

Source: Snyder, Mark and Steve Gangestad. 1986 "On the Nature of Self Monitoring." *Journal of Personality and Social Psychology*, 51(1). Copyright © 1986 by the American Psychological Association. Reprinted with permission.

Self-Monitoring: Interpretation of Responses

Circled responses indicate high self-monitoring responses. If you have 11 or more responses that match those circled below, this indicates that you may have a high self-monitoring orientation. If you have 10 or fewer responses that match those circled below, this indicates that you may have a low self-monitoring orientation. Remember that one style (low or high self-monitoring) is not generally better than the other. Each style has benefits and costs.

T ⒡ 1. I find it hard to imitate the behavior of other people.

T ⒡ 2. At parties and social gatherings, I do not attempt to do or say things that others will like.

T ⒡ 3. I can only argue for ideas that I already believe.

⒯ F 4. I can make impromptu speeches even on topics about which I have almost no information.

⒯ F 5. I guess I put on a show to impress or entertain others.

⒯ F 6. I would probably make a good actor.

T ⒡ 7. In a group of people, I am rarely the center of attention.

⒯ F 8. In different situations and with different people, I often act like very different persons.

T ⒡ 9. I am not particularly good at making other people like me.

⒯ F 10. I am not always the person I appear to be.

T ⒡ 11. I would not change my opinions (or the way I do things) in order to please someone.

⒯ F 12. I have considered being an entertainer.

T ⒡ 13. I have never been good at games like charades or improvisational acting.

T ⒡ 14. I have trouble changing my behavior to suit different people and different situations.

T ⒡ 15. At a party, I let others keep the jokes and stories going.

T ⒡ 16. I feel a bit awkward in public and do not show up quite as well as I should.

⒯ F 17. I can look anyone in the eye and tell a lie with a straight face (if for a right end).

⒯ F 18. I may deceive people by being friendly when I really dislike them.

Endnotes

1. Church, Allan. 1997. "Managerial Self-Awareness in High-Performing Individuals in Organizations." *Journal of Applied Psychology*, 82(2): 281–292; Ashford, Susan, and Ann Tsui. 1991. "Self-Regulation for Managerial Effectiveness: The Role of Active Feedback Seeking." *Academy of Management Journal*, 34: 251–280.

2. Kiechel. 1989. "How to Spot an Empty Suit." *Fortune*. November 20: 22.

3. Ibid., p. 23.

4. Kaplan, Robert, Wilfred Drath, and Joan Kofodimos. 1991. *Beyond Ambition: How Driven Managers Can Lead Better and Live Longer*. San Francisco, CA: Jossey-Bass Publishers.

5. Kofodimos, Joan. 1993. *Balancing Act: How Managers Can Integrate Successful Careers and Fulfilling Personal Lives*. San Francisco, CA: Jossey-Bass Publishers.

6. Argyris, Chris. 1991. "Teaching Smart People How to Learn." *Harvard Business Review*, 69(3): 99–110.

7. Kaplan, Robert, Wilfred Drath, and Joan Kofodimos. 1985. *High Hurdles: The Challenge of Executive Self-Development* (Technical Report No. 125). Greensboro, NC: Center for Creative Leadership.

8. Kaplan, R. 1990. "The Expansive Executive: How the Drive to Mastery Helps and Hinders Organizations." *Human Resource Management*, 29(3): 307–327.

9. Hochschild, Arlie Russell. 1997. *The Time Bind: When Work Becomes Home and Home Becomes Work*. New York: Holt and Company.

10. Reuter, Anne. 2004. "Professor Puzzles Over Why Some Grow and Some Falter," citing Neal Krause. *Ann Arbor News*, pp. E1–E2.

11. Needleman, Sarah. 2009. "Staying in the Game with Help from the Sidelines. *Wall Street Journal*. September 1. http://coachingcommons.org/news/wall-street-journal-staying-in-the-game-with-help-on-the-sidelines; Sherman, Stratford, and Alyssa Freas. 2004. "Wild West of Executive Coaching." *Harvard Business Review*, November 1: 82-90; Johnson, Lauren Keller. January 2007. "Getting More from Executive Coaching," *Harvard Management Update*.

12. Bridges, William. 1997. *Creating You & Co.: Learn How to Think Like the CEO of Your Own Career*. Reading, MA: Addison-Wesley Longman; Peters, Tom. 1997. "The Brand Called You." *Fast Company*. August/September.

13. Peters, Tom. 1997. "The Brand Called You." *Fast Company*. August/September: 84.

14. Fisher, Ann. 2004. "Show Off, without Being a Blowhard." *Fortune*. March.

15. Peters, Tom. 1997. "The Brand Called You." *Fast Company*. August/September: 84.

16. Finder, Alan. 2006. "For Some, Online Persona Undermines a Resume," *New York Times Online*, June 11, http://www.nytimes.com/2006/06/11/us/11recruit.html?pagewanted=1&ei=5094&en=3886d00a08e539b5&hp&ex=1150084800&partner=home page

17. Johnston, Timothy, and Laura Edwards. 2002. "Genes, Interactions, and the Development of Behavior." *Psychological Review*, 109(1): 26–34; Olson, James, Philip A. Vernon, Julie Aitken Harris, and Kerry L. Jang. 2001. "The Heritability of Attitudes: A Study of Twins." *Journal of Personality and Social Psychology*, 80(6): 845–860; Borkenau, Peter, Rainer Miemann, Alois Angletner, and Frank M. Spinath. 2001. "Genetic and Environmental Influences on Observed Personality: Evidence from German Observational Study of Adult Twins." *Journal of Personality and Social Psychology*, 80(4):655–668; Dickens, William, and James R. Flynn. 2001. "Heritability Estimates Versus Large Environmental Effects: The IQ Paradox Resolved." *Psychological Review*, 108(2).

18. Dweck, Carol. 2008. "Can Personality Be Changed? The Role of Beliefs in Personality and Change." *Current Directions in Psychological Science*, 17(6): 391–394; Sin, Nancy, and Sonja Lyubomirsky. 2009. "Enhancing Well-Being and Alleviating Depressive Symptoms with Positive Psychology Interventions: A Practice-Friendly Meta-Analysis." *Journal of Clinical Psychology*, 65(5): 467–487.

19. Seligman, Martin. 1998. *Learned Optimism: How to Change Your Mind and Your Life*. New York: Free Press. Dunkel, Curtis and Jennifer Kerpelman (eds.). 2006. *Possible Selves: Theory, Research, and Application*. Hauppauge, NY: Nova Science Publishers.

20. Zweig, Jason. 2009. "Is Your Investing Personality in Your DNA?" *Wall Street Journal*, April 4: B1.

21. Athos, Anthony, and John Gabarro. 1978. *Interpersonal Behavior: Communication and Understanding in Relationships*. Upper Saddle River, NJ: Prentice Hall, 4.

22. Markus, Hazel, and Paula Nurius. 1986. "Possible Selves." *American Psychologist,* 41: 954–969.

23. Kitayama, Shinobu, Hisaya Matsumoto, Hazel Rose Markus, and Vinai Norasakkunkit. 1997. "Individual and Collective Processes in the Construction of the Self: Self-Enhancement in the United States and Self-Criticism in Japan." *Journal of Personality and Social Psychology,* 72(6): 1245–1267; Kitayama, Shinobu, Hyekyung Park, A. Timur Sevencer, Mayumi Karasawa, and Ayese K. Uskul. 2009. "A Cultural Task Analysis of Implicit Independence: Comparing North America, Western Europe, and East Asia." *Journal of Personality and Social Psychology,* 97(2): 236–255.

24. Sedikides, Constantine, Lowell Gaertner, and Yoshiyasu Toguchi. 2003. "Pancultural Self-Enhancement." *Journal of Personality and Social Psychology,* 84(1): 60–79.

25. Tillich, Paul. 1952. *The Courage to Be.* New Haven, CT: Yale University Press; Berg, David, and Kenwyn Smith. 1997. *Paradoxes of Group Life.* San Francisco, CA: Jossey-Bass Publishers.

26. Oyserman, Daphna, Heather Coon, and Markus Kemmelmeier. 2002. "Rethinking Individual and Collectivism: Evaluation of Theoretical Assumptions and Meta-Analysis." *Pyschological Bulletin,* 128(1): 3–72; Fiske, Alan Page. 2002. "Using Individualism and Collectivism to Compare Cultures—A Critique of the Validity and Measurement of the Constructs: Comment on Oyserman et al." *Psychological Bulletin,* 128(1): 78–88.

27. Sedikides, Constantine, Lowell Gaertner, and Yoshiyasu Toguchi. 2003. "Pancultural Self-Enhancement." *Journal of Personality and Social Psychology,* 84(1): 60–79.

28. Spence, Janet T. 1985. "Achievement American Style: The Rewards and Costs of Individualism." *American Psychologist,* 40(12): 1285–1295.

29. Triandis, Harry C. 1989. "The Self and Social Behavior in Differing Cultural Contexts." *Psychological Review,* 96: 507.

30. Ibid.

31. Iyengar, Sheena, and Mark R. Lepper. 1999. "Rethinking the Value of Choice: A Cultural Perspective on Intrinsic Motivation." *Journal of Personality and Social Psychology,* 76(3): 349–366.

32. Sedikides, Constantine, Lowell Gaertner, and Yoshiyasu Toguchi. 2003. "Pancultural Self-Enhancement." *Journal of Personality and Social Psychology,* 84(1): 60–79.

33. Marks, Gary. 1984. "Thinking One's Abilities Are Unique and One's Opinions Are Common." *Personality and Social Psychology Bulletin,* 10(2): 203–208.

34. Kitayama, Shinobu, Hisaya Matsumoto, Hazel Rose Markus, and Vinai Norasakkunkit. 1997. "Individual and Collective Processes in the Construction of the Self: Self-Enhancement in the United States and Self-Criticism in Japan." *Journal of Personality and Social Psychology,* 72(6): 1245–1267.

35. Kim, Heejung S. 2002. "We Talk, Therefore We Think? A Cultural Analysis of the Effect of Talking on Thinking." *Journal of Personality and Social Psychology,* 83(4): 828–842.

36. Triandis, Harry C. 1989. "The Self and Social Behavior in Differing Cultural Contexts." *Psychological Review,* 96: 510.

37. Markus, Hazel, and Shinobu Kityama. 1991. "Culture and the Self: Implications for Cognition, Emotion, and Motivation." *Psychological Review,* 98: 224–253.

38. Triandis, Harry C. 1989. "The Self and Social Behavior in Differing Cultural Contexts." *Psychological Review,* 96: 507.

39. Sedikides, Constantine, Lowell Gaertner, and Yoshiyasu Toguchi. 2003. "Pancultural Self-Enhancement." *Journal of Personality and Social Psychology,* 84(1): 60–79.

40. Kitayama, Shinobu, Hisaya Matsumoto, Hazel Rose Markus, and Vinai Norasakkunkit. 1997. "Individual and Collective Processes in the Construction of the Self: Self-Enhancement in the United States and Self-Criticism in Japan." *Journal of Personality and Social Psychology,* 1245–1267.

41. Ibid.

42. Markus, Hazel Rose, and Shinobu Kitayama. 1991. "Culture and the Self: Implications for Cognition, Emotion, and Motivation." *Psychological Review,* 98(2): 224.

43. Klidas, Antonios. October 31-November 2, 2002. "The Cultural Relativity of Employee Empowerment: Findings From the European Hotel Industry." The Netherlands: Institute for Research on Intercultural Cooperation.

44. Gilligan, Carol. 1982. *In a Different Voice.* Cambridge: University Press.

45. Weick, Karl. 1996. *Sensemaking in Organizations.* Thousand Oaks, CA: Sage Publications, 23.

46. 2001. "Personal Histories: Leaders Remember the Moments and People Who Shaped Them." *Harvard Business Review,* 34: 27–38.

47. Ibid.

48. Bryant, Adam. 2009. "Imagining a World of No Annual Reviews." *New York Times.* October 18: B2.

49. Brady, Diane. 2004 Act II: Ann Fudge's Two-Year Break from Work Changed Her Life. Will Those Lessons Help Her Fix Young & Rubicam? *BusinessWeek*, 72–82.

50. Meacham, John. "I Had to Learn to Fight." *Newsweek*, September 1, 2008. http://www.newsweek.com/2008/08/22/i-had-to-learn-to-fight.html

51. Ibid.

52. Herrara, Nicholas, R. B. Zajonc, Grazyna Wierczorkowska, and Bogdan Cichomski. 2003. "Beliefs About Birth Rank and Their Reflection in Reality." *Journal of Personality and Social Psychology*, 85(1): 142–150.

53. Sulloway, Frank J. 1996. *Born to Rebel: Birth Order, Family Dynamics, and Creative Lives*. New York: Pantheon Books.

54. Ibid., xiii.

55. Dunkel, Curtis, Colin R. Harbke, and Dennis Papini. 2009. "Direct and Indirect Effects of Birth Order on Personality and Identity: Support for the Null Hypothesis." *The Journal of Genetic Psychology*, 170(2): 159–176.

56. Rosenthal, Robert, and Lenore Jackson. 1968 and 1992. *Pygmalion in the Classroom: Teacher Expectations and Pupils' Intellectual Development*. New York: Irvington Publishers, vii–viii.

57. Alderfer, Clayton. 1983. "Intergroup Relations and Organizations." In J. Richard Hackman, Edward W. Lawler, and Lyman W. Porter (eds.). *Perspectives on Behavior in Organizations*. New York: McGraw-Hill, 408–416.

58. Harquail, Celia Virginia Felicia. 1996. "When One Speaks for Many: The Influence of Social Identification on Group Advocacy in Organizations." Unpublished dissertation. Ann Arbor, MI: University of Michigan, 29.

59. Ibid.

60. Markus, Hazel, and E. Wurf. 1989. "The Dynamic Self-Concept: A Social Psychological Perspective." *Annual Review of Psychology,* 38: 307–308.

61. Markus, Hazel, and E. Wurf. 1989. "The Dynamic Self-Concept: A Social Psychological Perspective." *Annual Review of Psychology,* 38: 299–337; Weick, Karl E. 1995. *Sensemaking in Organizations*. Thousand Oaks, CA: Sage; Fiske, Susan T., and Shelley E. Taylor. 1991. *Social Cognition*, 2nd ed. New York: McGraw-Hill.

62. Weick, Karl E. 1996. *Sensemaking in Organizations*. Thousand Oaks, CA: Sage.

63. Druian, P., and R. Catrambone. 1966. "Cognitive Accessibility of the Self Concept in Person Perception." Behavioral Science Research Foundation. Unpublished.

64. Harquail, Celia Virginia Felicia. 1996. "When One Speaks for Many: The Influence of Social Identification on Group Advocacy in Organizations." Unpublished dissertation. Ann Arbor: University of Michigan, 270.

65. Gilligan, Carol. 1992. *In a Different Voice*. Cambridge, MA: Cambridge University Press.

66. Weick, Karl E. 1995. *Sensemaking in Organizations*. Thousand Oaks, CA: Sage.

67. Albert, Stuart, Blake Ashforth, and Jane Dutton. 2002. "Organizational Identity and Identification: Charting New Waters and Building New Bridges." *Academy of Management Review,* 25(1): 13–18; Frankl, Viktor. 1959. *Man's Search for Meaning*. New York: Simon and Schuster.

68. Baumeister, Roy, and Mark Leary. 1995. "The Need to Belong: Desire for Interpersonal Attachments as a Fundamental Human Motivation." *Psychological Bulletin,* 117(3): 497.

69. Bowlby, John. 1988. *A Secure Base: Parent-Child Attachment and Healthy Human Development*. New York: Basic Books, 11. Kahn, William A. 2002. "Managing the Paradox of Self-Reliance." *Organizational Dynamics*, 30: 239–256.

70. Bandura, Alfred. 1986. *Social Foundations of Thoughts and Action: A Social Cognitive Theory*. Upper Saddle River, NJ: Prentice Hall. Paunonen, Sampo and Ryan Hong. 2010. "Self-Efficacy and the Prediction of Domain Specific Cognitive Abilities." *Journal of Personality*, 78(1): 339–360.

71. Ashforth, Blake, and Alan M. Saks. 2000. "Personal Control in Organizatons: A Longitudinal Investigation with Newcomers." *Human Relations,* 53(3): 311–339; Krause, Neal, and Benjamin Shaw. 2000. "Role-Specific Feelings of Control and Mortality." *Psychology and Aging,* 15(4): 617–626. Bandura, Albert. 2001. "Social Cognitive Theory: An Agentic Perspective." *Annual Review of Psychology*, 52: 1–26.

72. Feldman, Martha, and Anat Rafaeli. 2002. "Organizational Routines as Sources of Connections and Understandings." *Journal of Management Studies*, 39(3): 309–329; Kelvin, Peter. 1977. "Predictability, Power and Vulnerability in Interpersonal Attraction." In Duck, Steven (ed.). *Theory and Practice in Interpersonal Attraction*, London: Academic Press, 355–378.

73. Gergen, Kenneth. 1991. *The Saturated Self, Dilemmas of Identity in Contemporary Life*. New York: Basic Books.

74. Ibid.

75. Judge, Paul. 1997. "Is the Net Redefining Our Identity?" *Business Week.* May 12: 100–102.

76. Turkle, Sherry. 1995. *Life on the Screen: Identity in the Age of the Internet.* New York: Simon and Schuster, 51.

77. Subrahmanyam, Kaveri, Robert E. Kraut, Patricia M. Greenfield, and Elisheva F. Gross. 2000. "The Impact of Home Computer Use on Children's Activities and Development." *Children and Computer Technology,* 10(2), http://www.futureofchildren.org

78. Turkle, Sherry. 1995. *Life on the Screen: Identity in the Age of the Internet.* New York: Simon and Schuster.

79. Greenfield, Patricia. 2009. "Technology and Informal Education: What Is Taught, What Is Learned." *Science,* 323(5910): 69–71.

80. Taylor, Jim, and Watts Wacker. 1997. *The 500 Year Delta: What Happens after What Comes Next.* New York: HarperBusiness.

81. Festinger, Leon. 1954. "A Theory of Social Comparison Processes." *Human Relations,* 7: 117–140.

82. Cooley, C. H. 1956. *Human Nature and the Social Order.* New York: Free Press.

83. Lockwood, Penelope, and Ziva Kunda. 1997. "Superstars and Me: Predicting the Impact of Role Models on the Self." *Journal of Personality and Social Psychology,* 73(1): 93.

84. Markus, Hazel, and Paula Nurius. 1986. "Possible Selves." *American Psychologist,* 41: 954, 965–966.

85. Ibid.

86. 1997. "Perspectives." *Newsweek* October 13: p. 27.

87. Shapiro, Eileen. 1995. *Fad Surfing in the Boardroom: Reclaiming the Courage to Manage in the Age of Instant Answers.* Reading, MA: Addison-Wesley.

88. Jackson, Bradley. 1996. "Reengineering the Sense of Self: The Manager and the Management Guru." *Journal of Management Studies,* 33(5): 571–590.

89. Ibid., p. 572.

90. Ibid.

91. Taylor, Jim, and Watts Wacker. 1997. *The 500 Year Delta: What Happens after What Comes Next.* New York: HarperBusiness.

92. Gergen, Kenneth. 1991. *The Saturated Self, Dilemmas of Identity in Contemporary Life.* New York: Basic Books, 34.

93. Doan, Robert E. 1997. "Narrative Therapy, Postmodernism, Social Constructionism, and Constructivism: Discussion and Distinctions." *Transactional Analysis Journal: Special Theme Issue on Transactional Analysis and Constructivism,* 27(2): 128.

94. Anderson, Walter Truett. 1997. *The Future of the Self: Exploring the Post-Identity Society.* New York: Tarcher Putnam, xvi.

95. Dougherty, Deborah, and Cynthia Hardy. 1996. "Sustained Product Innovation in Large, Mature Organizations: Overcoming Innovation-to-Organization Problems." *Academy of Management Journal,* 30(5): 1120–1153.

96. Turkle, Sherry. 1995. *Life on the Screen: Identity in the Age of the Internet.* New York: Simon and Schuster, 51.

97. Weick, Karl E. 1993. "The Collapse of Sense-making in Organizations: The Mann Gulch Disaster." *Administrative Science Quarterly,* 38: 628–652.

98. Smircich, Linda, and Gareth Morgan. 1982. "Leadership: The Management of Meaning." *Journal of Applied Behavioral Science,* 18(3): 258.

99. Ibid., p. 260.

100. Knight, M., and Robert Doan. 1994. *The Stories We Tell Ourselves: I-Spi: A Technique for Narrative Assessment.* Orlando, FL: Harcourt Brace.

101. Doan, Robert E. 1997. "Narrative Therapy, Postmodernism, Social Constructionism, and Constructivism: Discussion and Distinctions." *Transactional Analysis Journal: Special Theme Issue on Transactional Analysis and Constructivism,* 27(2): 131.

102. Ibid., p. 129.

103. Goffman, Erving. 1959. *The Presentation of Self in Everyday Life,* New York: Anchor Books; Andrzej Nowak, Robin Vallacher, Abraham Tesser, and Wojceich Borkowski. 2000. "Society of Self: The Emergence of Collective Properties of Self-Structure." *Psychological Review,* 107(1): 39–61.

104. Hurtado, Aida. 1996. "Strategic Suspensions: Feminists of Color Theorize the Production of Knowledge." In Goldberg, Nancy, Blythe Clinchy, Mary Belenky, and Jill Mattuck Tarule (eds.). *Knowledge, Difference and Power.* New York: Basic Books, 384.

105. Bell, Ella. 1990. "The Bicultural Life Experiences of Career-Oriented Black Women." *Journal of Organizational Behavior,* 11: 459–477; Brannen, Mary Yoko. 2000. *Your Next Boss Is Japanese: Recontextualization, Negotiated Culture, and Organizational Change.* New York: Oxford University Press.

106. Hurtado, Aida. 1996. "Strategic Suspensions: Feminists of Color Theorize the Production of

Knowledge." In Goldberg, Nancy, Blythe Clinchy, Mary Belenky, and Jill Mattuck Tarule (eds.). *Knowledge, Difference and Power.* New York: Basic Books. Schleicher, D. J., and A. R. McConnell. 2005. "The Complexity of Self-Complexity: An Associated Systems Theory Approach." *Social Cognition*, 23, 387–416.

107. Settles, Iris, Robert Sellers, and Alphonse Damas, Jr. 2002. "One Role or Two? The Function of Psychological Separation in Role Conflict." *Journal of Applied Psychology*, 87(3): 574–582.

108. Ibid.

109. Ibid., p. 387.

110. Beyer, Janice, and David R. Hannah. 2002. "Building on the Past: Enacting Established Personal Identities in a New Work Setting." *Organization Science,* 13(6): 636–652; Ruderman, Marian, Patrica Ohlott, Kate Panzer, and Sara King. 2002. "Benefits of Multiple Roles for Managerial Women." *Academy of Management Journal,* 45(2): 369–386; Settles, Iris, Robert Sellers, and Alphonse Damas, Jr. 2002. "One Role or Two? The Function of Psychological Separation in Role Conflict." *Journal of Applied Psychology,* 87(3): 574–582, 57; Rothbard, Nancy. 2001. "Enriching or Depleting? The Dynamics of Engagement in Work and Family Roles." *Administrative Science Quarterly,* 46(4): 655–685; Ibarra, Herminia. 2003. *Working Identity: Unconventional Strategies for Reinventing Your Career.* Boston: Harvard Business School Press, 35; Moen, Phyllis, Donna Dempster-McClain, and Robin M. Williams Jr. 1992. "Successful Aging: A Life Course Perspective on Women's Multiple Roles and Health." *American Journal of Sociology*, 97(6): 1612–1638; Schleicher, D. J., and A. R. McConnell. 2005. "The Complexity of Self-complexity: An Associated Systems Theory Approach." *Social Cognition, 23,* 387–416.

111. Rothbard, Nancy. 2001. "Enriching or Depleting? The Dynamics of Engagement in Work and Family Roles." *Administrative Science Quarterly,* 46(4): 655–685.

112. Beyer, Janice, and David R. Hannah. 2002. "Building on the Past: Enacting Established Personal Identities in a New Work Setting." *Organization Science,* 13(6): 636–652.

113. Ruderman, Marian, Patricia Ohlott, Kate Panzer, and Sara King. 2002. "Benefits of Multiple Roles for Managerial Women." *Academy of Management Journal,* 45(2): 369–386.

114. Rothbard, Nancy. 2001. "Enriching or Depleting? The Dynamics of Engagement in Work and Family

Roles." *Administrative Science Quarterly,* 46(4): 655–685.

115. Ibarra, Herminia. 1999. "Provisional Selves: Experimenting with Image and Identity in Professional Adaptation." *Administrative Science Quarterly,* 1999: 764–791.

116. Hill, Linda. 1992. *Becoming a Manager: Mastery of a New Identity.* Boston: Harvard Business School Press, 173–174. Cited in Ibarra, Herminia. 1999. "Provisional Selves: Experimenting with Image and Identity in Professional Adaptation." *Administrative Science Quarterly,* December: 764–791.

117. Ibarra, Herminia. 2003. *Working Identity: Unconventional Strategies for Reinventing Your Career.* Boston: Harvard Business School Press, 35.

118. Brinkman, Rick, and Rick Kirschner. 2002. *Dealing with People You Can't Stand.* New York: McGraw-Hill, 221.

119. Breen, Bill. 2003. "Desire, Connecting with What Customers Want." *Fast Company*, 86–89.

120. Blustein, David L. 1994. "Social Cognitive Orientations and Career Development: A Theoretical and Empirical Analysis." *Journal of Vocational Behavior,* 31: 63–80. Cited in Kilduff, Martin and David Day. 1994. "Do Chameleons Get Ahead? The Effects of Self-Monitoring on Managerial Careers." *Academy of Management Journal,* 37(4): 1047–1060.

121. Snyder, Mark, and S. Gangestad. 1982. "Choosing Social Situations: Two Investigations of Self-Monitoring Processes." *Journal of Personality and Social Psychology,* 43: 123–135. Cited in Kilduff, Martin and David Day. 1994. "Do Chameleons Get Ahead? The Effects of Self-Monitoring on Managerial Careers." *Academy of Management Journal,* 37(4): 1047–1060. Day, David and Deidra Schleicher. 2006. "Self-Monitoring at Work: A Motive-Based Perspective." *Journal of Personality,* 74(3): 685–713; Leone, Christopher. 2006. "Self-Monitoring: Individual Differences in Orientations to the Social World." *Journal of Personality*, 74(3): 633–658.

122. Ibid.

123. Snyder, Mark. 1979. "Self-Monitoring Processes." In Berkowitz, L. (ed.). *Advances in Experimental Social Psychology,* Vol. 12, New York: Academic Press, 35–128. Cited in Kilduff, Martin, and David Day. 1994. "Do Chameleons Get Ahead? The Effects of Self-Monitoring on Managerial Careers." *Academy of Management Journal,* 37(4): 1047–1060.

124. Mehra, Ajay, Martin Killduff, and Daniel J. Brass. 2001. "The Social Networks of High and Low

Self-Monitors: Implications for Workplace Performance." *Administrative Science Quarterly*, 46: 121–146; Gangestad, Steven, and Mark Snyder. 2000. "Self-Monitoring: Appraisal and Reappraisal." *Psychological Bulletin,* 126(4).

125. Day, David and Deidra Schleicher. 2006. "Self-Monitoring at Work: A Motive-Based Perspective." *Journal of Personality,* 74(3): 685–713.

126. Nathan, John. 1999. *Sony: The Private Life*. Boston: Houghton-Mifflin.

127. Day, David and Deidra Schleicher. 2006. "Self-Monitoring at Work: A Motive-Based Perspective." *Journal of Personality,* 74(3): 685–713.

128. Mehra, Ajay, and Mark T. Schenkel. 2007. "The Price Chameleons Pay: Self-Monitoring, Boundary Spanning and Role Conflict in the Workplace." *British Journal of Management,* 19(2): 138–144; Day, David, and Deidra Schleicher. 2006. "Self-Monitoring at Work: A Motive-Based Perspective." *Journal of Personality*, 74(3): 686–713.

129. Knowles, Malcolm. 1990. *The Adult Learner: A Neglected Species,* 4th ed. Houston, TX: Gulf Publishing.

130. Gutner, Toddi. 2008. "Applicants' Personalities Put to the Test." *Wall Street Journal*. August 26: D4.

3

■ ■ ■

Building Trust

This chapter will help you:

- Understand how trust contributes to individual and organizational success.
- Develop a working definition of trust.
- Learn how to build trust.
- Learn how to repair trust once broken.
- Learn how to create "swift trust" when needed.
- Learn how positive emotions and behaviors build trust and enhance personal and organizational effectiveness.

The importance of trust becomes clear
when we try to imagine a world without it.

—ROBERT BRUCE SHAW
Author of *Trust in the Balance*

WHY TRUST MATTERS

In the office in which I work, there are five people of whom I am afraid. Each of these five people is afraid of four people (excluding overlaps), for a total of twenty, and each of these twenty people is afraid of six people, making a total of one hundred and twenty people who are feared by at least one person. Each of these one hundred and twenty people is afraid of the other one hundred and nineteen, and all of these one hundred and forty-five people are afraid of the twelve men at the top who helped found and build the company and now own and direct it.[1]

So begins the chapter "The Office in Which I Work" in Joseph Heller's classic book, *Something Happened*. I begin this chapter with Heller's words not because they necessarily reflect everyday work life today (although they do for some people and ring true, at least in part, for many others). Rather, I begin this chapter with Heller's words because they illustrate the fundamental importance of trust in our lives.

Why is trust so important to us? We need trust because we must live in a complex world that we cannot fully understand, depend on people whom we can never completely know, and rely on organizations that do not exist for the sole purpose of meeting our personal needs. Therefore, we must rely on trust—essentially a leap of faith—that "some things will remain as they are or ought to be,"[2] that other people will not take unfair advantage of us,[3] and that we will not be harmed by the organizations in which we invest our future. In short, trust helps us face the inevitable risks of everyday life so that we can rise above our fears; take productive action; and experience tranquility and happiness in a complex, unpredictable, and sometimes threatening world.

Despite the importance of trust in everyday work life, many managers see it as a nice-to-have quality rather than a necessity. In her study of new managers, Harvard professor Linda Hill found that "most new managers put their efforts into demonstrating their technical competence" rather than building trust. One of the managers in her study explained:

> The first thirty days were critical . . . I had to demonstrate that I had ability. I kept looking for a big win, picking the right stock, stealing a big producer from the competition. I had to demonstrate that I worked hard. I stayed late and came in on weekends. It was hard to get relief from the pressure of it all.

However, Hill found that employees "were making judgments using a different set of standards. They wanted to find out if the new manager deserved their trust and respect. Staff members were clearly sizing up the new boss—and their criteria weren't always fair." By emphasizing their technical competence and ignoring trust-building activities, managers often "missed opportunities for building goodwill among their subordinates, just when they needed it most."[4]

Bosses also make judgments about the trustworthiness of the managers who work for them. In a study of middle- and upper-level executives, researchers found that executives who derailed were viewed by their managers as less trustworthy and as having less integrity than were their more successful peers. What criteria did these bosses use to determine trustworthiness? The bosses focused on whether the manager blamed others or took personal responsibility for mistakes, put personal desires over organizational needs, and denied or admitted personal shortcomings.[5]

It is not surprising that managers who earn the trust of others tend to have better job performance, have more satisfied and committed employees, have stronger networks, get more challenging job assignments, and get promoted more often than those who don't inspire trust.[6] Specifically, they are better able to do the following:

- Attract and retain followers because employees prefer to work with people they believe are trustworthy.
- Promote a sense of belonging because employees are more likely to identify with organizational goals and values; invest psychologically in their jobs; and feel pride, loyalty, and affection toward their managers and organizations.[7]
- Build support for their goals because employees who trust their managers are less likely to question their managers' competence, goodwill, direction, and intentions.[8]

- Develop more productive employees because people in trusting relationships tend to exhibit increased emotional stability, self-control, creativity, and flexibility, as well as less stress and defensiveness.[9]
- Inspire employees to go "beyond the call of duty" and contribute to their organizations in ways that add value but that are not in their job descriptions.[10]
- Enhance the quality of customer service because employees who trust their managers are more likely to engage in the kinds of helping behaviors that result in high-quality service.[11]
- Focus on value-added work because they do not need costly employee control systems that can consume both managers' and employees' time, distract them from focusing on fundamental work objectives,[12] and reduce innovation and cooperation.[13]
- Enhance communication because employees are more likely to speak openly and honestly, listen carefully, and give bad news upward if they trust the boss.[14]
- Increase the "speed and efficiency in the creation and transfer of knowledge" because employees are more willing to cooperate with each other in the sharing of information.[15]
- Reduce conflict and the costs of negotiation because employees are more likely to give each other the benefit of the doubt and be open-minded, flexible, and willing to be influenced by each other.[16]
- Have more effective group decision-making processes because group members feel free to focus on organizational tasks and goals rather than defend themselves from what they perceive to be threatening. Team members who don't trust their bosses are more likely to have difficulty concentrating on their tasks, are more likely to engage in self-protecting and low-risk behaviors, have more difficulty dealing with uncertainty, and are less likely to support and implement the ideas of their leaders.[17]
- Promote organizational change because employees are more likely to feel secure, be flexible, take risks, and cope productively with complexity, ambiguity, and uncertainty.[18]
- Collaborate more across organizational boundaries.[19]
- Survive organizational crises because they are more likely to receive undistorted information from employees, enable decentralized decision making that allows employees to react quickly to crises, and encourage collaboration within and across organizations affected by the crisis.[20]
- Help employees accept unfavorable information and decisions that adversely affect them because employees who trust their managers are more likely to assume that their managers did the best that they could under the circumstances, were fair in their decision-making process, and will do whatever it takes to turn the situation around. The more unfavorable and unexpected the situation, the more important trust becomes.[21] For example, researchers Aneil Mishra and Gretchen Spreitzer found that employees who trust their organizations are more likely to cope effectively during downsizings.[22]

In addition to the aforementioned benefits of employees' trust in their managers, there are many other benefits to trust in organizations. For example, managers who trust the employees who work for them tend to behave in ways that help their employees succeed. They are more likely to have higher expectations for what employees can achieve, challenge employees with assignments that will help them grow, empower employees, and provide encouragement to employees.[23] Teams with members that trust each other tend to outperform those with members that have low trust. Researcher Li-Fang Chou and her colleagues found that trusting relationships among team members enhance the quality and speed of the team's outcomes, as well as the performance of individual team members. Members of high-trust teams tend to have common values about what needs to be done and how to do it. They are able to predict each other's behavior, which makes it easier to coordinate with each other. They are more willing to share information, cooperate with each other, manage team stress, and adapt to changing environmental conditions.[24] Virtual teams benefit from trust among team members because they are better able to handle the "uncertainty, complexity, and expectations of the virtual environment."[25] For all of these reasons, trust has been called a "social lubricant,"[26] "invisible asset,"[27] "collaborative capital,"[28] "hidden source of wealth,"[29] and the "heart of relationships."[30] Rather than simply being nice to have, trust in organizations is increasingly being viewed as a source of competitive advantage. This is because high-quality relationships—those built on trust—provide economic value to organizations, take a long time to develop, and cannot be easily copied by other organizations.[31]

> **Trust is like the air we breathe. When it's present, nobody really notices. But when it's absent, everybody notices.**
> —WARREN BUFFETT,
> *American investor,*
> *industrialist, philanthropist*

For example, Southwest Airlines has been consistently on *Fortune* magazine's annual lists of most admired companies. Since its first flight in 1971, Southwest Airlines has been ranked among the most successful in terms of safety, customer service, on-time performance, and stock performance. The company has had no pay cuts, employee layoffs, or strikes in its history, and company leaders support unionization. LUV is Southwest's stock symbol. The success of the company has been attributed in large part to founder and former CEO Herb Kelleher's outstanding "people skills" and his ability to build trust among employees and customers.[32] When asked about the secrets to the company's success, Kelleher explained:

> The intangibles are more important than the tangibles. Someone can go out and buy airplanes from Boeing and ticket counters, but they can't buy our culture, our esprit de corps. We've had people come in to see how we turn around planes. (Southwest's time to get planes in and out of gates is about half the industry average.) They keep looking for gimmicks, special equipment. It's just a bunch of people knocking themselves out.[33]

Although Kelleher is no longer the CEO of Southwest Airlines, the foundation of trust that he helped build continues to serve the company well, and it inspires Southwest's leaders and employees to celebrate the company's successes in good times and work through problems together in bad times.[34]

WHAT IS TRUST?

Researchers John Cook and Toby Wall define trust as "a willingness to ascribe good intentions to and have confidence in the words and actions of other people," especially when doing so would put one at risk if one's trust is misguided.[35] Three characteristics are fundamental to our understanding of trust: uncertainty, risk, and perceptions.

Uncertainty

We need to trust—take a leap of faith—only if we have partial information about a person or situation and cannot entirely control the outcome. If we have complete knowledge and control of a situation, we have no need to trust because we can anticipate and ensure the outcome that we desire. For example, if we are willing and able to monitor all aspects of an employees' work-related behavior (e.g., through cameras, electronically counting computer keystrokes, or monitoring phone calls), then we do not need to rely on trust to ensure that the employees are doing their jobs. However, if we choose to delegate or create self-managing (or virtual) teams, then we must trust that employees are focusing on their tasks and working together toward organizational goals without subjecting them to various forms of overt control or covert surveillance.

Risk

When we trust a person or organization, we assume that the benefits of our relationship with them will outweigh any costs to us. Indeed, trust is necessary only if the cost of trusting will be greater than the possible gain.[36] To illustrate this point, researcher Dale Zand provides this fine example:

> [A] parent is exhibiting trusting behavior in hiring a baby-sitter so he can see a movie. The action significantly increases his vulnerability, because he cannot control the baby-sitter's behavior after leaving the house. If the baby-sitter abuses that vulnerability, the penalty may be a tragedy that may adversely affect the rest of his life; if the baby-sitter does not abuse that vulnerability, the benefit will be the pleasure of seeing a movie.[37]

Thus, when we decide to give our boss bad news, we trust that our boss will not kill the messenger. When we give employees confidential organizational information that enables them to make appropriate decisions quickly, we trust that they will not pass on this information to our competitors. When we invest our money through investment advisors and firms, we assume that they will act ethically on our behalf.

Perception

Trust is necessary in situations where we do not have complete information about another person's intentions. Therefore, our trust in someone is based in large part on our perceptions of that person's trustworthiness. We base these perceptions on several factors, including the person's reputation,[38] our prior experiences with the person,[39] and our stereotypes about that person's identity group memberships (e.g., gender, race, religion, and nationality)[40] and organizational group memberships (e.g., department or hierarchical level).[41] Researcher Michele Williams notes that we are more likely to believe that someone is trustworthy and are likely to cooperate with them when we see them as belonging to the same group(s) as ours. Furthermore, we are more likely to rely on stereotypes about who we can and cannot trust when we are under time pressure.[42]

The importance of perception in the development of trust and mistrust cannot be overstated because our perceptions often turn into self-fulfilling prophecies. Researcher Sandra Robinson explains that we tend to look for and focus on information that confirms our prior perceptions about a person's trustworthiness and ignore or minimize information that disconfirms our prior perceptions. Consequently, when we mistrust someone, we are "more likely to look for, find, and remember incidents of breach, even in the absence of an objective breach" because it is consistent with our prior perceptions.[43] We are also less likely to invest emotionally in the relationship because we may doubt that there will be a payoff for our investment. Consequently, the relationship is likely to be characterized by avoidance, conflict, or a "veneer of civility," each of which can increase mutual mistrust.[44] In contrast, when we trust someone, we are "more likely to overlook, forget, or not recognize an actual breach when it does occur" and invest more emotionally in the relationship. Trust is a cognitive and emotional "filter" that influences our interpretations of another person's behavior, as well as our expectations of how we believe the person will act in the future.[45]

In short, if we have complete information about a person or organization, if we can completely control a situation, if we can perfectly predict an outcome, and if we have nothing or little to lose, then trust is not necessary. However, such situations are increasingly rare in our everyday work life, so the ability to trust and to be trustworthy is essential to our effectiveness and well-being. The antecedents and consequences of trusts are described in more detail on the following pages and are summarized in Figure 3-1.

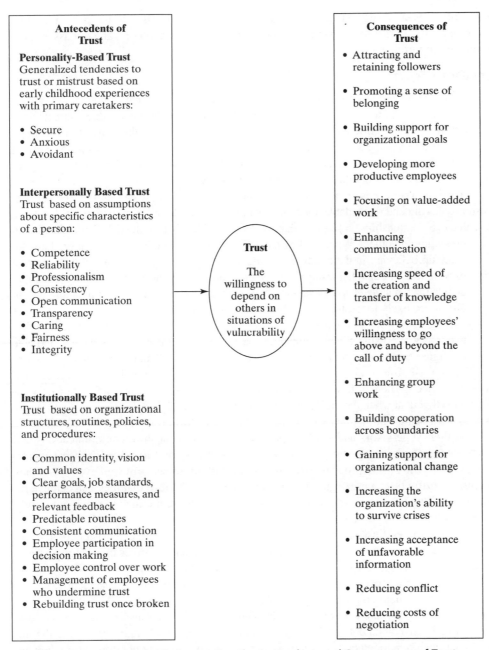

Antecedents of Trust

Personality-Based Trust
Generalized tendencies to trust or mistrust based on early childhood experiences with primary caretakers:

- Secure
- Anxious
- Avoidant

Interpersonally Based Trust
Trust based on assumptions about specific characteristics of a person:

- Competence
- Reliability
- Professionalism
- Consistency
- Open communication
- Transparency
- Caring
- Fairness
- Integrity

Institutionally Based Trust
Trust based on organizational structures, routines, policies, and procedures:

- Common identity, vision and values
- Clear goals, job standards, performance measures, and relevant feedback
- Predictable routines
- Consistent communication
- Employee participation in decision making
- Employee control over work
- Management of employees who undermine trust
- Rebuilding trust once broken

Trust

The willingness to depend on others in situations of vulnerability

Consequences of Trust

- Attracting and retaining followers
- Promoting a sense of belonging
- Building support for organizational goals
- Developing more productive employees
- Focusing on value-added work
- Enhancing communication
- Increasing speed of the creation and transfer of knowledge
- Increasing employees' willingness to go above and beyond the call of duty
- Enhancing group work
- Building cooperation across boundaries
- Gaining support for organizational change
- Increasing the organization's ability to survive crises
- Increasing acceptance of unfavorable information
- Reducing conflict
- Reducing costs of negotiation

FIGURE 3-1   Framework for Understanding the Antecedents and Consequences of Trust

WHY SHOULD I TRUST THEE? LET ME COUNT THE REASONS

If trust is based on our willingness to put ourselves in a vulnerable position in situations in which we have limited control and in which the hazards of a broken trust will be greater than the potential gains, then how do we determine whom we should trust? Our choice to trust or mistrust is both a rational decision and an emotional reaction. As researchers Gary Fine and Lori Holyfield explain, "one not only thinks trust, but feels trust."[46]

Substantial research suggests that our tendency to trust or mistrust another person has two roots: our propensity to trust (our general tendency to trust or mistrust others) and our assessment of a person's trustworthiness.

Propensity to Trust

Some people, it seems, are simply more—or less—trusting than are others. Indeed, many psychologists believe that our tendency to trust or mistrust others is a relatively stable characteristic rooted, in part, in our early childhood experiences. Psychiatrist John Bowlby argued that through our infant and childhood experiences with our parents and other early attachment figures who act as primary caretakers, we develop a general working model of others that affects how willing we are to trust ourselves and others throughout the rest of our lives.[47]

If our earliest experiences with the significant caretakers on whom we depend for our survival are consistently loving and dependable, then we develop a "secure base" from which we develop a comfort with close relationships and believe that we "can confidently take the risks" associated with depending on others. When we begin our lives with a secure base, we are more likely to grow up believing in the goodwill of others, remembering more positive than negative experiences in our relationships with others, and having constructive coping skills that enable us to handle everyday stresses.[48] When we have a secure base to build on, we are also more likely to trust our own competence and judgment, and this faith in ourselves enables us to work well independently as well as with others. Researcher William Kahn explains that organizational members, in part, "must be effectively self-reliant" and able to "figure things out with minimal supervision, develop collaborations and coalitions to move their projects along, and work comfortably amid the ambiguity and insecurity that surround those projects. There is, however, a paradox at the heart of self-reliance: people are only capable of being self-reliant when they feel securely attached to others."[49]

> We're never so vulnerable than when we trust someone—but paradoxically, if we cannot trust, neither can we find love or joy.
> —WALTER ANDERSON, *Political scientist, futurist, and author*

People with secure attachments bring several benefits to the workplace. They are more likely to trust their supervisors and attribute positive intent to managerial communications and actions. This trust, in turn, motivates employees to achieve better performance for their supervisors.[50] Employees who have a propensity to trust are also likely to perform well even when they have an untrustworthy boss, perhaps because it enables them to believe that they can achieve results regardless of the hurdles before them. They may also be more inclined to reach out to others to gain the support they need to succeed.[51]

In contrast, if our earliest experiences with significant caregivers are inconsistent (e.g., caregivers who sometimes respond to our needs in a loving way and at other times in an angry or aloof way) or undependable (e.g., caregivers who are consistently distant or punitive toward us), we are more likely to develop an insecure or avoidant working model of others. Consequently, we are more likely to grow up believing that we generally cannot rely on the goodwill of others or their willingness and ability to take care of our needs. Thus, when in relationships, we are likely to engage in self-protective behaviors such as trying too hard to please others or dismissing the importance of relationships altogether; becoming overdependent on others in our effort to gain their approval or distancing ourselves from others in an effort to avoid the risk of being let down; avoiding confrontation or consistently challenging others; and under- or overcontrolling our environment.[52]

Furthermore, people with insecure or avoidant working models of others tend to have "more rigid and narrow expectations" of relationships and, through their behavior, tend "to provoke the very reactions they fear."[53] For example, managers who do not trust their employees may micromanage their employees. By doing so, they may encourage dependency, lack of initiative, increased resentment, and decreased commitment to the task. This leads the managers to believe that these employees indeed cannot be trusted, and then they micromanage these employees even more, which creates a vicious cycle of mutual mistrust. In contrast, managers who trust their employees are more likely to give them the information, training, resources, and emotional support that they need to act independently and successfully accomplish their tasks, which creates a virtuous cycle of mutual trust.

In short, the seeds of our propensity to trust or mistrust may be sown early in our lives. Furthermore, our decisions to trust others may be based as much in our emotional reactions to past experiences as they are based in the particular circumstances of the current situation.

Assessment of a Person's Trustworthiness

People assess another person's trustworthiness based on three general characteristics: ability, benevolence, and integrity.[54] More specifically, people look for the following characteristics to determine whether you are worthy of their trust:[55]

- *Competence.* Do you have a track record of getting results at work?
- *Reliability.* Can others count on you to follow through on your commitments in ways that make their jobs easier rather than harder?
- *Professionalism.* Do you show that you are dedicated to your work and professional in your interactions?
- *Consistency.* Is your behavior predictable over time and across situations?
- *Open communication.* Are you accessible, willing to share accurate information freely, and open to the opinions of others?
- *Transparency.* Are you clear about what people need to do to be successful? Do you give explanations for your decisions?
- *Caring.* Do people believe that you will listen with care and concern if they share their ideas, hopes, feelings, and problems with you?
- *Fairness.* Do you make decisions based on fairness rather than favoritism?
- *Integrity.* Are you honest, moral, and consistent in your words and deeds?

See Figure 3.2 to assess the degree to which you are acting in ways that enhance your employees' trust in you. The relative importance of each of these characteristics in determining

1. Competence: Do you have an expertise and track record of success?	1	2	3	4	5
2. Reliability: Can people count on you to follow through in ways that make their jobs easier rather than harder?	1	2	3	4	5
3. Professionalism: Do you show that you are dedicated to your work and professional in your interactions?	1	2	3	4	5
4. Consistency: Can people predict how you will react in different situations?	1	2	3	4	5
5. Open Communication: Are you accessible, willing to share information freely, and open to the opinions of others?	1	2	3	4	5
6. Transparency: a) Do people know what they need to do to be successful around you? b) Do you give explanations for your decisions?	1 1	2 2	3 3	4 4	5 5
7. Caring: Do people believe that you will listen with care and concern if they share their ideas, hopes, feelings, and problems with you?	1	2	3	4	5
8. Fairness: Do you make decisions based on fairness rather than favoritism?	1	2	3	4	5
9. Integrity: Are you honest, moral, and consistent in your words and deeds?	1	2	3	4	5
(1 = Not at all; 5 = Very much so)					

FIGURE 3-2   Relational Power: Build Trust

whether one should trust another person is situation specific. For example, if I'm going for life-saving surgery, then I'm likely to base the choice of physician primarily on his or her reputation for technical competence and a consistent record of success. However, if I'm choosing a day care for my child, then I'm likely to base my choice on its reputation for being a caring place that is responsive to children and parents as much as for its technical expertise.

Optimal Trust: Is There Such a Thing as Trusting Too Much?

It is naïve and ineffective to break our social world into either/or categories of people whom we trust unconditionally and people whom we do not trust at all. Trusting others too much can lead us to harm our own and our organizations' performance by taking unnecessary risks, unwittingly ignoring or discounting information that suggests that our trust has been misplaced, saying more than is politically wise, misusing organizational resources, failing to monitor people and situations closely when appropriate, and ignoring our own judgment. Trusting others too little can cause us to be overly suspicious, miss out on opportunities that require risk, limit our sphere of relationships to a chosen few, minimize our dependence on others, resist others' attempts to influence us, withhold or distort information, develop a defensive orientation to the world, engage in costly monitoring activities to ensure compliance, and make us generally unpleasant to be around. In short, trusting too much leads to blind faith and gullibility; trusting too little leads to cynicism and suspicion. Both diminish our effectiveness. Researcher Andrew Wicks and his colleagues recommend that managers develop "optimal trust," which they describe as "knowing whom to trust, how much to trust them, and with respect to what matter."[56]

One of the biggest mistakes we can make is to invest too much trust in too few people. We tend to trust people with whom we have frequent positive interactions and with whom we share significant similarities, yet these criteria can significantly limit our circle of trusted people.[57] One problem with trusting too few people too much is that we may become overdependent on their interpretations and advice and fail to reach out to others who can provide a more complex view of the situations that we face and the problems we must solve. Asking a few trusted confidants for advice may be fine when trying to understand a simple situation or solve a straightforward problem. However, limiting input to that which is provided by a few trusted colleagues can be a recipe for disaster when trying to solve complex problems for which you have insufficient expertise.[58] For example, Alexandra Penney, former editor of *Self Magazine*, lost a significant part of her life savings to Bernie Madoff's Ponzi scheme after taking her psychiatrist's advice to invest in Madoff's funds. Although she may have been wise to trust her psychiatrist's therapeutic expertise, she was unwise to assume his expertise in psychiatry also made him a good judge of investment opportunities.[59]

Researchers Gabriel Szulanski, Robert Jensen, and Rossella Cappetta explain that the problem with trusting too few sources is that "we take far too much for granted with a trustworthy source . . . We assume that the source knows the many factors related to the situation, understands all the interconnections that influenced the results, and comprehends the whole interplay of subtle actions by many people leading to decision making . . . With a trustworthy source, we may unwittingly suspend our own power of observation and judgment." These tendencies can lead to simplistic and misguided interventions to complex problems.[60]

How can you avoid trusting too much in too few sources? First, you should take time to informally develop relationships with a broad and diverse group of people so that they are willing to provide you with honest and useful inputs when you need it. Second, you should approach complex problems with a systematic decision-making process that involves the inputs of many people who represent different perspectives.

CREATING TRUST: INTERPERSONAL STRATEGIES

Effective managers see building trust as an essential part of their everyday work life. They realize that although trust is critical to managerial effectiveness, it cannot be enforced,[61] cannot be created instantaneously,[62] takes ongoing effort to maintain,[63] and is difficult to rebuild once broken. We build interpersonal trust in two ways: by developing personal credibility and by creating a work environment that promotes trust throughout the organization. To develop a personal reputation for being trustworthy:

- *Be competent at what you do.* Make sure that employees know what you are good at and find opportunities to demonstrate your competence. Acknowledge rather than deny your limitations so that others can help compensate for your limitations.
- *Be clear about what values are important to you and model these values.* Employees want to know that you stand for something beyond self-interest and instrumental concerns.[64]
- *Have frequent positive interactions with employees.* The more positive contact you have with employees, the more opportunity you have to build familiarity and mutual understanding—both of which help to build mutual trust.[65]
- *Communicate regularly.* Be accessible to employees and provide ongoing information, status reports, and feedback. Keep employees informed of decisions and the processes by which decisions are made.
- *Listen to employees and take their opinions seriously.* Employees who feel that they can voice their opinions and believe that these opinions are taken seriously are more likely to trust their leaders, have greater commitment to the leaders' decisions, and are more likely to implement these decisions.[66] Don't "kill the messenger" of bad news.
- *Be predictable and consistent.* Abrupt and arbitrary changes in behavior confuse people, make it difficult for people to know what you want, and increase anxiety.[67]
- *Provide unsolicited help.* Take time to listen to others' problems, give useful information to others, help others even at some cost to you, and take others' needs into account when making decisions.[68]
- *Show understanding, concern, and appreciation for employees.* Show respect for style and cultural differences. Recognize employees' needs to take care of family obligations. Express gratitude. Says Amazon's founder and CEO Jeff Bezos, "I try to use Tuesdays and Thursdays to say thank you to people. I still don't do that nearly enough. It's a classic situation of something that's never the most urgent thing to do. But it's actually very important, in a soft way, over a long period."[69]
- *Follow through on commitments.* Don't promise more than you can deliver.

In short, effective managers see every encounter—large or small—as an opportunity to build trust. One manager described how his trust for his boss influenced his motivation and ability to achieve results:

> My boss's trustworthiness is a huge positive factor in my work effectiveness. I am definitely more motivated, my time is focused on doing my job, and I will go the extra mile to do it better. Because of this trust, I am not afraid to voice

> People with humility don't think less of themselves, they just think of themselves less.
> —KEN BLANCHARD AND NORMAN VINCENT PEALE, *Power of Ethical Management*

my opinion and propose new solutions. At the same time, I also engage in the same way with open and honest communication and collaboration within and outside of the team. For the entire team, there is a strong sense of belonging and high motivation, increased speed of knowledge creation and transfer (very important in high-tech job), and very little energy wasted on confliction resolution. At crunch time (for example, at the end of a product release), there is never a lack of resources to get the job done, and we usually have more volunteers than necessary to take on the additional work.

The most common ways to break trust are advancing your own interests at the expense of others, being blatantly and pompously self-promoting, using inconsistent standards to evaluate employees, allowing some people to break rules while expecting other people to follow the rules, not taking care of performance problems quickly, enabling employees who continue to perform poorly to stay with the organization, not giving employees opportunities to grow, taking credit for employees' work, withholding information, being close-minded, acting disrespectful toward others, lying, breaking promises, betraying confidences, consistently underperforming, and acting inconsistently in what you say and do.[70]

How to Repair Trust Once It Is Broken: The Art of Apologizing

Apology is a lovely perfume; it can transform the clumsiest moment into a gracious gift.
—MARGARET LEE RUNBECK, *Time for Each Other*

Despite our best efforts, sooner or later we all do something that breaks someone's trust in us. Sometimes it is intentional, and we regret it afterward. Sometimes it is unintentional, and we may not even notice our transgression until it is pointed out to us. But regardless of whether our transgression is intentional or not, it can undermine our relationship with a person who loses faith in us or feels harmed by our actions. Therefore, it is important to take steps to rebuild the trust that has been broken.

To rebuild trust, both parties must believe that the relationship is worth saving and must be willing to invest the time and emotional energy into repairing the relationship.[71] However, organizational researchers Roy Lewicki and Barbara Benedict Bunker recommend that the "perpetrator" of the broken trust—the person who has done the real or perceived misdeed—take the first step toward rebuilding trust. They explain:

> If the victim has to do the confrontation, the victim bears a double burden: the consequences of the trust violation and the social awkwardness and embarrassment that may be entailed with confronting the other about his or her actions. In addition, if the victim has to do the work, it may imply that the violator is insensitive and out of touch with his or her actions and the consequences . . . Denying that the act happened, claiming that there weren't any consequences, denying any responsibility for it, or claiming that the act was unimportant and should have no impact on the trust level will likely intensify the others' anger and contribute to further trust deterioration rather than to trust repair. If trust has been broken "in the eye of the beholder," it has been broken.[72]

Psychiatrist Aaron Lazare says that the apology is critical because it is "at the heart of the healing process."[73] Lazare explains that when we apologize, we take the shame off the person whom we hurt by our actions and put the shame on ourselves for having hurt that person. When we admit to someone that we did something inappropriate, we are saying to the person, "I'm the one who was wrong, mistaken, insensitive, or stupid" and "You were not wrong or stupid for having trusted me." By acknowledging that we caused the problem and are taking responsibility for the harm that we caused, we give the offended person "the power to forgive."[74]

Although apologies are critical for maintaining relationships, many people find it difficult to apologize. Says Lazare:

> Despite its importance, apologizing is antithetical to the ever-pervasive values of winning, success, and perfection. The successful apology requires empathy and security and the strength to admit fault, failure, and weakness. But we are so busy winning that we can't concede our own mistakes.[75]

When we do something that breaks someone's trust in us, how we describe our wrong doing, the sincerity of our apology, and the genuineness of our offer to make amends influence that person's willingness to forgive.[76] If the apology is not seen as sincere, then the person who felt harmed by us may be hypervigilant in future interactions with us, and the road to rebuilding trust will be steep.[77] For your apology to be viewed as sincere:

- You should acknowledge that a breach of trust has occurred. People who feel harmed and who can clearly place responsibility on the transgressor are more likely to forgive than are people who feel the attribution of harm-doing is more ambiguous.[78]
- Your apology should be specific rather than general ("I'm sorry that I didn't give you credit for all the work that you did on the project" rather than "I'm sorry for what I did."). By being specific, you acknowledge that you understand what you did that hurt the other person.
- Your apology should acknowledge that you know that you hurt the other person by your actions ("I'm very sorry that I hurt you by not acknowledging your contribution to the success of the project at the meeting.") and that you are troubled by your actions ("It bothers me that I could have been so insensitive, especially after all the work you did on the project."). By doing so, you assure the other person that you share a common moral ground and are disappointed that you have not lived up to your mutual moral standards. Never trivialize the transgression by saying or implying that "it was nothing" or "no harm was done."
- Explain why you did what you did ("I was rushing through the presentation and I'm sorry that because of my haste I failed to acknowledge the team's contributions" or "I recently had a bad interaction with the boss and I took credit for the team's work in order to make myself look better—and that was wrong for me to do."). Doing so tells the other person that you are a generally trustworthy person and that your behavior in the situation was an exception to your normal behavior.
- Say that you are willing to do whatever it takes to repair the trust, even at some discomfort to yourself ("At the next meeting, I'll be sure to publicly acknowledge your contributions. I already mentioned them to the boss and explained my oversight. I also recommended that you take the lead on the next project because it's an interesting and highly visible project."). Doing so lets the other person know that you are willing to endure personal sacrifices on his or her behalf as a consequence of your actions and that you are looking out for his or her best interests.

By taking the preceding steps in your apology, you assure the other person that you emphathize with him or her, that you are genuinely sorry, that the other person and the relationship are important to you, that you share similar moral values, and—most important—that the person can feel safe with you in the future.

Lazare warns that "pseudoapologies" are unlikely to work. In a pseudoapology, the wrong-doer fails to show empathy for those who feel harmed or to take responsibility for what he or she has done. Saying "I'm sorry that you feel that way" is less likely to incur forgiveness than saying "I'm sorry that I've broken your trust in me by my actions." Former U.S. Senator Robert

Packwood gave a pseudoapology when he was accused of sexually harassing several women while in office. His apology: "I'm apologizing for the conduct that it was alleged that I did."[79]

Undoubtedly, people should apologize for their mistakes and transgressions simply because it's the right thing to do. However, there's evidence that sincere and thoughtful apologies can pay off as well. Hospitals have traditionally practiced a "deny and defend" strategy when accused of medical error, in part to try to protect themselves against lawsuits. Recently, some medical institutions have adopted a strategy of full disclosure and apologizing in the aftermath of medical error. After the University of Michigan Health System (UMHS) began addressing medical malpractice claims openly and collaboratively with the claimants and attorneys, malpractice claims were reduced by 55%, litigation costs were decreased by 50%, and claim processing time decreased from 20.3 to eight months between 1999 and 2006. To institutionalize this strategy of full disclosure, the UMHS and other medical organizations have developed the following principles:

- Communicate clearly and honestly with patients and families following "adverse patient events."
- Apologize and compensate "quickly and fairly" when inappropriate medical care causes harm.
- "Defend medically appropriate care vigorously."
- Reduce future patient injuries and claims by learning from past experience.[80]

The goal of this process is to engage in an open and collaborative problem-solving process so that (1) families of those harmed by medical error feel that the hospital leadership and staff have taken responsibility for mistakes that were made and recognize the pain and suffering of the family; (2) the patients, their attorneys, and the hospital administrators can come to a fair conclusion and possible compensation based on a strategy of full disclosure; and (3) the hospital leadership and staff can learn from past errors so that they can give patients better care in the future. This helps the families rest assured that the lessons learned from their loved one's death might save others.[81]

Forgiveness

Forgiveness rebuilds trust and restores relationships. Forgiveness is defined as the willingness to rise above negative feelings associated with a person who we believe has harmed us and instead view the person with goodwill.[82] Forgiveness also involves choosing to repair the relationship or moving forward without ill will instead of taking revenge even when it may seem that retaliation could be justified. In short, forgiveness is a "cancellation of debt."[83]

> The weak can never forgive. Forgiveness is the attribute of the strong.
> —MAHATMA GANDHI

Notably, forgiveness is associated with greater well-being for the forgiver as well as the forgiven. People who are willing to forgive others tend to have better social relationships, fewer illnesses, less stress, and lower rates of depression. For example, gerontologist Neal Krause found that older people who unconditionally forgave others (and themselves) and made peace with their past tended to have better mental health (e.g., less depression, fewer anxieties about death, and greater life satisfaction) than did those who held grudges or forgave reluctantly.[84]

Forgiveness is an effective coping mechanism because it gives the forgiver a greater sense of control. Researcher Karl Aquino and his colleagues explain that "forgiveness is not easy and should not be confused with resignation. . . . Forgiveness is control rather than escape oriented because it involves an active effort on the part of the victim to change his or her feelings about and behavior toward the offender. This distinguishes it from simply avoiding or denying the problem. Forgiveness is *not* forgetting that a wrong occurred. . . . Rather, it involves a deliberate effort to alter how one thinks, feels, and behaves toward the offender, even when it may be within one's moral right to pursue retribution and experience anger and resentment."

Forgiveness liberates us from negative emotions and the desire for revenge. It also helps us see the world in more sophisticated ways rather than in black and white. People who don't forgive may use less effective coping strategies such as distancing themselves from others and retaliating in ways that may damage themselves, others, and the organization.[85] It is not surprising that the more important the relationship is to the people involved, their organizations, and the people they serve, the more important it is to forgive.[86]

> Resentment is like drinking poison and waiting for the other person to die.
> —*Actress and writer Carrie Fisher*

CREATING TRUST: ORGANIZATIONAL STRATEGIES

Interpersonal trust is necessary but insufficient for creating high-trust organizations. In addition to trusting their peers, direct reports, and bosses, employees must also trust their organizations. To build a foundation of trust, employees must believe that their organization's strategies are appropriate, that the people in charge know what they are doing, that the organizational policies and processes are fair and ethical, and that the work is designed to help employees achieve organizational goals.[87] Effective managers create trust-sustaining mechanisms—institutional norms, policies, procedures, and structures—that promote trust throughout the organization.[88] The following help create a work climate that fosters trust:

- *Develop a collective identity.* Bring employees together psychologically by articulating a common vision, promoting shared values, creating joint products, emphasizing similarities among employees and departments and the benefits of the differences that exist, giving employees opportunities to interact with each other, developing feelings of mutual obligation and dependence, and encouraging norms that promote cooperation.[89]
- *Provide clear goals, job standards, performance measures, and relevant feedback.* Employees need to know how they create value, what is and is not in their job descriptions, how they will be evaluated and on what criteria, and the consequences of their behavior.
- *Provide predictable routines.* Employees need shared routines, habits, and rituals that they can count on in their everyday work life. Particularly during times of change, employees need a "safe haven of predictability"[90] that provides feelings of stability, promotes a collective memory, and enables cooperation and coordination among employees.[91]
- *Communicate consistent messages.* Consistency in words and deeds in good times and in bad times minimizes confusion, cynicism, and rumors.
- *Encourage employee participation in decision making.* When employees feel that they are involved in the decision making and that their input is taken seriously, they are more likely to believe that the decision-making process is fair and are thus more likely to be committed to the leader, the organization, and the decisions that are made.[92]
- *Enable employees to control their work and their time.* After performance expectations have been made clear, give employees the freedom, information, and training to make many of their own decisions about the day-to-day details of their work, including how they will manage work–life balance issues. Remember that trust begets trust.
- *Watch for employees who undermine trust.* These include people who are incompetent, unmotivated, unethical and deceptive, as well as people who are micromanagers and cynics who promote negative attitudes toward the organizations. Offer training to employees who undermine trust. If they don't change, remove them from the organization or at least get them out of the way of employees who are trying to move the organization forward.[93]

- *Rebuild organizational trust once broken.* When something happens that damages employee trust, immediately work to rebuild trust by identifying the source of the mistrust, owning up to being part of the problem if that is the case, identifying what you and others will do to rebuild trust, and replacing people who were involved in creating the mistrust.[94]

In short, work environments that promote trust are those that provide employees with a common direction, competent and dependable colleagues, opportunities to interact with each other, clear work structures and task expectations, predictable routines, and some freedom to control their own environment within these boundaries. A work climate that is unpredictable or consistently out of control will undermine trust because it threatens employees' basic human needs to predict and control their environment. When these needs are not met, employees are more likely to react defensively rather than productively to their managers, each other, their customers, their tasks, and their organizations.

How can you tell if mistrust is festering? In his article "Nobody Trusts the Boss," researcher Fernando Bartoleme provides several questions that can help you determine whether trust is waning: Are employees communicating with you or each other less often? Do employees avoid giving you bad news? Do employees avoid meetings? Do some employees rarely speak up at meetings? Does morale seem to be deteriorating? Do employees lack enthusiasm and increasingly complain about their workload? Is there an increase in absenteeism and turnover? Are employees blaming other people and departments for problems?[95]

> Few things help an individual more than to place responsibility upon him, and to let him know that you trust him.
> —BOOKER T. WASHINGTON

If your answers to these questions are "yes," then you may want to consider that you or the work climate (rather than the employees themselves) may be at fault. To rebuild trust, you can focus on changing your own behavior or the work environment by heeding the advice in the previous sections.

Organizational Structure and Swift Trust

In today's organizations, organizational members are becoming more dispersed, work assignments are becoming more project based, short-term work relationships are becoming more common (e.g., relationships with subcontractors, consultants, and temporary workers), and temporary task teams are becoming the norm rather than the exception. Consequently, our professional effectiveness and success depend on our ability to work quickly, competently, and often virtually on complex problems with people whom we don't know very well and with whom we have never worked before.

In such situations, we must depend on what organizational researchers Debra Meyerson, Karl Weick, and Rod Kramer call "swift trust." This is a kind of trust that is developed when "there isn't time to engage in the usual forms of confidence-building activities that contribute to the development and maintenance of trust in more traditional and enduring forms of organization." Meyerson explains that developing swift trust in these situations is critical because "unless one trusts quickly, one might never trust at all."[96]

Consider the case of temporary groups such as new product development teams, emergency room medical teams, and airplane cockpit crews. A temporary group is a collection of individuals with diverse skills who have never worked together before (and may not work together in the future) and who must depend on each other to accomplish a complex task successfully and quickly. A high degree of mutual trust is necessary because the outcome of their work is uncertain, group members must depend on each other for a successful outcome, and people risk serious consequences if the group fails.[97] For example, if all group members do not work together effectively, a new product development team's products may never get launched, an emergency medical team's patients may die, and an airplane cockpit crew's plane may crash.

However, members of temporary groups do not have time to develop a history of shared experiences that can lead to trust. Instead, to be successful, they must presume that each member of the group is trustworthy. On what bases do members of temporary groups presume trust? Rather than rely on personal relationships and a common history with each other, members of temporary groups base their mutual trust on the system in which the group does its work. Researcher Robyn Dawes explains:

> We trust engineers because we trust engineering and believe that engineers are trained to apply valid principles of engineering; moreover, we have evidence every day that these principles are valid when we observe airplanes flying. We trust doctors because we trust modern medicine, and we have evidence that it works when antibiotics and operations cure people.[98]

In short, temporary groups depend, in large part, on "depersonalized trust."[99] Members of effective temporary groups trust each other because they trust that they share a set of standard operating procedures and expectations about how to define and solve problems, what information and tools are needed to solve problems, who has the authority to make certain decisions and take particular actions, how to deal with routine and nonroutine events, what behaviors are appropriate and inappropriate, what accountability measures should be used, and how to define success. Such trust is developed not through interpersonal relationships, but through the cultures, policies, and procedures of the institutions of which they are a part.[100]

Researcher Robert Ginnett illustrates the importance of institutional trust-building mechanisms using airplane cockpit crews as an example:

> Even though the particular members of a given crew may never have worked together as a team before, when they come together, they step into a preexisting "shell" (Hackman, 1986a; Ginnett, 1987) that defines much of what is expected of them as a team. This shell includes not only the context and design factors. . . . but also a set of expectations about the roles of each individual in the crew. It is as if the definitions of the captain, the first officer, the engineer, and the rest of the crew (and, to some degree, the boundaries of the group as a whole) are already in place before any individual enters the setting.[101]

In short, trustworthy systems are as important as trustworthy interpersonal relationships, particularly when employees need to quickly develop into fast-moving temporary teams that can handle both the day-to-day routines as well as the unexpected emergencies that may arise.

BEYOND TRUST: POSITIVE EMOTIONS AND SUCCESS

Researchers agree that it pays to feel good and to do good. People who feel and express positive emotions tend to be more effective at their jobs; have more successful careers; and lead happier, healthier, and longer lives. You may be thinking, "Sure, if I had a great job, worked for a devoted boss, made more money, and had perfect health, I'd feel pretty positive, too." However, researchers have found that it's not what you have that counts, but whether you appreciate what you have and share your goodwill with others. After all, many people have similar jobs, incomes, material belongings, health status, opportunities, and tragedies. However, some of these people wake up

> The mind is its own place, and in itself can make a heaven of hell, a hell of heaven.
> —JOHN MILTON

each morning thankful for what they have, whereas others wake up miserable despite what they have.

How Positive Emotions and Behaviors Lead to Professional Success and Well-Being

Positive feelings such as joy, hope, love, compassion, generosity, gratitude, optimism, pride, serenity, and forgiveness serve many purposes.[102] When we feel these positive emotions, we tend to think more broadly and creatively, seek out new information and experiences, behave more flexibly, have more confidence in our abilities and the abilities of others, be more persistent, get over bad experiences and negative emotions more quickly, and give and get the social support we need to solve problems and implement solutions. We are also better able to both engage in the moment and plan for the future. In contrast, negative emotions, such as fear, anger, envy, resentment, frustration, worry, guilt, and shame, tend to narrow our focus and flexibility, often limiting our options just when we need them most. For example, fear tends to lead to the desire to escape or to hoard resources, anger can lead to the desire to attack or take revenge, and guilt and shame can result in the desire to withdraw rather than engage. Frederickson explains that although negative emotions narrow our ability to think and act in complex ways, positive emotions broaden these abilities and create an upward spiral that increases our effectiveness and well-being in the short and long term.[103]

To understand how positive emotions affect our problem-solving abilities, researcher Alice Isen and colleagues designed a simple experiment to see how positive emotions might influence physicians' decision-making abilities. They gave some teams of physicians a small bag of candy and asked them to think out loud as they tried to understand a case of a patient with liver disease. When compared with teams of physicians who did not receive candy, the physicians who received the bag of candy were able to integrate facts faster and were less likely to get stuck with premature conclusions. The researchers concluded that even a simple act of goodwill, such as giving candy, can create positive emotions in ways that enhance effectiveness. Other studies have shown that employees who express positive emotions tend to be evaluated more highly by their supervisors, receive greater pay increases, and receive more support from their supervisors and coworkers. In one study of MBAs, those who reported that they experience more positive emotions tended to be more careful during a decision-making simulation and were perceived to be more effective interpersonally in team discussions.[104] Studies have also shown that teams that have significantly more positive than negative interactions (those teams with a ratio of approximately 5.5 positive to each negative interaction) tend to outperform other teams in terms of profitability, customer satisfaction, and evaluations from bosses, peers, and direct reports. Positive interactions included "support, encouragement, or appreciation" and negative interactions included "disapproval, sarcasm, or cynicism."[105]

In addition to contributing to our effectiveness and career success, many studies have shown that positive emotions can help us bounce back from adversity, build stronger immune systems, and live longer and healthier lives.[106] People who experience positive emotions, especially during the most difficult periods of life, tend to tolerate pain better, cope with and recover from illness faster, and experience less depression. For example, people who experience the death of a loved one and yet find positive meaning amid their suffering are more likely to create long-term plans and have greater well-being a year after their loss. In a landmark study of aging nuns, researchers found that nuns who had expressed positive emotions in essays they wrote when they were young had a lower incidence of Alzheimer's disease decades later and lived up to 10 years longer than nuns who expressed fewer positive emotions through their writing.[107] For more information about this fascinating study, go to www.nunstudy.com.

Despite the emphasis on positive emotions, we should not assume that positive emotions always lead to success or that negative emotions always lead to poor outcomes. For example, teams made up of members who are overwhelmingly positive and do not engage in necessary task-related conflict may engage in groupthink and get stuck in other dysfunctional patterns that no longer serve the team well. Researchers have found that teams begin to lose effectiveness once they reach 11.5 positive interactions for each negative interaction. There is considerable research that suggests that although optimism leads to higher performance and success for many people, it does not bring out the best in all people. In her research, Julie Norem found that some people—particularly people who tend to be more anxious than others—use a strategy called "defensive pessimism" to enhance their performance. They worry about what might go wrong, overprepare, and fret over the smallest details. Although pessimism can be paralyzing for some people, defensive pessimists harness their anxiety in ways that lead to higher performance. They succeed by preparing for the worst and hoping for the best. Furthermore, advising them to relax or "look on the bright side" may undermine, rather than enhance, their performance.[108]

How Positive Emotions Lead to Organizational Effectiveness

Overall, positive emotions are not only good for individuals, they are also good for organizations. Researchers have found that organizational leaders who express positive emotions encourage their organizational members to feel positive emotions as well. When employees feel positive emotions, they are more likely to set higher goals, see and fix mistakes, feel more competent and empowered, have greater problem-solving capabilities, act more flexibly, feel more job satisfaction and loyalty to their organizations, go above and beyond the call of duty, interact with each other more frequently, give and get social support, share resources, resolve conflict and negotiate more reasonably, and rebound from hurdles and crises more quickly.[109]

Researcher Kim Cameron found that when employees in recently downsized organizations viewed their leaders as "virtuous" ("compassionate, forgiving, trusting, and optimistic"), the organization "had significantly higher productivity, higher quality outputs and lower employee turnover." Employees in virtuous organizations also believed that their organizations were more profitable, offered higher quality products or services, were better able to retain customers, and paid employees more than the competition.[110] How important is organizational loyalty? As noted in an *MIT Sloan Review* article about loyalty in organizations worldwide, "the truly loyal exhibit the kinds of behaviors that make business successful—they work hard, stay late, go the extra mile to delight the customer, and recommend the company to their friends as a good place to work. . . . High risk employees are spending their working hours clicking through Monster.com."[111]

> The trust of the people in the leaders reflects the confidence of the leaders in the people.
> —PAULO FREIRE

How Positive Emotions Help People Manage Organizational Crises

It is not surprising that positive emotions are particularly critical during a crisis because they enable employees to be mindful of what is happening around them, improvise behaviors that increase their chances for success in the crisis, broaden rather than constrain their perceptions of available options, and—rather than focus only on themselves—take care of others who are also affected by the crisis.[112] Managers' and employees' reactions during a crisis are often a moment of truth for organizations. As the following examples illustrate, positive emotions such as compassion and empathy during crises enoble as well as enable.

I never trust people's
assertions. I always judge
them by their actions.
—ANN RADCLIFFE,
British Author

After the Twin Towers in New York City were devastated by a terrorist attack on September 11, 2001, employees at a Starbucks located near the Towers were told by their manager that they could leave to protect their own safety. Instead, employees and the store manager compassionately chose to stay and bring stunned people passing by into the store, giving them food and drink, shelter from falling debris, and emotional support.[113] During the September 11 tragedy, says Sue Shellenbarger of the *Wall Street Journal*, "Employees . . . believed they were seeing their bosses' true colors. Their conclusions about what they saw either deepened their commitment or damaged it beyond repair. . . . At a Chicago consulting firm, a senior supervisor ordered employees on September 11 to return to business as usual. A consultant who worked at the firm said, 'What we needed was to stop and say, OK, we're going to take a deep breath and think about this . . . I will remember this situation and how my firm dealt with it.'" Shellenbarger concludes: "Embedded in a crisis is an opportunity for employers to rebuild damaged loyalty. Loyalty shapes people's choices not only about where to work, but also about how long, hard, and wholeheartedly to apply their mental energies."[114] Kenneth Chenault, CEO of American Express Co., ensured that employees and customers felt the care and concern they needed during the September 11 crisis. *BusinessWeek* described Chenault's leadership:[115]

> AmEx helped 560,000 stranded cardholders get home, in some cases chartering airplanes and buses to ferry them across the country. It waived millions of dollars in deliquent fees on late-paying cardholders and increased credit limits to cash-starved clients. . . . Most telling, Chenault gathered 5,000 American Express employees at the Paramount Theater in New York on September 20 for a highly emotional "town hall meeting." During the session, Chenault demonstrated the poise, compassion, and decisiveness that vaulted him to the top. He told employees that he had been filled with such despair, sadness, and anger that he had seen a counselor. Twice he rushed to spontaneously embrace grief-stricken employees. Chenault said he would donate $1 million of the company's profits to the families of the AmEx victims. "I represent the best company and the best people in the world," he concluded. "In fact, you are my strength, and I love you." It was a poignant and unscripted moment. Says AmEx board member Charlene Barshefsky, a partner at Wilmer Cutler & Pickering, who viewed a video of the event, "The manner in which he took command, the comfort and direction he gave to what was obviously an audience in shock was of a caliber one rarely sees."

During the economic crisis of 2009, Paul Levy, CEO of Beth Israel Deaconess Medical Center, stood in front of the employees in Sherman auditorium and appealed to their compassion, saying:

> I want to run an idea by you that I think is important, and I'd like to get your reaction to it . . . I'd like to do what we can to protect the lower-wage earners—the transporters, the housekeepers, the food service people. A lot of these people work really hard, and I don't want to put an additional burden on them. Now, if we protect these workers, it means the rest of us will have to make a bigger sacrifice. It means that others will have to give up more of their salary or benefits.

On hearing this, employees began applauding. After the sustained applause ended, he asked the employees for ideas that would help the medical center weather the economic storm. The flood of e-mails from employees included offers to work one day fewer each week and give up pay raises, bonuses, vacation time, sick time, and some benefits.[116]

In good times and in bad times, positive emotions and behaviors create positive upward spirals in organizations because they can create a "contagion effect" in which people copy each other's emotions. Furthermore, when employees feel gratitude for the goodwill they receive, they want to repay this goodwill with greater loyalty and effort and pass this goodwill on to others such as coworkers and customers. Consequently, positive emotions in organizations can be a competitive advantage that is not easily copied by competitors. How can you cultivate positive emotions in your workplace?

- Express positive emotions—gratitude, generosity, optimism, trust—regularly at work. Start meetings with sincere words of appreciation. Walk around the hallways and notice who is there, what they are doing, and why you should be thankful. Be appreciative to the clients that you serve. Help other people. Remember that positive emotions are contagious, especially when expressed by direct supervisors and organizational leaders.
- Engage in positive deviance. Give unexpected kindnesses and reach out to others when it is least expected. When you engage in positive emotions and behaviors when it goes against the norm, the element of surprise and courage becomes a powerful example to others, both strengthening people's trust in you and role-modeling behavior for others to follow.[117]
- Help people find positive meaning in their day-to-day work lives, including in the mundane, the sad, and the crises. Help employees see how their work contributes to a greater good and whom they are helping through their efforts.
- Provide opportunities for people to help each other and to express appreciation for the help they receive from others.
- Celebrate small wins so that employees experience ongoing success and the associated positive emotions.
- In a crisis, enable employees to experience and express what it feels like to rise to the occasion and find the strength and resources they never knew they had.
- And the next time someone says, "have a nice day," you'd be wise to heed their advice.

CONCLUSION

Effective managers realize that one of their most important jobs is to earn the trust of their employees, colleagues, bosses, customers, and other constituents. They also realize that it is equally important to create organizational structures and processes that promote trust at all levels of the organization. They know that trust is necessary for managing the routine interactions of everyday life and vital for initiating organizational change and responding to crises. Most important, says ethics researcher LaRue Hosmer, they recognize that people in organizations pay attention to issues concerning "what is right, just, and fair as well as what is efficient, effective, and practical."[118]

The ability to earn trust and create work environments that promote trust throughout the organization is becoming increasingly valuable in today's global, diverse, and technology-driven economic environment. Managers must be able to help people who don't share a common culture (and whose cultural groups may share a history of animosity and distrust toward each other) learn to work together productively to serve organizational goals. They must be able to help employees involved in alliances, mergers, and acquisitions build trust and interdependence quickly. They must be able to develop trust and respect among employees who work in virtual teams and who rarely, if ever, see each other. They must be able to trust employees enough to provide them with the training, resources, and support that empower employees to take independent action so that their organizations can be responsive, flexible, and fast. And because of the business and political scandals that have dominated the media in recent years, managers must work harder than ever to build trust. Undoubtedly, in today's work environment, trust is a must-have, not a nice-to-have, quality.

Chapter Summary

Trust in organizations is a source of competitive advantage. A high-quality network of internal and external relationships that is built on trust provides economic value to the organization, takes a long time to develop, and cannot be easily copied by other organizations.

Managers who are able to inspire trust tend to be more effective, have stronger networks, and get promoted more often than those who do not inspire trust. They are better able to attract and retain followers, promote loyalty and a sense of belonging, build support for their goals, develop more productive employees, focus on value-added work rather than costly employee control systems, enhance communication, reduce conflict, reduce the costs of negotiation, inspire employees to go beyond their job descriptions to serve organizational goals, enhance group decision making, encourage cooperation across boundaries, promote organizational change, survive organizational crises, and help employees accept unfavorable decisions.

Teams in which the members trust each other tend to outperform teams with low trust because trusting relationships enable team members to get higher-quality results in less time because of their common values, ability to predict each other's behavior, coordinate with each other, share information, cooperate with each other, manage team stress, and adapt to changing environmental conditions. Virtual teams benefit significantly from trust among team members because they are better able to handle the uncertainty and complexity of the virtual environment.

When we trust someone, we are willing to ascribe good intentions to that person and have confidence in his or her ability to act on these intentions. Our belief in a person's trustworthiness will influence how we behave toward that person, the task, and the organization.

Trust is only necessary in conditions of vulnerability, risk, and uncertainty. If we can perfectly predict and control a situation, or if we have nothing to lose if our assumptions about the person's or organization's good intentions or actions are wrong, then trust is not necessary.

Our willingness to trust is also based on our perceptions of a person's or organization's trustworthiness. These perceptions are based on the person's or organization's reputation, our past experiences with the person or organization, and our stereotypes about that person. Perceptions are important because they can turn into self-fulfilling prophecies.

Our propensity to trust—or mistrust—others may be influenced by our early childhood experiences. If our earliest experiences with primary caregivers (parents, day-care providers, and significant others) are consistently loving and dependable, we are more likely to become comfortable trusting and depending on others. If our earliest experiences with primary caregivers are inconsistent or undependable, we are more likely to grow up believing that we cannot rely on the goodwill of others and their ability to take care of our needs. Our early experiences with caregivers also influences our ability to trust our own competence and judgment later in life.

We determine whether to trust another person based on our assessments about that person's ability, benevolence, and integrity. Specifically, we make assumptions about whether that person is competent, reliable, professional, consistent, open to communication, transparent, fair in his or her decision making, concerned about our welfare, and acting with integrity.

It is important to develop optimal trust—knowing when it's wise to trust someone and when it's wise to be cautious about their judgment. It's unwise to have too much trust in too few people. When we have too few people to count on for ideas and support, we narrow our perception of problems and solutions and thus inhibit our ability to make and implement high-quality decisions. To make decisions based on optimal trust, (1) develop a broad network of people you can trust so that you can view the situations and solve problems from different perspectives and (2) create a systematic decision-making process that enables you to integrate and assess the strengths and weaknesses of different views.

When we break someone's trust in us, we may be able to rebuild that trust by offering a sincere apology and making amends. Apologies are important because they assure the person who feels harmed that we are genuinely sorry, share similar moral values, and can be counted on to be trustworthy in the future. Forgiveness is also important because it enables the relationship to move forward and it increases the psychological and physical well-being of the forgiver.

Our willingness to trust is also based in the organizational environment in which we work. High-trust organizations create a collective identity among employees, opportunities for employees to interact, clear job structures and processes, predictable routines, and opportunities for employees to control their own work environment and make their own decisions about their day-to-day work.

Clear structures and processes are particularly critical in organizations that routinely depend on temporary teams because members of such teams tend not to know each other very well and do not have the time to build interpersonal trust. Therefore, they must rely on "depersonalized trust"—shared goals, knowledge, operating measures, and performance standards—to become an effective team quickly.

In good times and in bad times, positive emotions and behaviors create positive upward spirals in organizations because they can create a "contagion effect" in which people copy each other's emotions. Positive emotions broaden people's perspectives, enhance decision-making abilities, and increase flexibility. Furthermore, when employees feel gratitude for the goodwill they receive, they want to repay this goodwill with greater loyalty and effort and pass this goodwill on to others, such as coworkers and customers. Consequently, positive emotions in organizations can be a competitive advantage that is not easily copied.

Food for Thought

1. What is the most useful thing you learned in this chapter, and why?
2. Based on the personal strategies described in this chapter (and that you assessed in Figure 3.2), what can you do to increase your own trustworthiness? Practice this behavior, and note any benefits and progress you make.
3. How does trust contribute to individual and organizational success?
4. Think of two people, one you trust and one you don't trust. List the reasons that lead to your trust or distrust of each person. What are the three most important lessons about gaining and losing trust that you learned from these people? What, if anything, could the person you don't trust do to earn your trust?
5. If you are a manager, what kinds of specific organizational interventions can you make to create a more trustworthy organizational environment (i.e., one that enhances trust among employees, clients, and other constituents)?
6. Imagine the following situation. Last week, you inadvertently mentioned at a meeting that a colleague was undergoing chemotherapy for cancer. Your colleague had told you about the illness and the chemotherapy in confidence just a few weeks ago. Your colleague heard that you had mentioned the illness at a meeting and was angry that you did so, particularly in such a public way.

Today, your colleague came to your office to discuss this breach of confidence and mentioned several concerns, not the least of which was that his or her own children did not know about the illness and were likely to hear of it from other employees who knew the family personally. You feel that an apology is necessary. Describe how you would apologize. Specifically, what would you say to your colleague who is undergoing cancer treatment? What else can you do to rebuild trust with this person?
7. Watch an apology of a well-known figure on YouTube. Examples include professional golfer Tiger Woods' apology for his infidelity, Akio Toyoda's apology for Toyota's safety lapses, and Marian Jones' apology for using steroids during the Olympics and then denying her use of steroids. Describe (1) whether you believe the person's apology meets the criteria for a sincere apology, (2) whether you believe the apology is credible, and why or why not, and (3) what you learned from your observation about apologies that you can use in your own life.
8. Think about someone from your past to whom you are grateful. Write a note of appreciation to that person, explaining what they did and why you are thankful.
9. Write down five things that you are thankful for today. Do this for the next week, and see if it enhances your general mood and behavior.

Endnotes

1. Heller, Joseph. 1966. *Something Happened.* New York: Alfred A. Knopf, Scapegoat Productions, 13.

2. Hosmer, Larue. 1995. "Trust: The Connecting Link between Organizational Theory and Philosophical Ethics." *Academy of Management Review,* 20(2): 379–403.

3. McAllister, Daniel J. 1995. "Affect- and Cognition-Based Trust as Foundations for Interpersonal Cooperation in Organizations." *Academy of Management Journal,* 38(1): 24–59.

4. Hill, Linda. 2003. *Becoming a Manager: Mastery of a New Identity, 2nd ed.* Cambridge, MA: Harvard Business Press.

5. Lombardo, Michael, Marian Roderman, and Cynthia McCauley. "Explanations of Success and Derailment in Upper Level Managerial Positions." *Journal of Business and Psychology*, 2(3): 199–216.

6. Dirks, Kurt, and Donald L. Ferrin. 2001. "The Role of Trust in Organizational Settings." *Organizational Science,* 12(4): 450–467; Clapp-Smith, Rachel, Gretchen R. Vogelgesang, and James B. Avey. 2009. "Authentic Leadership and Positive Psychological Capital: The Mediating Role of Trust at the Group Level of Analysis." *Journal of Leadership and Organizational Studies*, 15(3): 227–240; Yang, Jixia and Kevin W. Mossholder. 2010. "Examining the Effects of Trust in Leaders: A Bases-and-Foci Approach." *The Leadership Quarterly*, 21: 50–63.

7. Cook, John, and Toby Wall. 1980. "New Worker Attitude Measures of Trust, Organizational Commitment and Personal Need Nonfulfillment." *Journal of Occupational Psychology,* 53: 39–52; citing Buchanan, B. 1974. "Building Organizational Commitment: The Socialization of Managers in Work Organizations." *Administrative Science Quarterly,* 19: 533–546.

8. Podsakoff, Philip, Scott MacKenzie, Robert Moorman, and Richard Fetter. 1990. "Transformational Leaders Behaviors and Their Effects on Followers' Trust in Leader, Satisfaction, and Organizational Citizenship Behaviors." *Leadership Quarterly*, 1: 107–142.

9. Rogers, Carl. 1961. *On Becoming a Person.* Boston MA: Houghton Mifflin.

10. Dirks, Kurt, and Donald L. Ferrin. 2001. "The Role of Trust in Organizational Settings." *Organizational Science*, 12(4): 450–467; Chiaburu, Dan S., and Audrey S. Lim. 2008. "Manager Trustworthiness or Interactional Justice? Predicting Organizational Citizenship Behaviors." *Journal of Business Ethics*, 83: 453–467; Grant, Adam, and John Sumanth. 2009. "Mission Possible? The Performance of Prosocially Motivated Employees Depends on Manager Trustworthiness." *Journal of Applied Psychology*, 94(4): 927–944.

11. Yoon, Mahn Hee, and Jaebeom Suh. 2003. "Organizational Citizenship Behavior and Service Quality as External Effectiveness of Contact Employees." *Journal of Business Research*, 56: 597–611.

12. McAllister, Daniel J. 1995. "Affect- and Cognition-Based Trust as Foundations for Interpersonal Cooperation in Organizations." *Academy of Management Journal,* 38(1): 24–59.

13. Hosmer, Larue. 1995. "Trust: The Connecting Link between Organizational Theory and Philosophical Ethics." *Academy of Management Review,* 20(2): 379–403.

14. Mishra, Aneil. 1996. "Organizational Responses to Crises: The Centrality of Trust." In Kramer, Roderick, and Tom Tyler (eds.). *Trust in Organizations: Frontiers of Theory and Research.* Thousand Oaks, CA: Sage Publications, 261–287.

15. Nahapiet, Janine, and Sumantra Goshal. 1998. "Social Capital, Intellectual Capital, and the Organizational Advantage." *Academy of Management Review,* 23(2): 242–266; McNeish, Joanne, and Inder Jit Singh Mann. 2010. "Knowledge Sharing and Trust in Organizations." *Institute of Chartered Financial Analysts of India (Hyderabad). The ICFAI Journal of Knowledge Management*, 8(1/2):18–39.

16. Butler, John K. 1995. "Behaviors, Trust and Goal Achievement in a Win-Win Negotiating Role Play." *Group and Organization Management,* 20(4): 486–501.

17. Zand, Dale E. 1971. "Trust and Managerial Problem Solving." *Administrative Science Quarterly,* 17: 229–239; Dirks, Kurt. 1999. "The Effects of Interpersonal Trust on Work Group Performance." *Journal of Applied Psychology,* 84(3): 445–455.

18. Nahapiet, Janine, and Sumantra Goshal. 1998. "Social Capital, Intellectual Capital, and the Organizational Advantage." *Academy of Management Review,* 23(2): 242–266; Colquitt, J. A., B. A. Scott, and J. A. LePine. 2007. "Trust, Trustworthiness, and Trust Propensity: A Meta-

Analytic Test of Their Unique Relationships with Risk Taking and Job Performance.*" Journal of Applied Psychology*, 92: 902–927.

19. Vangen, Siv, and Chris Huxham. 2003. "Nurturing Collaborative Relations: Building Trust in Interorganizational Collaboration.*" The Journal of Applied Behavioral Science,* 39(1): 5–31.

20. Mishra, Aneil. 1996. "Organizational Responses to Crises: The Centrality of Trust." In Kramer, Roderick, and Tom Tyler (eds.). *Trust in Organizations: Frontiers of Theory and Research.* Thousand Oaks, CA: Sage Publications, 261–287.

21. Korsgaard, M. Audrey, David M. Schweiger, and Harry Sapienza. 1995. "Building Commitment, Attachment, and Trust in Strategic Decision-Making Teams: The Role of Procedural Justice." *Academy of Management Journal,* 38(1): 60–84; citing Folger, Robert, and Mary Konovsky. 1989. "Effects of Procedural and Distributed Justice on Reactions to Pay Raise Decisions." *Academy of Management Journal,* 32: 115–130; McFarlin, Dean, and Paul Sweeney. 1992. "Distributive and Procedural Justice as Predictors of Satisfaction with Personal and Organizational Outcomes." *Academy of Management Journal,* 35: 626–637.

22. Mishra, Aneil, and Gretchen M. Spreitzer. 1998. "Explaining How Survivors Respond to Downsizing: The Role of Trust, Empowerment, Justice, and Work Redesign." *Academy of Management Review,* 23(3): 567–588.

23. Brower, Holly, Scott Lester, M. Audrey Korsgaard, and Brian Dineen. 2009. "A Closer Look at Trust between Managers and Subordinates: Understanding the Effect of Both Trusting and Being Trusted on Subordinate Outcomes." *Journal of Management,* 35(27): 325.

24. Chou, Li-Fang, An-Chih Wang, Ting-Yu Wang, Min-Ping Huang, and Bor-Schiuan Cheng. 2008. "Shared Work Values and Team Member Effectiveness: The Mediation of Trustfulness and Trustworthiness." *Human Relations,* 61(12): 1713–1742.

25. Jarvenpaa, Sirkka, and Dorothy Leidner. 1999. "Communication and Trust in Global Virtual Teams." *Organizational Science,* 10(6): 791–815.

26. Gambetta, Diego. 1988. "Can We Trust Trust?" In Gambetta, Diego G. (ed.). *Trust.* New York: Basic Blackwell, 213–237.

27. Nooteboom, Bart, Hans Berger, and Niels G. Noorderhaven. 1997. "Effects of Trust and Governance on Relational Risk." *Academy of Management Journal,* 40(2): 308–338.

28. Shaw, Robert. 1997. *Trust in the Balance.* San Francisco, CA: Jossey-Bass.

29. Lipnack, Jessica, and Jeffrey Stamps. 1997. *Virtual Teams: Reaching across Time, Space, and Technology.* New York: John Wiley, 228–229.

30. Robinson, Sandra. 1996. "Trust and the Breach of the Psychological Contract." *Administrative Science Quarterly,* 41: 574–599.

31. Barney, Jay, and M. Hansen. 1994. "Trustworthiness as a Source of Competitive Advantage." *Strategic Management Journal,* 15: 175–190.

32. Serwer, Andy, and Kate Bonamici. 2004. "The Hottest Thing in the Sky." *Fortune,* 149(5): 86–94.

33. Lancaster, Hal. 1999. "Herb Kelleher Has One Main Strategy: Treat Employees Well." *The Wall Street Journal,* August 31: B1.

34. Blanchard, Ken, and Terry Waghorn. March 23, 2009. "Make Sure Your Employees Trust You—Or Else." *Forbes.com.* http://www.forbes.com/2009/03/23/trust-respect-employees-leadership-managing-blanchard.html

35. Cook, John, and Toby Wall. 1980. "New Work Attitude Measures of Trust, Organizational Commitment and Personal Need Nonfulfillment." *Journal of Occupational Psychology,* 53: 39–52.

36. Deutsch, Morton. 1958. "Trust and Suspicion." *Journal of Conflict Resolution,* 2: 26–279.

37. Zand, Dale E. 1971. "Trust and Managerial Problem Solving." *Administrative Science Quarterly,* 17: 229–239.

38. Burt, R., and M. Knez. 1995. "Kinds of Third-Party Effects on Trust." *Rationality and Society,* 7: 255–292.

39. Bartolome, Fernando. 1989. "Nobody Trusts the Boss, Now What?" *Harvard Business Review,* 67: 135–143.

40. Williams, Michele. 1999. "In Whom We Trust; Social Categorization, Affect and Trust Development." Unpublished paper. Ann Arbor, MI: University of Michigan; citing Cox and Taylor. 1993. *Cultural Diversity in Organizations.* San Francisco, CA: Berrett-Koehler; Adler, Nancy. 1997. *International Dimensions of Organizational Behavior,* 2nd ed. Cincinnati, OH: South-Western College Publishing.

41. Smith, Kenywn. 1982. *Groups in Conflict: Prisons in Disguise.* Dubuque, IA: Kendall Hunt.

42. Williams, Michele. 2001. "In Whom We Trust: Social Group Membership as an Affective-Cognitive Context for Trust Development." *Academy of Management Review,* 26(3): 377–396.

43. Robinson, Sandra. 1996. "Trust and the Breach of the Psychological Contract." *Administrative Science Quarterly*, 41: 574–599.

44. Ross, Michael, and John G. Holmes. 2001. "Trust and Communicated Attributions in Close Relationships." *Journal of Personality and Social Psychology*, 81(1): 57–64.

45. Ibid.; Dirks, Kurt T., and Donald L. Ferrin. 2001. "Trust in Organizational Settings." *Organizational Science*, 12(4): 450–467.

46. Fine, Gary, and Lori Holyfield. 1996. "Secrecy, Trust and Dangerous Leisure: Generating Group Cohesion in Voluntary Organizations." *Social Psychology Quarterly*, 59: 22–38.

47. Mikulincer, Mario. 1998. "Attachment Working Models and the Sense of Trust: An Exploration of Interaction Goals and Affect Regulation." *Journal of Personality and Social Psychology*, 74(5): 1209–1225; Bowlby, John. 1988. *A Secure Base: Clinical Applications of Attachment Theory.* London: Routledge.

48. Mikulincer, Mario. 1998. "Attachment Working Models and the Sense of Trust: An Exploration of Interaction Goals and Affect Regulation." *Journal of Personality and Social Psychology*, 74(5): 1209–1225; Holmes, John G., and John K. Rempel. 1989. "Trust in Close Relationships." In Hendrick, Clyde (ed.). *Review of Personality and Social Psychology*, 10: 187–220.

49. Kahn, William. 2002. "Managing the Paradox of Self-Reliance." *Organizational Dynamics*, 30(3): 239–256.

50. Simmons, Bret, Janaki Gooty, Debra Nelson, and Laura Little. 2009. "Secure Attachment: Implications for Hope, Trust, Burnout, and Performance." *Journal of Organizational Behavior*, 30: 233–247; Bernerth, Jeremy, and H. Jack Walker. 2009. "Propensity to Trust and the Impact on Social Exchange." *Journal of Leadership and Organizational Studies*, 15(3): 217–226.

51. Grant, Adam, and John Sumanth. 2009. "Mission Impossible? The Performance of Prosocially Motivated Employees Depends on Manager Trustworthiness." *Journal of Applied Psychology*, 94(4): 927–944.

52. Mikulincer, Mario. 1998. "Attachment Working Models and the Sense of Trust: An Exploration of Interaction Goals and Affect Regulation." *Journal of Personality and Social Psychology*, 74(5): 1209–1225.

53. Holmes, John G., and John K. Rempel. 1989. "Trust in Close Relationships." In Hendrick, Clyde (ed.). *Review of Personality and Social Psychology*, 10: 187–220.

54. Yakovleva, Maria, Richard Reilly, and Robert Werko. 2010. "Why Do We Trust? Moving Beyond Individual to Dyadic Perceptions." *Journal of Applied Psychology*, 95(1): 79–91; Schoorman, David, Mayer, Roger, and James H. Davis. 2007. "An Integrative Model of Organizational Trust: Past, Present, and Future." *Academy of Management Review*, 32(2):344–354.

55. Mayer, Roger, James H. Davis, and F. David Schoorman. 1995. "An Integrative Model of Organizational Trust." *Academy of Management Journal*, 20(3): 709–734; Clark, Murray, and Roy L. Payne. 1997. "The Nature and Structure of Workers' Trust in Management." *Journal of Organizational Behavior*, 18: 205–224; Whitener, Ellen, Susan Brodt, M. Audrey Korsguaard, and Jon Werner. 1998. "Managers as Initiators of Trust: An Exchange Relationship Framework for Understanding Managerial Trustworthy Behavior." *Academy of Management Review*, 23(3): 513–530; McAllister, D. J. 1995. "Affect- and Cognition-Based Trust as Foundations for Interpersonal Cooperation in Organizations." *Academy of Management Journal*, 38: 24–59.

56. Wicks, Andrew C., Shawn L. Berman, and Thomas M. Jones. 1999. "The Structure of Optimal Trust: Moral and Strategic Implications." *Academy of Management Review*, 24(1): 99–116.

57. Cialdini, Robert. 2001. *Influence: Science and Practice.* Needham Heights, MA: Allyn & Bacon; McAllister, Daniel. "Affect and Cognition Based Trust as Foundations for Interpersonal Cooperation in Organizations." *Academy of Management Journal*, 38(1): 24–59.

58. Sweetman, Kathrine. 2001. "The Perils of Trusting Too Much." *MIT Sloan Management Review*, Spring: 10.

59. Penney, Alexandra. 2010. The Bag Lady Papers: The Priceless Experience of Losing It All. New York: Voice/Hyperion.

60. Szulanski, Gabriel, Rossella Cappeta, and Robert Jensen. 2002. "When Trustworthiness Matters: Knowledge Transfer and the Moderating Effect of Causal Ambiguity." Working Paper. Wharton School.

61. Hosmer, Larue. 1995. "Trust: The Connecting Link between Organizational Theory and Philosophical

Ethics." *Academy of Management Review*, 20(2): 379–403.

62. Nooteboom, Bart, Hans Berger, and Niels G. Noorderhaven. 1997. "Effects of Trust and Governance on Relational Risk." *Academy of Management Journal*, 40(2): 308–338.

63. Nahapiet, Janine, and Sumantra Goshal. 1998. "Social Capital, Intellectual Capital, and the Organizational Advantage." *Academy of Management Review*, 23(2): 242–266.

64. Clawson, James. 1987. "The Role of Trust and Respect in Developmental Relationships." Charlottesville, VA: Teaching Note, Colgate Darden Graduate Business School.

65. McAllister, Daniel. 1995. "Affect- and Cognition-Based Trust as Foundations for Interpersonal Cooperation in Organizations." *Academy of Management Journal*, 38(1): 24–59; Nooteboom, Bart, Hans Berger, and Niels G. Noorderhaven. 1997. "Effects of Trust and Governance on Relational Risk." *Academy of Management Journal*, 40(2): 308–338.

66. Korsgaard, M. Audrey, David M. Schweiger, and Harry J. Sapienza. 1995. "Building Commitment, Attachment, and Trust in Strategic Decision-Making Teams: The Role of Procedural Justice." *Academy of Management Journal*, 38(1): 60–84; Zaheer, Akbar, Bill McEvily, and Vincenzo Perrone. "Does Trust Matter?" *Organization Science*. March–April, 9(2): 1998.

67. Stevenson, H, Howard and Mihnea Moldoveanu. 1995. "The Power of Predictability." *Harvard Business Review*, July–August: 140–143.

68. McAllister, Daniel. 1995. "Affect- and Cognition-Based Trust as Foundations for Interpersonal Cooperation in Organizations." *Academy of Management Journal*, 38(1): 24–59.

69. *Wall Street Journal*. 1999. B1.

70. Bartoleme, Fernando. 1989. "Nobody Trusts the Boss Completely, Now What?" *Harvard Business Review*; Galford, Robert, and Ann Seibold Drapeau. 2003. "The Enemies of Trust." *Harvard Business Review*, 89–95.

71. Lewicki, Roy, and Barbara Benedict Bunker. 1996. "Developing and Maintaining Trust in Work Relationships." In Kramer, Roderick, and Tom R. Tyler (eds.). *Trust in Organizations: Frontiers of Theory and Research*. Thousand Oaks, CA: Sage Publications, 114–139.

72. Ibid., p. 132.

73. Lazare, Aaron. 1995. "Go Ahead, Say You're Sorry." *Psychology Today*. January/February: 40–78.

74. Ibid.

75. Ibid., p. 40.

76. Lewicki, Roy, and Barbara Benedict Bunker. 1996. "Developing and Maintaining Trust in Work Relationships." In Kramer, Roderick, and Tom R. Tyler (eds.). *Trust in Organizations: Frontiers of Theory and Research*. Thousand Oaks, CA: Sage Publications, 114–139.

77. Ibid.

78. McCullough, Michael, Frank Fincham, and Jo-Ann Tsang. 2003. "Forgiveness, Forbearance, and Time: The Temporal Unfolding of Transgression Related Interpersonal Motivations." *Journal of Personality and Social Psychology*, 84(3): 540–557.

79. Lazare, Aaron. 1995. "Go Ahead, Say You're Sorry." *Psychology Today*. January/February: 40–78.

80. Boothman, Richard, Amy Blackwell, Darrell Campbell, Jr., Elaine Commiskey, and Susan Anderson. January 2009. "A Better Approach to Medical Malpractice Claims? The University of Michigan Experience." *Journal of Health & Life Sciences Law*, 2(2): 125–159.

81. Boothman, Richard, Amy Blackwell, Darrell Campbell, Elaine Commiskey, and Susan Anderson. January 2009. "A Better Approach to Medical Malpractice Claims? The University of Michigan Experience." *Journal of Health and Life Sciences Law*, 2(2): 125–159. Premier Safety Institute. 2009. Honesty and Apology Result in 55% Reduction in Malpractice Claims, http://www.premierinc.com/quality-safety/tools-services/safety/safety-share/09-09-full.jsp#story-01

82. McCullough, Michael, Frank Fincham, and Jo-Ann Tsang. 2003. "Forgiveness, Forebearance and Time: The Temporal Unfolding of Transgression-Related Interpersonal Motivations." *Journal of Personality and Social Psychology*, 84(3): 540–557.

83. Exline, J. J., and R. F. Baumeister. "Expressing Forgiveness and Repentance: Benefits and Barriers." In McCullough, M. E., K. I. Pargament, and C. E. Thoresen (eds.). *Forgiveness: Theory, Research, and Practice*. New York: Guilford Press, 133–155.

84. Rueter, Anne. 2002. "Prescription for Health: Forgive Freely." *Ann Arbor News:* E1–E2; Aquino, Karl, Steven Grover, Barry Goldman, and Robert Folger. 2003. "When Push Doesn't Come to Shove: Interpersonal Forgiveness in Workplace

Relationships." *Journal of Management Inquiry*, 12: 209–216.

85. McCullough, M. E., K. C. Rachal, S. J. Sandage, E. Worthington, S. W. Brown, and T. L. Hight. 1998. "Interpersonal Forgiving in Close Relationships: Theoretical Elaboration and Measurement." *Journal of Personality and Social Psychology*, 75: 1586–1603.

86. Karremans, Johan, and Paul Van Lange. 2003. "When Forgiving Enhances Psychological Well-being: The Role of Interpersonal Commitment." *Journal of Personality and Social Psychology*, 84(5): 1011–1026.

87. Galford, Robert, and Anne Seibold Drapeau. 2003. "The Enemies of Trust." *Harvard Business Review*, 89–95.

88. Shaw, Robert. 1997. *Trust in the Balance*. San Francisco, CA: Jossey-Bass.

89. Lewicki, Roy, and Barbara Benedict Bunker. 1996. "Developing and Maintaining Trust in Work Relationships." In Kramer, Roderick, and Tom Tyler (eds.). *Trust in Organizations: Frontiers of Theory and Research*. Thousand Oaks, CA: Sage Publications, 114–139; Nahapiet, Janine, and Sumantra Goshal. 1998. "Social Capital, Intellectual Capital, and the Organizational Advantage." *Academy of Management Review*, 23(2): 242–266.

90. Stevenson, Howard H., and Mihnea Moldoveanu. 1995. "The Power of Predictability." *Harvard Business Review*. July–August: 140–143.

91. Nahapiet, Janine, and Sumantra Goshal. 1998. "Social Capital, Intellectual Capital, and the Organizational Advantage." *Academy of Management Review*, 23(2): 242–266.

92. Korsgaard, M., Audrey David Schweiger, and Harry Sapienza. 1995. "Building Commitment, Attachment and Trust in Strategic Decision-Making Teams: The Role of Procedural Justice." *Academy of Management Journal*, 38(1): 60–64.

93. Galford, Robert, and Anne Seibold Drapeau. 2003. "The Enemies of Trust." *Harvard Business Review*, 89–95.

94. Ibid.

95. Bartoleme, Fernando. 1989. "Nobody Trusts the Boss: Now What?" *Harvard Business Review*. March–April: 135–142.

96. Meyerson, Debra, Karl Weick, and Roderick Kramer. 1996. "Swift Trust and Temporary Groups." In Kramer, Roderick, and Tom R. Tyler (eds.). *Trust in Organizations: Frontiers of Theory and Research*. Thousand Oaks, CA: Sage Publications, 166–197.

97. Ibid.

98. Meyerson, Debra, Karl Weick, and Roderick Kramer. 1996. "Swift Trust and Temporary Groups." In Kramer, Roderick, and Tom R. Tyler (eds.). *Trust in Organizations: Frontiers of Theory and Research*. Thousand Oaks, CA: Sage Publications, 166–197; citing Dawes, Robyn. 1994. *House of Cards: Psychology and Psychotherapy Built on Myth*. New York: Free Press, 24.

99. Brewer, M. B. 1981. "Ethnocentrism and Its Role in Interpersonal Trust." In Brewer, M. B., and B. E. Collins (eds.). *Scientific Inquiry and the Social Sciences*. San Francisco, CA: Jossey-Bass.

100. Zucker, Lynn. 1986. "Production of Trust: Institutional Sources of Economic Structure, 1840–1920." In Shaw, Barry, and Larry Cummings (eds.). *Research in Organizational Behavior*. Greenwich, CT: JAI Press, 53–111; Meyerson, Debra, Karl Weick, and Roderick Kramer. 1996. "Swift Trust and Temporary Groups." In Kramer, Roderick, and Tom R. Tyler (eds.). *Trust in Organizations: Frontiers of Theory and Research*. Thousand Oaks, CA: Sage Publications, 166–197.

101. Ginnett, Robert. 1990. "Airline Cockpit Crew." In J. Richard Hackman (ed.). *Groups That Work (and Those That Don't)*. San Francisco, CA: Jossey-Bass, 427–448.

102. Isen, Alice. 2003. "Positive Affect as a Source of Human Strength." In Aspinwall, Lisa, and Ursula Staudinger (eds.). *A Psychology of Human Strengths*. Washington, D.C.: American Psychological Association, 179–195; Cameron, Kim, Jane E. Dutton, and Robert Quinn (eds.). 2003. *Positive Organizational Scholarship: Foundations of a New Discipline*. San Francisco: Berrett, 263–278; Snyder, C. R., and Shane J. Lopez (eds.). 2002. *Handbook of Positive Psychology*. Oxford: *Oxford University Press*.

103. Fredrickson, Barbara. 2003. "Positive Emotions and Upward Spirals in Organizations." In Cameron, Kim, Jane E. Dutton, and Robert Quinn (eds.). *Positive Organizational Scholarship: Foundations of a New Discipline*. San Francisco: Berrett Koehler, 163–175; Fredrickson, Barbara, and Marcial Losada. 2005. "Positive Affect and the Complex Dynamics of Human Flourishing." *American Psychologist*, 60(7): 678–686.

104. Staw, Barry, Robert Sutton, and Lisa Pelled. 1994. "Employee Positive Emotion and Favorable

Outcomes at the Workplace." *Organization Science*, 5(1): 51–72; Staw, Barry, and Sigal Barsade. 1993. "Affect and Managerial Performance: A Test of the Sadder-but-Wiser and Happier-and-Smarter Hypothesis." *Administrative Science Quarterly*, 38(2): 304–332.

105. Losada, Marcial. 1999. "The Complex Dynamics of High Performance Teams." *Mathematical and Computer Modeling*, 39(9–10): 179–192; Losada, Marcial, and Emily Heaphy. 2009. "The Role of Positivity and Connectivity in the Performance of Business Teams: A Nonlinear Dynamics Model." *American Behavioral Scientist*, 47(6): 740–765.

106. Taylor, Shelly. 1991. *Positive Illusions: Creative Self-Deception and the Healthy Mind*. New York: Basic Books.

107. Danner, D. D., D. A. Snowdon, and W. V. Friesen. 2001. "Positive Emotions Early in Life and Longevity: Findings from the Nun Study." *Journal of Personality and Social Psychology*, 80: 804–813.

108. Norem, Julie. 2001. *The Positive Power of Negative Thinking: Using Defensive Pessimism to Harness Anxiety and Perform at Your Peak*. New York: Basic Books.

109. Cameron, Kim, Jane Dutton, and Robert E. Quinn (eds.). 2003. *Positive Organizational Scholarship: Foundations of a New Discipline*. San Francisco: Berrett-Koehler Publishers.

110. Cameron, S. Kim 2003. *Organizational Virtuousness and Performance*. In Cameron, Kim, Jane E. Dutton, and Robert Quinn (eds.). *Positive Organizational Scholarship: Foundations of a New Discipline*. San Francisco: Berrett-Koehler, 48–65.

111. Sweetman, Katherine. 2001. "Employee Loyalty around the Globe." *MIT Sloan Management Review,* Winter: 16.

112. Sutcliff, Kathleen, and Timothy Vogus. 2003. "Organizing for Resilience." In Cameron, Kim, Jane E. Dutton, and Robert Quinn (eds.). *Positive Organizational Scholarship: Foundations of a New Discipline*. San Francisco: Berrett-Koehler, 94–110.

113. Argenti, Paul. 2002. "Crisis Communication: Lessons from 9/11." *Harvard Business Review*. 80(12): 103–109.

114. Shellenbarger, Sue. 1999. "Some Bosses Fumbling in Crisis Have Bruised Loyalty of Employees." *Wall Street Journal*. B1.

115. Byrne, John, and Heather Timmons. 2001. "Tough Times for a New CEO." *Business Week Online*.

116. Cullen, Kevin. March 12, 2009. "A Head with a Heart." *Boston Globe*. http://www.boston.com/news/local/massachusetts/articles/2009/03/12/a_head_with_a_heart/?s_campaign=8315

117. Spretizer, Gretchen, and Scott Sonenshein. 2003. "Positive Deviance and Extraordinary Organizing." In Cameron, Kim, Jane E. Dutton, and Robert Quinn (eds.). *Positive Organizational Scholarship: Foundations of a New Discipline*. San Francisco: Berrett-Koehler, 207–224.

118. Hosmer, Larue. 1995. "Trust: The Connecting Link between Organizational Theory and Philosophical Ethics." *Academy of Management Review*, 20(2): 379–403.

4

. . .

Communicating
Effectively

This chapter will help you:

- Understand how communication influences managerial effectiveness.
- Learn techniques for active listening.
- Learn how to give and receive effective feedback.
- Learn how to make 360-degree feedback effective.
- Enhance your cross-cultural communication.
- Understand how language reflects and perpetuates status and power differences in organizations, and learn strategies for inclusive communication.
- Understand why stories are one of the most effective ways to mobilize people, and learn how to tell a story that engages people and moves them to take action.
- Learn how the simple checklist can help you avoid costly mistakes.
- Learn how to use e-mail effectively.

Have I reached the party to whom I am speaking?

—GERALDINE, the telephone operator character created by Lily Tomlin

Communication is a contact sport. We communicate to comfort and hurt, influence and resist, co-ordinate and create chaos, bring people together and pull them apart, make ourselves known and hide behind our words. Yet we often worry so much about speaking clearly and concisely that we overlook the power of language to transform ourselves, our relationships, and our organizations.

Not that speaking clearly and concisely isn't important. Indeed, researchers and businesspeople agree that people who communicate clearly tend to be more effective and more valued in organizations than those who do not.[1] Our efforts to communicate clearly and concisely help us organize our thoughts, avoid misunderstandings, and focus employees' attention on important organizational goals and issues. But the ability to articulate a clear and concise message is only one of many communication skills that we can use to enhance our personal and organizational performance. To better understand the power of language in organizations, consider the following assumptions.

- Communication creates, as well as reflects, reality. Great leaders communicate in ways that change people's view of what is real, true, right, worthy, and possible. Steven Jobs of Apple Computer and Pixar Films, the Reverend Martin Luther King of the civil rights movement, Mahatma Gandhi of the Indian independence movement, and Gloria Steinam of the women's movement all used the power of words to create new realities and convince others that these new realities were worth pursuing.

> **Language. I loved it. And for a long time I would think of myself, of my whole body, as an ear.**
> —MAYA ANGELOU, *American Writer*

- Communication is the real work of managers. In a study of *Fortune* 1,000 workers commissioned by Pitney Bowes, "84 percent of the employees polled [said they] were interrupted more than three times an hour by messages; 71 percent said that they feel 'overwhelmed' by the onslaught. Each employee in the survey said that he or she receives an average of 178 messages and documents every day. Because of the deluge of communications, many of the workers said that 'real work' often has to wait until after hours or weekends."[2] Although communication may distract some employees from their "real work," it *is* the real work of managers. Researchers have concluded that effective managers spend much of their time in informal and unplanned communication. Rather than viewing this as a distraction, they depend on this communication to obtain timely information, build relationships, and develop support for their ideas.[3]

Many of us have been taught that communication is a linear process in which our goal is to get a clear message to the listener and to have this message understood in the way it was intended. But Robert Holland, communications consultant to Fortune 500 companies, gives a more realistic picture of communication in complex organizations:

> As long as communication is a human activity, there will be chaos in communication. The fact is that we cannot control information, and those who try will be frustrated. The only sane alternative is to manage information and the communication of it. . . . Management is all about creating the message, evaluating the media at your disposal, assessing the benefits and risks of using each, deciding which media to use, and then closing the loop by monitoring the results and responding to them. It sounds like it will work, but as we all know, there are hundreds of variables that can throw our best plans into chaos.[4]

In short, organizational communication lies somewhere between order and chaos, requiring continuous adjustment and adaptation.[5] Even if we could make everything perfectly clear, would we want to? Not always: Ambiguity in communication leaves room for new interpretations, creative thinking, and experimentation, all of which are fundamental to personal and organizational innovation, change, and growth.

But even though communication cannot always be controlled, it can—and should—be managed. In this chapter, I focus on communication skills that can increase your effectiveness. I begin with two classic communication skills that are as relevant today as they were when they were introduced decades ago: active listening and giving and receiving feedback, including 360-degree feedback. I then move to five communication skills that are getting increasing attention in organizations today: using motivating language, communicating across cultures, being aware of how power dynamics are reinforced and changed through communication at work, telling stories that create meaning and mobilize action, and communicating through e-mail and other technologies. I also address an increasingly useful tool that helps avoid costly mistakes and, more importantly, saves lives—the simple and underrated checklist.

BOX 4-1 Say What? Great Moments in Communication

On Literacy

"You teach a child to read, and he or her will be able to pass a literacy test." *President George W. Bush.*[6]

On Clarity

The U.S. space agency NASA lost its $125 million Mars Climate Orbiter when it flew too close to Mars because of a communication breakdown between two teams of engineers that worked together on the project. The team of engineers from Lockheed Martin in Denver used English measurements—pounds and feet—when they built the Orbiter. However, the team of engineers that controlled the Orbiter from NASA's jet propulsion laboratory in Pasadena, California, assumed the measurements were in metric terms, an error that caused the Orbiter to fly too close to Mars, where it either burned or broke up.

On Confidentiality

"Be careful!!—I wouldn't want this to get out. I would strongly recommend Never to put this in writing!!" Notes written in the margin of an internal memo commissioned by an outside lawyer in which Tyco International LTD managers were urged to "create stories" that would support accounting decisions. The memo—and the warning written in the margins—was found during an investigation of the company and used in the conspiracy, grand larceny, and falsifying business records case against Tyco executives.[7]

On E-Mail

Defense contractor Lockheed Martin suffered a costly six-hour e-mail system crash caused by an employee who sent 60,000 coworkers a nonwork-related e-mail message about a national prayer day. The employee was fired.[8]

ACTIVE LISTENING

The Swiss psychiatrist Paul Tournier wrote that "it's impossible to overemphasize the immense need human beings have to be really listened to, to be taken seriously, to be understood."[9] Yet in a "Brand Called You" economy in which being able to sell oneself is seen as the mother of all skills, the value of listening does not seem to get the respect it deserves. Indeed, the old saying that "the opposite of talking isn't listening, it's waiting to talk"[10] seems increasingly relevant. However, the *Wall Street Journal* columnist Hal Lancaster warns:

> It's time to stop promoting yourself and start listening. . . . To get what you want in your career, stop talking and start listening and observing. Instead of aggressively selling yourself, learn how others communicate, how they process information, and what their needs are.[11]

The act of listening is often confused with the exercise of waiting for one's turn to speak.
—Anonymous

Whether starting your career or standing on the pinnacle of success, the ability to listen to others in ways that make them feel heard and understood is an essential managerial skill. The more you listen to others, the more likely you are to hear what employees need to do their jobs, learn what customers want, hear good ideas, receive bad news, avoid mistakes, and build stronger relationships. Researcher Sachiko Mineyama and colleagues studied the impact of supervisors' active listening on employees' psychological stress. They found that employees who worked for supervisors who scored high on active listening skills reported more workplace support, greater feelings of job control, and less stress than those who worked for supervisors who scored lower on active listening skills.[12]

Managers who don't listen to others are unlikely to hear important information, especially cautionary information or bad news that can help them manage high-risk situations.[13] Disgruntled Yale University employees publicly chastised the university's former president Benno Schmidt by creating this unflattering ditty: "Benno doesn't listen; and when he listens, he doesn't hear; and when he hears, he doesn't understand; and when he understands, he's against it."[14] Critics blamed Jill Barad, former CEO of Mattel, for the company's steep decline in shareholder earnings in the late 1990s. Although they credited Barad's marketing savvy and persistence with building Barbie from a $250 million brand in the mid-1980s to a $1.7 billion brand a decade later, they also argued that her ego was too caught up in the Barbie brand, that she suffered from "an inability to accept an alternative point of view," that executives at Mattel were afraid to contradict her, and that customers and dealers felt that they weren't being listened to.[15] In contrast, when Ann Fudge took the CEO position at Young & Rubicam, Inc., she was asked what she would do when she stepped into the role. "The first thing I'm going to do is listen," said Fudge who, according to the *Wall Street Journal*, is "known as a coalition builder with the ability to rally loyal troops around her." Given her exceptional ability to listen to all constituents, it's not surprising that U.S. President Barack Obama appointed Fudge to the bi-partisan Fiscal Responsibility and Reform Commission in 2010.[16]

> Everything that needs to be said has already been said. But since no one was listening, everything must be said again.
> —ANDRE GIDE,
> *Nobel Laureate in Literature*

Why is listening so hard to do? There are several opinions on this. Harvard's John Kotter says that "the problem with people who are very successful is that they suffer ego expansion. It crushes everything in its path. It also becomes a wall."[17] The Brazilian educator Paulo Freire put it this way: "Dialogue cannot exist without humility. How can I [talk developmentally with others] if I always project ignorance onto others and never perceive my own?"[18] Psychologist Carl Rogers argued that listening to others is difficult because it takes courage: "If you really understand another in this way, if you are willing to enter his [sic] private world and see the way life appears to him [sic], without any attempt to make evaluative judgments, you run the risk of being changed yourself."[19]

When we're in everyday conversation with another person, how do we hinder active listening? Sometimes our impressions or stereotypes of a person shape how we interpret his or her comments. We may emphasize certain things and downplay other things the person says. Sometimes we get carried away with our own ideas and start thinking about how we would respond (while the other person is speaking) rather than really listening to the other person. Sometimes our emotions get in the way, especially during difficult conversations. And sometimes we just let our mind drift while the other person is speaking. As one manager recently told me, "If I had a dollar for every time I nodded my head at someone without having heard most of what he or she said, I'd be a millionaire today."

"Active listening" refers to listening to understand another person's point of view without evaluating or judging the person or his or her views. It requires empathy, which is both a perception and behavioral skill. As a perception skill, empathy means understanding that each person has a different view of the world, accepting that this perspective may be different from one's own, and respecting that difference. As a behavioral skill, empathy means responding to another person in ways that validate that person's perspective.[20] Nearly 50 years after psychologist Carl Rogers coined the term "active listening," Steven Covey, author of the book *Seven Habits of Highly Effective People*, explains: "Seek first to understand, then to be understood . . . when others feel understood first, they feel affirmed and valued, defenses are lowered, and opportunities to speak openly and to be understood come much more naturally and easily."[21] The benefits of active listening are summarized in Figure 4.1.

> Our meeting had that quality of sweetness that lasts for a lifetime; even if you never speak to the person again, see their face, you can always return in your heart to that moment when you were together to be renewed.
> —bell hooks,
> *Teaching to Transgress*

In their wonderful book *Difficult Conversations*, Douglas Stone and his colleagues at the Harvard Negotiation Project explain that most conversations, especially difficult ones, are really

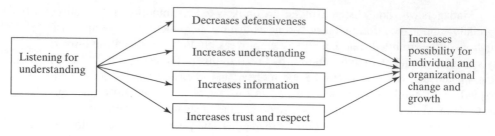

FIGURE 4-1   Active Listening

three conversations happening at once. Some of these conversations are happening out loud, but the others are happening inside the participants' heads and hearts. The "*what happened conversation*" focuses on perceptions of the facts—who did what to whom, when, why, who is right, what was meant, who gets credit, and who's to blame? The "*feelings conversation*" focuses on emotions—how do I feel about this, how does the other person feel, how much should I protect the other person's feelings, and do I show or hide my feelings? The "*identity conversation*" focuses on the impact of the discussion on the participants' identity and self-esteem—am I competent or incompetent, how am I being perceived by the others, what impact will how I handle this conversation have on my future? By listening actively to the other person, you may gain valuable insights at each of these levels of conversation, which can help you and the other person identify the best outcomes.[22] To listen actively, the following are important:

1. *Listen with intensity.* Give the speaker your full attention. This means:
   - Don't get distracted. Turn off the phone, ignore the computer screen, and don't check the time.
   - Don't assume that the issue is uninteresting or unimportant.
   - Don't listen only for what you want to hear.
   - Don't think ahead to what you plan to say next.
   - Don't interrupt, talk too much, or finish people's sentences for them.
   - Don't engage in fake listening techniques, such as nodding your head, saying "I see," or smiling even though you aren't really paying attention.
   - Don't let the person's status, appearance, or speaking style distract you from hearing the message.
2. *Listen with empathy.* Try to understand the message from the speaker's point of view. Empathy does not mean agreeing with the other person, but it does mean respecting the person's perspective and feelings.
   - Suspend thoughts (e.g., counterarguments, stereotypes, and preconceptions) and feelings (e.g., defensiveness) that can distract you from hearing the speaker's perspective.
   - Don't relate everything you hear to your own experience, such as "That reminds me of the time. . . ."
   - Listen for feeling as well as content.
   - Pay attention to body language that can provide clues to the speaker's concerns and emotional state.
3. *Demonstrate acceptance.* Show that you are listening with an open mind.
   - Avoid killer phrases, such as "You've got to be kidding," "That will never work," and "Yes, but. . . ." These responses belittle and discount what the other person thinks and feels. See Box 4.2 for a list of other killer phrases.

BOX 4-2   Killer Phrases

You can't teach an old dog new tricks.
Don't rock the boat.
It will never work.
Don't be silly.
The boss (or employees) will never go for it.
People don't want to change.
We tried that before.
You've got to be kidding.
Prove it.
If it ain't broke, don't fix it.
You must be kidding.
Be realistic.
Yes, but . . .

Fill in other killer phrases:

_____

_____

_____

- Avoid judgmental body language. Condescending grins and rolling one's eyes can have the same effect as killer phrases.
- Use encouraging language and body language.

4. *Take responsibility for completeness.* Encourage the speaker to give complete information.
   - Ask open-ended questions, such as "What do you think the critical issues are?" "Why do you think so?" "What do other people think about this?" "What other choices do you have?" "How do you think this will affect your future choices?" and "Do you have any more concerns?"
   - Confirm your understanding by paraphrasing what you heard, summarizing the main points, and asking if what you summarized was the message that the speaker intended. Doing so ensures that you have understood the message, gives the speaker an opportunity to clarify his or her ideas, and lets the speaker know that you are sincerely interested in understanding the key issues.

5. *Be yourself.* Be natural and don't come across as a compulsive, an artificial, or an overly trained active listener.[23] Remember that active listening is based more on a sincere attitude of openness, respect, and learning than on a set of rigid techniques.

How important is it to develop a reputation for being a good listener? In one study of executive promotion, researcher Peter Meyer and his colleagues concluded that "the most common factor that differentiated the successful candidates for promotion was this: The executive was seen as a person who listens."[24] Both Benno Schmidt of Yale University and Jill Barad of Mattel may have been listening to their constituents, but some of their most important constituents didn't think that they were.

How do people determine whether someone is listening? They consider how much time the person spends listening, whether the person asks questions about what they're hearing, whether they interrupt when others are speaking, whether they use body language that suggests they are listening, and whether they actually do something about what they hear.

> A new idea is delicate. It can be killed by a sneer or a yawn; it can be stabbed to death by a joke or worried to death by a frown on the right person's brow.
> —CHARLES BROWER,
> *U.S. advertising executive*

GIVING AND RECEIVING FEEDBACK

Simply stated, feedback is "any information that answers the question 'How am I doing?'"[25] At its best, feedback answers employees' questions, sets clear expectations, reduces uncertainty, encourages desired behaviors, helps employees learn new skills, enhances employee performance, and is a necessary part of coaching.

Researchers have found that although receiving feedback is an important developmental opportunity, managers often resist giving feedback. A conference board study found that 60% U.S. and European companies that participated in the study "identified improper or insufficient performance feedback [as] a primary cause of deficient performance."[26] Why do managers resist giving feedback? Harvard professor Lou Barnes wisely stated:

> The biggest problem usually found in organizations is the problem of excess caution. All too often people are not told things that would help them behave more effectively because of our fear of "not wanting to hurt them." As a result, the problem is perpetuated, and people get hurt later when . . . they are fired, demoted, or suddenly told that they are worth far less to the organization than they had thought.[27]

How can you promote effective feedback in your organization? First, you can create a feedback-friendly work environment. Second, you can promote effective feedback techniques.

Creating a Feedback-Friendly Work Environment

Remember that employees are more likely to seek out feedback if they feel that they will not be negatively evaluated for doing so and that it will help improve their performance.[28] To create such a work environment:

- Set clear, measurable performance standards so that people can judge for themselves when they are and are not meeting performance standards.
- Give ongoing feedback rather than only during performance reviews or when something goes wrong.
- Find opportunities to give positive feedback. Spencer Johnson and Ken Blanchard, authors of the book *The One Minute Manager*, call this "catching people doing something right."[29]
- Set a tone of openness. Let employees know that giving feedback—not only from managers to direct reports but also from direct reports to managers and peers to peers—is an important part of their job.
- Make sure that organizational managers and leaders are role models of feedback seeking and feedback giving.
- Make sure that managers know the feedback policies concerning potential discrimination, sexual harassment, or other activities that may be illegal. The way such feedback is given (or not given) has legal implications.
- Institutionalize the feedback process by providing employees with ongoing feedback regarding unit, industry competition, and industry performance. This can be provided through an organization's intranet in a way that employees can access this feedback whenever they want.

Promoting Effective Feedback Techniques

GIVING FEEDBACK   Effective feedback is motivated by the desire to genuinely help another person, a relationship, or an organization. To be most helpful, feedback should enable the receiver to understand, accept, and do something about the information. The following advice can increase your effectiveness in giving feedback:[30]

- Choose the right moment. In general, feedback is most useful when the person is ready to hear it (when the person is not too busy, tired, or upset), when the recipient has solicited the information and as soon as possible after the event that triggers the feedback.
- Choose the right place. A useful, though not universal, guideline is to praise in public and criticize in private. Remember, however, that in some cultures people enjoy receiving positive feedback in public and in others, they prefer receiving it in private.
- Use an appropriate communication style. Understand your own communication style as well as that of the receiver, and adapt your message to the receiver's style as much as possible. For example, if the person appreciates data, then emphasize data when giving the person feedback. If the person prefers to focus on the big picture, then emphasize the impact on the organization's goals or a greater good.
- State the purpose of the feedback session and where it fits into the broader organizational goals. For example, say, "I've had two complaints from customers this month, and I want to discuss these complaints with you. As you know, customer satisfaction is one of our top five quality indicators for your department" or "I've noticed that profits in your area have increased by 5 percent since last quarter. Because profitability is an important measure of success in our company, I want to let you know how much I appreciate your efforts and the efforts of the employees who work for you." If it's a delicate issue and you are uncertain how to frame it, be honest and say, "I don't know how to say this, yet it's important that we discuss this because . . . "[31]
- Focus on key performance issues, behavior that the receiver can do something about, and only one or two issues at a time. Frustration is only increased when the receiver is faced with too much information, concerns that are irrelevant to the job, or situations over which he or she has no control.
- Be specific rather than general. Provide observable, recent examples of behaviors. Avoid using general statements, such as "You always" or "You never." Don't present perceptions as facts or present one person's opinion as everyone's opinion.
- Be descriptive rather than evaluative. If possible, present data graphically. Doing so provides "a readily understandable comparative benchmark" for future discussions.[32] For example, show monthly figures and say, "As the figures here show, six months ago the customer service department was among those with the lowest turnover in our division. Over the last six months, the customer service department has developed the highest turnover in the division and is above the industry norm as well." Avoid evaluative language such as "bad" or "worse" that can create defensiveness. For example, don't say, "The turnover rate in your department is awful."
- Provide positive feedback, not just criticism.[33] For example, say, "I've noticed that although employee turnover has increased by 15%, customer satisfaction has also increased by 10%. What do you think is going on?"
- Describe your feelings, if appropriate. For example, say, "I worry that the customer service department will get a reputation as a difficult place to work, and we won't be able to get top-caliber employees to work there."
- Check that the receiver has understood the feedback as intended. Ask the receiver to rephrase what he or she heard you say.

- Encourage a response. Ask open-ended questions, such as "What do you think is going on?" "What do you think needs to be done to curtail the turnover?" and "How can I help?"
- Give time to react. If a person gets defensive or emotional, let him or her react. You may even learn something new and be better able to help the person find effective solutions.
- Encourage the receiver to check the accuracy of the feedback with others. Is this just your impression, or is it shared by others?
- End on an encouraging note. Discuss how the organization will benefit from the recipient's efforts to change and show confidence in the recipient's abilities. Let the employee know that you are available to help and ask what resources he or she needs to succeed. This may include training, equipment, staff, information, or additional funding.
- Follow up on the feedback session. Remember to notice and acknowledge when the recipient's behavior has changed. Avoid holding onto previous perceptions of the recipient once he or she has changed the behaviors discussed.

Finally, if you are giving feedback—particularly negative feedback—to someone in a lower level of the organizational hierarchy, be aware that the employee may be particularly sensitive to the information. For example, you may think an employee is generally very effective, yet you may give the employee feedback on one area of his or her performance that you feel could be improved. The employee may incorrectly generalize your feedback to other areas and assume that you are unhappy with his or her performance in general. Rather than focus on improving that one area, the employee may decide to look for a new job, and you may lose a valuable employee because of a misunderstanding. Therefore, it is important to understand the power of your position and help employees, particularly those over whom you have significant power, keep feedback in perspective.

> There are only two people who can tell you the truth about yourself—an enemy who has lost his temper and a friend who loves you dearly.
> —ANTISTHENES

RECEIVING FEEDBACK   Receiving helpful feedback is an important developmental opportunity, yet most of us do not actively pursue it. We may not ask for feedback because we are afraid that asking for feedback may draw attention to our weaknesses or make us look "insecure, uncertain, or incompetent."[34] Researchers Susan Ashford and Greg Northcraft suggest that these concerns are not unfounded. In a study of middle managers, they found that when managers who were perceived as high performers asked for feedback (particularly negative feedback), their boss's and direct reports' positive impressions of them increased. But when managers who were perceived as average or below average performers asked for feedback (particularly negative feedback), the results were less positive. This suggests that although average or below-average performers are more likely to benefit from the learning that comes from receiving negative feedback, they need to be particularly sensitive to how they obtain this feedback.

So, should you ask for feedback? Absolutely. Receiving feedback is a critical developmental opportunity that you shouldn't forgo—but request feedback wisely. Remember that you are managing impressions as well as looking for information that can enhance your performance. There are many people who can give you useful feedback—your bosses, peers, direct reports, customers, friends, and professional coaches—so select your sources carefully and get feedback from multiple sources. You also can monitor your environment for insights into how you are doing. For example, you can pay attention to trends in customer or employee satisfaction surveys, note whether people are coming to you for help and advice more or less often than in the past, and compare your performance on key performance indicators to those of your peers.

Also, remember to time your requests for feedback carefully. Ashford and Northcraft warn that sometimes it is wise to avoid asking for feedback, at least for a while, when you are trying a new or risky task that requires persistence. They say that a strategy of avoiding feedback may be useful "for maintaining a necessary level of self-efficacy to allow some level of persistence at [the] tasks."[35]

Once you decide to ask for feedback, the following guidelines can help you make the most of the feedback.[36]

- Request feedback from people whom you trust and who will be honest with you.
- If the feedback is too general ("You're doing a fine job" or "There's room for improvement"), ask for examples of specific, recent behavior.
- Don't be defensive, make excuses, or blame others when you hear criticism. Listen carefully, let the person finish speaking, and try to understand what the person is trying to tell you. Even if you disagree with the feedback, you may learn something new. For example, you may learn that you need to better manage people's perceptions of you, be more clear about your needs or accomplishments, or use a different management style to be more effective.
- Do not overreact or underreact to feedback. Be aware that you may overreact to the feedback, particularly when the person giving you feedback is your boss or has power over you. Conversely, you may not take feedback as seriously as you should if the person giving you feedback is in a lower hierarchical position than you are.
- Once the feedback is complete, summarize what the speaker said to make sure that you understand the key points. Ask for (or develop together) clear performance measures so that you both can evaluate future performance. Thank the person for his or her concern and advice.
- Explain what you are going to do in response to the feedback. Then do it, evaluate the consequences of your actions on performance, and then let the feedback giver know of the outcome, particularly if you can show that your performance has improved.
- Follow up with the feedback provider to let him or her know how you are doing in the future.

The Effectiveness of Multirater Feedback

We often think about feedback as process in which one person gives feedback to another person. Yet almost all Fortune 500 companies use multirater feedback, often spending millions of dollars to implement multirater feedback programs.[37] The most commonly used form of multirater feedback is 360-degree feedback that involves anonymously surveying direct reports, peers, bosses, and others (e.g., customers and suppliers) to gain information about a specific manager's performance across a standard set of competencies (e.g., communicating effectively, providing clear direction, setting clear performance measures, showing care and concern, and inspiring creativity). A survey of the Society of Human Resource Managers members found that 360-degree feedback is used almost exclusively for managers, and most often used for executives and middle- to upper-level managers.[38]

These surveys often include a self-assessment as well so that managers can compare their self-assessments with how they are perceived by others. Notably, researchers have found that the most effective managers tend to rate themselves more similarly to their raters, which suggests that having an accurate perception of your skills is associated with high performance. People who rate themselves significantly higher than others rate them tend to be poorer performers.[39] In one study, individuals whose feedback from raters was significantly lower than their own were more likely to believe that the feedback they received was less accurate and less useful than did those with smaller gaps in self–other perception.[40] Some research suggests that the larger the gap between self-perception and raters' perceptions, the more likely the person being rated will believe that the feedback was not useful and become discouraged.

Organizational leaders are willing to spend a considerable amount of time, effort, and money on such multirater programs because they expect these to help managers improve their on-the-job performance and enhance organizational results. This assumption is intuitively appealing and is based on several assumptions. First, obtaining feedback from a variety of people who interact with the manager on a regular basis should provide a well-rounded and more accurate view of the manager's performance in specific areas that matter to organizational performance. Second, because the feedback is typically anonymous and combined with other sources, there is reason to believe that raters will feel comfortable enough to provide more honest feedback. Third, once a manager knows how he or she is perceived by others, the manager will be motivated to improve his or her performance in ways that will enhance bottom-line results.

When it is implemented effectively, 360-degree feedback provides managers with information about what they are doing well and what they need to improve. Once they have this information, managers can work toward leveraging their strengths and minimizing their weaknesses so that they can give their boss, peers, and direct reports what they need to do their best work and achieve their work goals. Research suggests that 360-degree assessments can provide accurate feedback. Studies have shown that feedback recipients who receive higher feedback ratings tend to receive more favorable annual reviews from their bosses; are rated as having higher overall performance (e.g., productivity and profitability) using objective measures; and inspire higher employee satisfaction, lower turnover, higher service quality, greater customer loyalty, and higher compensation.[41] Unfortunately, researchers have found that multirater feedback enhances managerial performance in only about one-third to one-half of the cases and has no effect or a negative effect on performance in the rest of the cases (regardless of whether the manager received high or low ratings).[42] Although multirater feedback has the potential for enhancing performance, it is no guarantee, and the success of such interventions depends on the characteristics of the person who receives the feedback and the way the feedback process is implemented.[43]

Who is less likely to respond positively and proactively to 360-degree feedback? Research suggests that people who receive extremely negative feedback may become discouraged and give up on changing their behavior.[44] In addition, people who are distrustful, cynical, low in emotional stability, and overly concerned with protecting their ego tend to react negatively to feedback.[45] Individual improvement is more likely to occur when recipients:

- feel positive about the feedback process;
- are high in feedback-orientation (e.g., they proactively seek out and appreciate feedback),[46] conscientiousness (e.g., being planful, reliable, responsible, organized, and achievement oriented),[47] and openness to experience, as well as when they see themselves as continuous learners;[48]
- have a sense of personal control and believe that personal change is possible;[49]
- follow-up with the raters after receiving their feedback; and
- set achievable and meaningful goals for self-development.

If you use 360-degree feedback in your organization, what can you do to increase the possibility that the feedback will lead to changes in behavior, as well as better performance and bottom-line results?

- Select assessments that evaluate performance on skills that are related to bottom-line results.
- Choose an appropriate time to conduct the 360-degree feedback so that the process will be successful. For example, avoid collecting feedback when employees are cynical or when the organization is in the midst of a significant and possibly threatening transition.

- Prepare feedback providers. Explain what the feedback process entails, ask that they provide honest responses, ensure anonymity, let them know what the feedback will be used for, and answer any questions they have about the process.
- Tell the person who completes a self-assessment that it doesn't pay to inflate their scores. Gently warn them that people who do so may be out of touch with how others perceive them and, consequently, may not be performing at their best.
- Tell the person what the ratings will be used for. People are likely to react positively to feedback when they believe it is to be used for personal development rather than for promotion or salary decisions.[50]
- Help the person interpret the feedback he or she receives. Keep explanations simple, and focus on specific skills (e.g., "It sounds like your employees want you to delegate more.") rather than personal characteristics (e.g., "You are a micromanager"). Present feedback in a way that doesn't threaten the person's self-concept. You can ask the recipient what he or she thinks the feedback providers are saying they need from the recipient to do the best work. For example, are direct reports saying they need more direction, more delegation, or more feedback on their performance?
- Help the recipient create a goal-setting plan that focuses on specific skill development and measurable results. Focus the plan on areas that the person wants to develop. Again, keep it simple.
- Provide training and development opportunities (including coaching) in the relevant skill areas.
- Encourage the recipient to follow up with the feedback providers to explain what he or she has learned and to gain additional insights and support.
- Repeat the 360-degree feedback process again to determine whether there has been any improvement.

MANAGERIAL LANGUAGE THAT MOTIVATES EMPLOYEES

Considerable research has shown that a manager's communication style is related to employee loyalty, motivation, stress level, job satisfaction, and job performance.[51] Managerial communication that motivates others falls into three categories:

Language, as symbol, determines much of the nature and quality of our experience.
—SONIA JOHNSON,
The Ship that Sailed into The Living Room

> ***Direction Giving and Uncertainty Reducing:*** Using language that minimizes employee role and task ambiguity. This includes clarifying goals, tasks, performance measures, and rewards.

> ***Relationship Building:*** Using language that develops an emotional connection with employees (e.g., sharing feelings, showing care and concern, and expressing appreciation).

> ***Meaning-Making:*** Using language, stories, and personal examples that explain the organization's vision, values, culture, structure, challenges, and opportunities (what our organization does, how we do it, and why we do it) so that employees can make sense of the organization and their place in it. This is most useful during periods of organizational entry, change, or uncertainty.

Managers who use these three forms of communication in their everyday interactions with employees are more likely than others to create a work environment that motivates and enables employees to do their best work. The assessment in Box 4.3 lists a series of questions you can ask employees to determine whether you are communicating in a way that brings out the best in them (and whether your manager is communicating in a way that motivates you).

BOX 4-3 Motivating Language Scale

The examples below show different ways that your boss might talk to you (or you might talk to employees). Please choose the answer that best matches your perceptions. Be sure to mark only one answer for each question.

Very Little	Little	Some	A Lot	A Whole Lot
VL	L	S	A	WL

Direction-Giving/Uncertainty-Reducing Language

1. Gives me useful explanations of what needs to be done in my work.   VL L S A WL
2. Offers me helpful directions on how to do my job.   VL L S A WL
3. Provides me with easily understandable instructions about my work.   VL L S A WL
4. Offers me helpful advice on how to improve my work.   VL L S A WL
5. Gives me good definitions of what I must do in order to receive rewards.   VL L S A WL
6. Gives me clear instructions about solving job-related problems.   VL L S A WL
7. Offers me specific information on how I am evaluated.   VL L S A WL
8. Provides me with helpful information about forthcoming changes affecting my work.   VL L S A WL
9. Provides me with helpful information about past changes affecting my work.   VL L S A WL
10. Shares news with me about organizational achievements and financial status.   VL L S A WL

Empathetic Language

11. Gives me praise for my good work.   VL L S A WL
12. Shows me encouragement for my work efforts.   VL L S A WL
13. Shows concern about my job satisfaction.   VL L S A WL
14. Expresses his/her support for my professional development.   VL L S A WL
15. Asks me about my professional well-being.   VL L S A WL
16. Shows trust in me.   VL L S A WL

Meaning-Making Language

17. Tells me stories about key events in the organization's past.   VL L S A WL
18. Gives me useful information that I couldn't get through official channels.   VL L S A WL
19. Tells me stories about people who are admired in my organization.   VL L S A WL
20. Tells me stories about people who have worked hard in this organization.   VL L S A WL
21. Offers me advice about how to behave at the organization's social gatherings.   VL L S A WL
22. Offers me advice about how to "fit in" with other members of this organization.   VL L S A WL
23. Tells me stories about people who have left this organization.   VL L S A WL
24. Tells me stories about people who have been rewarded by this organization.   VL L S A WL

Source: Mayfield Rowley, Jacqueline, Milton Ray Mayfield, and Jerry Kopf. 1998. "The Effects of Leader Motivating Language on Subordinate Performance and Satisfaction." *Human Resource Management*, 37(3): 235–248. Used with permission.

Are You Getting Enough Bad News?

Undoubtedly, managers who are unable to see problems quickly and accurately face a "major liability in our increasingly complex and fast-paced world."[52] Effective managers find out that trouble is brewing through employees who are willing to give them frequent, honest information—including bad news. Unfortunately, employees are often reluctant to give their boss unfavorable information.

For example, early in former President Bill Clinton's administration, political analysts concluded, "No one in the Clinton operation has the stature, guts, and willingness to rein in the president when his own judgment is faulty."[53] Says researcher Walter Scott, "All of us have had our share of bonehead ideas. Having someone tell you it's a bonehead idea before you do something about it is really a great blessing."[54] Walter Kiechel III of *Fortune* magazine puts it more bluntly: "You can't afford to become isolated at the top, hearing only agreeable tidings borne by simpering yea-saying subordinates."[55]

> The day soldiers stop bringing you their problems is the day you have stopped leading them. They have either lost confidence that you can help them or concluded that you do not care. Either case is a failure of leadership.
> —GENERAL COLIN POWELL

There are several reasons that managers don't get bad news from their subordinates. Researcher Fernando Bartolome explains:

> Candor depends on trust, and in hierarchical organizations, trust has strict natural limits. In a hierarchy, it is natural for people with less power to be extremely cautious about disclosing weaknesses, mistakes, and failings—especially when the more powerful party is also in a position to evaluate and punish. Trust flees authority and, above all, trust flees a judge.[56]

In organizational hierarchies, employees are likely to promote and exaggerate good news and hide or minimize bad news.[57] Even the most kind-hearted and well-intentioned boss may not get the bad news he or she needs. Why not? Employees may not want to bother a boss who seems too busy to listen. They may be trying to protect a boss who seems to prefer hearing good news and is overly sensitive to bad news. They may try to solve the problem themselves or hope that the problem will correct itself over time. They may be afraid that asking for help to solve a problem will make them look incompetent. Or, there may be too many levels of the hierarchy that impede upward communication. Ultimately, however, small problems can grow into big ones, and bosses can get blindsided when they should have seen the problems coming.

Because hierarchy has such a powerful effect on employee behavior, managers must take proactive steps to encourage the communication of bad news. The most important thing you can do is to build a reputation as someone who can be trusted with bad news. Building such a reputation takes time, but there are many steps you can take to speed up the process.[58]

> Much unhappiness has come into the world because of bewilderment and things left unsaid.
> —DOSTOYEVSKY

- *Be accessible.* Don't surround yourself with gatekeepers. Take employees out to breakfast, lunch, or dinner. Visit employees' work areas and establish regular times when people can come to see you.
- *Be approachable.* Create an atmosphere in which employees feel comfortable speaking up. Avoid intimidating surroundings.
- *Surround yourself with independent minds.* In many organizations, people move ahead by adhering to the status quo and not challenging the way things are being done, even if they have ideas about how things could be done more effectively. Top performers who feel secure in their jobs are more likely to feel comfortable giving bad news, so ask them first.

- *Run meetings that encourage independent thinking and honest feedback.* Don't give your opinions first; develop processes that ensure that all views are heard; create a devil's advocate role; and regularly ask questions such as "What do you think of this?" "Has anyone seen or heard of any problems?" "Can this backfire in any way?" and "Is there any other way to look at this?" Publicly support employees who express contrary opinions or provide bad news.
- *Be discreet about sources.* Don't betray confidences. Provide ways for employees to give information anonymously, including suggestion boxes, questionnaires, online bulletin boards, and 360-degree feedback.
- *Never shoot the messenger.* Many employees have learned through experience that people who give bad news can get punished. When people come to you with bad news, you should spend most of your time listening, not speaking. Walter Kiechel wisely advises that managers should respond with three statements when they hear bad news: Can you tell me more about what happened? What do you think we should do? Thanks for letting me know. And then, of course, managers should do something about what they hear.

COMMUNICATING ACROSS CULTURES

Most of us have heard stories of humorous, embarrassing, and costly cross-national communication blunders. For example, when Coca-Cola introduced the soft drink to the Chinese market, "the bottles were marked with Chinese characters that presented the sounds of 'Coca-Cola' but that in fact meant 'Bite the wax tadpole.'"[59] When Kentucky Fried Chicken first introduced its "finger lickin' good" slogan to China, it was translated as "eat your fingers off."

> The sum of human wisdom is not contained in any one language, and no single language is capable of expressing all forms and degrees of human comprehension.
> —EZRA POUND,
> *The ABC of Reading*

Even the same words can mean different things in different cultures. It's commonly said, "Even though the British and Americans speak English, this doesn't mean that they speak the same language." For example, when Americans say that they want to "table an idea," it means that they want to put it aside for the moment. When the British say that they want to "table an idea," it means that they want to attend to it immediately. The meaning of gestures and body language may differ from culture to culture as well. For example, Anglo Americans show that they are paying attention to another person by making eye contact and using fillers such as "uh huh" or "I see." But many cultures don't use eye contact or fillers routinely in conversation.[60] Hand motions used in one country (e.g., the hand signals commonly used to say "OK" or "come here" in the United States) may be considered obscene in another.

One manager described his perception of the difference between Japanese and North American communication styles this way: "The Japanese probably will never become gabby. We're a homogeneous people and don't have to speak as much as you do here. When we say one word, we understand 10, but here you have to say 10 to understand one."[61] Table 4-1 describes one of the most common communication differences across national cultures: low context versus high context communication.

Effective managers enhance communication across cultures not by stereotyping but by paying attention to potential cultural differences in communication. By doing so, they show respect, avoid misunderstandings, and build common ground. The following guidelines can help you enhance your cross-cultural communication when people speak different languages:

- Speak clearly, use commonly known words and short sentences, but don't be patronizing.
- Avoid slang, jargon, buzzwords, and abbreviations that may not be understood.
- Avoid sarcasm and use humor carefully. Never criticize nationalities or other cultures.

TABLE 4-1	Differences between High Context and Low Context Communication	
Low Context	**High Context**
Message is carried primarily by words ("Read my lips.").	Message is carried in large part through nonverbal signals and situational cues (such as status).
Communication is direct ("Get to the point.").	Communication is indirect.
Primary purpose of communication is to exchange information.	Primary purpose of communication is to build relationships.
Conflicts are depersonalized. It is possible to separate the person from the issues.	Conflicts are personalized. Face-saving is important.
Business relationships start and end quickly and do not require trust.	Business relationships are developed slowly and are built on trust.

- Don't judge people or their message because of the way that they speak.
- Do your homework and learn preferred communication styles, including body language.
- Do not assume that "yes" and "no" are straightforward responses. "Yes" may mean "I understand" or "I'm saying 'yes' to help you save face, but you should be able to tell from my body language that I really mean to say no."
- Learn to decipher silence.
- Be flexible, especially with time. Consider norms regarding pace and punctuality.
- Learn some words in the language of the country you are visiting.
- Learn appropriate greetings. For example, learn to pronounce people's names correctly; determine whether they prefer to be referred to by formal titles, first name, or last name; and determine whether they prefer to be met with a handshake, a bow, or other greeting.
- If you are unsure of the appropriate degree of formality, err on the side of being too formal. Dress formally at first meetings. Be punctual. In some cultures, it is appropriate to address higher status and older people first. Do not ask personal questions.
- Be aware of important social rituals. For example, remember that in some cultures, people want to "get down to business" quickly, whereas in other cultures business discussions should be avoided until relationships are developed. In the United States, the front passenger seat of the car is the seat of honor. In Japan, it's the back seat.
- When in doubt, follow the lead of people from the other culture.

Differences in communication are not limited to national borders. Many researchers argue that men and women tend to have different communication styles, although some researchers argue that these differences are small, others argue that these differences are more pronounced.[62] For example, research suggests that:

- Men are more likely to express themselves directly, and women are more likely to express themselves indirectly. In other words, a man is more likely to say "Turn in the report by tomorrow," and a woman is more likely to say "Would it be possible to get the report to me by tomorrow?" Yet both men and women expect the report to be turned in tomorrow.

- Women are more likely to emphasize relationship building in communication, and men are more likely to emphasize information giving and debate in communication. Communications researcher Deborah Tannen refers to this difference as "rapport talk" versus "report talk."[63]
- Women are more likely than men to give verbal and nonverbal signals that they are listening to others, such as making eye contact, nodding their heads, smiling, and saying "uh huh." Men are more likely to listen without such signals.[64]
- Both men and women are less likely to interrupt men, but men are more likely than women to interrupt women. This pattern has been found both in children and adults. Researcher Holly Craig notes that "this pattern is not limited to conversations among peers. Boys interrupt women as well as girls who are closer to their own age."[65]
- Men may be more likely than women to send e-mails with neutral or negative emotional content. This may lead to their e-mails being experienced by the receiver as being even more negative than intended.[66]

As always, when making generalizations about cultural patterns, an important caveat is in order. Our communication styles and preferences are the result of many factors, not only nationality, gender, or any other common cultural category. Personality, experience, training, and even family dynamics influence our communication styles. One woman, for example, explained, "At our house, we warn new friends to be careful because we treat conversation like a competitive sport. The first one to take a breath is considered the listener."

My goal in summarizing these patterns of differences is not to encourage stereotyping. Men and women in conversation are much more similar than different (in other words, men aren't from Mars and women aren't from Venus). That said, it's wise to be aware of potential differences in communication that can lead to misunderstanding so that both men and women are heard and understood as intended.[67]

Culture, Language, and Power

In the end, we will remember not the words of our enemies, but the silence of our friends.
—THE REVEREND MARTIN LUTHER KING JR.

The late anthropologist Edward Sapir once said, "All in all, it is not too much to say that one of the really important functions of language is to be constantly declaring to society the psychological place held by all of its members."[68] In other words, we signal and perpetuate our assumptions about status and power through our ways of communicating in our families, communities, and workplaces.

In organizations, we can see these assumptions in action by noting who speaks more often, who gets credit for ideas, who interrupts and who gets interrupted, who gets heard and who gets ignored, and which ways of speaking are assumed to signal confidence and competence and which are not.[69]

Changing how we communicate is a powerful way that we can influence assumptions about power and status. Change, of course, doesn't come easily. For example, in the 1970s, many women and men in the United States challenged the common practice of using male nouns and pronouns to refer to both men and women (e.g., "A manager should make sure that all employees communicate regularly with him.") and promoted gender-inclusive language (such as using "chairperson" rather than "chairman"). Researcher Wendy Martyna notes that efforts to promote the use of sex-unbiased language were met with significant resistance. Critics, she says, called these efforts "ardent Amazonian," and "sisspeak." *Time* magazine called these efforts "ms-guided," a syndicated columnist called them "linguistic lunacy," and linguistic faculty at Harvard called it "pronoun envy." Many argued that the use of male nouns and pronouns to refer to both men and women was simply a linguistic convention with no exclusion or offense intended; that using "he or she" rather than a simple "he" sounded awkward and "offends the traditional eye"; and that people who promoted gender-inclusive language were too sensitive, seeing injustice and inequality where none was intended.

However, research suggests that using male nouns and pronouns to refer to both men and women may indeed reinforce cultural beliefs that promote inequality (e.g., the belief that men, more so than women, are expected to become managers and executives). For example, in a study of male and female responses to employment advertisements, researchers Sandra Bem and Daryl Bem found that when employment advertisements used male pronouns in their text (e.g., "The applicant should have a degree in business administration. In addition, he should have strong communication skills."), women were less likely to apply for stereotypically male jobs than they were when the advertisement used sex-unbiased pronouns.[70]

The unnamed should not be taken for the nonexistent.
—CATHERINE MACKINNON,
Sexual Harassment of Working Women, 1979

In addition to its potential for supporting inequality, sex-biased language can be confusing, particularly as more women and men enter professions that were previously dominated by one gender. For example, it is unclear whether the statement "Businessmen are retiring later today than in the past" refers to a pattern of early retirement for businessmen only or for businesswomen as well. Sex-biased language can also sound silly. Martyna provides these clever examples:

> Startled laughter often greets such sentences as "Menstrual pain accounts for an enormous loss of manpower hours" or "Man, being a mammal, breast-feeds his young." We do a double take when hearing of the gynecologist who was awarded a medical award for "service to his fellowman."[71]

Increasingly, the business press, as well as the academic community, is moving away from sex-biased language. For example, most business communication textbooks in the United States, the *Harvard Business Review, the Wall Street Journal, the New York Times, Fast Company* magazine, *the Academy of Management Journal,* the Associated Press, the American Psychological Association, and many law and literature journals now require gender-inclusive language. What are the advantages of using nonsexist language at work? In a *Business Horizons* article, Bill Daily and Miriam Finch explain:[72]

> Nonsexist language puts the emphasis on roles and the work produced, not the gender. Dropping gender distinctions is one tangible method management can use to announce that these distinctions are unnecessary and, what is more important, inappropriate. Most employees, both male and female, will appreciate this overt gesture and follow the lead. Nonsexist language also helps employees reach their full potential . . . [because it] allows no false links between knowledge, skills, abilities, and gender. Nonsexist language helps create a supportive work climate. . . . When sexist language is the norm, management may falsely assume that everyone supports or at least accepts its use. Even though employees may not express their disapproval, however, they may vent it in some indirect manner, such as subtly withholding support or cooperation. This type of backlash can be avoided by using language that supports every employee, not just some. Nonsexist language unifies the workforce instead of dividing it.

Table 4-2 provides guidelines for using gender-inclusive language.[73] I realize that many, perhaps most, readers are already using gender-inclusive language. However, there are still many people who are willing to do so but find it challenging and who would appreciate advice. And there are still many people (you've seen them on television or you've read their articles and books) who think that using gender-inclusive language is unnecessary. For those who fall into the latter category, Martyna notes that philosopher and psychologist William James once said that a new idea moves through three stages: "It is first attacked as absurd; then admitted to be true, but seen as obvious and insignificant; and finally, seen as so important that its adversaries claim they discovered it."[74]

TABLE 4-2 Guidelines for Using Gender-Inclusive Language	
Don't	**Do**
Don't use the word "man" or "mankind" to refer to both men and women ("Let's get the best man for the job.").	Use words such as "person" or "humanity" that are gender inclusive ("Let's get the best person for the job.").
Don't use the generic terms "he" or "his" to refer to both sexes.	• Use "he or she" or "his or her" ("Every employee should check his or her e-mail daily.").
	• Use plural pronouns ("Employees should check their e-mail daily.").
	• Alternate the use of "he" and "she" (e.g., use "he" in one paragraph and "she" in the next).
	• Avoid pronoun use altogether ("E-mail should be checked daily.").[75]
Don't use gender-specific prefixes or suffixes such as "businessman," "chairman," "workman," "manpower," "man-made," and "man-hours."[76]	• Use gender-inclusive prefixes and suffixes such as "businessperson," "chairperson," "person-hours," or "work hours."
	• Use words such as *"employees"* (instead of "manpower") or *"manufactured"* (instead of "man-made").
Don't use "man" as a verb ("Someone needs to man the office over the holiday.").	Use generic terms ("Someone needs to be at the office over the holiday.").
Don't use nonparallel language ("I'd like to introduce Mr. Kim and Susan" or "Let's get the men and girls from the mailroom to join us for lunch today.").[77]	Use parallel language ("I'd like to introduce Bob Kim and Susan Park," "I'd like to introduce Mr. Kim and Ms. Park," or "Let's invite the men and women from the mailroom to lunch today.").
Don't use occupational stereotyping ("When the doctor writes a prescription, he should make sure the handwriting is legible.").	Use gender-inclusive language ("When the doctor writes a prescription, the doctor should make sure the handwriting is legible" or "When doctors write prescriptions, they should make sure their handwriting is legible.").
Don't use qualifiers that reinforce stereotypes ("male secretary" or "female CEO").	Use the appropriate title such as "the secretary" or "CEO."
When you don't know the gender of the recipient, don't begin written correspondence or telephone messages with gender-biased salutations ("Dear Sir" or "I'd like to leave a message for Mr. Smith.").	Use gender-inclusive salutations ("Dear Customer," "Dear Reader," or "I'd like to leave a message for customer service representative Smith.").

COMMUNICATING TO MOBILIZE ACTION

Effective managers mobilize employees to go above and beyond the call of duty not by instilling fear but by creating meaning that inspires collective action. As mentioned in Chapter 2, organizational researchers Linda Smircich and Gareth Morgan explain that effective leaders influence others by

> . . . framing experience in a way that provides a viable basis for action, e.g., by mobilizing meaning, articulating and defining what has previously remained implicit or unsaid, by inventing images and meanings that provide a focus for new attention, and by consolidating, confronting or changing prevailing wisdom. . . . The person that is most easily recognized as an organizational leader is one who rises above and beyond the specification of formal structure to provide members of the organization with a sense that they are organized, even amidst an everyday feeling that at a detailed level everything runs the danger of falling apart.[78]

Meaning-making is particularly important when employees first enter an organization, during times of transition, and during crises.[79] How do effective leaders inspire others? They use inspiring language, images, and stories.

Using Inspiring Language

When researchers compared the speeches of charismatic versus noncharismatic international leaders, they concluded that the speeches of charismatic leaders contained more references to:[80]

- Collective history and the continuity between the past and the present
- Collective identity and fewer references to individual self-interest
- Followers' worth and efficacy as individuals and as a collective
- The leader's similarity to followers and identification with the followers
- Values and moral justifications, and fewer references to tangible outcomes and instrumental justifications
- Distant goals and the distant future, and fewer references to short-term goals and the near future
- Hope and faith

In a study of presidential rhetoric, Purdue University researcher Cynthia Emrich and her colleagues found that U.S. presidents who used more image-based rhetoric in their most significant speeches were rated higher in both charisma and greatness. The researchers explain: "Leaders who use words that evoke pictures, sounds, smells, tastes, and other sensations tap more directly into followers' life experiences than do leaders who use words that appeal solely to followers' intellects. By engaging followers' senses, not only their minds, leaders make their messages more immediate, real, and appealing to followers." Imagery-based rhetoric works because it engages people's attention, helps them understand and remember key points, and engages their emotions. People who use only "abstract, concept-based rhetoric run the risk of delivering a message that will, in effect, 'go in one ear and out the other'"[81] or send listeners into a "state of what can feel like total sensory deprivation."[82]

Consider the Reverend Martin Luther King's 1963 "I Have a Dream" speech that he delivered in front of the Lincoln Memorial in Washington, D.C., as the keynote address on the March on Washington for civil rights. He did not say, "Racism is very bad, and I want us to end racism within the next generation," nor did he use bullet points in PowerPoint to summarize his message:

- Racism is bad.
- We're all in this together.
- Let's stop racism in one generation.[83]

Instead, he reminded us all that people should be judged by the "content of their character" rather than "the color of their skin"; he expressed his dream that all children, regardless of race, will play together as "sisters and brothers"; and he expressed his belief that we all share this "hope" for the future.[84]

> **What kind of people we become depends crucially on the stories we are nurtured on.**
> —CHINWEIZU,
> *Voices from Twentieth Century Africa*

As Emrich explains, the Reverend King could have repeatedly proclaimed in his speech, "I have an idea," but it's doubtful that it would have had the same moving and historical impact as repeatedly using the word "dream."[85] In his speech, the Reverend King used compelling rhetoric including creating a visual picture of the future, referring to God, appealing to the listeners' shared rights and responsibilities as U.S. citizens, and framing racial equality as a common hope. Note that he also used linguistic techniques such as rhythm, balance, and repetition, all of which can mesmerize an audience and increase retention.[86]

Telling Stories

Stories are not simply entertainment or escapism. We tell and listen to stories to make sense of our world and our place in it. Stories help us remember our past, make sense of our present, and create our futures. Some stories tell us who we are or who we can be. Other stories tell us what we should and shouldn't do. Some stories help us simplify an overwhelming and confusing world. Other stories help us rise above the details of everyday life to remind us how truly special the world is. Chip Bell of *Training and Development* magazine explains:

> People love stories. They love to tell them and they love to hear them. A really good story makes a campfire worth lighting, a cocktail party worth attending, and a reunion worth holding. A story can evoke tears and laughter. A good story can touch something familiar in each of us, and yet show us something new about our lives, our world, and ourselves."[87]

> **People don't ask for facts when making up their minds. They would rather have one good soul-satisfying emotion than a dozen facts.**
> —ROBERT KEITH LEAVITT

The most effective communicators know that most people are notoriously poor at remembering facts and statistics, yet quite adept at remembering and passing on interesting stories.[88] Yet, too many managers and professionals assume that the facts will speak for themselves and move people to take action. Indeed, Stanford researcher Chip Heath warns that all of us need to be careful of the "curse of knowledge," the assumption that people outside of our area of expertise understand the insider knowledge that we take for granted and that hinders our ability to speak in a way that others can easily understand.[89]

Academics, for example, speak their own language that is often difficult (pretty much impossible) to understand outside academia. Consider, for example, the title of communication researcher Deborah Tannen's address at the Annual Meeting of the Linguistic Society of America: "Abduction, Dialogicality and Prior Text: The Taking of Voices in Conversational Discourse." Although Tannen's message is valuable to our everyday lives, she is using a language that is understood and valued within her small community of scholars.[90] Although Tannen can speak and write in a manner that is conventional in the research community, she is an expert at speaking across audiences. Her best-selling books (in which she sheds the curse of knowledge and translates her research into catchy language we can all understand) include *Talking 9 – 5: Women and Men at Work, That's Not What I Meant: How Conversational Style Makes or Breaks Relationships,* and *I Only Say This because I Love You: Talking to Your Parents, Partner, Sibs, and Kids When You're All Adults.*

Ira M. Levin, managing partner of Workplace Innovation Consultants and former principal in Ernst and Young's Business Change Implementation Practice in California, says that many companies' visions are stated as "en vogue phrases, buzzwords, and managementese that . . . resemble bumper sticker slogans . . . [and] can be readily interchanged across companies with minimal editing." He argues that visions are more compelling when they are stated as a "highly lucid story of an organization's preferred future in action."[91] Some companies use stories to develop and promote products. Patagonia designs new products by listening to customers' stories about their outdoor adventures. Kimberly Clark invented Huggies Pull-Ups for toddlers and created a $500 million market by listening to parents' stories about what it was like to toilet train their toddlers.[92] The late Anita Roddick, social activist and founder of the Body Shop, used stories to show customers that the Body Shop's socially responsible products are worth using:

> We communicate with passion—and passion persuades. We preach and teach; we educate and inform. We do not, for example, train our staff to sell; I hate high-pressure sales techniques. The idea that everyone should walk out of our shops having bought something is an anathema to me. We prefer to give staff information about the products, anecdotes about the history and derivation of the ingredients, and any funny stories about how they came on to Body Shop themselves. We want to spark conversations with our customers, not browbeat them to buy.[93]

Why do stories work? Stories are natural "cognitive units" that human beings use to store, make sense of, and pass on information.[94] By giving us a clear beginning, middle, and ending, stories help us simplify a complex world and provide us with a sense of reason, order, and predictability among the chaos. They give us a way to express our fears, joys, and dreams that might otherwise be unspeakable or incomprehensible. They help us see through the eyes of others[95] and gain understandings we may not have had before.[96] And they help us preserve the wonder and mystery of the world by enabling us to believe in that which we cannot see. Stories work, in part, because they reach out to us at an emotional level, and emotions can influence our thinking and behavior more than logic can. That's why a scary movie frightens us even though we know "it's only a movie."[97]

> There is no agony like bearing an untold story inside you.
> —Zora Neale Hurston, *"Dust Tracks on a Road."*

Given the powerful way that stories shape our thinking and behavior, it's no surprise that they play an important role in employee socialization, organizational change, and public relations.[98] Stories are particularly useful for describing and explaining complex situations. Although stories are central to human understanding and motivation, our formal management education tends to "de-story" us, a point not lost on humorists.[99] One of my favorite New Yorker cartoons has the devil and a ghoul sitting across from each other at a job interview, and the devil asks the ghoul, "I need someone well-versed in the art of torture. Do you know PowerPoint?" Encouraged to depend on facts, theories, numbers, bullet points, and executive summaries, we tend to forget the power of stories in everyday work life. In the following sections, I hope to rekindle your desire and ability to tell stories at work.

Creating a Powerful Story

The most powerful organizational stories inform employees and inspire them to take action. A story doesn't have to be complex to be powerful. Indeed, some of the best stories are short and simple. Says David M. Armstrong, grandson of the founder of Armstrong International, "You don't need an MBA to tell stories—or to understand them."[100] Consider the following story that gets passed around Amazon.com.

> When an elderly woman e-mailed [Amazon.com] to say that she loved the service but had to wait for her nephew to come over and break through the packaging, Bezos

had it redesigned in a way that was no less protective of the goods, but required much less violence to open.[101]

CEO Jeff Bezos uses this simple one-sentence story to emphasize the importance of "Amazon.com's inordinate responsiveness to customers" and his belief that Amazon.com is "the most customer-obsessed company to ever occupy planet Earth." IBM employees sometimes tell the following story about its former CEO, Tom Watson, Jr.:

> A young executive had made some bad decisions that cost the company several million dollars. He was summoned to Watson's office, fully expecting to be dismissed. As he entered the office, the young executive said, "I suppose after that set of mistakes you will be wanting to fire me." Watson was said to have replied, "Not at all, young man, we have just spent a couple of million dollars educating you."[102]

The Watson story sends the message that IBM is committed to its employees and that employees can make mistakes as long as they learn from them. Are these stories true? No one knows for sure. Many powerful stories aren't necessarily based on verifiable facts. Organizations, like all communities, have myths. Over time, the details of the story may change, some points may get exaggerated, and other points may be forgotten. However, the essence of the story will survive if its message feels genuine and relevant to employees, customers, and other constituents. However, once the message is no longer seen as genuine or relevant, it loses its power. Powerful organizational stories have some or all of the following characteristics:

- *Simple.* Listeners are not overwhelmed by details.
- *Relevant.* They are told for a purpose that matters to organizational members. They reflect organizational beliefs, values, or goals, or help organizational members gain an understanding of complex or ambiguous situations.
- *Inclusive.* All organizational members can see themselves in the story. Everyone who hears it is able to say, "These are my people," "This is my story," and "I can delight customers too."
- *Concrete, temporal, and action oriented.* They have a protagonist(s) who faces a hurdle to be overcome or a dilemma to be resolved, a sequence of causally related events that evolve over time, a climax and resolution, and a moral or a lesson that people find useful for their day-to-day work lives.
- *Emotional.* They excite, delight, and otherwise move the listener at an emotional level. Powerful stories are not simply a series of facts strung together in a logical order. Researchers have found that stories that evoke the strongest emotions (positive or negative) spread farther and last longer.[103]
- *Unexpected.* They surprise the listener with an unexpected twist, and this surprise keeps people listening and makes the story memorable.[104]
- *Friendly, not cynical.* Even sad stories should leave the listener with feelings of hope, joy, or satisfaction.[105]
- *Appeal to uniqueness.* They make the people in the organization feel that the organization and the people in it are different and special in some important way (e.g., "We're the most customer-obsessed company on earth." "We are the most innovative organization." "We are helping people in a way that no one else can."). Even though the characteristics described in the story may not be truly unique to the organization—indeed, other organizations may tell similar stories—the story makes people feel as though their organization is unique in some important way.[106]

- *Shared by many people.* They are interesting and important enough to be told and retold throughout the organization and passed on to newcomers as well as outsiders.

What makes a story go viral? Stories that pass from one person to another quickly and repeatedly tend to have three things in common. First, the more the stories appeal to emotions, the more likely they are to get passed on. Second, stories are more likely to be told to others when the people telling them feel like they're helping others (e.g., "Let me give you an example of why this company is a great—or horrible—place to work."). Third, stories are more likely to be passed on when a trigger reminds the people to tell the story.[107] For example, if someone mentions Steve Jobs' controversial leadership style, this can trigger employees at Apple Computer to pass on some of the many stories about how they felt both threatened and inspired by his quirky leadership style.

When Stanford professor Bob Sutton told people he was writing his book, *The No Asshole Rule: Building a Civilized Workplace and Surviving One that Isn't* (which became a best seller), he said that many people immediately began telling stories about Steve Jobs. Sutton said, "As soon as people heard I was writing a book on assholes, they would come up to me and start telling a Steve Jobs story. The degree to which people in Silicon Valley are afraid of Jobs is unbelievable. He made people feel terrible; he made people cry. But he was almost always right, and even when he was wrong, it was so creative it was still amazing."[108]

Telling a Powerful Story

Telling a good story requires thinking clearly about the message that you want to convey, anticipating the reactions of the audience, and using rhetorical techniques that keep the listener listening.[109] To tell a good story:

- *Know why you're telling the story and the key beliefs or values that you want to express.* The audience should not be asking themselves, "What's the point?" "Why are you telling me this story?" "Where does this fit in?"[110]
- *Know how you want listeners to feel.* Do you want them to be worried about the competition? Humble and/or proud of their accomplishments? Connected to people in other parts of the organization? Strong, competent, and resilient when facing danger? Adaptable when facing change?
- *Know your audience.* Lee Iacocca, former CEO of Chrysler, explains that "it's important to talk to people in their own language. If you do it well, they say, '. . . he [sic] said exactly what I was thinking.'"[111] Adapting the message or language to the audience says, "We're in this together."
- *Be credible.* People need to believe the story is plausible and reflects not only the perspectives of leaders or a small group but of followers and others as well.[112]
- *Set the context.* Be visual so that people can watch the story unfold in their minds. ("It was five minutes before I was scheduled to go to the podium and speak. Three hundred angry people were in the audience. My hands were already sweating from nervousness, and then I realized that I had left my notes for my speech in my briefcase on the airplane that was on its way back to Singapore.")
- *Be dramatic.* Integrate well-placed pauses, vary your gestures, and mimic the characters' voices or actions. Build slowly to the climax or punch line to create a sense of mystery, excitement, irony, humor, joy, or warmth.
- *Don't fill in too many details.* Give listeners the space to use their imagination. A good principle is to use more detail in the beginning of the story to set the stage and then give fewer details as the story unwinds. Consider which points should be exaggerated and embellished and which points should be played down or excluded.[113]

- ***Don't overexplain.*** The story should be clear enough to speak for itself. You shouldn't have to explain what it means or why it's relevant.
- ***Don't preach.*** Remember that the best stories "don't tell people what to think, but create a space for them to think in."[114]

Are stories and storytelling in organizations really that straightforward? Well, yes and no. They do simplify a complex world, help us express organizational values, and play an important role in organizational socialization. But like most aspects of organizational life, we don't have as much control over our stories as we like to think.

History will be kind to me, for I intend to write it.
—Sir Winston Churchill

Researchers have found that organizations have multiple stories being told around the organization at the same time; not all of these stories are initiated by managers and executives; and not all of these stories support the organization's espoused beliefs, values, or goals. Furthermore, every story we tell, regardless of how carefully we choose our words, is open to multiple interpretations depending on the audience (e.g., hierarchical level or culture) and the particular context, and these interpretations can change over time.[115]

Researcher David Boje gives examples of competing stories at Disney World, the quintessential storytelling organization. Employees at Disney World tell as many stories about Walt Disney as they tell about princesses and princes, giants and elves. Some of the Walt Disney stories are the official stories started by Disney himself. In these stories, he frames himself as a pioneer in animation who brought happiness to millions of people. However, some of the Walt Disney stories were started by employees who frame him as an egotistical tyrant who took credit for the ideas of the underpaid animators who worked for him.

Power consists to a large extent in deciding what stories will be told.
—Carolyn Heilbrun, *Writing a Woman's Life*

Which stories are true? Was Walt Disney's organization a happy kingdom or oppressive workplace? Did Walt Disney really say, "I love Mickey Mouse more than any woman I have ever known?" and, if so, was this his real feeling or was he just trying to make a point? We may never know the complete truth. But we do know that each of the stories has a message that is designed to frame experience; that each story may have exaggerated some elements and left some things out; and that multiple stories, taken together, show a more complex and comprehensive picture than any one story can do alone. To assess whether a story is true or a myth, you can try finding it at snopes.com, a Web site that investigates whether a story is truth or fiction.

Be Wise When Listening to Stories

The previous section discussed how to tell a story so that people will support your ideas. In this section, I discuss the risks of being taken in by a good story. When you are listening to a well-crafted story that is designed to gain your support, how can you tell if the ideas illustrated by the story deserve your support? University of California researcher Kimberly Elsbach conducted a fascinating study of Hollywood executives who routinely received pitches from screenwriters who were trying to sell their ideas. Elsbach found that the way in which the ideas were presented were more influential than the quality of the ideas themselves (which, as she says, is probably one of the reasons why plenty of poor quality television shows get aired).

She explains, "We all like to think that people judge us carefully and objectively on our merits. But the fact is, they rush to place us into neat little categories—they stereotype us. . . . People on the formal end of pitches have no formal, verifiable, or objective measures for assessing that elusive trait—creativity . . . therefore [they] apply a set of subjective and often inaccurate criteria very early in the encounter, and from that point on, the tone is set." In other words, Hollywood executives make judgments about whether a person is creative, dependable, and so on within seconds of meeting the person. Then, the executive listens to the pitch with an either open or closed mind based on these stereotypes. Elsbach warns that we "should beware of relying on stereotypes. It's all too easy to be dazzled by pitchers who ultimately can't get their projects off the ground, and it's just as easy to overlook the creative individuals who can make good on their ideas."

We are all busy and often must make quick decisions based on limited information. So, it's easy to get wooed by a good story—and stereotypes about the storyteller—and then be seduced into supporting ideas that have little merit or backing people who can come up with good ideas but cannot implement them. There are several things you can do to minimize this risk. Most important, you should recognize that you are easily seduced by stereotypes about the credibility of the storyteller. Then, if you find yourself being swept away by a good story, a charming storyteller, or an engaging presentation, ask for data to support the idea. Ask the persons to provide concrete evidence of experience in the area of interest, and ask if they can show completed projects as proof that they have a track record of following through on their ideas. Ask them what kinds of failures and hurdles they have faced in the past and what they learned from these experiences. This will provide you with insights about how they will work when things don't go as planned. Ask to speak with people who have worked with them before. Get opinions from other people who may not share the same stereotypes that you have about what success, creativity, and professionalism look like.[116]

CHECKLISTS: AN UNDERRATED AND LIFE-SAVING COMMUNICATION TOOL

In contrast to the richness of stories, checklists provide a simplifying mechanism that can be very useful, particularly in complex situations. Yet, most of us tend to underestimate the power of checklists, relegating them to boring, routine, and unimportant tasks.

Physician Peter Pronovost, a critical care specialist at John Hopkins University School of Medicine, conducted a study to evaluate the effectiveness of checklists for reducing infections and mortality in hospitals. He was concerned that line infections (infections that occur because of inappropriate insertion of intravenous lines into patients to deliver medicine or nutrition) were relatively common in hospitals. Pronovost created a simple five-step checklist designed to ensure that nurses and physicians inserting lines into patients were following established protocol. The checklist included the following steps: (1) wash [your] hands with soap, (2) clean the patient's skin with chlorhexidine antiseptic, (3) put sterile drapes over the entire patient, (4) wear a sterile mask, hat, gown, and gloves, and (5) put a sterile dressing over the catheter site once the line is in.

Although these steps are well-known in the medical profession, Pronovost found that physicians skipped at least one of these critical steps in the process approximately one-third of the time, sometimes resulting in infections and, in the extreme, the death of a patient. A year after the checklist process was instituted at one hospital, the infection rate over the course of 11 days went from 11% to 0%. During 15 months of using the checklist, there were only two line infections. Researchers calculated that the checklist prevented 43 infections and eight deaths, and probably saved the hospital $2 million in costs over that period. When the five-step checklist was instituted in Michigan intensive care units over an 18-month period, line infections were nearly eliminated, approximately 1,500 lives were saved, $175 million was saved, and the intensive care units using the checklist outperformed 90% of intensive care units across the nation in reducing infections and death due to improperly inserted IV lines.

Why do checklists work? They work because mistakes are almost inevitable in today's complex world, regardless of how well educated and experienced we are. They work because they help us remember the important (yet often not exciting) things we need to do. They work because they help us ensure consistency and avoid blind spots that we may otherwise overlook when we're in a hurry or when we're facing complex situations. They work because they help multiple people coordinate their actions. And they work because they protect us from mistakes we might make out of ignorance (not knowing what to do), ineptness (knowing what to do and forgetting), and arrogance (thinking we're so smart that things will turn out fine even if we don't go through appropriate procedures).

If something as simple as a checklist can transform medical care and save lives, imagine how the simple checklist, when used appropriately, can transform your own work.[117]

TALK AND TECHNOLOGY

In 1943, Thomas Watson, founder of IBM, declared, "I think there is a world market for maybe five computers." In 1977, Ken Olsen, founder of Digital Equipment Corporation, predicted that "there is no reason anyone would want a computer in their home."[118] In 1981, Bill Gates said, "640K ought to be enough for anybody." Their predictions about the impact of computer technology on everyday life were wrong. Today, over 75% of U.S. households have home Internet access. Over 90% of U.S. households in which at least one person has a bachelors' degree have home Internet access.[119] Home Internet usage in Australia is just over 60%, Europe just over 50%, Latin America approximately 35%, the Middle East approximately 30%, Asia at just over 20%, and Africa at approximately 11%. Worldwide, home Internet usage was almost 29% in 2010.[120] Nearly three quarters of Millennials (people born between 1980 and 1995) use social networking sites daily, and 40% of adults in older generations do so.

> We are drowning in information but starved for knowledge.
> —JOHN NAISBITT, *Futurist*

Clearly, communication technologies are significantly changing our expectations about communication. For example, a Pew Research Study found that over 80% of Millennials said they sleep with their cell phone placed on or right next to their bed, compared with 68% for Generation X, and 50% of Boomers.[121] In addition to increasingly having (and wanting) access to communication technologies around the clock, we can communicate with a broader and more diverse audience through a wider range of communication channels than ever before. If we have something to say, we can say it face-to-face or through the phone, e-mail, chat technologies, texting, Twitter, Facebook, Skype, overnight mail, or snail mail (that's the old-fashioned stamped letter).

The availability of all these communication technologies has led to a behavior called "multicommunicating," the practice of having multiple conversations simultaneously while using different communication technologies.[122] For example, you can have a telephone conversation with someone while simultaneously checking your e-mail. Does multicommunicating increase effectiveness? It depends. On the one hand, you could be checking your e-mail to find information relevant to the conversation, and the person on the phone may be aware that you're checking your e-mail to research that relevant information. On the other hand, you could be engaging in two entirely different conversations, and the person on the phone may be wondering why there are unexpected periods of silence and a lack of common social cues (e.g., saying "I understand" or "uh huh") on your end of the conversation. The first scenario may enable you to make the phone conversation more efficient because you are able to quickly access relevant information from your e-mail. The second scenario may lead to inefficiency, confusion, and errors because you are distracted by your engagement in two different and nonoverlapping conversations. Consider this: Would you want a physician to be multicommunicating while discussing your case with a colleague? It probably depends on whether the physician is multicommunicating to find additional information about your case or whether the physician is discussing two different cases using two different communication media at the same time (or planning a child's soccer tournament while simultaneously discussing your case).

Not surprisingly, there is considerable interest in how communication technologies affect our social connections to each other. The Pew Internet and American Life Study found that people in the United States who use cell phones and participate in various online activities tend to have larger and more diverse core social networks. In addition, the study found that the use of the Internet has little or no effect on people's participation in their local communities, including visiting with their neighbors in person. In fact, the study found that Internet users were 40% more likely to visit a public park or café. The study found that the average number of people with whom participants in the study felt they could "discuss important matters or who they consider to be 'especially significant' in their life" has declined by approximately one-third since 1985. However, they also found that this decline wasn't related to cell phone or Internet use (the researchers did not speculate what may have caused the decline). Finally, the study found that, "People's mobile phone use outpaces their use of landline phones as a primary method of staying in touch with their closest family and friends, but face-to-face contact still trumps all other methods".[123]

Although several technologies are transforming the way we communicate and spend our time, I focus on e-mail in the following section because e-mail is now a taken-for-granted part of everyday work life in many organizations. E-mail is appealing because it is easy, accessible, relatively economical, and serves as a written record of organizational communication. We can send messages to many people simultaneously; overcome many barriers associated with time, distance, and physical disabilities; and work flexibly and productively from home (and from the beach, mountain, or airplane, for that matter).

Critics argue that e-mail can be too much of a good thing. Access to unlimited information can lead to information overload. Expectations of round-the-clock availability can lead to unrealistic demands on employees' time. And the speed at which the Internet operates may contribute to an unrealistic sense of time. Says Jerry Riftin:

> The computer introduces . . . a time frame in which the nanosecond is the primary temporal measurement. The nanosecond is a billionth of a second, and though it is possible to conceive theoretically of a nanosecond . . . it is not possible to experience it. Never before has time been organized at a speed beyond the realm of consciousness.[124]

Communication consultant David Ancel argues that the Internet may also give us an unrealistic sense of place. He explains:

> If you travel 18 hours and 10,000 miles to Asia and you step off the plane and are hit by the heat and humidity, you know that you're someplace different and you're going to have to make some adjustments. But if you send an e-mail from your desk or walk around the corner to a videoconference room, you haven't moved at all off of your cultural space.[125]

Other concerns about e-mail have been more highly publicized. Most of us are aware that the Internet has opened the doors to cyberthieves who steal company secrets; cyberhackers who bring organizations' information and communication systems to a standstill; cybermarketers whose unsolicited e-mail messages annoy people and clog computer networks; and cyberslackers who use company-provided computers and Internet services to shop, play games, download pornography, send personal messages, look for other jobs, or start their own business—all on company work time. The *Wall Street Journal* reported that "of 1,244 employees surveyed by Vault.com, a New York job-search Web site, 90.3 percent acknowledge surfing nonwork-related sites, a practice one respondent describes as 'the millennium cigarette break.'"[126]

Despite its annoyances and risks, most of us appreciate the convenience, speed, and ease of using e-mail. As with all communication tools, e-mail is most effective when used thoughtfully.

Rules for Effective E-Mail Communication

Rule 1: Use the right medium for the message. E-mail is not as effective as face-to-face communication if you are trying to build relationships, influence people, or deal with sensitive topics. The more important the message is, the more important face-to-face communication becomes.

- Use e-mail when you need to send simple messages to or retrieve simple messages from an individual, group, or large audience.
- Use e-mail for instrumental purposes, such as setting up meetings, sending agendas, or following up on action plans.
- Use e-mail when you want to keep a record of the communication.
- Do not use e-mail for sensitive topics, complex communications, urgent messages, or confidential information.

Rule 2: Think before you hit the "send" key. Before you send a message, ask yourself what would happen if your message was posted in a public place, sent to someone by mistake, or forwarded to someone by the receiver. If you have any concerns, use a more private communication method.

- Check all destination addresses.
- Don't forward any e-mails until you ask the sender for permission.
- Don't forward jokes and inspirational messages to everyone on your e-mail list.

Rule 3: Be professional. Because e-mail is fast and easy to use, it can lead to overuse, sloppiness, or inappropriate informality. To counter these tendencies:

- *Be sensible about distribution.* Send only pertinent e-mail and do not overdistribute. Use online bulletin boards for general-interest messages.
- *Be concise.* Make the subject heading brief and meaningful. Cover only one topic per message. Keep messages short. Use short paragraphs, with headings if necessary, for quick reading.
- *Be clear.* Use common language. Define all acronyms and jargon if you must use them. Avoid abbreviations. Identify the e-mail to which you are responding. When making requests, be clear about what you need, what form you need it in, and when you need it.
- *Be attentive to style.* Use proper grammar, spelling, and punctuation. Proofread e-mail before sending it. Don't type in all caps: It's seen as shouting.
- *Be respectful.* When in doubt, err on the side of formality rather than informality. Think before responding emotionally. Don't send e-mail when you are angry. Be cautious when using humor, and don't be sarcastic. Never send or forward any e-mail that has any sexist, racist, political, or other comments that may be perceived by some people as inappropriate.
- *Be sensitive to the emotional tone of your e-mails.* Be careful about the tone of your e-mails. Researchers have found that mail recipients may view e-mails that are neutral in tone as having a negative tone. The same studies have found that people perceive e-mails that express negative emotions to be even more negative than intended.[127]

- *Be sensitive to culture.* When in doubt, use formal titles. Be aware of time differences, work hours, and holidays. Be considerate of nonnative speakers. Don't assume that the meaning of emoticons transfers across cultures. North Americans use the emoticon : -) to express a smile. The Japanese (who call emoticons *kao maaku,* which means "face marks") use ^-^ to express a smile.[128]
- *Be accessible.* Read your e-mail regularly. Let people know how often you check your e-mail (e.g., Can they expect you to check your e-mail in the evenings or on weekends?). Respond to messages as soon as possible. Let people know when you are out of the office and whom they should contact if you are unavailable.
- *Be sensitive to power.* Remember that when you send e-mail messages to people with less power, they may read more into the messages than you intended. For example, if you send a message to a direct report that says, "Please see me in my office at 2:00 tomorrow," the employee may worry about the purpose of the meeting, even though you intend to surprise the employee with a promotion or pay raise.
- Use a signature file that includes your name, title, and contact information.

Rule 4: Be organized.

- Create folders for any e-mails that you want to keep.
- Delete or file messages as soon as you are finished with them.

Rule 5: Be careful.

- Assume all e-mail is as public as a postcard.
- Never give your password to anyone.
- Get top-quality antivirus software and use it regularly. Update the software so that new viruses are covered.
- Don't open unsolicited attachments from anyone you don't know because they may contain viruses.
- Be wary of opening attachments from people whom you know if the attachment did not originate with the sender (such as humorous attachments or chain letters) or if the subject or message is too general (i.e., "important information attached").
- Don't reply to unsolicited marketing e-mails (spam) because that lets the marketer know that they have reached an active address. Purchase antispam software or sign up for spam protection through your Internet service provider.[129]
- Be careful when posting your e-mail address or personal information on the Web. Always check Web sites' policies regarding privacy.
- If you are concerned about privacy, you may want to remove the "cookies" that are "small data files left on your hard drive by Web pages to track your surfing habits." Although they are mostly harmless, they can pose privacy concerns. Note that removing cookies can affect your ability to use some Web sites.[130]

Rule 6: Develop and distribute official organizational policies regarding e-mail.

- Be clear about what e-mail should and should not be used for; whether employees are allowed to send personal messages, jokes, and other nonwork-related messages over e-mail;[131] and what distribution policies (e.g., bulletin boards versus direct e-mails) are approved by the organization.
- Be clear about which Internet uses are approved and which are not (such as online shopping, games, or porn sites).

- Let employees know if the organization will be inspecting e-mail messages and monitoring Internet use. Make sure that employees know the laws related to electronic communications privacy. At this writing, employers can monitor Internet use and retrieve and read saved and deleted messages that employees send without getting employees' permission.
- Let employees know of the consequences for noncompliance with organizational e-mail policies.

Rule 7: Stay informed of new technologies. Software is routinely developed to manage some of the problems associated with e-mail, including "remote paper shredders"; technologies that prevent people from copying, printing, or forwarding messages to others; and "fire walls" that prevent recipients from forwarding messages outside the organization's intranet or approved destinations.[132] See Box 4.4 for tips for managing voice mail.

BOX 4-4   Tips for Managing Voice Mail

1. Update your greeting daily.
   - Include the name, date, and when you'll get back to the caller.
   - Give instructions on how to reach a live person or send you an e-mail.
   - Ask the caller to leave a brief message.
   - Speak slowly and clearly, especially when giving out numbers or names.
2. Let callers know when you are out of the office, when you will return, and with whom they can speak in the meantime.
3. Redirect calls to another person when you're out of the office. When you are not available, forward incoming calls directly to the phone mail system so that it will answer after only one ring.
4. Return calls promptly and check messages when you are out of the office if necessary.
5. Call yourself and listen to your own greeting. Is it clear and concise? Do you sound friendly and relaxed?
6. Don't overrely on voice mail to avoid human interaction.
7. When leaving a message on voice mail, prepare your message prior to making your call so that you can be thorough yet clear and concise and let the receiver know what you want him or her to do after hearing your voice mail. Remember that your voice mail message has an impact on how the receiver perceives you. People shouldn't have to call back for more information. State your name and organization's name; say why you're calling; tell the caller what you want her or him to do; say all names, numbers, and addresses (including e-mail addresses) slowly; repeat them; and spell names, if necessary.
8. Never leave angry voice mails or voice mails that criticize others. Remember that voice mail messages can be forwarded to others, so be certain that you'd be comfortable having your message heard by others.

BOX 4-5   Employee Resistance through Communication

Employees have always found subtle and clever ways to resist organizational power and exert their own power. Here are a few examples.

Buzzword Bingo

To express their frustration at the escalating use of buzzwords in organizations, employees at several organizations are playing a new game called "Buzzword Bingo." To play the game, employees create a

BOX 4-5 *Continued*

bingo-style sheet (say, a four-by-four matrix) and insert common buzzwords in each of the boxes. When they go to meetings, they bring their bingo sheets. When a buzzword is used during the meeting, employees check their bingo sheets to see if the word is in one of the boxes. If so, they check the box. When all the boxes in a horizontal row or vertical column are checked, the holder of the sheet shouts "Bingo!" Bill Ellet of *Training and Development* magazine explains that the game is a "lighthearted attempt to promote clear communication" and "have some fun." He also explains that employees use this game to react to what they may feel is an inappropriate use of power. He explains, "Buzzwords are often a tacit currency of power: 'I know what this means, and you don't. Therefore, I'm more important than you are.' Buzzwords are deliberately exclusive . . . [and] can dress up vacuousness."[133]

Panic Buttons and Other Diversions

Some Web sites, including the Dilbert Web site, have what are called "panic buttons." Employees who are using the site can click on the panic button if their boss, coworkers, or customers come near. A screen will appear that includes a fake spreadsheet, fake news report, or other fake but responsible-looking material.

CONCLUSION

Undoubtedly, organizational communication is becoming increasingly complex. Today's manager must communicate with people who don't speak the same language or share the same culture, align diverse employees toward shared organizational goals, and create synergy among many different kinds of communication media.[134] Despite the new communication challenges that managers face today, the basic lessons of communication have not changed nor will they change in the future. Employees will continue to want to be heard, understood, and respected. They will want to know what they should be doing, for whom, and by when. They will want to know how they're doing and where they stand. And they will want to find meaning in their work so that they can feel that they are giving their time and energy toward something worth doing.

Box 4.6 describes best the practices of organizations that take organizational communication seriously and leverage it to achieve organizational goals.

BOX 4-6 **Leadership Lessons in Communication**

Based on a study of ten leading U.S. corporations known for exemplary employee communications practices, researchers Mary Young and James Post identified the leadership's best practices:[135]

1. *They champion communication.* They are committed to communicating frequently and personally with employees. Notably, their success as communicators isn't necessarily tied to their style. One executive was described as "a bit wooden in front of television cameras," but he was praised for his willingness to "communicate often, frequently in person, display a willingness to address challenging questions, listen carefully, and respond quickly to sensitive topics."
2. *They have a clear employee communication strategy.* They systematically incorporate many different ways of communicating: presentations, television, online videos, newsletters, question-and-answer sessions, email, and Web broadcasting.

(*continued*)

> ## BOX 4-6 *Continued*
>
> 3. *They emphasize face-to-face communication, particularly in times of uncertainty and change.* They communicate quickly and candidly, even when the news isn't expected or favorable. They explain not only what happened but also who, why, when, where, and how. They don't tell people how people should feel about news. Says one manager, "It is insulting to tell people how they should feel about change."[136] Rather, they support different perspectives.
> 4. *They manage the bad news/good news ratio.* They make sure that they hear about failures, mistakes, and customer complaints. Employees in these organizations know that bad news is as important to hear as good news.
> 5. *They are committed to two-way communication.* They set up meetings, informal lunches, and interactive online sessions, and they regularly request and reward upward feedback—all designed to get important information, hear new ideas, and encourage bad news. In the best organizations, employees use these methods of communicating and take them seriously.
> 6. *They match their words and actions.* They know that when employees see a mismatch between what the leaders say and do, they stop listening.
> 7. *They know their audiences.* They are familiar with their various employee groups, customers, and other constituents. They know what kind of information their constituents want, when they want it, and in what form. They adapt their content and presentation to the needs and style of the audience.
> 8. *They share responsibility for employee communication.* They expect all managers to communicate personally and frequently with employees.
>
> ---
>
> *Source:* Adapted from Young, Mary, and James Post. 1993. "Managing to Communicate, Communicating to Manage: How Leading Companies Communicate with Employees." *Organizational Dynamics,* Summer: 31–43.

Chapter Summary

Communication is the real work of managers. Effective managers spend much of their time in informal and unplanned communication. This communication enables them to obtain timely information, build relationships, and develop support for their ideas.

Active listening refers to listening to understand another person's point of view without evaluating or judging the other person or his or her views. Active listening involves listening with intensity, listening with empathy, demonstrating acceptance, taking responsibility for completeness, and being yourself. Remember that active listening is more a sincere attitude of openness and respect than a set of rigid techniques.

Employees want feedback so that they can know how they are doing. Feedback answers employees' questions, sets clear expectations, reduces uncertainty, encourages desired behaviors, helps employees learn new skills, enhances employee performance, and is a necessary part of coaching. Effective feedback is given in a way that the receiver understands the information, accepts the information, and is able to do something about it.

Managers need to see problems quickly and accurately so that they can respond before the situation gets worse. However, employees are often reluctant to give their managers bad news. To encourage employees to bring you bad news, be accessible, be approachable, surround yourself with independent minds, run meetings that encourage independent thinking and honest feedback, be discreet about sources, and "never shoot the messenger."

Effective managers know how to communicate effectively across cultures. They pay attention to differences in the meanings of words and phrases, body language (e.g., the appropriateness of eye contact), and communication styles (e.g., high context versus low context).

Many researchers have concluded that men and women tend to have different communication styles. Specifically, they say that men tend to be more direct than women, women are more likely to emphasize relationship building and men are more likely to emphasize information giving, women are more likely to give verbal and nonverbal signals that they are listening to others, and men and boys are more likely to interrupt women and girls. In addition, men's e-mails tend to be more emotionally neutral, which can lead to these "e-mails being interpreted as more negative in tone than intended.

Communication practices perpetuate assumptions about power differences. You can see these assumptions in action by noting who speaks more often, who gets credit for ideas and who doesn't, who interrupts and who gets interrupted, and who gets heard and who gets ignored. Changing how people communicate is an effective way to change assumptions about status and power. Using gender-inclusive language is one technique that many managers, organizations, and business publications are using to create an inclusive workplace.

Effective leaders know that creating meaning that mobilizes action is an important part of their job. They know that bullet points and executive summaries aren't enough. They use influential language and compelling stories to create a common vision, encourage a collective identity, and inspire coordinated action toward common goals. Stories are powerful because they are convincing and memorable. They are natural cognitive units that human beings use to store, make sense of, and pass on information. In addition, they help human beings simplify a complex world, manage ambiguities and contradictions, see order among the chaos, see through the eyes of others, and gain new understandings. Stories that are memorable and move people to take action tend to have the following qualities: sim-

plicity, relevance, concreteness, temporality, action-orientedness, emotional, unexpectedness, friendliness rather than cynicism, and appeal to uniqueness.

Stories that go viral have three things in common. First, the more emotionally appealing the stories, the more likely they will be passed on to others. Second, the people who tell them feel like they are helping others. Third, they tend to be told when a trigger event happens that inspires them to tell the story.

Checklists are a useful tool for managing complex situations. They work because mistakes are almost inevitable in today's complex world, regardless of how well educated and experienced we are. They work because they help us remember the important (yet often not exciting) things we need to do. They work because they help us ensure consistency and avoid blind spots that we may otherwise overlook when we're in a hurry or when we're facing complex situations. They work because they protect us from mistakes we might make out of ignorance (not knowing what to do), ineptness (knowing what to do and forgetting), and arrogance (thinking we're so smart that things will turn out fine even if we don't go through appropriate procedures).

Computer technology, particularly the Internet, is significantly changing the way we communicate at work. People are more likely to "multicommunicate", which means that they use different technologies to communicate with different audiences simultaneously (e.g., being on a telephone conference while at the same time checking e-mail).

E-mail is appealing because it is easy, accessible, relatively economical, less intrusive than meetings or telephone calls, and serves as a written record of organizational communication. Because e-mail can be abused, effective users of e-mail know its advantages and risks and follow practices that increase their e-mail effectiveness.

Food for Thought

1. What is the most useful thing you learned in this chapter, and why?
2. Based on the personal strategies described in this chapter, what can you do to enhance your communication effectiveness? Practice this behavior, and note any benefits and progress you make.
3. How does effective communication contribute to individual and organizational success?
4. Consciously use active listening when you have a conversation with someone. What did it feel like? What were the consequences? How did the other person react? What did you like about it? What didn't you like about it?

5. Think about a time when you felt that you weren't listened to. Describe the situation, as well as the consequences. Describe how you may have contributed to the situation. What did you learn from the situation that can make you a better manager today?

6. Imagine that you have an employee named Pat Buonafeste. Pat is a supervisor in the customer service department of an online book retailer. You have heard from two of Pat's direct reports that the workload in Pat's area has been escalating over the past two months and that Pat is becoming increasingly stressed and difficult to work for. They also told you that Pat has been taking long lunches several times a week and leaving early every Friday. They said that they resent having to work so hard while Pat is taking extra time off. They are very responsible employees, yet they are threatening to leave the company and go work for a competitor if you don't solve the problem. You feel that you need to give Pat feedback on the employees' concerns and find out what is going on. What will you say to Pat?

7. Observe a team meeting or classroom discussion. Write down some of the conversation patterns that you observe. For example, who speaks most often, who interrupts most, who is most quiet, who gets taken most seriously, and how do people get themselves heard? Are any power dynamics being expressed through these communication patterns? What are the potential consequences of these patterns? If you were a communications consultant, what recommendations would you make to improve the performance of this team or class?

8. Meet with someone from another culture and discuss communication differences between your culture and this person's culture. What are the three most interesting communication differences? How might these differences lead to misunderstandings or hinder effectiveness?

9. Think about a story that gets told in your organization. What is the underlying message in the story? Are there other stories in the organization that support or contradict this message?

10. Think about one of the most inspiring speeches you've ever heard. Why was it so inspiring? Did it move you to take action? If so, what actions did you take?

11. Imagine that you are a manager named Fran. While you were reading your e-mail today, you received a copy of a message that was not intended for you to see. The employee sent the following e-mail to a peer and inadvertently copied you: "Can you believe it? No wonder Chris didn't want to work here anymore. Fran really doesn't seem to know what's going on and just cannot leave well enough alone." Would you tell the person who wrote and copied the e-mail that you received and read the message? Why or why not? If you did decide to speak with the person who wrote the e-mail, what would you say? What else might you do to manage the situation?

12. MIT Nobel Prize winner Robert Solow once said, "We see computers everywhere but in the productivity statistics."[115] Think about your organization's use of e-mail. In what ways does the use of e-mail add to your productivity? In what ways does it distract from your productivity? What can you do to make your own use of e-mail more productive?

13. Many employees are using the Internet at work to shop, browse favorite Web sites (e.g., on gardening, dating, or movie reviews), and send personal messages to their friends and family. Is this abusive "cyberslacking" or a legitimate "equivalent of the millennium coffee break?" Why? Is it appropriate for employees to use the organization's Internet access to look for new jobs or promote their own businesses? Why or why not?

14. Think of a particular activity that's important to your work that is complex and would benefit from a checklist that walks you and others through the critical steps. What would those steps be? How would the checklist make you and others more effective?

Endnotes

1. Murhy, Herta, and Herbert Hildebrandt. 1991. *Effective Business Communications,* 6th ed. New York: McGraw-Hill.

2. 1997. "Calling Mission Control." *Training and Development.* August: 9–10.

3. Mintzberg, Henry. 1990. "The Manager's Job: Folklore and Fact." *Harvard Business Review,* 68(2): 163–177.

4. Gayeski, Diane, and Jennifer Majka. 1996. "Untangling Communication Chaos: A Communicator's Conundrum for Coping with Change in the Coming Century." *Communication World,* 13(7): September 1.

5. Ibid.

6. "Perspectives." *Newsweek.* March 2001.

7. Maremont, Mark and Laurie Cohen. December 31, 2002. "Tyco's Internal Report Finds Extensive Accounting Tricks. WSJ Online. http://online.wsj.com/ad/article/SB1041284714352956633.html?mod=sponsored_by_findlaw

8. Naughton, Keith with Joan Raymond, Ken Shulman, and Diane Struzzi. 1999. "Cyberslacking." *Newsweek.* November 29: 62–65.

9. Crossen, Cynthia. 1997. "Blah, Blah, Blah: The Crucial Question for These Noisy Times May Just Be 'Huh?'" *Wall Street Journal,* July 10: B1.

10. Ibid.

11. Lancaster Hal. 1997. "It's Time to Stop Promoting Yourself and Start Listening." *Wall Street Journal.* June 10: B1.

12. Mineyama, Sachiko, Akizumi Tsutsumi, Soshi Takao, Kyoto Nishiuchi, and Norito Kawakami. 2007. "Supervisors' Attitudes and Skills for Active Listening with Regard to Working Conditions and Psychological Stress Reactions among Subordinate Workers." *Journal of Occupational Health*, 49(2): 81–87

13. Taleb, Nassim, Daniel Goldstein, and Mark Spitznagel. October 2009. "Six Mistakes Executives Make in Risk Management." *Harvard Business Review.*

14. Yale Ditty on Benno Schmidt. *New York Times Magazine*, 1992.

15. Morgenson, Gretchen. 1999. "Barbie Guru Stumbles: Critics Say Chief's Flaws Weigh Heavily on Mattel." *New York Times,* November 7.

16. Baskerville, Dawn M., and Sheryl Hilliard Tucker. 2003. "Ann Fudge Gets Top Y&R Post as Dolan Quits." *Wall Street Journal,* B1 and B4.

17. Kiechel, Walter. 1990. "How to Escape the Echo Chamber." *Fortune,* June 18: 12–13.

18. Freire, Paulo. 1994. *Pedagogy of the Oppressed,* (revised edition, first published in 1970). New York: Continuum Publishing, 71; cited in Dixon, Nancy. 1996. *Perspectives on Dialogue.* Greensboro, NC: Center for Creative Leadership, 6.

19. Rogers, Carl, and F. Roethlisberger. 1991. "Barriers and Gateways to Communication." *Harvard Business Review,* November–December.

20. Miller, Gerald R., and Mark Steinberg. 1975. *Between People.* Southampton, NY: Science Research Associates, Inc.

21. Covey, Steven. 1991. *Thirty Methods of Influence.* New York: Franklin Covey Press.

22. Stone, Douglas, Bruce Patton, and Sheila Heen. 2000. *Difficult Conversations: How to Discuss What Matters Most.* New York: Penguin Books.

23. Robbins, Stephen, and Phillip Hunsaker. 1989. *Training in Interpersonal Skills: Tips for Managing People at Work.* Upper Saddle River, NJ: Prentice Hall.

24. Meyer, Peter. 1998. "So You Want the President's Job." *Business Horizons.* January–February: 2–6.

25. Bell, Chip, and Ron Zemke. 1992. "On-Target Feedback." *Training,* June: 36–44.

26. Hequet, Marc. 1994. "Giving Good Feedback." *Training,* September: 72–76.

27. Barnes, Louis. 1989. "Managing Interpersonal Feedback (Course Note 483027)." Boston, MA: Harvard Business School .

28. Ashford, Susan, and Gregory Northcraft. 1992. "Conveying More (or Less) than We Realize: The Role of Impression-Management in Feedback Seeking." *Organizational Behavior and Human Decision Processes,* 53: 310–334.

29. Johnson, Spencer, and Kenneth Blanchard. 1993. *The One-Minute Manager.* Berkeley, CA: Berkeley Publishing Group.

30. Barnes, Louis B. 1982. "Managing Interpersonal Feedback." *Harvard Business Review,* September; Clawson, James. 1989. *Some Principles of Giving and Receiving Feedback.* Charlottesville, VA: Darden Graduate Business School Foundation.

31. Hequet, Marc. 1994. "Giving Good Feedback." *Training.* September: 72–76.

32. Bell, Chip, and Ron Zemke. 1992. "On-Target Feedback." *Training.* June: 36–44.

33. Ng, Michael. 1994. "Effective Feedback Skills for Trainers and Coaches." *HRFocus.* July: 7.

34. Ashford, Susan, and Gregory Northcraft. 1992. "Conveying More (or Less) than We Realize: The Role of Impression-Management in Feedback Seeking." *Organizational Behavior and Human Decision Processes,* 53: 310–334.

35. Ibid.

36. Barnes, Louis B. 1982. "Managing Interpersonal Feedback." *Harvard Business Review, September;* Clawson, James. 1989. *Some Principles of Giving and Receiving Feedback.* Charlottesville, VA: Darden Graduate Business School Foundation.

37. Ghorpade, Jai. 2000. "Managing Five Paradoxes of 360-Degree Feedback." *Academy of Management Executive,* 14(1): 140–154.

38. Lepsinger, Richard, and Antoinette D. Lucia. 1997. *The Art and Science of 360-Degree Feedback.* San Francisco: Jossey-Bass.

39. Brett, Joan, and Leanne Atwater. 2001. "360-Degree Feedback: Accuracy, Reactions, and

Perceptions of Usefulness." *Journal of Applied Psychology,* 86: 930–942; Church, Allan. 1997. "Do You See What I See? An Exploration of Congruence in Ratings with Multiple Perspectives." *Journal of Applied Social Psychology,* 27(1): 983–1020; Atwater, Leanne, Cheri Ostroff, Francis Yammarino, and John Fleenor. 1948. "Self-Other Agreement: Does It Really Matter?" *Personnel Psychology,* 51: 577–598; Van Velsor, Ellen, Sylvester Taylor, and Jean Leslie. 1993. "An Examination of the Relationship among Self-Perception Accuracy, Self-Awareness, Gender and Leader Effectiveness." *Human Resource Management,* 32(2–3): 249–264; Atwater, Leanne, David Waldman, and Joan Brett. 2002. "Understanding and Optimizing Multisource Feedback." *Human Resource Management,* 41(2): 193–208; Atwater, Leanne, and Francis Yammarino. 1992. "Does Self-Other Agreement on Leadership Perceptions Moderate the Validity of Leadership and Performance Predictions?" *Personnel Psychology,* 45: 141–164.

40. Brett Joan, and Atwater, Leanne. 2001. "360-Degree Feedback: Accuracy, Reactions and Percepons of Usefulness." *Journal of Applied Psychology,* 86: 930–942.

41. Smither, James, Manuel London, and Richard Reilly. 2005. "Does Performance Improve Following Multisource Feedback? A Theoretical Model, Meta-Analysis, and Review of Empirical Findings." *Personnel Psychology,* 58:33–66

42. Kluger, Avraham N., and Angelo DeNisi. 1996. "The Effects of Feedback Interventions on Performance: A Historical Review, A Meta-Analysis, and Preliminary Feedback Theory." *Psychological Bulletin,* 119: 254–284; Atwater, Leanne, A., Paul Rousch, and Allison Fischthal. 1995. "The Influence of Upward Feedback on Self- and Follower Ratings of Leadership." *Personnel Psychology,* 48: 35–60.

43. Smither, James, Manuel London, and Richard Reilly. 2005. "Does Performance Improve Following Multisource Feedback? A Theoretical Model, Meta-Analysis, and Review of Empirical Findings." *Personnel Psychology,* 58: 33–66; Goldsmith, Marshall, and B. Underhill. 2000. "Multisource Feedback for Executive Development." In Bracken, David, Carol Timmreck, and Allan Church (eds.). *The Handbook of Multisource Feedback.* San Francisco: Jossey-Bass, 275–288.

44. Kluger, A., and A. Nisi. 1996. "The Effects of Feedback Intervention on Performance: A Historical Review, a Meta-Analysis, and a Preliminary Feedback Intervention Theory." *Psychological Bulletin,* 119: 254–284.

45. Atwater, Leanne, David Waldman, David Atwater, and Priscilla Cartier. 2000. "Upward Feedback Field Experiment. Supervisors' Cynicism, Follow-up and Commitment to Subordinates." *Personnel Psychology,* 53: 275–297; Tuckey, Michelle, Neil Brewer, and Paul Williamson. 2002. *Journal of Occupational and Organizational Psychology,* 75: 195–216. DeNisi, Angelo, and Avraham Kluger, "Feedback Effectiveness: Can 360-Degree Appraisals Be Improved?" *Academy of Management Executive,* 14(1): 129–139.

46. Rutkowski, K., L. Steelman, and R. Griffith. 2004. "An Empirical Examination of Accountability for Performance Development." Paper presented at the 19th Annual Conference of the Society of Industrial and Organizational Psychology. Chicago, IL.

47. Domick, P., R. Reilly, and J. Byrne. 2004. "Individual Differences and Peer Feedback: Personality's Impact on Behavior Change." Paper presented at the 19th Annual Conference of the Society for Industrial and Organizational Psychology. Chicago, IL.

48. Vicere, A., and R. Fulmer. 1998. "Leadership By Design: How Benchmark Companies Sustain Success Through Investment in Continuous Learning." Boston: *Harvard Business Review.*

49. Heslin, Peter, Gary Lantham, and Don VandeWalle. 2005. "The Effect of Implicit Person Theory on Performance Appraisal." *Journal of Applied Psychology,* 90(5): 842–856.

50. Greguras, G., C. Robie, D. Schleicher, and M. Goff. "A Field Study of the Effects of Rating Purpose on the Quality of Multisource Ratings." *Personnel Psychology,* 56: 1–21.

51. Mayfield Rowley, Jacqueline, Milton Ray Mayfield, and Jerry Kopf. 1998. "The Effects of Leader Motivating Language on Subordinate Performance and Satisfaction." *Human Resource Management,* 37(3): 235–248.

52. Larson, Erik, and Jonathan King. 1996. "The Systematic Distortion of Information: An Ongoing Challenge to Management." *Organizational Dynamics,* 22(3): 49–61.

53. Birnbaum, Jeffrey. 1993. "Ex-Chief of Staff Ponders Clinton Woes and Urges Advisors to Stand Up to Boss." *Wall Street Journal.* May 27.

54. Kiechel, Walter. 1990. "How to Escape the Echo Chamber." *Fortune,* June 18: 12–13.

55. Ibid.

56. Bartolome, Fernando. 1994. "How to Get Bad News, Too." *Executive Female.* May/June: 15–18.

57. Fulk, Janet, and Sirish Mani. 1985. "Distortion of Communication in Hierarchical Relationships." In M. McLaughlin (ed.). *Communication Yearbook.* Vol 9. Beverly Hills, CA: Sage, 483–510

58. Kiechel, Walter. 1990. "How to Escape the Echo Chamber." *Fortune.* June 18: 12–13; Bartolome, Fernando. 1994. "How to Get Bad News, Too." *Executive Female.* May/June: 15–18; Bartoleme, Fernandes. 1989. "Nobody Trusts the Boss Completely, Now What?" *Harvard Business Review,* 67(2): 135–143.

59. *The Working Communicator.* Undated. New York: Japan Airlines.

60. Kennedy, Jim, and Anna Everest. 1991. "Put Diversity in Context." *Personnel Journal,* September: 50–54.

61. Ibid.

62. Tannen, Deborah. 1990. *You Just Don't Understand: Women and Men in Conversation.* New York: Ballentine Books.

63. Ibid.

64. Craig, Holly. 1991. *Gender Differences in Language.* Ann Arbor, MI: Communicative Disorders Clinic Publication.

65. Ibid.

66. Byron, Kristin. 2008. "Carrying Too Heavy a Load? The Communication and Miscommunication of Emotion by Email." *Academy of Management Review,* 33(2): 329–327.

67. Crossen, Cynthia. 1997. "Blah, Blah, Blah: The Crucial Question for These Noisy Times May Just Be 'Huh?'" *Wall Street Journal.* July 10: B1; Hyde, Janet. 2005. "The Gender Similarities Hypothesis." *American Psychologist,* 60(6): 581–592.

68. Sapir, Edward. 1963. *Selected Writings of Edward Sapir in Language, Culture, and Personality.* David Mandelbaum (ed.). Berkeley, CA: University of California Press; cited in Martyna, Wendy. 1980. "Beyond the He/Man Approach: The Case for Nonsexist Language." *Signs: Journal of Women in Culture and Society,* 5(3): 482–492.

69. Tannen, Deborah. 1995. "The Power of Talk: Who Gets Heard and Why." *Harvard Business Review.* September–October: 139–148.

70. Bem, Sandra, and Daryl Bem. 1973. "Does Sex-Biased Job Advertising Aid and Abet Sex Discrimination?" *Journal of Applied Social Psychology,* 3(1): 6–18.

71. Martyna, Wendy. 1980. "Beyond the He/Man Approach: The Case for Nonsexist Language." *Signs: Journal of Women in Culture and Society,* 5(3): 482–492.

72. Daily, Bill, and Miriam Finch. 1993. "Benefiting from Nonsexist Language in the Workplace." *Business Horizons.* March–April: 30–34.

73. The material for the figure was developed from a variety of sources including Daily, Bill, and Miriam Finch. 1993. "Benefiting from Nonsexist Language in the Workplace." *Business Horizons.* March–April: 30–34; Munter, Mary. 1986. *Business Communication: Strategy and Skill.* Upper Saddle River, NJ: Prentice Hall; Murphy, Herta, and Herbert W. Hildebrandt. 1991. *Effective Business Communications*, 6th ed. New York: McGraw-Hill; Lentz, Richard. 1984. "Job Aids: A Checklist for Nonsexist Writing." *Performance and Instruction Journal, 13.*

74. Martyna, Wendy. 1980. "Beyond the He/Man Approach: The Case for Nonsexist Language." *Signs: Journal of Women in Culture and Society,* 5(3): 482–492.

75. Daily, Bill, and Miriam Finch. 1993. "Benefiting from Nonsexist Language in the Workplace." *Business Horizons,* March–April: 30–34.

76. Murphy, Herta A., and Herbert W. Hildebrandt. 1991. *Effective Business Communications*, 6th ed. New York: McGraw-Hill, 79–80.

77. Munter, Mary. 1987. *Business Communication: Strategy and Skill.* New York: McGraw-Hill.

78. Smircich, Linda, and Gareth Morgan. "Leadership: The Management of Meaning."*The Journal of Applied Behavioral Science,* 18(3): 258.

79. Mayfield, Jacqueline Rowley, Milton Ray Mayfield, and Jerry Kopf. 1998. "The Effects of Leader Motivating Language on Subordinate Performance and Satisfaction." *Human Resource Management,* 37(3&4): 235–248.

80. Hartog, Den, Deanne N., and Robert M. Verburg. Winter 1997. "Charisma and Rhetoric: Communicative Techniques of International Business Leaders." *Leadership Quarterly,* 8(4): 355–391; citing Shamir, B., M. B. Arthur, and R. House. 1994. "The Rhetoric of Charismatic Leadership: A Theoretical Extension, a Case Study and Implications for Research." *Leadership Quarterly,* 5: 25–42.

81. Emrich, Cynthia, Holly Brower, Jack Feldman, and Howard Garland. 2001. "Images in Words: Presidential Rhetoric, Charisma, and Greatness." *Administrative Science Quarterly,* 46: 527–557.

82. Morgan, Nick. 2001. "The Kinesthetic Speaker: Putting Action into Words." *Harvard Business Review,* April: 113–120.

83. Conger, Jay. 1991. "Inspiring Others: The Language of Leadership." *The Academy of Management Executive,* February: 31–45.

84. Washington, James M. (ed.). 1986. *A Testimony of Hope: The Essential Writings and Speeches of Martin Luther King, Jr.* San Francisco, CA: Harper, 217–220.

85. Emrich, Cynthia, Holly Brower, Jack Feldman, and Howard Garland. 2001. "Images in Words: Presidential Rhetoric, Charisma, and Greatness." *Administrative Science Quarterly,* (46): 527–557.

86. Conger, Jay. 1991. "Inspiring Others: The Language of Leadership." *The Academy of Management Executive,* 5(1): 31–45.

87. Bell, Chip. 1992. "The Trainer as Storyteller." *Training and Development,* September: 53–56.

88. Heath, Chip, Chris Bell, and Emily Sternberg. 2001. "Emotional Selection in Mimes: The Case of Urban Legends." *Journal of Personality and Social Psychology,* 81; Kounios, John, and Philip J. Holcomb. 1994. "Concreteness Effects in Semantic Processing: ERP Evidence Supporting Dual-Coding Theory." *Journal of Experimental Psychology: Learning, Memory and Cognition,* 20: 804–823; Marsharck, Mark, Charles L. Richman, John C. Yuille, and R. Reed Hunt. 1987. "The Role of Imagery in Memory: On Shared and Distinctive Information." *Psychological Bulletin,* (102): 28–41.

89. Heath, Chip and Dan Heath. December 2006. "The Curse of Knowledge." *Harvard Business Review.*

90. Tannen, Deborah. January 8, 2010. "Abduction, Dialogicality and Prior Text: The Taking of Voices in Conversational Discourse." Plenary address at the 84th Annual Meeting of the Linguistic Society of America, Baltimore, Maryland.

91. Levin, Ira M. 2000. "Vision Revisited: Telling the Story of the Future." *Journal of Applied Behavioral Science,* 36(1): 92–93.

92. Lieber, Ronald. 1997. "Storytelling: A New Way to Get Close to Your Customer." *Fortune.* February 3: 102–108.

93. Roddick, Anita. 1991. *Body and Soul.* New York: Crown Trade Paperbacks, 25.

94. Schank, Roger, and Robert Abelson. 1995. "Knowledge and Memory: The Real Story." In R. J. Wyer, Jr. (ed.) *Advances in Social Cognition.* Vol. 8. Hillsdale, NJ: Erlbaum, 1–86.

95. Sander, Russell Scott. 1997. "The Most Human Art: Ten Reasons Why We'll Always Need a Good Story." *Utne Reader.* September–October: 54–56.

96. Hequet, Marc. 1992. "Poof! Myth and Fable Appear as Human Development Tools." *Training.* December: 46–50.

97. Decker, Bert with James Denney. 1992. *You've Got to Be Believed to Be Heard.* New York: St. Martin's Press.

98. Wilkins, Alan. 1989. "Corporate Culture: The Role of Stories." In Morgan, Gareth (ed.). *Creative Organizational Theory: A Resource Book.* Newbury Park, CA: Sage.

99. Zempke, Ron. 1990. "Storytelling: Back to a Basic." *Training,* March: 44–50; Conger, Jay. 1991. "Inspiring Others: The Language of Leadership." *Academy of Management Executive,* 5(1): 31–45.

100. Armstrong, David. 1992. "Management by Storytelling." *Executive Female,* May/June: 38–77.

101. De Jonge, Peter. 1999. "Riding the Wild, Perilous Waters of Amazon.com." *New York Times,* March 14: 36–81.

102. Schein, Edgar. 1997. *Organizational Culture and Leadership.* San Francisco, CA: Jossey-Bass, 13.

103. Heath, Chip, Chris Bell, and Emily Sternberg. 2001. "Emotional Selection in Mimes: The Case of Urban Legends." *Journal of Personality and Social Psychology,* 81.

104. Heath, Chip, and Dan Heath. 2007. *Made to Stick: Why Some Ideas Survive and Others Die.* New York: Random House.

105. Bell, Chip. 1992. "The Trainer as Storyteller." *Training and Development,* September: 53–56.

106. Martin, Joanne, Martha Feldman, Mary Jo Hatch, and Sim Sitkin. 1983. "The Uniqueness Paradox in Organizational Stories." *Administrative Science Quarterly,* 28: 438–453.

107. Heath, Chip, and Dan Heath. May 2009. "Three Secrets to Make Your Message Go Viral." Fast Company Online.

108. Elkind, Peter. March 5, 2008. "The Trouble with Steve Jobs." *Fortune Online.* http://money.cnn.com/2008/03/02/news/companies/elkind_jobs.fortune/index.htm

109. Bell, Chip. 1992. "The Trainer as Storyteller." *Training and Development,* September: 53–56.

110. Ibid.

111. Iacocca, Lee with William Novak. 1984. *Iacocca: An Autobiography.* Bantam Books.

112. Brown, Andrew, and Michael Humphreys. 2003. "Epic Tales and Tragic Tales: Making Sense of Change." *The Journal of Applied Behavioral Science,* 39(2): 121–144.

113. McGregor, Ian, and John Holmes. 1999. "How Storytelling Shapes Memory and Impressions of Relationship Events Over Time." *Journal of Personality and Social Psychology,* 76(3): 403–419; citing Shank, Roger, and Robert Abelson. 1995. "Knowledge and Memory: The Real Story." In

Robert J. Wyer, Jr. (ed.). *Advances in Social Cognition*. Vol. 8. Hillsdale, NJ: Erlbaum, 1–86.

114. Zempke, Ron. 1990. "Storytelling: Back to a Basic." *Training,* March: 44–50.

115. Boje, David. 1995. "Stories of the Storytelling Organization: A Postmodern Analysis of Disney as 'Tamara-Land'." *Academy of Management Journal,* 38(4): 997–1036; Brown, Andrew, and Michael Humphreys. 2003. "Epic Tales and Tragic Tales: Making Sense of Change." *The Journal of Applied Behavioral Science,* 39(2): 121–144.

116. Elsbach, Kimbery. 2003. "How to Pitch a Brilliant Idea." *Harvard Business Review*, 81(9): 117–122.

117. Pronovost, Peter, D. Needham, S. Berenholtz, D. Sinopoli, H. Chu, and S. Cosgrove. 2006. "An Intervention to Decrease Catheter-Related Bloodstream Infections in the ICU. *The New England Journal of Medicine,* 355(26): 2725–2732; Gawande, Atul. 2009. *The Checklist Manifesto: How to Get Things Right*. New York: Metropolitan Books.

118. Ibid.

119. U.S. Census. October 2009. *Internet Use in the United States*. http://www.sbdcnet.org/SBIC/demographics.php

120. Internet World Stats: Usage and Population Statistics. June 30, 2010. http://www.internetworld-stats.com/stats.htm

121. "Millennials: Confident, Connected, Open to Change." February 24, 2010. Social and Demographic Trends. Pew Research Center. http://pewsocialtrends.org/pubs/751/millennials-confident-connected-open-to-change

122. Reinsch, N. Lamar, Jeanine Warisse Turner, and Catherine Tinsley. 2008. "Multicommunicating: A Practice Whose Time Has Come?" *Academy of Management Review*, 33(2): 391–403.

123. Hampton, Keith, Lauren Sessions, Eun Ja Her, and Lee Rainie. November 2009. "Social Isolation and New Technology." *The Pew Internet and American Life Study*. http://pewresearch.org/pubs/1398/internet-mobile-phones-impact-american-social-networks

124. Veiga, John, and Kathleen Dechant. 1997. "Wired World Woes: www.help." *Academy of Management Executive,* 11(3): 73–86; citing Juliet Schorr. 1992. *The Overworked American*. New York: Basic Books.

125. Gundling, Ernest. 1999. "How to Communicate Globally." *Training and Development,* June: 28–31.

126. 1999. "A Special News Report about Life on the Job—and Trends Taking Shape There." *Wall Street Journal*. December 21: A1.

127. Byron, Dristin. 2008. "Carrying Too Heavy a Load? The Communication and Miscommunication of Emotion by Email. *Academy of Management Review*, 33(2): 309–327.

128. 1996. *Training and Development*. December: 7.

129. Abernathy, Donna. 1990. "Seven Ways to Work Smarter On-line." *Training and Development.* June: 20.

130. Ibid.

131. Stepanck, Marcia with Steve Hamm. 1998. "When the Devil Is in the E-Mails." *Business Week*. June 8: 72–74.

132. Gross, Neil. 1999. "Innovations." *Business Week,* October 25: 95.

133. Ellet, Bill. 1999. "Can't Beat 'Em? Play with 'Em." *Training and Development.* November: 84.

134. Gayeski, Diane, and Jennifer Majka. 1996. "Untangling Communication Chaos: A Communitator's Conundrum for Coping with Change in the Coming Century." *Communication World,* 13(7): September 1.

135. Young, Mary, and James Post. 1993. "Managing to Communicate, Communicating to Manage: How Leading Companies Communicate with Employees." *Organizational Dynamics.* Summer: 31–43.

136. Ibid.

5

•••

Gaining and Using Sustainable, Ethical Power and Influence

This chapter will help you:

- Develop a working definition of sustainable, ethical power.
- Understand the characteristics of people with sustainable, ethical power.
- Learn how to read and adapt to the styles of other people so that you can become more influential with many different types of people.
- Learn how to use (and resist) six universal forms of influence.
- Learn how ethical organizational politics can enhance organizational effectiveness.

Power is America's last dirty word. It is easier to talk about money—
and much easier to talk about sex—than it is to talk about power.

—Rosabeth Moss Kanter

From our first cry until our last will and testament, we try to influence the world around us. As toddlers, we try to assert our power with the emphatic use of the word, "No." We soon learn that we can influence people more successfully by charming them with a smile and heartfelt compliment ("You're my best friend."). As we get older, we try to impress the people with whom we have romantic aspirations through the way we dress and talk. When we become adults, we try to convince our children to do their homework, be polite, and go to college. We try to persuade the people we love to take good care of themselves. We try to negotiate a lower sales price when we want to buy the house of our dreams. And when we move into that dream house, we try to persuade our neighbors to stop mowing their lawn with their ear-shattering power mower at 7:00 on Saturday mornings.

In the working world, we try to prove to recruiters that we're exactly the kind of employee their organization needs. We try to persuade our boss that we deserve the training, mentoring, and high-profile assignments that will help us gain valuable experience, as well as career advantages such as promotions and salary increases. We try to encourage the employees who work for us to do their best work and to go above and beyond the call of duty when necessary. And we try to convince our colleagues and others over whom we have no formal control to pay attention to our ideas and help us when we need their support.

Although we all try to influence people throughout our lives, most of us don't take the time to learn the art and science of gaining power and influence. There are at least three reasons for this. First, some people mistakenly assume that only people with official positions of power have power (e.g., manager, director, principal, physician). However, there are several forms of power and influence that aren't related to one's official role in organizations. Second, some people are unaware that researchers have been studying best practices for gaining and using power and influence for over four decades. Third, some people are ambivalent about power. This ambivalence is due, in part, to having a mistaken and narrow view of power. They believe that power naturally corrupts. But for every scandal about the abuse of power, there are multiple stories about the ethical use of power that has transformed individuals, organizations, and the world for the better.

> **Power doesn't corrupt people; people corrupt power.**
> —WILLIAM GADDIS,
> *Author and journalist*

Undoubtedly, there will always be people who gain and use power in unscrupulous ways, but that shouldn't stop you from understanding and using power ethically. If you shy away from using power and influence, you leave the world in the hands of those who would abuse it. Indeed, Harvard Professor Linda Hill explains that powerlessness can corrupt. She explains that people with power can shape their environment, whereas the powerless are "destined to be molded and constrained by theirs. How often have we heard of people who believed they had 'no choice' but to engage in some unethical act because they did not have the 'power to change the way things are usually done?'"[1]

People who are skilled at influencing others reap significant rewards, including the ability to get better results at work more quickly, achieve their career goals, and enjoy greater well-being because they are better able to achieve the support and resources they need.[2] People who are not willing and able to influence others can pay dearly for their lack of influence skills. In addition to inhibiting your job effectiveness and career potential, believing that you cannot influence your environment can have negative effects on your psychological and physical well-being.[3] For example, researchers have found that people who feel that they have some control over the most important goals in their lives tend to live longer.[4] Researchers have also found that employees who feel that they lack control over their work and their workplace tend to have a higher incidence of stress, heart disease, and job dissatisfaction.[5] A lack of influence skills can also negatively affect your income. For example, in a *Wall Street Journal* article, Carnegie Mellon management professor Linda Babcock explained that "skipping or bungling a single negotiation can inflict a huge penalty. A 22-year-old woman who fails to get her first job offer of $25,000 boosted by $5,000 stands to lose more than $568,000 by age 60."[6]

Some people seem to have a natural talent for getting people to buy into their ideas, gaining support from others, and being at the right place at the right time. Fortunately for the rest of us, there is a science to gaining and using power and influence. This chapter helps you learn techniques that will help you gain sustainable, ethical power and influence. By using these skills, you will be better able to achieve the goals that are important to you, your organizations, your communities, and the people who depend on you. You will be able to use these skills at work or at home, whether you are a manager, individual contributor, salaried employee, consultant, or hourly employee. At the end of this chapter, I discuss how organizational politics can enhance organizational effectiveness and how you can ethically engage in politics to achieve the results that you desire.

FOUNDATIONS OF SUSTAINABLE, ETHICAL POWER AND INFLUENCE

Power refers to the willingness and ability of a person or group to influence the attitudes, beliefs, and behaviors of others so that they are willing to support the goals that the person or group believes are important.[7] In short, power enables people to influence their environment and get things done. Note that the use of power is necessary only when there is real or potential conflict over interests, goals, or the means by which to achieve those interests or goals.[8]

Although we often describe people or groups as "powerful," power is not a stable characteristic of a person or group. Rather:

- Power must be actively sought and continuously replenished.
- Power is negotiated in a relationship. You can only have power over another person if that person perceives you as having something that he or she wants or needs.[9]
- Power is situational. You may have power in one situation yet be powerless in another. For example, you may be in charge at your office, but the dentist is clearly in charge when performing a root canal.

Thus, to have sustainable power that transcends a particular time, position, and place, you must (1) have a variety of resources to offer people what they believe they need or want, (2) know many different strategies for gaining the support of others, and (3) adapt your strategy based on the situation.

Power can be gained and used ethically or unscrupulously. You are gaining and using power ethically when:[10]

- You explicitly tell people what you want to achieve and why.
- You put the interests of others and the organization at least a equal to your own interests and, when appropriate, put others' interests ahead of your own.
- You treat everyone with respect, administer organizational policies and procedures fairly, and do not abuse anyone's rights or exploit people.[11]
- You leave yourself reasonably open to be influenced by others.
- You back your requests with honest supporting data.

Why We Need Power and Influence Skills

Many people believe that if everyone simply focused on his or her jobs and followed standard organizational procedures, the most competent people would be promoted, the best ideas would rise to the top, and everyone would cooperate with each other to implement the best decisions for the greater good. Many people also believe that organizational decisions are typically made from a rational analysis of all available information and then implemented in a systematic way. But the organizational world doesn't—and will never—work this way for several reasons.[12]

OUR ENVIRONMENTS ARE INCREASINGLY COMPLEX   Organizations and the environment in which they operate today are so complex and fast changing that few job descriptions and organizational policies can account for every opportunity and problem that arises. Consequently, working within one's job descriptions and standard operating procedures can hold individuals and organizations back from achieving important goals with the highest quality and with the most efficient use of resources. People with influence skills are able to get better results in less time, using fewer resources, and with less stress, especially in challenging times.

PEOPLE ARE BOUNDEDLY RATIONAL   Although we like to think of ourselves as rational decision makers, all human beings are instead "boundedly rational"[13] and "lazy information processors."[14] Our human minds are incapable of taking in all the information that comes our way, remembering everything that we learn, and interpreting information from every conceivable angle. To further complicate things, the amount of information we feel we must process is increasing. Persuasion researcher Robert Levine warns that "the burden [on our ability to process information] is greater today than ever before. A recent study estimated that one week of the *New York Times* newspaper carries more information than a person in the sixteenth century digested in a lifetime."[15] Because of our inability to process all the information we believe we need to make decisions, we often (1) "satisfice"—we look for good-enough answers—rather than the best possible answers and (2) use cognitive shortcuts to determine the course of action we believe we should take. In other words, instead of systematically seeking out and sifting through all relevant information, we make decisions on the basis of questions such as "What have we done in the past?" "Who is the person with the most expertise?" "What are other people doing about this kind of problem?" and "Whose advice can I trust?" Sometimes these cognitive shortcuts serve us well, and sometimes they don't. For better and worse, people who understand these shortcuts leverage this knowledge to frame their requests in ways that are more likely to trigger these shortcuts and gain support.

UNCERTAINTY   In an increasingly complex world, we cannot predict all the consequences of the different courses of action we could take, nor can we accurately predict the costs of lost opportunities. And even if we had all the information we needed to make the best decision today, we cannot predict how future events will shape the consequences of our decisions in the long term. People with influence skills are able to help people make sense of information in ways that support their goals, even when information about the future is uncertain.

MUTUAL INTERDEPENDENCE   More often than not, people must make and implement organizational decisions together with others.[16] However, people in organizations tend to have different interests, perspectives, values, work styles, and objectives. Although these differences can lead to creativity, innovation, and higher quality decisions, these differences can also cause misunderstanding, conflict, and resistance. People with influence skills are better able to bring people together to collaborate toward common organizational goals.

LIMITED RESOURCES   Only so many projects can be funded, only so many people can be promoted, and only so many issues can be considered by organizational leaders. Consequently, organizational members sometimes must compete with each other to have their ideas heard and supported so that they can achieve their organizational and career goals.[17] People with influence skills know how to develop mutual support in ways that enable more people and groups to achieve their goals.

In short, we need to understand how to influence others because we compete for limited resources in an uncertain world with people who have imperfect decision-making abilities and conflicting interests (and over whom we have limited, if any, formal authority). Furthermore, our job descriptions and organizational policies are not sufficient to enable us to help our organizations address all the important opportunities and problems that come our way in an increasingly complex and fast-changing world.

Characteristics of People with Power

People who have sustainable power—power that transcends a particular time, position, and place—behave in ways that enable them to convince people that they are worth listening to, that

Power is not revealed by
striking hard or often, but
by striking true.
—HONORE DE BALZAC,
Journalist and writer

their ideas have merit, and that they deserve the support of others. Contrary to the battlefield or bully image of power, people with sustainable power realize that they don't gain power by hoarding it or beating people over the head with it. Instead, people with sustainable, ethical power gain and use their power subtly and respectfully. They pay attention to things that other people miss, see situations from multiple perspectives, adapt their behavior so that they can be successful in many different settings, spend a great deal of time trying to understand and support others, and make *other* people feel powerful.[18] One manager described his boss this way:

> Most of the people here would walk over hot coals in their bare feet if my boss asked them to. He has an incredible capacity to do little things that mean a lot to people. Today, for example, in his junk mail he came across an advertisement for something that one of my subordinates had in passing once mentioned that he was shopping for. So, my boss routed it to him. That probably took 15 seconds of his time, and yet my subordinate really appreciated it. To give you another example, two weeks ago he somehow learned that the purchasing manager's mother had died. On his way home that night, he stopped off at the funeral parlor. Our purchasing manager was, of course, there at the time. I bet he'll remember that brief visit for quite a while.[19]

The above example illustrates that sustainable power is accumulated through small but significant and sincere acts over time. Although people who develop sustainable, ethical power differ in many ways, they tend to share much in common. Specifically, they are achievement oriented, politically astute, competent, self-aware, socially skilled, interpersonally influential, well connected, and trustworthy.[20]

- *Achievement oriented:* They are action oriented and focus on achieving the goals that they believe are important. They believe that they can influence their environments and strategize ways for doing so.
- *Politically astute:* They understand strategies for gaining influence and are willing to use the informal organization that operates outside official policies, procedures, and chains of commands to achieve their goals. They think in shades of gray rather than black and white. Says Kathleen Reardon in her practical book *The Secret Handshake: Mastering the Politics of the Business Inner Circle,* "Their worlds are not a neat series of do's and don'ts, but rather avenues of extensive possibilities."[21] They are adaptable. Although they continuously focus on their objectives, they are willing to be flexible about how they achieve them.[22]
- *Competent:* They are competent, have the expertise required to do their job well, and can be counted on to follow through with their responsibilities and commitments.[23]
- *Self-aware:* They understand their styles, strengths, and weaknesses, as well as how they are perceived by others. They draw on their self-knowledge to understand (1) what kind of support they can offer to others and (2) how others' perceptions of them affect their willingness to provide support.
- *Socially skilled:* They are astute observers of human behavior and have solid social skills.[24] They show a genuine interest in others and are sensitive to the needs of others. They are great listeners. They know that they cannot obtain information, observe other people's reactions, and hear other people's perspectives unless they stop talking and start listening.
- *Interpersonally influential:* They communicate well and are able to build rapport with many different kinds of people. They are likable and know how to help people feel comfortable with them. They are willing to be flexible and frame their requests in ways that respect other people's point of view so that their ideas will be heard, understood, and supported.

- *Well connected:* They proactively develop mutually supportive connections with a broad network of colleagues and influential people so that they can build mutual support. They use these connections to achieve results.
- *Trustworthy:* They have integrity, a characteristic that builds trust and predicts job performance and leadership potential.[25] Consequently, they are viewed as authentic and giving rather than manipulative and self-interested.

Anyone who is committed to achieving their goals can adopt the mindset and learn the skills that will help them gain sustainable, ethical power. The rest of this chapter focuses on three types of influence skills: (1) being able to read other people and adapt your message in ways that will help you be understood and supported, (2) using six universal forms of influence, and (3) developing political savvy. Figure 5-1 summarizes these influence strategies. Before you read the following sections, consider at least three people whom you want to influence, and identify what you would like them to do. Write their names and what you would like them to do in Table 5-1. Then, as you read the following sections, write down several strategies that you can use to gain their support.

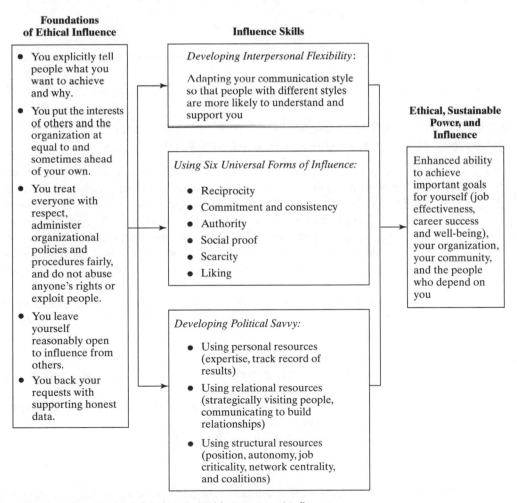

FIGURE 5-1 Developing Ethical, Sustainable Power and Influence

TABLE 5-1	Implementing Influence Strategies	
Person You Want to Influence	**What You Want That Person to Do**	**Strategies You Can Use to Influence the Person**
Person #1		
Person #2		
Person #3		

DEVELOPING INTERPERSONAL POWER: READING AND ADAPTING TO OTHER PEOPLE'S INTERESTS AND STYLES

You can change the way people listen to you. Altering the direction of your communication can change your today, tomorrow, and potentially the direction of your career.
—KATHLEEN KELLEY REARDON,
The Secret Handshake

Influential people have well-developed social skills. They enjoy watching people and figuring out why people do what they do. They understand that people who seem unreasonable may simply have different goals, perspectives, and ways of reasoning. They know that people are more likely to listen to, understand, and support someone they trust and who treats them well. They create positive interactions with others by building on similarities, respecting differences, aligning different interests toward common goals, and expressing their desires in ways that are understandable and palatable to others.

In this section, I describe a model that will help you understand and adapt to people with different styles so that you are more likely to achieve mutually supportive goals. Specifically, you will:

- Learn the Social Styles model that identifies four different types of behavioral styles.
- Identify your preferred behavioral style, as well as the strengths and weaknesses associated with that style.
- Understand how your style may be perceived by others and how those perceptions may influence whether people support or resist you.
- Develop strategies for influencing people with different styles.

The Social Styles Model

The Social Styles model provides a useful framework for understanding your own behavioral preferences and the preferences of others.[26] This model assumes that (1) we all have predictable and taken-for-granted ways of behaving, including how we make decisions, interact with others, and resolve conflicts; (2) if we understand our preferred styles, as well as the preferred styles of the others, we can avoid some of the problems that arise from the misunderstandings, conflicts, and frustrations that can occur when people with different styles interact; and (3) we are more likely to influence others if we build relationships based on mutual understanding and respect.

Note: Before you read any further, please take the Social Styles assessment in Box 5-2 at the end of this chapter.

The Social Styles model focuses on two dimensions:

- *Assertive/probing:* This refers to whether a person prefers to assertively push his or her ideas forward quickly (assertive) or patiently draw ideas out from other people or from careful analysis of data (probing).
- *High responsiveness/low responsiveness:* This refers to whether a person emphasizes rationality, objectivity, and task-focus (low responsiveness) or emotional expressiveness, intuition, and relationships (high responsiveness).

On the basis of these two dimensions, a person's social style can usually be categorized into one of four categories: driver (assertive/low responsiveness), expressive (assertive/high responsiveness), amiable (probing/high responsiveness), and analytic (probing/low responsiveness). Tables 5-2 through 5-6 describe the common characteristics of each style, the potential strengths and limitations of each style, how each style may be perceived by others, and how people with each style tend to react under stress. Table 5-7 describes influence strategies for each style. When using social styles to gain a better understanding of yourself and others, keep in mind the following:

- People are much more complex in their thinking and behaving than the Social Styles model (or any model for that matter) can portray.
- Style descriptions should be used as guidelines for understanding behavior and building mutually supportive relationships rather than as templates for stereotyping people into rigid and simplistic categories.
- One style is not generally better or worse than the others. All styles bring important perspectives and skills, as well as blind spots and limitations.
- Everyone uses all four of these styles at different times, but we tend to prefer one style more than the others and use that style most often, especially under stress.
- One's social style may change over time.
- Some styles may be more appropriate than others in particular situations.
- Successful people respect and leverage the strengths of each of the four styles.
- Everyone can learn how to be more flexible and use all four styles.

You can use the following tables to learn the strengths and weaknesses of each style, how people with each style may be perceived by others, and what strategies you can use to influence people with each style. As you read through these tables, return to Table 5-1 on which you listed the three people whom you identified as people you want to influence. How would you describe each person's social style? Based on what you've learned about the Social Styles model, write down the strategies that may be useful for each person. Remember that people give clues about how they can be influenced.[27] If you take the time to look for these clues, you will be much more successful in your influence attempts. For example, you can ask people questions (e.g. "What do you think the most important issues are in this organization and how

TABLE 5-2 General Characteristics of Each Social Style	
Analytic	**Driver**
Emphasizes facts, data, and procedures	Emphasizes goals and bottom-line results
Well organized	Decisive and direct
Systematic, logical, objective	Encourages risk taking
Careful, detailed, disciplined	Competitive
Conservative	Impatient
Reserved	Uses report talk (facts and information)
Uses report talk (facts and information)	Fast-talking and may interrupt
Asks questions	Focuses on content not style
Chooses words carefully	Uses bold gestures and direct eye contact
Focuses on content not style	Leans forward and may be loud
Uses limited gestures and facial expressions	May not praise others
Uses deliberate and slow decision making	May be formal
May need to be right	May not want to be told what to do
Amiable	**Expressive**
Emphasizes collaboration	Emphasizes positive vision of the future
Good listener and agreeable	Enthusiastic, energetic, can-do attitude
Uses rapport talk (building relationships)	Uses rapport talk (building relationships)
Tries to see others' perspectives	Likes to think out loud
Empathetic	Optimistic, dramatic, and spontaneous
Asks questions	Encourages innovation and risk taking
Wants to include everyone	Social, playful, and comfortable with most people
Prefers consensus	Leans forward, uses bold eye contact
Likes routine	Uses animated gestures/facial expressions
Often quiet, slow, and steady	Fast-talking
Easygoing and modest	Expresses emotions and concern
Uses open, unhurried gestures	Likes to be center of attention
May not give direct statements/opinions	May speak in generalities
May avoid making big decisions	May not seek out data to back up intuition

do you think we can solve them?"), observe their reactions (including body language), and listen carefully to the way that they speak. You can pay attention to what people say and how they interact at meetings. You can observe how people make presentations (do they emphasize the vision, results, data, or people?),[28] and you can ask someone who knows the people you want to influence to describe their styles and preferences. Although it's useful to understand others, it's equally useful to understand yourself. Therefore, you can use the Social Styles model to understand your strengths, your weaknesses, which strategies are effective and ineffective at influencing you, and what kinds of environments bring out the best in you. If you're curious about how you're perceived by others, you can also have someone else complete the

TABLE 5-3	Potential Strengths of Each Social Style

Analytic	Driver
Planning	Taking initiative
Analyzing	Getting things done fast
Organizing	Blocking out distractions
Ensuring accuracy	Focusing on results
Adhering to principles	Being decisive
Following procedures	

Amiable	Expressive
Getting along with others	Inspiring enthusiasm
Listening to others	Public speaking
Providing service	Building alliances
Being patient and dependable	Gaining support
Earning trust and cooperation	Generating ideas for breakthrough solutions
Keeping commitments	

TABLE 5-4	Potential Weaknesses of Each Social Style

Analytic	Driver
May miss the big picture	May be impatient
May assume data speaks for itself	May be too independent
May spend too much time on details	May assume they have best answer
May have inappropriate perfectionism	May underestimate need for building relationships
May be slow to make decisions	May be intimidating so people obey out of fear or may not give necessary bad news
May not share information	
May underestimate need for building relationships	

Amiable	Expressive
May be indecisive	May be disorganized
May not use time effectively	May be impulsive/unpredictable
May be slow to make decisions	May have short attention span
May be too dependent	May procrastinate
May have difficulty expressing opinions or disagreeing	May ignore data and details
May be taken advantage of by more assertive people	May make generalizations based on too little information
May overcommit	May underestimate reality of implementation
	May miss deadlines

TABLE 5-5	Potential Behavior under Stress for Each Social Style
Analytic	**Driver**
Avoiding	Fighting
May be too critical	May be autocratic and controlling
May obsess and get lost in the details (paralysis by analysis)	May rant and rave but bark may be worse than bite
May have excessive perfectionism	May forget what made them angry in the first place
Amiable	**Expressive**
Avoiding	Fighting
May close down/get stuck	May attack when challenged
May passively wait for someone else to take charge	May be unpredictable
	May say too much to too many (loose lips sink ships)

TABLE 5-6	Weaknesses as They May Be Perceived by Others
Analytic	**Driver**
Picky	Dominating
Indecisive	Pushy
Slow	Unpredictable
Moralistic	Bully
Stuffy	Scary and uncomfortable to be around
Too critical	Unappreciative and insensitive
Amiable	**Expressive**
Too conforming	Undisciplined
Uncertain	Impulsive
Little independent thinking	Egotistical
Too wishy-washy	Manipulative
Too emotional	Superficial

Social Styles assessment at the end of this chapter using you as the target when they answer the questions. This will enable you to see if your self-perceptions match those of others' perceptions of you.

When using the Social Styles model to influence others, keep the Platinum Rule in mind: Do unto others as they'd like done unto them.

TABLE 5-7 Influence Strategies for Different Social Styles	
Analytic	**Driver**
<u>Motivated by</u>: Control and security through accuracy, precision, consistency, and attention to process	<u>Motivated by</u>: Power, control, competence, achievement, winning (being #1), independence, competition, change, being right, results, action, promotions, salary
<u>Fears</u>: Being out of control, criticism, sudden or uncontrolled change, embarrassment, mistakes	<u>Fears</u>: Not being on top, being seen as "soft," being taken advantage of, falling into routines, not meeting deadlines
<u>What they don't like in others</u>: Lack of predictability, unsubstantiated claims, disorganization, too much emotion	<u>What they don't like in others</u>: Lack of motivation, weaknesses, indecision, inaction
<u>To influence</u>: Be formal, systematic, detailed, direct, precise, and organized; Provide facts, data, and examples to back up claim; Explain how to do things; Show how plan fits with existing policies, practices, procedures; Ask for their advice; Focus on process; Schedule extra time for meetings; Support the person's principles; Give reasons for need for speed	<u>To influence</u>: Be decisive, directive, controlled, confident, and efficient; Emphasize immediate actions and measurable results; Explain what needs to be done; Support person's priorities; Focus on future "wins"; Schedule short, direct meeting; Be viewed as someone who gets results
<u>What they need from you to succeed</u>: Provide deadlines; Break large projects into smaller steps; Refocus on big picture as appropriate; Refocus on importance of speed and results as well as data and process	<u>What they need from you to succeed</u>: Provide candid feedback even if they don't ask for it; Don't take criticisms from drivers personally (they simply may not be tactful); Provide independence yet focus on working with others as appropriate; Refocus on importance of relationships and process as well as results and speed
Amiable	**Expressive**
<u>Motivated by</u>: Belonging, acceptance, involvement, stability, security, attention to process	<u>Motivated by</u>: Meaning, dreaming, making a positive difference, change, popularity, recognition, prestige, compliments, applause, approval
<u>Fears</u>: Conflict, not being liked, sudden change, risk	<u>Fears</u>: Loss of prestige, not being where the action is, being isolated, not being liked, public humiliation, falling into routines
<u>What they don't like in others</u>: Insensitivity, people not keeping their commitments, pushy people, aggressiveness, conflict seekers	<u>What they don't like in others</u>: Lack of enthusiasm, inattention to values/people, naysayers, pessimism, and lack of vision
<u>To influence</u>: Be friendly, agreeable, and specific; Proceed gently; Explain why; Show concern for people and feelings; Support need for inclusion; Focus on process for making decisions	<u>To influence</u>: Be stimulating, enthusiastic, creative, inspiring, optimistic, flexible; Explain who needs to be brought on board; Support person's desires, accomplishments; Focus on results; Focus on feelings and the distant future
<u>What they need from you to succeed</u>: Provide opportunity to show initiative; Provide clear deliverables and deadlines; Offer assistance with time management; Refocus on speed and results as well as relationships and processes	<u>What they need from you to succeed</u>: Provide structure and discipline; Provide clear deliverables and deadlines; Refocus on processes (attending to details and data gathering) as well as vision and breakthrough ideas

USING THE SIX UNIVERSAL FORMS OF INFLUENCE

Although human beings differ in many ways, we all share some fundamental human needs. People who understand these common needs and help people fulfill these needs are more likely to be successful in their attempts to influence others. After reviewing decades of research, social psychologist Robert Cialdini concluded that "persuasion works by appealing to a limited set of deeply rooted human drive and needs, and it does so in predictable ways."[29] In his thoughtful and practical book *Influence: Science and Practice*, Cialdini identifies six universal forms of influence that transcend personality and culture:[30]

- *Reciprocation:* People feel obligated to pay back favors, gifts, and help that they receive from others. ("If you scratch my back, I'll scratch yours.")
- *Commitment/consistency:* People are more likely to agree with a request if they feel it is consistent with a commitment they have made (especially a commitment that they make publicly or write down) or a behavior they have taken in the past.
- *Authority:* People tend to obey people they perceive to be authorities and experts.
- *Social proof:* People are more willing to support an idea if they know that other people support it, especially if they perceive the other people to be similar to them.
- *Scarcity:* People tend to want what they believe is unique, rare, or in limited supply.
- *Liking:* People want to support the people they like.

Cialdini explains that these forms of influence work because they act as cognitive shortcuts that help us bypass more complicated and costly decision-making processes. As mentioned earlier, we cannot gather all the data we need for every decision we make, nor can we interpret all the data we gather from every possible angle. So, we use cognitive shortcuts to help us make both the small and large decisions we face every day. For example, we help someone out because he helped us out last week (reciprocation). We donate money every year to the same charities (commitment and consistency). We buy a particular brand of toothpaste because an advertisement says that 90% dentists recommend this toothpaste (authority). We agree to a costly proposal at work because everyone else at the meeting seems to support it (social proof). We purchase an item in response to a "limited time offer" (scarcity). We select a physician because someone we trust recommends her (liking).

We are more likely to use cognitive shortcuts under particular conditions: when we are confused, uncertain, surprised, faced with too little or too much information, or feeling pressured, as well as when we trust the person requesting our support.[31] Cialdini warns that we are more likely to use cognitive shortcuts today than we were in the past. He explains:

> The evidence suggests that the ever-accelerating pace and informational crush of modern life will make this particular form of unthinking compliance even more and more prevalent in the future. . . . The issues may be so complicated, the time so tight, the distractions so intrusive, the emotional arousal so strong, or the mental fatigue so deep that we are in no cognitive condition to operate mindfully.[32]

Cialdini adds, "All this leads to an unnerving insight: With the sophisticated mental apparatus we have used to build world eminence as a species, we have created an environment so complex, fast-paced, and information-laden that we must increasingly deal with it in the fashion of the animals we long ago transcended."[33]

"Triggers" tend to set these cognitive shortcuts in motion. Seeing someone in a white lab coat triggers us to believe that the person is a scientist, so we assume that the person is a credible expert and we are more likely to comply with his or her request. Hearing that a book is on a "best seller" list or is recommended in a book review triggers us to purchase that book. It is not surprising that people who understand these triggers are more likely to be influential than are people who don't understand these triggers.

Note that something as simple as a well-placed word can trigger compliance. Psychologist Ellen Langer and her colleagues conducted an experiment in which they had people use different verbal strategies for cutting into a line of unsuspecting people waiting to make copies at a copy machine. Some people who tried to cut in line said, "Excuse me, I have five pages. May I use the Xerox machine *because I'm in a rush?*" Ninety-four percent of the people waiting in line complied. Other people who tried to cut in line said, "Excuse me, I have five pages. May I use the Xerox machine *because I have to make some copies?*" In this condition, 93% of the people in line complied with the request to cut in line, even though the person making the request did not offer any specific reason for cutting in line. The simple use of the word "*because*", not the actual reason given, seemed to act as a trigger for compliance.[34] Note that when the word "because" wasn't used, only 60% of the people in line let the person who wanted to make copies cut in line. Langer and her colleagues explain that we often respond mindlessly—without thinking and as if we are on automatic pilot—to certain triggers. In contrast, mindfulness means that we think before we act, and we think in complex ways.

Much of the time, responding automatically to cognitive shortcuts serve us well, but sometimes it doesn't. If you know these six universal forms of influence and are mindful of the triggers that set them in motion, not only will you be more influential than someone who is unaware of them, but you will also be less likely to be on automatic pilot—and be an easy target—when someone tries to influence you.

Some readers of this book believe that they are quite resistant to persuasion attempts. If you are one of these people, you should keep in mind that researchers have found that people who feel invulnerable to influence attempts may be more susceptible to influence attempts than are others because they are less likely to take precautions. They may not take precautions because they often have the mistaken belief that people who try to influence others are obvious and pushy in their attempts. They don't realize that the most effective influencers are subtle and indirect in their approach. To make this point, advertising critic Jean Kilbourne says:

> "You should have an open mind, but not so open that your brain falls out."
> —JACOB NEEDLEMAN, *Philosopher*

> Almost everyone holds the misguided belief that advertisements don't affect them, don't shape their attitudes, don't help define their dreams. . . . What I hear more than anything else, as I lecture throughout the country, is "I don't pay attention to ads . . . I just tune them out. . . . They have no effect on me." Of course, I hear this most often from young men wearing Budweiser caps.[35]

In the following sections, you will learn about each of six universal forms of influence in more detail. You will learn why they work, gain specific strategies for using each form of influence, and learn strategies for resisting mindless compliance to each of the influence strategies so that you can make more mindful and informed decisions. As you read these sections, you can return to Table 5-1 to write down additional strategies you can use to gain the support of the three people whom you would like to influence.

Be aware that each of these forms of influence can be used ethically or unethically. Ethical persuaders ask themselves, "How can I genuinely present the *honest* merits of my case in a way that is more likely to gain compliance?" They never provide false information or artificially inflate the merits of their case. They do not pretend to be authorities or experts if they are not. They do not engage in false flattery. They do not promise what they cannot deliver. Remember that using unethical influence attempts may get you what you want in the short term, but will harm your credibility and often the reputation of the organizations that you represent in the long term. In Cialdini's words, "Time wounds all heels."[36]

The Reciprocation Rule

If you don't go to other people's funerals, they won't come to yours.
—YOGI BERRA, *Hall of Fame baseball player and former manager of New York Mets*

Simply stated, the reciprocation rule is this: If you give me something—help, favors, information, gifts, support, concessions—I will feel obligated to give you something in return.[37] If you pay for my lunch today, I will feel obligated to pay for your lunch in the future. If you give me a gift on my birthday, I will feel obligated to give you a gift on your birthday. If you send me a holiday card, I will feel obligated to send you a holiday card. If you invite my child to your house for a play date, I will feel obligated to invite your child to my house for a play date. If you support my ideas at today's meeting, I will feel obligated to support your ideas at a future meeting. If you give me information when I request it, I will feel obligated to give you information when you request it. If you come to an event that I am sponsoring, I will feel obligated to come to a future event that you are sponsoring. If you give me a concession in our negotiation, I will feel obligated to give you a concession, too.

Because the reciprocation rule is shared by all cultures, researchers believe it is based, in part, on a universal survival instinct. Individuals and societies can survive only if people cooperate with each other and help each other when help is needed. Therefore, we are willing to support others because in the long run (consciously or unconsciously) we want to be able to count on others when we need something. The late philosopher Erich Fromm explained that all human beings believe and support the wisdom, "Inasmuch as we are all human, we're all in need of help. Today I, tomorrow you."[38] It is not surprising that people who do not participate in the social give and take of mutual obligation are less likely to receive support when they need it.

For several decades, researchers have illustrated the power of the reciprocation rule through experiments. The research design typically involves someone doing someone else a small, often unexpected favor, and then asking the recipient of the favor for some help to see if the act of giving would increase compliance. One often cited experiment by social psychologist Dennis Regan is described below:

> Regan had subjects work in pairs on a bogus task supposedly measuring art appreciation. One of the subjects, let's call him Andy, was actually a paid actor working as Regan's assistant. During a short rest period in the middle of the experiment, Andy left for a couple of minutes. For half the subjects (the gift group), Andy returned with two Cokes, handing one to the subject and keeping one for himself, explaining, "I asked him [the experimenter] if I could go get myself a Coke and he said it was ok, so I brought one for you, too." For the other half (the control group), Andy returned without a gift. In both conditions, Andy later asked the subject to do him a favor. Andy said that he was selling raffle tickets for his high school back home and that he'd get a prize if he sold the most tickets. Would the subject be willing to buy one or more tickets? In clear support of the reciprocation theory, Andy sold almost twice as many tickets to people he'd given a free Coke earlier.[39]

Most examples of the power of reciprocation are found outside the experimental lab. During the Civil War, nurse Clara Barton delivered medical supplies to the front line, cared for wounded soldiers, helped locate missing soldiers, and helped create the Red Cross. Later, Clara Barton became an active supporter of the suffrage movement and hoped to gain women's right to vote. As she campaigned for women's right to vote, she told men who had been soldiers during the Civil War, "When you were weak and I was strong, I toiled for you. Now you are strong and I am weak. Because of my work for you, I ask your aid. I ask the ballot for myself and my sex. As I stood by you, I pray you stand by me and mine."[40]

After the 2002 terrorist attack in Bali, the Australian government donated two medical centers to thank the Balinese for taking care of Australian citizens after the attack. A South China *Morning Post* newspaper article, "Repaying a Debt of Gratitude," described the gift this way:

> Australian Prime Minister John Howard yesterday inaugurated two medical centers to thank the Balinese who cared for so many Australians after the terrorist bombings one year ago. Mr. Howard officially opened an intensive care and burn unit at the Sangla hospital, in Bali, which treated most of the victims. Australia has donated A\$4.5 million (HK \$24 million) toward the intensive care unit, which is still under construction. Another A\$2.94 million is building and equipping the Bali Memorial Eye Centre, a small specialist hospital. "This is the most practical and tangible way to express our gratitude to the people of Bali," Mr. Howard said.[41]

Not all acts of reciprocation are noble. Although stock market analysts are supposed to be objective, researchers James Westphal and Michael Clement studied thousands of analysts and found that almost 63% of those analysts received favors from chief executive officers, chief financial officers, and other senior executives. Executives tended to increase the number of favors given when their firms performed worse than expected. The researchers found that analysts who received at least two favors from executive officers were half as likely as analysts who did not receive favors to downgrade a company after reports of poor company earnings were released. Westphal and Clement found that these favors included putting an analyst in touch with a top manager of another company, providing industry information, offering to meet with an analyst's clients, giving career and personal advice, recommending an analyst for a job, and helping the analyst obtain entry to a private club or nonprofessional organization.[42] Clement warns, "The bottom line is that favor-rendering to analysts is evidently widespread and that it seems to be compromising the value of the guidance these experts provide to investors. . . . While there may be no simple solution to the problem, our findings certainly suggest that it deserves to be taken seriously."[43]

Because the feeling of obligation is an extremely powerful source of influence, its power does not diminish over time. The following are several examples that illustrate how people will feel obligated to repay a favor decades and generations later. In 1956, the International Rescue Committee (IRC) helped a 20-year-old Jewish man named András Gróf emigrate to the United States to escape oppression and persecution related to the Hungarian Revolution. Gróf arrived in the United States with significant hearing loss from having had scarlet fever as a child, as well as serious dental problems. An IRC worker gave Andras money to get his teeth fixed and a blank check to purchase a hearing aid. Shortly after arriving in the United States, András changed his name to Andrew Grove and later became the CEO and chairman of Intel Corporation, one of the world's most successful producers of microprocessors. In 2001, Grove donated the proceeds from his book, *Swimming Across: A Memoir*, to the International Rescue Committee in appreciation for its help over 40 years earlier.[44]

Pharmaceutical giant Merck became the first non-Japanese company to enter the highly protected Japanese pharmaceutical market in the early 1980s. Why was Merck granted access?

Because immediately following World War II, Merck provided Japan with free medical support. In his book *The Leadership Moment*, leadership researcher and professor Michael Useem described Merck's entry into the Japanese market as follows:

> Tuberculosis, for example, had surged in Japan in the years after World War II, and the war's devastation left few in a position to pay for a powerful Merck product that worked wonders against it: streptomycin. The company finally decided to donate a large supply to the Japanese public. Coming at a moment of great hardship, Merck's generosity has long been remembered. When the company sought access to Japan's domestic market in 1983, Japanese authorities took the rare step of approving Merck's $300 million purchase of 50.02 percent of Banyu Pharmaceutical, Japan's tenth largest drug maker. At the time it was the largest direct investment by a foreign company in a notoriously closed market. "We received help from the Japanese government in making the first acquisition of this kind to be allowed," remembers [former Merck CEO] Vagelos, and it should come as no surprise that Merck is the largest American pharmaceutical company in Japan today.[45]

When American journalists Euna Lee and Laura Ling were imprisoned in North Korea in 2009, the U.S. government sprung into action to secure their release. Of all the diplomats available, The North Korean government chose to meet with former president Bill Clinton. A North Korean official explained, "As president, Mr. Clinton had sent [North Korean Leader] Mr. Kim a letter of condolence on the death of his father, Kim Il-sung . . . For Mr. Kim . . . freeing the women was a 'reciprocal humanitarian gesture.'"[46]

Cialdini explains that even concessions can trigger the desire to reciprocate. For example, imagine that you go to a meeting with your boss and ask for a raise. The boss says, "No." Rather than leave the office immediately, this moment provides an opportunity to draw on the reciprocation rule.[47] Your gracious acceptance of your boss's refusal of a raise is likely to be seen by your boss as a concession. So, rather than simply leave the office immediately, you could use that moment to thoughtfully ask for a concession in return. If you can't have the raise, perhaps you can have something else of value to you: a new laptop computer, a high-profile assignment, or additional training in a new skill that will help you get the raise the next time (and boost your marketability should the raise not come through next year either). The *Wall Street Journal* gave this example of a young woman's smart negotiation when she accepted her job as a human resource manager. "In hiring the human resources manager, a suburban Boston biotech concern balked at giving her more than its promised 10% raise. But the company agreed to immediately pay all expenses so she could complete graduate school. Official policy partly covered tuition after six months of service. She also got time off to study. '[She said] it was a mutual gain for both of us.'"[48]

If you give me a cup of tea, I'll give you a glass of wine.
—CHINESE PROVERB

The most important lesson to learn from the reciprocation rule is this: If you want to have sustainable influence over time, you must be willing to give often—and be the first to give. When you walk into a new setting—neighborhood, work organization, school—your immediate instinct should be to learn what other people need and then help them meet those needs.

LEVERAGING THE RECIPROCATION RULE

- Give generously and sincerely to others, and give first.
- Remember that gifts, favors, assistance, and concessions are most influential when they are perceived as sincere and valuable by the receiver (not gratuitous, manipulative, or trivial).

- Remember that you'll get what you give. If you give kindnesses, favors, help, and concessions, you are more likely to get these in return. If you are unwilling to help others when requested to do so, others will be unwilling to help you when you need help.
- Do not negate the value of your help or concessions with statements such as "it was nothing" or "no problem." Such statements imply that you have given nothing and thus reciprocation is not warranted in return. Instead, when someone acknowledges having received something from you (such as favors or help), respond with a straightforward "Thank you" or "I'm glad it was helpful. I was happy to help."[49]
- Remember to enjoy the pleasures of giving freely with no intent of gaining something in return.

RESISTING THE RECIPROCATION RULE

- If you accept a favor, frame it as generosity freely given and do not assume obligation, particularly in advertising or marketing attempts.
- When you do feel obligated, remember that you can choose when and how you repay the favor. Just be sure to repay it.

The Scarcity Rule

People tend to value things that are unique, rare, or in limited supply. The scarcity rule works because the belief that something is scarce arouses our panic emotions and "now or never thinking" so we tend to pursue that which appears to be in short supply.[50] This is why advertisers regularly use statements such as "one time offers," "limited edition," "24-hour sale," "once-in-a-lifetime opportunity," and "only 15 items left in stock."

Guy Laliberté, founder of the Canadian Circus Company, Cirque Du Soleil, uses the scarcity rule to continue to build demand for his avant-garde circus featuring opulent sets, colorful costumes, and gifted performers. Born to a middle-class family in Quebec City, Canada, Laliberté left home at the age of 18 to work in Europe as a street performer, often living hand-to-mouth to learn the basics of fire-breathing, stilt-walking, and other circus talents. Today, he is a billionaire who has founded the One Drop Foundation that provides access to water to help fight poverty in developing countries. More than 90 million people have attended at least one of Cirque Du Soleil's performances worldwide, resulting in an estimated yearly revenue of over $800 million in revenues. *Newsweek* reported that Laliberte, concerned about overexposure:

> insists that despite the Cirque boom, he is strictly following a business policy of slightly undersatisfying the public's appetite. Laliberte likens his strategy to that of Enzo Ferrari, explaining, "When Enzo Ferrari was putting out a new car model, he would ask how many cars he could sell. . . . If it came to, say, 250, he'd say, 'OK, we'll do 249.' At every performance, I want there to be at least one person who hits his nose on the closed door of the theatre because it's sold out."[51]

A clever business strategy perhaps, although the *Newsweek* reporter who reported the story lamented, "Who said running a circus was about keeping the kids smiling?"[52]

Clothing marketers also leverage the scarcity rule. One national clothing chain orchestrated its own shortage of a heavily advertised $198 jacket to enhance the chain's reputation as a merchandiser of hip and highly desirable clothing. The *Wall Street Journal* reported, "Hoping to make the item a 'fashion moment,' the company featured it heavily in its fall advertising campaign and promoted it with fashion glossies. Then it limited its shipments to just 5,000 jackets, no more than half the normal run for such a product. The result, a flurry of waitlists, which didn't move the company to reorder. 'When we sell out, we sell out,' said [one of the clothing chain's executive vice presidents]. 'It adds to the allure.'"[53]

The above examples illustrate how some businesses use the scarcity rule to increase customer demand. But these examples also illustrate a problem with this strategy. If people feel as though they've been manipulated, the strategy can backfire, and the people who artificially create scarcity may lose the credibility and support they seek to gain for their organization.

LEVERAGING THE SCARCITY RULE

- Highlight real (not contrived) unique benefits, scarcity, and exclusive information.
- Highlight real (not contrived) scarcity
- Point out unique features
- Emphasize exclusive information

RESISTING THE SCARCITY RULE

- Don't rush to a decision because you feel pressured or respond to claims of scarcity with "panic emotions." Take time to get the facts, use a systematic decision-making process, determine alternative courses of action, and weigh the costs and benefits of rushing to a decision.

The Authority Rule

Most of us are taught in childhood to obey authority figures (e.g., parents, teachers, religious leaders, bosses, and social leaders) and respect the advice and talents of experts (e.g., physicians, scientists, and researchers). Therefore, even as adults we're more likely to comply with a request if the person making the request is an authority figure or expert. Although we like to think that we'd know talent and expertise when we see it, we tend to assess a person's expertise by looking for cues such as titles, style of dress (e.g., lab coats, formal attire), claimed expertise, degrees posted on the wall, and initials following their name that signal that someone is an authority or expert. See Box 5-1 for a fascinating example of how we can be very poor judges of expertise without such cues.

Because of our trust in authority and experts, we often want management gurus to tell us how we should manage our organizations, financial advisers to tell us how we should invest our money, and restaurant critics to tell us where we should dine. Usually our reliance on experts and authority figures serves us well. But our willingness to obey authority figures and be impressed by experts can backfire. Authority figures and experts are fallible human beings. People may claim to be experts when they are not. An expert in one area (e.g., engineering) may not be an expert in another (e.g., understanding customer needs). We may disregard our own instincts when listening to authority figures and experts. In a classic study of obedience to authority, researcher Stanley Milgram designed an experiment in which naïve subjects were asked by a "scientist" (who was actually an actor in a white lab coat) to deliver electric shocks to another human being (who, unknown to the subject, was another actor and not really receiving the shocks) under the pretense that the scientist was studying the effect of punishment on learning. Over half of the experimenter's research subjects complied with the authority figure's request to deliver electric shocks even though the victim screamed for them to stop and said he was having heart problems during the experiment.[54] Milgram concluded that the subjects' desire to obey authority superseded their desire to stop delivering shocks to the suffering victim.

BOX 5-1   The Power of Cognitive Shortcuts: The Case of Violinist Joshua Bell in the Subway

To test the power of dress and other cues on people's ability to assess talent and expertise, *Washington Post* reporter Gene Weingarten had 39-year-old Joshua Bell, one of the world's most renowned violinists, play classical music in the L'Enfant Plaza subway station in Washington, DC, while unassumingly dressed in jeans, a T-shirt, and a baseball cap. During the morning rush hour on that January day in 2007, Bell gingerly removed one of the most rare and valuable violins in existence—one that was handcrafted by Antonio Stradivari in 1713 and is today worth about $3 million—from its case. He placed the violin case in front of him and threw a few dollars in the case to encourage others to reward his subway performance with money. He then began to play elegant classical masterpieces.

On that busy morning in the subway, Bell looked like any other street musician rather than the virtuoso who just days before filled symphony halls in Boston and North Bethesda with people who were willing to pay $100 to hear him perform. Bell's reputation was (and is) stellar. When composer John Corigliano accepted the Oscar for the musical score to the movie, *The Red Violin*, he honored Bell by saying, "He plays like a god." A few days after the subway experiment, Bell was awarded the Avery Fisher prize, the highest honor for a musician in the United States. However, without the external signals of expertise (such as a tuxedo or a concert hall) to inform them that Bell was an internationally known virtuoso, only seven of the 1,070 people who passed him stopped to listen to him in the subway. Approximately $37 was thrown into the violin case at his feet throughout his performance. Weingarten's experiment is a stunning example of human beings' inability to assess expertise without taken-for-granted external cues. In fact, Weingarten earned the Pulitzer Prize for Journalism for his *Washington Post* article, "Pearls before Breakfast," in 2007. You can read the *Washington Post* article and see a video online of Bell playing in the subway while people pass by.

Source: Weingarten, Gene. April 8, 2007. "Pearls before Breakfast." Washington Post. http://www.washingtonpost.com/wp-yn/content/article/2007/04/04/AR2007040401721.html

---

Another experiment illustrates that we may be more likely to believe that someone is an expert if that person uses incomprehensible jargon rather than language that is simple to understand. In this mock jury experiment:

Subjects were asked to evaluate a plaintiff's claim that the company he'd worked for exposed him to a dangerous chemical that caused his cancer. Some jurors listened to the supposed expert witness, Dr. Thomas Fallon, a professor of biochemistry, explain in simple terms that the chemical in question causes the type of liver cancer the plaintiff had been stricken with. Fallon described, for example, how previous studies found that the chemical "caused not only liver disease but also cancer of the liver and . . . diseases of the immune system as well." Other subjects heard Dr. Fallon go off on the dangers of the chemical in complicated, often incomprehensible language. He explained how the chemical led to "tumor induction as well as hepatomegaly, hepatomegalocytosis, and lymphoid atrophy in both spleen and thymus." The results of the study found that when Dr. Fallon was presented as a man of outstanding credentials, the jury was almost twice as likely to be convinced if he spoke in obscure jargon than if he presented in simple and straightforward language. The researchers concluded that when the witness spoke simply the jurors could evaluate his argument on its merits. But when he was unintelligible, they had to resort to the mental shortcut of accepting his title and reputation in lieu of comprehensible facts. And so, another paradox: Experts are sometimes most convincing when we don't understand what they're talking about.

The researchers also found that using cryptic language works only if one has the title and credentials to be seen as a credible expert. In the same mock jury experiment, when Dr. Fallon was introduced with "shakier credentials," jurors were less convinced by his jargon than when he spoke in straightforward terms.[55] The lesson is this: Although we often rely on other people's expertise to make decisions, we are not always the best judges of expertise.

LEVERAGING THE AUTHORITY RULE

- Develop real expertise in something that people value, need, and want.
- Do not assume your authority or expertise is obvious to others. If you have a title, use it. If you have degrees or if you have won awards, post them. If you are an expert in an area, tell people. If there are people who can endorse your expertise, have them do so.[56]
- Show that high-status people and known experts support your ideas.
- Present a professional image.

RESISTING THE AUTHORITY RULE

- Remember that trust in authority figures and experts is often useful, but should not be given uncritically.
- Be reasonably cautious with claims of expertise. Check credentials to determine if the person who claims to be an expert is truly an expert in the area in which you need advice.
- Be careful of the halo effect. Recognize that an expert in one area is not necessarily an expert in another area.

The Rule of Social Proof

Many of us remember our parents telling us when we were growing up: "If everyone jumped off a cliff, would you jump off a cliff, too?" Our parents were trying to warn us of the universal tendency to follow the crowd, even when it is against our best interest. They knew intuitively what researchers have spent years studying: For better and worse, we look to other people to make decisions about how to act, particularly when we are uncertain about what to do, when we are seeking the approval of others (e.g., when we want to fit in), and when we believe that the people moving in a particular direction are similar to us.[57] Parents have every right to be concerned about the influence of peer behavior on their teens because researchers have found that teenagers are more likely to engage in alcohol consumption when their peers do so.[58]

Television show producers use this rule when they add laugh tracks to sitcoms, knowing that we are more likely to laugh if we hear other people laughing. Bartenders use this rule when they put a few dollars in the tip jar at the beginning of their shift to encourage customers to add new tips. Management team members use this rule when they go along with a decision at a meeting because they believe that everyone else in the meeting wants to go along with the decision. So, if you want to convince your boss, colleagues, employees, neighbors, parents, or children to accept one of your ideas, you are more likely to get their buy-in if you show them that other people they respect already support the idea, especially if they see themselves as similar to the people who support the idea.

In one interesting study of the power of social proof, researchers convinced a hotel manager to put two different signs in randomly chosen hotel rooms asking guests to re-use towels to reduce unnecessary laundering as a way of being environmentally responsible. In some rooms, the sign asked guests to "help save the environment" by re-using their towels. In other rooms, the sign asked guests to "join their fellow guests in helping to save the environment" by re-using their towels. Guests who stayed in rooms with the signs that informed them that their fellow guests re-used their towels were 26% more likely to reuse their towels than were those who were in rooms that had the standard appeal to be environmentally responsible. In a follow-up study, the researchers found that people who stayed in hotel rooms that had a sign saying that 75% of the people who stayed in the same hotel room re-used their towels were 33% more likely to re-use their towels.[59] Because we cannot (and sometimes do not want to) analyze every situation in depth, we watch others to get a sense of the best (or at least good-enough) decision. This rule usually serves us well because most people we follow are not headed in a direction that would harm them or others. But, as with all cognitive shortcuts, following the crowd can also lead us down the wrong path, as the people who invested in Bernie Madoff's fraudulent investments painfully learned.

LEVERAGING THE RULE OF SOCIAL PROOF

- Show that other people already support your idea or request.
- Obtain testimonials from satisfied people, especially people who are experts or similar to the people you want to influence.
- Show how others have succeeded by complying with your request (or similar request).

RESISTING THE RULE OF SOCIAL PROOF

- Realize that you are more susceptible to following others when you perceive them to be similar to you, when you want to fit in, and in times of uncertainty.
- Remember that "when birds of a feather flock together, they can turn into sitting ducks."[60]

The Commitment and Consistency Rule

We all have a desire to maintain a positive and consistent self-concept. So, we all want to believe that our actions are consistent with our values, that people can count on us to live up to our commitments, and that once we choose a course of action we will follow through with it. This is especially true when we believe that the commitments we make are freely chosen rather than coerced. So, once we freely say we are committed to a belief, we are likely to act in ways that support that belief. And once we freely choose a course of action (e.g., voting for a particular political party, supporting a particular charity), we are likely to follow that course again and again.

The commitment and consistency rule is indeed powerful. Once we begin going in a certain direction, we are unlikely to stop or change course even if evidence suggests that we are making a mistake. Researchers call this phenomenon "escalating commitment to a failing course of action."[61] For example, couples get married even though they do not love each other because they publicly announced their engagement, had an engagement party, purchased the wedding attire, reserved the reception hall, and hired the caterer. People stay in careers that no longer satisfy them because they have already invested a lot of money to obtain a degree in that profession or spent several years of their lives in that profession. People and groups make business decisions that do not serve their organizations well because they have already invested substantial organizational funds into the project. Governments persist with losing courses of action in part to justify their past commitments and investments in these courses of action.[62]

The implications of this rule are clear: If you want someone to take a particular course of action, you will be more successful if you link your request to a publicly made voluntary commitment. Another way to leverage the consistency rule is to ask for compliance with a small request and then build to a larger request (this is known as the "foot-in-the-door technique").[63] Restaurants advertise free appetizers because they know that once people are in the restaurant, they are more likely to order the full meal, including expensive drinks and desserts. The commitment and consistency rule is even more powerful if you can convince people to put their commitment in writing.[64] Cialdini describes an experiment in which "college students in one group were asked to fill out a printed form saying they wished to volunteer for an AIDS education project in the public schools. Students in another group volunteered for the same project by leaving blank a form stating that they didn't want to participate. A few days later, when the volunteers reported for duty, 74% of those who showed up were students from the group that signaled their commitment by filling out the form."[65]

Cialdini explains that "people live up to what they have written down."[66] So, if you want a team to meet a deadline, have them put their agreement to meeting the due date in writing. If you want an employee to perform to a higher standard or develop a new skill, get his or her commitment in writing. If you want to achieve a goal (e.g., eat healthier, get a new job, be a kinder person), put your commitment in writing and post it where you will be reminded of your commitment—better yet, tell other people of your commitment as well. But remember that the commitment rule of persuasion only works if the commitment is important to the person and is made voluntarily. The rule is unlikely to work if people feel they were coerced into making a commitment or if they don't really care.

LEVERAGING THE COMMITMENT AND CONSISTENCY RULE

- Connect your request to *voluntary* commitments, publicly stated beliefs, and existing behaviors.
- Begin with small requests and build up to bigger requests.
- Have people voluntarily put their commitments in writing.

DEFENSE

- Be careful of what you promise, because you will hold yourself accountable.
- Do not feel obligated to commit to a large request just because you made a small commitment.
- Remember that you can disengage from a commitment at any time, no matter how far you've gone down a path. Learn to say "I changed my mind," "I have a different perspective now," "I learned something," and "I was wrong." Remember the sage advice of Warren Buffett, one of the richest men in the world: "When you find yourself in a hole, the best thing you can do is stop digging."[67]
- You can help other people change direction from a failing course of action by helping them save face and reminding them that they now have more information than they had when they initially began that course of action and help them link the change to a commitment that they had publicly made.[68]

The Liking Rule

The liking rule is based on the simple principle that we tend to be drawn to people we like and away from people we do not like. This rule is powerful because human beings are quick to judge people as good or bad, competent or incompetent, motivated or unmotivated, smart or stupid, strong or weak, and trustworthy or dishonest. Indeed, most of the approximately 18,000 adjectives English speakers use to describe each other are either complimentary (e.g., "competent," "honest," or "motivated") or noncomplementary (e.g., "incompetent," "dishonest," or "lazy").[69] Our tendency to evaluate people positively or negatively influences who we listen to and who we ignore, who we interact with and who we avoid, who we promote and who we pass over, and whose ideas we support and whose ideas we resist.[70]

We support people we like for at least three reasons. First, we assume the people we like will be benevolent toward us, will cooperate with us, and will not harm us. Because we believe in their goodwill, we are more likely to seek out and follow their advice, support their interests, and agree to their requests. For example, researchers estimate that 70% people in the United States ask for advice in choosing a physician, 53% moviegoers ask for recommendations from people they know, and 91% people who make a major purchase obtain recommendations from people they know.[71] The second reason that liking is such a powerful form of influence is that we want to please the people to whom we are attracted so that they will like us back. The third reason we support people we like is that we want to be associated with them. This is why teenagers spend so much money buying clothing advertised by well-known sports figures and pop idols.

What makes people likable? We are attracted to people who reward us in some way. We like people who raise our self-esteem; pay positive attention to us; and make us feel comfortable, happy, heard, competent, successful, proud, powerful, and safe. The late Mary Kay Ash, founder and CEO of Mary Kay cosmetics, put it simply: "Everyone has an invisible sign hanging from their neck saying: Make me feel important." We dislike people when we feel punished by our association with them. So, we avoid or resist people who make us feel uncomfortable, unhappy, unheard, incompetent, unsuccessful, insignificant, embarrassed, or afraid. Notably, some researchers have concluded that people from North America tend to be particularly drawn to three types of rewards: attention, approval, and success.[72]

The smallest acts can increase liking. Seeing another person smile, for example, makes us feel good. Successful waiters and waitresses who depend on tips from customers for much of their income are exceptionally skilled in the art of being likable. For example, they know that they are likely to earn larger tips simply by smiling. In one study, researchers "examined the effects of smiling on the tips earned by cocktail waitresses who served 48 male and 48 female customers. Although the number of drinks ordered was not affected by the smiling, the amount of tips was. A broad smile brought in $23.20, while a minimal smile earned only a total of $9.40."[73] Successful waiters and waitresses also engage in small acts such as acting as allies ("Let me see if I can get you an extra serving of rice at no extra charge."), repeating what the customer wants so that the customer feels heard and understood ("Let me make sure I have your order right. You said that you want a large pizza with red, not green, peppers. Is that correct?"), writing "thank you" on the check, and giving a piece of candy with the bill. All these small acts tell customers that they are liked and in return customers express their appreciation to their server with larger gratuities.[74]

Researchers have found that attractiveness, positive interactions, proximity, perceived similarity, and flattery predict whether we like someone, and thus how much influence this person has with us. Each of these predictors of likability is described below.

Attractive Physical Appearance.   We tend to be drawn to people we perceive to be physically attractive. However, this form of influence can be short-lived. For example, what is considered

> If you could master one element of personal communication that is more powerful than anything . . . it is the quality of being likable. I call it the magic bullet, because if your audience likes you, they'll forgive just about everything else you do wrong. If they don't like you, you can hit every rule right on target and it doesn't matter.
> —ROGER AILES,
> *Public relations adviser to Presidents Ronald Reagan and George Bush, Sr.*

> Don't open a shop unless you like to smile.
> —CHINESE PROVERB

attractive in one setting may be viewed as unattractive in another setting. A person wearing a sharp designer business suit may draw positive reviews on Wall Street but may be seen as pretentious, flashy, and untrustworthy in a more modest setting. Being thin is viewed as attractive in some cultures, but carrying more weight is viewed as a sign of wealth and health in other cultures.[75] Youth is valued in some cultures, but age is valued in others. Another limitation of attractiveness is that although people who are perceived as attractive are more likely to get their foot in the door more quickly, other characteristics such as expertise, helpfulness, and reciprocation will quickly override attractiveness as a form of influence.[76]

Positive Experiences.   We tend to like people with whom we share positive experiences.[77] We like people who are accessible, who cooperate with us, who help us, who like us, who are considerate, and who are open, genuine, and spontaneous.[78] Likable people behave in ways that make others feel good. A nod of approval, a warm smile, a few words of agreement, and an accepting tone of voice all make other people feel as though they are seen, heard, and appreciated. We also are inclined to like people with whom we share an enjoyable experience.[79] For example, we tend to feel good when we are dining, so we tend to transfer those good feelings to the people with whom we share an enjoyable dining experience.[80] We don't have to share the same positive experience with someone else simultaneously to feel a common bond. For example, alumni from the same university will often help each other out if they attended the university years, even decades, apart.

Proximity.   The closer we are to each other physically, the more likely we will be attracted to each other. Proximity gives us the opportunity to gather information about and experience with someone. Because social norms dictate that people be polite and helpful, it is likely that we will have more positive than negative interactions with the people who are near us—and this will increase our liking of them. Furthermore, if we work near someone, live near someone, or attend the same social functions, it is likely that we share significant similarities (e.g., culture, income, educational level, attitudes), and similarity breeds attraction as well.[81]

Perceived Similarity.   We tend to be attracted to people whom we perceive to be similar to us on characteristics such as attitudes, values, status, work style, personality characteristics, physical characteristics, dress, culture, and life experience.[82] We are attracted to people who we believe are similar to us in significant ways for many reasons. First, we want to protect and enhance our self-image, so we want to see people whom we believe are similar to us as having positive characteristics. Second, we want to invest in the success of people whom we believe are similar to us because we believe that doing so may enhance our own chances for success.[83] Third, we want to be around similar others because we believe that we are more likely to expect goodwill, interact easily, and predict their behavior.[84]

Researchers have found that children as young as three years old are influenced by similarity. In an interesting study, they found that three-year-olds tended to select puppets whose food preferences or appearance was similar to the child's preferences and appearance. They also found that three-year-olds in the study preferred to play with children who shared their preference in toys.[85] In other studies, researchers have found that supervisors give higher performance ratings to employees they like and perceive to be similar to them.[86]

The power of perceived similarity was illustrated in an experiment in which researchers gave subjects a scenario in which a car was parked on a hill with the hand brake securely set. Unknown to the driver, the brake cable was in poor repair. The subjects were told that the car "rolled down the hill, crashed into a store window, slightly injured a small girl, and caused a merchant to be hospitalized for a year." When subjects were told to assume that the driver's characteristics were either "very much like your own" (rather than "not at all like your own"), they believed that he was less responsible for the accident and assigned more lenient penalties to him.[87]

Understanding the liking rule is particularly important for people who are demographically different from the people they want to influence. In one study, researchers found that "demographically different people may have more control over the impressions others form of them than has been considered in previous research."[88] People who are in a demographic minority are more likely to be viewed through stereotypical assumptions. However, they can break down unfavorable stereotypes and build opportunities to build connections if they "individuate" themselves from these stereotypes, interact often, communicate personal information, reveal in subtle and explicit ways who they are and who they are not, emphasize their commitment to common goals and a common fate, and build on the similarities they have with the people with whom they want to connect. The researchers found that people who were demographically different from others in their group and who took steps to separate themselves from stereotypes were perceived more positively, connected more with their group, felt more satisfied, and performed better than those who didn't actively differentiate themselves from stereotypes.

Praise and Flattery.   Cialdini explains that praise "both charms and disarms."[89] Most of us respond positively to flattery because we all want to feel good about ourselves.[90] So, we tend to be attracted to and support people who confirm our positive impressions of ourselves. We are particularly susceptible to flattery when it focuses on characteristics that we care about (I am likely to be more impressed if you praise my presentation skills than if you say you like my socks.), when our self esteem needs a boost (I am more likely to appreciate a compliment when I'm having a bad day.), and when we are uncertain of our skills (I am more likely to appreciate praise for my talent at building an innovative Web site if I am a novice rather than if I am an expert at building Web sites.).[91] We are also more susceptible to flattery when we believe it is sincere. In fact, if we know that we are not good at something, we are more likely to respect the person who gives us honest feedback rather than the person who gives us false feedback because we may believe that the latter person may be manipulative or lacking in judgment.[92]

> Goodwill is the one and only asset that competition cannot undersell or destroy.
> —MARSHALL FIELD,
> *American merchant,*
> *1834–1906*

The most important lessons from the liking rule are these: People are more likely to support you if they like you. They are more likely to like you if they perceive you to be attractive, if they have positive experiences with you, if you are near them, if they perceive you to be similar to them, and if you genuinely compliment characteristics that are important to them.

There's an important caveat to the liking rule. Although liking is a powerful form of influence, reciprocation appears to be even more powerful. For example, in one experiment, researchers wanted to determine whether subjects would be more likely to support someone they liked or someone who had done them a favor. In the experiment, they manipulated liking by having the naïve subject overhear a confederate talking on the telephone either pleasantly or in an insulting and unattractive way. In one experimental condition, the confederate left the room but returned with two drinks and told the subject that he was given time to buy himself a drink so he brought one to the subject as well. In another experimental condition, the experimenter brought drinks to both the confederate and the subject. In the third experimental condition, neither the confederate nor the experimenter brought any drinks to the subject. Toward the end of the experiment, the confederate asked the subject to help him gather data for a survey. In the experimental condition in which the subject received no drink from the experimenter or confederate, the subject was more likely to comply with the requests by the confederate who was pleasant (more likable), rather than unpleasant (less likable), during the alleged telephone conversation. However, in the experimental condition in which the subject received a drink from the confederate, he was more likely to comply with the confederate's request for help regardless of whether the confederate was pleasant (likable) or unpleasant (unlikable) during the telephone conversation. In other words, the sense of obligation to repay a favor (help with collecting data for a survey in return for a free drink) outweighed attraction as a form of influence.[93]

LEVERAGING THE LIKING RULE

- Be kind, genuine, and respectful to everyone.
- Use body language that shows approval and interest.
- Create opportunities to have positive cooperative interactions with others.
- Offer sincere compliments when you have the opportunity to do so.
- Individuate yourself from stereotypes and build on similarities with others, especially if you are in a minority.
- Repair damaged relationships by building on similarities, offering sincere compliments, creating opportunities for positive interactions, and using body language that shows goodwill.

RESISTING THE LIKING RULE

- Separate your attraction to a person from the merits of the case that is being made.
- Broaden your perception of attractiveness as well as the diversity of your network so that you are not overly dependent on the knowledge, viewpoints, resources, or influence of a few people or groups. Notably, some research suggests that the more "psychologically secure" a person is, the more likely that person will want to go beyond associating with people who are similar and associate with a diverse group of people.[94]

SUMMARIZING THE SIX UNIVERSAL FORMS OF INFLUENCE   If you know the six universal forms of influence, you are more likely to achieve the goals that you set out for yourself, your organizations, your communities, and the people who depend on you. Taking time to strategize how you will present your case to others can make the difference between gaining and losing the support you desire. Cialdini explains, "One more breath, a few more words, a carefully crafted request, and you can increase people's willingness to say yes."[95]

In addition, if you are aware of these forms of influence, you will be less likely to react mindlessly to other people's attempts to influence you. Remember that you are more likely to use cognitive shortcuts when you are under time pressure, during periods of uncertainty, when you lack critical information, and when you are feeling distracted, stressed, or tired. To avoid responding mindlessly to influence attempts, give yourself time before you make a decision so that you can (1) reduce ambiguity by gathering more information from multiple and diverse sources, (2) identify the actual merits of the case as well as alternative choices, (3) consider the costs and benefits of compliance, (4) use a systematic process for gathering information and making decisions, and (5) remember that you have the right to say "no" gracefully. Persuasion researcher Robert Levine warns that you should be particularly cautious when "the intensity of your reaction exceeds the seeming importance of the situation."[96] Levine also warns, "Be careful when the same people who want to fill your expectations are also in the business of creating them," noting that the same corporation that owns Ben and Jerry's luxury ice cream brand also owns the Slimfast diet brand.[97]

Finally, remember that ethical influence is based on *honestly* telling people what you want to accomplish, presenting the real merits of your case in a genuine way, and following through on

- *Reciprocation:* People feel obligated to pay back favors, gifts, and help that they receive from others. ("If you scratch my back, I'll scratch your back.").
- *Commitment/consistency:* People are more likely to agree with a request if they feel it is consistent with a commitment they have made (especially a commitment that they volunarily make publicly or write down) or a behavior they have taken in the past.
- *Authority:* People tend to obey people they perceive to be authorities and experts.
- *Social proof:* People are more willing to support an idea if they know that other people support it, especially if they perceive the other people to be similar to them.
- *Scarcity:* People tend to want what they believe is unique, rare, or in limited supply.
- *Liking:* People want to support the people they like, and they tend to like people they perceive as attractive or similar to them, people who are near them, people with whom they've shared positive experiences, and people who compliment them.

FIGURE 5-2   The Six Universal Forms of Influence
Adapted from: Cialdini, Robert. 2006. Influence: Science and Practice. New York: Harper.

your promises.[98] Robert Cialdini and Noah Goldstein explain the importance of ethically implementing the six universal forms of influence:

> It is imperative to stress that knowledge of the fundamental principles of social influence does not carry with it the right to use this information unscrupulously. In trying to persuade others, one can ethically point to the genuine expertise, accurate social validation, real similarities, truly useful favors, legitimate scarcity and existing commitments. Those who do attempt to dupe or to trap others into compliance are setting themselves up for a double-barreled whammy—by breaking the code of ethics and by risking getting caught—that can produce the disagreeable consequences of diminished self-concept and diminished future profit.[99]

DEVELOPING POLITICAL SAVVY

In 1920, Winston Churchill said, "Politics are almost as exciting as war, and quite as dangerous. In war you can be killed only once, but in politics many times."[100] Churchill's statement reflects how many people feel about organizational politics. Although some individuals and organizations follow the "kill or be killed" and "eat or be eaten" school of organizational politics, successful people engage in a more ethical and productive form of organizational politics that is based on building mutual support and that promotes organizational effectiveness as well as personal success.[101]

Political behavior in organizations refers to activities that (1) people engage in to influence important personal or organizational outcomes, (2) are not part of one's official job description, and (3) are not carried out through official and explicitly stated organizational policies and procedures.[102] Political behavior is often called "knowing the ropes," "working the system," and "greasing the wheel." When not taken to extremes and when used ethically to serve organizational and personal goals, political behavior in organizations enhances productivity. Many researchers argue that political behavior is an inevitable and desirable part of organizational life because it helps people get things done faster—and often better—than if they operated solely within the constraints of their official job descriptions and standard organizational procedures.[103] Furthermore, researchers have found that some forms of political behavior increase innovation in organizations.[104]

> Politically adept people recognize that they're at least 75 percent responsible for how others treat them.
> —KATHLEEN KELLY REARDON,
> *The Secret Handshake*

Job descriptions and standard procedures, while necessary and useful, share two limitations. First, they are rarely detailed or flexible enough to cover all the situations that employees must handle when navigating the complex and ambiguous realities of organizational life. Consequently, the most effective employees know that they sometimes must work outside official job descriptions and organizational procedures to get their work done to the best of their ability. Second, job descriptions and standard procedures are based on the assumptions that human beings always think and act rationally, that the environment will stay relatively stable over time, and that conflicts over goals and resources will be minimal. However, people are not rational despite their best intentions, change is a constant in most organizations, and multiple agendas and limited resources guarantee that conflict will always be an organizational reality.

Therefore, it should come as no surprise that people who understand the informal and unwritten rules in their organizations—and who are competent at their work—tend to be more successful than those who don't understand these rules.[105] Says one astute political player, "There's a formal set of rules and an informal set. You need to learn the informal set or you're only playing on half the court."[106]

In a *Business Week* article, MBA program graduates lamented that they received few, if any, lessons in business school about managing organizational politics and thus were caught unaware and unskilled when faced with the real world of organizations:

> Perhaps the loudest complaint was about just how ill-prepared alums felt when faced with the politics and challenges of managing in the middle. Many said they should have been forced to take more organizational behavior classes, though, "it's like trying to get someone to eat their spinach," concedes 40-year-old Charles W. Breer, . . . who has spent most of his post-MBA career working for Northwest Airlines Corp. [and is now with Delta Airlines]. Still, actual office politics—the tricky mix of sociology, personality, and corporate culture that exists in every workplace—can make a mockery of B-School theory. Breer says his hardest times were managing a 12-person staff. "At a minimum, I wish someone had told me this would be one of the biggest challenges, and then given me some tips," said Breer.[107]

Can you survive without understanding and engaging in organizational politics? Probably. Can you thrive without a general understanding and at least a limited engagement in organizational politics? Unlikely. As *Fortune* magazine says, "If you simply follow the rules, do your job well, and wait to be promoted, it could be a very long wait."[108] This view has been supported by substantial research.[109] If you choose to work only within the specific guidelines of your job and connect only with people who are directly related to your job, then you are most likely performing below your potential. If you are a manager, you also are inhibiting the performance of the people who work for you. Why? Because you may not have the influence you need to give the employees who work for you access to contacts, information, and resources that can help them do their job better and obtain the assignments, promotions, and salary increases they may desire.[110]

Because of the important role that political behavior plays in organizations, some organizations hire coaches to teach new high-potential employees how to use the informal organization to get their work done better and faster. Korn/Ferry International, the world's largest executive search firm, charges companies as much as $10,000 to teach new employees the ropes over an intensive six-week period. The *Wall Street Journal* reported that one of Korn/Ferry's biggest challenges is helping new employees answer the following question: "How can you champion enough change to justify your hiring—without rocking the boat so much that you endanger your latest gig? Failure to strike the right balance often derails newcomers. 'They push too hard, too fast, and do it in an undiplomatic way,' says Ben Dattner, a New York industrial psychologist. Rather than jump in . . . full speed ahead, it makes more sense to understand the kind of organizational culture you're working in, and then strategize accordingly."[111]

The rest of this chapter helps you understand which political strategies are likely to work, why they work, and how to avoid dysfunctional organizational politics. In the following sections, I discuss the characteristics of politically savvy people, as well as techniques for gaining political influence. I also discuss what managers can do to minimize dysfunctional organizational politics.

Characteristics of Politically Savvy People

Researcher Robert Sternberg in his book *Why Smart People Do Stupid Things*, likes to tell this story about Jack, a bully who delights in making others feel stupid, and Jack's target Irvin who subtly and cleverly achieves his own goals.[112]

> Jack, who considers himself smartest in his class, likes to make fun of Irvin, the boy he has identified as the stupidest in the class. Jack pulls aside his friend Tom and says, "You want to see what 'stupid' means, Tom? Watch this. Hey Irvin, here are two coins. Take whichever one you want. It's yours." Irvin looks at the two coins, a nickel and a dime, for a while and then selects the nickel. "Go ahead, Irv, take it, it's yours," Jack laughs. Irvin takes the larger coin and walks away. An adult who has been watching the transaction from a distance walks up to Irvin and gently points out that the dime is worth more than the nickel, even though it is smaller and that Irvin has just cost himself five cents. "Oh, I know that," replies Irvin. "But if I picked the dime, Jack would never ask me to choose between the two coins again. This way, he'll keep asking me again and again. I've already collected over a dollar from him, and all I have to do is keep choosing the nickel."

Jack thinks that he's clever and that he made a fool out of Irvin. However, Irvin is the wiser and more successful of the two—especially if his goal is to make money off of Jack's nasty desire to make Irvin look stupid. Irvin, more so than Jack, is a budding political player. People who have finely tuned political skills know how to conduct themselves in different situations so that they are more likely to achieve their goals. They certainly don't make other people feel stupid. They take time to read situations before jumping in. They know what they want to achieve and, with their goals in mind, they decide which battles to fight, which battles to avoid, and when to give in. They decide when to confront directly, when to be subtle, and when to back off completely. They know that timing matters.[113] Irvin may eventually let Jack know that he understands that the dime is worth more than the nickel, but not yet. He still wants to earn more money off of Jack's foolish attempt to be a bully.

A hallmark characteristic of political savvy people is that they focus on understanding people (their styles, needs, and wants) and situations and then use this knowledge to devise strategies that will help them advance themselves, others, and the organization. In her practical and engaging book, *The Secret Handshake: Mastering the Politics of the Business Inner Circle*, University of Southern California professor Kathleen Reardon explains: "The politically astute don't assume—they assess. They read each significant situation in terms of the benefits to those involved. They nurture a healthy skepticism regarding easy answers, and choose instead to study human nature. They are not casual observers; they are *professional* observers."[114]

A common misconception is that if you want to get ahead in your organization, you must sometimes engage in activities that are not consistent with your interests, talents, or values.

Savvy political actors realize that there are many ways to find opportunities to interact with others, build relationships, find common ground, get information, and be visible. Consequently, they do not feel constrained if they choose not to participate in certain activities. They realize that they don't have to play golf or tennis if they do not play the game, go out drinking if they don't want to, miss all of their children's soccer games, or participate in activities that may not be consistent with their interests or values. As Reardon explains,

> Politically astute people know there is more than one way to solve a problem; when one method doesn't work, they switch to another way. They know that there is more than one way to handle any situation. For every locked entrance, there is a back door, window—or even a chimney.

Because politically adept people have developed a broad range of political strategies for achieving their goals, they are not tied to simplistic assumptions about what they must do to achieve their goals. And if they ever do feel pressured to do something that is against their values, savvy political players are often in better shape than are others to leave the situation and find work environments in which they can thrive without compromising their fundamental values.

Politically savvy people draw on three sets of resources to achieve the goals they desire for themselves, others, and their organizations: personal, relational, and structural. Personal resources refer to characteristics that build one's reputation and credibility such as expertise, experience, education, job tenure, likability, and professional activity.[115] Relational resources refer to one's willingness and ability to create mutually supportive relationships with a broad and diverse group of people. Structural resources refer to one's formal position in the organizational hierarchy (e.g., hourly worker, manager, senior manager, and president) or informal position in important organizational networks.[116] Each of these resources is described in more detail in the following sections. As you read these sections, consider the many opportunities you have for enhancing your political influence in your organization.

Personal Power

The most savvy political players make sure that they have knowledge, skills, and experience that are valuable and visible to others. Harvard professor John Kotter advises, "The larger the achievement and the more visible it is, the more power the manager tends to develop."[117] Therefore, you will have more power in your organization if you are an expert in something that people need and if you show how your expertise adds significant value to the organization.[118]

Most of us know some people who spend so much time focusing on politicking and advancing their careers that they forget to focus on achieving measurable results and helping others as well. Gerry Roche, senior chairman of of the executive search and development firm Heidrick and Struggles International, explains:[119]

> I have 400 recruiters working for me here, and they're all trying to "get ahead." This one fellow goes off to a five-day conference on career development, and while he's there he doesn't bother to check his voice mail back at the office. And all week long a very big, important client is trying and trying to reach him and getting more and more frustrated. Finally, this client calls me, furious, and he says, "What's the deal with this guy?" So naturally when he gets back from his career-development conference, I call him into my office, and I explain it to him very carefully: "Stop worrying about your career, and return your damn phone calls."

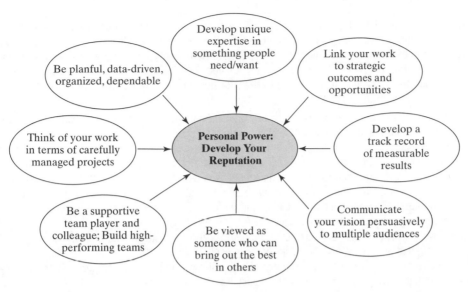

FIGURE 5-3   Personal Power: Develop Your Reputation

The lesson is this: Don't focus so much on getting ahead that you forget to take care of the business at hand and the people who depend on you to achieve their goals. If you are in a new position—whether it's a new job, a recent promotion, or a new assignment as a team or project leader—you'll want to build your reputation for having expertise that adds bottom-line value early. In his book *The First 90 Days: Critical Success Strategies for New Leaders at All Levels*, Harvard professor Michael Watkins advises readers to secure early wins with tangible and visible results. He says, "The best candidates [for early wins] are problems that you can tackle reasonably quickly with modest expenditure and that will yield visible organizational operational or financial gains. . . . Identify two or three key areas, at most, where you will seek to achieve rapid improvement."[120] Figure 5-3 summarizes the key areas you must focus on to build a personal reputation from which you can build your personal power. People with these characteristics are more likely to be seen as valuable in good times and bad times because they can be counted on to bring visible, meaningful, and measurable results to the organization, and they help others do so as well.

Relational Power

If you're one of the few experts at something that everyone needs, you're in a very good position indeed. And if you are socially skilled and invested in the success of others as well, you will be nearly irreplaceable.[121] Politically sophisticated people understand others and use this knowledge to develop mutually supportive relationships and draw on these relationships to achieve their personal and organizational goals.[122] They develop these relationships by strategically identifying and interacting with people who can help them achieve their goals and by communicating in ways that draw people toward them and toward their ideas.

Strategically Visiting People.   Savvy political players seem to have a "radar" that enables them to get themselves in the right place, at the right time, with the right people. But, as Reardon explains, "this radar comes from having done their homework. Before conferences and dinners, they find out who will be attending, and by the time the conference starts they know whom

<u>A word of warning</u>: You want to be sure that your expertise and reputation don't backfire. One of the biggest complaints I hear from very competent and results-oriented professionals is that their boss wants to keep them in their current position rather than promote them. Explicitly or implicitly, their boss is telling them, "I can't afford to lose you from your current position" or "You're a great individual contributor but I just don't see you as a leader." If you find yourself in this position, there are several ways to deal with your boss's resistance to promoting you.

- Help the boss find someone else who can perform your responsibilities so that you can be free to move ahead without leaving a gap in expertise in your current position.
- Ask your boss to tell you which specific steps you must take to get promoted to the next level. Ideally, you should get your boss to write down his or her advice, perhaps as part of your performance review, because your boss will want to behave consistently with what he or she commits to do in writing. For example, your boss may say that you need to demonstrate advanced technical skills, presentation skills, or leadership skills such as coaching and mentoring others, motivating others, leading teams, and navigating the political environment.
- Make sure that you let your boss and other influential people outside of your area know that you want to be promoted and that you want to take on new responsibilities.
- Be visible and create opportunities for interacting positively and cooperatively throughout the organization so that your name comes up when discussions of promotions are raised.
- Ensure that your boss and other influential people see you as someone with leadership potential rather than solely as an individual contributor. This means:
  - having relevant leadership (not only technical) skills; in other words, being able to create a context in which *others* can do their best work;
  - being seen as someone who possesses the characteristics that predict success, including conscientiousness (hard work and dependability); proactivity (a "can-do" attitude); interpersonal awareness; adaptability; social skills; and positive emotions, such as hope, optimism, and resilience;
  - being someone that other leaders in the organization know, understand, and are comfortable with—and breaking down any stereotypes they may have of you that may interfere with their ability to see you as someone with leadership potential; and
  - volunteering to lead projects, interact with customers and people outside of your unit, mentor newcomers in your area, and engage in other activities that demonstrate your leadership potential and enable you to increase your visibility throughout the organization.
- If you have done the above and you still cannot get promoted within your department or organization, you may have to leave your current job and get a new one through which you can build the reputation and opportunities that you want from the start.

FIGURE 5-4   Getting a Promotion: When Expertise Backfires

they'll try to arrange or 'strategically chance' to meet. A true mover and shaker works the room—any room—intelligently. While others are spinning their wheels, they're zeroing in on those they need to attract to their web of relationships."[123] Note, however, that Reardon warns that these relationships are effective "only to the extent that the people you're accessing consider you reliable, consistent, and professional."[124]

Says one successful employee, "I make myself get up from this desk a few times each day to visit with people. I always go in with something to ask or say of interest, and then I read the situation and decide how long to stay. I got ahead by doing this when other people wouldn't."[125] By visiting people outside her immediate work area, she learns about different parts of the organization, gains insight into other people's interests and skills, builds common ground, figures out how she can help others, gets visibility with key people, identifies who is likely to support and resist her, and gains support in case she may need it in the future.[126]

Communicating with Others.   Savvy political players communicate with others not only to give and get information, but to build relationships, make sense of situations, and promote their ideas in ways that increase the probability that their ideas will be understood and supported. They understand that each time they communicate with someone, they have an opportunity to build a relationship and deepen mutual commitment. Reardon explains, "Making valuable connections involves conveying to others a sense of having truly noticed them. . . . Politically adept people find something intriguing about each person they meet. . . . With the ones potentially helpful to them in the future, politically savvy are especially attentive. They ask questions of them, seek elaboration of their comments identify mutual interests about which they can comfortably converse, and express a good reason why they should share business cards to enable future interactions."[127]

Savvy political players also communicate in ways that help them make sense of situations. They listen to people with different points of view to get a well-rounded picture of a situation. They seek out opinions from senior executives, employees working on the front line, people from different departments, people outside of the organization with whom they interact on a regular basis, and customers who use the products or services they provide. By doing so, they not only get the information they need, but also build connections along the way. Researcher Michael Watkins suggests that when you get a new job or take on a new project, you visit people from many different areas inside and outside of the organization and ask them the same set of questions so that you can get a well-rounded view of the situation: "What are the biggest challenges this organization is facing (or will face) in the near future? Why is this organization facing (or going to face) these challenges? What are the most promising unexploited opportunities for growth? What would need to happen to exploit the potential of these opportunities? If you were me, what would you focus attention on?"[128]

Savvy political players also know that they must communicate their ideas in ways that other people will understand and support. Although they do not change the honest merits of their message, they do adapt the way they express these merits based on the interests of their audience. For example, they will emphasize a compelling vision of the future, bottom-line results, data-driven decisions, or concern for employees and customers depending on their audience's primary focus.

Structural Power

Location, location, location. Politically savvy people place themselves where they can have the greatest impact. They understand the complex web of relationships inside and outside of the organization, and they know that their ability to influence others is based, in part, on their location in this network of relationships. Some of this power comes from having a formal position in the organization (e.g., being a manager or director) that gives them control over information, decisions, and resources.[129] Much structural power comes not from where one sits in the organizational hierarchy, but rather where one places oneself in the informal social networks inside and outside of the organization.[130] Five avenues for gaining structural power are described subsequently: position, autonomy, criticality, centrality, and coalitions.

Position.   Power is associated with particular roles in organizations and thus is attributed to people hired into those roles. People at higher organizational levels have more official sources of power than people at lower levels because they can control resources that people value at lower levels of the hierarchy. For example, if you are a manager, then you can control important resources such as information and budgets, as well as important career benefits such as training opportunities, high-profile assignments, promotions, and salary increases. Furthermore, people in most societies are socialized to view hierarchical power as legitimate, so people are likely to listen to you because of the position you hold. Position power has two notable limits. First, your position gives you power with the employees who work for you, but it does not necessarily give you power to control resources and outcomes outside your immediate chain of command. Second, when you leave a position in which power is invested, you lose the power associated with that position as well (although you may still be respected for having held that position, particularly if you were competent and developed goodwill).[131]

Autonomy. People who work in positions that allow discretion over how, when, and where their work is done are more likely to be able to create opportunities in which they can leverage and showcase their skills, develop new talents, and interact and build relationships with many different kinds of people outside their own area who can offer them information, opportunities, and support. In contrast, people who work in a routine job that offers little autonomy, requires limited judgment, and provides few opportunities to develop new skills or interact with others are more easily replaced.[132]

Criticality. People who work on tasks that have a direct impact on organizational performance or that are critical links in the workflow are likely to have more influence than if they work on tasks that are perceived to be peripheral to organizational performance.[133]

Centrality. People who are central to important organizational networks have access to and control many organizational resources and are integral to the flow of information, funding, and other resources that other people need to achieve their goals. There are many ways in which you can increase your centrality. You can take a job that gives you control over resources that others need. You can place your office physically close to where things are happening so that you stay "in the know" and maintain visibility. You can get to know many people inside and outside of the organization and thus play an important role in linking people together, providing advice, offering support, and managing the information flow between people and places.[134]

> Never doubt that a small group of thoughtful, committed citizens can change the world. Indeed, it is the only thing that ever has.
> —MARGARET MEAD, *Anthropologist*

Coalitions. A coalition is an informal group of people who work together to promote issues that are important to them.[135] People in coalitions support each other's goals and provide information, resources, and connections that can make things happen for each other. These "influence networks" are particularly powerful when you need the support of people over whom you have no direct authority. Coalitions are also useful when the voice of one or a few people isn't enough to influence people who have the power to change the ways things are done. For example, if a few people in an organization say they want flextime, they may get little response. But if hundreds of people say they want flextime to be offered in the organization, they are more likely to get a response. A common mistake of new professionals and managers is that they spend too much time focusing up and down the organizational hierarchy and not enough time building coalitions with colleagues and other constituents who can help them achieve common goals over time.[136]

The main point to remember about developing personal, relational, and structural power is this: Your power is based, in large part, on your ability to control resources that are important to others. The more that people are dependent on your expertise, connections, and access to information and financial resources, the more power you have.[137] The less dependent you are on others to achieve your goals, the more choices and flexibility you have, and the more power you have. It's important to realize that people with power aren't necessarily the people with the most impressive job titles or the most visibility. The people who have the most power are those who have resources that other people need and want, regardless of their job title.

Remember that you must create *multiple* bases of power if you want to achieve the goals that are important to you, your organizations, your communities, and the people who depend on you. It is a mistake to become dependent on only a few sources of power. For example, a job that is critical to the organization today may be obsolete tomorrow. Expertise that is in demand today

Goals: Have you identified the goals you want to achieve for your unit, career, and life in general?

Personal influence:

- Do you have expertise that is valued by the organization?
- Do you have a track record of achieving results?
- What do you have that people want and need in order to achieve their goals?
- What can you do to increase your visibility? Consider volunteering for task forces and high-profile assignments, engaging in organizationally sponsored community services, participating in professional meetings, publishing articles (including publishing on the Internet and creating your own Web site), speaking up appropriately at meetings, giving presentations, meeting people in person rather than sending e-mails, helping others achieve their goals, and sending thank-you notes and congratulatory messages. Even seemingly insignificant things like wearing name tags or reintroducing yourself when you see someone you've met before ensures that people are more likely to remember your name.

Relational influence:

- *Strategic visits:* Have you identified whose support you need, as well as who is likely to support or resist you? Have you planned visits to these people to begin building mutually supportive relationships? Have you asked people how you can help them achieve their goals?
- *Strategic communication:* Have you identified people's styles, wants, and needs so that you can help them achieve their goals and describe the merits of your case in ways that are likely to gain their support?

Structural influence:

- *Position:* Do you have a hierarchical position that controls people's access to resources such as information, contacts, budgets, training and development opportunities, promotions, or salary increases?
- *Autonomy:* Can you build autonomy into your job so that you have more freedom in terms of where, when, and with whom you do your work?
- *Criticality:* Can you ensure that your job is perceived as critical to the workflow of the organization? Can you measure how your job contributes to important organizational outcomes? How many people are dependent on you to get their job done? Do you work in a unit that is central to organizational success? How specialized are the knowledge and skills required for your job? How easily can you and others in your unit be replaced? If your organization were in a crisis, would you be able to help it get out of that crisis?
- *Centrality:* Do people come to you for advice, to gain access to other people, or to gain access to other resources that help them accomplish their tasks? Can you increase your centrality to organizational networks by gaining control of information, expertise, connections, and other resources that people need to achieve their goals? Can you join projects and teams that are central to the organization's goals?
- *Coalitions:* What coalitions can you join and create to promote common interests?

Also remember to know several influence strategies and be able to use the strategies that are appropriate for the situation rather than your favored approach.

FIGURE 5-5 Increasing Your Political Power

may be old news six months from now. A mentor who supports you today may leave or be demoted. A reorganization in your workplace or industry can shift the configuration of your network and your place in it. Politically savvy people follow the sage and simple advice, "don't put all of your eggs in one basket."

Minimizing Dysfunctional Organizational Politics

Undoubtedly, some people are uncomfortable engaging in organizational politics—and sometimes for good reason. If taken too far, engaging in organizational politics can promote self-interest, distract people from their jobs, and become an end in itself. But engaging in organizational politics wisely and ethically can encourage innovation, increase flexibility, speed up decision making and implementation, build networks of mutually supportive relationships inside and outside of the organization, and help the organization adapt to an increasingly complex environment.

Although some political behavior is inevitable and desirable in organizations, excessive political behavior can result in dysfunctional behaviors that are unethical and disrupt effective organizational functioning. People who work in highly politicized organizations can spend too much time, energy, and resources engaging in self-protective political activity rather than focusing on serving customers, creating high-quality products, and enhancing shareholder value. Politically charged environments tend to be characterized by me-first thinking, lack of trust, divisiveness between people and groups, secretive decision-making processes, limited flow of information, fear of providing honest opinions and negative feedback, and unwillingness to help others. Consequently, highly politicized organizations tend to have less cooperation, flexibility, and innovation than organizations whose politics are kept in check.[138]

If you are a manager in a highly politicized organization (or if you want to prevent your organization from becoming dysfunctionally politicized), you can take steps to minimize dysfunctional political behaviors. Employees are more likely to engage in political behavior when organization goals and performance measures are uncertain, when organizational decision-making processes (including decisions about career advancement) are not transparent, when employees feel that they do not have inputs for decisions that affect them, and when trust in people and organizational processes is lacking.[139] You can minimize dysfunctional political behavior by doing the following:

- Provide clear goals, performance measures, and feedback so that employees stay focused on the task and can link their behavior to important organizational results.[140]
- Reward individuals and groups for achieving not only personal and unit results, but also overall organizational results.
- Provide clear guidelines for the attitudes and behaviors that can lead to promotions, salary increases, and other forms of career advancement.
- Provide training in how to demonstrate these attitudes and behaviors—and visibly promote people based on these characteristics.
- Use a systematic and transparent process for making important organizational decisions, including those about career advancement, and ensuring that employees understand how these decisions are made.
- Provide people with opportunities to participate in decision making, as well as with the information they need to make and implement effective decisions.
- Make it clear that dysfunctional political behavior will not be tolerated, especially excessive self-promotion, turf building, and other behaviors that harm other employees, departments, customers, shareholders, or the organizational goals.
- Encourage critical thinking and the reporting of bad news so that employees don't feel silenced by fear.

CONCLUSION

Some people are more adept at gaining and using power and influence than are others. However, what looks like natural talent or street smarts is the result of thoughtful and systematic day-to-day efforts designed to gain the willing support of others. Successful people know that they must translate their intelligence, expertise, and experience into resources that are of value to others. They know that power is not something they have, but rather something that they must nurture and grow every day through small acts that build trust and support. People who develop ethical and sustainable power know that people listen to them not because they *have* to but because they *want* to.

Regardless of your position in your organization, you have resources that you can draw on to gain the willing support of others so that you can be more effective and increase your career potential. Undoubtedly, some people are more inclined than others to seek out power and influence. But if you are in a managerial or leadership role, it is your responsibility—not a choice—to know how to influence others so that you can help the employees who depend on you achieve their goals.

> I'm no longer afraid of storms, for I am learning how to sail my own ship.
> —LOUISA MAY ALCOTT, *Author*

Remember that both the politically naïve and the politically abusive can self-destruct, one with a whimper and the other with a bang. People who are politically naïve assume that they don't have power and aren't aware of the many resources that they have to offer, so they don't try to influence others. Consequently, they are unlikely to achieve their potential because their skills, efforts, and contributions tend to go unnoticed and unappreciated. In addition, they are unable to fully support their staff who need their boss's influence and political sophistication to achieve their goals. People who are politically abusive treat people as adversaries rather than allies, focus on getting rather than giving, want to be right rather than effective, and try to force or trick people into compliance rather than earn support through honest means. More often than not, their influence is short lived because they do not gain the sustained support they need to be successful in the long term. It's usually just a matter of time before their strategies backfire.

My hope is that by reading this chapter you can avoid falling into the trap of political naïveté or abuse. By using the strategies for gaining and using ethical, sustainable influence described in this chapter, you will be better able to gain and use power and influence ethically and wisely so that you can achieve the goals that are important to you, your organizations, your communities, and the people who depend on you.

Chapter Summary

Power refers to a person's willingness and ability to influence the attitudes, beliefs, and behaviors of others so that they are willing to support the goals that the person believes are important.

It is necessary only when there is real or potential conflict over interests, goals, or the means by which to achieve those interests or goals.

It is not a stable characteristic of a person or group. Rather, it must be actively sought and continuously replenished, is negotiated through relationships (to be powerful, you must have something the other person wants), and is situational because you may be powerful in one situation yet not in another.

People who have sustainable power—power that transcends a particular time, position, and place—communicate and behave in ways that convince people that

they are worth listening to, that their ideas have merit, and that their ideas will be mutually beneficial.

You need power and influence skills because you often must try to gain support from people over whom you have no official power. People who have well-developed power and influence skills, as well as competence and a track record of results, are better able to achieve goals that are important to them, their organizations, their communities, and the people who depend on them.

To have sustainable power that transcends a particular time, position, and place, you must (1) have a variety of resources to offer that people believe they need or want, (2) know many different strategies for gaining the support of others, and (3) adapt your strategies based on the situation.

You have many opportunities to influence others because human beings are boundedly rational. We all live in an uncertain world in which we can't predict the outcome of our decisions and rarely have enough information on which to make rational decisions nor can we remember and make sense of all the complex information that comes our way. People who are influential help others make sense of the environment and make decisions in ways that support their goals.

You are gaining and using power ethically when you explicitly tell people what you want to achieve and why; you put the interests of others and the organization at least equal to a your own interests and, when appropriate, are able to put others' interests ahead of your own; you treat everyone with respect, administer organizational policies and procedures fairly, and do not abuse anyone's rights or exploit people; you leave yourself reasonably open to be influenced by others; and you back your requests with supporting data.

Although people with sustainable power differ in many ways, they share much in common: they focus on achieving the goals that they believe are important; they are action-oriented and want to shape their environment; they are competent, dependable, and have the expertise required to do their job well; they do their homework and develop systematic strategies for gaining support; they are willing to use the informal organization that operates outside official policies, procedures, and chains of commands to achieve their goals; they are astute observers of human behavior and have solid social skills; they love information, are great listeners, and have an open mind; they realize that managing perceptions is at least as important as managing reality; they frame their requests in ways that don't change the merits of their case but that respect other people's point of view so that their ideas will be heard, understood, and supported; they are flexible in the ways that they think and act; although they continuously focus on their objectives, they are willing to be flexible about how they achieve them; and they have integrity.

The Social Styles model provides a useful framework for understanding your own behavioral preferences and the preferences of others. This model assumes that (1) we all have predictable and taken-for-granted ways of behaving, including how we make decisions, interact with others, and resolve conflicts; (2) if we understand our preferred styles as well as those of others, we can avoid some of the problems that arise from the misunderstandings, conflicts, and frustrations that can occur when people with different styles interact; and (3) we are more likely to influence others if we build relationships based on mutual understanding and respect. The Social Styles model focuses on two dimensions:

- *Assertive/probing:* This refers to whether a person prefers to assertively push his or her ideas forward quickly (assertive) or quietly draw ideas out from other people or from careful analysis of data (probing).
- *Low responsiveness/high responsiveness:* This refers to whether a person emphasizes rationality, objectivity, and task-focus (low responsiveness) or emotional expression, intuition, and relationships (high responsiveness).

On the basis of these two dimensions, a person's social style can usually be categorized into one of the four categories: driver (assertive/low responsiveness), expressive (assertive/high responsiveness), amiable (probing/high responsiveness), and analytic (probing/low responsiveness). You can use this model to understand other people, how other people may perceive you, how you and others may act under stress, and how you can influence people with each of the different styles.

Although human beings differ in many ways, we all share some fundamental human needs. People who understand these common needs and help people fulfill these are more likely to be successful in their attempts to influence others. Social psychologist Robert Cialdini says, "Persuasion works by appealing to a limited set of deeply rooted human needs, and it does so in predictable ways." According to Cialdini, there are six universal forms of influence:

- *Reciprocation:* People feel obligated to pay back favors, gifts, and help that they receive from others.
- *Commitment/consistency:* People are more likely to agree with a request if they feel it is

consistent with a commitment they have made (especially a commitment that they make publicly or write down) or a behavior they have taken in the past.

- *Authority:* People tend to obey people they perceive to be authorities and experts.
- *Social proof:* People are more willing to support an idea if they know that other people support it, especially if they perceive the other people to be similar to them.
- *Scarcity:* People tend to want what they believe is unique, rare, or in limited supply.
- *Liking:* People want to support the people they like. People tend to like people they perceive to be attractive, people they believe to be similar to them in important ways, people with whom they have positive interactions, people they are near, and people who flatter them.

These forms of influence work because they act as cognitive shortcuts that help us bypass more complicated and costly decision-making processes. We are more likely to use cognitive shortcuts under particular conditions: when we are confused, uncertain, surprised, faced with too little or too much information, or feeling pressured, as well as when we trust the person requesting our support. "Triggers" tend to set these cognitive shortcuts in motion.

Much of the time responding automatically to cognitive shortcuts serve us well, but sometimes it doesn't. If you know the six universal forms of influence and are mindful of the triggers that set them in motion, not only will you be more influential than someone who is unaware of them but you will also be less likely to be on automatic pilot—and be an easy target—when someone tries to influence you.

Each of these forms of influence can be used ethically or unethically. Ethical persuaders ask themselves, "How can I genuinely present the *honest* merits of my case in a way that is more likely to gain compliance?" They never provide false information or artificially inflate the merits of their case. They do not pretend to be authorities or experts if they are not. They do not engage in false flattery. They do not promise what they cannot deliver.

To avoid responding mindlessly to influence attempts, give yourself time before you make a decision so that you can (1) reduce ambiguity by gathering more information from multiple and diverse sources, (2) identify the actual merits of the case as well as alternative choices, (3) consider the costs and benefits of compliance, (4) use a systematic process for gathering data and making decisions, and (5) remember that you have the right to say "no" gracefully.

Political behavior in organizations refers to activities that (1) people engage in to influence important personal or organizational outcomes, (2) are not part of one's official job description, and (3) are not carried out through official and explicitly stated organizational policies and procedures.

Political behavior in organizations can enhance productivity, innovation, flexibility, and speed when not taken to extremes and when used ethically to serve organizational, as well as personal, goals because it helps people go beyond the constraints of their official job descriptions and standard operating procedures.

If taken too far, engaging in organizational politics can promote self-interest, distract people from their jobs, create fear and self-protecting behaviors, promote divisiveness between people and groups, limit the flow of information, and foster an unwillingness to help others. Consequently, highly politicized environments tend to have less cooperation, flexibility, and innovation than organizations in which politics are used to promote the greater good rather than self-interest alone.

Employees are more likely to engage in dysfunctional political behavior when organizational goals and performance measures are uncertain, when organizational decision-making processes (including decisions about career advancement) are not transparent, when employees feel that they do not have input into decisions that affect them, and when trust in people and organizational processes is lacking.

You can minimize dysfunctional political behavior by providing clear goals, performance measures, and feedback; rewarding individuals and groups for achieving not only personal and unit results, but also overall organizational results; providing clear guidelines for the attitudes and behaviors that can lead to promotions, salary increases, and other forms of career advancement; providing training in how to demonstrate these attitudes and behaviors—and visibly promoting people on the basis of these characteristics; using a systematic and transparent process for making important organizational decisions; providing people with opportunities to participate in decision making, as well as with the information they need to make and implement effective decisions; making it clear that dysfunctional political behavior—self-promotion, turf building, and other behaviors that harm other employees, departments, customers, shareholders, or the organizational goals—will not be tolerated; and encouraging critical thinking and communicating bad news so that employees don't feel silenced by fear.

Using political skills ethically adds value to organizations. If you choose to work only within the specific guidelines of your job and connect only with people who are directly related to your job, then you are most likely performing below your potential. If you are a manager, you also are inhibiting the performance of the people who work for you because you may not have the influence you need to give the employees who work for you access to contacts, information, and resources that can help them do their job better and obtain the assignments, promotions, and salary increases they may desire.

Politically savvy people draw on three sets of resources to achieve the goals they desire for themselves, others, and their organizations: personal, relational, and structural. Personal resources refer to characteristics that build one's reputation and credibility such as expertise, experience, education, job tenure, likability, and professional activity. Relational resources refer to one's willingness and ability to communicate with and strategically create mutually supportive relationships with a broad and diverse group of people. Structural resources refer to one's position in the organizational hierarchy, job autonomy, job criticality, job centrality, and membership in coalitions.

The main point to remember about developing personal, relational, and structural power is this: Your power is based, in large part, on your ability to control resources that are important to others. The more that people are dependent on your expertise, connections, and access to information and financial resources, the more power you have. The less dependent you are on specific others to achieve your goals, the more choices and flexibility you have.

Remember that you must create *multiple* bases of power if you want to achieve the goals that are important to you, the people who depend on you, and the organizations and societies to which you belong. It is a mistake to become dependent on only a few sources of power.

Some people are more adept at gaining and using power and influence than are others. However, what looks like natural talent or street smarts is the result of thoughtful and systematic day-to-day efforts designed to gain the willing support of others. They know that power is not something they have, but rather something that they must nurture and grow every day through small acts that build trust and support. People who develop ethical and sustainable power understand that people listen to them not because they *have* to but because they *want* to.

BOX 5-2   Social Styles

Used with permission of *Leadership Development Associates*, Canton, GA, 770-479-8643.

Directions

Please respond to each statement in the survey on how well it describes the person you are assessing (or yourself). On a scale of "1" to "7," circle the number that best fits the person you are describing (This could be yourself or someone else). Try to use the ratings of "1" and "7" only in exceptional cases.

As a guide:

"1" means that I have never or rarely observed this behavior in this individual."4" means that I have observed this behavior to an average extent."7" means that I have observed this behavior very often or always.

Of course, you may use the other ratings:

"3" and "2" represent varying degrees between average and little.
"5" and "6" represent varying degrees between average and often.

To start, please check one of the following to indicate your work relationship with the person you are assessing.

☐ You are the person named   ☐ This person reports to you   ☐ Other
☐ You report to this person   ☐ This person is your peer

This person

1. Tends to focus on immediate goals and objectives	**1.**	1	2	3	4	5	6	7
2. Is detailed-oriented	**2.**	1	2	3	4	5	6	7
3. Sees the big picture	**3.**	1	2	3	4	5	6	7
4. Comes across in a friendly manner	**4.**	1	2	3	4	5	6	7
5. Is organized	**5.**	1	2	3	4	5	6	7
6. Makes friends quickly	**6.**	1	2	3	4	5	6	7
7. Is talkative	**7.**	1	2	3	4	5	6	7
8. Usually makes quick decisions	**8.**	1	2	3	4	5	6	7
9. Is spontaneous	**9.**	1	2	3	4	5	6	7
10. Is trusting	**10.**	1	2	3	4	5	6	7
11. Is methodical	**11.**	1	2	3	4	5	6	7
12. Is conscious of time	**12.**	1	2	3	4	5	6	7
13. Prefers facts and logic to opinion and instinct	**13.**	1	2	3	4	5	6	7
14. Is very considerate of others	**14.**	1	2	3	4	5	6	7
15. Has a lively imagination; thinks creatively	**15.**	1	2	3	4	5	6	7
16. Prefers to make decisions without consulting others	**16.**	1	2	3	4	5	6	7
17. Prefers to work alone	**17.**	1	2	3	4	5	6	7
18. Is very cooperative and easy to work with	**18.**	1	2	3	4	5	6	7
19. Likes being the center of attention	**19.**	1	2	3	4	5	6	7
20. Aggressively pursues goals	**20.**	1	2	3	4	5	6	7
21. Opinion and feeling enter into decision-making process	**21.**	1	2	3	4	5	6	7

(continued)

BOX 5-2 *Continued*

22. Is deliberate in making decisions	**22.**	1	2	3	4	5	6	7
23. Expresses strong opinions	**23.**	1	2	3	4	5	6	7
24. Can be very impatient	**24.**	1	2	3	4	5	6	7
25. Is loyal to friends and organization	**25.**	1	2	3	4	5	6	7
26. Likes to have all the facts before making a decision	**26.**	1	2	3	4	5	6	7
27. At times makes snap decisions	**27.**	1	2	3	4	5	6	7
28. Likes to be in control	**28.**	1	2	3	4	5	6	7
29. Has a warm and pleasant personality	**29.**	1	2	3	4	5	6	7
30. Is persuasive	**30.**	1	2	3	4	5	6	7
31. Does not allow emotion to influence decisions	**31.**	1	2	3	4	5	6	7
32. Weighs ideas and suggestions carefully	**32.**	1	2	3	4	5	6	7
33. In pursuit of goals can come across as uncaring	**33.**	1	2	3	4	5	6	7
34. Takes a personal interest in people	**34.**	1	2	3	4	5	6	7
35. Is open to new ideas or change	**35.**	1	2	3	4	5	6	7
36. At times appears deep in thought	**36.**	1	2	3	4	5	6	7
37. Can be loud or even boisterous	**37.**	1	2	3	4	5	6	7
38. Likes facts and figures and bottom-line results	**38.**	1	2	3	4	5	6	7
39. Takes things seriously, does not "kid around"	**39.**	1	2	3	4	5	6	7
40. Is easy to get along with	**40.**	1	2	3	4	5	6	7
41. Is articulate; gets right to the point	**41.**	1	2	3	4	5	6	7
42. Tends to be quiet and reserved	**42.**	1	2	3	4	5	6	7
43. Thinks and expresses self in broad terms	**43.**	1	2	3	4	5	6	7
44. Is very tolerant and forgiving	**44.**	1	2	3	4	5	6	7
45. Conforms to change	**45.**	1	2	3	4	5	6	7
46. Is perceptive in "reading" a situation	**46.**	1	2	3	4	5	6	7
47. Takes a practical approach	**47.**	1	2	3	4	5	6	7
48. Can be stubborn	**48.**	1	2	3	4	5	6	7
49. Is competitive	**49.**	1	2	3	4	5	6	7
50. Seeks accommodation to resolve or avoid conflict	**50.**	1	2	3	4	5	6	7
51. Is business-like	**51.**	1	2	3	4	5	6	7
52. Finds it difficult to admit error	**52.**	1	2	3	4	5	6	7
53. Easily adapts to change	**53.**	1	2	3	4	5	6	7
54. Can be blunt at times	**54.**	1	2	3	4	5	6	7
55. Is insightful	**55.**	1	2	3	4	5	6	7
56. Easily voices opinions	**56.**	1	2	3	4	5	6	7
57. Is a reasonable person	**57.**	1	2	3	4	5	6	7
58. Likes to argue the point	**58.**	1	2	3	4	5	6	7
59. Is tactful	**59.**	1	2	3	4	5	6	7
60. Reacts defensively to negative feedback	**60.**	1	2	3	4	5	6	7
61. Respectful towards others	**61.**	1	2	3	4	5	6	7
62. Finds it difficult to concede to other person's views	**62.**	1	2	3	4	5	6	7
63. Tends to be critical of others	**63.**	1	2	3	4	5	6	7
64. Not quick to accept change	**64.**	1	2	3	4	5	6	7
65. Is very resourceful	**65.**	1	2	3	4	5	6	7
66. Usually sees things in black or white; right or wrong	**66.**	1	2	3	4	5	6	7
67. Tends to blame others for own shortcomings	**67.**	1	2	3	4	5	6	7
68. Looks for compromise to resolve issues	**68.**	1	2	3	4	5	6	7

BOX 5-2   *Continued*

Scoring—Part One

Enter the rating for each item 1 through 44 in the corresponding numbered spaces in the columns below

I	**II**	**III**	**IV**
1. _____	3. _____	2. _____	4. _____
8. _____	7. _____	5. _____	6. _____
12. _____	9. _____	11. _____	10. _____
16. _____	15. _____	13. _____	14. _____
20. _____	19. _____	17. _____	18. _____
24. _____	23. _____	22. _____	21. _____
28. _____	27. _____	26. _____	25. _____
31. _____	30. _____	32. _____	29. _____
33. _____	35. _____	36. _____	34. _____
38. _____	37. _____	39. _____	40. _____
41. _____	43. _____	42. _____	44. _____

TOTALS _____ _____ _____ _____

(Add or subtract   (−2)   (+1)   (+2)   (−6)
to total)

Net Total _____ _____ _____ _____

Place totals from each column in the
appropriate quadrant.

Interpreting Your Style

The quadrant having the highest score is your dominant style. The quadrant with the lowest score is your least used style. A tie score in two or more quadrants indicates equal dominance in those styles.

III_____	I_____
ANALYTICAL	DRIVER
IV_____	II_____
AMIABLE	EXPRESSIVE

(continued)

BOX 5-2 *Continued*

Scoring—Part Two—Versatility Scale

Now enter the ratings for items 45 through 68 in the appropriate spaces in Columns A and B

Column A	Column B
45._____	48._____
46._____	49._____
47._____	52._____
50._____	54._____
51._____	56._____
53._____	58._____
55._____	60._____
57._____	62._____
59._____	63._____
61._____	64._____
65._____	66._____
68._____	67._____

TOTALS _____   _____

Total each column and enter the sum for each in the space provided. Calculate the net difference between the sums. If the sum of column A is greater than the sum of column B, plot the net difference in the left side of the scale. For example, if A is greater than B by 15 points, draw an arrow at the number 15 just below the word "High" on the left side of the scale. If column B is greater than column A by a net difference of 15, then place an arrow pointing at 15 on the right side of the scale. People with high versatility are more likely to be able to "read" and adapt to different social styles.

35 ___ 30 ___ 25 ___ 20 ___ 15 ___ 10 ___ 5 ___ 0 ___ 5 ___ 10 ___ 15 ___ 20 ___ 25 ___ 30 ___ 35

High   Moderate   Low

Food for Thought

1. Identify someone whom you believe has sustainable, ethical influence. What does this person do to develop and maintain power and influence? If possible, interview this person and ask (1) how they've developed influence and (2) what advice they can offer you for gaining sustainable, ethical influence.

2. Identify three sources of power that you have and when they are useful. Identify three sources of power that you

need to develop to have an even greater positive impact on your environment.

3. On the basis of the Social Styles Assessment, identify your primarily Social Style. Then, answer the following questions: (1) What kind of work environment brings out the best in me? (2) What strengths do I bring to the workplace (and how can I leverage those strengths)? (3) What weaknesses do I bring to the workplace (and how can I

manage those weaknesses)? (4) If someone wanted to influence me, how would they do so (e.g., what words or phrases would they use)? (5) What words or phrases would not influence me? (6) What song reflects my style?

4. Identify a person that you want to influence.

   a. Using the Social Styles model, identify that person's dominant style, identify three strategies that you will use to try to influence this person, and develop a plan of action for implementing these strategies. Review your progress after one week, then again at one month. Did you get the support you wanted? Why or why not?

   b. On the basis of the six universal forms of influence, identify three strategies that you will use to try to influence this person and develop a plan of action for implementing these strategies. Review your progress after one week, then again at one month. Did you get the support you wanted? Why or why not?

5. Over the next few days, watch commercials and read advertisements, and identify as many of the six universal forms of influence that you can (reciprocity, authority, scarcity, social proof, commitment and consistency, and liking).

6. Consider the last time you did something you didn't want to do. Why did you do it? Were you influenced by any of the six universal forms of influence? Could you have resisted the influence better if you had understood your susceptibility to these forms of influence? List at least four things you can do to protect yourself from being mindlessly influenced by others.

7. Think about someone with whom you have a difficult relationship, yet whose support you need now or may need in the future. Identify at least three strategies for building mutual trust and respect in the relationship, and develop a plan of action for implementing these strategies. Review your progress after one week, then again at one month. Is the relationship better after implementing these strategies than it was in the past? What did you gain by taking steps to improve the relationship?

8. Likability is one of the most powerful forms of influence. List at least five ways you can make yourself more likable to others. Remember that people are drawn to people who make them feel good and away from people who make them feel bad about themselves. Consider that attractiveness, positive interactions, proximity, perceived similarity, and genuine compliments build attraction.

9. If you are currently working in an organization, identify at least six steps you can take to increase your political influence in the next six months.

10. Imagine that you and a colleague are both interested in obtaining a high-profile assignment. In general, you have the same set of skills, same educational background, and have been with the organization for the same amount of time. On the basis of what you've learned in this chapter, what can you do to increase the probability that you will get the assignment?

Endnotes

1. Hill, Linda. 1995. "Power Dynamics in Organizations." *Harvard Business School Case Note*, 9-494-083, March 22.

2. Breland, Jacob, Darren Treadway, Allison Duke, and Garry Adams. 2007. "The Interactive Effect of Leader–Member Exchange and Political Skill on Subjective Career Success." *Journal of Leadership and Organizational Studies*, 13(3): 1–14; Ferris, Gerald, Darren Treadway, Pamela Perrewe, Robyn Brouer, Ceasar Douglas, and Sean Lux. 2007. "Political Skill in Organizations." *Journal of Management*, 33(3): 290–320.

3. Perrewe, Pamela, Kelly Zellars, Gerald Ferris, Ana Maria Rossi, Charles Kacmar, and David Ralston. 2004. "Neutralizing Job Stressors: Political Skill as an Antidote to the Dysfunctional Consequences of Role Conflict Stressors." *Academy of Management Journal*, 47: 141–152; Hochwater, Wayne, Gerald Ferris, Mark Gavin, Pamela Perrewe, Angela Hall, and Dwight Frink. 2007. "Political Skill as Neutralizer of Felt Accountability—Job Tension Effects on Job Performance Ratings; A Longitudinal Investigation." *Organizational Behavior and Human Decision Processes*, 102(2): 226–239.

4. Fry, Prem S. 2004. "Protecting the Quality of Life of Older Adults." *Geriatric Times*. July/August, Vol. II, http://www.cmellc.com/geriatrictimes/g010719.html; Krause, Neale, and Benjamin Shaw. 2000. "Role-Specific Feelings of Control and Mortality." *Psychology and Aging*. American Psychological Association, http://apa.org/journals/pag/pag 154617.html

5. Sutton, R., and Kahn, R. L. 1984. "Prediction, Understanding, and Control as Antidotes to Organizational Stress. In J. Lorsch (ed.). *Handbook*

of Organizational Behavior. Boston, MA: Harvard University Press; Sauter, S., J. Hurrell, and C. Cooper (eds.). 1989. *Job Control and Worker Health.* New York: Wiley.

6. Lublin, Joann. 2003. "Women Fall Behind When They Don't Hone Negotiation Skills." *Wall Street Journal.* November: B1.

7. Hill, Linda. 1995. "Power Dynamics in Organizations." *Harvard Business School Case Note*, 9-494-083, March 22; French, John R., and Bertram Raven. 1959. "The Bases of Social Power." In Dorwin Cartwright (ed.). *Studies in Social Power.* Ann Arbor, MI: University of Michigan Institute for Social Research, 159–167; Tushman, Michael T. 1977. "A Political Approach to Organizations: A Review and Rationale." *Academy of Management Review*, 2: 206–216.

8. Pfeffer, Jeffrey. 1977. "Power and Resource Allocations in Organizations." In Barry Staw and Gerald Salancik (eds.). *New Directions in Organizational Behavior.* Chicago, IL: St. Clair Press, 235–266.

9. Fiol, C. Marlene, Edward J. O'Connor, and Herman Aguinis. 2001. "All for One and One for All? The Development and Transfer of Power Across Organizational Levels." *Academy of Management Review*, 26(2): 224–242.

10. Tedeschi, James. 1974. "Attributions, Liking, and Power." In Ted Huston (ed.). *Foundations of Interpersonal Attraction.* New York: Academic Press, 193–215; DeLuca, Joel R. 1999. *Political Savvy: Systematic Approaches to Leadership Behind-the-Scenes.* Berwyn, PA: Evergreen Business Group; Reardon, Kathleen Kelley. 2001. *The Secret Handshake: Mastering the Politics of the Business Inner Circle.* New York: Currency.

11. Cavanaugh, Gerald, Dennis J. Moberg, and Manuel Velasquez. 1981. "The Ethics of Organizational Politics." *Academy of Management Review*, 6(3): 363–373.

12. Kotter, John. 1985. *Power and Influence.* New York: Free Press; Pfeffer, Jeffrey. 1992. *Managing with Power: Politics and Influence in Organizations.* Boston: Harvard Business School Press; DeLuca, Joel R. 1999. *Political Savvy: Systematic Approaches to Leadership Behind-the-Scenes.* Berwyn, PA: Evergreen Business Group.

13. March, James, and Herbert Simon. 1993. *Organizations.* 2nd ed. Oxford: Blackwell; March, James. 1994. *A Primer on Decision Making: How Decisions Happen.* New York: Free Press.

14. Langer, Ellen. 1978. "Rethinking the Role of Thought in Social Interactions." In H. Harvey, W. Ickes, and R. Kidd (eds.). *New Directions in Attribution Research.* Vol 2. Hillsdale, NJ: Erlbaum, 35–50; Reardon, Kathleen Kelley. 2001. *The Secret Handshake: Mastering the Politics of the Business Inner Circle.* New York: Currency.

15. Levine, Robert. 2003. *The Power of Persuasion: How We're Bought and Sold.* Hoboken, NJ: John Wiley and Sons.

16. Kotter, John. 1977. "Power, Dependence and Effective Management." *Harvard Business Review.* July/August: 125–136; Pfeffer, Jeffrey. 1992. *Managing with Power: Politics and Influence in Organizations.* Boston, MA: Harvard Business School Press.

17. Pfeffer, Jeffrey. 1992. *Managing with Power: Politics and Influence in Organizations.* Boston, MA: Harvard Business School Press.

18. Bennis, Warren, and Burt Nanus. 1985. *Leaders.* New York: Harper and Row.

19. Kotter, John. 1977. "Power, Dependence and Effective Management." *Harvard Business Review.* July/August: 125–136.

20. Ferris, Gerald, Darren Treadway, Pamela Perrewe, Robyn Brouer, Ceasar Douglas, and Sean Lux. 2007. "Political Skill in Organizations." *Journal of Management*, 33(3): 290–320.

21. Reardon, Kathleen Kelley. 2001. *The Secret Handshake: Mastering the Politics of the Business Inner Circle.* New York: Currency.

22. Kanter, Rosabeth. 1984. *The Change Masters: Innovation and Entrepreneurship in the American Corporation.* New York: Touchstone Books; cited in Reardon, Kathleen Kelley. 2001. *The Secret Handshake: Mastering the Politics of the Business Inner Circle.* New York: Currency, 204.

23. Stapleton, R., P. L. Nacci, and J. T. Tedeschi. 1973. "Expertise Power Interpersonal Attraction and the Reciprocation of Benefits." *Journals of Personality and Social Psychology*, 27(2): 199–205; French, John R., and Bertram Raven. 1959. "The Bases of Social Power." In Dorwin Cartwright (ed.). *Studies in Social Power.* Ann Arbor, MI: University of Michigan Institute for Social Research, 150–167.

24. Reardon, Kathleen Kelley. 2001. *The Secret Handshake: Mastering the Politics of the Business Inner Circle.* New York: Currency.

25. Becker, Thomas E. 1998. "Integrity in Organizations: Beyond Honesty and Conscientiousness." *Academy of Management Review*, 23(1): 154–161.

26. Alessandra, Tony, Michael O'Connor with Janice Van Dyke. 1994. *People Smarts: Bending the Golden Rule to Give Others What They Want*. San Francisco, CA: Jossey Bass; Alessandra, Tony, and Michael O'Connor. 1996. *The Platinum Rule: Discover the Four Basic Business Personalities and How They Can Lead You to Success*. New York: Warner Books; Merrill, David, and Roger Reid. 1999. *Personal Styles and Effective Performance*. New York: CRC Press; Social Styles Survey. *Leadership Development Associates*. Canton, GA, (800) 258-5987; Caproni, Paula. 2003. *Enhancing Productivity through Relationships*: The Social Style Model. Teaching Note.

27. Reardon, Kathleen Kelley. 2001. *The Secret Handshake: Mastering the Politics of the Business Inner Circle*. New York: Currency.

28. Douglas, Eric F. 2001. *Straight Talk: Turning Communication Upside Down for Strategic Results at Work*. 2nd ed. Sacramento, CA: LRI Publishing, 60–61.

29. Cialdini, Robert B. 2001. "Harnessing the Science of Persuasion." *Harvard Business Review*. October: 72–79; Cialdini, Robert B. 2001. *Influence: Science and Practice*. Needham Heights, MA: Allyn and Bacon, 47.

30. Cialdini, Robert B. 2001. *Influence: Science and Practice*. Needham Heights, MA: Allyn and Bacon.

31. Levine, Robert. 2003. The *Power of Persuasion: How We're Bought and Sold*. Hoboken, NJ: John Wiley and Sons; Cialdini, Robert B. 2001. *Influence: Science and Practice*. Needham Heights, MA: Allyn and Bacon; P. Worchel, and B. McCormic. 1963. "Self-concept and Dissonance Reduction." *Journal of Personality*, 31: 588–599.

32. Cialdini, Robert B. 2001. *Influence: Science and Practice*. Needham Heights, MA: Allyn and Bacon, x, 9.

33. Ibid., p. 235.

34. Langer, Ellen, A. Blank, and B. Chanowitz. 1978. "The Mindlessness of Ostensibly Thoughtful Action: The Role of 'Placebic' Information in Interpersonal Interaction." *Journal of Personality and Social Psychology*, 36: 635–642; cited in Cialdini, Robert B. 2001. *Influence: Science and Practice*. Needham Heights, MA: Allyn and Bacon, 4.

35. Kilbourne, Jean. 1999. *Deadly Persuasion*. New York: Free Press, 127; cited in Levine, Robert. 2003. The *Power of Persuasion: How We're Bought and Sold*. Hoboken NJ: John Wiley and Sons, 18.

36. Cialdini, Robert. 1999. "Of Tricks and Tumors: Some Little-Recognized Costs of Dishonest Use of Effective Social Influence." *Psychology and Marketing*, 16(2): 91–99.

37. Gouldner, Alvin. 1960. "The Norm of Reciprocity: A Preliminary Statement." *American Sociological Review*, 25: 161–178.

38. Fromm, Erich. 1956. *The Art of Loving*. New York: Harper, 48; cited in James T. Tedeschi. 1974. "Attributions, Liking, and Power." In Huston, Ted Huston (ed.). *Foundations of Interpersonal Attraction*. New York: Academic Press, 193–215.

39. Levine, Robert. 2003. The *Power of Persuasion: How We're Bought and Sold*. Hoboken, NJ: John Wiley and Sons, 66; citing Dennis Regan. 1971. "Effects of a Favor and Liking on Compliance." *Journal of Experimental Social Psychology*, 7: 627–639.

40. "Eminent Opinions on Woman Suffrage." *The Women's Suffrage Cookbook*. 1886. Published in Aid of the Festival and Bazaar, Boston, December 13–19: 146.

41. Agence France-Presse. 2003. "Repaying a Debt of Gratitude." *South China Morning Post*. October 13: A8.

42. Westphal, James, and Michael Clement. 2008. "Sociopolitical Dynamics in Relations between Top Managers and Security Analysts: Favor Rendering, Reciprocity, and Analyst Stock Recommendations." *Academy of Management Journal*, 51(5): 873–897.

43. "Favors to Wall Street Analysts Can Help Stock Ratings, McCombs Professor Says." McCombs School of Business Press Release, August 14, 2007. http://www.mccombs.utexas.edu/news/pressreleases/clement_res07.asp

44. Tedlow, Richard. 2006. *Andy Grove: The Life and Times of an American Icon*. New York: Penguin Group.

45. Useem, Michael. 1998. *The Leadership Moment: Nine True Stories of Triumph and Disaster and Their Lessons for Us All*. New York: Random House.

46. Lander, Mark, and Peter Baker. August 4, 2009. "In Release of Journalists, Both Clintons Had Key Roles." http://www.nytimes.com/2009/08/05/world/asia/05korea.html

47. Cialdini, Robert B. 2001. *Influence: Science and Practice*. Needham Heights, MA: Allyn and Bacon.

48. Lublin, Joann. 2003. "Women Fall Behind When They Don't Hone Negotiation Skills." *Wall Street Journal*. November: B1.

49. Cialdini, Robert B. 2001. "The Power of Persuasion." *Executive Briefings: Strategies for the*

Competitive Edge. Mill Valley, CA: Kantola Productions.

50. Cialdini, Robert B. 2001. "Harnessing the Science of Persuasion." *Harvard Business Review*. October: 72–79.

51. "Cirque Dreams Big." 2003. *Newsweek*. July 14: 42–44.

52. Ibid.

53. Daspin, Eileen. 2003. "The T-Shirt You Can't Get." *Wall Street Journal*. October 10: W1 and W10.

54. Milgram, Stanley. 1969. *Obedience to Authority*. New York: Harper and Row.

55. Levine, Robert. 2003. The *Power of Persuasion: How We're Bought and Sold*. Hoboken, NJ: John Wiley and Sons; citing J. Cooper, E. Bennett, and H. Sukel 1996. "Complex Scientific Testimony: How Do Jurors Make Decisions?" *Law and Human Behavior*, 20: 379–394.

56. Cialdini, Robert B. 2001. *Influence: Science and Practice*. Needham Heights, MA: Allyn and Bacon, 77.

57. Festinger, Leon. 1957. "A Theory of Social Comparison Process." *Human Relations*, 7: 117–140.

58. Ali, Mir, and Debra Dwyer. 2010. "Social Network Effects in Alcohol Consumption Among Adolescents." *Addictive Behaviors*, 35: 337–342.

59. Goldstein, Noah, Robert B. Cialdini, and Vladas Griskevicius. 2008. "A Room with a Viewpoint: Using Social Norms to Motivate Environmental Conservation in Hotels." *Journal of Consumer Research*, 35: 613–624.

60. Levine, Robert. 2003. The *Power of Persuasion: How We're Bought and Sold*. Hoboken, NJ: John Wiley and Sons.

61. Staw, Barry. 1976. "Knee-deep in the Big Muddy: A Study of Escalating Commitment to a Chosen Course of Action." *Organizational Behavior and Human Performance*, 16: 27–44.

62. Ibid.

63. Freedman, J. L., and S. C. Fraser. 1966. "Compliance without Pressure: The Foot in the Door Technique." *Journal of Personality and Social Psychology*, 4: 195–202.

64. Cialdini, Robert B. 2001. "Harnessing the Science of Persuasion." *Harvard Business Review*. October: 72–79.

65. Cialdini, Robert B. 2001. "Harnessing the Science of Persuasion." *Harvard Business Review* October: 72–79.

66. Ibid.

67. Levine, Robert. 2003. The *Power of Persuasion: How We're Bought and Sold*. Hoboken, NJ: John Wiley and Sons, 186.

68. Goldstein, Noah, Steve J. Martin, and Robert Cialdini B. 2008. *Yes! 50 Scientifically Proven Ways to Be Persuasive*. NY: Free Press. See esp. p. 82.

69. Berscheid, Ellen, and Elaine Hatfield. 1978. *Interpersonal Attraction*. 2nd ed., New York: Random House, 22.

70. Berscheid, Ellen, and Elaine Walster. 1974. "A Little Bit About Love." In Ted Huston (ed.). *Foundations of Interpersonal Attraction*. New York: Academic Press, 355–381; Walster, Elaine, and G. W. Walster. 1976. "Interpersonal Attraction." In Bernard Seidenberg and Alvin Snadowsky (eds.). *Social Psychology: An Introduction*. New York: Free Press, 276–308.

71. Levine, Robert. 2003. *The Power of Persuasion: How We're Bought and Sold*. Hoboken, NJ: John Wiley and Sons, 54.

72. Lott, Albert, and Bernice Lott. 1974. "The Role of Reward in the Formation of Positive Interpersonal Attitudes." In Ted Huston (ed.). *Foundations of Interpersonal Attraction*. New York: Academic Press, 174–192.

73. Jidd, K. J., and J. S. Lockard. 1978. "Monetary Significance of the Affiliative Smile." *Bulletin of Psychonomic Society* 11: 344–346; cited in Pfeffer, Jeffrey. 1992. *Managing with Power: Politics and Influence in Organizations*. Boston. MA: Harvard Business School Press.

74. Lynn, M., and M. McCall. 1998. "Beyond Gratitude and Gratuity." Unpublished manuscript. Ithaca, NY: Cornell University, School of Hotel Administration; cited in Cialdini, Robert B. 2001. *Influence: Science and Practice*. Needham Heights, MA: Allyn and Bacon; Rind, Bruce, and Prashant Bordia. 1996. "Effect of Restaurant Tipping of Male and Female Servers Drawing a Happy, Smiling Face on the Backs of Customers' Checks." *Journal of Applied Social Psychology*, 26(3): 218–225; cited in Cialdini, Robert, and Noah Goldstein. 2002. "The Science and Practice of Persuasion." *Cornell Hotel and Restaurant Administration Quarterly*, 43(2): 40–50.

75. Rosenblatt, Paul. 1974. "Cross-Cultural Perspective on Attraction." In Ted L. Huston (ed.). *Foundations of Interpersonal Attraction*. New York: Academic Press, 79–95.

76. Tedeschi, James. 1974. "Attributions, Liking, and Power." In Ted L. Huston (ed.). *Foundations of Interpersonal Attraction*. New York: Academic Press, 193–212.

77. Ibid.

78. Le Gaipa, J. J. 1974. "Testing a Multidimensional Approach to Friendship." In Steve Duck (ed.). *Theory and Practice in Interpersonal Attraction*. London: Academic Press, 249–270.

79. Lott, Albert J., and Bernice B. Lott. 1974. "The Role of Reward in the Formation of Positive Interpersonal Attraction." In Ted L. Huston (ed.). *Foundations of Interpersonal Attraction*. New York: Academic Press, 171–189.

80. Razran, G. H. S. 1938. "Conditioning Away Social Bias by the Luncheon Technique." *Psychological Bulletin*, 35: 693; cited in Cialdini, Robert B. 2001. *Influence: Science and Practice*. Needham Heights, MA: Allyn and Bacon, 167.

81. Berscheid, Ellen, and Elaine Hatfield. 1978. *Interpersonal Attraction*. 2nd ed. New York: Random House, 34.

82. Byrne, Donn. 1971. *The Attraction Paradigm*. New York: Academic Press; Tim Emswiller, Kay Deaux, and Jerry E. Willits. 1971. "Similarity, Sex, and Requests for Small Favors." *Journal of Applied Social Psychology*, 1: 284–291.

83. Byrne, Donn, and Gerald L. Clore. 1967. "A Reinforcement Model of Evaluative Responses." *Personality: and International Journal*, 1: 103–128; Tajfel, H., and Turner J. "The Social Identity Theory of Intergroup Behavior." In Worchel, S., and W. G. Austin (eds.). 1986. *The Psychology of Intergroup Relations*. Chicago, IL: Nelson-Hall, 7–24; Tsui Ann, Terri Egan, and Charles O'Reilly. 1992. "Being Different: Relational Demography and Organizational Attachment." *Administrative Science Quarterly*, 37: 549–579.

84. Kelvin, Peter. 1977. "Predictability, Power and Vulnerability." In Steve Duck (ed.). *Theory and Practice in Interpersonal Attraction*. London: Academic Press, 355–378.

85. Fawcett, Christine, and Lori Markson. 2010. "Similarity Predicts Liking in 3-Year-Old Children." *Journal of Experimental Child Psychology*, 106(4): 345.

86. Kolodinsky, R. W., Treadway, D. C., and Ferris, G. R. 2007. "Political Skill and Influence Effectiveness: Testing Portions of an Expanded Ferris and Judge (1991) model." *Human Relations*, 60: 1747–1777.

87. Tedeschi, James. 1974. "Attributions, Liking, and Power." In Ted L. Huston (ed.). *Foundations of Interpersonal Attraction*. New York: Academic Press, 193–212.

88. Flynn, Francis, Chatman, Jennifer, and Sandra Spataro. 2001. "Getting to Know You: The Influence of Personality on Impressions and Performance on Demographically Different People in Organizations." *Administrative Science Quarterly*, 46: 414–442.

89. Cialdini, Robert B. 2001. "Harnessing the Science of Persuasion." *Harvard Business Review*. October: 72–79.

90. Brass, Daniel, and Marlene E. Burkhardt. 1993. "Potential Power and Power Use: An Investigation of Structure and Behavior." *Administrative Science Quarterly*, 36(3): 441–470.

91. Dutton, D. G. 1972. "Effect of Feedback parameters on Congruency versus Positivity Effects in Reactions to Personal Evaluations." *Journal of Personality and Social Psychology*, 24: 366–371.

92. Shrauger, J. S. 1972. "Response to Evaluation as a Function of Initial Self-Perception." *Psychological Bulletin*, 82: 581–596.

93. Regan, D. T. 1971. "Effects of a Favor and Liking on Compliance." *Journal of Experimental Social Psychology*, 7: 627–639; cited in Tedeschi, James. 1997. "Attributions, Liking, and Power." In Ted L. Huston (ed.). *Foundations of Interpersonal Attraction*. New York: Academic Press, 193–212.

94. Goldstein, J. W., and H. Rosenfeld. 1969. "Insecurity and Preference for Persons Similar to Oneself." *Journal of Personality*, 37: 253–268; Berscheid, Ellen, and Elaine Hatfield. 1978. *Interpersonal Attraction*. 2nd ed. New York: Random House, 89.

95. Cialdini, Robert B. 2001. "The Power of Persuasion." *Executive Summaries: Strategies for the Competitive Edge*. Mill Valley, CA: Kantola Productions.

96. Levine, Robert. 2003. *The Power of Persuasion: How We're Bought and Sold*. Hoboken, NJ: John Wiley and Sons, 241.

97. Ibid., 238.

98. Cialdini, Robert B. 2001. "Harnessing the Science of Persuasion." *Harvard Business Review* October: 72–79.

99. Cialdini, Robert B., and Noah Goldstein. 2002. "The Science and Practice of Persuasion." *Cornell Hotel and Restaurant Administration Quarterly*, 43(2): 40–50.

100. Witt, L. Alan. 2003. "Influences of Supervisor Behaviors on the Levels and Effects of Workplace Politics." In Lyman Porter, Harold L. Angle, and Robert W. Allen (eds.). *Organizational Influence Processes*. Armonk, New York: M.E. Sharpe, 209–228.

101. Pfeffer, Jeffrey. 1992. *Managing with Power: Politics and Influence in Organizations*. Boston, MA: Harvard Business School Press; Kotter, John. 1977. "Power, Dependence and Effective Management." *Harvard Business Review*. July/August: 125–136; DeLuca, Joel R. 1999. *Political Savvy: Systematic Approaches to Leadership Behind-the-Scenes*." Berwyn, PA: Evergreen Business Group; Reardon, Kathleen Kelley. 2001. *The Secret Handshake: Mastering the Politics of the Business Inner Circle*. New York: Currency.

102. Ibid.

103. Pfeffer, Jeffrey. 1981 "Management as Symbolic Action: The Creation and Maintenance of Organizational Paradigms." In Larry L. Cummings and Barry M. Staw (eds.). *Research in Organizational Behavior*, Greenwich, CT: JAI Press, 1–52; Schein, V. (ed.). 1977. "Individual Power and Political Behavior." *Academy of Management Review*, 2: 64–72.

104. Kanter, Rosabeth. 1983. The Change Masters: Innovations and Entrepreneurship in the American Corporation. New York: Simon and Schuster; Ibarra, Herminia. 1993. "Network Centrality, Power and Innovation Involvement: Determinants of Technical and Administrative Roles." *Academy of Management Journal*, 36: 471–501; Frost, Peter, and Carolyn Egri. 1991. "The Political Process of Innovation." In Lawrence L. Cummings and Barry M. Staw (eds.). 1991. *Research in Organizational Behavior*. 13: Greenwich, CT: JAI Press, 229–295.

105. Pfeffer, Jeffrey. 1992. *Managing with Power: Politics and Influence in Organizations*. Boston, MA: Harvard Business School Press; Reardon, Kathleen Kelley. 2001. *The Secret Handshake: Mastering the Politics of the Business Inner Circle*. New York: Currency; Kanter, Rosabeth Moss. 1979. "Power Failure in Management Circuits." *Harvard Business Review*. July/August: 65.

106. Reardon, Kathleen Kelley. 2001. *The Secret Handshake: Mastering the Politics of the Business Inner Circle*. New York: Currency.

107. Merritt, Jennifer with Kate Hazelwood. 2003. "What's an MBA Really Worth?" *Business Week*. September 17: 90.

108. Stewart, Thomas. 1997. "Get with the New Power Game." *Fortune*. January 13: 58–59; Pfeffer, Jeffrey. 1992. *Managing with Power: Politics and Influence in Organizations*. Boston, MA: Harvard Business School Press.

109. Brass, Daniel, and Marlene Burkhardt. 1993. "Potential Power and Power Use: An Investigation of Structure and Behavior." *Academy of Management Journal*, 36(3): 441–471; Kipnis, David, Stewart Schmidt, and Ian Wilkinson. 1980. "Intraorganizational Influence Tactics: Explorations in Getting One's Way." *Journal of Applied Psychology*, 65: 440–452.

110. Kanter, Rosabeth. 1979. "Power Failures in Management Circuits." *Harvard Business Review*, 57: 65–75.

111. Lublin, Joann. 2003. "Women Fall Behind When They Don't Hone Negotiation Skills." *Wall Street Journal*. November: B1.

112. Sternberg, Robert. 2002. *Why Smart People Can Be So Stupid*. New Haven, CT: Yale University Press.

113. Pfeffer, Jeffrey. 1992. *Managing with Power: Politics and Influence in Organizations*. Boston, MA: Harvard Business School Press.

114. Reardon, Kathleen Kelley. 2001. *The Secret Handshake: Mastering the Politics of the Business Inner Circle*. New York: Currency, 95.

115. Ibarra, Herminia. 1993. "Network Centrality, Power and Innovation Involvement: Determinants of Technical and Administrative Roles." *Academy of Management Journal*, 36: 471–501.

116. Ibid.

117. Kotter, John. 1977. "Power, Dependence and Effective Management." *Harvard Business Review*. July/August: 125–136.

118. French, John R., and Bertram Raven. 1959. "The Bases of Social Power." In Dorwin Cartwright (ed.). *Studies in Social Power*. Ann Arbor, MI: University of Michigan Institute for Social Research, 150–167.

119. Stewart, Thomas. 1997. "Get with the New Power Game." *Fortune*. January 13: 58–59.

120. Watkins, Michael. 2003. *The First 90 Days: Critical Success Strategies for New Leaders at All Levels*. Boston, MA: Harvard Business School Press, 93.

121. Pfeffer, Jeffrey. 1992. *Managing with Power: Politics and Influence in Organizations*. Boston, MA: Harvard Business School Press.

122. Ferris, Gerald, Darren Treadway, R. Kolodinsky, W. Hockwarter, C. Kacmar, C. Douglas, and D. Frink. 2005. "Development and Validation of the Political

Skills Inventory." *Journal of Management*, 31: 126–152.

123. Reardon, Kathleen Kelley. 2001. *The Secret Handshake: Mastering the Politics of the Business Inner Circle*. New York: Currency, 77.

124. Ibid., 78.

125. Ibid., 63.

126. Watkins, Michael. 2003. *The First 90 Days: Critical Success Strategies for New Leaders at All Levels*. Boston, MA: Harvard Business School Press; Reardon, Kathleen Kelley. 2001. *The Secret Handshake: Mastering the Politics of the Business Inner Circle*. New York: Currency.

127. Reardon, Kathleen Kelley. 2001. *The Secret Handshake: Mastering the Politics of the Business Inner Circle*. New York: Currency, 79.

128. Watkins, Michael. 2003. *The First 90 Days: Critical Success Strategies for New Leaders at All Levels*. Boston, MA: Harvard Business School Press, 46.

129. French, John R., and Bertram Raven. 1959. "The Bases of Social Power." In Dorwin Cartwright (ed.). *Studies in Social Power*. Ann Arbor, MI: University of Michigan Institute for Social Research, 150–167.

130. Ibarra, Herminia. 1993. "Network Centrality, Power and Innovation Involvement: Determinants of Technical and Administrative Roles." *Academy of Management Journal*, 36: 471–501.

131. Brass, Daniel. 1984. "Being in the Right Place: A Structural Analysis of Individual Influence in Organizations." *Administrative Science Quarterly*, 29: 518–553; French, John R., and Bertram Raven. 1959. "The Bases of Social Power." In Dorwin Cartwright (ed.). *Studies in Social Power*. Ann Arbor, MI: University of Michigan Institute for Social Research, 150–167.

132. Kanter, Rosabeth. 1979. "Power Failure in Management Circuits." *Harvard Business Review*. July/August 65–75; Reardon, Kathleen Kelley. 2001. *The Secret Handshake: Mastering the Politics of the Business Inner Circle*. New York: Currency.

133. Pfeffer, Jeffrey. 1992. *Managing with Power: Politics and Influence in Organizations*. Boston, MA: Harvard Business School Press; Freeman, L. C. 1979. "Centrality in Social Networks: Conceptual Clarification." *Social Networks*, 1: 215–239; Brass, Daniel, and Marlene Burkhardt. 1993. "Potential Power and Power Use: An Investigation of Structure and Behavior." *Academy of Management Journal*, 36(3): 441–471; Ibarra, Herminia. 1993. "Network Centrality, Power and Innovation Involvement: Determinants of Technical

and Administrative Roles." *Academy of Management Journal*, 36: 471–501.

134. Freeman, L. C. 1979. "Centrality in Social Networks: Conceptual Clarification." *Social Networks*, 1: 215–239; Brass, Daniel, and Marlene Burkhardt. 1993. "Potential Power and Power Use: An Investigation of Structure and Behavior." *Academy of Management Journal*, 36(3): 441–471; Ibarra, Herminia. 1993. "Network Centrality, Power and Innovation Involvement: Determinants of Technical and Administrative Roles." *Academy of Management Journal*, 36: 471–501.

135. Robbins, Stephen. 2000. *Organizational Behavior*. 9th ed. Upper Saddle River, NJ: Prentice Hall; citing W. B. Stevenson, J. L. Pearce, and L. W. Porter. 1985. "The Concept of Coalition in Organizational Theory and Research." *Academy of Management Review*. April 10(2): 261–263; Watkins, Michael. 2003. *The First 90 Days: Critical Success Strategies for New Leaders at All Levels*. Boston, MA: Harvard Business School Press.

136. Watkins, Michael. 2003. *The First 90 Days: Critical Success Strategies for New Leaders at All Levels*. Boston, MA: Harvard Business School Press.

137. Pfeffer, Jeffrey, and Alison Konrad. 1991. "The Effects of Individual Power on Earnings." *Work and Occupation*, 18: 385–414.

138. Eisenhardt, Kathleen, and L. J. Bourgeous III. 1998. "Politics of Strategic Decision Making in High Velocity Environments: Toward a Mid-Range Theory." *Academy of Management Journal*, 31: 737–770.

139. Tushman, Michael E. 1977. "A Political Approach to Organization: A Review and Rationale." *Academy of Management Review*, 2: 206–216; Cobb, A. T. 1986a. "Informal Influence in the Formal Organization." *Group and Organizational Studies*, 11: 229–253; March, James, and Herbert Simon. 1958. *Organizations*. New York: Wiley. Pfeffer, Jeffreys. 1978. *Organizational Design*. Arlington Heights, IL: AHM Publishing; Robbins, S. E. 1976. *The Administrative Process: Integrating Theory and Practice*. Englewood Cliffs, NJ: Prentice-Hall; Madison, D. L., Allen, R. W., Porter, L. W., Renwick, P. A., and Mayes, B. T. 1980. "Organizational Politics: An Exploration of Managers' Perceptions." Human Relations, 33: 79–100; Eisenhardt, Kathleen, and L. J. Bourgeous III. 1998. "Politics of Strategic Decision Making in High Velocity Environments: Toward a Mid-Range Theory." *Academy of Management Journal*, 31:

737–770; Witt, L. Alan. 2003. "Influences of Supervisor Behaviors on the Levels and Effects of Workplace Politics." In Lyman Porter, Harold L. Angle, and Robert W. Allen (eds.). *Organizational Influence Processes*. Armonk, NY: M.E. Sharpe, 209–228.

140. Pfeffer, Jeffrey. 1978. *Organizational Design*. Arlington Heights, IL: AHM Publishing; cited in

Witt, L. Alan. 2003. "Influences of Supervisor Behaviors on the Levels and Effects of Workplace Politics." In Lyman Porter, Harold L. Angle, and Robert W. Allen (eds.). *Organizational Influence Processes*. Armonk, NY: M.E. Sharpe, 209–228.

6

■ ■ ■

Managing Relationships with Your Direct Reports, Bosses, and Peers

This chapter will help you:

- Understand how managing your relationships with your direct reports, bosses, and peers influences your effectiveness, as well as your career success and well-being.
- Understand how authority dynamics influence your relationship with your boss and direct reports.
- Create a context that empowers and motivates employees.
- Learn how organizational contexts can bring out the best and worst in employees.
- Improve your relationship with your boss, including a difficult boss.
- Enhance your mentoring and networking skills.
- Understand the importance of building high-quality connections and being viewed by others as an energizer in networks.
- Understand the role of impression management in everyday work life.

At the end of the day you bet on people, not strategies.

—LARRY BOSSIDY, *Former CEO of Allied Signal*

Decades of research on organizational effectiveness have led to the same conclusion: The quality of your relationships with direct reports, bosses, and peers has a significant impact on your work effectiveness, career success (in terms of promotions, salary increases, and job satisfaction), and personal well-being. For example, researchers have found the following:

- Social skills are a stronger predictor of executive success than are technical skills, and the need for social skills increases as one moves higher in the organizational hierarchy.[1]
- Employees' commitment to their supervisors is a stronger predictor of their productivity than is their commitment to their organization.[2]

- Employees in "high-quality, trusting relationships with managers" are likely to receive higher performance ratings than those who are not in such relationships.[3]
- People who are willing and able to understand other people's needs and adapt their behavior in response to other people's needs tend to get promoted more, receive higher salaries, and have more mentors than do those who don't do so.[4]
- People who have a strong network of relationships tend to live happier, healthier, and longer lives.[5]

Undoubtedly, investing in relationships with your direct reports, bosses, and peers is one of the most important things that you can do for yourself, others, and the organization. Indeed, if you are a manager, it's your job to manage your relationships proactively and systematically. After all, the manager's job is to get work done with and through others. But, it's not only managers who benefit from building high-quality relationships. Researchers have found that technical professionals who have strong networks tend to receive higher salaries than do technical employees who don't have strong networks.[6] This is not surprising because today's problems are too complex for even the smartest person to solve alone, and most jobs are designed to be interdependent with others. Unfortunately, many of us get so busy with the technical details of our day-to-day tasks that we don't invest enough time to build relationships with others who can help us become more effective.

In this chapter, we focus on developing high-quality relationships with your direct reports, bosses, and peers. Regardless of whether you are managing up, down, or sideways, remember the following two assumptions about human relationships:

- High-quality relationships are built on trust, respect, and reciprocity.
- We are all fallible human beings who depend on each other for our professional effectiveness, career success, and personal well-being.[7]

With these assumptions in mind, we move on to the rest of this chapter. We first focus on how we develop our attitudes toward boss–employee relationships and the consequences of these attitudes on our effectiveness. Next, we focus on strategies for managing your relationships with your direct reports and bosses. We then look at three skills (mentoring, networking, and impression management) that are useful regardless of whether we are managing up, down, or sideways.

AUTHORITY RELATIONS AT WORK

Despite all the talk about flattened organizations, participative management, and empowerment, hierarchy is alive and well in most work organizations today. Indeed, one of the most important lessons that effective managers learn is that their everyday behaviors get interpreted "through the lens of authority relations."[8] In other words, our assumptions about boss–employee relationships influence what (and who) we pay attention to, how we interpret what (and who) we attend to, and how we behave toward others. We develop our attitudes toward authority in at least two ways: our place in the organizational structure (e.g., whether we are in a boss or direct report role at work) and our personality (e.g., the attitudes about authority that we unconsciously develop early in our lives).

Organizational Structure and Authority Relations

Research suggests that people with lower power in the organization (e.g., your direct reports) tend to pay more attention to and develop more complex interpretations of the behavior of people who are higher than they are in the organizational hierarchy.[9] In contrast, bosses tend to pay less attention to individuals at lower hierarchical levels, develop relatively simplistic interpretations of their behavior, think less about individual differences among direct reports, and often don't realize how their behaviors affect those at lower hierarchical levels.[10] Direct reports' keen interest in their boss's attitudes, feelings, and behaviors is understandable because the boss has a significant impact on his or her direct reports' effectiveness, career development, job satisfaction, and psychological well-being. Certainly, direct reports have an impact on the boss's effectiveness, career development, and well-being, as well. However, as psychologist Marty Grothe, coauthor of *Problem Bosses: Who They Are and How to Deal with Them*, explains, when things go wrong in a relationship, "the person who has the least power will hurt more."[11]

Harvard researcher Linda Hill says that bosses tend to be particularly unaware of "how their everyday behaviors get scrutinized and amplified by subordinates" and how "seemingly insignificant actions can have broad consequences."[12] Picture the boss who calls an employee into his or her office without an explanation ("Smith, I'd like to see you in my office at 11:00 tomorrow morning."). Not knowing what to expect, Smith may imagine a variety of reasons for the meeting ("What did I do?" "Am I in trouble?" "Is there going to be a downsizing, and am I going to be laid off?"). The manager may have called Smith to the office to offer a promotion, challenging job assignment, or reward for a job well done. However, Smith may imagine at least some worst-case scenarios unless he or she is given information about the purpose of the meeting in advance. Although the manager probably won't give the meeting another thought until the next morning, Smith may lose a little sleep over the purpose of the meeting.

Although direct reports tend to have less official power than their boss, they also tend to underestimate how much the boss depends on them and how much power direct reports have in the relationship. Researchers who study power in organizations explain that all groups in an organizational hierarchy have power, albeit different kinds.[13] People at upper levels have the power to define the organization's reality (by setting the organization's direction, rules, policies, procedures, and quality standards). People at lower levels have the power to support or resist that reality (by offering or withholding support, psychologically or physically withdrawing from the organization, joining unions, and engaging in public protest). People at middle levels have the power to either bring the people at the lower and upper levels together or keep them apart, often by acting as filters for information and resources. Notably, the people in the middle may be invested in keeping those at upper and lower levels apart, because if people at upper and lower levels could figure out how to work directly and effectively with each other, the people at the middle level would lose a significant base of power. Indeed, the security of the people in the middle is often dependent on maintaining distance between people at upper and lower levels.

> Nobody is as powerful as we make them out to be.
> —ALICE WALKER,
> *In Search of Our Mother's Gardens*

In short, organizational structure creates psychological and physical boundaries within and between hierarchical groups and shapes the way people at lower, middle, and upper levels of the hierarchy try to exert their influence with those across hierarchical levels, as well as with customers and other external constituents. Researcher Bob Sutton likes to tell this story that he heard from Jason Zweig, a writer for *Money* magazine:[14]

Some years back, [Zweig] was standing behind an irate passenger at the check-in line in New York. Jason described how the passenger went on and on insulting the airline employee, and how impressed he was at her ability to remain cool, calm, and professional in the face of such abuse. Jason told me, and confirmed later over e-mail, that although it was years ago, "It is her words that have stuck forever in my memory: 'Oh, he's going to [L.A.], but his luggage is going to Nairobi'—and the faint but unmistakable firmness in her smile that made me realize, half with a chill and half with a thrill, that she wasn't kidding."

The point to remember here is this: It's wise to remember that where we sit in the organizational hierarchy influences how we think and act within our group and toward others, even though we may attribute our behavior and that of others to personality. The most successful managers understand how their own and others' place in the hierarchy influences perceptions and behavior. They then use this knowledge to develop more sophisticated interpretations of others' behavior and act more effectively in response.

Personality and Authority Relations

We develop our attitudes toward authority long before we enter the world of work, and we bring these attitudes into every boss–direct report relationship that we have.[15] Psychoanalysts argue that we develop our beliefs about authority through our experiences with our earliest authority figures—our parents and primary caretakers. These experiences influence our relationships toward authority figures throughout our lives primarily by unconsciously shaping our assumptions about the goodwill and dependability of authority figures. Researchers William Kahn and Kathy Kram describe three orientations toward authority:[16]

- *Interdependent.* If our primary caretakers are responsive toward our needs in our earliest years, we are likely to develop the belief that we are worthy of their goodwill and can depend on them to take care of us. Consequently, our attitudes toward authority figures will be that authority figures are likely to be trustworthy and dependable unless proven otherwise. Whether we are in the boss or employee role, we are likely to view the authority relationship as being built on mutual respect and responsibility ("We're in this together." "How can we help each other?"). Kahn and Kram argue that interdependent attitudes are likely to lead to the most effective and satisfying boss–employee relationships.

- *Dependent.* If our primary caretakers are inconsistent in their care of us (e.g., sometimes being accessible and caring, while at other times being distant and uncaring), we may develop the belief that we can sometimes count on authority figures and sometimes not. Because we see that our caretakers are able to care for us at least some of the time, we attribute their inconsistency not to their willingness or ability to take care of us but to our own worthiness. In other words, we believe it is our fault when the caretaker does not respond to us. Consequently, we spend much of our time and effort trying to win the caretaker's attention and affection. When we become adults, our attitude toward authority figures is likely to be one of dependence, and we will try to do whatever it takes to please authority figures to earn their goodwill and support. Whether we are in the boss or employee role, we will expect that the boss's job is to take care of the employee and the employee's job is to agree with and please the boss ("Whatever you say, boss." "The boss is always right.").

- *Counterdependent.* If our primary caretakers are psychologically or physically absent in our early years, we may develop the belief that we cannot depend on authority figures to take care of our needs and that we can only count on ourselves to get what we need in life. Consequently, as adults, we are likely to view authority figures as irrelevant or hurdles to overcome. Whether we are in the boss or employee role, we are likely to resist authority by assuming that the role of the boss is irrelevant and that the boss should stay out of their employees' way even when employees may need our support ("You can't count on the boss to get anything done." "You don't need the boss to help you accomplish your goals.").

Simply stated, we unknowingly bring our childhood attitudes toward authority into our roles as bosses and direct reports at work when we are adults. Because we see certain types of authority relations as "normal" (interdependent, dependent, or counterdependent), we are likely to act in ways that create the authority dynamics that we expect. For example, if we have a dependent attitude toward authority, then we are likely to act more help-less than we really are and expect our bosses to take care of us. When we are in the boss role, we are likely to encourage the people who work for us to be dependent on us, often by withholding important information, training, or material resources that would enable employees to become more independent.

> No one can make you feel inferior without your consent.
> —ELEANOR ROOSEVELT

If we have a counterdependent attitude toward authority, we are likely to reject the authority of our boss, which will further strain our relationship with the boss. When we are in the boss role, we are likely to dismiss our own authority and responsibility toward employees and not offer sup-port and assistance even when employees want and need our help. If we have an interdependent attitude toward authority, we are likely to act in ways that bring out the best in the boss–direct re-port relationship. These different orientations toward authority are illustrated in Figure 6-1.

In short, our personality and our place in the organizational hierarchy significantly shape what we notice, how we interpret what we notice, and how we behave toward our bosses and direct reports. To avoid falling into dysfunctional patterns of boss–employee relationships, remember the following:

- The boss–employee relationship is a partnership between two fallible human beings who are dependent on each other's expertise, support, and goodwill for their professional effec-tiveness, career success, and psychological well-being.[17]
- Our position in an organizational hierarchy (lower, middle, upper) and our childhood atti-tudes toward authority may pull us into unconscious and often misguided assumptions and behaviors that can undermine our effectiveness, as well as that of our bosses, our direct reports, and the organization.

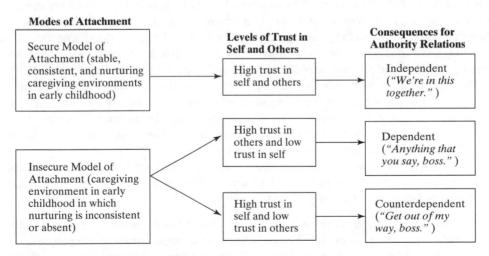

FIGURE 6-1 Authority Relations at Work
Source: Model based on Kahn, William, and Kathy Kram. 1994. "Authority at Work: Internal Models and Their Organizational Consequences." *Academy of Management Review*, 19(1): 17–50. Reprinted by permission of *Academy of Management Review*; Bernerth, Jeremy, and H. Jack Walker. 2009. "Propensity to Trust and the Impact on Social Exchange." *Journal of Leadership and Organizational Studies*, 15(3): 217–226; Simmons, Bret, Janaki Gooty, Debra Nelson, and Laura Little. 2009. "Secure Attachment: Implications for Hope, Trust, Burnout, and Performance." *Journal of Organizational Behavior*, 30: 233–247; Kahn, William, 2002. "Managing the Paradox of Self-Reliance." *Organizational Dynamics*, 30(3): 239–256.

- Both bosses and direct report have power in the relationship. Indeed, the higher we go in the organizational hierarchy, the more dependent we are on others to get our work done.

The best steps you can take to develop effective relationships with your bosses and direct reports are to develop an understanding and appreciation for authority relations at work; be aware of your own attitudes toward authority and how they influence your ability to have an effective relationship with your boss; learn strategies that are likely to enhance the quality of your relationship with your bosses and direct reports; and systematically apply these techniques in your everyday work life.

MANAGING AND MOTIVATING DIRECT REPORTS

You must genuinely like and respect those who are performing under your command, for neither the liking nor the respect can be successfully faked.
—BENJAMIN DAVIS

People tend to get promoted to managerial positions because they are excellent individual contributors. In other words, they are effective engineers, marketers, salespeople, teachers, nurses, social workers, and so on. They accomplish their day-to-day tasks thoughtfully, thoroughly, and quickly. But when they are rewarded with a promotion to a managerial position, they are often surprised that the skills that helped them succeed as individual contributors are insufficient for success in their managerial roles. They have to make the transition from getting jobs done themselves to getting the jobs done with and through others. They often find that their biggest challenges are forming effective work relationships with employees[18] and creating a work environment that enables the people who work for them to succeed.

When people are promoted to managerial positions, their immediate concern is "How do I motivate the people who work for me?" One of the most important lessons that you will learn in this chapter is that you cannot motivate anyone because people must motivate themselves. *Instead, your job is to create a work context in which people will be inspired and enabled to do their best work.* Be aware that creating a context for high performance doesn't necessarily mean spending more money. Rather, it means being aware of what drives people (e.g., meaning, belonging, competence, control, and consistency) and creating opportunities to enable them to fulfill these drives at work. Another critical lesson you will learn is that the direct manager or supervisor—not just top leadership or organizational culture—is one of the most important determinants of an employee's commitment and productivity.[19] In other words, if you are a manager, *you* can help your employees add value to the organization through your everyday actions even if you and your team don't have the complete support of your manager.

Although some managers struggle in the managerial role, others thrive. Consider the case of automotive supervisor Pat Kerrigan. The former public school psychologist and successful plant manager explains what being a manager means to her:

> I have to say I've never made a part in my life and I don't really have any plans to make one. That's not my job. My job is to create an environment where people who do make them can make them right, make them right the first time, can make them right at a competitive cost, and can do so with some sense of responsibility and pride in what they're doing. And I don't have to know how to make a part to do any of those things. . . . My role is supporting, enabling, and empowering.[20]

Paul Orfalea, founder and Chairperson Emeritus of Kinko's, echoes Kerrigan's view. The son of Lebanese immigrants, Orfalea is severely dyslexic, was frequently expelled from school, graduated eighth from the bottom of his high school class of 1,200 students, and barely made it through college. He admits that even today he cannot read very well, is not mechanically inclined, and hasn't quite figured out how a computer works. He began his business in 1970 in 100 square feet of space near the University of Southern California with a $5,000 loan, naming his business Kinko's after his boyhood nickname that referred to his curly hair. When Orfalea stepped down as CEO of Kinko's at age 52, he had a personal worth of $225 million, more than 23,000 employees, and a stellar reputation for corporate responsibility. Kinko's has been listed in *Fortune* magazine's 100 best companies in America, *Forbes* magazine's 500 biggest private companies, and *Working Mother* magazine's best companies for working mothers. He attributes his success to his passionate commitment to taking care of employees and customers, his ability to make the complex simple, and his drive to hire good people, give them what they need to serve the customers well, and then let them do their work.

What do effective managers like Pat Kerrigan and Paul Orfalea do to ensure that employees are both willing and able to perform at their best so that they can add value to the organization? Although they have different work styles, strengths, and weaknesses, they share the ability to create a work context that enables people to excel at their work. They understand that all people everywhere are driven by fundamental needs for meaning, belonging, competence, control, and consistency. They also understand that each person has his or her unique interests, needs, life situations, and definitions of success—and these must be attended to in order for the employee to feel committed to and effective in the organization.

In order to attend to employees' unique and changing needs, successful leaders are cognitively and behaviorally complex.[21] Rather than using one-size-fits-all management styles, they analyze problems from a variety of perspectives, determine the most appropriate management style for each situation, and adapt their behaviors accordingly. They can be inspirational visionaries and detail-driven policy makers, hands-off delegators and hands-on technical advisors, participative managers, and buck-stops-here decision makers—all depending on the needs of the situation.

In this section, I present two models of leadership that are based on the assumption that effective managers are able to diagnose the managerial style that is most appropriate for a given situation and adapt their management style to the needs of the situation so that they can bring out the best in others. The first model is Situational Leadership, created by Paul Hersey and Ken Blanchard. The second model is the Denison Leadership Development Model, created by Daniel Denison.

The Situational Leadership Model

Situational leadership is one of the most widely known employee-centered models of leadership. It has been used in training programs in more than 400 of the *Fortune* 500 companies, and more than one million managers have been exposed to it.[22] According to the Situational Leadership Model, the manager's goal is to develop employees so that the employees become increasingly competent and confident in their work and less dependent on the manager for technical and psychological support.[23] In short, Situational Leadership is about developing employees through appropriate degrees of delegation. To determine the appropriate delegation style to use, Hersey and Blanchard advise managers to focus on three criteria:

Don't be irreplaceable. If you can't be replaced, you can't be promoted.
—ANONYMOUS

- *Leadership style.* Effective managers develop employees by using both task-focused and relationship-focused behaviors. Task-focused behaviors reflect a "concern for production" (e.g., clearly stating task goals, procedures, policies, and performance measures).

Relationship-focused behaviors reflect a "concern for people" (e.g., praising people and showing personal concern).[24] Both task- and relationship-focused behaviors are essential to getting work done effectively and efficiently, although one or the other may be more appropriate at any given time, depending on the developmental level of the employee.

- *Employee readiness.* Employees must be both psychologically willing (be motivated and confident) and technically able (have the necessary skills, knowledge, and experience) to accomplish a task effectively and independently.[25] When an employee is doing a task for the first time, the employee may need to be told what to do, how to do it, and when to do it. The employee also typically requires training, assistance, and follow-up. As the employee becomes more confident and competent at performing the task independently, he or she needs less technical assistance (task-focused behaviors) and more encouragement (relationship-focused behaviors) to build confidence and independence.

- *The characteristics of the task.* Every task has its own demands. Each of us excels in some tasks, needs help in others, and resists some tasks altogether. For example, a professor may be very effective at research, but not very effective at teaching, or vice versa. An engineer may be very adept at writing technical reports but less able to convey his or her ideas in a compelling way when faced with a nontechnical audience. A salesperson may be excellent at getting orders from clients but less effective in filling the orders correctly and on time. Consequently, managers need to adapt their style on the basis of employees' willingness and ability to do a particular task.

In short, each employee has different developmental needs, and these needs change with the situation. If an employee is able and willing to effectively handle a task, the manager should offer the employee significant independence to do that task. If an employee is unable and unwilling to effectively handle a task, the manager should reduce the employee's independence on that task. Hersey and Blanchard describe four managerial styles, each based on employees' willingness and ability to accomplish a particular task.[26] Each style is most effective when matched to the needs of the situation.

- *Telling or directing.* This style is low on relationship-focused behaviors and high on task-focused behaviors (e.g., telling the employee what to do, how to do it, and when to do it, as well as closely supervising and following up on the employee's performance). This style is best used when an employee is lacking in specific skills and lacks the confidence or motivation to complete the specific task independently. This does not mean that the manager should offer no relationship-focused behaviors. However, these are secondary to task-focused behaviors. When an employee is unwilling and unable to do a task, the best way to boost that employee's motivation, confidence, and skill is to teach the employee how to do the job well. If a manager does not provide enough structure and direction, the employee is likely to flounder, perform substandard work, and lose confidence in his or her ability to perform the task.

- *Persuading or coaching.* This style is high on both task- and relationship-focused behaviors. This style is best used when an employee may have some relevant skills but still needs technical support and follow-up but is gaining in ability and motivation. At this point, the employee needs encouragement to maintain his or her confidence, particularly as the manager begins to encourage more independence.

- *Participating or supporting.* This style is low on task-focused behaviors and high on relationship-focused behaviors. This style is best used when an employee is experienced and capable with a particular task but lacks the confidence to complete the job successfully without help or psychological support from the manager. For example, an employee may be able to do an excellent job preparing and making a presentation to senior managers, but still wants the manager to attend the presentation for backup and to provide feedback after the presentation.

- **Delegating.** This style is low on both task- and relationship-focused behaviors. This style is best used when an employee is both willing and able to perform a particular task independently with no input or follow-up needed or wanted from the manager. Indeed, the employee may be more proficient at the task than the leader is. A manager's attempts to intervene by offering either technical or psychological support may be viewed by the employee as micromanaging or meddling.

How can you tell if the employee is willing and able to successfully complete a particular task?[27] To assess *ability*, find out whether the person has the necessary job knowledge. Does the person know what needs to be done, why it needs to be done, where to get appropriate resources and support, who should be involved, level of quality standards, and appropriate performance measures? Does the person have the skills and experience to successfully complete the project without supervision? Does the person tend to seek out help when needed? Does the person consistently show high levels of performance with this type of task? Remember that high performance in one type of task does not necessarily predict high performance in another. Does the person consistently meet deadlines? On basis of your responses, would you rate the person as high or low on ability to take on this task?

To assess *willingness*, determine whether the person shows the confidence and motivation to take on the responsibility for the task. Does the person proactively seek out accountability in terms of asking for deadlines, quality standards, and other performance standards? On the basis of your responses, would you rate the person as high or low on willingness and confidence to take on this task?

The simplicity and intuitive appeal of the Situational Leadership Model have contributed significantly to its becoming one of the most well-known and appreciated models used in management training. Some researchers have concluded that the model is useful for managing recently hired employees[28] and employees at low to moderate readiness levels,[29] but less useful for managing employees at high readiness levels. Researchers generally agree that the Situational Leadership Model is valuable because it reminds managers to avoid one-size-fits-all management styles, to adapt their styles to the needs of employees and the situation, to take advantage of opportunities to build direct reports' skills and confidence, and, most importantly, to take seriously their role as teachers and developers of others.

The Denison Leadership Development Model

On the basis of more than 25 years of research with more than 1,000 organizations and 40,000 individuals, researcher Daniel Denison concluded that effective managers are able to analyze situations from a variety of perspectives and adapt their behavior accordingly. Furthermore, they focus their attention on creating an organizational culture that inspires and enables high performance.[30] He argues that managers create effective organizational cultures by focusing on four critical areas: communicating a clear and engaging mission; ensuring consistency through clear policies, procedures, and norms; encouraging employee involvement; and promoting adaptability. He found that attention to these four areas has significant bottom-line results in terms of productivity, quality, profitability, and growth.

As you can see in Figure 6-2, effective managers focus on both the internal organization (consistency and employee involvement) and the external environment (mission and adaptability).

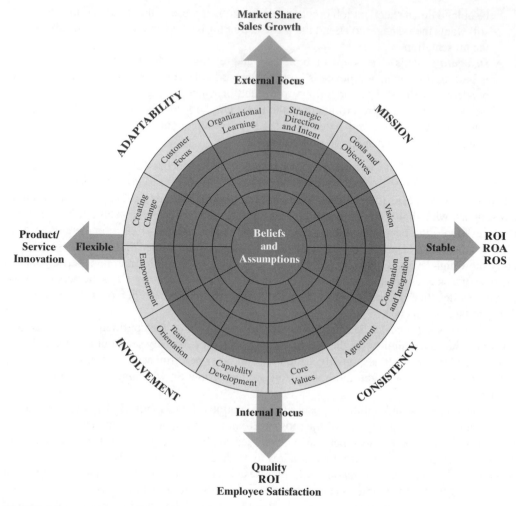

FIGURE 6-2 Denison Model: Linking Culture and Leadership to Performance
Source: Used with the permission of Daniel Denison and William Neale, creators of the Denison Leadership Development Survey. For a more in-depth look at the questions and to obtain an on-line analysis of your personal leadership style or organization culture, see www.denisonculture.com

They also promote both stability (mission and consistency) and change (employee involvement and adaptability). Each of the four critical areas is divided into three skills.

> **You manage things; you lead people.**
> —ADMIRAL GRACE MURRAY HOPPER, *U.S. Navy*

MISSION   Managers who communicate a clear and engaging mission know that people want purpose and meaning in their day-to-day work lives. A clear and engaging mission provides direction and makes the work worth doing. Effective managers know that every employee needs to see how he or she contributes to the organizational mission. The three skills associated with creating a clear and engaging mission are:

- defining strategic direction and intent by communicating the organization's long-term strategies to all employees so that everyone can see where the organization is headed, why it is going in that direction, and how they can help the organization get there;

- focusing on goals and objectives by articulating ambitious yet realistic goals, ensuring that employees know why these goals and objectives are important, and tracking progress against these goals so that employees can see the consequences of their efforts; and
- creating shared vision by promoting an engaging view of the organization's desired future state so that employees feel excited about the future and can see the link between short-term results and achieving the long-term vision.

CONSISTENCY Managers who promote consistency understand that employees need a sense of predictability and control in their day-to-day work lives. This is particularly important during times of change and when coordination across different parts of the organization is needed. Managers promote consistency by clearly communicating a set of values, methods for doing business, and a code of ethics that employees collectively use to support their day-to-day decisions and actions. By providing clear procedures, policies, values, and norms, effective managers promote a sense of predictability, control over the environment, a distinct way of doing business, and organization-wide coordination. The three skills associated with building consistency include:

- defining core values by clearly communicating the organizational values and living by those values;
- working to reach agreement among different people and parts of the organization by creating a cohesive culture, encouraging diverse opinions, supporting constructive conflict, and promoting win–win solutions; and
- managing coordination and integration by encouraging people from different parts of the organization to work together toward common organizational goals and providing a clear set of policies, procedures, and values to guide day-to-day decisions.

HIGH INVOLVEMENT Managers who create high-involvement work cultures understand that employees will be more likely to invest their energy in organizations in which they feel like they have some control, opportunities for personal development, and opportunities to make an impact on the organization. These managers emphasize employee participation, autonomy, and growth, which in turn enhance employees' sense of ownership in the organization and responsibility for the organization's success. The three skills associated with creating a high-involvement work environment include

> Remember that change is most successful when those who are affected are involved in the planning.
> —Warren Bennis, *Why Leaders Can't Lead*

- empowering others by sharing information, encouraging participation in organizational decisions, and enhancing employees' belief that they personally can make a difference in the organization;
- building a team orientation by encouraging teamwork (both within and across organizational units), cooperation toward common goals, and a sense of collective accountability for the achievement of goals; and
- developing organizational capability by investing in the ongoing development of employee knowledge and skills, delegating authority so that employees can use their skills to make and implement decisions, and viewing employees' capabilities as an important source of competitive advantage.

ADAPTABILITY Managers who promote adaptability know that an organization's growth and survival depends on its ability to align its internal policies, practices, and norms with the external environment. Consequently, effective managers pay attention to customers, competitors, and other critical constituents—and adapt their internal policies, practices, and norms in response. The three skills associated with promoting adaptability are:

- creating change by encouraging flexibility, responsiveness, continuous improvement, adaptability, and cooperation across organizational units;
- emphasizing customer focus by enabling all employees to attend to customer needs, understand what customers want, and respond quickly to customer input; and
- promoting organizational learning by encouraging and rewarding innovation and risk, seeing failure as opportunity for learning, and sharing learning across organizational units.

Through his research, Denison concluded that managers who are skilled at creating mission, consistency, high-involvement, and adaptability are likely to create organizational cultures that positively influence the bottom line. All four areas are positively correlated with return on assets. Mission and consistency tend to have a positive impact on financial performance measures, such as return on assets, return on investment, and return on sales. Consistency and involvement tend to have a positive impact on product and service quality (fewer defects, less rework, efficient use of resources), employee satisfaction, and return on investment. Involvement and adaptability tend to have a positive impact on creativity, innovation, product development, and adaptability. Adaptability and mission tend to have a positive impact on revenue, sales growth, and market share.

Routine is not organization, any more than paralysis is order.
—SIR ARTHUR HELPS,
English historian

Denison's Leadership Development Model reinforces the assumption that effective managers are cognitively and behaviorally complex. That is, they are able to see the organization from a variety of perspectives, diagnose the needs of a particular situation, and adapt their behavior in response. Most important, the Leadership Development Model reminds managers that their effectiveness depends on their ability to create a work culture that inspires high performance. Box 6-1 provides a list of questions that you can answer to determine how well you are doing in each of the four critical areas (mission, consistency, involvement, and adaptability).

A Note on Empowerment: It's More Than a Feeling

There is a lot of talk about empowerment these days, but few managers understand what it is and how they can create conditions that inspire it. When employees feel empowered, they believe that they can influence their work environment, and this belief motivates them to take actions to make an impact on their environment. Employees who feel empowered show initiative, flexibility, innovation, and openness to change. They are committed to helping the organization achieve its goals even if that means going beyond their job descriptions.

On the basis of a review of several studies of empowerment, researchers Gretchen Spreitzer and Robert Quinn concluded that employees who feel empowered share four beliefs about themselves and the work that they do, and these are nurtured and supported by their managers and organizational leaders:[31]

- *Meaning.* Employees believe that the organization's missions and goals are important and are aligned with their values and preferred ways of behaving. People who find meaning in their work care about what they are doing and expect their work to be challenging. They understand how their work contributes to the achievement of the mission and goals.
- *Competence.* Employees have confidence in their ability to do the work associated with their work roles. They have the basic skills they need, believe in their capacity to grow, and

BOX 6-1   Denison's Leadership Development Model: How Effective Are You at Creating an Organizational Culture That Inspires High Performance?

This is a sample of the items that comprise the Denison Leadership Development Survey. The entire survey consists of 96 items.

Mission Trait: Creates Shared Vision

1. I help create a shared vision of what this organization will be like in the future.
2. I translate the vision into reality in a way that helps guide individual action.
3. I encourage others in ways that ensure buy-in and commitment.

Consistency Trait: Defines Core Values

1. I do the "right thing" even when it is not popular.
2. I practice what I preach.
3. I live up to my promises and commitments.

Involvement Trait: Empowers People

1. I see that decisions are made at the lowest possible level.
2. I create an environment where everyone feels that his/her efforts can make a difference.
3. I delegate authority so that others can do their work more effectively.

Adaptability Trait: Promotes Customer Focus

1. I encourage direct contact with customers.
2. I actively seek feedback from customers.
3. I respond quickly and effectively to customer feedback.

Source: Used with the permission of Daniel Denison and William Neale, creators of the Denison Leadership Development Survey. For a more in-depth look at the questions and to obtain an on-line analysis of your personal or organization's profile, see www.denisonculture.com. Reprinted with permission of Denison Consulting.

---

want to learn new skills so that they can meet the challenges ahead of them. They are supported by managers who encourage learning by mistakes as well as by successes.

- *Self-determination.* Employees believe that they are trusted and have the freedom to make choices about how they do their work and accomplish their work goals. This enables them to make necessary decisions and take relevant actions thoughtfully and quickly, all within clear boundaries set by the manager (e.g., clear goal, milestones, performance measures, quality standards, and feedback processes). To support employees' independence, empowering managers provide them with the information, training, technology, and other resources they need to do their job well. These boundaries and resources enable employees to act independently (instead of being micromanaged) while aligning their work with the manager's and organization's goals.
- *Impact.* Employees believe that they can influence the work environment. They believe that their manager and organizational leaders listen to them and invite them to participate in decision-making. Consequently, employees feel they have a say regarding organizational

decisions, actions, and outcomes that matter to them, their organizations, and the people they serve.[32]

Taken together, these beliefs help create an active rather than passive orientation toward shaping their work role and their organization.[33]

You can take the empowerment assessment in box 6.2 to assess how empowering your job is. You can assess a job from your past as well.

Can you empower employees? The answer is "no." You can't force empowerment on anyone, but you can create conditions and work relationships that increase the possibility that employees will feel empowered and behave accordingly. Spreitzer's research suggests that six conditions are likely to inspire employees' feelings of empowerment:[34]

1. *Low role ambiguity.* Clear boundaries, goals, and performance measures, as well as clearly defined tasks and lines of responsibility, are likely to increase employees' feelings of control over their work environment, and thus reduce feelings of insecurity and stress that can block action. Spreitzer found that this condition had the strongest relationship to feelings of empowerment.
2. *Working for a boss who has a wide span of control.* When a boss is responsible for managing several employees, he or she is likely to be too busy to micromanage them. Consequently, employees are likely to have more freedom to make and implement decisions on their own.
3. *Sociopolitical support.* When employees feel like they are "integrated into the key political channels for getting work done in organizations," they feel as if they have more power to influence the organization.[35]
4. *Access to information.* When employees have access to information, they feel that they can make higher quality decisions and thus are more optimistic that they will succeed in their efforts to have an impact on their environment.
5. *A participative unit climate.* When employees believe that their opinions are sought after and valued, they feel that they can have a direct influence on their environment.
6. *Education and training.* When employees receive work-related training, they feel as though the organization is investing in them (and thus values them). They also are likely to feel (and be) more competent and more willing to take the risks involved in trying to influence their work environment.

Spreitzer and others have concluded that access to abundant resources is not significantly related to empowerment.[36] The stories of the humble beginnings of Apple Computer, Microsoft, and Kinko's in garages and other sparse environments illustrate this point. Indeed, people who feel empowered may see lack of resources as a challenge to be overcome with ingenuity rather than a block to performance.

Who is responsible for creating conditions that inspire employees to do their best work? A Gallup Organization study of more than 100,000 employees and almost 8,000 business units in 36 companies found that the direct manager or supervisor, more so than the top leadership or organizational culture, influenced whether employees were committed to and added value to the organization. They also found that organizations whose employees could answer the following six questions positively

---

BOX 6.2   Empowerment Assessment

Using the following scale, please indicate the extent to which you agree or disagree that each one describes how you see yourself in relation to your workplace.

1 = Strongly Disagree   3 = Neutral   5 = Strongly Agree

2 = Disagree   4 = Agree

a. ____ I am confident about my ability to do my job.

b. ____ The work that I do is important to me.

c. ____ I have significant autonomy in determining how I do my job.

d. ____ My impact on what happens in my unit is large.

e. ____ My job activities are personally meaningful to me.

f. ____ I have a great deal of control over what happens in my unit.

g. ____ I can decide how to go about doing my own work.

h. ____ I have considerable opportunity for independence and freedom in how I do my job.

i. ____ I have mastered the skills necessary for my job.

j. ____ The work I do is meaningful to me.

k. ____ I have significant influence over what happens in my unit.

l. ____ I am self-assured about my capabilities to perform my work activities.

Scoring Directions

Scoring the empowerment instrument requires simple arithmetic calculations. Use the worksheet provided below.

Please fill in your scores for the items in the order shown.

Meaning

b. ☐ +

e. ☐ +

j. ☐
___
☐ Sum (total of responses)

Competence

a. ☐ +

i. ☐ +

l. ☐
___
☐ Sum (total of responses)

Self-Determination

c. ☐ +

g. ☐ +

h. ☐
___
☐ Sum (total of responses)

Impact

d. ☐ +

f. ☐ +

k. ☐
___
☐ Sum (total of responses)

(continued)

BOX 6-2 *Continued*

Profiling Your Own Empowerment

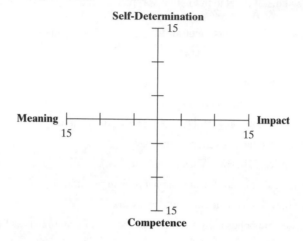

Map your score on each dimension on this graph and connect the dots to create a kite shape.

Source: Gretchen Spreitzer and Robert Quinn. Reprinted by permission of Professor Gretchen Spreitzer.

were significantly more likely to have increased customer satisfaction, productivity, and profitability, as well as less turnover:[37]

> "Do I know what is expected of me at work? Do I have the materials and equipment I need to do my work right? Do I have the opportunity to do what I do best every day? In the last seven days, have I received recognition or praise for good work? Does my supervisor, or someone at work, seem to care about me as a person? Is there someone at work who encourages my development?"

The most important point to remember from the above studies is that you cannot empower anyone. Rather, you can create conditions that are likely to help employees feel empowered,

FIGURE 6-3 Dilbert Cartoon by Scott Adams
Source: Dilbert © Distributed by United Features Syndicate. Reprinted by permission.

which will in turn influence their commitment to the organization and their willingness and ability to proactively try to add bottom-line value.

A CAUTIONARY NOTE: OBEDIENCE TO AUTHORITY

Most people in positions of authority (e.g., managers, teachers, and parents) spend time worrying about how they will get employees, students, and children to listen to them and obey them. Yet few people in positions of authority worry about an equally troubling problem: People are likely to obey those in positions of authority even when doing so is unethical and against their own conscience.

In the 1960s, Yale psychologist Stanley Milgram conducted one of the most well-known and disturbing experiments on human behavior. Born in 1933, Milgram grew up during World War II. Like many psychologists of his era, he wanted to understand why so many seemingly normal people were willing to follow Hitler's orders to systematically imprison and kill millions of Jews and others who didn't fit into Hitler's vision of the ideal future. In search of an answer, Milgram conducted a series of experiments designed to understand the dynamics of obedience to authority. He described his experiment as follows:

> In order to take a close look at the act of obeying, I set up a simple experiment at Yale University. Eventually, the experiment was to involve over 1,000 participants and would be repeated at several universities, but at the beginning, the conception was simple. A person comes to a psychological laboratory and is told to carry out a series of acts that come increasingly into conflict with conscience. The main question is how far the participant will comply with the experimenter's instructions before refusing to carry out the actions required.[38]

Milgram recruited about 1,000 participants through newspaper advertisements and direct mail solicitation. On entering the laboratory, each recruit met an "experimenter" and another "recruit" who was waiting to participate in the experiment. The "experimenter" wore a professional-looking gray lab coat when he greeted the participants and told them that they would be participating in a study on memory and learning. What the recruit who responded to the advertisement or direct mail solicitation didn't know was that the other recruit and the experimenter were confederates of the experiment. The confederate recruit was a 47-year-old white male accountant of Irish American descent who was trained to act out his role in a mild-mannered and likable way. The experimenter was a 31-year-old high school teacher who was trained to act stern and impartial. The real purpose of the study was to determine how many of the actual recruits would obey the experimenter's requests to inflict harm on another human being against that person's will.

The experimenter told the naïve recruit and the confederate recruit that one person would be the "teacher" in the experiment and the other would be the "learner." Unknown to the naïve recruits, they were always given the role of the teacher, and the confederate recruit was always given the role of the learner. The experimenter then told the naïve teacher and the learner that the teacher's goal was to test the learner's memorization of a series of word pairs (such as "blue box" and "nice day"). For example, the teacher was to say the world "blue," and the learner was supposed to respond with the word "box." If the learner gave the correct answer, the teacher would move on to the next word pair. If the learner gave the wrong answer (e.g., if the learner said "blue sky" when the correct answer was "blue box"), the teacher was directed to punish the learner by subjecting him to increasingly intensive electrical shocks.

After describing the teacher's duties, the experimenter brought the teacher and learner to a small windowless room where the learner would stay during the experiment. He then showed the teacher and learner a "shock machine" that was designed to give the learner the electrical shocks. He seated the learner in a chair, strapped his arms to a machine to "prevent excessive movement," and attached an electrode to the learner's wrist. The experimenter then took the teacher to another room and showed him an impressive "shock generator" that had "a horizontal line of 30 switches, ranging from 15 volts to 450 volts, in 15-volt increments." Each switch was labeled with a verbal designation ranging from "slight shock" to "danger—severe shock." The experimenter then told the teacher to quickly move on to the next question whenever the learner gave a correct answer. When the learner made a mistake, the teacher was to give the learner a shock by pushing the appropriate switch on the shock generator, beginning with the lowest shock level and then increasing the shock level with each successive mistake. The experimenter then gave the teacher a sample shock so that the teacher could experience what the shocks would feel like to the learner.

Unknown to the teacher, the learner wasn't really going to receive electrical shocks. Instead, the learner (confederate of the experiment) was pretending to receive the shocks. The learner gave approximately three wrong answers for each correct answer and had the same programmed response for each level of shock for each experiment. For example, the learner grunted at 75 volts, complained that the shocks were getting painful at 120 volts, groaned in pain at 135 volts, demanded to be released from the experiment at 150 volts, said "I can't stand the pain" at 180 volts, screamed out in pain at 270 volts, stated he would no longer respond to questions at 300 volts, shouted "Let me out of here, my heart's bothering me" at 330 volts, and gave no response at all after 330 volts.[39]

When Milgram asked a group of psychiatrists to predict at what level of shock the teacher would refuse to continue with the experiment, the psychiatrists predicted that most teachers would stop at 150 volts (the point at which the learner began demanding to be released). They also predicted that less than one-tenth of a percent of the subjects would shock the learner up to the maximum 450 volts. However, approximately 65% of the teachers continued to shock the learner up to 450 volts. The mean maximum shock level was 350 volts, and the earliest break-off point was 135 volts. Why were so many of the teachers willing to subject the learner to painful and potentially dangerous shocks at the request of an experimenter? Milgram offered this explanation:

> A commonly offered explanation is that those who shocked the victim at the most severe level were monsters, the sadistic fringe of society. But if one considers that almost two-thirds of the participants fall into the category of "obedient" subjects, and that they represented "ordinary" people drawn from working, managerial, and professional classes, the argument becomes very shaky. . . . This is, perhaps, the most fundamental lesson of our study: Ordinary people, simply doing their jobs, and without any particular hostility on their part, can become agents in a terribly destructive process. Moreover, even when the destructive effects of their work become patently clear, and they are asked to carry out actions incompatible with fundamental standards of morality, relatively few people have the resources needed to resist authority.[40]

Relativity applies to physics, not ethics.
—Albert Einstein

Remember that the "scientist" used no coercive power (such as threats of punishment) to ensure the teacher's obedience. Any of the research subjects had the right to walk away from the experiment at any time. The "scientist" simply explained the experiment and the participant roles and then urged the teacher to continue to perform the task with polite but firm and impassive statements such as "The experiment must go on," "Continue, teacher," "It is absolutely essential that you continue," and "You have no other choice, you must continue." He also provided assurances that "although the shocks may be painful, there is no permanent tissue damage."[41] Milgram and other researchers suggest that subtle but very powerful forces were at play, including:

- *Trappings of legitimacy.* The experiment looked legitimate. The language of "scientific experiment" was trustworthy. The experimenter, always a Caucasian male in Milgram's experiments, wore a lab coat and spoke with authority. The laboratory was clean and professional-looking.

- *Emphasis on technical rather than human aspects of the interaction.* The experimenter repeatedly emphasized the technical aspects of the "procedure" and encouraged the teacher to carry out the procedures as quickly as possible. The experimenter also deperson-alized the learner by always referring to him as "learner" and never by his name. By as-suming an unemotional demeanor and focusing on procedures, the experimenter reduced the interactions to a technique rather than a human interaction with consequences.

- *Abdication of personal responsibility.* One of the most poignant interactions in the series of experiments was when one of the teachers hesitated before shocking the distraught learner and asked the experimenter who would take responsibility if anything happened to the learner. When the experimenter responded, "I will take responsibility," the teacher con-tinued to shock the learner as instructed. Later analysis showed that teachers who adminis-tered the lowest shock levels were more likely to believe that they, not the learner or exper-imenter, were more responsible for their own actions.

- *Group dynamics.* In a variation of the study, Milgram found that teachers were more in-clined to participate in shocking the learner if they were playing a subsidiary role in a group (e.g., if another "teacher" actually pushed the lever on the shock machine while the subject stood by). Milgram also found that teachers were more likely to refuse to obey if others in the group refused to obey.

- *Proximity to authority figure and victim.* In other variations of the study, Milgram found that the farther away the experimenter was from the teachers, the less likely they were to obey him. For example, obedience declined substantially when the experimenter gave his orders from a different room. Milgram also found that the closer the teacher was to the learner, the less likely the teacher was to comply with the experimenter's orders.

- *Cultural norms.* One study conducted with Australian citizens found a significantly lower rate of obedience (28%) than Milgram found with his U.S. subjects (62.5%). The re-searcher suggested that this difference may reflect "national differences in obedience ide-ology that contribute to a predisposition to obey or defy authority."[42]

- *Personality.* Some researchers argue that personality characteristics and "enduring be-liefs" may play a role in obedience to authority.[43] These characteristics include social in-telligence, tendencies toward hostility, attitudes toward authority figures, internal versus external locus of control, and degree of belief in scientific authority.

Researcher Thomas Blass suggests that self-awareness can lessen the risk that someone may blindly follow authority down a path that goes against their conscience. He explains:

> The conditions that prevail within the setting of a Milgram obedience experiment are typically conducive of an inhibition of self-awareness, rather than enhancement of it. The subject's attention is focused outward rather than inward, absorbed in the me-chanical details of the procedure. In fact . . . [t]he considerable amount of physical activity to work a shock machine might actually artificially depress the subject's

self-awareness. . . . Also drawing attention away from the self is the subject's attunement to the experimenter's commands and to the learners' answers and complaints. . . . Features of the typical Milgram-type obedience experiment are anything but promotive of self-awareness.[44]

Lessons for Everyday Work Life

The most important lesson of the Milgram experiments is that each of us may be more prone to obeying the orders of a legitimate authority than we think we are. Situational pressures such as the presence of authority figures, symbols of legitimacy, organizational routines, and the actions of our peers can exert significant influence on our behavior. Now that you know the results of the Milgram experiment, it may not surprise you to know that the National Transportation Safety Board concluded that up to 25% of all plane crashes are caused by dysfunctional obedience to authority. In December 1993, all 16 people on board a Northwest Airlink Flight died when the plane crashed in Hibbing, Minnesota, after descending too quickly. The National Transportation Safety Board determined that the "captain flew the airplane inappropriately and did not 'exercise proper crew coordination'; the first officer did not properly monitor and alert the captain of the problematic descent [accepting the authority's definition of the situation]; the captain intimidated his first officer; the airline failed to adequately supervise the captain, who had a history of intimidating his first officers; and the FAA did not provide adequate surveillance of the airline. . . Most of the captain's communication with the first officer was either to correct him or to tell him what to do." The National Safety Board believes that at least 25% of plane accidents could be prevented if first officers monitored the captain's decisions more carefully and challenged these decisions when they seem inappropriate, a practice researcher Eugen Tarnow calls "obedience optimization."[45]

Fortunately, there are people who resist and do the right thing when faced with unethical and immoral situations. There are also leaders who ensure that their employees have the courage to question them about organization policies when they are headed down the wrong path. Undoubtedly, there are actions that you can take to minimize the risk of blind obedience to authority. For example, when you are in a position of authority, assume that people will take your authority and the authority of the organization seriously. In other words, be careful of what you ask people to do (or what followers may think you want them to do even if you haven't asked them to do so explicitly) because they may do it, even if it is unethical, illegal, or goes against their conscience. Indeed, researchers have found that "the behavior of one's superiors is among the strongest influences on ethical behavior, playing a larger role than the behavior of peers or even one's personal ethical frameworks."[46] In addition, you can:

- Keep symbols of authority at a minimum.
- Regularly encourage employees to speak their mind and question the status quo.
- Reward employees when they challenge and resist what they perceive to be troublesome requests or behaviors. Reward small acts of courage so that employees will be more likely to engage in large acts of courage when necessary.
- Create a work context that promotes self-awareness and "obedience optimization" rather than blind obedience.

When you are in a follower position:

- Be aware of your own attitudes toward authority and how they may influence your behavior. Remember that authority figures are fallible human beings and that you have more choices in any given situation than may immediately seem obvious.

- Recognize that when it comes to immoral acts, you—not anyone else (not a leader or organization)—are responsible for your behavior.
- Prime yourself to be ready to leave or expose a morally questionable situation.
- When you find yourself in a morally questionable situation, try to get yourself a peer who will join you in resistance. People are more likely to resist when others are doing so as well.
- If possible, distance yourself from the situation for a while to get perspective. Make sure that you have "walk money" in the bank so that you feel you can walk away from any job or situation if you feel felt it is necessary.
- Practice small acts of courage. Says Professor Peter Vaill, "Courage is at bottom the capacity and process of maintaining one's identity and values in the face of psychic challenge. . . . [I]f one has not made a habit of turning toward a situation courageously, no matter how small and mundane, one will not know how to turn toward the big situations courageously."[47]

Notably, Milgram has been widely praised for the profound insights his experiment offers into human behavior. He also has been widely criticized for conducting an experiment that may have had troubling consequences for the people who participated in the study, particularly those who learned that they were willing to inflict harm on another human being against his or her will. Some people have argued that Milgram's well-intended willingness to put the "teachers" through significant psychological trauma illustrated his own theory of obedience to authority. Simply stated, even scientists may engage in unethical behaviors in the service of science. In the 1970s, the American Psychological Association instituted national guidelines to protect research subjects from intended or unintended negative consequences of experiments. The Milgram experiment, as designed in the 1960s, does not meet those guidelines.

BOX 6-3   Bad Apples and Bad Barrels

When the images of the horrific abuse by U.S. military personnel at Abu Ghraib prison in the aftermath of the 2003 Iraq War emerged in 2004, people worldwide were appalled. Yet psychologists, though appalled, were not surprised. Experiments (and historical events) repeatedly have shown that, regardless of nationality, many normal human beings, when placed in certain contexts, will engage in abusive behaviors that they would not otherwise do.

For example, in August 1971, Stanford psychologist Philip Zimbardo conducted the now-famous prison experiment in which he recruited male college students from various colleges to participate in a prison simulation for which the students would receive $15 per day. The recruits were given personality tests, and the experimenters selected 21 students who they considered to be normal and healthy. Through a random selection process, 12 students were chosen to act as guards and nine were chosen to act as prisoners. The guards were given mirrored sun glasses, khaki uniforms, a whistle, and sticks. The prisoners were picked up at their homes by Palo Alto police, handcuffed, deloused, forced to wear prison outfits and chains, and brought to the makeshift prison in a Stanford University basement.

Zimbardo's original purpose was to study the "prisoners," but his interest soon shifted to the "guards" as they quickly began abusing the prisoners. The guards began to use the prisoners as playthings for their amusement, especially as they became increasingly bored and at night when they thought they weren't being observed. They amused themselves in several ways, including stripping the prisoners, putting them in solitary confinement, putting bags over their heads, sexually humiliating

(*continued*)

BOX 6-3 *Continued*

them, waking them up repeatedly in the middle of the night, and degrading them in a variety of other ways. Although the experiment was scheduled to last for two weeks, Zimbardo cancelled it after six days because the guards' abuse and prisoners' distress escalated to unpredicted levels. Zimbardo explains that he stopped the experiment after Christina Maslach, a recently graduated Ph.D., visited the simulated prison and strongly protested against continuing the experiment. Zimbardo notes that she was the only visitor out of 50, including a priest, who had asked to stop the experiment. He also notes that he, too, found himself thoroughly engaged in his role as scientific researcher and thus didn't stop the experiment earlier.

Zimbardo concluded that the demands of the situation in the prison experiment were more powerful than the personalities of the students involved. After the abuses at Abu Ghraib prison were exposed, Zimbardo argued that, even though we'd like to think more kindly of human nature, the abuses were practically inevitable because the situation was conducive to bringing out the worst in guards. Zimbardo identified the following precipitating conditions: Secrecy, dehumanization of the prisoners, lack of accountability from top down, vague or changing rules, lack of standard operating procedures or lack of enforcement of those that existed, ambiguous requests from authorities, a seemingly legitimizing ideology, lack of proper training of the guards, diffusion of responsibility, obedience to authority, few visits by senior leaders to the site, a "lack of supervision that conveys a sense of permissiveness," a few bad apples who act as role models to others, subtle social pressure to conform, bystanders who chose not to intervene, and significant power differentials. When these conditions are present, says Zimbardo, "hell becomes the ordinary situation"—so ordinary that prison guards felt comfortable taking photos of their abuse, often with the guards looking into the camera and smiling in the background.

This experiment, as well as historical events, teaches us that we must recognize the power of situations to bring out not only the best in us, but the worst in us as well—regardless of our gender, nationality, or religious orientation. If we changed the guards in the Zimbardo experiment or Abu Ghraib prison, it is likely that some of those who took their place would have been abusive as well because the conditions created a context that was likely to bring out the worst in many people. This doesn't absolve individuals of personal responsibility for their actions, but Zimbardo warns that it is misleading to assume that the problem was caused by a few "rotten apples" rather than a "rotten barrel." Note also that there were some people who resisted and reported the abuses at Abu Ghraib prison, and these people illustrate that just as some individuals fall into abusive behaviors under certain conditions, others develop the courage to resist.

To see slides and text by Zimbardo describing the 1971 Stanford Prison experiment, go to http://www.prisonexp.org

Source: Zimbardo, Philip. 2004. "Power Turns Good Soldiers Into Bad Apples." May 9. http://users.crocker.com/~afsc/statements/APPLES.HTML; "Stanford Prison Experiment Foretold Iraq Scandal." 2004. May 8. www.religionnewsblog.com; Stanford Prison Experiment. 2004. www.prisonexp.org/links.htm; "Why Did They Do It? Are Those Charged with Abuse a Few Bad Apples, or Are They Just Like the Rest of Us?" *Time*. May 17; O'Connor, Anahad. 2004. "Pressure to Go Along with the Abuse Is Strong, but Some Soldiers Find the Strength to Refuse." *New York* Times. May 14.; Zimbardo, Philip. 2008. *The Lucifer Effect: Understanding How Good People Turn Evil.* New York: Random House Trade Paperbacks.

AN OPTIMISTIC TALE: ORGANIZING FOR COMPASSION

Too often, we hear about organizations that fail to live up to their moral obligations to their members and society. We are less likely to hear about organizations that show extraordinary generosity and compassion in times of need. All organizations have members who experience serious illness, death of family members, and other events that create human suffering. Yet there is great variety in how organizations respond to this suffering. In some organizations, employees are empowered to reach out and quickly do whatever it takes to help those in need. In other organizations, employees' efforts to help others in need are hindered with a "stick-to-business" culture and paralyzing red tape.

Researchers Jane Dutton, Monica Worline, Jacoba Lilius, and Peter Frost studied organizations that show extraordinary compassion.[48] To illustrate compassionate organizing, they described how a business school responded when some students lost all of their belongings in an apartment fire. Through a variety of coordinated actions on the part of instructors, students, support staff, and the dean, the students quickly received the resources and emotional support they needed to heal from the experience, continue with their studies, and move on with their lives.

For example, all of the students immediately received the clothing, university identification cards, laptops, and other items they needed (e.g., eye glasses). The Office of Student Services ensured that two non-U.S. students had their immigration papers replaced within days. An instructor and staff from the Student Services offices volunteered to coordinate monetary donations, which included making daily trips to cash checks so that they could quickly give the money to the students in need and ensure that the students wouldn't be burdened with this additional task. One student coordinated efforts to create backpacks that were customized with the relevant supplies, books, readings, and notes each student needed to continue his or her studies. The business school's executive education center housed and fed the students until they were able to find their own housing.

How does an organization activate a cascade of collective compassion? What systems need to be in place to enable organizational members to improvise unofficial yet useful roles (e.g., money coordinator, backpack creator), coordinate actions across multiple groups, and customize the care they offer in ways that address the unique circumstances of those in need, especially when there are no official rules to follow for addressing such situations? Certainly, it's important to have some compassionate individuals who are drawn to helping others. In this case, an instructor was driving down the street when she saw the students standing outside the burning building, and she felt compelled to stop and help rather than drive by. This instructor then took the initiative to contact the dean's office and enlisted the support of a trusted colleague she knew who worked in Student Services. However, as the researchers note, the acts of a few kind and proactive individuals aren't enough to provide the scale (the amount of resources provided), scope (the breadth and variety of resources provided), customization (attention to unique needs of individuals), and speed of response required to provide all the necessary support. The researchers concluded that organizations that inspire and enable organizational members to proactively provide coordinated and compassionate responses to their members' suffering have several characteristics in common:

- *Values that support caring for others.* In this case, the business school explicitly promotes the value that taking care of others is not only legitimate, but expected. On entering the MBA program, all incoming students spend one day of their orientation program providing service to local communities in need. Not only do these values create an environment in which help is more likely to be offered, but they also create an environment in which organizational members feel free to ask for help rather than to hide or minimize their own suffering. For example, one of the students did not hesitate to go to the Student Services offices in her overcoat, smoky pajamas, and winter boots to seek out support immediately after the fire. Explicitly stated values of care and service also enable organizational members to encourage others who resist efforts to offer support to get on board. In this case, the executive education residence staff initially resisted housing the students in their hotel rooms because they felt it was against school policy. However, their resistance was overcome by pressure from others who convinced the executive education staff that not helping these students was (1) a violation of the business school's explicitly stated values of care and service and (2) a deviation from the outpouring of support that was being shown by other organizational members, including staff in the dean's office.

- *Symbolic leadership and stories.* Organizational leaders role model an ethic of care and compassion through their actions. In this case, the dean was scheduled to give his annual "state-of-the-school" speech shortly after the fire. Early into the speech, he deviated from his planned comments to stop and give a personal check for $300 to help the students in need and to encourage others to help out as well. By publicly doing so, he role modeled the school's commitment to caring for its members in times of need and demonstrated how individual acts of compassion can make a difference. Stories about the students' plight and the many ways people helped (e.g., the instructor's proactive compassion, the way student services had the students' immigration papers replaced quickly, the dean's personal contribution, the students who created the fully-equipped backpacks) inspired others to help and to view the organization as a place in which people are responsible for each other's care.

- *Networks and relationships.* Organizations that provide the scale, scope, customization, and speed of response in times of need depend on the coordination of multiple networks and personal connections throughout the organization. In this case, the instructor who first came to the students' aid had contacts in many different networks (e.g. the dean's office, Student Services, the women's faculty support group, student sections, student clubs), each of which (1) had access to different resources and (2) created links to other networks that could provide a wider and more diverse set of resources.

- *Compassionate routines.* Compassionate organizations have a history of using established routines that enable people to provide support to those in need. Established routines help organizational members focus on what the organization believes is important and to act quickly and automatically without overthinking their actions or worry about negative consequences. In this case, it is normal practice for the dean's office to e-mail the business school community when one of its members is ill, has a death in the family, or is facing another type of crisis. Consequently, it was perceived as normal and expected for organizational members to use e-mail to reach out and coordinate with each other to provide the students with the support and resources they needed.

- *Systems that support caregiving.* Compassionate organizations have existing systems in place that are designed to support an ethic of care and customization. In this case, the Student Services office has staff in place to help students who need psychological support and other assistance in times of need, so helping these students was seen as part of the job rather than an exception to their responsibilities.

The lesson for leaders who want to promote compassionate organizing is that it's not enough to be a compassionate leader. Rather, leaders need to see themselves as social architects who create organizational cultures and systems that generate patterns of thinking and acting that motivate and enable organizational members to provide the "scale, scope, speed, and customization that is likely to reduce pain and suffering."[49]

MANAGING YOUR BOSS

Your relationship with your boss plays a critical role in your task effectiveness, performance ratings, career progress, and psychological well-being.[50] Although most people take it for granted that it is the boss's job to manage employees, fewer people realize that it's equally important for employees to manage their boss. When they do realize the importance of managing their boss, their strategy is often one of "cautious adaptation."[51]

Why is managing up so important? It is not only important to you in terms of your effectiveness, promotions, salary, and well-being, but it's important to your boss and the people who work for you as well. Your boss *needs* you to give him or her information, advice, and support in order to make the right decisions and achieve organizational goals. Your employees *need* you to manage your boss so that they can get the information, support, and resources they need to do their best work, and so that they can get the visibility and credibility they need for their own career advancement. In short, by proactively managing your boss, you increase your ability, your boss's ability, and your employees' ability to achieve results.

In her book, *The Secret Handshake: Mastering the Politics of the Business Inner Circle*, researcher Kathleen Kelly Reardon profiles Beth Klein, vice president and general manager of General Electric's nuclear medicine systems business:

> As a leader, you have to pick the best people and give them the tools to be successful and help them realize their dreams . . . so it's my responsibility to get visibility for my team at the senior management level. To ensure this, Ms. Klein, who oversees several hundred employees in the U.S., France, Sweden, and Israel, stays in close communication with her direct reports. Each Friday, her top managers e-mail her notes about competitive gains or improvements that they have achieved that week. She in turn consolidates their reports into a "global weekly highlights" e-mail, which she then shares with her superiors, as well as her far-flung employees. "It's a way for me to keep in touch and to let them know how we are doing." Every time she is assigned a new boss, she tries to determine exactly what method of communication he or she prefers—and she advises junior managers on her staff to do the same. "I tell them to sit down and have a discussion about how to best communicate and when," she says, "Some bosses prefer very regular communications while others prefer to be contacted only with specific problems."

Unfortunately, many employees believe that there is little that they can do to influence their boss directly, so they use indirect means that are often ineffective. They try to guess what the boss wants, bend over backward to try to please the boss, or keep a low profile to avoid the boss. These self-protective strategies rarely bring out the best in the boss–employee relationship. Instead, these strategies are likely to detract from the task, inhibit honest communication, and hinder upward feedback.[52]

These self-protective strategies are not surprising. In an organizational hierarchy, it is easy for employees to forget the power that they have in the relationship. Bosses need employees' talent and support to accomplish their goals. After all, the boss, the employee, and the organization gain from high-quality boss–employee relationships that are based on high levels of trust, communication, and interaction between the manager and employees.[53] Thus, it makes sense to manage your relationship with your boss in a way that benefits you, your boss, and the organization.

The first step toward managing your boss is understanding your own attitudes toward authority and how these attitudes may help or hinder your relationship with your boss. For

---

BOX 6-4   How Effective Are You at Managing Your Boss?

To see how well you are managing your boss, answer the following questions:

1. Do I know my boss's goals?
2. Do I give the boss what he or she needs to achieve these goals?
3. Do I know my boss's preferred styles of working, and do I adapt my behavior accordingly? For example, is my boss a reader (someone who prefers to receive information in writing) or a listener (someone who prefers to receive information face-to-face)?
4. Do I know my boss's strengths and weaknesses so that I can build on the strengths and compensate for the weaknesses?
5. Does my boss trust me? In other words, have I built a reputation for being honest, loyal, and dependable?
6. Do I keep the boss informed of important information and events so that he or she is never taken by surprise?
7. Do I show appreciation to the boss when appropriate?
8. Do I use the boss's time and resources sensibly?
9. Do I help the boss look good in the eyes of others?
10. Do I tell the boss what my goals, wants, and needs are and what I need to be successful in my job and career?

Source: Adapted from Drucker, Peter. 1986. "How to Manage the Boss." *The Wall Street Journal.* August 1; Gabarro, John, and John Kotter. 1993. "Managing Your Boss." *Harvard Business Review*, 150–157; Gabarro, John, and John Kotter. 2007. "Managing Your Boss." *Harvard Business Online.* October 2, http://www.businessweek.com/managing/content/oct2007/ca2007102_963954.htm; Randall, Iris. 1992. "How to Manage Your Boss." *Black Enterprise.* September: 86–92.

---

example, do you have an interdependent, dependent, or counterdependent attitude toward authority, and what are the consequences on the effectiveness of the relationship? The next step toward managing your boss is to answer the questions in Box 6-4 to identify areas in your relationship with your boss that need improvement. The third step, of course, is to change your behaviors based on your assessment so that you and your boss can enjoy a more productive relationship.

Managing Abrasive Bosses

Although most of us have been blessed with one or more wonderful bosses during our career, most of us also have faced the agony of working with a boss who behaves badly. Indeed, in their study of the developmental experiences of successful executives, researchers Michael Lombardo, Morgan McCall, and Ann Morrison found that most of these executives had worked for a bad boss at one time or another, and these executives viewed their experience with a troublesome boss as important to their professional growth.[54]

For example, an article reported that the president of one company sent the following e-mail to 400 managers:

> We are getting less than 40 hours of work from a large number of EMPLOYEES. The parking lot is sparsely used at 8am; likewise at 5pm. As managers, you either do not know what your EMPLOYEES are doing or you do not CARE. You have created

expectations of the work effort which allowed this to happen inside [this company], creating a very unhealthy environment. In either case, you have a problem and you will fix it or I will replace you. NEVER in my career have I allowed a team which worked for me to think they had a 40-hour job. I have allowed YOU to create a culture which is permitting this. NO LONGER.

One report noted that "His tirade continued, adding that hell would freeze over before he increased employee benefits. He wanted to see the car park nearly full by 7:30 A.M. and half full at weekends. The missive concluded, 'You have two weeks. Tick Tock.'" The company's stock fell 22% after a manager who received the e-mail posted it on Yahoo. The company president promptly apologized, beginning his e-mail this way, "Please treat this memo with the utmost confidentiality. It is for internal dissemination only. Do not copy or e-mail to anyone else."

There are many ways in which bosses can behave badly, but I will focus on highly authoritarian and abrasive bosses. These bosses have been described as "psychobosses from hell,"[55] organizational vampires who "suck the life blood out of the organization,"[56] Dr. Jekyll and Mr. Hyde personalities whose erratic behavior can drive employees crazy,[57] "toxic bosses," and "petty tyrants" who micromanage and belittle employees.[58] Although these characterizations may seem extreme, they represent an intimidating managerial style built on the abuse of power. Whether loud and in-your-face forceful or low key and simmering with intensity, authoritarian and abrasive bosses share several characteristics. Researcher Blake Ashforth offers the following profile:

> Recurring elements appear to include close supervision, distrust and suspicion, cold and impersonal interactions, severe and public criticism of others' character and behavior, condescending and patronizing behavior, emotional outbursts, coercion, and boastful behavior; they suggest an individual who emphasizes authority and status differences, is rigid and inflexible, makes arbitrary decisions, takes credit for the efforts of others and blames them for mistakes, fails to consult with others or keep them informed, discourages informal interaction among subordinates, obstructs their development, and deters initiative and dissent. Pervasive themes in these descriptions are a tendency to overcontrol others and to treat them in an arbitrary, uncaring, and punitive manner.[59]

Their hallmark characteristic is that they tend to lack empathy and believe that employees cannot be trusted. This characteristic is illustrated by the story of a manager who "demanded that employees taking time off for funerals show a copy of the obituary to verify their relationship to the deceased."[60] Abrasive bosses usually believe that employees are not motivated or capable of doing their job well, and so must be carefully supervised, controlled, and forced into obedience. It is not surprising that their bad behavior tends to escalate during times of stress such as deadlines and crises.[61]

I have learned silence from the talkative, toleration from the intolerant; and kindness from the unkind; yet strange, I am ungrateful to these teachers.
—KAHLIL GIBRAN, *Lebanese novelist*

Psychiatrist Harry Levinson says that abrasive bosses often are technically very capable, action-oriented, and achievement-driven. Consequently, organizational leaders often tolerate their interpersonal shortcomings. But this tolerance is costly.[62] Employees who feel abused by their boss report greater dissatisfaction with their jobs and life, greater psychological distress, and greater intentions to leave their job. They are also less likely to engage in organizational citizenship behaviors—going above and beyond the call of duty—that organizations depend on to achieve their goals.[63] Feelings of fear can discourage employees' creativity and initiative, minimize risk taking, decrease information flow (especially to the petty tyrant who needs information to make effective decisions), suppress healthy conflict, hinder task performance, inhibit cooperation among employees and across departments, and increase employee absenteeism.[64] Furthermore, abusive bosses can be lawsuits waiting to happen.

The petty tyrant can make employees nervous, distracted, and more prone to mistakes and accidents. For example, in a study of airline flight crew performance, researchers found that the crews made fewer mistakes when their captains were "warm, friendly, self confident, and able to stand up to pressure (i.e., agreeable and emotionally stable)" and made more mistakes when their captains were "arrogant, hostile, boastful, egotistical, passive aggressive, or dictatorial."[65] Although authoritarian and abrasive bosses often see themselves as perfectionists who only want what's best for the organization, their behavior tends to cause many of the problems they claim they want to solve.

Seagull manager: A manager who flies in, makes a lot of noise, dumps over everything, and then leaves.
—Ken Blanchard

Why do abrasive bosses act the way that they do? Research suggests that abrasive bosses may have had childhood difficulties that resulted in problems with self-esteem and self-confidence, lack of trust in others, lack of impulse control, lack of empathy, and high needs for control.[66] Research also suggests that people with an authoritarian personality tend to be domineering, rigid, impersonal, focused on status, and prefer strict adherence to policies.[67] Some abrasive bosses act the way that they do because their behavior is consistent with that of the organizational culture and they are rewarded for their behavior (or at least not disciplined for it). After all, it's hard to swim with the sharks over a long period of time and not start to act like one in the process.

What can you do if you have a bad boss? You're not going to ask your boss if he or she grew up in a dysfunctional family. You're not a psychologist, and it's really none of your business. You're going to have to deal with the boss's current behaviors with the best tools you have—your self-awareness and social skills.

Before focusing on the boss, you need to think first about yourself. Have all your bosses been jerks? If you have never had a good boss, then it is likely that you are part of the problem. Perhaps your attitude or behavior brings out the worst in bosses. Maybe you have an unrealistic expectation of what your bosses can and should do for you, in which case they are guaranteed to disappoint you. Maybe you developed a counterdependent attitude toward authority early in life and carry that attitude of distrust of authority into your adult relationships with bosses at work. Maybe you're bashing the boss to relieve stress, but this can be a problem if it undermines your relationship with your boss.

Let's say that your boss is indeed abrasive, and you are not a significant cause of his or her behavior. Even if you're not part of the problem, you can be part of the solution. Remember that your relationship with your boss is built on mutual dependence, and you have some power to influence the situation.[68] Also remember that you can't change another person, but you can change yourself (which may inspire the other person to change). Most important, remember to never let your boss "take away your dignity and self-respect."[69] To help improve your relationship with a troubling boss, first answer the questions in Box 6-4, and then consider the following strategies:

- *Analyze the situation.* Does the boss act badly primarily with you (in which case it's probably personal) or with all employees? Is the problem really the boss, or might it be that the boss is simply following organizational policies or procedures? Is it possible that your boss is socially inept but is well intentioned, technically competent, and has no ill will toward you or others? What specifically makes the boss angry or stressed? Your analysis of the situation will influence your strategy to improve the relationship.

- *Get clear expectations.* Together with your boss, identify goals, quality standards, and performance measures.
- *Keep careful records.* Document the goals, quality standards, performance measures, and requests that your boss has made so that you both can refer to them to evaluate your performance. Also document any contributions you have made to the department or organization, including quantifiable data, employee and customer comments, and 360-degree feedback results. Keep records of any abusive behavior from your boss. Some of this behavior, such as sexual harassment or other discriminatory practices, may be illegal.
- *Look for something good in your boss.* Inside a rough exterior, you may find a gem of a human being. Perhaps your boss has great technical skills, brings in a lot of business, or tenderly takes care of his or her elderly parents. Remember that most difficult bosses welcome any appreciation and kindness you show toward them because they probably don't get a lot of positive interpersonal feedback. Although your boss may come across as insensitive, it may be that the boss is socially inept and may not mean to be distant or disrespectful.
- *Determine your boss's goals, needs, wants, styles, and pressures, and adapt accordingly.* What can you do to adapt to your boss's style? What do you have in common with your boss that you can build on? What can you offer the boss that is of value to him or her? What do you do that may annoy the boss?
- *Create and celebrate small wins.* Look for small opportunities for you and your boss to succeed together—creating an outstanding report or presentation, getting a new client, or developing a new strategy. When you succeed together, take time to acknowledge your joint success. Doing so reminds your boss that you are loyal and capable, that he or she can count on you, and that the two of you make an effective team.
- *Ask friends and colleagues how to handle your relationship with your boss.* People who have developed a good relationship with the difficult boss can be particularly helpful. Learn what you can do to help the boss trust you and see you as a competent ally.
- *"Don't invest your ego in the relationship.* Don't look for empathy, interest in your life, or praise. You won't get it," says Michael Maccoby, author of *The Productive Narcissist: The Promise and Peril of Visionary Leadership.*[70]
- *Confront your boss.* If you decide to challenge your boss, do it professionally. When planning your strategy, be clear about what you want to accomplish from the meeting and what you need from the boss. Remember to consider the boss's goals and style, and have data available to support your concerns.
- *Learn a lesson.* If you cannot improve your relationship with a difficult boss, then think of your experiences with this boss as an education in persistence, stress management, conflict management, and how not to treat people.[71]
- *If all else fails, leave.* Always keep your resume updated, your network in place, and money in the bank so that you can leave your job. Before you accept a new job, pay attention to the potential new boss's character. *Wall Street Journal* columnist Susan Shellenbarger suggests that, when considering a new position, you should ask people what it's like to work for the boss. Does the boss have a reputation as a people developer? Do employees seem intimidated? Is there a lot of turnover in that boss's area? How does this manager work in a crisis or under stress?[72]
- *Have empathy for the boss.* Psychologist Harry Levinson says that the sad truth is that, sooner or later, tyrannical bosses pay a high price for their behavior. Bosses with abrasive personalities are "vulnerable to coronaries," and your boss's behavior—particularly hostility—may cause his or her own demise.[73]

Finally, while you are thinking about your own bad boss, it's a good time to ask yourself if you are a difficult boss. Although most of us complain about our bad bosses, few of us think about how we may be a burden to our own direct reports.

MANAGING MENTOR–PROTÉGÉ RELATIONSHIPS

A recent *Wall Street Journal* article provided the following advice: "In this economy, you need to take advantage of every available resource to propel your career. Finding a mentor—and preferably a network of mentors—is an easy and smart way to get you started."[74] Mentoring is a partnership through which a person with more experience (a mentor) consciously helps a person with less experience (a protégé) learn and achieve his or her professional goals. Researchers Kathy Kram and Lynn Isabella explain that mentors help protégés by offering two kinds of support:[75]

> *Instrumental support.* This includes helping protégés develop their technical and political skills, providing opportunities for challenging and high-visibility assignments, providing feedback on performance, role-modeling appropriate attitudes and behaviors, connecting protégés to people who can help their careers, and protecting protégés from people and situations that can hurt their careers.
> *Psychosocial support.* This includes providing emotional support, giving career advice, inviting protégés to informal social activities (e.g., lunch, dinner, or golf), and helping protégés manage the stresses of everyday work life. Psychosocial support is critical because it influences the protégés' self-esteem, self-confidence, and motivation, which in turn influences the protégés' effectiveness.[76]

Both mentors and protégés benefit from high-quality mentoring relationships. Mentors benefit from the increasing effectiveness of the protégés, the organizational insights and information that protégés provide, and the protégés' increasing power and influence. Mentors also benefit from the personal satisfaction that comes from helping others and gaining a reputation for being effective people developers.[77] Research suggests that employees who have mentors are more likely to have greater self-confidence, more influence over organizational policies, more access to important people and organizational resources, higher salaries, more promotions, greater job mobility, and more satisfaction with their jobs and careers.[78]

This does not mean that people who don't have dedicated mentor relationships can't reap the same organizational advantages; however, mentors can make some advantages easier and faster to come by. Harvard professor Linda Hill argues that most employees do not have mentors, and those who do soon realize that their mentors cannot solve all of their career problems.[79] In her study of new managers' experiences during their first year on the job, Hill found that few of the new managers "relied on their current bosses as resources" during that time, perhaps because they wanted their boss to perceive them as competent, and they didn't want their bosses to know that they needed help.[80] For most of these new managers, peers tended to be the greatest source of support because they are likely to be more accessible than are bosses and they can be useful sources of technical information, political advice, empathy, and emotional support, particularly if the peer relationships aren't overly competitive.[81]

In today's complex and unpredictable environment, you can no longer afford to depend on one or two mentors found only at higher hierarchical levels. Instead, you need to develop a network of mentors at different levels of the hierarchy, inside and outside the organization, who provide access to different contacts, skills, resources, and types of support. Researchers Monica Higgins and Kathy Kram point out that people who proactively develop a network of developmental relationships tend to benefit more than others in the areas of career change, personal learning (e.g., learning about oneself, one's professional identity, and what one needs to do to achieve one's goals), organizational commitment, and work satisfaction.[82]

Mentoring relationships, like all relationships, carry risks as well as benefits. Mentors may have unrealistic or unclear expectations for the protégé, making it difficult for the protégé to succeed. Mentors may take unfair advantage of their protégés or feel threatened by their protégés' increasing skill and influence. They also may invest too much time in their protégés and ignore the needs of other employees who also need their help.[83] Protégés may become overdependent on their mentors and may be perceived by others as being unable to stand alone (known as the "sidekick" effect).[84] Protégés may become dependent on too few mentors and fail to develop a diversity of mentoring relationships that are important to their effectiveness and success. And their reputations may be harmed if their mentors get caught in political battles, fall out of favor, or leave the organization (known as the "guilt by association" effect).[85]

Recent research has found that "bad mentoring may be worse than no mentoring at all" and may negatively affect the protégé's self-esteem, reduce job satisfaction, increase stress, increase absenteeism, and inspire the protégé to quit. Understanding the consequences of poor mentoring is important because many organizations are instituting formal mentoring programs in which mentors and protégés are matched by the organization. In some of these cases, the mentor may not want the mentoring role, may not be trained in appropriate mentoring practices, may be out of touch with the issues faced by the employee, or may have dysfunctional behaviors (e.g., may be tyrannical, selfish, deceitful, manipulative, or sabotaging) that inhibit rather than support the protégé's development.[86]

It is not surprising that building a network of developmental relationships can minimize many of these risks.

Diversity and Mentoring

Mentoring relationships that cross cultural groups, such as gender, race, and nationality, can be more complex than mentoring relationships in which the mentor and protégé belong to similar cultural groups. The challenges that mentors and protégés with different cultural identities (e.g., race, gender, or nationality) face can make these relationships more enjoyable, result in greater learning for both the mentor and protégé, and inspire pride in overcoming any real or perceived challenges associated with such mentoring relationships. Furthermore, people who are in the minority at managerial levels can benefit from mentors from the dominant cultural group who help them overcome the emotional and structural barriers to advancement.[87] When mentors and protégés manage their relationship effectively, they enhance their reputations as effective managers of diversity and serve as role models for the rest of the organization.

Research suggests that cross-cultural mentoring relationships may be more difficult to develop. Human beings tend to feel more attracted to, more positively toward, and more comfortable with people whom they perceive to be similar to themselves (known as the similarity-attraction effect).[88] Researcher Stacy Blake-Beard, in her research on male mentors and female protégés, explains that perceived similarity "provides a foundation for identification to occur between mentor and protégé. Identification is the process by which the mentor is able to see something of himself in the protégé that he would like to nurture and support; the protégé also sees something in the mentor that she would like to role model and emulate." Blake-Beard advises mentors and protégés to look below surface differences and identify "deep-level" similarities such as values, attitudes, knowledge, and skills. Identifying similarities is important because, as Blake-Beard notes, "Past studies have found that attitudinal similarity is a 'catalyst for effective communication' and has been associated with higher group cohesiveness, satisfaction, performance ratings, and pay ratings."[89] In addition, identifying and building on other surface-level similarities such as having grown up in the same part of the country, having attended the same college, having some common interests, or having some of the same acquaintances can build attraction.[90] And showing ability and a track record of success are important ways to attract a mentor.[91]

When mentors and protégés cannot find similarities to build upon, they may find it difficult to identify with and trust each other because of real or perceived differences in values, lifestyles, and organizational experiences. Consequently, they may consciously or unconsciously avoid developing a mentoring relationship with each other.[92] When they do engage in a mentoring relationship, they may be less likely to initiate conversations with each other, confide in each other, spend time together, and have confidence in each other.[93] They also may be excessively cautious with each other. For example, the mentor may be overly concerned about being politically correct and fail to give the protégé critical feedback. The protégé, on the other hand, may attribute critical feedback to the mentor's stereotypes or attitudes toward the protégé's identity group rather than as a helpful critique of the protégé's work performance.

Furthermore, protégés may find it difficult to view mentors from a different gender, race, nationality, or other identity groups as role models. Mentors may find it difficult to give protégés the psychosocial support that can enhance the protégés' self-esteem, confidence, and motivation.[94] Consequently, protégés who are of a different identity group than their mentor often must get their role-modeling and psychosocial needs met elsewhere.[95] Indeed, research suggests that cross-race and cross-gender developmental relationships are more likely to be "sponsor" relationships that provide primarily instrumental support rather than "mentor" relationships that provide both instrumental and psychosocial support.[96]

Cross-race and cross-gender mentoring relationships may also be subject to more intense public scrutiny, as well as rumors, sexual innuendo, and claims of reverse discrimination.[97] Finally, when there are relatively few minorities in higher organizational levels, the few who are in these positions may be expected to be mentors, sponsors, and role models to the other minorities coming up the ranks. This can create an additional burden of responsibility on minorities, distract them from their other responsibilities, create excessively high expectations of them, and reinforce stereotypes that they are helpful primarily to people who share their cultural groups rather than to all employees.[98] When asked if she feels an "obligation to be a role model for other women," Donna Dubinsky, former president and CEO of Palm Computing, responded:

> I like being a role model to a certain extent. But what I try to do is to be very successful and [have] very high integrity and [be] a real contributor to my field. By doing so I believe that it sets an example for other women that they too can achieve that. That's what it means to be a role model, as opposed to the idea that I have an obligation to help every person who comes through the door who happens to be a woman. I'm going to help the high performers in my organization, men and women alike.[99]

How to Make the Most of Mentoring Relationships

Like all effective professional relationships, successful mentor–protégé relationships are built on trust and respect between two imperfect human beings who have multiple demands on their time. Furthermore, successful mentor–protégé relationships are based on reciprocity, change over time, and can take considerable planning, risk, and hard work on the part of the mentor and protégé.[100] The following advice can help you find and make the most of your mentoring relationships.

Advice for Protégés

- *Develop a network of developmental relationships.* As Ellen Ensher, co-author of the book, *Power Mentoring* says, "Unlike a marriage, mentoring relationships do not have to be monogamous."[101] Identify your goals for achieving results that matter at work, the expertise you want to develop, and the career progression you desire. Then develop a network of mentors who can help you achieve these goals. These would include peers, subject matter experts, people who are one step ahead of you in your career, and people at more senior levels. Develop a good relationship with your boss so that your boss will want to be one of these mentors. Michael Fenlon, Managing Director of Human Resources Strategy at PricewaterhouseCoopers says, "There is nothing like having a boss who is your biggest fan and who will advertise your abilities and potential to management and other senior leaders."[102] If you are unable to find mentoring opportunities in the organization, go outside of the organization for support or hire a professional career coach. And remember that you don't need to have all these mentors at the same time because it takes time and effort to be an effective protégé and you don't want to have so many mentors that you can't manage their expectations.
- *Have realistic expectations.* Mentors are not "guardian angels who dedicate their careers to the altruistic mission of nurturing protégés."[103] Remember that there are risks as well as rewards in any mentoring relationship and that each mentor is only one of many resources that you have to enhance your effectiveness, career development, and job satisfaction.
- *Develop a reputation as a high-potential protégé.* Mentors want to invest their time and resources in protégés whom they believe will be successful. Indeed, research has shown that mentors are more likely to select a protégé based on his or her perceived ability rather the protégé's need for help.[104] Therefore, show that you are committed to your professional development, develop a reputation as someone who works well with others, ask for help when you need it, and be open to feedback.
- *Be sensitive to your mentors' goals, needs, and style.* Mentors want to be successful, achieve their work goals, look good to others, and enjoy the time they spend with others. Therefore, you should do your best to make it effective and pleasurable, not painful, for mentors to work with you. At a minimum, this means understanding and adapting to your mentors' goals and preferred work styles.
- *Be pleasant to be around.* Make it pleasant and easy to work with you, and bring a positive, as well as thoughtful, attitude to the relationship. You want your mentors to look forward to seeing you and helping you out.
- *Give to mentors.* Remember that mentor–protégé relationships are based on reciprocity.[105] Think about what you can offer your mentors, and make sure that you take time to show appreciation. Go above and beyond the call of duty for your mentors, follow-through on their advice, let them know how their advice and support has helped you, and show appreciation for their efforts. As one mentor said of one of her protégés, "Unlike other [mentoring relationships] I've had, that one I thought really worked nicely because she took it very seriously and spent time thinking through what she wanted to cover. . . . Then, she would come back the next time and say, 'You know how we talked about this? . . . I did that. I

talked to [so and so], and it actually worked out great. That was good advice, thank you. I learned something there.'"[106]

- ***Do your best to get out of dysfunctional mentoring relationships.*** These include those in which the mentor is tyrannical, selfish, deceitful, manipulative, distancing, neglectful, trying to clone you into his or her self-image, clueless about the challenges that you face, sabotaging rather than supporting your success, inappropriate in other ways, or simply a bad fit.[107]

- ***Consider being a mentor for others.*** If you are a manager, mentoring others is your responsibility. It's also a great way to pay it forward, to give back to the organization, and to show appreciation to the people who have helped you along the way. Mentoring is also a way to clarify your own values and best practices that you want to pass onto others and to learn new skills (e.g., teaching, coaching, learning to listen).

- ***Realize that mentor–protégé relationships will change over time.*** Be ready to notice when a mentoring relationship is—or should be—transitioning to a new stage, and then move forward gracefully. On the basis of her observations of several mentoring relationships, researcher Kathy Kram concluded that mentoring relationships tend to go through four stages: (1) initiation, in which the parties show an initial interest in each other and get to know each other; (2) cultivation, in which the interactions between the mentor and the protégé become more frequent and increasingly based on trust; (3) separation, in which the mentor and the protégé begin to go their own ways; and (4) redefinition, in which the mentor and the protégé redefine their relationship (e.g., the protégé and the mentor may become peers, or the protégé may leave the organization and hire the former mentor as a consultant or employee).[108]

- ***Be prepared to accept additional complexity and greater learning in mentor–protégé relationships that cross cultural identity groups (e.g., race, gender, and nationality).*** If you are in the minority in an organization, remember that you may face more barriers in getting mentors. Therefore, you may have to work harder and more proactively to demonstrate your competence, clearly articulate your desire for challenging and high-visibility assignments, put more effort into making mentors and protégés feel comfortable, manage external perceptions, and get more of your social and emotional needs through different kinds of mentoring relationships.[109] In their research on the developmental experiences of successful minority executives, researchers David Thomas and John Gabarro concluded that successful minority executives attributed much of their early success to their broad range of developmental relationships early in their careers, and they had "many more such relationships and with a broader range of people [than white executives in the study had], especially early in their careers."[110]

Advice for Mentors

What does it take to be an effective mentor? Research suggests that people who become effective mentors are likely to have reputations for being good "people developers" who enjoy helping others. They tend to be known as informal, even tempered, and good listeners who interact frequently with employees. They also tend to have high standards, hold employees accountable, are comfortable delegating, provide developmental experiences and useful feedback, give employees the room to make their own mistakes, and share political insights about their organization. In short, they are committed to the long-term development of employees.[111]

There are many reasons for you to be a mentor. Someone may have caught your eye as a particularly high-potential employee. You need good employees and believe that mentoring is one way to develop competent, loyal employees. Perhaps you are at a life stage where you want to invest in the next generation. Mentoring may be an official part of your job, so you do it because you have to mentor employees, not because you really want to. Regardless of the reasons you choose to become a mentor, there are several steps that you can take to make your relationships with protégés mutually rewarding. See Table 6-1 for mentoring dos and don'ts.[112]

TABLE 6-1 Mentoring Dos and Don'ts	
Do	**Don't**
Be yourself and share your knowledge and experience.	Don't expect the protégé to follow in your footsteps. He or she may not share your career goals.
Set realistic expectations and boundaries for the mentoring relationship. Explain your role as a mentor, how much time you can offer, the best times to meet, the best way to reach you, and your preferred working style.	Don't neglect the protégé. Don't delay requests, even if it's just to say that you can't meet right away. Let the protégé know where he or she can go for information and assistance if you can't help. Don't make promises you can't keep.
Plan what you intend to say, particularly at first meetings. What points do you want to cover and in what order? How do you want the protégé to feel?	Don't wing it, particularly at first meetings.
Ask good questions: What are your goals? What do you want to know? How can I know? How can I help? Listen carefully to the answers.	Don't dominate the conversation or spend too much time talking about yourself.
Encourage the protégé's long-term as well as short-term growth.	Don't limit your discussion to the protégés current job.
Provide a "safe haven" where the protégé can be free from judgment and free to express his or her concerns and opinions. Give positive feedback. Remind the protégé that learning comes from overcoming hurdles and failures, as well as from successes.	Don't judge the protégé or breach a confidence.
Be sensitive to style and cultural differences. Differences influence the relationship most in the beginning. Over time, sharing common values and a common organizational identity can override real or perceived differences. Focus on commonalties as professionals and members of the organization.	Don't give in to stereotypes. Don't give up if the "chemistry" isn't there immediately. Remember that an effective mentoring relationship is built on trust, caring, and commitment, all of which can be proactively developed over time.
If you have a long-distance mentoring relationship, systematically plan telephone meetings, e-mail check-ins, and similar communication strategies to keep in touch. Schedule extra time to spend together when you happen to be at the same location.	Don't assume that distance should end the relationship.

NETWORKING

Many hardworking and high-achieving professionals think that interpersonal relationships often get in the way of their work performance, particularly when they are busy or when a relationship doesn't add immediate instrumental value. Their thinking—and the potential consequences of this thinking—goes somewhat like this:

> I thought it was enough to know my job and to work hard. I stayed on top of the new developments in my field. I even won a few industry awards for my designs. I came in early and worked late. Heck, I rarely went out to lunch—I just kept working. Sometimes I worked so hard that I didn't even have enough time to return phone calls or email messages, especially those messages from people who I didn't know very well or who were asking for favors that I didn't have time to do. Priorities, priorities, priorities, you know. Frankly, I don't have much in common with many of the people here anyway, nor do I ever expect to. I barely have enough time to get to know my own family. I have two children, one in the second grade and one in the fourth grade. Or is it the third and fifth grade? And friends, who has time for friends? So, you ask me if I was surprised when my colleague was promoted and I wasn't? Definitely. I don't get it. Hasn't anyone noticed how hard I work and the contributions that I make to this company? Maybe it's true what they say: "It's not what you know, it's who you know."

The preceding passage reflects a common naïveté about professional life. The assumption is that it's either what you know or who you know. But in reality, it's both. Researcher Wayne Baker explains that "success depends on two factors: what a person knows (his or her human capital) and the network of relationships he or she has developed (the person's social capital). The world has changed in such a way that no one person can know enough about his or her profession anymore, so he or she has to draw on information, knowledge, and resources that other people offer. One of the biggest lessons people need to unlearn as they enter the world of business is that success is an individual matter."[113]

Your network enables you to develop the social capital—the resources (e.g., information, ideas, skills, knowledge, goodwill, material goods, and financial resources) and opportunities (e.g., recommendations, job leads and promotions) you gain through your relationships with others. The following example, told by former Secretary of Labor Robert B. Reich, illustrates the ironic power of connections.

> A few years ago, a woman named Marcia Lewin used a political connection to help secure a job for her daughter. Lewin contacted her friend Walter Kaye, a retired insurance executive from New York who was a major donor to the democratic party, having enriched its coffers by between $300,000 and $350,000. Not incidentally, Kaye was a friend of Hillary Rodham Clinton, the First Lady. With the help of Kaye, Marcia's daughter Monica got a job as a White House intern, and the rest, sad to say, is history.[114]

Networking is the deliberate, systematic process of building and maintaining relationships based on mutual benefit. Some of these relationships are with people inside the organization, and others are with people outside the organization. Some of these relationships provide immediate instrumental benefits, whereas others have no immediate or apparent work-related benefits.

Some of these relationships are based on formal organizational ties such as those with direct bosses, direct reports, colleagues, and customers. Others are based on informal ties such as those with people from other departments and people you meet at professional conferences, social events, clubs, religious institutions, schools, child or elder care, and so on. Some are close relationships with people with whom you interact often and who provide emotional, as well as instrumental, support. Others are relationships that are based on little more than the exchange of a business card.

All of these relationships can contribute to your professional effectiveness, career advancement, and psychological well-being. Research suggests that people with well-developed networks have access to more information and material resources, are more central to organizational innovations, are perceived as more powerful, are better able to influence others and implement ideas, get more support, have stronger and more far-reaching reputations, and hear about job leads more quickly and more often. Team leaders who network with individuals and groups beyond their own team tend to be more likely to be promoted, in part because their teams are likely to perform better because of the additional resources and support they get from people outside the team.[115] Research also suggests that people with strong networks have access to more social and emotional support that can enhance their psychological well-being, particularly in times of change or crisis.[116]

> If the organization man defined the workplace of the 1950s, the individual networker will be the model of the 2000s.
> —ANN REILLY DOWD

Unfortunately, many people associate networking with superficial schmoozing, taking advantage of people, or playing politics, so they find the idea of systematically building relationships for mutual benefit distasteful. Certainly, networking—like all good things—can be abused. Some people try to use their network as a substitute for personal competence, spend so much time networking that they pay little attention to their day-to-day tasks, overinvest in superficial relationships, or use people for their own ends without offering anything in return. Others see every social event as an opportunity to meet people who can help them instrumentally in their jobs or careers. Indeed, someone once suggested that I join a local church not because it could fulfill my spiritual needs but because it's a "great place to network." (Personally, I wasn't impressed with the idea of joining a religious institution for the networking, rather than spiritual, opportunities.)

Networking, when done responsibly, is ethical for many reasons. It is ethical because we all have the responsibility to make our organizations and ourselves more effective. Building and nurturing a broad range of high-quality work relationships enables us to do so. It is ethical because high-quality relationships are built on trust, respect, and reciprocity. Indeed, a fundamental assumption of effective networking is that networks are built not only on what you get from the people in your network but from what you give to the people in your network. It is ethical because building our network inspires us to reach out and interact with people with whom we wouldn't normally interact, which broadens our worldview and experience. And it is ethical because people who have effective networks are likely to be competent, as well as connected.[117]

Characteristics of Effective Networks

There is no such thing as an ideal network. Your ideal network depends on what you want to accomplish.[118] Nonetheless, the most effective professional networks have several characteristics in common. They are broad, diverse, include high-status contacts, and include both strong ties (people you are close to and interact with often) and weak ties (people you don't know very well and interact with infrequently).

DIVERSITY: The diversity of your network matters because if your network is made up of people who are similar to you in identity (e.g., race, gender, nationality, religion, sexual orientation, or class) or organizational (e.g., hierarchical level and departmental affiliation) group memberships, they are more likely to have similar experiences, perceptions, and networks as you have.[119] If you have a diverse network, you are likely to have access to a greater range of resources that can provide task, career, and social support.[120] For example, someone who has a network that includes positive relationships with peers, bosses, bosses of bosses, direct reports, people from many different departments, and people from outside the organization is likely to be perceived as more powerful and is likely to have an easier time implementing a new idea than someone whose network is limited to peers or to people in his or her own department. As Baker explains, this is because "repeated interaction encourages cooperation."[121] Unfortunately, the comfort associated with similarity tends to get stronger in turbulent and uncertain times—ironically, just when new ways of thinking and interacting among different groups in the organization are needed most. Consequently, you need to build real connections with a diverse network of people *before* you need the support.[122]

STATUS: The status of people in your network matters because people who are perceived to have high-status contacts in their network are viewed as more competent and powerful.[123] The key word here is "perceived." In an intriguing study, researchers Martin Kilduff and David Krackhardt concluded that a person's "performance reputation" is based in part on that person's ability to do high-quality work and in part on people's perceptions that the person has a prominent friend. Kilduff and Krackhardt note that their study suggests that it is the perceptions of a person's relationship with an influential person, not the actual existence of the relationship, that matters.[124] They refer to this as the "basking-in-reflected-glory effect."[125] It is not surprising that we base our assumptions about a person's competence on whom we think they know. It is often difficult to assess a person's performance, so we look for other signals that they are competent. If we think that an influential person believes that someone is competent, then we are likely to use this information to make assumptions about that person's competence as well, given no evidence to the contrary.

STRONG AND WEAK TIES: Having both strong ties and weak ties in your network matters because both types of ties offer particular kinds of benefits. Tie strength refers to the degree of intimacy, interaction, emotional investment, and expectations of reciprocity in a relationship.[126] Strong ties offer more trust, closeness, and emotional support than do weak ties, and they tend to last longer.[127] Although strong ties provide deeper levels of ongoing instrumental and emotional support, weak ties provide broader exposure and a wider range of resources (e.g., job leads from someone that you met briefly at a conference). You need the ongoing instrumental and emotional support that you get from strong ties, but you also need the broad exposure and access to resources that you get from weak ties. After all, you can't know everyone well, so your effectiveness, career growth, and general well-being depend on the cooperation and support of people whom you don't know very well, if at all.

Diversity and Networks

In today's global and diverse economic environment, researchers are becoming increasingly interested in how the networks of people from various cultural groups differ, why they differ, and whether these differences have consequences. As of this writing, most researchers who study networks agree that people from different organizational groups (e.g., department and hierarchical level) and identity groups (e.g., race, gender, and nationality) tend to develop different kinds of networks and take different approaches to gaining instrumental, career, and emotional support.[128]

Even differences across hierarchical levels influence networking patterns. For example, research suggests that managers, in contrast to nonmanagers, tend to have more relationships outside their immediate work group, belong to more clubs and societies (e.g., chambers of commerce), and have more coworkers in their informal networks.[129] This is not surprising because managers depend on a greater number and variety of people to get their work done. Indeed, a broad and diverse network is increasingly being seen as a basic requirement of a manager's job.

A growing body of research suggests that successful women and people of color in the United States tend to have a more diverse network of relationships and more ties outside their departments and organizations than do their equally successful white peers and less successful women and people of color in the United States.[130] Why is this so? Researchers use two theories to explain this pattern: the similarity-attraction hypothesis and distinctiveness theory. Drawing on the similarity-attraction theory, researchers argue that people in the majority are less likely to seek out, interact with, and feel a connection with people who are in the minority. Consequently, when women and people of color are underrepresented at upper levels of the hierarchy, they often have to go outside their departments and organizations to find other women and people of color with whom to develop strong ties that offer both instrumental and psychosocial support.[131]

Drawing on distinctiveness theory, researchers argue that "people in a social context tend to identify with others with whom they share characteristics that are relatively rare in that context."[132] In other words, those in the minority in an organization, department, or hierarchical level, are more likely to notice the similarity between themselves and other minorities and thus be more attracted to and seek out each other. Thus, two women in a crowd of men will tend to notice, identify with, and interact with each other on the basis of gender. However, the same two women will be less likely to notice and seek out each other in a predominantly female group. Distinctiveness theory assumes that the same would hold true for any member of other underrepresented groups in a group or organization.

The similarity-attraction and distinctiveness dynamics have several implications for the networks of people in the minority in organizations. They suggest that if people in the minority tend to be located primarily at lower levels of the organizational hierarchy, they are likely to have more relationships with people who also have lower organizational status and fewer relationships with people who have higher organizational status. They also are more likely to be viewed as more marginal to the organization.[133] Consequently, they may have less access to important information and material resources, feel more alienated from the organization, and be less satisfied with their work.

Given these dynamics, it's important for people who are in the minority or in lower hierarchical levels to proactively develop their network by seeking out commonalities and connections with people outside their identity and hierarchical group. In addition, some research suggests that people who in the minority in organizations benefit from joining effective minority network groups. Researcher Raymond Friedman describes network groups as groups that bring together people in who are minorities in organizations "for the purpose of meeting each other, helping each other succeed, and identifying issues within the organization that are a common concern."[134]

One of the first and most well-known network groups is the Black Caucus Group at Xerox. Decades ago, this group was formed by older and experienced African American salespeople to socialize, promote, and provide support to younger and less experienced African American salespeople at Xerox. In the early 1970s, the African American salespeople typically were not integrated into critical informal organizational networks that existed among white employees, even though these networks often provided mentoring relationships and access to unofficial information that helped employees navigate organizational politics, enhance their work performance, and manage their careers. By forming the Black Caucus Group, the senior African American salespeople were able to provide the younger African American salespeople with these informal yet critical advantages, as well as role models for success within Xerox. Within the Black Caucus Group, African American sales representatives felt they were able to ask questions and discuss issues that they felt uncomfortable asking outside the group. By creating this separate group for African American salespeople, they were able to develop the perspective and skills that would enable them to add more value, achieve more career success, and ultimately more fully integrate into Xerox.

On the basis of their research, Friedman and his colleagues concluded that well-managed network groups provide several benefits.[135] Minority managers who join network groups are more likely to stay with the organization, in part because network groups provide professional and psychological support, increase job satisfaction, and strengthen organizational commitment. Network groups, when well run, provide greater access to information about the company (e.g., new technologies, corporate strategy, and career systems), enable more opportunities for mentoring and presentations by senior people, promote social gatherings, offer seminars and workshops, provide contacts that may lead to other prospects, and provide opportunities to give back to one's community (e.g., through mentoring programs or fundraising for minority scholarships). Each of these benefits can increase the minority member's power base and enhance job effectiveness, career opportunities, and general well-being. Notably, one study found that racial minorities (in U.S. companies that supported network groups) were more likely to have a white mentor, in part because effective network groups help members create more cross-race ties.[136]

Network groups tend to be initiated and managed by members of minority groups who reach out to the organizational leaders for support and legitimacy. Friedman and his colleagues recommend the following strategies for building an effective network group:

- Be sure that the group does not become "factionized" or too political. Focus on helping members achieve the success that they desire.
- Create an effective means of selecting network group leaders and managing the transition between leaders.
- Provide many different kinds of activities so that the network group meets the needs of members with different goals, life situations, and interests.
- "Attract high potential minority employees" and make "membership in the group a symbol of success."
- Regularly reach out to organizational members who are not members of the network group, and maintain positive relationships with organizational leaders.
- Include high-level and successful minority managers who can provide the network group with influence, legitimacy, and connections with important organizational networks.

Note that when not well managed, network groups can run the risk of being perceived as promoting "symbolic separation," rather than greater integration into the organization.[137] In other words, people who join network groups may be perceived as taking a separatist strategy at work. In contrast, when people in the minority join *effective* network groups that separate them at times from the majority for the purpose of professional development and emotional support, they are also more likely to succeed in the organization, which promotes their integration into the majority. To take advantage of the benefits of network groups, while simultaneously managing perceptions of separatism, the most useful strategy for people who are minorities in organizations is to maintain ties to network groups and simultaneously develop a broad network of relationships with members of the majority group both within and outside the organization.[138]

Networking Advice

Wayne Baker says that "there's virtually no correlation between personality type and social network. People can change their networks more easily than they can change their personality. Everyone can learn new skills." The most important things that you can do to build your network are to be systematic and proactive—and remember that "small steps can have a big payoff.[139] Remember that your network grows by what you *give* to people." Also remember that your ideal network depends on what you want to gain from your network. At a minimum, determine what you want and need in three areas:

- *Task accomplishment.* Who can help you get your work done? What experts do you need to know? What kinds of influential people can help your reputation, offer you support, and provide you with opportunity and visibility? Who can provide you with critical information, material resources, and support? Who can you talk with about organizational politics? Who can you help do their own work better?
- *Career advancement.* Who can help you with your career? Who would make a good mentor and role model? Who can you call on if your company is downsized and you lose your job? Who can give you leads about job opportunities? Who can you help with their career-advancement?
- *Psychological and social support.* What kinds of people do you enjoy being around? Do you know people who appreciate you primarily for who you are, not just for your professional accomplishments? Do you know people who will support you when you are down and not only when your career is going well? Do you know people who will provide help and emotional support if you have a medical emergency, need help caring for children or aging parents, need to discuss delicate organizational problems, or lose your job? Do you help people when they need support? Do people trust you enough to turn to you for help?

Once you have analyzed what you want from your network and what you can offer people in your network, identify who is in your current network and identify the strengths and weaknesses of your network. To what degree does your current network help you achieve your task, career, and psychosocial goals? How diverse is your network? Do you have high-status people in your network? Do you have both strong and weak ties? Are you reaching out to people outside your immediate work group? The assessment in Box 6-5 can help you identify your networking strengths and weaknesses.

Next, take steps to systematically develop your network. In addition to face-to-face networking, consider online social networking opportunities such as LinkedIn and Facebook, as well as creating your own Web sites, writing blogs, and joining online communities related to your professional and personal goals. Search online to find the best advice for creating an online presence that is inviting, clarifies your brand and expertise, and helps you join and contribute to relevant online communities. Most important, remember that developing your network is an

BOX 6-5   How Skilled Are You at Networking?

Answer the following questions to identify your networking strengths and weaknesses.

	Not at All	Rarely	Some-times	Frequently	Always
I have a reputation for excelling at what I do.					
I have an expertise that I am known for.	___	___	___	___	___
I am reliable. I keep my word and don't promise more than I can deliver.	___	___	___	___	___
I do my work on time, within budget, and I do it right the first time.	___	___	___	___	___
I'm the kind of person people want to be around.					
I show genuine respect for everyone.	___	___	___	___	___
I am optimistic and positive.	___	___	___	___	___
I am a good listener.	___	___	___	___	___
I invest in the success of others.	___	___	___	___	___
I give more than I receive from others.	___	___	___	___	___
I reach out to people outside my cultural or organizational groups.					
My network includes people from many different cultural and organizational groups.	___	___	___	___	___
I help people from other cultures feel comfortable.	___	___	___	___	___
I am considerate of other people's cultures.	___	___	___	___	___
I seek out common ground between myself and others.	___	___	___	___	___
I am aware of the impact of my culture on how others may perceive me and relate to me.	___	___	___	___	___
I am loyal and trustworthy.					
I am discrete and protect the confidentiality of others.	___	___	___	___	___
I support others when they are going through difficult as well as successful periods.	___	___	___	___	___
I return messages (telephone calls, mail, e-mail, text messages) quickly.	___	___	___	___	___
I am visible.					
I know several high-status people who are aware of my strengths.	___	___	___	___	___
I participate in committees and positions of responsibility.	___	___	___	___	___

BOX 6-5 *Continued*

	Not at All	Rarely	Some-times	Frequently	Always
I attend professional meetings and conferences.	____	____	____	____	____
I participate in community events (e.g., neighborhood events, political events).	____	____	____	____	____
I have a professional online presence (e.g., social networking sites such as LinkedIn, Facebook).	____	____	____	____	____
I systematically plan my network.					
I know what I want to achieve from my network.	____	____	____	____	____
I know what people I need in my network.	____	____	____	____	____
I know what I can offer people in my network.	____	____	____	____	____
I keep in touch with people in my network.	____	____	____	____	____
I actively fill the gaps in my network.	____	____	____	____	____
I use my network.					
I request information and materials resources from people when I need them.	____	____	____	____	____
I let people know when I need their support.	____	____	____	____	____
I manage the downside of networking.					
I can say "no" to requests gracefully to avoid getting overcommitted.	____	____	____	____	____
I set personal boundaries gracefully.	____	____	____	____	____
I manage my time well.	____	____	____	____	____
I make time to spend time with the people I love.	____	____	____	____	____

1. Based on your assessment of your networking skills, what are your strengths?
2. What are your weaknesses?
3. Identify three things that you will do in the next week to improve your network.
4. Identify three things that you will do in the next three months to improve your network.
5. Identify three things that you will do in the next year to improve your network.

ongoing process, and your needs may change over time. Having a systematic plan of action will help you prioritize your networking strategy so that it is focused, manageable (remember that effective networks are built thoughtfully over time, and you don't have to do everything at once), and enjoyable. Box 6-6 describes several small steps that you can take to develop and nurture your network.

When systematically developing your network, remember that the *quality*, not only the quantity, of the relationships you have with others matters. Positive organizational scholarship

---

BOX 6-6   Fifteen Steps toward Developing and Nurturing Your Network

1. Always treat everyone with respect.
2. Always carry your business card. Know the norms for giving and receiving business cards in different cultures; for example, the Japanese consider it rude to write on a business card.
3. Invest in your social skills. Attend workshops that enhance your social skills. Practice these skills every day.
4. During conversations, ask people about themselves, their work, or their interests and listen carefully. Remember to thank people when the conversation is over.
5. Give sincere compliments. People like to be appreciated.
6. Follow up with people you have recently met or contacted. For example, send notes thanking people for their time or assistance. Pass on articles or information that may be of interest to them. One consultant sends three notes of appreciation each workday, which takes approximately 15 minutes a day. At the end of a workweek, she's nurtured at least 15 relationships, which add up to 750 relationships a year if she works 50 weeks a year.[144]
7. Take time to meet with people with whom you wouldn't normally interact. Get out of your office. Volunteer for committees and assignments that take you out of your immediate work area. Invite different people to breaks, breakfast, lunch, or dinner.
8. Participate in company events and functions.
9. Don't overrely on e-mail. Face-to-face interactions are still the best way to build relationships, particularly new relationships.
10. Find the time to help others. Offer unsolicited help.
11. Help people meet others outside their network who can help them.
12. Join professional groups such as alumni associations, network groups, and community groups.
13. Attend conferences, trade shows, and other professional gatherings. Choose your conferences carefully. Prior to attending a conference: (1) set objectives for what you want to achieve; (2) write out your agenda, including events you want to attend and people you want to meet; (3) attend social events; (4) sit with people you don't know during the event and with a different group at different times; (5) plan your conversations (e.g., plan on asking questions such as "What are the greatest challenges your organization—or profession—has today?" "How did you first get involved with your organization?" and (6) always wear a name tag and exchange business cards when appropriate.
14. Be organized. Start a network file that lists the names and contact information for people you want in your network.
15. Don't burn any bridges. Whenever possible, leave relationships on a positive note. If you ask someone for help and they say "no," remember to thank them anyway.

---

researchers describe two ways in which the quality of relationships matters: the development of high-quality connections and the role of energizers in networks.

HIGH-QUALITY CONNECTIONS Researchers Jane Dutton and Emily Heaphy define high-quality connections as those that are based on vitality, mutual support, and positive regard.[140] These connections can be brief (such as when two people meet at a conference and immediately find themselves immersed in a fascinating conversation) or long-term (such as when colleagues work together for several years). What are the characteristics of a high-quality connection? In a high-quality connection, both parties feel emotionally connected, energized, and appreciated. They find it easy to think broadly and come up with new ideas together. They are adaptive and resilient when faced with hurdles and setbacks because they believe in their ability to successfully address challenges together. Researchers have found that people who experience high-quality connections tend to feel physically better, are more engaged at work, connect more often and more successfully with people from other organizational areas, are more open to learning, are more attached and committed to their organizations, and have better performance.[141]

ENERGIZING RELATIONSHIPS Researcher Wayne Baker and his colleagues found that some people in networks are "energizers."[142] Energizers inspire people with their visions, provide people with opportunities to contribute to something they believe is meaningful, and offer hope when needed. In contrast, de-energizers sap people's energy through their negative attitudes, promotion of their personal agendas, and lack of follow-through on the commitments they make to others. People are drawn toward energizers because they feel more engaged, motivated, and positive when they are around them. In particular, they feel they have meaningful goals in common, are hopeful that they can make a difference, feel engaged in the moment (Note that it's hard to feel energized by someone who is distracted by a laptop or smart phone.), and can see progress from their shared efforts.[143] When interacting with energizers, people believe that they can think more creatively, process information more quickly, remember more about the conversation, and behave more proactively. Consequently, energizers play a critical role in helping organizations learn, adapt, and achieve organizational objectives. Not surprisingly, people who are described as energizers in organizations tend to be higher performers because they are able to bring out the best in themselves and others.

The point here is that it's worth thinking about the quality of your relationships, not only the quantity of your relationships. Are your relationships characterized by vitality, mutual support, and positive regard? Do people look forward to seeing you and do you look forward to seeing others? Are you someone who people feel energized by when they're around you, or do they feel as though their energy is depleted when around you? Finally, what can you do to increase the number of energizing and high-quality interactions and energizing relationships in your everyday work?

IMPRESSION MANAGEMENT

No discussion of managing up, down, and sideways would be complete without a discussion of impression management. After all, says researcher Susan Ashford, organizations "are made up of people who observe and make judgments about each other."[145] The judgments people make about us influence our ability to achieve results at work, attain the career success that we desire, and have interactions that enhance our self-esteem. Consequently, it is not surprising that we sometimes use impression management strategies to influence other people's judgments of us in order to achieve these goals.[146]

We sometimes use impression management to get something for ourselves— organizational resources, a high performance rating, or a job promotion. Or we may use impression management to help someone else feel comfortable ("The people at the office are looking forward to meeting you because they've heard many good things about your work."), save face ("No, I really don't think anyone on the board noticed that you were reading your e-mail during the meeting."), or feel joy ("What a beautiful baby!")—all of which help build the trust from which goodwill, cooperation, and coordination grow.

> If you ever do a survey, you'll find that people prefer illusion to reality, ten to one.
> —JUDITH GUEST, *Ordinary People*

In short, impression management is both a self-preservation technique in hierarchical organizations and an important social ritual that helps make organizational relationships more satisfying and productive. Indeed, impression management is so taken for granted in everyday organizational life that we often don't notice when we or others are doing it. We consciously and unconsciously use a variety of impression management strategies, and we can employ many of them sincerely.[147] For example:

- We use *ingratiation* to make others feel better in the hope that doing so will enhance their perceptions of us.[148] Ingratiation strategies include flattering, doing favors, conforming to other people's opinions, and smiling to show support, agreement, or friendliness. Although ingratiation is usually associated with someone who is trying to influence someone who is higher in the organizational hierarchy ("buttering up the boss"), we also use ingratiation with our peers, direct reports, clients, and others.

- We use *self-enhancement* to promote a positive image of ourselves to enhance other's impressions of us.[149] We may, for example, actively promote our strengths ("Did I ever tell you I was the valedictorian of my class?"), take credit for a job well done ("The team helped out so much after I got that million-dollar contract."), or "dress for success" ("Dress for the job you want, not the job you have.").

- We use a *basking-in-reflected-glory* strategy when we associate ourselves with someone or something that is viewed positively by others to enhance others' impression of us. We often refer to this as "riding someone else's coattails" or "being seen in the right places with the right people." To illustrate, the story is told that a businessman once asked the wealthy financier Baron de Rothschild for a loan. De Rothschild is reported to have responded, "I won't give you a loan myself; but I will walk arm-in-arm with you across the floor of the stock exchange, and you soon shall have willing lenders to spare."[150]

- We use *intimidation* when we want to force someone to do something. Examples include threatening to quit, fire someone, or tell a boss about someone's undesirable action. We are more likely to use these strategies when we have power over someone, when the target is not in a position to retaliate, and when our goal isn't to be liked by the person we are intimidating.[151]

- We use *self-deprecation and self-handicapping* strategies when we want to make ourselves look bad to achieve a desired goal.[152] For example, we may say, "I'm sorry I acted discourteously at yesterday's meeting" to increase our chances of getting forgiveness from someone whom we offended. We may excuse ourselves from playing in the company's annual volleyball tournament by explaining that we have a bad back. We may use excuses to explain why we did a poor job ("I was just getting over the flu and I probably should have stayed home but I stayed at work because I really wanted to finish the job on time."). We may avoid learning a new skill or pretend to be incompetent in order to get someone else to do something that we don't want to do ("Can you make the 50 copies of the report, please? I can never get that copier to work.").

Research suggests that "playing dumb" at work is quite common. Researchers conducted a telephone survey of 2,247 working adults from 48 states in the United States and asked them if they ever "pretended to be less intelligent or knowledgeable than they were" at work. More than 25% of the respondents admitted to doing so. Almost 15% of the male workers admitted to playing dumb with their bosses, and 7% of the women workers admitted to doing so. Seventeen percent of the men admitted to playing dumb with their coworkers, and 9% of the women admitted to doing so. Younger workers reported playing dumb more often than did older workers.[153]

    It appears that many of our efforts at impression management work. Several studies suggest that direct reports who use ingratiation tend to be better liked by their bosses; have more positive communication with their supervisors; receive more favorable performance evaluations; and receive more feedback, resources, challenges, pay raises, and promotions than their equally qualified coworkers who do not use ingratiation.[154]

Why does impression management work? In part, it's because we are social animals and, as such, have a natural desire to be liked by others. Flattery, favors, and other ingratiating behaviors make us feel noticed and appreciated. Impression management techniques also work because we often need to make judgments based on limited information, and sometimes the only information we have about someone is the image that they project. The more ambiguous the situation and the less objective data we have about a person, the more likely we are to "judge the book by its cover," even though doing so can sometimes lead us down the wrong path.

Impression management can be risky business. People who invest too much time in impression management may not devote enough time to their job duties.[155] People who oversell themselves may have trouble living up to the expectations that they raise.[156] People who routinely engage in opinion conformity (i.e., going along with the opinions of others even when they privately disagree) may withhold important information, feedback, and bad news that is critical to effective decision making, and they may come across as unable to take a stand or promote their own ideas. People who use flattery too often may come across as smarmy or manipulative. Self-promotion can come across as conceited and tiresome.[157] Indeed, research suggests that ingratiation techniques such as flattery are more likely to be successful than self-enhancement techniques. And note that what may be perceived as flattery in one culture may be inappropriate in another culture.

> The aim of flattery is to sooth and encourage us by assuring us of a truth of an opinion we have already formed about ourselves.
> —EDITH SITWELL

So, what can you do to avoid some of the risks associated with impression management? To avoid being swayed by others' attempts at impression management, look for objective measures of performance by setting clear performance standards and performance measures, and routinely assess whether your impressions match the person's actual performance. If possible, use a 360-degree feedback system to learn how people at all levels of the hierarchy perceive this person. Remember, we tend to evaluate people whom we perceive to be similar to ourselves more positively, so be careful to monitor your own biases.

To avoid being seen as an empty suit (someone who makes all the right moves but does not perform well when it comes to completing assignments and contributing to the organization), make sure that you are competent at your work, focused on completing tasks as well as developing relationships, and are able to articulate how you add measurable value to the organization and help others achieve their work goals. Be respectful and sincere toward everyone and not only toward people who you feel can help you achieve your career goals. Perhaps most important, remember that although impression management is necessary for developing effective and rewarding work relationships, being overdependent on other people's judgments for your self-esteem and career success can be a stressful and fragile existence.

CONCLUSION

Regardless of our role in organizations (direct report, peer, boss), we are all fallible human beings who depend on each other's help to get results, have the careers we desire, and enjoy our lives and work. Each of our relationships—whether we are managing up, down, or sideways to our peers—is based on building mutual trust and goodwill. It's wise to remember that every interaction with your boss, peers, and direct reports is an opportunity to build a more productive and more enjoyable relationship that adds value to those in the relationship, your organization, and the people your organization serves.

Chapter Summary

The quality of your relationships with your direct reports, bosses, and peers significantly influences your task effectiveness, career development (promotions and salary), job satisfaction, and personal well-being.

Regardless of whether you are managing up, down, or sideways, remember the following assumptions about human relationships: High-quality relationships are built on trust, respect, and reciprocity. We are all fallible human beings who depend on each other for our professional effectiveness, career success, and personal well-being.

Our relationships with bosses and direct report are shaped by our attitudes toward authority relationships (i.e., our beliefs about whether authority figures are competent, trustworthy, and caring). Our attitudes toward authority are shaped by where we sit in the organizational hierarchy as well as our earliest experiences with authority figures—our parents and primary caretakers.

Effective managers are cognitively and behaviorally complex. They are able to perceive situations from a variety of perspectives, assess the appropriate action required for each situation, and adapt their behavior accordingly.

Managers who use the Situational Leadership Model adapt their task and relationship-focused behaviors to the willingness and ability of employees to accomplish specific tasks.

Managers who use the Denison Leadership Development Model adapt their behavior to the needs of the situation as well. They base their behavior on their analysis of the internal and external organizational environment, as well as the employees' and organization's needs for stability and change. They respond to this analysis by focusing on four areas: creating a clear, engaging mission; ensuring consistency across organizational units (e.g., through policies, procedures, and norms); promoting teamwork within and across units; and empowering employees. Research suggests that managers who focus on these areas contribute to performance measures, such as organizational growth, profitability, customer service, and employee satisfaction.

Empowerment refers to an employee's belief that he or she can have an impact on the organizational environment. Employees are likely to feel empowered when they believe that the work is meaningful; that they have the competence to do the work; that they have the freedom to choose the way to achieve goals; and that they can influence organizational outcomes."

Although you cannot ensure that employees will feel empowered, you can create a context that promotes empowerment by providing clear boundaries, goals, and performance measures, and provide sociopolitical support, information, education and training, and a participative work climate. Notably, abundant resources are not related to empowerment.

Research suggests that many employees are likely to obey the wishes of authority figures, even if doing so is unethical. Both the Milgram experiment and the Stanford prison experiment, as well as events in the "real world," remind us that people may blindly follow authority even when asked to do things that are unethical.

While some organizations are known for promoting unethical and abusive behavior, others are known for promoting compassion. Organizations that have a history of responding compassionately when their members are suffering or are in need of personal support tend to have the following characteristics in common: values that support caring for others rather than simply "sticking to business," networks and relationships through which calls to action can move quickly, a history of established routines that enable people to help others (e.g., sending out e-mails when someone is ill), and systems that support caregiving. Leaders who want to promote compassionate organizing know that it's not enough to be a compassionate leader or to have a few compassionate employees. Rather, leaders who build compassionate organizations see themselves as social architects who create organizational cultures and systems that generate patterns of thinking and acting that motivate and enable organizational members to provide the scale, scope, speed, and customization of support and resources needed to help people when they are suffering.

The ability to manage your boss is a critical managerial skill. Managing your boss involves understanding your boss (goals, styles, strengths, and weaknesses), understanding yourself (goals, styles, strengths, and weaknesses), and adapting your behavior in ways that bring out the best in you, your boss, and your organization.

Mentor–protégé relationships provide the protégé with both instrumental and psychosocial support. To benefit most from mentoring relationships, remember that they are built on trust and respect between two imperfect human beings who have multiple demands on their time; are based on reciprocity; change over time; and take considerable planning, risk, and hard work on the part of the mentor and protégé.

Research suggests that mentors and protégés from different cultural groups may be less likely to interact with each other, confide less in each other, and have less confidence in each other. The protégé may find it difficult to see the mentor as a role model, and the mentor may find it difficult to provide appropriate psychosocial support. However, both mentors and protégés may benefit from overcoming the challenges together, developing a broader worldview, and being role models for managing diversity in the organization.

Networking is the deliberate, systematic process of building and maintaining relationships based on mutual benefit. The best kind of network depends on what you want to accomplish. However, a general rule is that your network should be broad and diverse, have high-status people in it, and include both strong and weak ties.

Research suggests that people who are in the minority in organizations are likely to benefit from maintaining ties to network groups (e.g., same-gender or same-race groups) while simultaneously developing a broad network of relationships with people who are in the majority in the organization.

When systematically developing your network, remember that the quality, not only the quantity, of the relationships you have with others matters. Positive organizational researchers have found that energizers and high-quality connections enhance individual and organizational effectiveness.

We use impression management when we behave in ways designed to influence another person's feelings toward us to get a desired end. Impression management techniques include ingratiation, self-enhancement, basking-in-reflected-glory, intimidation, self-deprecation, and self-handicapping. Remember that although impression management is taken for granted, unavoidable, and often useful, in everyday organizational life, it also carries risks.

Food for Thought

1. What is the most useful thing you learned in this chapter, and why?
2. With the strategies for managing up, down, and sideways described in this chapter, what can you do to increase your own effectiveness? Practice one of these behaviors over the next week, and note any benefits and progress you make.
3. Think about the best and worst boss (or authority figure) you ever had. What were the characteristics of the best boss? Worst boss? How might you have contributed to the situation with your worst boss? What lessons did you learn from the best boss and worst boss that you can use to make yourself a better manager?
4. Think of a time when you felt empowered at work. What did it feel like? What were the consequences?

Did your boss, colleagues, organizational leadership, or others do anything that helped you feel this way?

5. Think of a time when you were courageous enough to resist what you believed was an unethical or immoral situation. What made you resist and what were the consequences? How can you ensure that you will have the courage to resist a slippery moral slope in the future?
6. If you wanted to create a context in which your employees would react compassionately to others in need, what steps would you take so that they would feel compelled and empowered to offer support and resources to those in need?
7. As you read earlier in this chapter, Donna Dubinsky, former president and CEO of Palm Computing, stated that although she likes being a role model, she downplays

any general sense of obligation to developing women in her organization any more than she feels obligated to develop men in her organization. In contrast, the founders of the Black Caucus Group at Xerox felt a general sense of obligation to African American salespeople at Xerox. Do you agree with Dubinsky? The founders of the Black Caucus Group? Why or why not?

8. Do you have a network of developmental relationships? If so, describe who is in it and what benefits the different relationships offer you. Also describe what benefits you provide in the different relationships. If you don't have a network of developmental relationships, what can you do to create one? Who should be in it and why?

9. When you are in the protégé role, what can you do to ensure that the mentor values working with you?

10. Complete the networking assessment in this chapter. What are your networking strengths and weaknesses?

What steps can you take this week, this month, and this year to improve your network?

11. Think about a high-quality connection that you've had with someone at work. What were the characteristics of this connection? What were the consequences of having this high-quality connection?

12. Identify someone you know who is an energizer in their organization. What do they do that draws people to them? How does being an energizer help this person's organization? What steps can you take to be an energizer in your organization?

13. Think back over the past week. Identify three impression management techniques that you used at work or at home. What were you trying to accomplish? Do you think you were effective? Why or why not? Describe any benefits and risks associated with using these techniques.

Endnotes

1. Goleman, Daniel. 1998. "What Makes a Leader?" *Harvard Business Review*. November–December: 93–102; Rosenbaum, James E. 1984. *Career Mobility in a Corporate Hierarchy*. Orlando, FL: Academic Press.

2. Becker, Thomas, Robert Billlings, Daniel Eveleth, and Nicole Gilbert. 1996. "Foci and Bases of Employee Commitment: Implications for Job Performance." *Academy of Management Journal*, 39(2): 464–482.

3. Duarte, Neville, Jane R. Goodson, and Nancy Klich. 1994. "Effects of Dyadic Quality and Duration on Performance Appraisal." *Academy of Management Journal*, 37(3): 499–521.

4. Kilduff, Martin, and David Day. 1994. "Do Chameleons Get Ahead? The Effects of Self-Monitoring on Managerial Careers." *Academy of Management Journal*, 37(4): 1047–1060; Turban, Daniel, and Thomas W. Dougherty. 1994. "Role of Protégé Personality in Receipt of Mentoring and Career Success." *Academy of Management Journal*, 37: 688–702.

5. Baker, Wayne. 1994. *Networking Smart: How to Build Relationships for Personal and Organizational Success*. New York: McGraw-Hill, xv.

6. Carroll, Glenn, and Albert Teo. 1996. "On the Social Network of Managers." *Academy of Management Journal*, 39(2): 421–440.

7. Gabarro, John, and John Kotter. 1993. "Managing Your Boss." *Harvard Business Review*. May–June: 150–157.

8. Hill, Linda. 1992. "Why Won't They Do What I Ask?" *Executive Female*. September/October: 13–20.

9. Bartolome, Fernando, and Andre Laurent. 1988. "Managers: Torn between Two Roles." *Personnel Journal*, 6(10): 72–83; Hill, Linda. 1992. *Becoming a Manager: Mastery of a New Identity*. 2nd ed. Boston, MA: Harvard Business School Press; Smith, Kenwyn K. 2003. *Groups in Conflict: Prisons in Disguise*. Dubuque, IA: Kendall Hunt Publishers.

10. Oshry, Barry. 1996. *Seeing Systems: Unlocking the Mysteries of Organizational Life*. San Francisco, CA: Berrett-Koehler Publishers; Smith, Kenwyn K. 1992. *Groups in Conflict: Prisons in Disguise*. Dubuque, IA: Kendall Hunt Publishing Company.

11. Kiechel, Walter. 1991. "Dealing with the Problem Boss." *Fortune*. August 12.

12. Hill, Linda. 1992. "Why Won't They Do What I Ask?" *Executive Female*. September/October: 13–20.

13. Smith, Kenwyn K. 1982. *Groups in Conflict: Prisons in Disguise*. Dubuque, IA: Kendall Hunt Publishers; Oshry, Barry. 2007. *Seeing Systems: Unlocking the Mysteries of Organizational Life*.2nd ed. San Francisco, CA: Berrett-Koehler Publishers, Inc.)

14. Sutton, Robert. 2007. "The No-Asshole Rule: Part 1." *The Huffington Post.* May 28. http://www.huffingtonpost.com/robert-sutton/the-no-asshole-rule-part-_b_49678.html

15. Bowlby, John. 1988. *A Secure Base: Parent-Child Attachment and Healthy Human Development.* London: Basic Books; Kahn, William, and Kathy Kram. 1994. "Authority at Work: Internal Models and Their Organizational Consequences." *Academy of Management Review,* 19(1): 17–50.

16. Kahn, William, and Kathy Kram. 1994. "Authority at Work: Internal Models and Their Organizational Consequences." *Academy of Management Review,* 19(1): 17–50.

17. Gabarro, John, and John Kotter. 1993. "Managing Your Boss." *Harvard Business Review.* May–June: 150–157.

18. Hill, Linda. "Why Won't They Do What I Ask?" *Executive Female.* September/October: 13–20.

19. Buckingham, Marcus, and Curt Coffman. 1999. *First, Break All the Rules: What the World's Greatest Managers Do Differently.* New York: Simon and Schuster.

20. Marx, Robert, Todd Jick, and Peter Frost. *Management Live: The Video Collection.* Upper Saddle River, NJ: Prentice Hall. Excerpts from the leadership alliance with Tom Peters.

21. Denison, Daniel R., Robert Hoojiberg, and Robert Quinn. 1995. "Paradoxes and Performance: Toward a Theory of Behavioral Complexity in Managerial Behavior." *Organization Science,* 6: 524–539.

22. Fernandez, Carmen, and Robert P. Vecchio. 1997. "Situational Leadership Theory Revisited: A Test of an Across-Jobs Perspective." *Leadership Quarterly,* 8(1): 67–84.

23. Hersey, Paul, and Kenneth Blanchard. 1993. *Management of Organizational Behavior: Utilizing Human Resources.* 6th ed. Upper Saddle River, NJ: Prentice Hall.

24. Blake, Robert, and Jane Mouton. 1981. *The Managerial Grid.* Houston, TX: Gulf Publishing.

25. Hersey, Paul, and Kenneth Blanchard. 1996. "Revisiting the Life-Cycle Theory of Leadership." *Training and Development,* 50(1); Blake, Robert, and Jane Mouton. 1981. *The Managerial Grid.* Houston, TX: Gulf Publishing.

26. Hersey, Paul, and Kenneth Blanchard. 1993. *Management of Organizational Behavior: Utilizing Human Resources.* Upper Saddle River, NJ: Prentice Hall.

27. Hersey, Paul. 1992. *Situational Leader.* New York: Warner Books.

28. Vecchio, Robert. 1987. "Situational Leadership Theory: An Examination of a Prescriptive Theory." *Journal of Applied Psychology,* 72(3): 444–451.

29. Norris, William, and Robert Vecchio. 1992. "Situational Leadership Theory." *Group and Organization Management,* 7(3): 331–342.

30. Denison, Daniel. 1990. *Corporate Culture and Organizational Effectiveness.* New York: John Wiley & Sons; Denison, Daniel, and Aneil Mishra. 1995. "Toward a Theory of Organizational Culture and Effectiveness." *Organization Science,* 6(2): 204–223.

31. Spreitzer, Gretchen. 1996. "Social Structural Characteristics of Psychological Empowerment." *Academy of Management Journal,* 39(2): 483–504; Spreitzer, Gretchen, and Robert Quinn. 2001. *A Company of Leaders: Five Disciplines for Unleashing the Power in Your Workforce.* San Francisco, CA: Jossey-Bass Publishers.

32. Ibid.

33. Spreitzer, Gretchen, Suzanne De Janasz, and Robert E. Quinn. 1999. "Empowered to Lead: The Role of Psychological Empowerment in Leadership." *Journal of Organizational Behavior,* 20: 511–526; Ergeneli, Azize, Guler Sag, Iam Ari, and Selin Metin. 2007. "Psychological Empowerment and Its Relationship to Trust in Immediate Managers." *Journal of Business Research,* 60(1): 41.

34. Spreitzer, Gretchen 1996. "Social Structural Characteristics of Psychological Empowerment." *Academy of Management Journal,* 39(2): 483–504.

35. Ibid.

36. Spreitzer, Gretchen. 1996. "Social Structural Characteristics of Psychological Empowerment." *Academy of Management Journal,* 39(2): 483–504; Katzenbach, Jon, and Douglas Smith. 1993. *The Wisdom of Teams.* New York: Harper Row; Lipman-Blumen, Jean, and Harold J. Leavitt. 1999. *Hot Groups: Seeding Them, Feeding Them, and Using Them to Ignite Your Organization.* New York: Oxford; Biederman, Patricia, and Warren Bennis. 1998. *Organizing Genius: The Secrets of Creative Collaboration.* New York: Perseus Press.

37. Buckingham, Marcus, and Curt Coffman. 1999. *First, Break All the Rules: What the World's Greatest Managers Do Differently.* New York: Simon and Schuster; Harter, James, Theodore Hayes, and Frank Schmidt. 2002. "Business-Unit-Level Relationship between Employee Satisfaction, Employee Engagement, and Business Outcomes: A Meta-Analysis." *Journal of Applied Psychology,* 87(2): 268–279

38. Milgram, Stanley. 1969. *Obedience to Authority.* New York: Harper and Row.
39. Ibid.
40. Ibid.
41. Ibid.
42. Blass, Thomas. 1991. "Understanding Behavior in the Milgram Obedience Experiment: The Role of Personality, Situations, and Their Interactions." *Journal of Personality and Social Psychology,* 60(3): 398–413; citing Kilham, W., and L. Mann. 1974. "Level of Destructive Obedience as a Function of Transmitter and Executant Roles in the Milgram Obedience Paradigm." *Journal of Personality and Social Psychology,* 29: 697–702.
43. Blass, Thomas. 1991. "Understanding Behavior in the Milgram Obedience Experiment: The Role of Personality, Situations, and Their Interactions." *Journal of Personality and Social Psychology,* 60(3): 398–413; citing Adorno, Thomas, Elise Frenkel-Brunswick, and Daniel Levinson. 1950. *The Authoritarian Personality.* New York: Harper and Row.
44. Blass, Thomas. 1991. "Understanding Behavior in the Milgram Obedience Experiment: The Role of Personality, Situations, and Their Interactions." *Journal of Personality and Social Psychology,* 60(3): 398–413.
45. Tarnow, Eugen. 2000. "Self-Destructive Obedience in the Airplane Cockpit and the Concept of Obedience Optimization." In Thomas Blass (ed.). *Obedience to Authority: Current Perspectives on the Milgram Paradigm.* Mahwah, NJ: Lawrence Erlbaum Associates, Publishers, 111–124.
46. Schminke, Marshall, Deborah Wells, Joseph Peyrefitte, and Terrence Sebora. 2002. "Leadership and Ethics in Work Groups." *Group & Organization Management,* 27(2): 272–293; Arlow, P., and T. Ulrich. "A Longitudinal Study of Business School Graduates' Assessments of Business Ethics." *Journal of Business Ethics,* 7: 295–302.
47. Vaill, Peter. 1997. "A Note on the Idea of Courage." *Organizational Behavior Teaching Review.*
48. Dutton, Jane, Monica Worline, Peter Frost, and Jacoba Lilius. 2006. "Explaining Compassion Organizing." *Administrative Science Quarterly,* 51: 59–96.
49. Ibid., p. 84.
50. Duarte, Neville, Jane Goodson, and Nancy Klich. 1994. "Effects of Dyadic Quality and Duration on Performance Appraisal." *Academy of Management Journal,* 37(3): 499–521; Wayne, Sandy, Robert C. Liden, Maria L. Kraimer, and Isabel Graf. 1999. "The Role of Human Capital, Motivation, and Supervisor Sponsorship in Predicting Career Success." *Journal of Organizational Behavior,* 20: 577–595.
51. Bartolome, Fernando, and Andre Laurent. 1988. "Managers: Torn between Two Roles." *Personnel Journal,* 6(10): 72–83.
52. Tepper, Bennett. 1995. "Upward Maintenance Tactics in Supervisory Mentoring and Nonmentoring Relationships." *Academy of Management Journal,* 38(4): 1191–1205.
53. Dienesch, R. M., and R. C. Liden. 1986. "Leader-Member Exchange Model of Leadership: A Critique and Further Development." *Academy of Management Review,* 11: 618–634.
54. Lombardo, Michael, and Morgan McCall, Jr. 1984. "The Intolerable Boss." *Psychology Today.* January: 44–48.
55. Dumaine, Brian. 1993. "America's Toughest Bosses." *Fortune.* October 18: 44.
56. Jardin, Andrew. 1992. "Frankenstein and Other Monsters We Love to Hate." *Supervision.* October: 8–26.
57. Lee, Tony. 1996. "Are You More of a Street Fighter or a Jeckle and Hyde?" *Wall Street Journal.* June 11:B1.
58. Ashforth, Blake. 1994. "Petty Tyranny in Organizations." *Human Relations,* 47(7): 755–778.
59. Ibid.
60. 1993. "Psychobosses from Hell." *Fortune.* October 18:44.
61. Ashforth, Blake. 1994 "Petty Tyranny in Organizations." *Human Relations,* 47(7): 755–778.
62. Levinson, Harry. 1978. "The Abrasive Personality at the Office." *Psychology Today.* May: 78–84.
63. Zellas, Kelly, Bennett Tepper, and Michelle Duffy. 2002. "Abusive Supervision and Subordinate's Organizational Citizenship Behavior." *Journal of Applied Psychology,* 87(6); 1068–1076.
64. Hall, Francine. 1991. "Dysfunctional Managers: The Next Human Resource Challenge." *Organizational Dynamics.* Autumn: 48–57; Tepper, Bennett. 2000. "Consequences of Abusive Supervision." *Academy of Management Journal,* 43(2): 178–190.
65. Chidester, T. R., R. L. Helmreich, S. E. Gregorich, and C. E. Geis. 1991. "Pilot Personality and Crew Coordination." *International Journal of Aviation Psychology,* 25–44.
66. Ashforth, Blake. 1994. "Petty Tyranny in Organizations." *Human Relations,* 47(7): 755–778; Levinson, Harry. 1978. "The Abrasive Personality at the Office." *Psychology Today.* May: 78–84.

67. Ashforth, Blake. 1994. "Petty Tyranny in Organizations." *Human Relations,* 47(7): 755–778.

68. Gabarro, John, and John Kotter. 1993. "Managing Your Boss." *Harvard Business Review.* May–June 150–157.

69. Miller, James R. 1996. *Best Boss/Worst Boss.* Arlington, TX: The Summit Publishing Group, 30.

70. Maccoby, Michael. 2003. *The Productive Narcissist: The Promise and Peril of Visionary Leadership.* Broadway Books.

71. Lombardo, Michael, and Morgan McCall, Jr. 1984. "The Intolerable Boss." *Psychology Today.* January: 44–48.

72. Shellenbarger, Susan. 1999. "Spotting Bad Bosses before You Get Stuck Working for Them." *Wall Street Journal.* September 29:B1.

73. Levinson, Harry. 1978. "The Abrasive Personality at the Office." *Psychology Today.* May: 78–84.

74. Garone, Elizabeth. 2009. "Pile on Mentors in Tough Times." *Wall Street Journal.* October 6: D6.

75. Kram, Katherine. 1985. *Mentoring at Work.* Glenville, IL: Scott, Foresman.

76. Scandura, T., and R. Viator. 1994. "Mentoring in Public Accounting Firms: An Analysis of Mentor-Protégé Relationships, Mentorship Functions, and Protégé Turnover Intentions." *Accounting Organizations and Society,* 19(8): 717–734; cited in Blake, Stacy Denise. 1996. *The Changing Face of Mentoring in Diverse Organizations.* Unpublished Doctoral Dissertation, University of Michigan.

77. Erikson, Eric. 1963. *Childhood and Society.* New York: W. W. Norton; Levinson, Dan. 1978. *Seasons of a Man's Life.* New York: Alfred Knopf.

78. Wayne, Sandy, Robert C. Liden, Maria L. Kraimer, and Isabel K. Graf. 1999. "The Role of Human Capital, Motivation, and Supervisor Sponsorship in Predicting Career Success." *Journal of Organizational Behavior,* 20: 577–595; Fagenson, Ellen A. 1988. "The Power of a Mentor: Protégés and Non-protégés' Perceptions of Their Own Power in Organizations." *Group and Organization Studies,* 13(2): 182–194; Whitely, William, and Pol Coetsier. 1993. "The Relationship of Career Mentoring, Early Career Outcomes." *Organization Studies,* 14(3): 419–441; Cox, Taylor, and Stacy Blake. 1991. "Managing Cultural Diversity: Implications for Organizations." *Academy of Management Executive,* 5(3): 45–52; Burlew, L. D. 1991. "Multiple Mentor Model: A Conceptual Framework." *Journal of Career Development,* 17: 213–221.

79. Hill, Linda, and Nancy Kamprath. 1998. "Beyond the Myth of the Perfect Mentor." Boston, MA: Harvard Business School Note 9-491-096; McCall, Morgan, Michael Lombardo, and Ann Morrison. 1989. *Lessons of Experience: How Successful Executives Develop on the Job.* New York: The Free Press.

80. Hill, Linda. 1992. *Becoming a Manager: Mastery of a New Identity.* Boston, MA: Harvard Business School Press.

81. Hill, Linda, and Nancy Kamprath. 1998. "Beyond the Myth of the Perfect Mentor: Building a Network of Developmental Relationships." Boston, MA: Harvard Business School Press, Note 9-491-096.

82. Higgins, Monica, and Kathy Kram. 2001 "Reconceptualizing Mentoring at Work: A Developmental Network Perspective." *Academy of Management Review,* 26(2): 264–288.

83. Howell, Baum. 1992. "Mentoring: Narcissistic Fantasies and Oedipal Realities." *Human Relations,* 45(3): 223–318.

84. Ibid.; Higgins, Monica, and Nitin Nohria, in press; cited by David Thomas and John Gabarro. 1999. *Breaking Through: The Making of Minority Executives in Corporate America.* Boston, MA: Harvard Business School Press.

85. Lancaster, Hal. 1996. "You Might Need a Guide to Lead You around Career Pitfalls." *The Wall Street Journal.* July 30: B1.

86. Ragins, Belle Rose, John L. Cotton, and Janice S. Miller. 2000. "Marginal Mentoring: The Effects of Type of Mentor, Quality of Relationship, and Program Design on Work and Career Attitudes." *Academy of Management Journal,* 43(6): 1177–1194; Scandura, Terri A., "Dysfunctional Mentoring Relationships and Outcomes." *Journal of Management,* 24: 449–467; Eby, Lillian; and Tammy Allen. 2002. "Further Investigation of Protégés' Negative Mentoring Experiences." *Group & Organization Management,* 27(4): 456–479; Blake-Beard, Stacy. 2001. "Taking a Hard Look at Formal Mentoring Programs: A Consideration of Potential Challenges Facing Women." *The Journal of Management Development,* 20(4): 331–345; Scandura, Terri. 1998. "Dysfunctional Mentoring Relationships and Outcomes." *Journal of Management,* 24(3): 449–67; Eby, Lillian, and Tammy Allen. 2002. "Further Investigation of Protégés' Negative Mentoring Experiences." *Group & Organizational Studies,* 27(4): 456–479. Scandura, Terri. 1998. "Dysfunctional Mentoring

Relationships and Outcomes." *Journal of Management,* 24(3): 449–67; Eby, Lillian, and Tammy Allen. 2002. "Further Investigation of Protégés' Negative Mentoring Experiences." *Group & Organizational Studies,* 27(4): 456–479.

87. Kanter, Rosabeth Moss. 1977. *Men and Women of the Corporation.* New York: Basic Books; Ragins, Belle Rose. 1997. "Barriers to Mentoring: The Female Manager's Dilemma." *Human Relations,* 42: 1–22; Blake, Stacy Denise. 1996. "The Changing Face of Mentoring in Diverse Organizations." Unpublished Doctoral Dissertation, University of Michigan.

88. Isen, Alice M., and Robert A. Baron. 1991. "Positive Affect as a Factor in Organizational Behavior." In Cummings, Larry, and Barry Staw (eds.). *Research in Organizational Behavior.* Vol. 13. Greenwich, CT: JAI Press, 1–53; Pffeffer, Jeffrey. 1984. "Organizational Demography." In Cummings, Larry, and Barry Staw (eds.). *Research in Organizational Behavior.* Vol. 5. Greenwich, CT: JAI Press.

89. Blake-Beard, Stacy. 2001. "Taking a Hard Look at Formal Mentoring Programs: A Consideration of Potential Challenges Facing Women." *The Journal of Management Development,* 20(4): 331–345; Harrison, D. A., K. H. Price, and M. P. Bell. 1998. "Beyond Relational Demography: Time and the Effects of Surface- and Deep-Level Diversity on Work Group Cohesion." *Academy of Management Journal,* 41(1): 96–107; Tsui, Ann, and Charles O'Reilly. 1989. "Beyond Simple Demographic Effects: The Importance of Relational Demography in Superior-Subordinate Dyads." *Academy of Management Journal,* 32(2): 402–23.

90. Cialdini, Robert B. 2001. *Influence: Science and Practice.* Needham Heights: Allyn and Bacon.

91. Allen, Tammy, Mark Poteet, and Joyce E. Russell. 2000. "Protégé Selection by Mentors: What Makes the Difference?" *Journal of Organizational Behavior,* 21: 271–282.

92. Feldman, Daniel, William R. Folks, and William H. Turnley. 1999. "Mentor-Protégé Diversity and Its Impact on International Internship Experiences." *Journal of Organizational Behavior,* 20: 597–611.

93. Jackson, Susan, V. Stone, and E. Alverez. "Socialization amidst Diversity: The Impact of Demographics on Work Teams, Old-Timers, and Newcomers." In Staw, Barry, and Larry Cummings (eds.). *Research in Organizational Behavior.* Vol. 15.

Greenwich, CT: JAI Press; Kram, Kathy. 1985. *Mentoring at Work.* Glenview, IL: Scott Foresman.

94. Ragins, Belle Rose, and D. McFarlin. 1990. "Perceptions of Mentor Roles in Cross-Gender Mentoring Relationships." *Journal of Vocational Behavior,* 37: 321–339; Blake, Stacy Denise. 1996. "The Changing Face of Mentoring in Diverse Organizations." Unpublished Doctoral Dissertation, University of Michigan; Thomas, David, and John Gabarro. 1999. *Breaking Through: The Making of Minority Executives in Corporate America.* Boston, MA: Harvard Business School Press.

95. Ragins, Belle Rose. 1997. "Diversified Mentoring Relationships in Organizations: A Power Perspective." *Academy of Management Review,* 22(2): 482–521; Clawson, James, and Kathy Kram. 1984. "Managing Cross-Gender Mentoring." *Business Horizons.* May–June: 222–232.

96. Kram, Kathy. 1988. *Mentoring at Work: Developmental Relationships in Organizational Life.* New York: University Press of America.

97. Hill, Linda, and Nancy Kamprath. 1998. "Beyond the Myth of the Perfect Mentor: Building a Network of Developmental Relationships." Boston, MA: Harvard Business School Press, Note 9-491-096.

98. Ragins, Belle Rose, and D. McFarlin, 1990. "Perceptions of Mentor Roles in Cross-Gender Mentoring Relationships." *Journal of Vocational Behavior,* 37: 321–339; Ragins, Belle Rose, and John Cotton. 1991. "Easier Said than Done: Gender Differences in Perceived Barriers to Gaining a Mentor." *Academy of Management Journal,* 34(4): 939–951; Thomas, David. "The Impact of Race on Managers' Experiences of Developmental Relationships (Mentoring and Sponsorship): An Intraorganizational Study." *Journal of Organizational Behavior,* 11: 479–492.

99. Interview with Donna Dubinsky, co-founder and CEO, Handspring. 2000. *Careers and the MBA.* Cambridge, MA: Crimson and Brown Associates 32(1).

100. Hill, Linda, and Nancy Kamprath. 1998. "Beyond the Myth of the Perfect Mentor: Building a Network of Developmental Relationships." Boston, MA: Harvard Business School Press, Note 9-491-096.

101. Ensher, Ellen, and Susan Murphy. 2005. *Power Mentoring: How Successful Mentors and Protégés Get the Most Out of Their Relationships.* San Francisco: Jossey Bass.

102. Garone, Elizabeth. 2009. "Pile on Mentors in Tough Times." *Wall Street Journal.* October 6: D6.

103. Ibid.

104. Allen, Tammy, Mark Poteet, and Joyce E. Russell. 2000. "Protégé Selection by Mentors: What Makes the Difference?" *Journal of Organizational Behavior,* 21: 271–282.

105. Hill, Linda, and Nancy Kamprath. 1998. "Beyond the Myth of the Perfect Mentor: Building a Network of Developmental Relationships." Boston, MA: Harvard Business School Press, Note 9-491-096.

106. Chandler, Dawn, Douglas T. Hall, and Kathy E. Kram. 2009. "How to Be a Smart Protégé." *Wall Street Journal Online.* August 17. http://online.wsj.com/article/SB10001424052970203937504574252141852898888.html

107. Scandura, Terri. 1998. "Dysfunctional Mentoring Relationships and Outcomes." *Journal of Management,* 24(3): 449–67; Eby, Lillian, and Tammy Allen. 2002. "Further Investigation of Protégés' Negative Mentoring Experiences." *Group & Organizational Studies,* 27(4): 456–479.

108. Kram, Kathy. 1985. *Mentoring at Work.* Glenview, IL: Scott, Foresman.

109. Ragins, Belle Rose. 1989. "Barriers to Mentoring: The Female Manager's Dilemma." *Human Relations,* 42: 1–22; Hill, Linda, and Nancy Kamprath. 1998. "Beyond the Myth of the Perfect Mentor: Building a Network of Developmental Relationships." Boston, MA: Harvard Business School Press, Note 9-491-096; Thomas, David. 1990. "The Impact of Race on Managers' Experiences of Developmental Relationships (Mentoring and Sponsorship): An Intraorganizational Study." *Journal of Organizational Behavior,* 11: 479–492; Blake, Stacy Denise. 1996. *The Changing Face of Mentoring in Diverse Organizations.* Unpublished Doctoral Dissertation, University of Michigan, 1996.

110. Thomas, David, and John Gabarro. 1999. *Breaking Through: The Making of Minority Executives in Corporate America.* Boston, MA: Harvard Business School Press.

111. Hill, Linda, and Nancy, Kamprath. 1998. Boston, MA: Harvard Business School Press, Note, 9-491-096; Clawson, James, and Kathy Kram. 1984. "Managing Cross-Gender Mentoring." *Business Horizons.* May–June: 22–32.

112. Lindenberg, Judith, and Lois Zachary. 1999. "Play 20 Questions to Develop a Successful Mentoring Program." *Training and Development.* February: 13–14.

113. Baker, Wayne. 1999. "How Rich are You? Wayne Baker on the Value of Social Capital." *Dividend.* Fall: 21–26.

114. Reich, Robert B. 2002. *The Future of Success: Working and Living in the New Economy.* New York: Vintage Books, p. 136.

115. Andona, Deborah, and Henrik Bresman. 2007. *How to Build Teams that Lead, Innovate, and Succeed.* Harvard Business School Press; Ibarra, Herminia. 1993. "Network Centrality, Power, and Innovation Involvement: Determinants of Technical and Administrative Roles." *Academy of Management Journal,* 36(3): 471–501; Baker, Wayne. 2000. Achieving Success through Social Capital: Tapping the Hidden Resources in Your Personal and Professional Networks. Jossey Bass; Seibert, Scott, Maria Kraimer, and Robert Liden. 2001. "A Social Capital Theory of Career Success." *Academy of Management Journal,* 44(2): 219–238; Oh, Hongseok, Giuseppe Labianca, and Myung-ho Chung. 2006. "A Multilevel Model of Group Social Capital." *The Academy of Management Review,* 31(3): 569

116. Wellman, B., P. J. Cartington, and A. Hall. 1988. "Networks as Personal Communities." In B. Wellman, and S. D. Berkowitz (eds.). *Social Structures: A Network Approach.* New York: Cambridge University Press.

117. De Souza, Gita. 2002. "The Influence of Inclusion in Influential Networks: Perceptions of Ability and Personality Traits on Promotions within Management." *Journal of Behavioral and Applied Management,* 4(1).

118. Baker, Wayne. 1999. "How Rich Are You? Wayne Baker on the Value of Social Capital." *Dividend.* Fall: 21–26.

119. Ibarra, Herminia. 1993. "Personal Networks of Women and Minorities in Management: A Conceptual Framework." *Academy of Management Review,* 18(1): 56–87.

120. Ibarra, Herminia. 1995. "Race, Opportunity, and Diversity of Social Circles in Managerial Networks." *Academy of Management Journal,* 38(3): 673–703;

121. Ibid

122. Baker, Wayne. 1999. "How Rich Are You? Wayne Baker on the Value of Social Capital." *Dividend.* Fall: 21–26.

123. Ibarra, Herminia. 1995. "Race, Opportunity, and Diversity of Social Circles in Managerial Networks." *Academy of Management Journal,* 38(3): 673–703.

124. Kilduff, Martin, and David Krackhardt. 1994. "Bringing the Individual Back In: A Structural Analysis of the Interaction Market for Reputation in Organizations." *Academy of Management Journal,* 37(1): 87–106.

125. Cialdini, Robert B., R. J. Borden, A. Thorne, M. Walker, R. Freeman, and L. R. Sloan. 1976. "Basking in Reflected Glory: Three (Football) Field Studies." *Journal of Personality and Social Psychology,* 34: 366–375.

126. Granovetter, Mark. 1982. "The Strength of Weak Ties: A Network Theory Revisited." In P. V. Masden and N. Lin (eds.). *Social Structure and Network Analysis.* Beverly Hills, CA: Sage.

127. Ibarra, Herminia. 1993. "Personal Networks of Women and Minorities in Management: A Conceptual Framework." *Academy of Management Review,* 18(1): 56–87.

128. Ibarra, Herminia. 1995. "Race, Opportunity, and Diversity of Social Circles in Managerial Networks." *Academy of Management Journal,* 38(3): 673–703.

129. Carroll, Glenn, and Albert Teo. 1996. "On the Social Network of Managers." *Academy of Management Journal,* 39(2): 421–440.

130. Thomas, David, and John Kotter. 1999. *Breaking Through: The Making of Minority Executives in Corporate America.* Boston, MA: Harvard Business School Press; Ibarra, Herminia. 1993. "Personal Networks of Women and Minorities in Management: A Conceptual Framework." *Academy of Management Review,* 18(1): 56–87; Ibarra, Herminia. 1997. "Paving an Alternative Route: Gender Differences in Managerial Networks for Career Development." *Social Psychological Quarterly,* 60(1): 91–102.

131. Thomas, David, and John Kotter. 1999. *Breaking Through: The Making of Minority Executives in Corporate America.* Boston, MA: Harvard Business School Press; Ibarra, Herminia. 1993. "Personal Networks of Women and Minorities in Management: A Conceptual Framework." *Academy of Management Review,* 18(1): 56–87.

132. Mehra, Ajay, Martin Kilduff, and Daniel Brass. 1998. "At the Margins: A Distinctiveness Approach to the Social Identity and Social Networks of Under-represented Groups." *Academy of Management Journal,* 41(4): 441–452.

133. Ibid.

134. Friedman, Raymond A. 1996. "Defining the Scope and Logic of Minority and Female Network Groups." *Research in Personnel and Human Resources Management,* 14: 307–349.

135. Friedman, Raymond A., and Brooks Holtom. 2002. "The Effects of Network Groups on Minority Employee Turnover Intentions." *Human Resource Management,* 41(4): 405–421.

136. Friedman, Raymond A., Melinda Kane, and David Cornfield. 1998. "Social Support and Career Optimism: Examining the Effect of Network Groups on Black Manager." *Human Relations,* 51(9): 1155–1178.

137. Friedman, Raymond A. 1996. "Defining the Scope and Logic of Minority and Female Network Groups." *Research in Personnel and Human Resources Management,* 14: 307–349.

138. Ibid.; Thomas, David, and John Kotter. 1999. *Breaking Through: The Making of Minority Executives in Corporate America.* Boston, MA: Harvard Business School Press; Ibarra, Herminia. 1993. "Personal Networks of Women and Minorities in Management: A Conceptual Framework." *Academy of Management Review,* 18(1): 56–87; Cox, Taylor, and Stella Nkomo. 1990b. "Factors Affecting the Upward Mobility of Black Managers in Private Sector Organizations." *Review of Black Political Economy,* 13(3): 39–48; Ibarra, Herminia. 1995. "Race, Opportunity, and Diversity of Social Circles in Managerial Networks." *Academy of Management Journal,* 38(3): 673–703.

139. Baker, Wayne. 1999. "How Rich Are You? Wayne Baker on the Value of Social Capital." *Dividend.* Fall: 21–26.

140. Dutton, Jane, and Emily Heaphy. 2003. *The Power of High Quality Connections: Positive Organizational Scholarship.* San Francisco: Berrett-Koehler Publishers.

141. Baker, Wayne, and Jane Dutton. 2007. "Enabling Positive Social Capital in Organizations." In Jane Dutton and Belle Rose Ragins (eds.). *Exploring Positive Relationships at Work: Building a Theoretical and Research Foundation.* Mahwah, NJ: Lawrence Erlbaum Associates, 325–345.

142. Baker, Wayne, Rob Cross, and Melissa Wooten. In Kim Cameron, Jane Dutton, and Robert Quinn (eds.). *Positive Organizational Scholarship: Foundations of a New Discipline.* San Francisco: Berrett Koehler Publishers 328–342.

143. Cross, Rob, Wayne Baker, and Andrew Parker. 2003. "What Creates Energy in Organizations?" *MIT Sloan Management Review,* 44(4): 51–56.

144. Nierenberg, Andrea. 1999. "Masterful Networking." *Training and Development,* February: 51–53.

145. Ashford, Susan, and Gregory Northcraft. 1992. "Conveying More (or Less) than We Realize: The Role of Impression Management in Feedback-

Seeking." *Organizational Behavior and Human Decision Processes,* 53: 310–334.

146. Wayne, Sandy J., and Robert Liden. 1995. "Effects of Impression Management on Performance Ratings: A Longitudinal Study." *Academy of Management Journal,* 38(1): 232–260.

147. Gardner, William. 1992. "Lessons in Organizational Dramaturgy: The Art of Impression Management." *Organizational Dynamics.* Summer: 33–46.

148. Liden, Robert, and Terence Mitchell. 1988. "Ingratiatory Behaviors in Organizational Settings." *Academy of Management Review,* 13(4): 572–587; Wortman, C. B., and Linsenmeier, J. A. 1977. "Interpersonal Attraction and Techniques of Ingratiation in Organizational Settings." In Barry Staw and Gerry Salancik (eds.). *New Directions in Organizational Behavior.* Chicago, IL: St. Clair Press.

149. Gardner, William. 1992. "Lessons in Organizational Dramaturgy: The Art of Impression Management." *Organizational Dynamics.* Summer: 33–46.

150. Kilduff, Martin, and David Krackhardt. 1994. "Bringing the Individual Back In: A Structural Analysis of the Internal Market for Reputation in Organizations." *Academy of Management Journal,* 37(1): 87–108; citing Cialdini, R. B. 1989. "Indirect Tactics of Image Management: Beyond Basking." In Robert A. Giacolone and Paul Rosenfeld (eds.). *Impression Management in the Organization.* Hillsdale, NJ: Erlbaum.

151. Gardner, William. 1992. "Lessons in Organizational Dramaturgy: The Art of Impression Management." *Organizational Dynamics.* Summer: 33–46.

152. Liden, Robert, and Terrence Mitchell. 1988. "Ingratiatory Behavior in Organizational Settings." *Academy of Management Review,* 13(4): 572–587.

153. Becker, Thomas, and Scott L. Martin. 1995. "Trying to Look Bad at Work: Methods and Motives for Managing Poor Impressions in Organizations." *Academy of Management Journal,* 38(1): 174–199.

154. Gardner, William. 1992. "Lessons in Organizational Dramaturgy: The Art of Impression Management." *Organizational Dynamics.* Summer: 33–46; Wayne, Sandy, and Robert Liden. 1995. "Effects of Impression Management on Performance Ratings." *Academy of Management Journal,* 38(1): 232–261.

155. Baumeister, Roy F. 1989. "Motive and Costs of Self-Presentation in Organizations." In Robert A. Giacalone, and Paul Rosenfeld (eds.). *Impression Management in the Organization.* Hillsdale, NJ: Erlbaum, 57–71.

156. Ibid.

157. Leary, Mark R., Patricia A. Rogers, Robert Canfield, and Celine Coe. 1986. "Boredom in Interpersonal Encounters: Antecedents and Social Implications." *Journal of Personality and Social Psychology,* 51(5): 968–975.

7

■ ■ ■

Managing Cultural Diversity

This chapter will help you:

■ Understand why effectively managing cultural diversity is a competitive advantage.

■ Understand why some well-intentioned diversity efforts fail.

■ Learn a definition of culture that goes beyond simplistic demographic categories.

■ Identify important cultural differences that affect work behavior.

■ Improve your multicultural competence.

■ Create a workplace that leverages diversity.

> *Diversity calls for managing people who aren't*
> *like you and who don't aspire to be like you. It's taking*
> *differences into account while developing a cohesive whole.*
>
> —R. ROOSEVELT THOMAS, JR., AUTHOR
>
> *Beyond Race and Gender*

Understanding the impact of culture on behavior in organizations is important because we live and work in a social and organizational world that is increasingly global and diverse and offers more "opportunities for interaction among people who do not share a common history or culture."[1] Diversity, both within and across nations, also offers more opportunities to capitalize on multiple perspectives, styles, expertise, and experiences in ways that add significant value to organizations—if the diversity is well managed. Consequently, it is not surprising that top companies agree that managing cultural diversity across and within and across nations is a critical managerial skill.[2]

In a recent survey of 1,500 CEOs conducted by IBM's Institute for Business Value, the CEOs expressed their concern that "global complexity is the foremost issue confronting [them] and their enterprises. The chief executives see a large gap between the level of complexity coming at them and their confidence that their enterprises are equipped to deal with it." The CEOs said that the "most important leadership competency" they look for in managers today is the ability to *creatively* find opportunities, adapt business practices, and connect with a "massively integrated world"—and to enable employees at all levels of the organization to do so as well.[3] Furthermore, in a Harvard Business School study designed to explore the future of MBA education, executives and business school deans told the researchers that "MBAs need to develop cultural intelligence, specifically a better understanding of which practices, strategies, and behaviors are universal and which are contingent" and how to be most effective when working with people and groups from different cultures.[4]

Not surprisingly, the ability to effectively manage diversity within nations, as well as across nations, significantly contributes to organizational success. In one study, researchers found that the stock price of companies that received awards for their affirmative action programs increased after the awards were announced. Conversely, the stock prices of companies that were charged with discrimination lawsuits decreased after the settlements were announced. The researchers concluded that organizations that have "high-quality affirmative action programs" are likely to place high value in the "effective management of diverse human resources" and that these programs "contribute to sustaining a competitive advantage and are valued in the marketplace."[5] Other researchers have found that companies that have more women represented in senior leadership roles and on corporate boards tend to financially outperform those that don't.[6]

Unfortunately, according to research conducted by the International Association of Colleges and Schools of Business, business leaders are concerned "that business school graduates are not leaving school with the cultural competence they need to work effectively in a diverse and global business environment."[7] This chapter is designed to respond to this call to improve managers' multicultural competence. It is divided into three parts. Part I answers the following questions: (1) What are the competitive advantages of a well-managed diverse workforce? and (2) What inhibits many organizations from achieving the potential that their diverse workforce offers? Part II addresses the following questions: (1) What is culture? and (2) What are some of the most common cultural differences that affect employees' ability to understand each other and work together effectively? Part III offers strategies for increasing your personal multicultural competence, as well as strategies for creating an organizational culture that helps employees turn the diversity of talent they offer into a competitive advantage.

Before we move on, I'll provide a brief definition of culture (and will provide a more in-depth definition later in this chapter) that you will find useful. "Culture" refers to the distinct ways that people who share a group identity are socialized to experience and interact with the world around them. Our cultural identity groups include—but are not limited to—nationality, race, gender, and religion. Through our socialization experiences within our identity groups, we learn what to value and ignore, what experiences (and people) to seek out and avoid, how to make sense of our experiences, how to interact with others, how to make decisions, and how to define effectiveness and success at work and in life in general.

It's wise to acknowledge that there are other kinds of diversity that influence organizational effectiveness that may or may not be related to culture, such as cognitive style.[8] Although we don't explicitly refer to cognitive style throughout this chapter, many of the ideas are relevant to understanding and leveraging cognitive styles (and other differences that people bring to organizations) as well. Cognitive style refers to ways of processing information that are based in experiences such as educational or functional background (and may be related to cultural socialization as well). It affects what we pay attention to (e.g., big picture or details, task or relationships), what we emphasize (e.g., change or stability), how we interpret information (e.g., relevant or irrelevant), how we use this information when making and implementing decisions, and how much we desire for challenges that stretch our abilities. The Myers–Briggs assessment and Social Styles assessment are among the many tools used to understand one's cognitive style. Although this chapter focuses on cultural diversity, it's important to acknowledge that there are many kinds of diversity that individuals bring to their teams and organizations.

PART I: DIVERSITY AS A COMPETITIVE ADVANTAGE

Business leaders are wise to be concerned about business schools not producing graduates with expertise in managing cultural diversity because the research is clear that organizations that *effectively* manage diverse human resources gain several competitive advantages over those that don't.

POSITIVE PUBLICITY   In addition to being viewed as a welcoming place for people of different cultural groups to work, positive publicity about diversity management may send a signal to the market that the organization is leveraging its human resources effectively and is likely to be progressive with other important and complex organizational initiatives as well.

RECRUITMENT, DEVELOPMENT, AND RETENTION OF THE BEST TALENT   Organizations with high-quality diversity programs and policies are able to draw from a wider pool of potential recruits and, thus, may be able to obtain and train the best and the brightest employees. Eastman Kodak's former CEO George Fisher explains, "We can no longer afford to discount the talents, skills, and contributions of any employee. We must instead create an environment where every person matters and every person is fully enabled to contribute to his or her maximum potential."[9]

MORE EFFECTIVE PROBLEM SOLVING, DECISION MAKING, AND WORK PROCESSES Researchers David Thomas and Robin Ely explain that groups that are traditionally "outside the mainstream . . . bring different, important, and competitively relevant knowledge and perspectives about how to actually do work—how to design processes, reach goals, frame tasks, create effective teams, communicate ideas, and lead. When allowed to, members of these groups can help companies grow and improve by challenging basic assumptions about an organization's functions, strategies, operations, practices, and procedures."[10]

ENHANCED TEAM PERFORMANCE   Diverse teams, *when well managed*, tend to make better decisions than relatively homogeneous groups, particularly when dealing with non routine, complex problems in which the diversity of team members provides resources that are relevant to the teams' tasks.[11] In one U.S. study, researchers Taylor Cox, Sharon Lobel, and Poppy McLeod contrasted the performance of homogeneous groups of all Anglos versus groups made up of Asians, African Americans, Anglos, and Hispanics on a creative task that required that they generate multiple ideas. Although there was no significant difference in the quantity of ideas, a group of external judges rated the ethnically diverse groups' ideas "an average of 11 percent higher than those of the homogeneous groups on both feasibility of implementation and overall effectiveness."[12] In another study, researchers contrasted the decision-making quality of homogeneous groups made up of all Japanese nationals versus diverse groups made up of members from different nations. They found that the cross-national groups tended to outperform the homogeneous teams. The researchers concluded that "exposure to different points of view may have triggered alternative cognitive processes in group members, which in turn improved performance."[13] They also found that the diverse groups tended to continue to improve over time at a greater rate than did the performance of the relatively homogeneous groups.[14]

LOWER LEGAL COSTS   Not surprisingly, discrimination suits, in addition to sending signals to the market that the organizations charged with these suits treat some employees unfairly, are expensive. In the United States, the average cost of a discrimination lawsuit is over $44 million. The median cost is $28 million. Among the largest discrimination settlements in the United States are Coca-Cola ($192 million), Texaco ($176 million), and State Farm insurance ($157 million).[15]

LOWER OPERATING COSTS   Effectively managing diversity can reduce costs associated with turnover. Organizations that effectively manage diversity may have lower operating costs because people in minority groups are more likely to be more satisfied with the organization, are better able to use their abilities at work, and are less likely to leave the organization to look for better opportunities elsewhere.[16] In addition, organizations that effectively prepare and manage employees on global assignments are less likely to be faced with the high cost of expatriates returning home from their assignments early because of their inability to adjust to a different culture.[17]

SUCCESS IN SERVING UNTAPPED MARKETS   Increasing consumer affluence in traditionally lower-income groups and emerging global markets offer substantial opportunities for organizations that have the capacity to understand and respond to understand the needs and wants of these markets. Researcher C.K. Prahalad presented the revolutionary case that there's a "fortune at the bottom of the pyramid," and businesses could both make profits and alleviate poverty while creating sustainable economic growth in these markets.

EFFECTIVE RESPONSE TO ADVOCACY GROUPS   Many minority groups are harnessing their growing economic power, asking organizations "What have you done for me lately?" and holding organizations accountable for the answers. Advocacy organizations publish listings of the best and worst places for minorities' and women's employment. They also publish listings of the best business schools for minorities and women. Organizations looking to recruit and retain employees take these listings seriously. For example, KPMG, the audit, tax, and advisory services firm, lists the awards it has received from several organizations on its college recruitment Web site. Among the many awards listed are DiversityInc's top 50 companies to work for, *Working Mother Magazine's* best companies to work for, *Working Mother Magazine's* best companies for multicultural women, Hispanic Business's Diversity Elite, Catalyst's award for exceptional programs to support and advance women in organizations, the Gay, Lesbian, Straight Education network's respect award, and *WorkLife Matters Magazine's* Disablity Matters Award.[18] In its rankings of the top 100 companies to work for, *Fortune* magazine provides additional information about how each of these companies fares in terms of employing the most or fewest women and minorities.[19]

As part of its Fair Share Program, the National Association for the Advancement of Colored People (NAACP) assesses organizations (including the hotel, automotive, banking, merchandizing, and telecom industries) on their responsiveness to the African American community in terms of jobs and business opportunities (e.g., vendors), and publishes their findings in popular business publications and online. The assessment criteria include five categories: the percentage of African Americans in managerial and professional positions, marketing and advertising to African

Americans, the number of relationships with African American vendors, investment opportunities and franchise ownership, and philanthropic giving that benefits African Americans.

In short, organizations that *effectively* manage diversity are better able to recruit, retain, and leverage the talent of the best and the brightest employees; lower costs by increasing productivity and avoiding expensive legal suits; tap into diverse markets both nationally and globally; and enhance their reputations among their constituents. Despite the many valuable advantages a diverse workforce can bring to organizations and the people they serve, many organizations miss the opportunity to leverage diversity.

Why Don't Many Organizations Achieve the Potential That Their Diverse Workforce Offers?

Several studies designed to assess the success of diversity programs found that having a diverse workforce does not necessarily predict positive organizational outcomes. Rather, how effectively organizations manage their diverse workforce determines whether organizations reap the potential rewards and minimize the associated risks. When poorly managed, a diverse workforce can increase the risks of dysfunctional processes such as lack of cohesion, miscommunication, increased conflict, poor decision-making processes, lack of coordination, dysfunctional "we–they" distinctions and biases, and increased employee absenteeism and turnover.[20] This section discusses two reasons why organizations' diversity efforts sometimes don't live up their potential: (1) Increasing the diversity of the workforce but not changing the way work gets done and (2) not managing the emotional and power issues associated with a diverse workforce.

INCREASING THE DIVERSITY OF THE WORKFORCE BUT NOT CHANGING THE WAY WORK GETS DONE Many organizations focus their diversity efforts primarily on achieving recruitment and retention targets for diverse groups. While they may achieve their demographic targets, they fail to draw on the new resources (e.g., values, perspectives, knowledge, skills, and experiences) that members of these diverse groups bring to the organization in ways that

People are easier to control when they are all alike.
—Lynn Maria Laitala,
In the Aftermath of Empire

can help the organization assess and creatively improve taken-for-granted work processes. Researchers Robin Ely and David Thomas explain that "the staff . . . gets diversified, but the work does not."[21] Although these organizations may have good intentions, their narrow focus on changing the "numbers" without changing their fundamental assumptions about how work gets done (e.g., how decisions should be made, how work hours should be arranged) can backfire. Without a change in the organizational culture, employees who are in the minority in these organizations may feel marginalized, unable to identify with the organization, and become frustrated at their inability to use their perspectives and talents in ways that add the most value to their organizations.[22] In their research, Ely and Thomas identified three different strategies that organizations use to manage their diverse workforces, with the "integration and learning strategy" offering the most benefits.[23] They describe the three perspectives as follows:

> *Integration and learning.* Organizations that use this perspective to manage diversity go beyond achieving demographic targets. These organizations view the "the insights, skills, and experiences" employees from multiple groups offer as valuable resources that enable the organization to "rethink its primary tasks and redefine its markets, products, strategies, and business practices in ways that will advance its mission. This perspective links diversity to work processes—the way that people do and experience work—in a manner that makes

diversity a resource for learning and adaptive change" in ways that can enhance organizational performance.[24] The ability to use the "integration and learning" perspective is relevant because, as I stated at the beginning of this chapter, in an IBM study of 1,500 CEOs, researchers concluded that the ability to think creativity and adapt quickly to a complex global environment is the most critical skill that CEOs are looking for in their leaders today.

Access and legitimacy. Organizations that use this perspective to manage diversity are guided by the assumption that the workforce demographics should reflect the diversity of the markets and constituencies served by the organization. The diverse workforce is viewed as a way to gain legitimacy within and access to these markets and constituents. Ely and Thomas argue that organizations "in which this perspective prevails use their diversity only at the margins, to connect with a more diverse market; they do not incorporate the cultural competencies of their diverse workforces into their core functions" in ways that can actually improve the way work gets done and enhance organizational performance.[25]

Discrimination and fairness. Organizations that use this perspective to manage diversity view a diverse workforce as "a moral imperative to ensure justice and the fair treatment of all members of society. It focuses diversification efforts on providing equal access opportunities in hiring and promotion, suppressing prejudicial attitudes, and eliminating discrimination." As with the access and legitimacy perspective, the focus—while well intentioned—is primarily on increasing the pool of diverse talent without necessarily using the resources this diverse pool of talent brings to the organization in ways that can improve organizational performance.

In short, organizations that use the integration and learning perspective to manage diversity have a competitive advantage because they enable *all* members of the organization to work together to learn from each other, broaden their perspectives, increase their adaptability, and expand their behavioral repertoires in innovative ways that help their organizations meet the demands of an increasingly diverse, complex, and fast-paced competitive environment.

MISMANAGING EMOTIONS AND POWER RELATIONS ASSOCIATED WITH A DIVERSE WORKFORCE   Efforts to manage diversity in organizations are often emotional journeys steeped in a nation's turbulent history of inequality and animosity among various groups within and across nations. Consequently, efforts to promote diversity are met with both passionate support and equally passionate resistance. When *Fortune* magazine ran a cover story about the 50 most powerful women in the United States, managing editor John Huey lamented: "I have learned that no matter how good our intentions are on this subject, the truth is, we are damned if we do and damned if we don't."[26] On the one hand, he argued, the article would be applauded as timely, relevant, and representing women's progress into the executive ranks. On the other hand, the article would be seen as marginalizing successful women, treating them as special cases, and misrepresenting the progress (or lack of progress) that women have made into the executive ranks.

In 2009, an emotionally laden controversy blossomed in the U.S. media after U.S. President Barack Obama bowed to Japan's Emperor Akihito during a weeklong tour of Asia. While some political pundits argued that President Obama's bow was "a gesture of kindness . . . [to show] goodwill between two nations that respect each other," other political pundits expressed concern that the U.S. president's bow to the emperor, rather than showing respect, made the U.S. appear "weak." Said conservative William Kristol, "I don't know why President Obama thought that was appropriate. Maybe he thought it would play well in Japan. But it's not appropriate for an American president to bow to a foreign one." This sentiment was reinforced in titles of media articles such as "How Low Will He Go?" and "Outrage in Washington over Obama's Japan Bow."[27] As illustrated by this controversy over the meaning of a greeting, the challenge of managing diversity goes beyond simply understanding different cultural beliefs and behaviors. The challenge of managing diversity also includes understanding how emotions and assumptions about power relations affect everyday interactions among people from different cultural groups.

> What worried me about coming out was that I would be marginalized, I'd be a one-issue person.
> —ALLAN GILMORE,
> *Former vice chairman of the board at Ford Motor Company*

Researcher Rae Andre argues that increased diversity in organizations can lead to "diversity stress," which she describes as "the discomfort [people] feel when they face a situation in which, because of the presence of multicultural factors, their usual modes of coping are insufficient."[28] Some employees, for example, may be uncomfortable in cross-cultural interactions because they are concerned that they will say or do something inappropriate or that they may be misunderstood. Thus, they may avoid cross-cultural interactions in an effort to minimize the possibility of discomfort, embarrassment, and conflict. Others may hide parts of their identity such as their religious affiliation or sexual orientation because they fear that they would be discriminated against if they revealed these identities. Given the potential for emotional stress, misunderstanding, and defensiveness, it's not surprising that some researchers have found that diverse work groups, unless they are well managed, can perform worse and have higher turnover than relatively homogeneous groups.[29]

Some research suggests that effective training is critical to the success of diversity programs.[30] For example, in one study, researcher Joycelyn Finley found that African Americans and Anglo Americans who were trained in skills designed to help them discuss emotionally hot topics felt that they were able to have more productive discussions about affirmative action than were those who did not have the training. Furthermore, the people who received the training also experienced the discussions as less stressful than did those who did not receive the training.[31]

Although training is important to an organization's diversity efforts, well-intentioned training programs can be undermined by poor facilitation. Diversity training programs are likely to backfire when facilitators make sweeping statements about cultural differences, suppress divergent opinions, assume one group alone is the cause of all the problems, and do not state the business case for diversity in a language that employees and executives can understand and value.[32]

The important point to take away from this chapter so far is that diversity, when understood (beyond a superficial level) and well managed (beyond achieving numerical targets), can provide organizations with a competitive advantage. In the following section, I provide an explanation of culture that is more in-depth than that which is typically presented in management books. I also provide information about cultural differences that are relevant to everyday work life. When these differences are well managed (e.g., integrated and used to enhance the way work gets done), they can add value to organization. When these differences are ignored or mismanaged, they can result in increased stress and misunderstandings that may inhibit organizational performance.

PART II: UNDERSTANDING CULTURE AND CULTURAL DIFFERENCES

> We didn't all come over on the same ship, but we're all in the same boat.
> —BERNARD BARUCH,
> *American financier and statesman*

Most of us tend to see culture through the lens of demographic categorizations such as nationality, race, and gender. In addition, many of us tend to view demographic categories such as race and gender as having been created by nature, clearly bounded, stable over time, and objectively observable. However, most categories used by societies to classify people are in large part created by human beings rather than by Mother Nature. Anthropologist and sociologist Lawrence A. Hirschfield explains that our use of demographic categories helps us make sense of our social world, but these categories don't necessarily represent an objective reality. Using racial categorizations as an example, he explains that:

> It is important to begin by talking about what race is not. Regardless of what our senses seem to tell us, race is not a biologically coherent story about human variation simply because the races we recognize and name are not biologically coherent populations. There is as much genetic variation within racial groups as there is between them. Now, this does not mean that race is not real psychologically or sociologically. It is obvious that race is real in both these senses. People believe in races, and they use this belief to organize important dimensions of social, economic, and political life. But this does not make race a real thing biologically. . . . In view of this, it makes more sense to think of race as an idea, not as a thing.[33]

Viewing demographic categories as ideas created by human beings rather than by natural categories makes these categories no less potent. Indeed, it explains why demographic categorizations such as gender, race, nationality, sexual orientation, and class are often extremely important to individuals and societies. They are important because they carry historic, economic, and political meanings that have significant implications for people's sense of identity, relationships with others, and assumptions about what is normal, moral, effective, and worth doing. Thus, although our categorizations are not objectively real, our emotional reactions to our categorizations are genuine. In the workplace, our reactions to these socially constructed demographic categorizations influence our ability to do our best work, bring out the best in others, and add value to our organizations.

You may be asking, "What about gender or age?" "Aren't those real?" Yes, of course, babies are born with either male or female parts, and people certainly do get older. Some human functions and abilities are biologically determined (e.g., giving birth to babies, although science is gaining some control over of how that happens). But our cultures provide us with the meanings that people attribute to physiological parts and natural life processes such as birth, aging, and death. For example, societies perpetuate beliefs about how boys and girls should dress, communicate, and behave. Societies also perpetuate assumptions about what paths boys and girls should choose in life, what jobs they should reach for, and how much they should get paid for their work. Regarding age, societies perpetuate beliefs about when childhood ends, when old age begins, how people of different ages should relate to each other, and what people of different ages are—and are not—capable of accomplishing (e.g., Should a 13-year-old boy or girl old have a job? Is someone who is 12 years old considered a child or adult? What kind of value can an 80-year-old adult offer to organizations and societies?).

Some researchers argue that it is useful to think of demographic categorizations such as gender, race, and age, in large part, as something that we *do* as a consequence of our socialization rather than something that we naturally *are* as a consequence of biological givens. Researchers Candace West and Don Zimmerman illustrate this distinction by using the word "sex" to refer to biological parts and functions (we have male/female parts) and by using the word "gender" to refer to the roles men and women take as a consequence of social expectations (we do gender).[34]

All human beings inevitably divide people into what we perceive to be natural and relevant categories in order to make sense of themselves, the world, and their place in it. Without the desire and ability to divide people (and things) into categories, we'd be paralyzed by the amount of overwhelming and incomprehensible information

The crucial differences which distinguish human societies and human beings are not biological. They are cultural.
—RUTH BENEDICT, *in Margaret Mead, An Anthropologist at Work*

the world presents to us. However, we need to carefully monitor our instincts to sort people into categories for several reasons. First, we often don't simply assume that people are different from each other. We also assume that some people are better (more effective, more moral) or worse (less effective, less moral) than others based on the categories in which our societies and organizations place them. Consequently, we promote and rationalize inequities, and we fail to appreciate and leverage human diversity to improve our organizations and societies. Second, when we sort human beings into what we perceive to be natural categories, we tend to see people within a demographic category as more similar than they are ("That's just like a man.") and see people from different cultural categories as more different than they really are ("Men are from Mars; women are from Venus."). However, there is much diversity among people within demographic groups, and there is much similarity among people between demographic groups. Third, when we overemphasize demographic categories, we can lose sight of many other "factors that make up the essence of who we are as human beings."[35] Novelist Gish Jen explains:

> From all of this, we may learn that there are two races of men [sic] in this world, but only these two— the "race" of the decent man and the "race" of the indecent man [sic]. Both are found everywhere; they penetrate into all groups of society. No group exists entirely of decent or indecent people.
> —VIKTOR FRANKL,
> *Psychologist and Holocaust survivor*

The way I am defined from the outside . . . is as Asian-American. To most people, that's who I "obviously" and "naturally" am, even though in my daily life, it's not always the most obvious thing about my identity. In fact, probably more of me is shaped by my temperament and rebelliousness. And my talkativeness. And my being a mother. And being a woman is a big, big, big shaping thing, probably more than my race . . . I resent all efforts to pigeonhole [me]. . . .[36]

Gish Jen is not alone in her concerns about being categorized. The U.S. Census Bureau is finding that more and more people, particularly young adults, see the Census Bureau's demographic categories as "arbitrary or offensive." In one census, nearly 10 million people surveyed by the Bureau "refused to describe themselves as white, black, Asian, or American Indian."[37]

So, how should we view culture? Rather than thinking of culture as being based on natural, stable, clearly bounded, and objectively identifiable categories, we may best be served by thinking of culture as a form of social identity that carries certain meanings and social expectations. A cultural-identity group (e.g., race, gender, nationality, religion, age, or sexual orientation) is a categorization that has meaning to a society, that people identify themselves as members of, that shapes how people within that group make sense of the world and relate to others, and that shapes how people outside the group perceive and relate to members of that group. Note that even if you don't identify yourself as a member of a particular cultural-identity group, people inside or outside the cultural-identity group may do so and then relate to you based on their stereotypes about people in that cultural-identity group. In some sense, our cultural-identity groups are inescapable and have consequences on our relationships with others whether or not we intend them to. The differences between defining demographic categories as natural versus socially constructed ideas are summarized in Table 7-1.

When we assume that demographic categories are based on cultural meaning systems, we assume the following:

- *Culture is learned, not natural.* All human beings have the desire and ability to learn about their culture and their place in it. As a result of socialization, human beings develop cultural identities that they view as meaningful and distinctive (e.g., race, gender, nationality, religion, and class) and to which they are emotionally attached. They develop these

TABLE 7-1 Differences between Defining Demographic Categories as Natural versus Socially Constructed	
Demographic Categories (e.g., race and gender) as Natural	**Demographic Categories (e.g., race and gender) as Socially Constructed**
Belief that demographic categories are natural, stable, clearly bounded, and objectively observable.	Belief that demographic categories are, in large part, socially created and reinforced by social institutions.
Rooted in biology.	Rooted in ideology (social beliefs, history, economic conditions, politics).
Demographic categories are something we *are* ("I *am* a woman" or "*I am* a man").	Demographic categories are, in large part, something we *do* (we *do* gender).
Focus on physical attributes, traits, and behaviors that are assumed to be specific to a particular cultural group.	Focus on the meanings of cultural group membership and the consequences of these meanings on identity, worldview, status, and behavior.

cultural identities through teachings and expectations from cultural group members, through teachings and expectations from people outside the cultural group, and by sharing a common history and social context.[38] Cultural identities influence one's self-concept, relationships with people within and outside one's cultural groups, and assumptions about what is true, moral, normal, effective, and appropriate.[39]

- *Cultural meaning systems are taken for granted.* Cultural meaning systems are often so taken for granted that members of cultural-identity groups typically don't think about them, particularly if they're members of a dominant cultural group. Although these meaning systems are culture specific, group members tend to be ethnocentric (i.e., they tend to see their meaning systems as universal standards for what is normal, moral, and effective behavior). Cultural-identity group members tend to interpret—and often misinterpret—the worldview and behaviors of others through their own cultural lenses.[40]
- *Cultural meaning systems are "dynamically stable".*[41] To survive, all cultures must change over time. However, deep cultural change happens slowly. Change happens when members of the culture view change as necessary for survival or when a critical mass of cultural group members are repeatedly exposed to alternative ways of thinking and acting that they find appealing.
- *Cultural meaning systems do not affect all members of the culture equally.* There is significant diversity within cultures. Each person's worldview, values, and behavior are significantly influenced by factors other than culture. These factors include (but are not limited to) family history and experience.

In short, cultural meaning systems are simplified models of the world that help us make sense of the world and provide guidelines for our behavior. These meaning systems and behavioral norms are valuable because they give us a sense of identity and feelings of belonging, and they make coordinated social action possible. However, cultural meaning systems can cause problems when they create blinders that prevent us from seeing alternative points of view or when they create dysfunctional dynamics within or across cultural-identity groups. As managers, it is important to understand our cultural meaning systems as well as those of others because these meaning systems influence the ways that we think, the expectations that we have of others, the way we do our work, and how we define effectiveness and success. When we use our understanding of these meanings systems to create work places that bring out the best in all employees, we are able to leverage the advantages of a diverse workforce and minimize some of the dysfunctional dynamics that can emerge when diversity is not well managed.

DIMENSIONS OF CULTURE

Mr. Akio Morita, the late cofounder and CEO of Sony, said that people are 95% the same and 5% different. In this section, we focus on the cultural differences that matter in the workplace because managers not only must understand and manage the similarities human beings from all cultures share, but the variation in values that different cultures promote. Cultural values can be defined as the "consciously and unconsciously held set of beliefs and norms—often anchored in the morals, laws, customs, and practices of a society—that define what is right and wrong and specify general preferences."[42]

This lesson was put into practice by Orin Smith, former CEO of Starbucks, the well-known upscale coffee bar chain. Smith explained Starbucks' strategies for adapting the stores to global markets:[43]

> The biggest lesson is not to assume that the market or the customers are just like Americans, even if they speak English or otherwise behave as if they were. They're not. This happened in the U.K. [and] it has been happening in Canada . . . [We] took to some of these English-speaking countries the same operating concerns and practices [as in the U.S.] and they just don't work the same way in all markets. . . . We have green tea frappucino in Taiwan and Japan. It's the largest-selling frappucino in these countries. . . . We don't offer it anywhere else. . . . The vanilla frappuccino was popularized in Asia [and is now in the U.S.]. We will be introducing strawberries and creme [frappuccino] out of the U.K. next year. That one will be extremely popular here. . . . Frappuccino type products are popular everywhere . . . You have a little bit less drip coffee in some markets because there are more espresso drinkers. In other countries, we don't sell as much whole-bean coffee. They're not into as much home brewing as we are here. We are trying to change that.

This section summarizes several cultural differences that are relevant to managing in a multicultural context. I discuss several dimensions on which cultures differ (e.g., preferences for independence or interdependence). This list of dimensions is not exhaustive. Rather, it focuses on cultural dimensions that have been particularly well researched, that have implications for behavior at work, that are likely to create misunderstandings at work if not understood and managed, and that provide opportunities for individual and organizational growth if understood and well managed. I have categorized the dimensions on the basis of the following issues that people in all cultures and work organizations must address: Who am I? How do I relate to others? How do I communicate with others? How do I deal with time? What is truth? How do I relate to my environment? What is the relationship of work to life?

When you read about the various dimensions of culture, it will be useful to think about the differences mentioned (e.g., independence versus interdependence, formality versus informality) as extreme ends of a continuum rather than discrete categorizations. Cultures and the individuals within them fall somewhere between these extremes. For example, all human beings need and express both independence and interdependence in their day-to-day life. However, people tend to emphasize one over the other, in part, because of the influence of their culture. After you have read this section, you may want to complete Box 7-1, "Work-Related Cultural Preferences," to identify some of your own preferences and compare them with those of the people with whom you work.

BOX 7-1   Work-Related Cultural Preferences

After reading the description of these dimensions in this chapter, circle the number that represents where you feel you are on each dimension.

Who am I?

Independent	1	2	3	4	5	Interdependent
Doing	1	2	3	4	5	Being
Status through achievement	1	2	3	4	5	Status through ascription

How do I manage relationships?

Low power distance	1	2	3	4	5	High power distance
Universalistic	1	2	3	4	5	Particularistic
Informal	1	2	3	4	5	Formal

How do I communicate?

Low context	1	2	3	4	5	High context
Report talk	1	2	3	4	5	Rapport talk
Neutral	1	2	3	4	5	Emotional
Think while talking	1	2	3	4	5	Think while quiet

How do I relate to time?

Fixed	1	2	3	4	5	Fluid
Monochronic	1	2	3	4	5	Polychronic
Linear orientation	1	2	3	4	5	Cyclical orientation
Future focus	1	2	3	4	5	past and present focus

Standards for truth

Inductive	1	2	3	4	5	Deductive
Seek consistency	1	2	3	4	5	Maintain contradictions

How do I relate to my environment?

Control environment	1	2	3	4	5	Adapt to environment
Change	1	2	3	4	5	Stability
Make my own choices	1	2	3	4	5	Have choices made for me

What is the relationship of work to life?

Live to work	1	2	3	4	5	Work to live
Work unlimited work hours	1	2	3	4	5	Work limited work hours
Business open around the clock	1	2	3	4	5	Business hours limited

Who Am I?

One of our most basic human drives is to make sense of ourself, the world, and our place in it. Through socialization in our cultures, we learn whether we should view ourselves as primarily independent from or dependent on others, whether we should emphasize our quality of life (being) or our achievements (doing), and how we attain status (e.g., power, promotions) in our culture.

INDEPENDENCE AND INTERDEPENDENCE One of the most fundamental differences between cultures is the degree to which they emphasize independence (individualism) or interdependence (collectivism). Independence emphasizes taking care of oneself, separating from others, making one's own decisions, rewarding personal accomplishments, and putting one's own interests and well-being above those of the group. In contrast, interdependence emphasizes connecting with others, taking care of others, making collective decisions, rewarding group accomplishments, and putting the group's interests and well-being above one's own. An MBA student from Japan noted this difference, saying: "When I was learning English at 'my' junior high school, one of the things I couldn't understand was that Americans refer to 'our school' as 'my school,' 'our teacher' as 'my teacher,' and so on. It seemed selfish to me."

Compared with employees from interdependent cultures, employees from independent cultures are likely to be more competitive with their colleagues, to appreciate being singled out for praise, and to be more comfortable with open conflict. In cultures that emphasize interdependence, employees are more likely to emphasize cooperation with their colleagues, be embarrassed by being singled out for praise, and believe that open conflict is rude.

Research suggests that North American, Northern European, and Western European cultures tend to emphasize independence. Southern European, Central and South American, African (with the exception of South Africa), Middle Eastern, and Asian cultures tend to emphasize interdependence. Some research suggests that, in the United States, women and people of color tend to emphasize interdependence more so than do Anglo American men.[44]

DOING AND BEING In action-oriented cultures that emphasize "doing," people tend to focus more on personal achievements, task accomplishments, and improving their standards of living. In cultures that emphasize "being," people tend to focus more on personal qualities, relationships, and the quality of life (that may not be measured in the acquisition of material goods or financial gains).[45] In their book *Doing Business Internationally*, Terence Brake, Danielle Walker, and Thomas Walker give the following example:

> In cross-cultural training seminars, we will often ask the participants, "Who are you?" not just once, but several times. Invariably, Americans will answer with their job titles, and only later with family information or personal interests. Latin Americans, Africans, and those from the Middle East will tend to answer with an affiliation-type answer, such as family, clan, or tribe name. Europeans, in their first three answers, will often answer with a brief description of their humanistic or philosophical outlook.[46]

STATUS: ACHIEVEMENT AND ASCRIPTION All cultures have different ways in which people earn status. In achievement-based cultures, people earn status primarily through personal achievements such as educational attainment, technical skills, and personal talents. In ascription-based cultures, people earn status primarily through their age, family, social connections, and the class into which they were born. Researcher Fons Trompenaars explains that "in an achievement culture, the first question is likely to be 'What did you study' while in a more ascriptive culture the question will more likely be 'Where did you study?'"[47] Achievement-based cultures are likely to encourage more individualistic, less formal, and more competitive behaviors and often value youth over age. Ascription-based cultures are likely to encourage the use of formal titles, respect social and organizational hierarchies, and value age over youth.

In his research, Trompenaars concludes that North America is primarily an achievement-based culture, although he finds less consistency with the other continents. However, he notes that "there is a correlation between Protestantism and achievement orientation, with Catholic, Buddhist, and Hindu cultures scoring considerably more ascriptively."[48]

How Do I Relate to Others?

All cultures have norms regarding appropriate ways of relating to others, including how people should relate to authority, how strictly people should interpret and enforce rules of social conduct (e.g., policies or laws), and the degree of formality that people should use in various social contexts.

HIGH AND LOW POWER DISTANCE   Different cultures have different norms for managing authority relations. Some tend to promote high power distance (more hierarchical), and others tend to promote lower power distance (more egalitarian).[49] Beliefs about power distance influence how we expect managers and direct reports to act toward each other. In cultures that are high in power distance, people are likely to expect social inequality and expect managers to know the right answers, make decisions for employees, and tell employees what to do. In addition, relationships across levels of the hierarchy tend to be more formal. Managers are likely to be called by their formal titles, hierarchies tend to be highly developed, and following the chain of command is likely to be important protocol. In cultures that are low on power distance, inequalities (although they exist) tend to be minimized, denied, and resisted. Managers are expected to draw on the expertise of direct reports, empower employees to make their own decisions, and encourage employees to take independent action. Relationships with managers tend to be less formal and organizational hierarchies flatter. Employees are more likely to bypass the formal hierarchy if they feel it is necessary to get things done.

In cultures with high power distance, managers who overzealously try to empower employees may make employees uncomfortable, get the answers that the employees think the managers want, and lose the respect of direct reports who believe that managers should be able to solve organizational problems on their own. In cultures with low power distance, managers who do not involve workers may be seen as dictatorial, power-hungry micromanagers and may face employee resistance and loss of employee support. Research suggests that Asian, Arab, Central and South American (with the exception of Argentina and Costa Rica), and Southern European cultures tend to have higher power distance orientations compared with Israel, Northern European, and North American cultures.[50]

UNIVERSALISM AND PARTICULARISM   Organized action depends on shared rules for social behavior. Not only do all cultures have rules about right and wrong behavior but they also have norms about how strictly those rules should be interpreted and enforced. In cultures with a universalistic orientation, "a rule is a rule," and it holds for all people and circumstances. In cultures with a particularistic orientation, rules are meant to be symbolic or general guidelines to be adapted to a particular person or situation. In such cultures, people are likely to be more

TABLE 7-2 Differences between Universalism and Particularism

Universalist Perspective	Particularist Perspective
Focuses on rules.	Focuses on relationships and circumstances.
Believes in one right way: Morality is based on universal principles and consistent standards that are independent of the person and context.	Believes in relativity: Morality is situational and standards depend on the person and context.
Assumes all people should be treated the same.	Assumes some people (e.g., family and friends) should be treated differently from others.
Emphasizes legal contracts: A trustworthy person is someone who honors his or her contract.	Emphasizes personal promises: A trustworthy person is someone on whom you can depend to look out for you.
"A deal is a deal."	"Things change" and "It depends."

flexible when applying rules to friends, relatives, or people inside their cultural groups than they are with others. People with a universalistic perspective fear that the system will collapse if they make exceptions to the rules. People with a particularist perspective fear that the system will collapse if they don't make exceptions to the rules.[51] North American, Northern European, and Western European cultures tend to be more universalistic relative to Asian, Central and South American, and Southern and Eastern European cultures. Some research suggests that in the United States, women and people of color tend to be more particularistic than are Anglo American men.[52] Table 7-2 summarizes the differences between universalist and particularist cultures.

FORMALITY AND INFORMALITY   In some cultures, people show respect for others by adhering to decorum—dressing appropriately for occasions, choosing words carefully, and attending to protocol. In other cultures, people are more casual in how they dress, speak, and act. For example, Central and South American, Arab, Asian, and European cultures are more formal relative to Australia and North America.

The following is one of my favorite stories about U.S. tendencies toward informality. The first time I taught in Helsinki, a colleague gave me a tour of the city. Coming from the United States, I told my colleague that I was surprised that I didn't see any homeless people in Helsinki. My colleague replied that few people lived on the street because of Finland's extensive social services. She then pointed to a man with a scraggly beard, patched corduroy jacket, baggy pants, and scuffed shoes and said, quite seriously, "Well, he could be a homeless person or he could be an American professor."

How Do I Communicate with Others?

Communicating effectively across cultures means paying attention to the meaning of the words, the intent of the speaker, and the social context in which communication takes place. Cultures differ in the degree to which they emphasize the spoken word or reading between the lines; whether the primary purpose of communication is to convey facts, assert status, or develop relationships; and whether expressing emotions supports or undermines the credibility of the speaker and the message.

HIGH- AND LOW-CONTEXT COMMUNICATION STYLES   People with low-context communication styles emphasize the spoken word. They tend to focus on the facts, get right down to business, and directly express their views and wants. Because they value facts and directness, communication is likely to move along quickly, and conflicts tend to be depersonalized. In contrast, people with high-context communication styles emphasize the intent behind the words and pay careful attention to the context in which the communication takes place. They emphasize the credibility and trustworthiness of the speaker and the relationship as much as the facts and the spoken word. They take time to get to know a person before getting down to business and look for cues that help them determine whether they should trust the person and invest in the relationship. Consequently, communication takes more time, and conflicts are likely to be personalized. In cultures in which face-saving is important, direct criticism can seriously damage a relationship.

In low-context cultures, the surrounding social context is seen as noise or static that gets in the way of clear communication. In high-context cultures, the surrounding social context is seen as sending important signals that enhance communication. Furthermore, in low-context cultures, harmony is sometimes sacrificed for directness. In high-context cultures, directness is sometimes sacrificed for harmony. The use of the word "yes" is commonly used to illustrate the difference between high- and low-context cultures. In high-context cultures, the word "yes" doesn't always mean agreement or affirmation. Therefore, when working with people from high-context cultures, you may want to phrase your questions so that you avoid "yes" or "no" answers. Box 7-2 summarizes the differences between high- and low-context communication styles.

BOX 7-2   High- and Low-Context Communication Styles

High-Context Communication Style	Low-Context Communication Style
Direct: Message carried primarily by words and less influenced by context (e.g., Saying "I am in agreement with you" means that the person is indeed in agreement and will support the idea.)	Indirect: Message highly influenced by context. It's important to be able to read the context and body language (e.g., Who's in charge? Might the meaning intended be different than the words expressed? Saying, "I am in agreement with you" may mean "I heard what you said" or "I don't want to embarrass you by disagreeing with you publicly" and may not mean that the person supports the idea.)
Purpose is to exchange information, focus on the task, and determine whether the words being expressed are being clearly understood as intended	Purpose is to build relationships, maintain harmony, and determine whether the people communicating can be trusted
Disagreements and criticisms are depersonalized (e.g., "Don't take this personally, but your presentation wasn't' very clear")	Disagreements and criticisms feel personal; therefore, face-saving and being tactful are important (e.g., "I'm embarrassed because you questioned the usefulness of the data I presented in front of the boss.")
Business relationships start and end quickly, and the ability to communicate effectively does not require time to build relationships and trust (e.g., "Now that we've come to an agreement, we'll have our lawyers look this over before we move forward.")	Business relationships can take a long time to develop because the ability to communicate effectively depends on the quality of the relationship (e.g., "Now that we've come to an agreement, we can count on each other to come through as promised.")

A personal example may be helpful here. A few years ago, I taught in an executive education program for a group of South Korean executives who, like many people from Asian cultures, tend to emphasize high-context communication. I developed a respectful relationship with the leader of the group who, consistent with cultural norms, was also the oldest person in the group. One day, I asked him if he thought the program was going well. Rather than answering "yes" or "no," he tactfully answered, "It is all going as planned." I understood from his ambiguous response that he might not have been completely pleased with the program and that he was reluctant to tell me so directly. By reading possible dissatisfaction into his ambiguous response, I was able to look into the matter further, make appropriate changes, and develop a successful program that better met the participants' needs. Researcher Jeffrey Sanchez-Burks provides another example:[53]

> Imagine an exchange between two people working together on a project. One person explains to a colleague an idea for how to present the results of the report in an upcoming departmental meeting. The colleague strongly dislikes the idea. However, in an effort to save face for the person, the colleague responds that "it's an interesting idea" and relies on relational cues such as vocal intonation and body language to convey the actual unfavorable opinion. If the person who proposed the idea is not attentive to these relational cues, the person will infer a positive response. . . . [As] the person moves toward implementing the idea, the colleague may withdraw from the project, offended that the person ignored the negative feedback. The person may then resent what appears to be an unannounced change in support for the idea.

North American and Northern European cultures emphasize low-context communication. Southern European, Central and South American, African, and Asian cultures emphasize high-context communication. Notably, understanding and adapting to the differences between low- and high-context cultures is particularly important in the United States today because an increasing number of immigrants and people entering the United States workforce come from high-context cultures, whereas executives are predominantly from low-context cultures.[54]

REPORT AND RAPPORT TALK   In her best-selling book *Talking from 9 to 5: Women and Men at Work*, communications researcher Deborah Tannen refers to two different styles of communicating: report talk and rapport talk.[55] Similar to low-context communication style, the goal of report talk is to state the facts. However, report talk is also associated with a desire to stand out, to exhibit knowledge and expertise, to reinforce or maintain status, and to win. In contrast, the goal of rapport talk is to establish connection with another person by looking for "similarities and matching experiences" or by deferring to others to establish connection. Tannen's research suggests that North American men are more likely to use report talk and North American women are more likely to use rapport talk. She attributes this difference in communication styles to socialization practices that begin in childhood. She notes that boys are encouraged to emphasize status and winning in their games and interpersonal relationships, and girls are encouraged to emphasize connection.

NEUTRAL AND EXPRESSIVE EMOTIONAL DISPLAYS   In some cultures, displays of emotion are used to emphasize a point, display interest, and show commitment. In such cultures, acting neutral can be seen as disinterest, a lack of understanding, or a lack of motivation. In other cultures, people are expected to show restraint and moderation during communication, particularly in business settings. Japan and many Northern European cultures tend to be less demonstrative of emotions than are Southern European cultures and the United States. In such cultures, displays of extreme emotions—happiness, disappointment, anger—are seen as immature and inappropriate. In their book *Managing Diversity*, Lee Gardenswartz and Anita Rowe tell a story about a North American employee of a Japanese organization. During a business meeting, she expressed her satisfaction with the company's success in achieving its goals with the enthusiastic exclamation, "Yeah!" Her boss later told her that her zealous expression of emotion was unprofessional in a business meeting.[56]

THINKING OUT LOUD OR THINKING WHILE SILENT   Some cultures, particularly Western cultures that value individualism, assume that being talkative is a positive trait because it enables people to assert their individuality and to put their ideas—even uninformed or incomplete ideas—out in the open for others to assess. For example, in some cultures, people who speak openly and often at meetings are viewed as being interested in gaining an understanding of the situation under discussion and motivated to solve problems. In other words, talking is viewed as a signal that the person is engaged and usefully contributing to the group discussion. In other cultures, people who think through problems carefully before speaking up are viewed as being attentive and motivated to understand problems in depth in order to add the most value when they do put their ideas out for others to hear. In other words, silence is viewed as a signal that the person is engaged and adding value to the group discussion. Researcher Heejung Kim explains, "East Asians believe that states of silence and introspection are considered beneficial for high levels of thinking, such as the pursuit of truth. This assumption is well expressed in Buddhist and Taoist practices, such as meditation."[57] This difference may be rooted in the way parents from different cultures raise their children. Parents from Western cultures are encouraged to talk to their children frequently and to encourage their children to speak up as well (e.g., to let people know what you're thinking while you're thinking it). Parents from East Asian cultures speak to their children less frequently and encourage their children to value silence as a way to learn and express self-control (e.g., to think carefully before speaking up).

This cultural difference is important because teachers and team leaders in the United States and other countries that value speaking up often try to encourage the more silent individuals in classes and teams to speak up more often. However, this emphasis on speaking frequently, especially when someone is still thinking through an issue, may actually impair the quality of the reasoning of people who prefer to think problems through before speaking because they process information better when they are quiet and need more time to translate their internal thoughts into the words they want to share with others. Similarly, asking people who prefer to think out loud to instead think silently before speaking may impair the quality of their thinking and problem-solving abilities because they tend to process information more verbally and in interaction with others. That said, in a global economy, it's wise for people to put the effort into learning skills that enable them to both think out loud and silently so that they can use either skill depending on the context and the needs of the situation (e.g., being quiet so that others can speak up; speaking up so that others have more ideas to work with, even if the ideas aren't yet fully formed). Understanding the difference in whether people engage in ideas silently or verbally will also help avoid misunderstandings across cultures (e.g., "People who talk before thinking through an idea are immature" or "People who don't speak up are uninterested or don't understand the situation").

How Do I Deal with Time?

Regardless of their culture, all human beings must deal with the passing of time. However, different cultures emphasize different ways of understanding and managing time, including whether time is viewed as a scarce resource to be saved and spent wisely or a series of moments to be savored; whether people should manage their time by doing one thing at a time or many things at once; whether people should focus primarily on the past, present, or future; and whether time progresses in a linear or circular fashion. For managers, these assumptions have implications for day-to-day time management and coordination, as well as for strategic planning.

FIXED AND FLUID TIME ORIENTATION People from cultures with a fixed orientation toward time tend to manage time with the clock and calendar in mind. They manage their time carefully, adhere to schedules, and expect punctuality. In addition, cultures with a fixed orientation tend to view time as a scarce resource to be managed. North Americans and Northern Europeans tend to prefer a fixed orientation. North Americans, for example, speak of saving time, borrowing time, wasting time, spending time, and running out of time. Businesspeople are warned, "The early bird gets the worm," "If you snooze, you lose," "Invest time wisely," and "Time is money." To better control their time, people invest in time management courses, buy time-saving devices, and eat fast food. Many North Americans schedule social lunches with friends weeks in advance and schedule "quality time" with their children.

Japan and other industrialized Asian cultures also tend to have a fixed orientation toward time, although the proper use of time, rather than speed, is likely to be the main concern. In Japan, it often takes a long time to make a decision because it is important to follow protocol. However, once the decision is made, implementation happens quite quickly.[58] In Japan, it is also important to pay attention to "properness, courtesy, and tradition" when managing time. Many Japanese business and social gatherings unfold carefully and ritually from one phase to another. Successful time management in such an environment means doing the "right thing at the right time."[59]

In Central and South America, the Middle East, Africa, and some Asian cultures, time tends to be experienced as more fluid. A focus on relationships is more likely to drive people's use of time more so than do clocks and calendars. The clock and calendar matter little if someone is engaged in a relationship or an important event. Serendipity and savoring the moment take precedent over schedules. Successful time management means fully attending to the people and matters in the moment, even if that means being late for a scheduled appointment.

It is not surprising that conflict may result between people who expect strict adherence to punctuality, agendas, schedules, and deadlines and people who see punctuality, agendas, schedules, and deadlines as loose guidelines for behavior. Someone with a fixed orientation toward time may see being late for a meeting as rude and irresponsible. In contrast, someone with a fluid orientation toward time may see cutting off a good conversation or leaving a meeting that is in progress to rush off to another meeting as rude and irresponsible.

MONOCHRONIC OR POLYCHRONIC TIME ORIENTATION All managers have multiple demands on their time, but they differ in the way that they manage these time demands. Researcher Allen Bluedorn and his colleagues explain that people with monochronic time orientations prefer to do one thing at a time, focus on the immediate task, and adhere to schedules. People with a polychronic time orientation prefer to do many things simultaneously, focus on relationships and process, and are likely to change plans often.[60] Northern European, North American, and industrialized Asian cultures tend to be monochronic. Southern European, Central and South American, Middle Eastern, and nonindustrialized Asian cultures tend to be polychronic.

PAST, PRESENT, AND FUTURE FOCUS All people must learn from the past, live in the present, and plan for the future. However, managers from different cultures differ in the degree to which they emphasize the past, present, and future. Cultures that focus on the past pay significant attention to tradition, with the hope that they can repeat the successes and avoid the mistakes of the past. Cultures that focus on the present tend to "seize the day" and focus on short-term thinking and quick results. Many European businesspeople, for example, complain that "Americans always live by their quarterly results."[61] Cultures that focus on the future tend to emphasize long-term planning and results and are willing to sacrifice short-term gains for long-term success.

The following story from *U.S. News and World Report* illustrates different orientations toward time, as well as lessons in diplomacy. When Madeleine Albright was U.S. Secretary of State, she visited the foreign ministers from the Arab states of the Persian Gulf. Although she dressed conservatively in keeping with the local traditions for women, she couldn't resist asking the men, "How many women do you have in your cabinet?" Startled, the men, trying to be polite, stumbled for answers. After a while, Saudi Arabia's foreign minister replied, "In the Middle East, where we define time differently, you must be patient."[62]

LINEAR VERSUS CYCLICAL TIME   Some cultures experience time passing in a linear, sequential fashion, one event taking place after another. The manager's goal is to move systematically from one point in time to another toward the future. Other cultures experience time as more cyclical. Every hour, day, week, season, and year follows a predictable cycle. The manager's goal is to understand the cycle and harmonize with the particular rhythms of the cycle. North American cultures tend to experience time as linear, whereas many Asian cultures tend to experience time as cyclical.

When planning, managers who emphasize linear thinking tend to focus primarily on the end result. For example, business author Steven Covey advises managers to "begin with the end in mind." The assumption is that focusing on the end result will lead to an effective process for meeting that goal. Cyclical thinking tends to emphasize the process and finding ways to harmonize with current conditions (which most likely have been seen before because of the cyclical nature of time). From this perspective, the assumption is that focusing on developing an appropriate process will lead to an effective end result.

What Is Truth?

Our assumptions about what is to be considered true and how we determine what is true influence how we teach others, how we learn from others, what is "fact" and what is "fiction," and what kind of information we consider to be the most useful in guiding the decisions we make at work and in our personal lives.[63] Different cultures emphasize different ways of creating and using knowledge.

INDUCTIVE AND DEDUCTIVE REASONING   Cultures that value inductive reasoning emphasize data, facts, objectivity, proof, direct observation, cause and effect, breaking things down into small parts, and understanding the separate parts. People who emphasize inductive reasoning tend to prefer using measurements and scientific methods for investigating problems and justifying conclusions. In contrast, people who emphasize deductive reasoning take a more holistic approach, with many elements and perspectives being held at one time.[64] They tend to stress abstract thinking, symbolism, understanding the whole rather than individual parts, and often rely on analogies, metaphors, and stories for explanations.[65] For people who prefer inductive processes, the credibility of an explanation depends on claims of objectivity and the use of a systematic methodology. For people who prefer deductive reasoning, the credibility of an explanation often depends on the credibility of the speaker and the ability of the speaker to engage the imagination and emotional commitment of the audience. North American cultures tend to emphasize inductive reasoning, whereas French, East Asian, and Central and South American cultures tend to emphasize deductive reasoning.[66]

SEEKING CONSISTENCY AND MAINTAINING CONTRADICTIONS   In some cultures, people tend to categorize the world and their experience in it into clear dichotomies. They believe something is either one way or another—true or false, right or wrong, real or unreal. Contradictions must be resolved for the situation to make sense and for a decision to be made. In other cultures, something can be simultaneously true and false, right and wrong, real and unreal. Contradictions must be maintained to see the complexity of the situation more clearly and to make a well-reasoned decision. This difference in perspective is nicely illustrated in the following statement: "In the West, we consider consistency a virtue. In the East, consistency is an attribute of small minds and children. For example, in the West a person who acts inconsistently with their attitudes are called hypocrites; in the East they are thought to be sophisticated, i.e., they do what they must rather than what they like to do."[67]

How Do I Relate to the Environment?

Regardless of their culture, all human beings and organizations must manage their relationship with the environment to survive. Managing this relationship involves assumptions about the degree to which human beings can (and should) control or adapt to the environment, whether change and uncertainty are welcome or threatening, and how much having multiple choices is viewed as necessary for making decisions that enhance the quality of work and life.

CONTROLLING, HARMONIZING WITH, AND BEING CONSTRAINED BY THE ENVIRONMENT
To survive, people must sometimes take control of their environments and at other times adapt to their environments. Cultures tend to differ in the degree to which they prefer to control, harmonize with, or adapt to their environment. In his book *Riding the Waves of Culture*, Fons Trompenaars gives the following example of the difference between preferences for controlling versus harmonizing with the environment.

> The late chairman of Sony, Mr. Akio Morita, once explained how he came to conceive of the Walkman [Yes, CD players were widely available long before MP3 players]. He loved classical music and wanted to have a way of listening to it on his way to work without bothering any fellow commuters. The Walkman was a way of not imposing on the outside world, but of being in harmony with it. Contrast this to the way most Westerners think about using the device. "I can listen to music without being disturbed by other people." Another obvious example is the use of face masks that are worn over the nose and mouth. In Tokyo, you see many people wearing them, especially in winter. When you inquire why, you are told that when people have colds or a virus, they wear them so they will not pollute or infect other people by breathing on them. In New York they are worn by bikers and other athletes who do not want to be polluted by the environment.[68]

The example above illustrates the use of Walkman (or MP3 players) and face masks to either take control of the impact of one's environment (e.g., to not be bothered by others and to not get sick from the environment) or adapt to one's environment (e.g., to not bother others and to not make others sick).

CHANGE: HIGH AND LOW UNCERTAINTY AVOIDANCE   Organizational success requires integrating both change and stability. Uncertainty avoidance refers to the degree to which people feel comfortable with change and ambiguity.[69] For example, some cultures encourage people to see personal and organizational change as productive and stimulating. Such cultures warn that people and organizations must "change or die." In this view, stability breeds complacency and complacency prevents us from seizing opportunities that are critical for survival. Other cultures encourage people to promote stability over change. Tradition, routines, predictability, and staying the course are the foundations of long-term survival. In this view, change and uncertainty create anxiety that can be damaging to important traditions and routines that are critical to achieving steady progress toward individual, organizational, and societal goals.

CHOICE   In the United States, having multiple choices is viewed as valuable and is taken for granted. This is most obvious when one looks at supermarket shelves and finds no fewer than 30 different brands of toothpaste, with each brand offering several options (e.g., "tartar control," "whitening," or "sensitive teeth"). Many researchers believe that choice is a universal human need, results in a greater sense of personal control, increases intrinsic motivation, and leads to positive outcomes such as greater satisfaction and higher performance.

Researchers Sheena Sethi Iyenger and Mark Lepper conducted a fascinating series of studies in which they contrasted the performance of Asian American and Anglo American children in high- and low-choice task situations. They found that the Asian American children were likely to perform better when the choices were made for them, particularly when the choices were made within a trusted situation (clear rules of the game) or by a trusted person (the child's mother). In contrast, the Anglo American children performed best when they were able to make their own choices.[70]

Sethi and Lepper suggest that the desire for choice may not be universal, nor does having choices always lead to the best performance. Instead, a desire for choice may be related to whether a person has an independent or interdependent sense of self. People from cultures that promote an independent self-concept (e.g., the United States) may prefer choice because it enables them to assert their independence and show their uniqueness. In contrast, people from cultures that promote an interdependent sense of self (e.g., China) may prefer to defer to a trusted person or institution to make choices on their behalf. Doing so enables them to show respect for protocol and authority, learn from the experience of others, and enhance their sense of belonging to a group.

Note that recent research suggests that the preference for choice, even in the United States, may be overstated.[71] Because of people's limited cognitive abilities (e.g., our ability to make sense of information), too much choice may inhibit effective decision-making and the ability to take action. For example, people—even in the United States where having multiple choices is valued—may become so overwhelmed by the trade-offs and cognitive effort that goes into choosing among alternatives that they may postpone decisions, decide to not choose at all, or be dissatisfied with the decisions they make because they wonder if they should have chosen the other alternatives.

This was illustrated in a simple but powerful study in which researchers Sethi Iyenger and Lepper set up two booths in a grocery store designed to entice shoppers to purchase jam. In one booth, the researchers placed 24 different kinds of jam (the "extensive choice condition"). In the other booth, the researchers placed only six different kinds of jam (the "limited choice condition"). Thirty-one (30%) of the consumers who passed the limited choice booth purchased jam compared with only three (1%) of the shoppers who passed the extensive choice booth. Interestingly, 60% of the customers who passed the extensive choice booth stopped at the booth, whereas only 40% stopped at the limited choice booth. This suggests that although the shoppers were drawn to having more choices, they were more likely to act on those choices—purchase the jam—when they were offered fewer choices. In another study, the researchers found that when they increased the number of topics students could choose from for a particular assignment, students were less likely to complete the assignment and performed poorer as the options increased.[72] The point here is that although cultures may promote differences in how much having choices should be valued, people across cultures may share similar cognitive limitations that influence how choice actually affects decision making.

What Is the Relationship of Work to Life?

It has been said that some people work to live, whereas others live to work. In some cultures, work is often viewed as a calling, passion, and even a spiritual quest. In other places, work is often viewed as a necessary evil or a means to an end such as survival or a comfortable life. Although these descriptions are extreme views, different cultures reinforce these views through vacation policies (e.g., some cultures offer two weeks each year; others offer five weeks each year), expected work hours (and norms about how long people who want to be successful should stay at the office after official work hours), how much time off—if any—parents should get after having a baby (and whether this time off should be paid or unpaid), and the degree to which someone's identity is defined by what their profession. For example, when you go to a party in some cultures, people try to get to know you by asking "What do you do?" In other cultures, this question wouldn't come up at a party because what you do for work is not as central to understanding who you are as a person in that culture.

The Difference between Stereotyping and Valuing Cultural Differences

When we discuss cultural differences, it is wise to keep in mind several caveats. First, all descriptions of differences across cultures are, of course, oversimplified. Cultural meaning systems are much more complex than the human mind can understand and the written word can express. Second, cultures change. Globalization, increased diversity within nations, and transportation and communication technologies are exposing us all to more cultures more often than ever before. Consequently, cultural norms that were prevalent 10 years ago may be less prevalent today, particularly among people from younger generations. Third, several scholars and practitioners worry that focusing on cultural differences can be divisive. Certainly this is the case when descriptions of cultural differences lead to stereotyping and discrimination.

The minority of one generation is usually the majority of the next.
*—*Gertrude Atherton,
The Aristocrats

Researcher Taylor Cox describes the differences between stereotyping and valuing diversity.[73] Stereotyping "involves the assumption that characteristics thought to be common in a cultural group apply to every member" (e.g., assuming that all Japanese are collectivists or all North Americans are individualists), and can imply negative judgments about these characteristics (e.g., thinking through ideas out loud is immature and wastes people's time; thinking through ideas before speaking not speaking up often in a meeting means that one is not engaged in the discussion). Furthermore, stereotyping tends to be one-dimensional. That is, when we stereotype, we tend to overemphasize a person's membership in one cultural-identity group and underemphasize other factors, including other cultural-group memberships, which also shape that person's worldview and behavior. For example, we may overemphasize people's race and underestimate how much their gender, class, religion, education, and nationality—even personality—influence their beliefs and behavior.

In contrast to stereotyping, valuing diversity "views cultural differences as positive or neutral." People who have this perspective are more likely to see the value in different perspectives and behaviors, and they are also more likely to learn from and leverage these differences to become more flexible and effective. The valuing diversity perspective also attends to people's multiple cultural-identity group memberships, and—instead of assuming all people from a particular culture inevitably share beliefs and behavioral styles—"is based on the concept of greater probability" that a person from a particular culture *may* share the worldview, values, and behavioral norms of their cultural-identity groups.[74] Stereotyping narrows our perspective and constrains our behavior; valuing diversity broadens our perspective, gives us multiple ways to interpret people's behaviors, expands our ability to make sense of complex situations, and enables us to build a broad and diverse network of relationships built on mutual trust and respect.

No matter how much we learn about the nuances of different cultures, managing across cultures is a constant process of sensemaking, trying out our assumptions to see if they're valid and useful, and adaptability. People are influenced by many factors other than their cultures, so there is no surefire way to predict another person's worldview, preferences, and behavior. However, increasing our knowledge of cultural influences on beliefs and behaviors enhances the possibility that we can "read" others' behavior more accurately, avoid misunderstandings, and interact with others more appreciatively and effectively.

> Fear of difference is fear of life itself.
> —MARY PARKER FOLLETT, *Creative Experience*

PART III STRATEGIES FOR LEVERAGING DIVERSITY

As mentioned earlier in this chapter, organizations that recruit, retain, and leverage the talent of the best and the brightest employees have a competitive advantage because all employees can learn from each other, think more creatively, be more adaptive, and continuously create more effective work processes that add value to their organizations and the people they serve. Furthermore, organizations that effectively manage diversity are more like to avoid expensive legal suits, tap into diverse markets both nationally and globally, and enhance their reputations as good places to work, support, and invest in. Organizations that don't manage diversity effectively lose opportunities to turn the talent of their diverse workforce into bottom-line results. This section describes best practices for achieving the benefits that a diverse workforce offers. We begin by discussing how you can enhance your personal multicultural competence. We then turn to how you can create a work environment that enables all employees to do their best work.

> Diversity without unity makes about as much sense as dishing up flour, sugar, water, eggs, shortening, and baking powder on a plate and calling it a cake.
> —C. WILLIAM POLLARD, *The Soul of the Firm*

Enhancing Your Personal Multicultural Competence

People with multicultural competence have particular attitudes and skills that travel well across cultures and that enable them to be effective—and add value—in multicultural settings. In a *Business Horizons* article, Thomas Fitzgerald describes an effective cross-cultural manager as someone "who can move in and out of social, cultural, and mixed-gender encounters with relative ease; one who is able to handle diversities of many sorts and to be flexible in the face of rapid social changes—in short, a psychologically secure person who believes in the common unity of humankind."[75] Hal Lancaster, columnist for the *Wall Street Journal*, interviewed executives about the qualities of effective global leaders. He concluded that an effective global leader "is someone who can handle more complexity and uncertainty than domestic managers are typically accustomed to, who relates well with diverse groups of people, who listens more than talks, who craves adventure over the status quo, and who accepts that there is more than one way to skin a business problem. As one executive put it, good global leaders like getting up in the morning and saying, 'I have no idea what's going to happen today.'"[76]

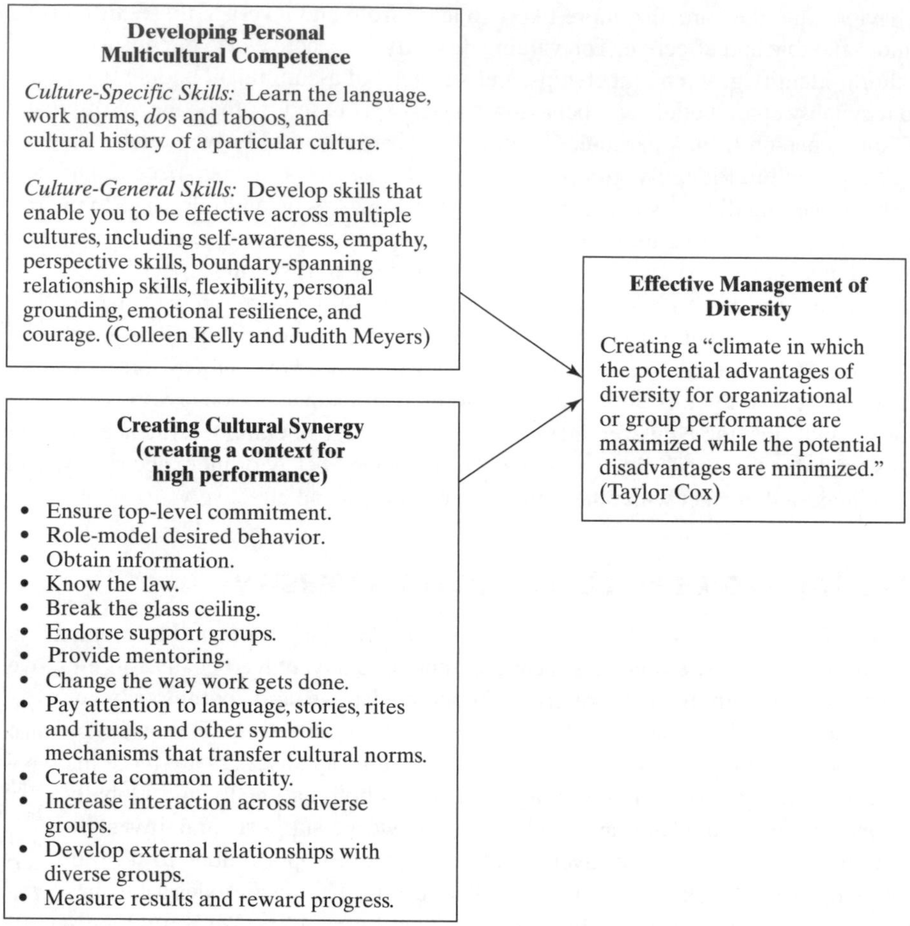

Developing Personal Multicultural Competence

Culture-Specific Skills: Learn the language, work norms, *do*s and taboos, and cultural history of a particular culture.

Culture-General Skills: Develop skills that enable you to be effective across multiple cultures, including self-awareness, empathy, perspective skills, boundary-spanning relationship skills, flexibility, personal grounding, emotional resilience, and courage. (Colleen Kelly and Judith Meyers)

Creating Cultural Synergy (creating a context for high performance)

- Ensure top-level commitment.
- Role-model desired behavior.
- Obtain information.
- Know the law.
- Break the glass ceiling.
- Endorse support groups.
- Provide mentoring.
- Change the way work gets done.
- Pay attention to language, stories, rites and rituals, and other symbolic mechanisms that transfer cultural norms.
- Create a common identity.
- Increase interaction across diverse groups.
- Develop external relationships with diverse groups.
- Measure results and reward progress.

Effective Management of Diversity

Creating a "climate in which the potential advantages of diversity for organizational or group performance are maximized while the potential disadvantages are minimized." (Taylor Cox)

FIGURE 7-1   Skills for Multicultural Competence

These perspectives support what researchers have found in their studies: People with high "cognitive complexity" (the degree of complexity with which a person takes in and makes sense of information and experiences), a high degree of "openness to experience" (being broad-minded and intellectually curious, enjoying novelty and exploration, and being able to go beyond conservative perspectives to consider new ideas and experiences), and a high degree of "need for cognition" (a tendency to participate in and enjoy experiences that take mental effort and stretch one's thinking) are more likely to manage diversity effectively and gain the benefits from doing so.[77]

> The curious are always in some danger. If you are curious you might never come home.
> —JEANETTE WINTERSON, *Oranges Are Not the Only Fruit*

It is not surprising that characteristics that inhibit the ability to effectively manage across cultures include rigidity, perfectionism, narrow-mindedness, self-centeredness, emotional immaturity, overemphasizing task and technical skills, underemphasizing relationships, lack of cross-cultural skills, and lack of interest in working across cultures.[78] Colleen Kelly and Judith Meyers, creators of the Cross-Cultural Adaptability Inventory, argue that effective multicultural managers have both culture-specific knowledge and culture-general skills.[79] Culture-specific knowledge helps a manager be effective in a specific culture. This includes knowledge such as how to manage a meeting with Brazilians, negotiate a deal with the Japanese, and conduct a presentation for North Americans. Culture-general skills, rather than focusing on the norms of a particular culture, refer to a frame of mind and set of competencies that enable you to be effective and at ease anywhere, with any culture, and with multiple cultures simultaneously (such as when managing a meeting attended by people who come from multiple cultures).

Culture-Specific Skills

To be an effective multicultural manager, you should make an effort to understand the particular cultures with which you are working. These efforts include the following:

- *Learn at least some of the language.* This shows respect for the culture, makes communication easier, and indicates to others that you have a willingness and ability to go outside your comfort zone. Pay attention to nonverbal communication such as body language, norms about who speaks first, and acceptable levels of formality or informality. For example, North Americans move their heads up and down to say yes. Bulgarians and Indians from the south of India tend to move theirs from side to side to say yes.[80] The common sign for "OK" in the United States is considered vulgar in many countries (including Brazil, Greece, Ghana, and Turkey) and means "worthless" in France and Belgium. The common "thumbs up" hand signal that suggests approval in the United States can be perceived as vulgar in many countries, including Iran, Afghanistan, and some parts of Italy.

- *Learn the work norms.* Learn which business practices tend to work best, how success is defined, and which behaviors people expect from a manager. Culture researcher Andre Laurent explains that "there is no such thing as Management with a capital M. The art of managing and organizing has no homeland. Every culture has developed through its history some specific and unique insight into the managing of organizations and of their human resources."[81] Remember that you need credibility, trust, and respect to be effective, and these are earned in different ways in different cultures. For example, in some nations managers are expected to be less involved in the technical details of their employees' work and more focused on being effective "people managers" and coaches who empower their employees, whereas in other nations managers are expected to be technical experts who take a more active role in helping employees solve technical problems.[82]

- *Learn the dos and taboos.* Effective multicultural managers learn appropriate business and social conventions that show respect for others in a culture. These include norms about how to dress for different functions, how to greet people, what kinds of conversations are appropriate, and what types of gifts are welcome. For example, in Japan, business cards are taken very seriously. Many Japanese businesspeople use business cards to determine the status of the person with whom they are dealing. Therefore, it is a good idea to list your degrees and honors on your business card and translate it into Japanese. In addition, it can be offensive to take a business card and put it away without reading it carefully. It also may be offensive to write on a person's business card—it would be like writing across the person's photograph.[83]

- *Understand the social context.* Try to understand how particular norms and customs reflect deeper assumptions and values of a culture. Specifically, take time to learn the history, politics, laws, religions, labor issues, and economic conditions of the cultures with which people work. To illustrate this point, cross-cultural consultant Fons Trompenaars describes a situation in which he and another Dutch consultant were conducting a change management seminar with Ethiopian managers. Initially, the seminar was going quite poorly. The seminar became successful only when the consultants took time to learn the history of Ethiopia. They learned that many Ethiopians' identity is tied to a wealthy and regal past. They integrated this treasured past into the seminar by asking participants, "What had Ethiopia done right in that period to make its cities and trade flourish?" For the participants, "the future was now seen as a way of recreating some of the greatest glories of the past; suddenly, the management of change seminar had captured the enthusiastic support of everyone."[84]

Understanding history, however, is not as simple as it may seem. When I told this story to an Ethiopian friend of mine, she noted that many Ethiopians, because of the history of intergroup conflicts in Ethiopia, would have been offended by the consultants' reference to Ethiopia's wealthy past. Discussing Ethiopia's wealthy past easily could have undermined the seminar, depending on which Ethiopians were in attendance.

Culture-General Skills

Culture-specific knowledge is necessary but insufficient for long-term managerial success because it is limited to specific cultural contexts. As cross-cultural interactions become the norm rather than the exception, you cannot always prepare for cross-cultural interactions in advance, nor can you learn all the nuances of every culture. Furthermore, you must know how to work with people from many different cultures simultaneously. For example, you may find yourself at a meeting with one Italian, one German, two Finns, one Indian, one North American, one Chinese, one Nigerian, and two Mexicans, all in the same room at the same time—with only two-hour notice. In short, you must be able to cross multiple cultural boundaries anytime and any place. Therefore, you need cultural-general skills that do not depend on in-depth culture-specific knowledge. At a minimum, these include a desire to work with people from diverse cultures.[85] In addition, you should:

- *Invest in self-awareness.* Take time to learn how your own culture affects how you see the world, why you do the things you do, and how your behavior affects others. Also take time to learn how you or your culture may be perceived by people whose cultures differ from your own.
- *Develop the ability to build connections across cultural boundaries.* Remember that every interaction is an opportunity to build a relationship. Try to make every cross-cultural interaction a positive one. Find ways to connect by identifying what you and others have in common (e.g., shared interests and experiences). Find opportunities to reach out beyond your culture to become increasingly comfortable and experienced working with people from cultures that differ from your own. Keep in mind the platinum rule: Treat others as they would like to be treated. By following the platinum rule, you will be better able to make others feel comfortable, develop mutual trust and respect with a wide variety of people, and get the support of people from many cultures.
- *Perception skills.* Pay attention to the social context in which you are working. Look for cues that can help you understand important business norms regarding how people want to

be treated at work, how they expect managers and professionals (including you) to act, and how decisions get made and implemented.[86]

- *Flexibility.* Develop cognitive flexibility, the ability to think in broad and complex ways, consider multiple goals and perspectives simultaneously, integrate divergent information, maintain rather than resolve contradictions, make sense out of ambiguity, and see uncertainty as an opportunity.[87] Also develop behavioral flexibility, which refers to the ability to view differences as opportunities rather than threats and to be able to adapt your perceptions and behaviors quickly in order to respond to others effectively.[88]

- *Personal grounding.* Remember that effective multicultural managers are not so flexible that they give up their personal values or standards and adapt indiscriminately to every situation.[89] Rather, they balance adaptability with a healthy respect for their own culture, personal beliefs, and treasured values. Mahatma Gandhi eloquently described the art of balancing adaptability with personal grounding when he said: "Let all my windows be open. Let all cultures blow in. But let not culture blow me off my feet."

- *Emotional resilience.* Cross-cultural encounters can be rewarding and invigorating, but they can also create feelings of anxiety, confusion, and embarrassment, especially when things don't go as planned and when people don't react in ways that you are used to.[90] Effective multicultural managers rebound quickly from stressful experiences, persist when faced with obstacles (often by trying different strategies or adjusting their goals), and maintain an optimistic attitude and sense of humor.

- *Courage and attention to inequities.* Most societies are stratified into hierarchies in which people from some cultural groups have more power than do people from other cultural groups, and these inequities tend to be replicated in organizations unless organizational leaders proactively take actions to resist these inequities.[91] Of course, this does not mean that people from some cultural groups are innately better or worse than are people from others; rather, societies and organizations promote these beliefs through policies and work practices.[92] To understand these inequities, pay attention to subtle and not-so-subtle patterns of inequities in everyday work life, such as who does and doesn't get taken seriously at meetings, who speaks and who doesn't, and which cultural groups tend to be over or underrepresented in various professions or at different levels of the hierarchy. Understanding and managing inequities is a particularly thorny issue when outside one's own country where sincere but naïve interventions in the spirit of equality can sometimes do more harm than good. Understanding the religion, laws, and history of intergroup relations is particularly critical.

Note that many of the culture-general skills also are important to success in relatively homogeneous settings. However, although managers may get by without some of these skills and attitudes in homogeneous settings, they are critical to success in multicultural settings. Remember that multicultural competence goes beyond learning a set of techniques, and is based on an attitude of humility, empathy, and respect for others and their beliefs.

Only equals can be friends.
—ETHOPIAN PROVERB

Developing Multicultural Competence

How can you develop culture-specific and culture-general skills? As always, experience is a good teacher. Meena Wilson and Maxine Dalton, researchers at the Center for Creative Leadership, found that successful expatriates often learned "lessons of difference and lessons of accommodation" at an early age. Many were exposed to diversity at a young age through "an immigrant parent, a foreign-born spouse, an international schooling experience, or childhood in a border town or ethnically diverse community. These individuals seemed to have learned early the lessons of difference—that there is more than one way to living one's life."[93] They also found that successful expatriates tend to have succeeded in handling disruptions earlier in their lives, such as moving several times as children. These experiences taught them how to take care of themselves, how to get along with new people, and how to survey the environment for cues that help them make sense of and succeed in new situations.

What if you haven't had some of these early experiences? It helps to remember that having these experiences doesn't guarantee that a person necessarily learns valuable lessons from them. Nor does it mean that people who don't have these early experiences lacked opportunities to develop attitudes and skills that help them become effective in cross-cultural situations. I know many people who have traveled the world over and failed to develop the emotional, cognitive, or behavioral flexibility that are the foundations of effective cross-cultural relationships. And I've known people who grew up in small, homogeneous communities who developed the qualities of curiosity, openness, empathy, and respect toward others—characteristics that are critical for cross-cultural effectiveness.

Structured activities, such as organized training programs and reading books about effective cross-cultural management, can help. In addition, you can learn a great deal by reading novels and watching movies about other cultures, particularly when they are created by the people from those cultures. Put yourself in a variety of cross-cultural situations that challenge your worldview and take you out of your comfort zone. Most important, you can develop mutually supportive relationships with people from different cultures. The more opportunities you have to be with people from other cultures, the more you can learn about yourself, others, and the world; the more practice you can get at enhancing your cross-cultural skills; the more humble and resilient you can become; and the more likely you will develop a reputation as someone who enjoys and succeeds in multicultural situations.

CREATING AN ORGANIZATIONAL CULTURE THAT VALUES AND LEVERAGES DIVERSITY

Effective managers not only pay attention to developing their own cultural competence, they also create an organizational culture that promotes diversity and enables all employees to work with and learn from each other in ways that add value to the organization and the people they serve. There are several steps that you can take to create an organizational culture that brings out the best in all employees.

Equality cannot be seized any more than it can be given. It must be a shared experience.
—JAMES FARMER,
All About CORE

ENSURE TOP-LEVEL COMMITMENT TO PROMOTING DIVERSITY AT ALL LEVELS   Leaders who are committed to cultural diversity take a public stand on their commitment, provide the strategic direction for creating an effective multicultural organization, and allocate the resources required to achieve their goals.[94]

ROLE-MODEL THE BEHAVIOR YOU WANT TO SEE   Although you may not be able to ensure commitment from all top-level executives, you can be a role model and look for opportunities to exhibit your commitment to diversity through your day-to-day interactions. Researcher Catherine Herr Van Norstrand explains that being a role model is particularly important when we are in a leadership role because others "may unquestioningly buy into our words and actions because they believe in us—we have more expertise and are expected to know what we are doing. They assume that we have gotten a grip on our own hang-ups and are ready to provide them with uncontaminated guidance. However, when our self-awareness is lacking, or even when we detect personal bias but neglect to stop it, the results of our collusion can be far-reaching."[95]

OBTAIN INFORMATION ABOUT HOW WELL YOUR COMPANY IS MANAGING DIVERSITY Take steps to understand how the current organizational culture helps and hinders diversity efforts. You can get this information in several ways, including written surveys, in-depth interviews, focus groups, and analysis of company data related to hiring, staffing, promotion, turnover, and employee and customer satisfaction. For example, you can assess the proportion of women, people of color, and people from different nationalities at different levels of the organizational hierarchy and use this information to explore whether everyone in the organization, regardless of culture, has a fair chance of rising up through the corporate ladder. You can also look to other organizations for best practices. Although most of the "best" companies admit that they still have a long way to go, they provide useful measures and data against which other organizations can judge their own efforts. For example, when *Fortune* magazine analyzed the companies that made their "Diversity Elite" list, they found that at the typical best company, minorities account for a greater percentage of representation in the boardroom, compared with the companies that didn't make their "Diversity Elite" list.[96]

> It is in the little actions of day-to-day work that employees will be testing to see if their leaders are respectful of the concerns and traditions of a particular gender or ethnic group.
> —JAY CONGER,
> *Leadership researcher*

You can also get information by establishing a diversity committee or task force. Many organizations create an internal advisory group consisting of a diverse group of employees who meet regularly, have access to top leadership, identify problems and opportunities, recommend interventions, and monitor progress toward diversity goals. The findings of these task forces can identify several opportunities for change that may otherwise go unnoticed. For example, when Avon developed a diversity task force, they identified several areas of concern. They found that Asian Americans were clustered in staff departments, women were becoming more satisfied with their advancement possibilities but were also becoming increasingly concerned about caretaker benefits, and gay and lesbian employees wanted benefits for their partners.[97]

KNOW THE LAW Make sure that all employees understand the legal environment at home and abroad.[98] Note that laws and interpretations of laws change often, so you should regularly check the status of discrimination laws in your own countries and in the countries in which you conduct business.

> I can't change my sex. But you can change your policy.
> —HELEN KIRKPATRICK,
> *Women of the World*

BREAK THE GLASS CEILING People, given the choice, will want to work in environments where they feel comfortable; have the opportunity to do their best work; and will be fairly rewarded for their efforts with growth opportunities, promotions, and salary increases. Organizations that lack a diverse workforce or have a high rate of turnover send signals that these conditions may not be met. If you don't already have a diverse workforce, you need to determine how to make your organization an employer of choice for diverse populations. One way to become an employer of choice is to break the glass ceiling. If your organization doesn't have diversity at all levels, including top management, executive, and director levels, it sends the message that opportunities to contribute and advance may not be available to people from all cultural groups. Consequently, some of the most high-potential people in those cultural groups will look to other organizations (e.g., your competition) to find these opportunities.

To break the glass ceiling, make sure that all employees have equal access to important developmental experiences that are stepping stones to professional development, promotions, and higher salaries. These opportunities include early experiences such as supportive mentoring relationships and challenging assignments that are important to a manager's later career success.[99] Challenging assignments include important projects or task forces, foreign assignments, line positions with direct profit and loss responsibility, and high-risk and high-visibility projects such as turning around a business or starting up a new division.[100] Such assignments enable employees to increase their visibility, take a strategic view of the organization, learn new technical and relationship management skills, prove themselves under difficult conditions, and develop the self-confidence and political savvy they will need at higher levels of the organization.

ELIMINATE REINDEER GAMES Law professor Theresa Beiner coined the term "reindeer games" to describe social activities that are not obviously work related, that provide work-related advantages, and that are made available to some employees but not others on the basis of their cultural-identity group membership.[101] These include activities such as lunches, dinners, and certain sports. Such activities can provide access to important executives, colleagues, customers, and other business contacts who can provide work-related information, support, and professional contacts. Participating in these social events may contribute to promotions and other career advantages as a consequence of the visibility, informal mentoring, and the other benefits they offer. Beiner uses the term "reindeer games" to refer to such activities because, as many people remember from childhood storybooks and songs, Santa Claus's reindeer excluded "poor Rudolf" from their reindeer games. She notes that "reindeer games" may be illegal in the United States under Title VII of the Civil Rights Act of 1964, which prohibits employment discrimination on the basis of sex, race, and religion because such "games" can result in "disparate treatment, exclusion, or psychological harm" to members of certain groups.[102]

ENDORSE SUPPORT GROUPS Research suggests that employees who are in the minority in organizations benefit (in terms of effectiveness and promotions) when they belong to support groups, also known as network groups (e.g., groups that specifically support women, African Americans, Latinos, and people from different nations in the organization).[103] As people who traditionally have been outside the managerial ranks move into higher levels of the organization, they often find themselves increasingly in the minority at those levels. Consequently, they often want and need support from others who share similar life and work experiences. Several organizations, including A. T. Kearney, the British Civil Service, and General Electric, promote "identity-based support groups" to provide support to their members and offer advice to the organization on how to make the organization more supportive and best use the talents of all employees.[104]

PROVIDE TRAINING Diversity training falls into two categories: awareness training and skill-based training.[105] Awareness training is often the starting point for diversity training programs and is designed to increase employees' awareness of and sensitivity toward diversity issues.[106] Such training focuses on helping employees understand the organization's commitment to developing a multicultural organization, the competitive advantages of multicultural organizations, the legal climate (e.g., affirmative action, equal employment opportunity, and sexual harassment laws), and the potential impact of cultural differences on individual behavior, interpersonal relationships, and group dynamics. One of the most important lessons from awareness training is that although people "share the same work environment," people from different cultural-identity groups often "experience that environment in very different ways."[107] Skill-based training provides employees with specific skills that help them manage diversity at work. Topics include understanding and managing one's own cultural biases, understanding different cultural norms, communicating and negotiating across cultures, and facilitating multicultural team meetings.

PROVIDE MENTORING OPPORTUNITIES   Researchers have found that providing mentoring to employees who are in the minority in organizations enhances their development and advancement in organizations. On the basis of his research of successful minority managers, Harvard researcher David Thomas concluded that "the people of color who advance the furthest all share one characteristic—a strong network of mentors and corporate sponsors who nurture their professional development."[108] Through mentoring, employees in the minority get advice about how to be successful in the organization, obtain visibility and contacts with people who can help them succeed, and obtain helpful psychological support.[109]

ENCOURAGE FORMAL EDUCATION   Encourage people of all cultural groups to pursue advanced education. The payoff of an MBA, for example, can be substantial. The Association to Advance Collegiate Schools of Business (AACSB), the organization that provides accreditation to MBA programs, found that the return on investment for MBA programs is as follows:[110]

- Day MBA programs: 15% return on investment, 5.1 years payback period, 59% salary increase
- Part-time MBA programs: 68% return on investment, 1.6 years payback period, 37% salary increase
- Executive MBA programs: 35% return on investment, 2.8 years payback period, 17% salary increase

Yet the enrollment of women in the top 15 MBA programs averages only around 35%, compared to approximately 50% in law and medical schools.[111] In one study, researchers found that 42% of the women they interviewed felt employers didn't encourage them to pursue the MBA, in contrast to 25% of men who felt this way. African American women were more likely to feel that they weren't encouraged to get an MBA degree than were Caucasian American women.[112] According to the AACSB, African Americans account for 5.3% of U.S. MBA students, Hispanic Americans account for 5.2%, and Native Americans account for less than 1%. Furthermore, only 3.6% of business school professors are black, 1.8% Hispanic, and less than 1% Native American.[113] It is notable that the ACT, a college entrance exam used in the United States, recently revised the exam questions and decided to "toss out essay questions in which one gender or ethnic group scored especially high or low."[114]

> Prejudice saves a lot of time, because you can form an opinion without the facts.
> —ANONYMOUS

> Unity, not uniformity, must be our aim. We attain unity only through variety. Differences must be integrated, not annihilated, nor absorbed.
> —MARY PARKER FOLLETT, *The New State*

CHANGE THE WAY WORK GETS DONE   Many organizational policies and routines were created for a bygone era. New perspectives can bring fresh ideas about how to improve quality, increase efficiency, decrease costs, inspire innovations, identify new markets, and meet customers' needs. Therefore, effective multicultural managers encourage employees to challenge current assumptions about when, where, and how work should be accomplished. They explore whether current organizational policies and norms are truly necessary for organizational effectiveness or whether they are rooted in taken-for-granted assumptions and routines that may add little value or even hinder progress.

For example, when I was pregnant with my second child, I was scheduled to teach a part-time MBA course. For 20 years, part-time MBA courses had been taught for three hours in the evening each week over 13 weeks. This schedule would have brought the last class precariously close to the date my daughter Leah was due to be born. So, I suggested to my department chairperson that I redesign the course to meet for four full days instead of 13 three-hour weekly sessions. The course would cover the same amount of material over the same number of classroom hours, but in a more compressed format. When the four-day course format was approved, more than 200 students signed up for only 50 seats (students said that they appreciated the reduced travel and reduced transition costs involved) and received top ratings from the students (students said that they appreciated the content, organization, and flow of the course material). Today, the business school where I teach has added several other courses in a compressed format because these courses are so well received by students and faculty.

PAY ATTENTION TO LANGUAGE AND OTHER FORMS OF ORGANIZATIONAL SYMBOLISM
Organizational assumptions about diversity are passed on through subtle, yet powerful symbolic mechanisms such as the taken-for-granted languages, stories, and rituals that are used in everyday organizational life. Consequently, be careful about what you communicate, intentionally or unintentionally, by the words that you use and the stories that you choose to tell. When you have people from many cultures in your organizational stories, for example, you show that you view people from all cultures as being able to succeed, fail, and make a difference in the organization. When you use inclusive language (e.g., using both "he" and "she" to refer to managers and secretaries), you send the message that you assume that both men and women can be effective in a variety of organizational roles.[115] When you avoid using "us versus them" language ("those Americans" or "those Germans"), you remind employees that "we are all in this together."

CREATE A COMMON IDENTITY   Research consistently shows that people who feel that they share a common identity see people in their group as more similar to themselves, see and remember more positive things about others in their group, see members of their group as more competent and, feel more comfortable with members of their group.[116] To develop a common identity among diverse employees, Ted Childs, who spent 15 years as IBM's vice president of global workforce diversity, regularly reminded employees that "the ties that bind us are stronger than the issues that divide us. . . . There is only one "ism" on which we need to focus—consumerism."[117]

INCREASE INTERACTION AMONG MEMBERS OF DIFFERENT GROUPS   Research suggests that people may overly focus on differences early in their relationships but often recognize and develop shared values when they spend more time together, particularly when they view each other as equals and as bringing different kinds of expertise to the organization. Therefore, create opportunities for members of different cultural groups to get to know each other personally, to see their common bonds as well as differences, view each other as equals and colleagues,[118] and appreciate the diverse talents and resources they bring to the organization.

DEVELOP EXTERNAL RELATIONS WITH DIVERSE GROUPS   Develop relationships with customers and vendors from a variety of cultures. Also support the various cultures in the community through organizational goodwill efforts and philanthropy. Many organizations develop alliances with advocacy groups (e.g., Catalyst and the NAACP, which focus on the advancement of women and people of color, respectively) that are committed to promoting diversity in organizations. Southwest, Delta, Comcast, Marriott, and Goldman Sachs are just a few of the corporations that are corporate partners with GLAAD, the Gay & Lesbian Alliance Against Defamation. Supporting advocacy groups shows your commitment to creating a diverse organization. It also helps you get information, ideas, support, and other resources that can help your organization achieve its goals.

MEASURE RESULTS AND REWARD PROGRESS   People tend to pay attention to what gets measured. Therefore, identify specific diversity areas that need improvement, set clear and measurable goals, adjust these goals as appropriate over time, develop ways to measure progress, hold employees accountable for meeting these goals, show employees how they personally contribute to achieving diversity goals, and reward small as well as big efforts and accomplishments.

CONCLUSION

Your job as a manager is to bring out the best in all employees so that everyone can add value to your organization. You can bring out the best in all employees in two ways. The first is to be a role model for effectively managing diversity. This involves understanding, respecting, and leveraging the different perceptions, values, and behaviors that people from different cultures and backgrounds bring to the organization. The second way is to bring out the best in all employees to create an organizational culture that enhances the potential advantages of diversity while minimizing the potential disadvantages. Creating an organizational culture that leverages diversity is an ongoing process. It doesn't happen overnight—or in one to two years. Like all major organizational interventions, it will include setbacks as well as advances. Keep in mind that small wins can have a big impact. Say researchers Debra Meyerson and Joyce Fletcher, "Small wins have a way of snowballing. One small change begets another, and eventually these small changes add up to a whole new system."[119] Thinking strategically, focusing on both the short and long term, and modeling the behaviors that you want to see will go a long way toward creating an organization that can recruit, retain, promote, and learn from the most talented people available, regardless of the cultural groups to which they belong.

Chapter Summary

As societies and organizations become more multicultural through within nation and global diversity, managers must view managing cultural diversity as a critical skill they will use every working day throughout their careers because doing so enables them to add increasing value to their organizations and the people they serve.

Effectively managing diversity can be a competitive advantage for several reasons, including positive publicity; recruitment, development, and retention of the best talent; better problem solving and decision making, enhanced team performance, lower legal costs, lower operating costs, success in serving diverse markets, and effective response to advocacy groups.

Although diversity can be a competitive advantage, not all organizations succeed in their efforts. There are many reasons that diversity programs fail to have the impact that organizations hope for, including lack of systematic planning and patience, overemphasizing numerical goals, not changing the way work gets done, emotional tensions from a history of conflictual relations across groups that carry over from society into the workplace, cultural ignorance that can make people uncomfortable working with each other and reduce personal commitment to a multicultural workplace, lack of training or poor quality training, and parochialism of management theories.

To turn the talents that a diverse workforce brings to an organization into enhanced performance and bottom-line results, leaders must go beyond focusing on the numbers (e.g., "How many people from different groups do we have and promote within the organization?"). To leverage diversity, organizational leaders must integrate the perspectives and behaviors these different groups bring to the workplace in ways that help the organization assess current practices and revise them as necessary to make them more effective and efficient. Effective managers of diversity use two sets of skills to enhance their ability to turn diversity into a competitive advantage: they invest in their own multicultural competence, and they create a work environment that brings out the best in all employees.

Demographic categories, such as race, gender, nationality, religion, and age, are socially constructed categorizations that have meaning to a society, that people identify themselves as members of, that may shape how people within that group make sense of the world and relate to people outside the group, and that shape how people outside the group make sense of and relate to people inside that group. This does not mean that categories such as age or sex don't have physiological roots, but that societies and organizations give these categories meanings that go beyond their physiological functions and characteristics.

Cultures promote different worldviews and behavioral norms that help people solve everyday problems and dilemmas of life such as: Who am I? How do I relate to others? How do I communicate with others? How do I deal with time? What is the truth? How do I relate to my environment? What is the relationship of work to life?

Effective multicultural managers understand the ways that cultural differences can influence people's preferences, expectations, and behaviors at work and adapt their managerial style accordingly. Doing so enables managers to grow personally and professionally, develop the trust and respect that is the foundation of effective work relationships, and leverage the diversity in the organization.

There are at least three perspectives that organizations that promote diversity may have: integration and learning (leveraging the different perspectives and behaviors the diverse workforce offers to increase innovation and adaptability with a focus on enhancing bottom-line results), access and legitimacy (believing that the workforce should reflect the demographics of the community, customers, and other constituencies, but not changing the way work gets done), and discrimination and fairness (believing that a culturally diverse workforce is a moral and social imperative to ensure justice). Organizations that promote the integration and learning perspective are more likely to reap the rewards of diversity in ways that add bottom-line value.

The job of the multicultural manager is to promote both the cultural diversity that broadens the organization's capabilities and the interdependence that aligns this diversity toward common organizational goals.

Effective multicultural managers continuously develop their own multicultural competence (their ability to be comfortable and effective in cross-cultural situations) and a work environment that promotes cultural synergy.

Personal multicultural competence requires both culture-specific knowledge and culture-general skills. Culture-specific knowledge enables managers to be effective in specific cultural contexts (e.g., doing business in Spain). Cultural-general skills enable managers to be effective with any culture and with multiple cultures simultaneously.

An effective multicultural work environment is one in which employees view people from different cultures as equals, believe that diversity contributes to the organization's effectiveness, and believe that all employees should have the opportunity to contribute to the organization's success and be rewarded for their contributions.

Creating an organizational culture that values and leverages diversity involves ensuring top-level commitment; having leadership role models that demonstrate valuing diversity in their everyday actions; obtaining data that enables leaders to assess whether their efforts are making a difference in the recruitment, selection, and promotion of people who are under-represented at different organizational levels; understanding the laws related to discrimination; taking actions to break the glass ceiling; avoiding reindeer games (limiting access to social activities that are not explicitly work related but that offer work-related advantages—e.g., invitations to dinners and clubs that provide access to senior leaders, customers, and others who provide information and opportunities); endorsing groups in the organization that provide support to people in minority groups; creating a common identity across groups; providing mentoring to people who are under-represented at higher organizational levels; encouraging people who are under-represented at higher organizational levels to advance their formal educations; attention to organizational symbolism (e.g., words, stories, and rituals) that encourages or discourages respect for diversity; and developing relationships with advocacy groups.

Food for Thought

1. What is the most useful thing you learned in this chapter, and why?

2. Based on the strategies for managing diversity in ways that contribute to your own success and organizational success for managing diversity described in this chapter, what can you do to increase your own effectiveness? Practice at least one of these behaviors, and note any benefits and progress you make.

3. Fill in the circles in Figure 7-2, "Identifying Cultural Influences." Which of these cultural identities are most important to you, and why? Which have the most impact on your everyday work life, and why? Do you ever "manage" these identity groups in any way and, if so, how? Compare your answers with someone else who has also completed Figure 7-2. How might your similarities and differences enhance and/or influence your ability to work effectively with each other?

4. If you could clone the ideal manager, what would that manager be like? Discuss your answer with someone else. How similar and different are your answers?

5. Interview someone who has lived, studied, or worked in another country. Ask them about the obstacles they faced, the skills they needed to be successful abroad, how their experience abroad affected their worldview and behavior, and the most important advice they have for others who want to live, study, or work abroad.

6. Select a country. Do some research on it and identify work-related norms, dos and taboos, and how the social context (e.g., history, laws, religion, economic context, and intergroup relations) shapes assumptions and behavior at work.

7. Complete the assessment shown in Box 7-1, "Work-Related Cultural Preferences." Have another person complete the assessment as well. Given your cultural profiles, what might the strengths be in your work relationship? What might the problems be in your work relationship? What can you do to ensure that you leverage the strengths and minimize potential weaknesses?

8. In what ways do you fit the stereotype of one of your cultural group memberships? In what ways do you not fit that stereotype, and why not?

9. Think of a time when you observed a situation involving a cultural bias or inequity in which you intervened. Discuss what motivated you to intervene. What did you do, and how did you feel? What were the consequences of your intervention? Now think of a time when you observed a situation involving a cultural bias or inequity but you did not intervene. Why didn't you intervene? How did you feel? What were the consequences?

10. Which perspective does your organization have toward diversity: integration and learning, access and legitimacy, discrimination and fairness, or "we don't think about it at all"? What are the consequences of your organization's perspective for you, others, and the organization? Given that research has shown that the integration and learning perspective is most likely to add bottom-line value to the organization, what can you do to promote this perspective in your part of your organization?

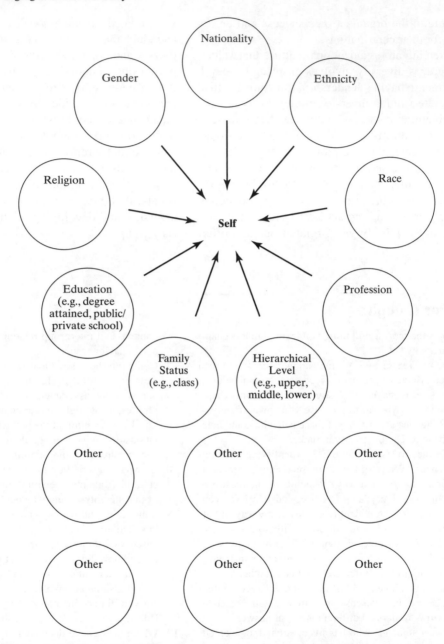

FIGURE 7-2 Identifying Cultural Influences
Fill in the information in each circle. How do your cultural identities influence your world view and behavior? How do they influence how others perceive you and act toward you? Do you ever actively "manage" any of your identities at work? If so, which ones and how?

Endnotes

1. Di'Tomaso, Nancy, Daria Kirby, Frances Milliken, and Harry Triandis. 1998. "Effective and Inclusive Learning Environments." A Report Commissioned by the International Association for Management Education (AACSB). St. Louis, MO: AACSB, 16.

2. 1995. "Survey Shows Many Companies Have Diversity Programs, Changes in Affirmative Action Perspectives." *Mosaics: Society of Human Resources Focus on Workplace Diversity,* 1(1): 1, 5.

3. Kern, Frank. 2010. "What Chief Executives Really Want." *Bloomberg Businessweek Online*: May 19. http://www.businessweek.com/innovate/content/may2010/id20100517_190221.htm

4. Legace, Martha. May 3, 2010. "What Is the Future of MBA Education: Interview with Srikant Datar and David Garvin." In *Working Knowledge: A First Look at Faculty Research.* Harvard Business School; http://hbswk.hbs.cdu/item/6363.html

5. Trompenaars, Fons. 1994. *Riding the Waves of Culture: Understanding Diversity in Global Business.* New York: Irwin Professional Publishing.

6. Desvaux, Georges, Sandrine Devillard-Hoellinger, and Pascal Baumgarten. 2007. *Women Matter: Gender Diversity, A Corporate Performance Driver.* McKinsey & Company Report; Carter, D., and W. Simpson. 2003. "Corporate Governance, Board Diversity, and Firm Value." *Financial Review*, 38(1): 33–53; Erhardt, N. L., J. D. Werbel, and C. B. Shrader. 2003. "Board of Director Diversity and Firm Financial Performance." *Corporate Governance: An International Review*, 11(2): 102–111.

7. Di'Tomaso, Nancy, Daria Kirby, Frances Milliken, and Harry Triandis. 1998. "Effective and Inclusive Learning Environments." A Report Commissioned by the International Association for Management Education (AACSB). St. Louis, MO: AACSB, 17.

8. Kearney, Eric, Diether Gebert, and Sven Voelpel. 2009. "When and How Diversity Benefits Teams: The Importance of Team Members' Need for Cognition." *Academy of Management Journal*, 52(3): 581–598.

9. Fisher, George. 1996. "Foreword." In Morrison, Ann (ed.). *The New Leaders: Leadership Diversity in America.* San Francisco, CA: Jossey-Bass.

10. Thomas, David, and Robin Ely. 1997. "Making Differences Matter: A New Paradigm for Managing Diversity." *Harvard Business Review*, 74(5): 79–90.

11. Van Knippenberg, C. K., W. De Dreu, and A. C. Homan. 2004. "Work Group Diversity and Group Performance: An Integrative Model and Research Agenda." *Journal of Applied Psychology*, 89: 1008–1022.

12. Cox, Taylor, Sharon Lobel, and Poppy McLeod. 1991. "Effects of Ethnic Group Cultural Difference on Cooperative versus Competitive Behavior on a Group Task." *Academy of Management Journal*, 34(4): 827–847.

13. Thomas, David C., Elizabeth C. Ravlin, and Alan W. Wallace. 1996. "Effect of Cultural Diversity in Work Groups." *Research in the Sociology of Organizations*, 14: 1–33.

14. Ibid., p. 26.

15. James, Erika Hayes, and Lynn Perry Wooten. 2006. "Diversity Crises: How Firms Manage Discrimination Lawsuits." *Academy of Management Journal*, 49(6): 1103–1118; Selmi, M. 2003. "The Price of Discrimination: The Nature of Class-Action Employment Discrimination Litigation and Its Effects." *Texas Law Review*, 81: 1249–1335.

16. Cox, Taylor H., and Stacy Blake. 1991. "Managing Cultural Diversity: Implications for Organizational Competitiveness." *Academy of Management Executive*, 5(3): 45–56.

17. Morrison, Ann. 1996. *The New Leaders*. Jossey-Bass. CA: San Francisco.

18. KPMG Campus: Awards and Recognition. http://www.kpmgcampus.com/whoweare/awards.shtml

19. "The 100 Best Companies to Work For: The Most Diversity," *Fortune Magazine*. 2007. http://money.cnn.com/magazines/fortune/bestcompanies/2007/diversity/index.html

20. Kochan, Thomas, Katrina Bezrukova, Robin Ely, Susan Jackson, Aparna Joshi, Karen Jen, Jonathan Leonard, David Levine, and David Thomas. 2003. "The Effects of Diversity on Business Performance: Report of the Diversity Research Network." *Human Resource Management*. Spring 42(1): 3–21. Joshi, Aparana, and Hyuntak Roh. 2009. "The Role of Context in Work Team Diversity Research: A Meta-Analytic Review." *Academy of Management Journal*, 52(3): 599–627; Kearney, Eric, Diether Gebert, and Sven Voelpel. 2009. "When and How Diversity Benefits Teams: The Importance of Team Members' Need for Cognition." *Academy of Management Journal*, 52(3): 581–598; van Knippenberg, C. K., W. De Dreu, and A. C. Homan. 2004. "Work Group Diversity and Group Performance: An Integrative Model and Research Agenda." *Journal of Applied*

Psychology, 89: 1008–1022; Williams, K. T., and C. A. O'Reilly. 1998. "Demography and Diversity in Organizations: A Review of 40 Years of Research." In B. M. Staw and L. L. Cummings (eds.), *Research in Organizational Behavior.* Greenwich, CT: JAI Press, Vol. 20: 77–140.

21. Prahalad, C. K. 2004. *The Fortune at the Bottom of the Pyramid: Eradicating Poverty through Profits.* Upper Saddle River, NJ: Wharton School Publishing. Thomas, David, and Robin Ely. 1996. "Making Differences Matter: A New Paradigm for Managing Diversity." *Harvard Business Review*, 74(5): 79–90.

22. Ibid., p. 82.

23. Ely, Robin, and David A. Thomas. 2001. "Cultural Diversity at Work: The Effects of Diversity Perspectives on Work Group Processes and Outcomes." *Administrative Science Quarterly*, 46: 229–273.

24. Ibid., p. 240.

25. Ibid., p. 243.

26. Huey, John. 1998. "Here We Go Again." *Fortune.* October 12: 26.

27. Griffith, Stephanie. 2009. "Outrage in Washington over Obama's Japan Bow." November 16. http://www.financialpost.com/entrepreneur/Outrage+Washington+over+Obama+Japan/2228035/story.html

28. Andre, Rae. 1995. "Diversity Stress as Moral Stress." *Journal of Business Ethics*, 14: 489–496.

29. Jackson, Susan, Joan Brett, Valerie Sessa, Dawn Cooper, Johan Julin, and Karl Peyronnin. 1991. "Some Differences Make a Difference: Individual Dissimilarity and Group Heterogeneity as Correlates of Recruitment, Promotion, and Turnover." *Journal of Applied Psychology*, 76(5): 675–689; O'Reilly, Charles, David Caldwell, and William Barnett. 1989. "Work Group Demography, Social Integration, and Turnover." *Administrative Science Quarterly*, 34: 21–37; Jackson, Susan E. 1991. "Team Composition in Organizational Settings: Issues in Managing an Increasingly Diverse Work Force." In S. Worchel, W. Wood, and J. Simpson (eds.). *Group Process and Productivity.* Beverly Hills, CA: Sage.

30. Jackson, Susan E. 1991. "Team Composition in Organizational Settings: Issues in Managing an Increasingly Diverse Workforce." In S. Worchel, W. Wood, and J. Simpson (eds.). *Group Process and Productivity.* Beverly Hills, CA: Sage.

31. Finley, Joycelyn. 1996. "Communication Double Binds: The Catch-22 of Conversations about Racial Issues in Work Groups." Dissertation Submitted to the University of Michigan.

32. Mulvaney, Tim. "Why Diversity Becomes Irrelevant." *Managing Diversity*, 7(6): 6.

33. Woodford, John. 1996. "Seeing Race: A New Look at an Old Notion." *Michigan Today.* June: 2.

34. West, Candace, and Don H. Zimmerman. 1987. "Doing Gender." *Gender & Society,* 1(2): 125–151.

35. Litvin, Deborah R. 1997. "The Discourse of Diversity: From Biology to Management." *Organization,* 4(2): 187–209.

36. Gilbert, Matthew. 1996. "Gish Jen, All-American." *The Boston Globe,* 4: 53, 58; quoted in Litvin, Deborah R. 1997. "The Discourse of Diversity: From Biology to Management." *Organization,* 4(2): 187–209.

37. 1995. "Increasing Diversity Creates Definition Issues." *Mosaics Society of Human Resources Focuses on Workplace Diversity,* 1(1): 3, 7.

38. Alderfer, Clayton. 1983. "Intergroup Relations and Organizations." In Hackman, Richard J., Ed Lawler, and Lyman Porter (eds.). *Perspectives on Behavior in Organizations.* New York: McGraw-Hill.

39. Ibid.

40. Wells, Leroy Jr. 1985. "Misunderstandings of and among Cultures: The Effects of Transubstantiative Error." In D. Vails-Weber, and J. Potts (eds.). *Sunrise Seminars,* 2: 51–57. Arlington, VA: NTL Institute.

41. Brake, Terence, and Danielle Walker. 1994. *Doing Business Internationally: A Workbook to Cross-Cultural Success.* New Jersey: Princeton Training Press.

42. Kirkman, Bradley, Gilad Chen, Jiing-Lih Farh, Zhen Xiong Chen, and Kevin Lowe. 2009. "Individual Power Distance Orientation and Follower Reactions to Transformational Leaders: A Cross-Level, Cross-Cultural Examination." *Academy of Management Journal*, 52(4): 744–764; Adler, Nancy. 2002. *International Dimensions of Organizational Behavior*, 4th ed. Cincinnati: South-Western College Publishing.

43. 2003. "It's a Grand Latte World." *Wall Street Journal.* December 15: b1 and b4.

44. Gilligan, Carol. 1993. *In a Different Voice: Psychological Theory and Women's Development.* Cambridge, MA: Harvard University Press.

45. Brake, Terence, Danielle Medina Walker, and Thomas Walker. 1995. *Doing Business Internationally: The Guide to Cross-Cultural Success.* Princeton, NJ: McGraw-Hill.

46. Ibid.

47. Trompenaars, Fons. 1994. *Riding the Waves of Culture: Understanding Diversity in Global Business.* New York: Irwin.

48. Ibid.

49. Kirkman, Bradley, Gilad Chen, Zhen Xiong Chen, and Kevin Lowe. 2009. "Individual Power Distance Orientation and Follower Reaction to Transformational Leaders: A Cross-Level Cross-Cultural Examination." *Academy of Management Journal*, 52(4): 744–764; House, R., P.J. Hanges, M. Javidan, P. W. Dorfman, and V. Gupta, & GLOBE Associates. 2004. Leadership, Culure and Organizations: The GLOBE study of 62 Societies. Thousand Oaks, CA: Sage; Farh, J. L., R.D. Hackett, and J. Liang. 2007. "Individual Level Cutural Values as Moderators of the Perceived Organizational Support-Employee Outcome Relationships in China: Comparing the Effects of Power Distance and Traditionality." *Academy of Management Journal*, 50: 715–729; Hofstede, Geert. 1984. *Culture's Consequences: International Differences in Work-Related Values*. Newbury Park, CA: Sage; Geert Hofstede. 1993. "Cultural Constraints in Management Theories." *Academy of Management Executive*, 7(1): 81–94.

50. Hofstede, Geert (2001). *Culture's Consequences: Comparing Values, Behaviors, Institutions, and Organizations across Nations* (2nd ed.). Thousand Oaks, CA: SAGE Publications.

51. Hampden-Turner, Charles, and Fons Trompenaars. 2000. *Building Cross-Cultural Competence: How to Create Wealth from Conflicting Values*. New Haven, CT: Yale University Press; Trompenaars, Fons. 1994. *Riding the Waves of Culture: Understanding Diversity in Global Business*. New York: Irwin.

52. Gilligan, Carol. 1993. *In a Different Voice: Psychological Theory and Women's Development*. Cambridge, MA: Harvard University Press.

53. Sanchez-Burks, Jeffrey. 2002. "Protestant Relational Ideology and (In)attention to Relational Cues in Work Settings." *Journal of Personality and Social Psychology*, 83(4): 919–929.

54. Kennedy, Jim, and Anna Everest. 1991. "Put Diversity in Context." *Personnel Journal*. September: 50–54.

55. Tannen, Deborah. 1995. *Talking from 9 – 5: Women and Men at Work*. Harper Paperbacks.

56. Gardenswartz, Lee, and Anita Rowe. 1993. *Managing Diversity: A Complete Desk Reference and Planning Guide*. San Diego, CA: Pfeiffer and Company.

57. Kim, Heejung. 2002. "We Talk, Therefore We Think? A Cultural Analysis of the Effect of Talking on Thinking." *Journal of Personality and Social Psychology*, 83(4): 824–842.

58. Copeland, Lennie, and Lewis Griggs. 1985. *Going International, How to Make Friends and Deal Effectively in the Global Marketplace*. New York: Plume Books.

59. Lewis, Richard. 1996. *When Cultures Collide*. London: Nicholas Brealey Publishing.

60. Bluedorn, Allen C., Carol Felker Kaufman, and Paul M. Lane. 1992. "How Many Things Do You Like to Do at Once? An Introduction to Monochronic and Polychronic Time." *Academy of Management Executive*, 6(4): 17–26.

61. Stone, Nan. 1989. "The Globalization of Europe: An Interview with Wisse Dekker." *Harvard Business Review*. May–June 67(3): 90–96.

62. 1997. *U.S. News and World Report*. December 1: 6.

63. Belenky, Mary Field, Blythe McVicker Clinchy, Nancy Rule Godberger, and Jill Mattuck Tarule. 1986. *Women's Ways of Knowing*. New York: Basic Books.

64. Kim, Heejung. 2002. "We Talk, Therefore We Think? A Cultural Analysis of the Effect of Talking on Thinking." *Journal of Personality and Social Psychology*, 83(4): 828–842; Fiske, A., S. Kitayama, H. Markus, and R. Nisbett. 1998. "The Cultural Matrix of Social Psychology." In D. Gilbert, S. Fiske, and G. Lindzey (eds.). *Handbook of Social Psychology*. New York: McGraw-Hill, 915–981.)

65. Brake, Terence, and Danielle Walker. 1994. *Doing Business Internationally: A Workbook to Cross-Cultural Success*. New Jersey, NY: Princeton Training Press.

66. Brake, Terence, Danielle Walker, and Thomas Walker. 1995. *Doing Business Internationally: The Guide to Cross-Cultural Success*. Princeton, NJ: McGraw-Hill.

67. Di'Tomaso, Nancy, Daria Kirby, Frances Milliken, and Harry Triandis. 1998. "Effective and Inclusive Learning Environments." St. Louis, MO: The International Association for Management Education (AACSB), 57; citing Triandis, Harry. 1994. *Culture and Social Behavior*. New York: McGraw-Hill.

68. Hampden-Turner, Charles, and Fons Trompenaars, . 2000. *Building Cross-Cultural Competence: How to Create Wealth from Conflicting Values*. New Haven, CT: Yale University Press.

69. Litvin, Stephen, John Crotts, and Frank Hefner. 2004. "Cross-Cultural Tourist Behavior: A Replication and Extension Involving Hofstedes's Uncertainty Avoidance Dimension." *International Journal of Tourism Research*. 6(1): 29–37. Hofstede, Geert. 1984. *Culture's Consequences: International*

Differences in Work-Related Values Newbury Park, CA: Sage; Geert Hofstede. 1993. "Cultural Constraints in Management Theories." *Academy of Management Executive,* 7(1): 81–94.

70. Sethi, Sheena, and Mark Lepper. 1999. "Rethinking the Role of Choice in Intrinsic Motivation: A Cultural Perspective on Intrinsic Motivation." *Journal of Personality and Social Psychology,* 76(3): 349–366.

71. Thompson, Debora, Rebecca Hamilton, and Petia Petrova. 2009. "When Mental Stimulation Hinders Behavior: The Effects of Process Oriented Thinking on Decision Difficulty and Performance." *Journal of Consumer Research,* 36: 562–574.

72. Iyenger, Sheena, and Mark Lepper. "When Choice Is Demotivating: Can One Desire too Much of a Good Thing?" *Journal of Personality and Social Psychology,* 79(6): 995–1006.

73. Cox, Taylor, Jr. 1997. "Distinguishing Valuing Diversity from Stereotyping." In Taylor Cox, Jr., and Ruby L. Beale (eds.). *Developing Competency to Manage Diversity: Readings, Cases, Activities.* San Francisco, CA: Berrett-Koehler Publishers.

74. Ibid.

75. Fitzgerald, Thomas. 1997. "Understanding Diversity in the Workplace: Cultural Metaphors or Metaphors of Identity?" *Business Horizons,* 40(4): 66–70.

76. Lancaster, Hal. 1998. "Learning to Manage in a Global Workplace (You're on Your Own)." *Wall Street Journal.* June 2: B1.

77. Kearney, Eric, Diether Gebert, and Sen Voelpel. 2009. "When and How Diversity Benefits Teams: The Importance of Team Members' Need for Cognition." *Academy of Management Journal,* 52(3): 581–598; Homan, Astrid, John Hollenbeck, Stephen Humphrey, Daan Van Knippenberg, Daniel Ilgen, and Gerben Van Kleef. 2008. "Facing Differences with an Open Mind: Openness to Experience, Salience of Intergroup Differences, and Performance of Diverse Work Groups." *Academy of Management Journal,* 51(6): 1204–1222.

78. Tung, Rosalie. 1987. "Expatriate Assignments: Enhancing Success and Minimizing Failure." *Academy of Management Executive,* 1(2): 117–126; Kelly, Colleen, and Judith Meyers. *Cross-Cultural Adaptability Inventory.* Minneapolis, MN: National Computer Systems.

79. Kelly, Colleen, and Judith Meyers. 1995. *Cross-Cultural Adaptability Inventory.* Minneapolis, MN: National Computer Systems.

80. Storti, Craig. 2007. *Speaking of India: Bridging the Communication Gap when Working with Indians.* Boston, MA: Intercultural Press, 35–79.

81. Laurent, Andre. 1986. "The Cross-Cultural Puzzle of International Human Resource Management." *Human Resource Management,* 25(1): 91–102.

82. Stewart, Rosemary. 1996. "German Management: A Challenge to Anglo-American Managerial Assumptions. *Business Horizons.* May–June: 52–54.

83. Kennedy, Jim, and Anna Everest. 1991. "Put Diversity in Context." *Personnel Journal.* September: 50–54.

84. Hampden-Turner, Charles, and Fons Trompenaars. 2000. *Building Cross-Cultural Competence: How to Create Wealth from Conflicting Values.* New Haven, CT: Yale University Press.

85. Kelly, Colleen, and Judith Meyers. 1995. *Cross-Cultural Adaptability Inventory.* Minneapolis, MN: National Computer Systems.

86. Ibid.

87. McGill, Andrew, Michael Johnson, and Karen Bantel. 1994. "Cognitive Complexity and Conformity: Effects on Performance in a Turbulent Environment." *Psychological Reports,* 75: 1451–1472.

88. Kelly, Colleen, and Judith Meyers. 1995. *Cross-Cultural Adaptability Inventory.* Minneapolis, MN: National Computer Systems.

89. Hodgetts, Richard. 1993. "A Conversation with Geert Hofstede." *Organizational Dynamics,* 57: 53–61.

90. Kelly, Colleen, and Judith Meyers. 1995. *Cross-Cultural Adaptability Inventory.* Minneapolis, MN: National Computer Systems.

91. Brief, Arthur, Elizabeth Umphress, Joerg Dietz, John Burrows, Rebecca Butz, and Lotte Scholten. 2005. "Community Matters: Realistic Group Conflict Theory and the Impact of Diversity." *Academy of Management Journal,* 48(5): 830–844.

92. Adler, Nancy J., and Susan Bartholomew. 1992. "Managing Globally Competent People." *Academy of Management Executive,* 6(3): 52–66.

93. Wilson, Meena S., and Maxine A. Dalton. 1997. "Understanding the Demands of Leading in a Global Environment: A First Step." *Issues and Observations,* 17(1, 2): 12–14.

94. Cox, Taylor, and Stacy Blake. 1991. "Managing Cultural Diversity: Implications for Organizational Competitiveness." *Academy of Management Executive,* 5(3): 45–56.

95. Herr Van Norstrand, Catherine. 1993. "Leaders in Collusion: How Leaders Perpetuate Male Privilege." In *Gender Responsible Leadership.* Newbury Park, CA: Sage, 3–29.

96. Daniels, Cora. 2004. "50 Best Companies for Minorities." *Fortune.* June 28, 149(13): 136–142.

97. Thomas, Roosevelt, Jr. 1992. *Beyond Race and Gender*. New York: Amacom.

98. Feltes, Patricia, Robert K. Robinson, and Ross L. Fink. 1993. "American Female Expatriates and the Civil Rights Act of 1991: Balancing Legal and Business Interests." *Business Horizons*. March–April: 82–86.

99. Kirchmeyer, Catherine. 1995. "Demographic Similarity to the Work Group: A Longitudinal Study of Managers at the Early Career Stage." *Journal of Organizational Behavior*, 16: 76–83.

100. Van Velsor, Ellen, and Martha W. Hughes. 1990. *Gender Differences in the Development of Managers: How Women Managers Learn from Experience*. Greensboro, NC: Center for Creative Leadership.

101. Beirman, Leonard. 1997. "Regulating Reindeer Games." *Academy of Management Executive*, 11(4): 92–93; citing Beiner, Theresa A. 1996. "Do Reindeer Games Count as Terms, Conditions, or Privileges of Employment under Title VII?" *Boston College Law Review*, 37: 643–690.

102. Ibid.

103. Friedman, Raymond A., and Kellina Craig. 2004. "Predicting Joining and Participating in Minority Employee Network Groups." *Industrial Relations*, 43(4): 793–816.

104. Cox, Taylor. 1994. *Cultural Diversity in Organizations: Theory, Research, and Practice*. San Francisco, CA: Berrett-Koehler Publishers.

105. Cox, Taylor, and Stacy Blake. 1991. "Managing Cultural Diversity: Implications for Organizational Competitiveness." *Academy of Management Executive*, 5(3): 45–56.

106. Carnevale, Anthony P., and Susan C. Stone. 1994. "Diversity: Beyond the Golden Rule." *Training and Development*. October: 22–39.

107. Fine, Marlene, Fern L. Johnson, and M. Sallyanne Ryan. 1990. "Cultural Diversity in the Workplace." *Public Personnel Management*, 19(3): 305–319.

108. Thomas, David. 2001. "The Truth About Mentoring Minorities: Race Matters." *Harvard Business Review*, April: 99–107.

109. Kronholz, June. 2004. "Graders Learn Fine Points of Scoring College-Exam Essays." *Wall Street Journal*. August 2: B1 and B4.

110. Holtom, Brooks, and Edward Inderrieden. 2007. "Investment Advice: Go for the MBA." *BizEd*. http://http://www.aacsb.edu/publications/archives/janfeb07/p36-41.pdf.

111. "Women in MBA Programs." 2008. *Business Week Online*. http://www.businessweek.com/bschools/content/nov2008/bs20081120_625488.htm.

112. University of Michigan Business School, Center for the Education of Women, and Catalyst. 2000. "Women and the MBA: Gateway to Opportunity." University of Michigan Business School, Center for the Education of Women, and Catalyst; Sellers, Patricia. 2003. "Power: Do Women Really Want It." *Fortune*. Oct 13: 80–100.

113. Alsop, Ronald, with Harris Interactive. 2006. *The Wall Street Journal: Guide to the Top Business Schools 2006*. New York: Random House.

114. Kronholz, June. 2004. "Graders Learn Fine Points of Scoring College-Exam Essays." *Wall Street Journal*. August 2: B1 and B4.

115. Martyna, Wendy. 1980. "Beyond the He-Man Approach: The Case for Nonsexist Language." *Signs. Journal of Women in Culture and Society*, 5(3): 482–493.

116. John Dovidio, Ana Validzic, and Samuel Gaertner. 1998. "Intergroup Bias: Status, Differentiation, and a Common Ingroup Identity." *Journal of Personality and Social Psychology*, 75(1): 109–120.

117. Childs, Ted, Jr. 1998. "Work Force Diversity in the United States: Diversity at IBM." http://www.empl.ibm.com/diverse/ltrchild.htm. September 9.

118. Dovidio, John, Ana Validzic, and Samuel Gaertner. 1998. "Intergroup Bias: Status, Differentiation, and a Common Ingroup Identity." *Journal of Personality and Social Psychology*, 75: 109–120.

119. Meyerson, Debra, and Joyce Fletcher. 2000. "A Modest Manifesto for Shattering the Glass Ceiling." *Harvard Business Review*. January–February: 126–136.

8

■ ■ ■

Creating High-Performing Teams

This chapter will help you:

■ Identify the characteristics of high-performing teams.

■ Understand when teams are and are not useful.

■ Develop leadership skills for creating work contexts that bring out the best in teams.

■ Learn why connecting teams externally is as important as building internal cohesion.

■ Understand predictable stages of a team's life cycle.

■ Prevent groupthink and other dysfunctional team dynamics.

■ Become a more effective team member and team leader.

> *When I started this business of teams, I was anxious to get it done and get back to my real job. Then I realized that, hey, this is my real job.*[1]

> —TEAM LEADER CITED IN *Fortune*

Teams are a fact of life for most organizations. We love them and we loathe them. Regardless of how we feel about teams, we know that most organizations cannot survive without them. People working in teams have the capacity to solve complex problems that cannot be solved by individuals working alone. People working in teams bring more resources to a task, including a variety of perspectives, knowledge, skills, and experience. When well managed, teams use these resources to create better results than any individual can accomplish working alone. When poorly managed, teams can waste people's time, deplete their energy, and achieve worse results than any of the team members could have achieved by working alone.

Every day, we put great faith in teams. Each time we drive a car, fly in an airplane, have surgery, or leave our children at school, we place our lives and the futures of our families in products and services created and delivered by teams. We put our faith not only in the talent of individuals but also in their ability to work together cohesively and competently as a team. Often, the teams in which we place our fate have never worked together before, as in the case of emergency medical teams and airplane cockpit crews.

Why do we put such faith in teams? In part, we just don't think much about it. When we fly in an airplane, for example, we sit down in our seat, buckle our seat belt, and we're off the ground. We take for granted the sophisticated interplay of intelligence and emotions, individual expertise and team coordination, and technological sophistication and human insight that enable the flight crew and air traffic controllers to respond to both the routine and unexpected events in our journey miles above the earth and safely back.

We also put our faith in teams because we instinctively understand that group life is necessary for human survival. We know that in many situations, "two heads (or more) are better than one" when solving problems and that "it takes a village to raise a child." This is as true today as it was in the nomadic ages when human beings depended on groups to forage for food, protect themselves and their offspring from predators, and move from place to place to find new resources to ensure their survival.

> Do you want a collection of brilliant minds or a brilliant collection of minds?
> —R. MEREDITH BELBIN,
> *British researcher and management theorist*

Undoubtedly, we have different challenges in the twenty-first century. Increasingly, our individual, organizational, and societal survival requires that we regularly solve complex problems that we have never faced before, that have no right answers, and for which the consequences of our decisions are uncertain. Furthermore, for our organizations to survive, we must work faster and better than the competition, creatively meet the rising expectations of a customer base that is increasingly more culturally diverse and globally dispersed, and deal with the new technologies that will continue to change the way that work gets done.

Given this complex and fast-paced environment, it's no surprise that more organizations are using teams to achieve their goals. But high-performing teams don't just happen. They are created from a group of talented individuals who are committed to a common goal that they believe is important, who have ways of working together that bring out the best in each other, who connect to relevant people and groups outside their team to gain resources and support, and who have leaders that create a work context that enhances rather than hinders the team's efforts.[2] In this chapter, I discuss the specific characteristics of high-performing teams and how you—as a team member and leader—can help create these characteristics. But first, I want to offer a reality check about teams.

BEYOND THE TEAM HYPE

Although teams are increasingly necessary for organizational success, it is a mistake to view them as the solution to all problems. As *Fortune* magazine journalist Kenneth Labich laments, "Weird fact of life: For every problem we face, someone has come up with a solution way too slick to be true. . . . In the corporate world, there's that supposed miracle cure for ailing organizations—team-based management."[3]

Like Labich, critical theorist Amanda Sinclair warns us against being seduced by the "tyranny of a team ideology."[4] She agrees that teams are not the solution to all organizational problems. However, she goes one step further and argues that an overzealous and naïve use of teams can reinforce some of the problems that teams are intended to solve. She explains:

> Teams can contribute to getting work of all kinds done, but not when their application is informed by a narrow framework that nurtures inappropriate expectations. Further, and more critically, the team ideology . . . tyrannizes because, under the

banner of benefits to all, teams are frequently used to camouflage coercion under the pretense of maintaining cohesion; conceal conflict under the guise of consensus; convert conformity into a semblance of creativity; give unilateral decisions a co-determinist seal of approval; delay action in the supposed interests of consultation; legitimize lack of leadership; and disguise expedient arguments and personal agendas.[5]

In short, both Sinclair and Labich agree that teamwork can significantly raise the level of individual, group, and organizational performance. But they also remind us that teamwork can lead to dysfunctional dynamics such as collective tunnel vision, inefficiencies, employee discontent, and moral lapses.[6] Most people reading this book can think of exceptionally ineffective, disastrous, and unethical decisions that were conceived and implemented by people working in teams.

> Our team is well balanced. We have problems everywhere.
> —TOMMY PROTHRO,
> *American football coach*

The point I want you to take away from these warnings is not that our optimism about teams is unwarranted. On the contrary, the *effective* use of teams is a significant competitive advantage for teams and organizations that use them. In addition, people who work in effective teams benefit personally because they develop new skills, increase their self-awareness, enhance their feelings of belonging, and expand their networks.[7] However, our optimism is more likely to lead to successful results if we use teams for appropriate tasks, understand both the positive behaviors (e.g., speed and creativity) and negative behaviors (e.g., free riding, groupthink) that can occur when people work together in teams, and develop leadership strategies that bring out the best rather than the worst in teams. In this chapter, I answer the questions (1) What is a team? (2) What are the characteristics of high-performing teams? and (3) What strategies do leaders use that enable teams to succeed?

WHAT IS A TEAM?

Teams come in many forms. They may be permanent, temporary, planned, or ad hoc. They may create products, provide services, or process people (as do human service agencies).[8] They may be formally chartered by organizational leaders or may emerge informally through employees' mutual interests and goals. They may be leader led or self-managed. Team members may routinely meet face-to-face at the same time and in the same place, or they may meet virtually and depend primarily on communication technologies to communicate and coordinate with each other. Regardless of their purpose and form, all teams are made up of "individuals interacting interdependently" to achieve common organizational goals.[9] Furthermore, all teams share the following characteristics:[10]

- *Clear boundaries.* Team members can identify who is and who isn't a member of the team. In addition, outsiders recognize the team as a legitimate organizational unit.
- *Collective responsibility for shared tasks.* Team members share collective responsibility for work outcomes, and feedback and rewards are given, in large part, to the team as a whole.
- *Differentiated member roles.* Each team member is expected to offer something distinctive and valuable to the team.
- *Autonomy.* Team members have some discretion over how they do their work.
- *Dependence on external people and resources.* Team members must depend on individuals and groups outside the team for information, resources, and support to accomplish their goals.

How do *teams* differ from work *groups*? Some researchers and practitioners see the difference as merely semantic and use the terms "group" and "team" interchangeably. Others, like myself, argue that although both work groups and teams are made up of individuals working interdependently toward common organizational goals, teams have several characteristics that differ from those of work groups, particularly if they are high-performing teams.

Members of high-performing teams tend to develop a collective purpose that goes beyond that which the organization has established for them.[11] Often, team members develop a purpose that gives them an opportunity to showcase and leverage their particular talents. For example, the organization may ask the team to develop a new product, yet team members may decide to go beyond the organization's request and create something that is the most technologically sophisticated or customer-friendly product on the market. Because they have personalized the team's goal, team members feel greater ownership of their work and believe that they are working for each other as well as for the team leader and the organization. In addition, people working in teams tend to have more say over how they do their work and expect a greater degree of personal learning and fulfillment from the team than do people working in groups. Furthermore, members of teams are not likely to see themselves as interchangeable or easily replaceable.[12] When someone leaves a team, the remaining team members feel a greater sense of loss (unless, of course, the person who leaves has been unproductive or disruptive, in which case the remaining team members celebrate the person's departure).

The leaders of high-performing teams spend less time in direct contact with the team and more time managing the context in which the team works. Rather than doing the work that the team members should be doing themselves, effective team leaders give the team a clear and meaningful purpose, provide it with needed resources, design a structure that helps team members achieve their collective goals, offer appropriate and well timed coaching to each member and the team as a whole, and connect the team to relevant external people and groups.

No two teams follow the exact same path to success. Every successful team has its unique goals, mix of team members, opportunities, and challenges. However, all high-performing teams have much in common. They consistently meet the three standards for effectiveness described in the next section (quality, individual learning, and team growth); they create processes for working together that enable members to work together successfully; and they have leaders who understand what they need to do (and not do) to bring out the best rather than the worst in their teams. Figure 8-1 summarizes the characteristics of high-performing teams, and these characteristics are discussed in detail in the following sections.

> Successful collaborations are dreams with deadlines.
> —WARREN BENNIS AND PATRICIA BIEDERMAN, *Organizing Genius: The Secrets of Creative Collaboration*

STANDARDS FOR TEAM EFFECTIVENESS

How can you distinguish a high-performing team from a mediocre one? High-performing teams meet three effectiveness criteria that enable them to have *sustained* success over time:[13]

- ***The team produces high-quality output.*** The team's products and services consistently meet—and often exceed—customers' expectations for quality products and services, timeliness, cost-savings, and other standards for success. It is able to achieve better results in less time using fewer resources than are lower-performing teams. It may not succeed in its efforts all of the time, but it succeeds most of the time.
- ***The team promotes the growth needs and well-being of each team member.*** All team members feel as though they benefit by being part of the team. Although some work

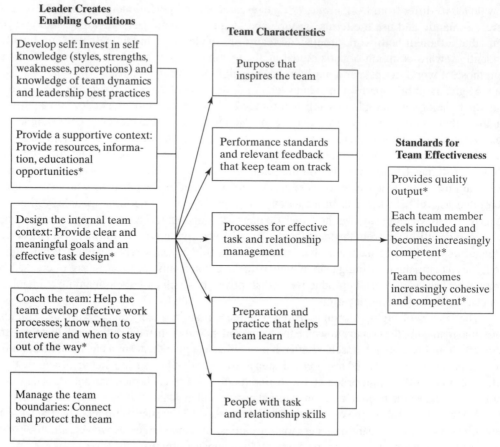

Leader Creates Enabling Conditions

Develop self: Invest in self knowledge (styles, strengths, weaknesses, perceptions) and knowledge of team dynamics and leadership best practices

Provide a supportive context: Provide resources, information, educational opportunities*

Design the internal team context: Provide clear and meaningful goals and an effective task design*

Coach the team: Help the team develop effective work processes; know when to intervene and when to stay out of the way*

Manage the team boundaries: Connect and protect the team

Team Characteristics

Purpose that inspires the team

Performance standards and relevant feedback that keep team on track

Processes for effective task and relationship management

Preparation and practice that helps team learn

People with task and relationship skills

Standards for Team Effectiveness

Provides quality output*

Each team member feels included and becomes increasingly competent*

Team becomes increasingly cohesive and competent*

*Based on Hackman, J. Richard. 2002. *Leading Teams: Setting the Stage for Great Performances.* Boston, MA: Harvard Business Press

FIGURE 8-1 Characteristics of High-Performing Teams

groups frustrate group members and block their ability to contribute and learn, a high-performing team motivates all team members and offers ample opportunities for each member to contribute to and learn from the team's work.

- *The team members collectively get smarter over time.* A high-performing team increases its collective competence over time. Team members take the time to reflect on their collective experience and learn from their successes and failures so that they continuously improve the team's performance.

Certainly, dysfunctional teams sometimes deliver successful products and services. However, their success is not sustainable over time because the team's problems will eventually hinder the team from achieving consistently successful results. For example, uneven participation by team members often leads to poor decisions because dominant (yet not necessarily more knowledgeable) team members overly influence the team's direction; the rest of the team colludes in this dynamic; and the team doesn't leverage the knowledge, experience, and resources of all members. Divisiveness among team members and lack of commitment to team goals can lead to free riding, settling for mediocre results, and team member turnover. Teams that don't take time to learn from their experience tend to repeat past mistakes, are more likely to engage in mindless routines, and may not be able to identify and recreate the processes that led to previously successful outcomes.

How large should a team be? A team should have on it only the people needed to accomplish the team's goal for two reasons. First, each additional member of a team increases the complexity of communication and coordination. Second, if people who are not needed to accomplish the team's goals are on the team, their time and effort can't be used elsewhere in the organization where they can add more value. Effective team leaders put the right number of people on the team. Some researchers argue that teams may operate best when they are slightly understaffed rather than overstaffed—referred to as "N-1 staffing" or "optimal understaffing." Slightly understaffing a team may inspire creativity, encourage the team to use their resources efficiently, discourage social loafing because everyone has a significant responsibility to contribute to the team, and result in greater team pride about achieving their goals. In addition to getting an appropriate number of people on the team, effective team leaders bring enough diversity into the team so that team members can offer different perspectives and approaches to the work, yet not so much diversity that team members are unable to pull together as a cohesive and coordinated unit.

FOUNDATIONS OF HIGH-PERFORMING TEAMS: PURPOSE, PERFORMANCE MEASURES, PEOPLE, PROCESS, AND PRACTICE

Most of us have been part of work groups that felt like a waste of time. We didn't know why we were included, our energy was sapped by attention to petty details and personal agendas that dominated team discussions, we accomplished little, and we lost valuable time that we could have spent on other important tasks. Most of us also have been part of work groups that energized us. We knew why we were called together, we felt we were contributing to a greater purpose, we looked forward to working with the people on the team, we could see the concrete results of our collective efforts, and we became wiser from our experiences with the team.

Why do some work groups drain us while others inspire us? Work groups are more likely to turn into high-performing teams when they are used for the right reason: to solve complex problems in which no one person has all the knowledge, skills, experiences, and other resources necessary to solve the problems and implement the solutions. If one person has all the resources to successfully solve a problem and implement the solution alone, then it is a waste of time, effort, and money to use a team to address the situation.

Work groups also are likely to turn into high-performing teams when they develop ways of working together that create *synergy*. Synergy occurs when the group's collective performance exceeds the potential of the most capable individual in the group. In short, the whole is greater than the sum of its parts. This increase is also referred to as *process gains*. In less effective work groups, the collective efforts of individuals don't result in improved quality, productivity gains, or team member growth.[14] Indeed, some work groups misuse individual resources so badly that group performance is less than that which individuals could have achieved by working alone on the problem. This decrease in performance is called *process losses*. A high-performing team that achieves synergy is built on five foundations:

> If you see a snake, just kill it. Don't appoint a committee on snakes.
> —H. ROSS PEROT,
> *Founder of EDS and Perot Systems*

- *Foundation 1: Purpose.* A clear and engaging *purpose* provides direction and inspires commitment toward common goals.
- *Foundation 2: Performance standards.* Clear and achievable measures of quality, quantity, speed, cost, and other performance standards help people focus their efforts

and provide a basis for relevant feedback that helps the team assess their progress toward these standards.

- *Foundation 3: People.* Team members who have a specific perspective and expertise to offer the team, as well as both task and relationship skills, provide the team with the intellectual and other resources needed for the team to solve complex problems that couldn't be solved by any one person alone.
- *Foundation 4: Processes.* Results-driven work processes enable team members to work together productively so that they can get better results in less time using fewer resources.
- *Foundation 5: Practice.* Opportunities to reflect what the team members are learning from their collective experiences, successes, and failures enable the team to continuously improve their competence as individuals and a team.

Each of these foundations is discussed in more detail in the following sections.

Foundation 1: Clear, Engaging Purpose

A high-performing team develops its sense of direction, inspiration, and momentum from a meaningful sense of purpose. A clear, engaging purpose lets the team know why it exists, and aligns the minds, hearts, and actions of team members toward a common goal that matters to them. A powerful purpose is clear yet broad (and concise) enough so that team members can determine how they can best use their unique talents, perspectives, and resources to achieve results that are linked to the purpose. It motivates team members to persist when faced with obstacles and hurdles. It enables them to create discrete and actionable steps that help them fulfill their purpose. Without a clear, engaging purpose, team members may pull apart, stray from the organization's expectations, waste time on activities that don't matter, or give up when they face hurdles.

As mentioned earlier, a high-performing team tends to create its own purpose that is at least as important to team members as is to the organization's purpose. Although the team's purpose is aligned with and supports that of the organization, the purpose that the team members create for themselves has a deeper meaning to them, enables them to better leverage team members' special interests and talents, and reinforces their collective identity as a unique and important entity.

POTENTIAL PROBLEMS WITH THE TEAM'S PURPOSE   Although a powerful team purpose is an important foundation for team success, it also can cause problems if the team's focus on the purpose is not well managed. Team members may become so committed to achieving their team's purpose that they lose sight of the larger organizational or societal goals and pursue their team's goals at the expense of the organization's goals. Team members may become so enamored with their purpose that they become willing to use any means necessary to achieve their goals, even if unethical. Team members who have invested so much of their time and effort pursuing the team's purpose may fail to notice that the environment has changed and their purpose is outdated. In addition, team members may become so cohesive and committed to their team's goals that they see people and groups from other parts of the organization as distractions, obstacles, or enemies rather than as mutually supportive partners committed to the common organizational mission. To avoid these risks, members of high-performing teams regularly review the appropriateness of their purpose and the means by which they go about achieving it. They are willing to adjust their purpose, and the means to achieving that purpose, as necessary to ensure that they are adding value in a way that is effective, efficient, and ethical.

Foundation 2: Performance Goals and Measures

A high-performing team develops specific and measurable performance goals by which it evaluates its progress. Effective performance goals are simultaneously challenging and achievable. Many organizations use the acronym SMART to design goals that enable teams to strategize how they will break the team's purpose into concrete and actionable steps. SMART goals are specific, measurable, aligned, realistic, and time-bound. These help team members prioritize their work, focus their energy and resources on actions that matter, and hold each other accountable. They help team members see how each contributes to achieving team goals, and they enable the team to experience small wins that build team members' confidence, commitment, and competence. SMART goals also help team members communicate the team's progress to people outside the team in a clear and measurable way. Sample SMART goals include:

- The team will increase our department's sales by 15% by the end of this fiscal year.
- The team will increase customer satisfaction, based on customer satisfaction surveys, by 10% by the end of the first quarter.
- The team will devise a system to complete the paperwork for each newly admitted patient within one hour by the end of the month.
- The team will ensure that everyone on our team has attended training and achieved certification in the new IT system by the end of this fiscal year.
- The team will identify and reach out to key people and departments who can help us achieve our goals within the next three weeks (and we will ask them how we can help them achieve their goals as well).
- As the team leader, I will meet with each person on the team to work with him or her to identify personal development goals by the end of the first quarter.
- As the team leader, I will take a workshop on effective delegation and implement three strategies for delegation by the end of the first quarter.

Box 8-1 contrasts the characteristics of the team's purpose and SMART goals. Together they ensure that the team has a meaningful purpose and a clear path toward achieving that purpose.

Foundation 3: People with Both Task and Relationship Skills

Members of a high-performing team aren't perfect. In today's complex and fast-changing environment, rarely do they join the team with all the technical, problem-solving, and relationship skills that their team needs for long-term success. However, members of a high-performing team take time to identify the skills that they need to help the team accomplish its goals, determine whether team members have those skills, and then find ways to fill the gaps, either by investing in the development of team members or by importing the skills from people outside the team. In addition, they tend to have the following characteristics:

> In crowds we have unison, in groups harmony. We want the single voice but not the single note.
> —MARY PARKER FOLLETT, *The New State*

- *Commitment.* They are committed to the team's purpose.
- *Specific expertise.* They have a specific expertise to offer the team, such as functional knowledge, technical abilities, or facilitation skills.
- *Open-mindedness.* They are not advocates of a particular method or function, even though they may be experts in a particular area. Open-mindedness increases people's ability to leverage diversity and connect to others they perceive to be different from themselves.[15]

BOX 8-1   Contrasting Engaging Purpose and SMART Goals

Engaging Purpose	Clear and Actionable Goals (SMART Goals)
• *Meaningful*: Team members need to believe the work is worth the effort.	• *Specific:* Describe what the team will do to achieve the team's purpose. Use action words such as "increase," "decrease," "develop," and "coordinate."
• *Positive*: Team members need to feel optimistic about the purpose and their ability to achieve their goals.	• *Measurable:* Provide clear performance standards so that team members will be able to assess their progress toward the goal.
• *Personalized*: Every team member needs to believe that he or she can personally contribute to the team's purpose.	• *Aligned:* Clearly link each goal to the team's overall purpose. Each person needs to be able to see how his or her individual and teamwork contributes to supporting the purpose.
• *Broad enough to be flexible*: Team members need to feel free to adapt their work strategies to address changes in the environment yet still stay aligned with the overall purpose.	• *Reachable:* Team members need to believe that they have enough knowledge, skill, and resources that enable them to achieve their goals. At the same time, goals should be challenging enough to keep team members engaged and stretch their skills.
• *Urgent*: Team members need to feel enough pressure to work efficiently, and they need to believe that their work is important enough to do quickly.	• *Time Bound:* Clear deadlines keep the team on track, provide a sense of urgency, and enable team members to hold each other and the team accountable for their assigned work.
• *Memorable*: The purpose needs to be stated in a way that is brief, understood by all, and easily remembered.	

- *General skills.* They have problem-solving, decision-making, and implementation skills.
- *Relationship skills.* They have skills that include willingness and ability to develop mutual trust and respect, communicate effectively, manage conflict, and respect diversity. As one Disney executive puts it, effective team members are able to "play in the sandbox with others."[16]
- *Adaptiveness.* Maryfran Hughes, who manages over 50 nurses in Massachusetts General Hospital's emergency area, says that "an adaptive personality can be as important as technical competence, particularly when 'people have to deal with situations where they have no control.'"[17]
- *Self-awareness.* They are aware of their own styles, strengths, and weaknesses; understand how they are perceived by others; understand how these styles, strengths, weaknesses, and perceptions affect team performance; and are willing to invest in ongoing personal development.

Must team members sacrifice themselves to the team and forego individual objectives? No, because a high-performing team finds ways to enable the individual, as well as the team, grow and develop. As Texas Instruments Vice President and Manager of Worldwide Facilities Shaunna Sowell found earlier in her career, a successful team experience can lead to individual learning, recognition, and promotions. Her experience was described in the *Wall Street Journal* as follows:

Ms. Sowell was leading a plant design team . . . when she was tapped for a product-quality steering committee that was loaded with bosses. She was intimidated at first, but her confidence grew with her experience. "I left one meeting thinking, my God, I've ruined my career," she recalls. "I'd just told a guy four levels above me he was wrong." Actually, she impressed an executive on the team who was casting about for a vice president of corporate environmental safety. . . . "You have to be a great individual contributor," she says. "That's how you get picked for the next team."[18]

Foundation 4: Results-Driven Processes

Teamwork involves managing a more complex set of tasks and relationships than does individual work. Team members must develop a shared understanding of their goals and their environment, identify multiple problems and opportunities, generate solutions, make trade-offs, agree on decisions, implement solutions, and evaluate the consequences of their decisions—all while managing the social dynamics that are inevitably part of everyday group life.

Leadership is at its best when the vision is strategic, the voice persuasive, the results tangible.
—MICHAEL USEEM,
The Leadership Moment

To manage these complex group tasks and relationships, effective teams develop systematic task and relationship processes for working together within the team and connecting with relevant individuals and teams outside the team. A process is an agreed-upon method (sequence of steps and behaviors) designed to help the team achieve its collective goals. Task processes refer to the systematic methods team members use to make decisions, implement solutions, maintain accountability, coordinate their efforts, build external support, manage conflict, and evaluate results. Relationship processes refer to the social skills that team members use to create a productive work climate that promotes a foundation of trust, openness, and psychological safety that leads to cohesiveness, commitment, creativity, critical thinking, and constructive conflict—all of which are necessary for effective group learning, decision making, and implementation of decisions.[19] Note that although effective task processes may enable a group with poor relationship skills to produce a high-quality product in the short run, effective relationship processes must be in place if group members are to remain committed to the team and produce high-quality results in the long run. The importance of creating high-quality relationships to the long-term success of teams is supported by considerable research that is finding that team members who feel positively toward their leader, each other, and the task are more likely to cooperate with each other, less likely to have dysfunctional conflict, less likely to be overly focused on the self over the team, more likely to manage the delicate balance between advocating and challenging each other's ideas, and more likely to have higher perceptions of the team's effectiveness.[20]

NORMS Norms refer to team members' collective implicit and explicit agreements about "how we do things around here." An effective team uses explicit and implicit norms to ensure that team member resources are well utilized, time isn't wasted, and team goals are achieved. Team norms express the team's central values (e.g., Is it acceptable to come late to meetings, or is timeliness expected? How should we manage conflict? Is it appropriate to use laptops and smart phones during meetings, or are all team members expected to focus their attention completely on the meeting's agenda? Is it acceptable for a few people to participate more often in meetings, or is equal participation expected?). Effective norms increase the predictability of team members' behaviors (e.g., Which kinds of e-mails are we supposed to respond to, and which are for information only and require no response?) and help team members coordinate their efforts (e.g., What kind of decision-making process should we use?). For example, a team may promote norms that team members are supposed to check their e-mail at least once each morning and again before leaving the office, be accessible by cell phone when they are not at the office, and return telephone calls from team members immediately.

Norms can be fun as well as instrumental. One Finnish executive development program that I worked with has the norm that if a cell phone rings during a meeting, the carrier of the phone must sing a song and buy all participants in the group a cognac that evening. I incorporated this norm into my classrooms (well, not the cognac). If a cell phone goes off in class, the student who owns the phone must sing a song for the rest of the class.

Explicit Norms. Explicit norms refer to behavioral guidelines that team members openly discuss, clearly understand, and explicitly communicate to new team members. Effective team norms:

- are consistent with the team's and organization's goals;
- address only those behaviors that affect team performance (such as quality standards, availability, accountability, communication, decision-making processes, conflict management, meeting management, and ways of showing respect for each other);
- address only those behaviors that each team member can control;
- are viewed as appropriate and achievable by all team members; and
- are revisited over time to make sure that they continue to help the team achieve its goals.

All team members should be involved in establishing explicit team norms for two reasons. First, each team member brings a particular set of values, personal goals, pressures, cultural norms, talents, perspectives, and work styles to the team. If these are not considered, the norms may undermine rather than enhance each team member's willingness and ability to perform well. Second, team members are more likely to be committed to norms that they help develop because they understand why each norm was created (e.g., how it helps the team achieve its goals) and how each norm will be enforced.

Explicitly developing team norms takes time and effort, but the payoffs are significant. Effective norms help a team get started quickly, keep behavior directed toward the team's purpose, provide clear standards against which members can judge their performance and be held accountable, increase predictability and coordination, enhance efficiency by helping team members use their collective resources (e.g., time, materials, knowledge, skills, and experience) wisely, and get the team back on track if it gets stuck or derailed.

Some teams have explicit consequences for team members who break an important norm (e.g., interrupting when someone is speaking). For example, some teams have team members donate a small amount of money to the team "bank" whenever someone breaks a norm (e.g., coming to a meeting late or interrupting while someone else is speaking). After a period of time, the team uses the money collected to go to dinner or to make a charitable donation.

Blamestorming: The practice of sitting around in a group discussing why a deadline was missed or a project failed and who was responsible.
—NEW MANAGEMENT WORDS,
Urban Dictionary

Implicit Norms. Many team norms are not explicitly planned or articulated. Rather, they evolve informally over time, are not written down, are rarely discussed, are often unconscious, and are reinforced through subtle and often unspoken means such as peer pressure. Implicit norms are unavoidable. No team can—or would want to—explicitly articulate all their norms. Doing so would waste precious time and feel oppressive.

Some implicit norms are functional. For example, a team may have unspoken norms that encourage team members to spend a few minutes socializing before each meeting. This implicit norm enables team members to build social bonds that enable them to build trust and work more quickly together. A team could have an implicit norm that enables a few team members to dominate meetings (e.g., team members who speak up more often, regardless of whether their comments are the most useful). This norm is likely to be dysfunctional if the team gives too much weight to a few team members' comments while under utilizing the knowledge of other team members who may be quieter yet have significant knowledge and skills to bring to the task.

Implicit norms can be problematic because, even when dysfunctional, they are usually not discussed—and all team members in their silence collude in perpetuating the problematic norm. Consequently, team members cannot assess the impact of these norms on the team's effectiveness or create more effective team norms. The most important lesson about team norms is this: Although team members cannot and should not regulate all team behaviors, they should develop explicit norms about behaviors that help the team engage in productive behaviors and minimize dysfunctional behaviors. The following tools will help you develop effective team norms.

Box 8-2 provides a checklist of guiding questions that you can use in developing your team's norms. Box 8-3 lists several questions that team members can discuss as part of a team review at critical stages of a team's life, particularly when a team completes a project. Box 8-4 helps you assess the direct financial costs of meetings. Box 8-5 provides guidelines for structuring effective team meetings.

BOX 8-2   Guidelines for Creating Team Norms

The following questions are designed to guide the development of your team's norms. Please rate each question on a scale of 1–5, with 1 being "not at all" and 5 being "Definitely"

Evaluating Team Effectiveness

_____ We have clear standards for quality.
_____ We have ways to help individual team members grow and develop.
_____ We have ways to ensure that the team as a whole engages in continuous learning.

Purpose

_____ We have a clear and engaging team purpose that is aligned with the organization's purpose.
_____ Every team member believes that the purpose is important.
_____ Every team member can see how he or she contributes to that purpose.

Performance Measures

_____ Every team member knows what his or her tasks are so that they can be held accountable for completing these tasks.
_____ Every team member has clear performance measures for standards of quality and timeliness.
_____ The team as a whole has clear performance measures for standards of quality and timeliness.
_____ The team receives regular feedback that helps team members assess how well they are progressing toward their goals.
_____ Each team member spends most of his or her time working on tasks that are important to achieving the team's purpose.
_____ Team members know the consequences of submitting substandard or late products.

People

_____ Team members have the task-related skills they need to do their work (e.g., technical skills, project management skills).
_____ Team members treat each other with respect
_____ All team members are comfortable expressing their ideas and also encourage others to speak up by asking for, and listening to, opinions from others.

(continued)

BOX 8-2 *Continued*

Process

_____ Team members are committed to each other in ways that build cohesion among all team members.

_____ Team members have predictable ways of coordinating with each other.

_____ Team members use an effective decision-making process.

_____ Team members have a systematic process for communicating with external people and teams (How often? For what reason? In what form?).

_____ Team members know how formal reports, presentations, and other written and verbal communication should be and what level of detail is important.

_____ Team members have norms for managing conflict so that it is constructive rather than destructive.

_____ Team members have more positive than negative interactions.

_____ Team members have a systematic way of integrating new members into the team.

Meetings

_____ Team members know how often they will meet and for what purposes.

_____ Team members know how meetings will be structured to maximize productivity.

Preparation and Practice

_____ Team members regularly take time to evaluate their performance and learn from the team's successes and failures.

_____ Team members have systems in place for identifying and filling skill gaps.

Leadership

_____ Team members know how leaders will be selected and whether leadership will be rotated.

_____ If leadership is rotated, team members know how leadership transitions will be made.

_____ Team members know the team leader's role—what he or she will and will not do for the team.

_____ Team members know how to communicate with the leader, including feedback and bad news.

Questions to Ask About the Team Norms

1. Are team norms consistent with the organization mission, values, and goals?
2. How will the team monitor team member compliance and uphold adherence to these norms?
3. How will we introduce new members to team norms?
4. How often will we reevaluate our norms to determine whether they are still appropriate and what our process will be?
5. How will we be sure that our norms are helping rather than hindering our process?

Foundation 5: Preparation and Practice

Researchers and practitioners often use sports teams as analogies for work teams. However, they often neglect one of the most critical factors for a sports team's success: preparation and frequent disciplined practice. High-performing teams routinely reflect on their performance. They systematically identify the skills they need to succeed, identify gaps between the skills that they have and those that they need, and then make the effort to learn and practice those skills. Coaching legend Bill Walsh, former head coach of the San Francisco 49ers and Stanford University's football team, believed the secret to his long-term success was in the way he helped his teams prepare for their games. He explained that preparation allowed the teams to "overcome the fact that we might not be the most physically talented team." His strategies for success included identifying the "essential skills" the team needed, establishing priorities and allocating time to systematically teach those skills, developing plans for multiple scenarios (even worst-case scenarios), and ensuring that the team systematically practiced those skills in the different scenarios. He explained, "It doesn't mean that [the plan] will always work; it doesn't mean that you will always be successful. But you will always be prepared and at your best."[21]

In short, disciplined preparation and practice helps team members acquire a broad repertoire of skills that they can use in a variety of situations, learn to anticipate each other's actions and contributions so that they can better coordinate their efforts in novel situations, and develop the confidence and ability to work under pressure without panicking or falling into dysfunctional behaviors.

BOX 8-3 Guidelines for Team Review

1. In what ways did we succeed? In what ways did we fail?
2. What did we do well that we should remember to do next time?
3. What could we have done better, faster, with higher quality, with fewer resources, and in less time?
4. Which team norms served us well?
5. Which team norms should we change?
6. Did anyone dominate our discussions, and why? Did anyone not speak up as much as the others, and why?
7. Did we have any sloppy hand-offs?
8. Did we listen to advice from anyone outside of the team who could have added value? If not, why not?
9. Did we miss any opportunities to build relationships or get support from people outside of our group? Who blocked our efforts? Whose support should we now build for the long-term?
10. Who outside of our team helped us and how should we thank them or reciprocate in some way?

BOX 8-4 Calculate the Cost of Your Meeting

How Much Does Your Meeting Cost?

Calculate the hourly salary and cost of benefits per attendee.

Attendee 1	_____
Attendee 2	_____
Attendee 3	_____
Attendee 4	_____
Attendee 5	_____
Total hourly salaries and benefits:	_____

Total hourly salaries and benefits multiplied by meeting length in hours equal the human cost of meetings. For example, if you have five people attending a meeting, each with salary and benefits worth $100 an hour, and the meeting lasts two hours, the human cost of the meeting would be $(\$100 \times 5) \times 2 = \$1,000$. Remember that effective meetings have the right people in the right place discussing the right issues in the right order.

BOX 8-5   Managing Meetings

To make sure that you make the best use of participants' time, consider the following questions:

- ✔ How will we notify team members and others of meetings?
- ✔ Will we expect all team members to attend all meetings?
- ✔ Will we expect all team members to be on time and attend the entire meeting?
- ✔ How will we deal with team members who miss meetings, don't meet performance standards in terms of quality and timeliness, or who are repeatedly late or leave early?
- ✔ How long will our meetings be?
- ✔ How will we structure meetings to best use team members' expertise, time, and resources? For example:
  - What materials, if any, will be made available in advance?
  - Will agendas be used, and who will make and distribute them?
  - How will we manage time so that it is not wasted?
  - Who will facilitate meetings, and will the facilitator role be fixed or rotated?
  - How will we manage task processes at meetings (gathering information, making presentations, making decisions, and evaluating results)?
  - How will we manage relationship processes at meetings (encouraging participation, openness, constructive conflict, creativity; resolving disputes; managing status dynamics—higher-status people tend to speak more and are taken more seriously than lower-status people; making sure all team members have influence in the group)?
  - Will team members have explicit roles to ensure that task and relationship processes are attended to? How will these roles be assigned? Will roles be rotated?
  - How formal/informal will meetings be?
  - How will we make sure that the meetings stay on track?
  - What will we do when we get stuck?
  - How will we discourage dysfunctional individual and group behaviors (under- or overparticipation; problematic status effects; marginalization of some team members; substandard performance)?
  - How will we identify action items and assign responsibilities?
  - Will we take time to reflect on our process and improve team performance?
  - Will we have minutes of the meetings taken and distributed? Who will take them, and who will receive them?

TEAM LEADERSHIP: CREATING A CONTEXT FOR HIGH-PERFORMING TEAMS

High-performing teams do not develop the five foundations—clear, engaging purpose; performance measures; skilled people with task and relationship skills; results-driven processes; and disciplined practice—without capable leadership. To be effective, team leaders must know how to create teams with a strong sense of collective identity, the motivation to achieve their goals, the skills needed to achieve those goals, and the ability to build effective relationships. Team leaders need to know when to intervene and when to stay out of the team's way, when to reward individuals and when to reward the team, and when to connect the team to external individuals and groups and when to protect the team from external influences. For team leaders, knowing what not to do is as important as knowing what to do.

People who seem to have natural leadership talent do not become effective team leaders overnight. Says David Nadler, chairman of Mercer Delta Organizational Consulting Group in New York City, "Corporations underestimate the shift in mindset and behavioral skills that team leaders need."[22] Team leaders must learn to do more than facilitate effective team meetings. They must learn how to proactively build trust with team members because they realize that team members' trust in the leader significantly contributes to the team's performance.[23] They also must learn to delegate tasks that they used to do themselves (and may still want to do, especially if they were successful individual contributors before they became team leaders); give out information that used to be confidential; turn over spending authority; share power, control, and credit; earn credibility with team members who have more customer or technical knowledge than the team leader has; enable team members who have different goals, personalities, and quirks to work together cohesively; encourage team members to coordinate their efforts with external individuals and groups; and develop rewards that motivate the team without demotivating the individual. Yet most organizations prepare team leaders with "little more than a handshake and a pat on the back."[24]

Effective team leaders know that *their most important job is managing the context in which the team works rather than directly intervening in the team's work.* Harvard researcher Richard Hackman explains:

> Rather than attempting to manage group behavior in real time, leaders might better spend their energies creating contexts that increase the likelihood (but cannot guarantee) that teams will prosper—taking care to leave ample room for groups to develop their own unique behavioral styles and performance strategies.[25]

This advice is echoed in a motto that physicist and former Xerox chief scientist Jack Goldman, who is credited for creating the Xerox Palo Alto Research Center, hung in his office: "There are two ways of being creative. One can sing and dance. Or one can create an environment in which singers and dancers flourish."[26] To help teams succeed, team leaders should develop skills in four key areas:

- Investing in ongoing personal development
- Designing a work context that enables the team to do its best work, including
  - a sense of identity as a bounded team
  - a supportive work context
  - clear, engaging goals
  - an enabling task design
  - appropriate and well-timed coaching
- Encouraging positive social interactions
- Connecting the team to external people and groups (and sometimes protecting the team from excessive external intervention)

Each of these team leadership skills is discussed in more detail in the sections that follow. As you read this section, remember that there are many kinds of team leader roles. Team leaders can be officially designated, or they can emerge informally in a team. The team leader role may be fixed, or it may rotate among different team members. Some teams are explicitly leader led, whereas others are self-managing. Regardless of the kind of leadership in the team, the most important task of the leader is to ensure that their teams have what they need to succeed.

Team Leadership Skill 1: Invest in Ongoing Personal Development

Effective team leaders know that team members pay particular attention to the attitudes, words, and behaviors of people in authority positions. Therefore, they invest in three kinds of personal development:

> A leader has a responsibility not just for his or her own sake, but for everyone else in the organization. Unless the leader has a degree of self-knowledge and self-understanding, there is a risk that he or she will use the organization to address his or her own neuroses.
> —PETER SENGE CITING ALAIN GAUTHIER

- *Developing self-awareness.* Effective leaders know that one of the best ways to change an individual's or team's behavior is to change their own behavior because team members will adapt their behavior in response to their leader's behavior. For example, if a team leader wants an individual or team to be more independent, then the team leader should provide the team with information, resources, and skills that encourage, rather than discourage, independence. If a team leader wants an individual or team to be more forthcoming with bad news, then the team leader should exhibit behaviors that welcome rather than inhibit bad news. If a team leader wants the team to leverage the diversity on the team, then the team leader should role-model these behaviors.
- *Understanding group dynamics.* Effective team leaders understand how social dynamics in groups affect team members' ability to use their collective resources effectively and achieve the team's goals. They understand that team members' biases and emotional lives—their hopes and fears—can significantly influence the effectiveness of the team's process and thus the quality of their decisions. They also understand that authority relations can affect how team members react toward the leader and how the leader acts toward the team members. Therefore, effective team leaders invest in understanding individual behavior as well as group dynamics so that they can anticipate problems, and then take steps to prevent or minimize dysfunctional behaviors and channel the team's energy toward productive ends.
- *Learning effective leadership techniques.* Effective team leaders develop good instincts. They do so by taking time to learn effective leadership practices, systematically implement these practices, and evaluate the impact of these techniques on the team's performance. In short, effective team leaders carefully plan their interventions and don't just "wing it."

Team Leadership Skill 2: Create a Work Context That Enables the Team to Do Its Best Work

In this section, I summarize research developed by Richard Hackman and his colleagues because they have spent over 25 years building a tested, cohesive, and practical set of best practices for leading high-performing teams.[27] To perform well, team members must be motivated to do their collective work, have the knowledge and skills that help them do it well, and develop ways of working together that enhance rather than inhibit their ability to reach their goals.[28]

> The problem is not shall groups exist or not, but shall groups be planned or not?
> —THEODORE LEAVITT

Hackman and colleagues have identified five conditions under which teams are likely to perform well: (1) having a clear identity as a bounded unit; (2) having a supportive organizational context; (3) having a clear, engaging goal; (4) having an enabling task design; and (5) having appropriate and well-timed coaching. Although team leaders can't guarantee that a team will succeed, teams are more likely to succeed when leaders ensure that these conditions are in place. Each is described in more detail later.

CREATE A TEAM IDENTITY AS A "REAL TEAM" Effective team leaders take time at the beginning of the team's life to ensure that team members are clear that they are part of a real team, "a reasonably stable unit with shared responsibility for a defined piece of work."[29] They know who is and is not a member of the team. They feel as though all team members were put on the team because each adds unique and significant perspectives and talents to the team. These clear boundaries enable team members to accept and fulfill their responsibilities to the team because there is no question that they are expected to be active members of the team. These boundaries also enable team members to identify their common goals, commit time and energy to the team, assign responsibilities to each other, hold each other accountable, keep track of individual and team performance, and create collective work norms that enable team members to communicate with each other and coordinate their work.

PROVIDE A SUPPORTIVE WORK CONTEXT   A team is more likely to succeed if team leaders provide information and educational opportunities that team members need to achieve their collective goals. Effective team leaders also provide rewards that encourage interdependence, are contingent on performance, and are given primarily to the team as a whole. Rewards can be financial (e.g., raises and bonuses), small and meaningful gifts of appreciation (e.g., trophies and gift certificates), professional development opportunities (e.g., education or attendance at conferences), enhanced team resources (e.g., increased team budgets for team use), or psychological (e.g., recognition and visibility).

A supportive organizational context does not necessarily mean having abundant resources. Research has found that high-performing teams do not always have the luxury of extra people or fine offices in which to do their work.[30] Indeed, researchers Patricia Ward-Biederman and Warren Bennis note:

> Great groups have some odd things in common. For example, they tend to do their brilliant work in spartan, even shabby surroundings. Someday someone will write a book explaining why so many pioneering enterprises, including Walt Disney Company, Hewlett-Packard, and Apple, were born in garages. . . . We can speculate on why great things are often accomplished in dull or tacky surroundings. Perhaps a bland or unattractive environment spurs creativity, functions as an aesthetic blank slate that frees the mind to dream about what might be. . . . But the truth is that most people in great groups spend very little time thinking about their surroundings. They have wonderful tunnel vision.[31]

Although high-performing teams tend not to have fancy surroundings, they do have ample support such as information, training, and access to people who can help them achieve their goals.

PROVIDE A CLEAR, ENGAGING DIRECTION   As mentioned earlier, effective team leaders clearly and enthusiastically articulate the organization's vision and their commitment to that vision. For example, Steve Jobs, founder of Apple Computer, told employees that Apple would "put a dent in the universe" and create something "insanely great." People who are loyal to the MacIntosh, iPod, and iPad would say that Apple has indeed achieved that mission. A clear, engaging direction energizes the team and helps team members align and organize their day-to-day work toward their collective goals. Creating a clear, engaging direction also enables the leader to design the overall framework in which the team can achieve their collective goals while simultaneously giving the team freedom within that framework to pursue those goals in ways that make sense to the team.[32]

DEVELOP AN ENABLING TASK DESIGN   Once team members are clear about and have invested in the team's goals, effective team leaders spend much of their time designing the structure, but not the details, of the team's work. An enabling design lets team members know what their responsibilities are and are not, as well as which decisions are made by the leader and which decisions they make themselves. An enabling design provides team members with the boundaries of their work (e.g., objectives, quality standards, milestones, feedback, required work processes) and freedom within those boundaries so that they can focus their efforts and use their collective energy to work effectively within those boundaries in their own way. When boundaries are unclear or constantly shifting, team members experience ongoing uncertainty that can distract the team and sap the team's energy. Having freedom within a well-designed framework gives team members a sense of ownership of their work, enables the team to use the unique talents of all team members, helps team members learn and grow from the decisions they must make, and frees the team to quickly adapt their work as needed to better meet the needs of situations as they arise (as long as they stay within the framework).[33]

Effective team leaders take time to identify which team tasks are critical to the team's success, eliminate tasks that add no value, and then design the critical tasks in a way that enhances the possibility that team members will be motivated and capable of doing those tasks well.[34] When a task is well designed, team members feel more motivated to do the work, more capable of achieving their goals, and more satisfied with the work that they do. They are less likely to experience free riders in the team and uneven participation among team members because all team members know what they are supposed to do and are held accountable for doing their share of the work. A well-designed task also prevents team members from getting stuck in mindless routines—doing things that don't matter much or doing things in inefficient ways—by helping the team prioritize their work and encouraging the team to continuously innovate and find better ways of doing their work as long as they stay within the boundaries set up by the leader. Hackman, together with his colleague Greg Oldham, identified five core job characteristics that predict these outcomes: skill variety, task identity, task significance, autonomy, and job-based feedback.[35] Each is described below. You can assess your own job (or that of your employees) with these job characteristics by taking the Job Diagnostic Survey at the end of this chapter.

> **We shape our dwellings and then our dwellings shape us.**
> —WINSTON CHURCHILL,
> *British politician and statesman*

- *Skill variety.* The job is designed so that team members are able to use a variety of talents, skills, and activities when doing their work.
- *Task identity.* The job is designed so that team members can do a whole piece of work from beginning to end.
- *Task significance.* The job is designed so that each team member believes the work that he or she does has a significant positive impact on others and contributes to the team purpose in a meaningful way. Toni Morrison, winner of the Nobel Prize in Literature, illustrates the importance of identification with a task with this story about her father who worked at U.S. Steel when she was a child: "I remember my Daddy taking me aside—this was when he worked as a welder—and telling me that he welded a perfect seam that day, and that after welding the perfect seam he put his initials on it. I said, 'Daddy, no one will ever see that. Sheets and sheets of siding would go over that, you know?' And he said, 'Yes, but I'll know it's there.'"[36]
- *Autonomy.* The job is designed so that team members feel that they are free to use their discretion in determining how they organize their work, make decisions, and take actions targeted at achieving the team's goals, as long as they work within the boundaries (e.g., goals, performance standards, essential work processes) agreed upon with the team leader. Team members who have significant control over how they do their

work are more likely to feel more ownership of their work and make appropriate decisions quickly.[37]

- *Job-based feedback.* The job is designed so that regular feedback about the effectiveness of team members' work is built into the job itself rather than being dependent on the team leader to provide the feedback. Team members are more likely to maintain direction and momentum if they have regular feedback that lets them know how they're progressing (e.g., in terms of quality or timeliness) and whether they need to adjust their individual and team strategies.

When team leaders put the first three core job characteristics in place (skill variety, task identity, and task significance), team members are more likely to experience their job as *meaningful.* When team leaders encourage and enable autonomy, employees are more likely to feel personal and collective *responsibility for the outcomes of their work.* When team leaders build ongoing feedback into the job itself (rather than expect team members to wait for the team leader or others outside the team to provide them with feedback), team members routinely *know the results of their efforts* quickly and can adjust their work accordingly on a regular basis. This sense of meaningfulness, responsibility for the work, and knowledge of their progress toward team goals through feedback inspires and enables team members to be more effective, feel more motivated, learn and grow from their collective work, and experience high job satisfaction.

Although a well-designed task is likely to motivate team members to do their best work, Oldham and Hackman acknowledge that the success of a well-designed task depends on several factors. For example, not everyone wants or needs to find their job meaningful, nor does everyone have a high need for growth from their job. There are also individual differences in the degree of team members' social skills and emotional maturity that affect their willingness and ability to work well with people inside and outside the team, regardless of how well the task is designed.[38] Not surprisingly, social dynamics in the team—the degree to which team members support each other—predict team members' commitment to the team and the team's ability to achieve collective goals.[39] Finally, a well-designed job can help the team succeed only if team members have the skills and talents that are relevant to the job. Consequently, team leaders need to be aware that although an effective job design increases the possibility that team member and the team as a whole will succeed, it can't guarantee success.[40]

PROVIDE EXPERT AND WELL-TIMED COACHING   Once the leader has created a real team, provided a supportive context, articulated a clear and engaging direction, and developed an engaging design that provides the team with both clear boundaries within which the team has the freedom to do the work, only then will the leader's efforts at coaching be effective. If a team doesn't have a clear direction and well-designed tasks, coaching is unlikely to have a significant impact on team performance. Indeed, researcher Ruth Wageman found that good coaching (e.g., asking the team useful questions that help the team think through strategic options, providing examples and best practices that the team can adapt for their own use, providing positive feedback when appropriate) can significantly help a well-designed team, but it has little or no impact on a poorly designed team. Furthermore, bad coaching (e.g., micromanaging the team, providing poorly timed interventions that distract the team from its work) can significantly harm a poorly designed team, but it has little impact on a well-designed team. In a well-designed team, poor coaching can distract the team and be an annoyance, but team members often avoid negative effects on performance because their clear goals and effective performance processes keep them on track.[41] In general, well-designed teams have less need for coaching in general, which leaves the team leader free to focus on strategic issues, obtain resources for the team, and connect the team to relevant external people and groups.

In most cases, the best types of interventions are those that support the team in doing its work rather than those that directly intervene in the day-to-day life of the team. Appropriate and well-timed interventions can propel the team forward, promote team learning, increase the team's confidence in itself, and enhance the team's long-term as well as short-term effectiveness. Supportive interventions include providing direction, providing resources (e.g., information, training, materials and equipment, access to relevant people, and rewards), removing obstacles, and helping the team coordinate its work with external people and groups. To the degree possible, the team should manage its own internal team dynamics, design its own task processes, and carry out its own work.[42] As researchers Patricia Ward Biederman and Warren Bennis say, "No great group was ever micromanaged."[43]

One of the most critical challenges team leaders have is to know when to intervene in the team's work and when to stay out of the team's way. Effective leaders know that the wrong interventions or badly timed interventions can wreak havoc on a team's performance. Such interventions can demotivate the team, inhibit team learning, undermine team members' confidence in themselves and the team, and increase the team's dependence on the leader—all of which can throw the team off track or slow it down.[44] Effective coaching practices include the following:

- Motivating the team by ensuring that team members know that their work is important and know how their work significantly affects the organization's ability to achieve its goals
- Providing educational opportunities for the team, especially by helping the team learn from its own experiences
- Providing information to the team, such as information about the competition, changes in the environment, and how their outcomes are influencing organizational outcomes
- Helping the team develop effective task and relationship-oriented work processes that can help them achieve better results in less time, using fewer resources
- Providing useful observations—based on clear data rather than speculation—that help team members notice and discuss patterns they may not otherwise address (e.g., "I noticed that Lee hasn't spoken up in the past two meetings." "I noticed that Chris has spoken up more than others during this meeting.")
- Asking useful questions to guide team learning and help the team members adjust their performance strategies (e.g., "What would be an appropriate strategy going forward?" "What has been working so far?" "What hasn't been working?" "What do you know now that you didn't know before that could change your performance strategies?")
- Encouraging the team to connect externally (e.g., "Who has contacts outside this team that will be helpful to achieving the team's goals?" "Whose support does the team need, and how can the team develop this support?")
- Encouraging team members to coach themselves by paying attention to their work processes, seeking out feedback on their performance, and creating and adjusting their work processes as appropriate
- Timing coaching interventions carefully with a special emphasis on coaching at the beginning, middle, and end of a project (Coaching interventions have the biggest impact at the beginning of the team's life to get the team off to a good start, in the middle to help the team evaluate and adjust work processes based on the information and experience team members gained during the first half of the project, and at the end to help the team learn from their experiences on the project)

- Using periods between the beginning, middle, and end of a project to identify what the team is doing right and providing positive feedback to reinforce those behaviors so that team members will feel motivated to continue their work and will learn which behaviors are most valued in the organization[45]

Knowing when to directly intervene in the team's work and when to stay out of the team's way is a "balancing act between action and patience."[46]

Team Leadership Skill 3: Encourage Positive Social Relationships

Although a well-designed task environment is critical to a team's success, a team's performance can be undermined by dysfunctional social relationships.[47] A well-designed task can't be expected to over-ride the negative effects of a team's social environment in which team members don't want to spend time together, don't listen to each other, don't support each other, and don't develop supportive relationships with people and groups outside the team. Team members do not need to become close friends, but they do need to respect each other and develop mutually supportive relationships.

Researchers Marcial Losada and Emily Heaphy found that the highest performing teams promote a more positive atmosphere than do lower performing teams. In their studies of 60 business unit teams for which they had performance data, Losada and Heaphy found that the "high-performing teams had about a six-to-one ratio of positive to negative statements, whereas [in] the low-performing teams . . . more than half of what was said was negative." Positive statements were supportive, appreciative, and encouraging (e.g., "That's a useful idea." "We did a good job answering questions after the presentation."). Negative statements were sarcastic, disapproving, and cynical (e.g., "That's a dumb idea." "The people in that department are all incompetent.")[48] Positive emotions and interactions pay off for teams because they provide an emotionally safe work context that encourages participation, open-mindedness, intellectual and behavioral flexibility, risk-taking, and resilience.

Notably, Barbara Fredrickson and Marcial Losada found that teams that were excessively positive (e.g., with a 11:1 ratio of positive to negative statements) were less likely to perform well.[49] Appropriate negative emotions, feedback, and experiences can help a team succeed because task-appropriate conflict and critique help teams refine their thinking, avoid groupthink, and fine-tune their performance strategies by carefully thinking through alternative scenarios and significant trade-offs involved when making decisions. Feeling disappointed that a project didn't turn out well can motivate team members to figure out what went wrong and take responsibility for errors. Feeling angry at a management decision can inspire team members to negotiate an alternative plan with management. Appropriate negative emotions protect the team from becoming "unrealistically Pollyannaish." Furthermore, learning to overcome negative situations is key to developing resilience, and overcoming negative situations and associated emotions together can strengthen team members' relationships (e.g., "What doesn't kill us makes us stronger.").

In their research, Losada and Heaphy also found that teams that balance both advocacy (e.g., each team member feels comfortable speaking up and advocating for his/her own ideas) and inquiry (e.g., each team member seeks out and listens to the ideas of others) tend to be more successful. In addition, they found that the most successful teams build cohesion internally yet they are not self-absorbed. High-performing teams avoid becoming insular and instead seek out perspectives, information, and resources from people and teams outside the team.

Team Leadership Skill 4: Connect the Team Externally to Relevant People and Groups

Teams don't operate in a vacuum. Rather, they depend on information, resources, cooperation, and goodwill from people and groups external to the team to progress in their work and achieve their goals.[50] Not surprisingly, researcher Deborah Ancona and colleagues found that teams that are both internally focused and externally connected achieve the highest performance ratings over time.[51] Today's problems are so complex that all teams must depend on the support of others to achieve their goals. Furthermore, the work that one team does has an effect on the work of other teams. Consequently, teams that connect externally are able to obtain more information, resources, and support—and they are likely to make better decisions that are more likely to get implemented—than teams that are primarily internally focused. Not surprisingly, leaders that connect their teams externally—who are seen as boundary spanners—tend to have more successful careers as well, in part because of their ability to help their teams achieve their goals and in part because of the visibility, information, and mutual support they gain through their external connections.

However, getting team members to seek out and work with external people and groups is often easier said than done.[52] Many well-designed, highly motivated teams fail because the walls they build around themselves intentionally or unintentionally limit their ability to get the information and support they need to make and implement decisions quickly and effectively. When Richard Parsons became CEO of Time Warner, he determined that he needed to turn "business units that feuded for more than a decade" into a cooperative whole so that he could give shareholders a superior return on their investment. Under the previous CEO, "sharp-elbowed divisional chiefs were freed to focus on their own businesses, without regard for the broader company, an approach that resulted in unresolved disputes between divisions like Warner Bros., and HBO." Parsons described his strategy simply: "We're trying to run the company to maximize the value of the whole company. You don't get credit [just] because you get good numbers. . . . You get credit for being a member of the team."[53]

The costs of intergroup conflict and lack of coordination became painfully apparent to Steve Case, former chairman of AOL Time Warner, when his brother Daniel was diagnosed with brain cancer. Says Case, "I was very surprised to learn that no one knows what causes brain cancer or how to cure it, despite decades of work." Before dying of brain cancer, Daniel founded the Accelerate Brain Cancer Cure (ABC^2) together with Steve, to promote collaboration among previously disconnected researchers and coordination of resources. As Steve told a Senate committee a few weeks before Daniel died, "the only way we can find a cure is by working together."[54]

The power of connecting people and groups together to solve complex problems quickly is a central focus of the Bill and Melinda Gates Foundation. Frustrated by the slow progress in producing an AIDS vaccine, the Gates Foundation provides funding only to researchers and research teams that share information and research findings. By requiring researchers to collaborate across labs, the foundation hopes to overcome the most significant obstacle that hinders efforts to find a vaccine: secrecy related to commercial interests and the desire to be the first to publish results in scientific journals. Says Dr. Nick Hellman, director of the foundation's HIV, TB, and Reproductive Health Initiative, "The whole field recognizes that in order to meet this humongous challenge, we have to change the way we work. . . . There have to be better networks and collaborations. [So] we require all grantees to collaborate across a spectrum of grants." By collaborating across groups and sharing information, formerly rival teams are able to build on each others' successes, avoid known pitfalls, and minimize redundancy. To promote collaboration and expedite the search for successful medical interventions, the Bill and Melinda Gates Foundation grants have brought together 16 research teams with a total of over 165 scientists from 19 countries. These teams are expected to fully collaborate by sharing data, findings, and other products of their research.[55]

The advantage of creating cross-team collaborations is illustrated by how quickly a worldwide team of researchers identified the deadly SARS virus, preventing what could have been a worldwide pandemic. Shortly after SARS began claiming lives in the Guangdong province in China in fall 2002, it was clear that SARS could become a global pandemic. By winter 2003, Dr. Klaus Stohr of the World Health Organization's influenza program created a collaboration among 12 labs worldwide with the mission of identifying the cause of SARS as quicky as possible. Dr. Stohr explained: "We needed people to share data and set aside Nobel Prize interests or their desire to publish articles in *Nature*." Within six months, the worldwide collaboration identified the deadly coronavirus as the cause of SARS, a discovery that helpcd put an end to the potential pandemic.[56]

Given the power of collaborating across teams, why is it often so difficult for different groups to work toward common goals? The roots of the difficulty in managing in-group/out-group relationships stem from our basic human needs to find meaning, to feel a sense of control and consistency, to belong, and to feel competent. Effective team leaders understand these human needs and develop strategies to help teams rise above their desire to focus internally at the expense of external connections that can help them be more successful.

MEANING   As human beings, we have a fundamental need to make sense of ourselves, the world, and our place in it. Our tendency to categorize our environment in terms of group memberships is a consequence of our need to make sense of the world. For example, we divide our work organizations into socially constructed professional groups such as engineers and accountants, hierarchical groups such as line workers and management, and functional groups such as production and marketing. Furthermore, we tend to see the world through the conceptual lenses provided by our groups, pay more attention to information that we believe is relevant to our group, and see our own group's goals as more important and positive than those of other groups.[57]

CONTROL AND CONSISTENCY   Categorizing our social world into groups gives us a sense of control, stability, and predictability in a complex and ambiguous environment. Without conceptual categories, we could not make sense of ourselves or others, nor could we take coordinated action with others. After all, Coca-Cola knows it is Cola-Cola because it is not Pepsi. Try to describe someone without using any categorizations (even eye color, height, and personality characteristics are based on socially approved categorizations). Imagine trying to organize and implement a project at work without using categorizations. Without our social categorizations, we would feel overwhelmed, confused, and paralyzed.

BELONGING   Because of our basic need to belong to a social group, we tend to identify strongly with the groups to which we belong and develop an emotional attachment to our group and our membership in it.[58] We are likely to see ourselves as more similar to people from our groups than to people from other groups;[59] are more likely to remember positive information and forget negative information about our in-groups;[60] and see members of out-groups in more homogeneous (e.g., "They're all alike."), stereotypical (e.g., "They all do this or that."), and negative ways (e.g., "They're less trustworthy or cooperative."[61]) than we see members of our own groups.[62]

COMPETENCE   Because we develop our identity in part from the groups to which we belong, we tend to define our personal success and failure partly in terms of our groups' successes and failures. Consequently, we want our groups to succeed and be viewed as competent by others. Furthermore, we develop a sense of responsibility for the status and success of our groups and thus are more likely to promote the interests of our groups[63] and help people from our groups.[64]

In short, our categorization of the world into social groups and our identification with our groups is positive because it helps us make sense of our social world and our place in it, gives us a sense of belonging, enables us to feel special and distinctive, and helps us take coordinated social action—all of which can increase our energy and involvement in tasks that we believe are relevant to our group. However, this categorization and identification becomes negative when it creates dysfunctional in-group dynamics and psychological barriers between groups that should be working together toward common organizational goals.[65]

For example, excessive in-group identification and cohesion can lead to isolation, conformity, overestimation of the in-group's competence (and underestimation of the out-group's competence), self-serving decisions, negative stereotyping and mistrust of outsiders, blindness to interdependencies with external individuals and groups, decreased communications with out-groups, and increased distortions of the communications that do take place.[66] These dynamics can lead to tunnel vision, moral lapses, groupthink, and other consequences that undermine individual, group, and organizational effectiveness. In short, teams that are overly focused internally and that do not build connections externally are unable to gain the information, resources, and support that are critical for solving complex problems quickly and effectively. Box 8-6 describes groupthink, one of the most well-known dysfunctional group processes that results from too much internal cohesion.

BOX 8-6   Groupthink: Symptoms and Solutions

Why is it that intelligent and competent individuals, when put in a group, can make terrible decisions? Researcher Irving Janis coined the term "groupthink" to refer to "the mode of thinking that persons engage in when concurrence seeking becomes so dominant in a cohesive in-group that it tends to override realistic appraisal of alternative courses of action."[67] In other words, individuals want so much to belong to a group and to maintain the cohesiveness of the group that they engage in behaviors designed to maintain cohesiveness rather than the critical thinking that can lead to high-quality decisions. Groups engaging in groupthink tend to:

- *Reinforce conformity.* They pressure group members who express disagreement to "get with the program."
- *Censor themselves.* Although group members may have concerns about the group's analysis or decisions, they don't express their concerns.
- *Create mindguards.* They shield the group or the group leaders from information or people who challenge the assumptions of the group.
- *Develop illusions of unanimity.* Because group members silence themselves and others in the group, they begin to share an illusion that everyone in the group agrees with the group's decisions.
- *Rationalize their decisions.* Because the group is invested in believing in the "rightness" of their decisions, they focus on data and arguments that support their position, and they minimize negative feedback or warnings from others.
- *Stereotype outsiders.* They develop negative stereotypes of outsiders so that they don't have to take the concerns of outsiders seriously.
- *Develop an unquestioned belief in the team's morality.* The group never questions the morality of their decisions. Indeed, they may justify their decisions on moral grounds.

BOX 8-6 *Continued*

- *Develop an illusion of invulnerability.* The group becomes overly optimistic about their capabilities and may take unreasonable risks.

These "concurrence-seeking" behaviors tend to increase when group members are under pressure to perform, such as when they are approaching deadlines or when they feel that a great deal is riding on their success. Some researchers argue that groupthink may have led to the decision to launch the Challenger space shuttle that failed less than two minutes after liftoff and killed all seven crew members in 1986.[68] Sadly, an investigation concluded that similar dynamics played a part in the Columbia disaster 17 years later in which all crew members died in 2003 as a consequence of damage from detached insulation foam. The 248-page investigative report asserted that "NASA's organizational culture had as much to do with this accident as the foam did." The report stated that NASA mission managers began to accept flaws in the shuttle system as normal and tended to ignore the fact that these flaws could result in a catastrophe. The report also blamed "reliance on past success as a substitute for sound engineering practice; organizational barriers that prevented effective communication of critical safety information and stifled differences of opinion, lack of integrated management across program elements; and the evolution of an informal chain of command and decision-making processes that operated outside the organization's rules." The report added "little by little, NASA was accepting more and more risk in order to stay on schedule."[69]

As a first step toward preventing groupthink, group members and leaders can learn to identify its symptoms: Group members may limit discussion to a few courses of action, fail to reexamine the desired course of action, fail to reexamine rejected alternatives, fail to consult experts or reject expert opinion that does not support the group's decision, filter out new information that is perceived as negative or threatening, and not develop contingency plans.[70]

Team leaders can take other steps to prevent groupthink. Team leaders should be aware of the intended and unintended consequences of their authority in the group. If they want honest opinions from team members, they may want to remove themselves from at least some of the meetings. When team leaders are at meetings, they should watch their body language and not state their preferences first. When they are not at meetings, they should keep personal staff who might filter information to a minimum. They should encourage team members to give them bad news by never "shooting the messenger." Instead, they should use three basic statements when hearing bad news: Can you tell me more? What do you think we should do? Thank you for bringing this to my attention.[71]

Alfred Sloan, Jr., who became president of General Motors in 1993 and continued on as Honorary Chairman of the Board until his death in 1966, was credited with saying the following when his senior team came to conclusions too quickly: "I take it that we are all in complete agreement with the decision here. . . . Then I propose we postpone further discussion of this matter until our next meeting to give ourselves time to develop disagreement and perhaps gain some understanding of what the decision is all about."[72]

In addition, team leaders should teach team members about groupthink and have team members assess their own potential for groupthink. They also should encourage team members to assign everyone the role of "critical evaluator," take warning signals seriously, seek outside opinions, consider worst case scenarios and develop contingency plans, and hold second-chance meetings to revisit decisions at a later date, if possible. They may also consider using outside consultants to facilitate meetings.

WHAT CAN A LEADER DO TO PROMOTE COOPERATION ACROSS TEAMS? The team leader's task is to help the team balance its need for internal cohesion and external integration. Team leaders must make sure that the team is both connected to and protected from external influences. For example, too little external communication can result in narrow-mindedness. Too much external communication can result in information

If a house be divided against itself, that house cannot stand.
MARK 3:25

overload. Too few external relationships can result in lack of support. Too many external relationships can interfere with a team's ability to complete its work in a timely manner. Effective team leaders help team members achieve the delicate balance between internal cohesion and external integration in several ways.

Start with Yourself: Clearly Demonstrate That You're a Boundary-Spanner Are you modeling behavior that promotes cooperation among various groups? Do you work cooperatively with leaders and members of other groups? Do you use language that says, "We're all in this together?" Notably, research has found that the use of words that suggest in-group or out-group status (such as "us" and "them") may perpetuate inter-group bias and conflict.[73]

Articulate a Common Vision That Inspires Interdependence Have you shared a common vision in a way that helps team members understand that, although their team's goals may be specific to the team, their goals overlap with those of other individuals and teams? Have you explained how connecting to other individuals and teams can help the team achieve their goals with higher quality, in less time, while using fewer resources?

Set Clear Expectations Have you clearly articulated your expectation that the groups will work together? Have you had each group clarify what it needs from other groups to do its work and what it can give other groups so that they can do their work?

Manage Communication and Coordination Across Groups Have you helped the team develop a clear strategy for communicating with people and groups external to the team so that they can obtain timely and useful strategic and political information, coordinate resources and activities, and build goodwill with people and groups whose support is needed? Research suggests that successful teams do not necessarily communicate more often with outsiders than do less effective teams, but they do have a clearer strategy regarding what they are trying to accomplish with their communication. In short, it's the quality, not only the quantity, of communication across team boundaries that enhances a team's performance.[74]

Promote Flexibility Coordinating resources, activities, and schedules with external people and groups requires flexibility. Have you encouraged team members to rethink and change their taken-for-granted routines, to modify normal division of labor, and to break down traditional boundaries between the team and outsiders? For example, researchers Deborah Ancona and Henrik Bresman found that the most effective teams alternated between connecting externally and then focusing internally to execute the ideas they learned through their connections. Specifically, they found that the most successful teams had an initial period of exploration in which they connected to others to gain as much information, resources, and support that they could. Then the teams shifted from connecting externally to focusing primarily (though not necessarily only) internally to use they learned to create their products or services. Then the teams shifted back to connecting externally to export their ideas outside of the team.[75]

Reward Cooperation Have you identified ways to encourage groups to invest in each other's success by rewarding cooperation? Profit-sharing or tying a percentage of bonuses to customer satisfaction or organizational performance (revenue and profit) can motivate different groups to work together.[76]

Have Teams Spend Time Together Have you identified ways that members of different groups can spend time together informally as well as formally? This can reduce bias and misunderstandings, increase positive feelings, and enhance cooperation if managed carefully. Note, however, that research suggests that having teams spend time together can backfire if groups already have animosity toward each other. In such cases, getting the groups together can fuel rather than reduce existing ignorance and hostility.[77] To encourage mutual respect and cooperation rather than fuel conflict, team leaders should be sure that common events are designed to promote feelings of equality among groups and emphasize the different—but equally valuable—expertise and resources that each group brings to the common tasks.[78] Shared positive experiences that can enhance cooperation include common training, meetings that are structured to maximize cooperation, and celebrations of efforts and victories.

Change Physical Layout   Have you considered changing the layout of a work site so that the teams can work more closely together? One study found that organizations that had physical layouts that enabled production employees from different areas "to see each other's work had cycle times 4.4 times faster than those with layouts that didn't. . . . This kind of layout . . . allows workers to share tasks easily, to observe when others are in trouble, and to offer assistance without letting their own performance deteriorate. . . . [It also enables employees from different areas] to analyze problems together, build prototypes, and discuss their individual and group-inspired ideas."[79]

Redefine Boundaries   Effective team leaders create new categorizations that integrate, rather than isolate or divide, groups that should be working together.[80] There are several ways to do this. Encourage employees to identify with the organization as a whole rather than with a function or department. Create a common enemy or external threat to help groups feel that they must combine their efforts to overcome this enemy or threat. Be forewarned, however, that creating a common enemy can backfire if the groups begin to overreact to the perceived enemy and focus their energy on beating the enemy rather than achieving their goals (e.g., meeting customers' needs).

Create Boundary-Spanning Roles in the Team   Teams that have team members who consider boundary-spanning as part of their roles and responsibilities tend to perform better than those that don't.[81] Boundary spanners tend to be high-performing team members who "communicate more often overall and with people outside their specialty."[82] Effective boundary spanners take on several roles, including the scout who gathers information and resources; the sentry who controls the flow of information and resources that goes out of the team; the ambassador who connects the team to relevant individuals and groups; and the guard who buffers the team from unwanted interruptions, premature judgment, and other influences that could slow the team down or take it off track.[83] These roles are summarized in Figure 8-2.

The main point to remember from this section is this: Team leaders create a context that brings out the best in their teams. They do so by helping their teams create a sense of identity as a real team, providing a supportive work context, creating an enabling task design, providing appropriate and well-timed coaching, encouraging positive social interactions and good will, and connecting the team to external people and groups who are relevant to the team's success.

THE TEAM LIFE CYCLE

Teams, regardless of their task, duration, or member characteristics, tend to go through predictable stages of development.[84] Researchers Jessica Lipnack and Jeffrey Stamps explain: "A team is first and foremost a process: It has a beginning, a

Failing organizations are usually over-managed and under-led.
—WARREN BENNIS,
American scholar, organizational consultant and author

Scout: Gets Information and Resources	Ambassador: Gets Support
•Sees through perspectives of key stakeholders (needs, wants, concerns, political issues) •Brings information and resources into the team	•Communicates upwards •Links to stakeholders'goals •Builds allies •Gets feedback •Manages impressions

Sentry: Filters Information	Guard: Protects the Team
•Screens information for relevance •Translates external information to make it useful to the team •Buffers team from distractions, including political agendas that can derail the team	•Protects against adversaries •Determines legitimacy and impact of external requests •Gives out legitimate information

FIGURE 8-2   Boundary-Spanning Behaviors that Manage Information, Resources, and Relationships
Source: Adapted from Ancona, Debra, and David Caldwell. 1992. "Bridging the Boundary: External Activity in Performance in Organizational Teams." *Administrative Science Quarterly,* 634–665.

middle, and an end. No team springs to life full-blown and none lives forever. Words such as conception, gestation, birth, childhood, adolescence, adulthood, midlife crisis, and old age all apply to a team's life."[85]

Each stage presents team members with particular challenges to be overcome and opportunities to grow. Some teams move slowly and tediously through the various stages, struggling to surmount obstacles and take advantage of opportunities. Other teams move relatively easily through the various stages, although struggling and getting stuck is common even in the most effective teams. Team leaders can help move the team successfully through each stage if they understand the emotions and behaviors associated with each stage, the impact of these emotions and behaviors on team effectiveness, and how and when to intervene so that they help rather than hinder team progress.

The most well-known theory of group development is based on the assumption that teams tend to go through five stages: forming, storming, norming, performing, and adjourning.[86] This theory, like many others, assumes that the passing of time significantly affects the way team members react emotionally and behaviorally toward the task, each other, and the leader. These stages are summarized in Figure 8-3.

Forming

Forming occurs when people first come together as a group. This is the most critical period in a team's life. Indeed, a National Traffic Safety Board study of "the circumstances in which cockpit crews were more likely to get into trouble" found that "73% of all incidences occurred on a crew's first day of flying together." Teams are most vulnerable during the very early stages of their life because they don't yet know each other and haven't yet created norms that help them

FIGURE 8-3 Stages of Team Development

Forming	Storming	Norming	Performing	Adjourning
Defining Characteristic: Pseudoteam	Defining Characteristic: Resistance	Defining Characteristic: Realistic appraisal of task, each other, and leader	Defining Characteristic: Task focus and productivity	Defining Characteristic: Closure and transition
Emotions: Ambivalence and anxiety	Emotions: Disillusionment, anger, and conflict	Emotions: Increased optimism and energy	Emotions: High energy, increased pride in their work, and confidence in each other	Emotions: Sadness and relief
Team Goal: Sense-making, dependence on leader	Team Goal: Resist task, each other, and leader	Team Goal: Create norms that enhance performance	Team Goal: Productivity and feedback on their efforts	Team Goal: Transfer learnings
Leader's Goals: • Get the team off to a good start. • Move team from dependence on leader to interdependence among each other.	Leader's Goals: • Channel team's emotional energy toward productive ends. • Help team members develop a realistic understanding of the task, each other, and the leader. • Make sure team members have the skills and resources they need to accomplish their task. • Continue to encourage interdependence among team members.	Leader's Goals: • Encourage team to focus on team goals and norms. • Provide resources team needs to do its work. • Stay out of team's way as much as possible.	Leader's Goals: • Keep team focused on goals. • Provide resources team needs to do its work. • Remind team of hazards of too much cohesiveness. • Connect the team to and protect the team from external individuals and groups. • Stay out of the team's way as much as possible.	Leader's Goals: • Help team get closure. • Transfer learning to new settings. Transfer relationships to new setting.

Adapted from: Tuckman, Bruce W., & Jensen, Mary Ann C. (1977). 'Stages of Small Group Development Revisited,' *Group and Organizational Studies, 2,* 419–427.

create predictable routines that enable them work together well (and safely in the case of airplane crews). In another study, researchers found that airplane crews that had spent several days working together, despite being fatigued from the long work hours, made fewer mistakes than crews of rested pilots who had just started working together. The benefits of experience in working together outweighed the costs of fatigue.[87]

During the early stage, team members must get to know each other, understand the tasks before them, figure out how to work together, develop a shared knowledge and skill base, understand their knowledge and skill gaps, develop mutually supportive relationships with each other, identify who they need to reach out to beyond the team members, and make sense of the leader's role. Because the dynamics that occur during this stage often set the tone for later stages, team members and leaders must pay careful attention to what early decisions are made and the processes by which they are made. Researchers have found that teams that develop *early* the positive belief they will be successful working together tend to be more effective later in the team's life. Specifically, when team leaders take time early in the team's life to build trust, effective communication processes, cooperative behavior among team members, and early successes, they are likely to create an upward spiral that propels the team toward continued success.[88]

At this stage, team members tend to be anxious and ambivalent about the potential benefits and costs of being part of the team. They are often unclear about the task, unsure of what obstacles lie ahead, and uncertain of their individual and collective abilities to achieve the team goals. Consequently, they tend to look to the leader to tell them what to do and how to do it. As team members will soon realize, this is a false hope because it is they and not the team leader who must figure out how to accomplish the tasks before them. One of the leader's main challenges at this stage is to help team members understand that the leader's job is to give team members the direction and resources they need to manage their own team process and solve their own problems. At this early stage, team members don't yet have enough information about the project to determine a comprehensive strategy, but they can develop a plan for outlining the situation; developing a preliminary plan of action; and identifying the resources they have within their team and for gathering the information, resources, and support they need from outside the team to explore the situation and then use what they learn to develop a realistic and more comprehensive strategy once they gain the information they need.

Furthermore, team members usually don't know each other very well at this stage. Consequently, they are unable to accurately assess each other's potential contributions, understand each other's intentions, or predict each other's behaviors. Team members' influence in the team tends to be based on stereotypes of outside roles (e.g., engineer or sales representative) rather than the variety of talents they bring to the team. They scrutinize the words and behaviors of team members and leaders carefully to look for cues that will help them make sense of the situation, although they often misinterpret those cues because of their lack of experience with each other. Misunderstandings are common, and discussions tend to be superficial, polite, and guarded. Furthermore, team members tend to ignore or minimize problems in an effort to promote team harmony, a decision that is likely to backfire later in the team's life if not addressed early on. Although the team may appear cohesive, it is a fragile cohesion based on what consultants Jon Katzenbach and Douglas Smith characterize as "pseudo relationships."[89]

Team members try to figure out whether they can trust the leader (Does the leader care about us? Is the leader competent?) and team members (Can I depend on other team members?), as well as the role they will play in the group (Will I belong? Will I have influence in this group?). They also are concerned about practical matters (How much time is this going to take? How hard am I going to have to work? What are the standards for performance? How will our work be measured?). However, they may not make these concerns explicit. Simply stated, team members try to figure out whether this is a team to which they want to belong.

The team leader's role at this stage is to get the team off to a good start by providing direction, structure, and resources and move the team from dependence on the leader to interdependence with each other. To this end, team leaders should do the following:

- Provide a clear, meaningful, and engaging direction with a sense of urgency.
- Encourage the group to develop their own purpose that is consistent with those of the organization, as well as SMART goals that will help them focus and assess their progress.
- Set an expectation of high performance standards and develop clear performance measures (quality standards, milestones, deadlines) because teams encounter problems when these are missing or constantly changing.[90]
- Give team members a chance to get to know each other, and ensure that everyone feels included (e.g., make sure each person feels he or she has something of value to offer the team and is respected by other team members).
- Provide a task design as described in the previous section that includes skill variety, task identity, task significance, autonomy, and feedback that is built into the team's work.
- Guide team members in their efforts to develop work processes (e.g., decision-making processes, internal and external communication) that will help them manage their task and relationship processes.
- Provide necessary resources (materials and equipment, information, education, and access to external people and groups who can help the team).
- Help team members realize that any ambivalence or anxiety that they feel is normal and that they have the direction, talent, and resources they need to succeed.
- Explain the team leader's role so that team members know what they can and cannot expect from the team leader.

Storming

No one ever said that becoming a team would be easy, and the storming stage proves it. This stage tends to be characterized by avoidance of the task, conflict among team members, and disillusionment with the leader. As team members become overwhelmed with the workload and upcoming deadlines, they may start questioning the validity of the task. As team members get to know each other better, personality conflicts may surface (e.g., the honeymoon period may be over). As team members begin to realize that the leader cannot solve their problems for them, they may become increasingly critical of the leader. Not all teams go through a storming stage, but those that do can come out of this stage even stronger if it is well managed.

Team members may express their resistance to the task, each other, and the leader both overtly and covertly. They may psychologically withdraw from the group (e.g., come to meetings late or miss meetings), question each other's and the leader's qualifications, become defensive, and form subgroup alliances. Although it may seem as though little is being accomplished, working through this conflict and developing a realistic (rather than overly optimistic or pessimistic) understanding of the task, each other, and the leader is the primary work of the team at this time.

The team leader's goal is not to eliminate the storming stage but to channel the emotional energy toward moving the team forward; help the team develop a realistic and appreciative understanding of the task, each other, and the leader; make sure that team members have the skills and resources they need to accomplish their task; and continue to move the team from dependence on the leader to dependence on each other. There are several ways that team leaders can help the team move through this stage:

- Encourage team members to focus on the team's purpose.
- Remind team members that, although the leader can't do the team's task for them, he or she can give the team the resources—training, information, and materials—that they need to accomplish the task.
- Encourage team members to use their emotional energy toward refining the task, creating norms, and developing open and candid communication.
- Encourage team members to develop communication, conflict, and decision-making strategies that can help them come to thoughtful agreements and decisions all team members can agree to support.
- Encourage team members to break the task into small steps so that they don't feel overwhelmed.
- Set up small wins so that team members feel a sense of accomplishment and movement toward completing the task, and remember that high-performing teams tend to have at least a 6:1 ratio of positive to negative interactions.

Norming

For teams that go through a storming stage, successfully passing through this stage and enter the norming stage realize the validity of the statement "What doesn't kill you can make you stronger." After debating and clarifying priorities, roles, and responsibilities, team members are now better able to create realistic norms. This stage tends to be characterized by increasing positive emotions, realistic optimism, and increasing group cohesion, particularly if team members have overcome a few hurdles and experienced some small wins together. Team members now have a more realistic view of the team task, each other, and the team leader. As team members begin to feel more familiar with each other and competent as a team, they focus less on interpersonal challenges and more on task challenges. They now have explicit norms for working together, disagreements are less likely to feel personal, and interactions become easier and more predictable. Team members may also develop a sense of humor and a vocabulary that's unique to the team. Rather than seeing each other as threats, they begin to feel more cohesive and see threats as external to the group (such as competitors).

At this stage, the team leader can help the team most by making sure that the team stays focused on its goals; encouraging the team to develop a performance strategy based on what they've learned about each other, the task, the opportunities, and the constraints; providing the resources the team needs to do its work and removing obstacles; and increasingly staying out of the team's way so that the team can determine how to best use their talents and resources to achieve the team's goals. Specifically, team leaders should practice the following:

- Show faith in the team's abilities.
- Foster commitment and interdependence by having team members spend formal and informal time together.

- Encourage the team to form norms that foster creativity, critical thinking, mindful decision making, and calculated risk taking now that team members are feeling increasingly secure with the leader, each other, and the task.
- Intervene directly in the team's work only if it is clear that team members cannot handle the problem themselves.
- Provide feedback, recognize important milestones, and acknowledge/reward successes so that team members see their progress.
- Provide opportunities for the team to reflect on their performance and learn from their successes and failures.
- Confront inadequate performance.

Performing

This is a high-energy and productive stage when the team begins to see significant payoffs from their shared history and the work norms that they developed. Team members know what they can and cannot expect from each other, are better able to anticipate each other's behaviors, and are able to coordinate with each other more easily and with less discussion. It is a time of increased creativity and confidence in the team's abilities. Team members take increasing pride in their work and become increasingly focused on getting results. They want to be able to measure the results of their efforts so that they can take necessary corrective actions quickly and effectively. Team members are likely to feel challenged rather than threatened by hurdles, and solutions come more quickly.

Some research suggests that a significant increase in performance tends to come around the midpoint of the team's life. Researcher Connie Gersick studied different project teams over several years. She concluded that, regardless of whether the project team lasted three months or three years, the teams tended to experience periods of inertia and struggle early in their lives followed by a "shift into high gear" and a "major jump in progress" around the midpoint of the team's life.[91] This midpoint was followed by a relatively smooth work period in which the teams felt the "consequences of its own past choices about how members would work together, about the amount of effort they had invested, and about how well they had attended to external requirements."

At this stage, the leader should continue to stay out of the team's way as much as possible; provide the resources it needs to do its work; focus on helping the team manage the boundaries between the team and external people and groups; provide appropriate positive feedback, and remind team members that their increased cohesion and confidence can lead to groupthink, particularly if team members begin to become insular and overconfident, suppress critical thinking, or make decisions that serve the team needs more than the needs of the organization.[92] Specifically, the team leader should:

- Continue to provide feedback on performance.
- Acknowledge when the team reaches important milestones.
- Remind the team of the potential negative consequences of excessive group cohesiveness.
- Revitalize the team by reminding team members of the greater purpose, providing "fresh facts and information," and connecting the team to people who can offer new perspectives and useful support.[93]
- Protect the team from too many external influences and distractions that could take them away from their team task.
- Give the team credit and visibility for their collective efforts.
- Help the team celebrate successes.

Adjourning

Sooner or later, most teams break up. Endings, like beginnings, must be carefully managed. When endings are well managed, team members feel a sense of accomplishment, reflect on the benefits of teamwork, transfer their team learning to future work settings, and solidify relationships with each other for future mutual benefit. When endings are poorly managed, the team experience may quickly fade into the background, disappointments may be remembered more than accomplishments, important learnings may be forgotten, and potential future relationships may be lost.

The team leader's goal at this stage is to help team members manage the psychological transition as they leave the team and help team members transfer learnings to new settings. To help team members manage endings, the team leader should:

- Clearly identify the team's accomplishments and what will happen with their work products.
- Relate these accomplishments to the greater organizational purpose.
- Provide opportunities to reflect on what lessons were learned from successes and failures that are applicable to other settings.
- Provide opportunities for team members to see each other as future resources.
- Celebrate.

MAKING SENSE OF TEAM LIFE CYCLE THEORIES Remember that theories of the team life cycle are just that—theories. The boundaries between one stage and another are, of course, not as clear as the theories make them appear. Not all teams will experience all of the the emotions and behaviors described in these theories or pass through all stages as described.[94] Furthermore, members of short-term project teams and ongoing teams may react differently to the task, each other, and the leader over time. Yet team life cycle theories are useful because they encourage us to view team life as a process, identify important psychological needs and milestones in a team's life, anticipate some of the emotions and behaviors that may affect a team's productivity, and design interventions that are appropriate for the team's changing needs.

CONCLUSION

Creating and managing high-performing teams is as much an art as it is a science. There is no magic formula that will guarantee team success, nor is there one best way to lead a team. Richard Hackman explains:

> There is no one best way to accomplish [team effectiveness], nor, despite volumes of research on the topics, is there any one leadership style that is optimal for coaching and helping work teams. . . . Coaching a group, like teaching a class, is done best when the leader exploits his or her own personality and style to get the lessons across. An active, energetic leader is likely to behave actively and energetically with his or her team, whereas a person who is generally soft-spoken and relaxed will tend to use that style. We would not have it any other way: When a leader tries to adopt a coaching style that is at variance with his or her personal style, leadership effectiveness inevitably suffers.[95]

In addition to leveraging your own style, there are several things that you can do to increase the probability that teams will succeed. You can remember that teams are not appropriate for all tasks, nor are they the cure-all for an organization's woes. However, teams are the best way to solve complex tasks that no one person can solve alone. You also can remember that high-performing teams are not blessed with flawless team members and leaders, nor do high-performing teams have perfect conditions in which to do their work. Rather, high-performing teams are able to rise to the challenges they face, have the persistence and skills to overcome obstacles, and leave the organization better off than it was before.

High-performing teams are able to do so because they have leadership that creates conditions that inspire and enable them to do their best work. Their leaders know when to step in and help the team and when to stay out of the team's way, as well as when to connect the team externally and when to protect the team. In short, teams are best served by leaders who have the knowledge, patience, and emotional maturity to do what's right for the team rather than react impulsively.[96]

Most important, keep in mind that leading teams is an ongoing process, not a one-shot deal. Recognize that the best things that you can do for the team are to help it get off to a good start; provide direction, structure, and resources; help the team manage relationships with external people and groups; carefully plan the type and timing of interventions; and then stay out of the team's way as much as possible. In spirit, effective team leaders live by the words of the Chinese philosopher Lao Tzu: "Leaders are best when people barely know that they lead. Good leaders talk little but when the work is done, the aim fulfilled, all others will say, 'We did this ourselves'."

Chapter Summary

A team is made up of individuals interacting independently to achieve common organizational goals. Furthermore, all teams share the following: clear boundaries, common tasks, differentiated member roles, autonomy, dependence on others, and collective responsibility.

The differences between a work group and a work team are these: Team members develop a purpose that is consistent with the organization's purpose but specific to the team members' interests and skills; team members have a greater sense of ownership of their work, develop a sense of mutual responsibility, and believe they are working for each other as well as for the team leader and organization; team members have more say over how they do their work and expect a greater degree of personal learning and fulfillment from the team; team members don't see each other as interchangeable or easily replaceable; team leaders spend less time directing the team's work and more time creating a context that enables team members to do their work.

Effective teams meet three criteria: (1) The team must consistently produce high-quality results. (2) The team must promote the personal growth needs and well-being of team members. (3) The team must grow and learn as a performing unit.

Team synergy occurs when the collective efforts of team members create output that exceeds the potential of the most capable team member. This increase in productivity of the team over the individual is called process gains. Process losses occur when teams misuse individual resources such that the team's output is less than that which individuals could have achieved on their own.

High-performing teams that achieve synergy are built on five foundations: a clear, engaging purpose that mobilizes action; clear performance goals and measures that encourage high standards; highly skilled people who add value; carefully developed work processes that enable team members to work together productively; and ample opportunities for team members to practice working together and learn from their successes and failures.

The most important task of the team leader is to create a work context that inspires and enables the team to do its work rather than directly intervening in the team's day-to-day work.

To create a context for high performance, team leaders should focus on five key areas: investing in personal development; providing team members with a supportive environment (e.g., resources and information); creating a work context that inspires and enables high performance (clear and engaging goals, a well-designed task, appropriate and well-timed coaching); encouraging effective social relations; and connecting the team externally.

A well-designed team task has the following five characteristics: skill variety, task identity, task significance, autonomy, and feedback.

High-performing teams tend to have at least a 6:1 ratio of positive/negative interactions (though not greater than an 11:1 ratio of positive/negative interactions because some critique and conflict is necessary for teams to develop a realistic and well-rounded view of situations). Team members also balance advocating for their own ideas and seeking out the ideas of other team members. In addition, high-performing teams balance building internal cohesion and connecting externally.

Groupthink occurs when team members' desire for belonging and cohesiveness leads to excessive concurrence seeking that overrides their ability to think critically and make effective decisions.

The team leader's task is to help the team balance its need for internal cohesion and external integration. Team leaders must make sure that the team is both connected to and protected from external influences. To manage cooperation across groups, team leaders should understand how their own attitudes and behaviors inspire or inhibit effective relationships across groups; articulate a common vision that inspires interdependence across groups; set clear expectations that the groups will work together; help the team develop strategies for communicating with external individuals and groups; reward team members' efforts to work with other groups; have teams spend time together, but be sure to emphasize equality and the expertise that each team brings to the task (otherwise, the time teams spend together can make relationships worse); change the physical layout in ways that promote interaction across teams; redefine boundaries by using language that integrates, rather than divides or isolates, teams; and create boundary-spanning roles in the team.

Boundary-spanners are high-performing individuals who communicate extensively with people and groups outside the team. Effective boundary-spanners engage in several activities, including gathering information and resources; controlling the flow of information and resources that go out of the team; connecting the team to relevant individuals and groups; and buffering the team from unwanted interruptions, premature judgment, and other influences that could slow the team down or take it off track.

Research suggests that teams tend to go through five stages of development: forming, storming, norming, performing, and adjourning. Each of these stages presents opportunities and hurdles for the team that the team leader can help the team manage. In particular, each stage has implications for team members' attitudes and behaviors toward the task, each other, and the team leader.

Effective leaders carefully manage the type and timing of interventions. They know when to intervene in the day-to-day activities of the team and when to stay out of the team's way. Team leaders can best manage the type and timing of interventions when they understand the team life cycle. Effective team leaders realize that creating high-performing teams is an ongoing process, not a one-shot deal.

Food for Thought

1. What is the most useful thing you learned in this chapter, and why?
2. Based on the strategies for managing teams described in this chapter, what is the most important thing you can do to increase your own effectiveness as a team member or team leader and the effectiveness of your teams? Practice this behavior, and note any benefits and progress you make.
3. Think about a team that you belonged to that you felt was particularly successful. What characteristics made it successful? How did you feel? What did you accomplish? What lessons can you take from this experience to become a better team member or leader?
4. Think about a team that you belonged to and felt was unsuccessful or a waste of time. What characteristics made it unsuccessful? How did you feel? What did you accomplish? What lessons can you take from this experience to become a better team member or leader?
5. Think about your most effective team leader. What are the five most important things he or she did that led to his or her effectiveness?

6. Think about your least effective team leader. What are the five most troublesome things he or she did that led to his or her ineffectiveness?

7. Take the Job Diagnostic Survey in Box 8-7 at the end of this chapter based on your current or previous job. Based on your survey results, would you say that your job is (or was) high or low on motivating potential? In which areas did you rate your job the highest (e.g., skill variety, task identity, task significance, autonomy, feedback)? In which areas did you rate your job the lowest? What can you do to increase the motivating potential of your job (or what could you have done)? What can your boss do to increase the motivating potential of your job (or what could your boss have done)?

8. In this chapter, you learned that high-performing teams have a ratio of at least 6 positive interactions for each negative interaction, a balance of advocacy (expressing one's own ideas) and inquiry (seeking out the ideas of others), and a balance between building internal cohesion and connecting externally. Observe a team and determine how the team is doing based on each of these three characteristics: positivity/negativity, advocacy/inquiry, and internal cohesion/external connection. Based on your assessment, what are the top three things this team could to enhance its performance?

9. Search for information about the BP oil spill disaster in the U.S. Gulf in 2010. What information can you find that gives insight into the decision-making processes and group/leadership dynamics that led to this disaster? What could BP have done to prevent the disaster? What lessons did you learn that will help you become a better team leader and decision maker?

10. Have you ever been involved in a team that engaged in groupthink? Describe the situation, the symptoms, and the consequences. What could the team leader and team members have done to prevent groupthink?

BOX 8-7 Job Diagnostic Survey

Richard Hackman and Greg Oldham developed a self-report instrument for managers to use in diagnosing their work environment. The first step in calculating the "motivating potential score" (MPS) of your job is to complete the following questionnaire.

1. Use the scales below to indicate whether each statement is an accurate or inadequate description of your present or most recent job. After completing the instrument, use the scoring key to compute a total score for each of the core job characteristics.

5 = Very descriptive
4 = Mostly descriptive
3 = Somewhat descriptive
2 = Mostly nondescriptive
1 = Very nondescriptive

_____ 1. I have almost complete responsibility for deciding how and when the work is to be done.

_____ 2. I have a chance to do a number of different tasks, using a wide variety of different skills and talents.

_____ 3. I do a complete task from start to finish. The results of my efforts are clearly visible and identifiable.

_____ 4. What I do affects the well-being of other people in very important ways.

_____ 5. My manager provides me with constant feedback about how I am doing.

_____ 6. The work itself provides me with information about how well I am doing.

_____ 7. I make insignificant contributions to the final product or service.*

_____ 8. I get to use a number of complex skills on this job.

_____ 9. I have very little freedom in deciding how the work is to be done.*

_____ 10. Just doing the work provides me with opportunities to figure out how well I am doing.

_____ 11. The job is quite simple and repetitive.*

_____ 12. My supervisors or coworkers rarely give me feedback on how well I am doing the job.*

_____ 13. What I do is of little consequence to anyone else.*

_____ 14. My job involves doing a number of different tasks.

_____ 15. Supervisors let us know how well they think we are doing.

_____ 16. My job is arranged so that I do not have a chance to do an entire piece of work from beginning to end.*

_____ 17. My job does not allow me an opportunity to use discretion or participate in decision making.*

_____ 18. The demands of my job are highly routine and predictable.*

_____ 19. My job provides few clues about whether I'm performing adequately.*

_____ 20. My job is not very important to the company's survival.*
_____ 21. My job gives me considerable freedom in doing the work.
_____ 22. My job provides me with the chance to finish completely any work I start.
_____ 23. Many people are affected by the job I do.

2. Scoring Key:
   Skill variety (SV) (items #2, 8, 11*, 14, 18*) = ___ /5 = ___
   Task identity (TI) (items #3, 7*, 16*, 22) = ___ /4 = ___
   Task significance (TS) (items #4, 13*, 20*, 23) = ___ /4 = ___
   Autonomy (AU) (items #1, 9*, 17*, 21) = ___ /4 = ___
   Feedback (FB) (items #5, 6, 10, 12*, 15, 19*) = ___ /6 = ___
   (Note: For the items with asterisks, subtract your score from 6.)
   Total the numbers for each characteristic and divide by the number of items to get an average score.

3. Now you are ready to calculate the MPS by using the following formula:

$$\text{Motivating Potential Score (MPS)} = \frac{SV + TI + TS}{3} \times AU \times FB$$

MPS scores range from 1 to 125.

4. You can compare your job characteristics with those of a classmate or with norms that your instructor has. Is the MPS of your job high, average, or low?

5. What could be done to increase the motivating potential of your job?

Source: J. Richard Hackman and Greg R. Oldham, _Work Redesign_ (adapted from pp. 80, 81, 90, and 303–306) © 1980 by Addison-Wesley Publishing Company, Inc. Reprinted by permission of Addison-Wesley Longman, Inc.

Endnotes

1. Dumaine, Brian. 1990. "Who Needs a Boss?" _Fortune_. May 7: 52–56.
2. Ancona, Deborah, and Henrik Bresman. 2007. _XTeams: How to Build Teams That Lead, Innovate and Succeed_. Watertown, MA: Harvard Business School Press; Hackman, J. R. 2002. _Leading Teams: Setting the Stage for Great Performances_. Watertown, MA: Harvard Business Press.
3. Labich, Kenneth. 1996. "Elite Teams." _Fortune_. February 19: 90–99.
4. Sinclair, Amanda. 1992. "The Tyranny of a Team Ideology." _Organizational Studies_, 13: 611–626.
5. Ibid.
6. Robinson, Sandra, and Anne M. O'Leary-Kelly. 1998. "Monkey See, Monkey Do: The Influence of Work Groups on the Antisocial Behavior of Employees." _Academy of Management Journal_, 41(6): 658–672.
7. Gilley, Ann, Jerry Gilley, C. William McConnell, and Abigail Veliquette. 2010. "The Competencies Used by Effective Managers to Build Teams: An Empirical Study." _Advances in Developing Human Resources_, 12(1): 29–45.

8. Hackman, J. Richard. 1990. _Groups That Work (and Those That Don't): Creating Conditions for Effective Teamwork_. San Francisco, CA: Jossey-Bass.
9. Lipnack, Jessica, and Jeffrey Stamps. 1997. _Virtual Teams: Reaching across Space, Time, and Organizations with Technology_. New York: John Wiley.
10. Alderfer, Clayton. 1983. "Intergroup Relations and Organizations." In Hackman, J. Richard, Edward Lawler, and Lyman Porter (eds.). _Perspectives on Behavior in Organizations_. New York: McGraw-Hill; Hackman, J. Richard. 1990. _Groups That Work (and Those That Don't): Creating Conditions for Effective Teamwork_. San Francisco, CA: Jossey-Bass; Hackman, J. Richard. 1987. "The Design of Work Teams." In Jay W. Lorsche (ed.). _Handbook of Organizational Behavior_. Upper Saddle River, NJ: Prentice Hall. 1987.
11. Katzenback, Jon, and Douglas K. Smith. 1993. _The Wisdom of Teams: Creating the High-Performance Organization_. New York: HarperBusiness.
12. Leavitt, Harold, and Jean Lipman-Bluman. 1995. "Hot Groups." _Harvard Business Review_. July–August: 109–116.

13. Hackman, J. Richard. 1990. *Groups That Work (and Those That Don't): Creating Conditions for Effective Teamwork*. San Francisco: Jossey-Bass.

14. Senge, Peter. 1990. *The Fifth Discipline: The Art and Practice of the Learning Organization*. New York: Doubleday.

15. Lancaster, Hal. 1997. "That Team Spirit Can Lead Your Career to New Victories." *Wall Street Journal*. January 14: B1.

16. Bennis, Warren, and Patricia Ward Biederman. 1997. *Organizing Genius: The Secrets of Creative Collaboration*. Reading, MA: Addison-Wesley Publishing Company.

17. Labich, Kenneth. 1996. "Elite Teams." *Fortune*. February 19: 90–99.

18. Lancaster, Hal. 1997. "That Team Spirit Can Lead Your Career to New Victories." *Wall Street Journal*. January 14: B1.

19. Edmonson, Amy. 1999. "Psychological Safety and Learning Behavior in Work Teams." *Administrative Science Quarterly*, 44(2): 350–383.

20. Barsade, Sigel. 2002. "The Ripple Effect: Emotional Contagion and Its Influence on Group Behavior. *Administrative Science Quarterly*, 47: 644–675; Losada, Marcial, and Emily Heaphy. 2004. "The Role of Positivity and Connectivity in the Performance of Business Teams." *American Behavioral Scientist*, 47(6): 740–765.

21. Rapaport, Richard. 1993. "To Build a Winning Team: An Interview with Head Coach Bill Walsh." *Harvard Business Review*. January/February: 110–120.

22. Caminiti, Susan. 1995. "What Team Leaders Need to Know." *Fortune*. February 20: 93–100.

23. Dirks, Kurt. 2002. "Trust in Leadership: Meta-Analytic Findings and Implications for Research and Practice." *Journal of Applied Psycyohology*, 87(4): 611–628.

24. Ibid.

25. Hackman, J. Richard. 1990. *Groups That Work (and Those That Don't): Creating Conditions for Effective Teamwork*. San Francisco, CA: Jossey-Bass.

26. Bennis, Warren, and Patricia Ward Biederman. 1997. *Organizing Genius: The Secrets of Creative Collaboration*. New York: Addison-Wesley.

27. Wageman, Ruth, Colin Fisher, and Richard Hackman. 2009. "Leading Teams when the Time Is Right: Finding the Best Moments to Act." *Organizational Dynamics*, 38(3): 192–203; Hackman, J. R. 2002. *Leading Teams: Setting the Stage for Great Performances*. Watertown, MA: Harvard Business Press.

28. Ibid.

29. Hackman, J. Richard. 2002. "New Rules for Team Building." *Optimize Magazine*. July: 50–62.

30. Hackman, J. Richard. 1990. *Groups That Work (and Those That Don't): Creating Conditions for Effective Teamwork*. San Francisco, CA: Jossey-Bass; Katzenback, Jon, and Douglas K. Smith. 1993. *The Wisdom of Teams: Creating the High-Performance Organization*. New York: HarperBusiness; Leavitt, Harold, and Jean Lipman-Bluman. 1995. "Hot Groups." *Harvard Business Review*. July–August: 109–116; Bennis, Warren, and Patricia Ward Biederman. 1997. *Organizing Genius: The Secrets of Creative Collaboration*. Reading, MA: Addison-Wesley.

31. Biederman, Patricia Ward, and Warren Bennis. 1997. *Organizing Genius: Secrets of Creative Collaboration*. New York: Addison-Wesley.

32. Imai, K., N. Ikujiro, and H. Takeuchi. 1985. "Managing the New Product Development Process: How Japanese Companies Learn and Unlearn." In R. H. Hayes, K. Clark, and Ed Lornez. (eds.). *The Uneasy Alliance: Managing the Productivity-Technology Dilemma*. Boston, MA: Harvard Business Review Press.

33. Eisenstat, Russell, and Susan Cohen. 1990. "Summary: Top Management Groups." In Hackman, J. Richard (ed.). *Groups That Work (and Those That Don't): Creating Conditions for Effective Teamwork*. San Francisco, CA: Jossey-Bass.

34. Oldham, Greg, and J. Richard Hackman. 2010. "Not What It Was and Not What It Will Be: The Future of Job Design Research." *Journal of Organizational Behavior*, 31: 463–479; Wageman, Ruth, Debra Nunes, James Burruss, and J. Richard Hackman. January 2008. "The Structure of Success." *Associations Now*, 4(1): 22–26.

35. Oldham, Greg, and J. Richard Hackman. 2010. "Not What It Was and Not What It Will Be: The Future of Job Design Research." *Journal of Organizational Behavior*, 31: 463–479; Hackman, J. Richard, and Gary Oldham. 1980. *Work Redesign*. Reading, MA: Addison-Wesley.

36. Hilton, Als. 2003. "Ghosts in the House." *New Yorker Magazine*. October 27: 54–69.

37. Ibid.

38. Mount, M. Barrick, and G. Stewart. 1998. "Five-Factor Model of Personality and Performance in Jobs Involving Interpersonal Interactions." *Human Performance*, 11:145–165.

39. Humphrey, S., J. Nahrgang, and F. Morgeson. 2007. "Integrating Motivation, Social, and Contextual

Design Features: A Meta-Analytic Summary and Theoretical Extension of the Work Design Literature." *Journal of Applied Psychology*, 92: 1332–1336.

40. Oldham, Greg, and J. Richard Hackman. 2010. "Not What It Was and Not What It Will Be: The Future of Job Design Research." *Journal of Organizational Behavior*, 31: 463–479.

41. Hackman, J. Richard, and Ruth Wageman. 2005. "A Theory of Team Coaching." *Academy of Management Review*, 30(2): 269–287; Wageman, Ruth. 2001. "How Leaders Foster Self-Managing Team Effectiveness: Design Choices vs. Hands-On Coaching." *Organizational Science*, 12: 559–577.

42. Ibid.

43. Biederman, Patricia Ward, and Warren Bennis. 1997. *Organizing Genius: Secrets of Creative Collaboration*. New York: Addison-Wesley.

44. Hackman, J. Richard. 1990. *Groups That Work (and Those That Don't): Creating Conditions for Effective Teamwork*. San Francisco, CA: Jossey-Bass.

45. Ibid., p. 12.

46. Katzenback, Jon, and Douglas K. Smith. 1993. *The Wisdom of Teams: Creating the High-Performance Organization*. New York: HarperBusiness.

47. Oldham, Greg, and J. Richard Hackman. 2010. "Not What It Was and Not What It Will Be: The Future of Job Design Research." *Journal of Organizational Behavior*, 31: 463–479.

48. Losada, Marcial, and Emily Heaphy. 2004. "The Role of Positivity and Connectivity in the Performance of Business Teams: A Nonlinear Dynamics Model." *American Behavioral Scientist*, 47(6): 740–765.

49. Fredrickson, Barbara, and Marcial Losada. 2005. "Positive Affect and the Complex Dynamics of Human Flourishing." *American Psychologist*, 60(7): 678–686.

50. Oh, Hongseok, Giuseppe Labianca, and Myung-Ho Chung. 2006. "A Multilevel Model of Group Social Capital." *Academy of Management Review*, 31(3): 569–582.

51. Ancona, Deborah, and Henrik Bresman. 2007. *XTeams: How to Build Teams That Lead, Innovate and Succeed*. Watertown, MA: Harvard Business School Press; Ancona, Deborah. 1990. "Outward Bound: Strategies for Team Survival in Organizations." *Academy of Management Journal*, 33(2): 334–365.

52. Alderfer, Clayton. 1983. "Intergroup Relations and Organizations." In Hackman, J. Richard, Edward Lawler and Lyman Porter (eds.). *Perspectives on Behavior in Organizations*. New York: McGraw-Hill; Stewart, Greg, Charles Manz, and Henry Sims. 1999. *Team Work and Group Dynamics*. New York: John Wiley and Sons; Brown, David. 1984. "Managing Conflict among Groups." In D. A. Kolb, I. M. Rubin, and I. N. McIntyre (eds.). *Organizational Psychology: Readings on Human Behavior in Organizations*. Upper Saddle River, NJ: Prentice Hall; Perdue, Charles, Michael Gurtman, John Dovidio, and Richard Tyler. 1990. "Us and Them: Social Categorization and the Process of Intergroup Bias." *Journal of Personality and Social Psychology*, 59(3): 475–486; Tajfel, Henri, and Turner, C. 1986. "The Social Identity Theory of Intergroup Behavior." In Stephen Worchel and William G. Austin (eds.). *Psychology of Intergroup Relations*. 2nd ed. Chicago, IL: Nelson-Hall.

53. Peers, Martin. 2003. "Tuning Up Time Warner." *Wall Street Journal*. December 11: B1 and B7.

54. Arnst, Catherine, John Carey, Arlene Weintraub, and Kerry Capell. 2002. "Cancer: The Hope. The Hype. The Reality." *Business Week* November 25.

55. Chase, Marilyn. 2006. "Gates Won't Fund AIDS Researchers Unless They Pool Data." *Wall Street Journal*. July 20: B1 and B4; Paulson, Tom. 2006. "Gates Foundation Awards $287 Million for HIV Vaccine Research." Seattle PI. July 19. http://www.seattlepi.com/local/278100_aidsvaccine19ww.html

56. Pottinger, Matt, Elena Cherney, Gautam Naik, and Michael Waldolz. 2003. "How Global Effort Found SARS Virus in Matter of Weeks." *Wall Street Journal*. April 16: A1 and A8.

57. Stewart, Greg, Charles Manz, and Henry Sims. 1999. *Team Work and Group Dynamics*. New York: John Wiley and Sons; Crocker, Jennifer, and Riia Luhtanen. 1990. "Collective Self-Esteem and In-Group Bias." *Journal of Personality and Social Psychology*, 58: 60–67; Turner J. C., M. A. Hogg, P. J. Oakes, S. D. Reicher, and M. S. Wetherell. 1987. *Rediscovering the Social Group: A Self-Categorization Theory*. Oxford, England: Basil Blackwell; Gaertner, Samuel L., Jeffrey Mann, Audrey Murrell, and John F. Dovidio. 1989. "Reducing Intergroup Bias: The Benefits of Recategorization." *Journal of Personality and Social Psychology*, 57: 239–249; Mullen, B., R. Brown, and C. Smith. 1987. "In-Group Bias as a Function of Salience, Relevance, and Status: An Integration." *European Journal of Social Psychology*, 22: 103–122; Maass, A., and M. Schaller. 1991. "Intergroup Biases and the Cognitive Dynamics of

Stereotype Formation." In W. Stroebe and M. Hewstone (eds.). *European Review of Social Psychology*. Vol. 2. New York: Wiley.

58. Tajfel, H. 1978. *Differential between Social Groups: Studies in the Social Psychology of Intergroup Relations*. London: Academic Press; Tajfel, Henri, and J. Turner. 1986. "The Social Identity of Intergroup Behavior." In S. Worchel and W. Austin (eds.). *Psychology and Intergroup Relations*. Chicago, IL: Nelson-Hall.

59. Allen, V. L., and D. A. Wilder. 1975. "Categorization, Belief Similarity, and Intergroup Discrimination." *Journal of Personality and Social Psychology*, 32: 971–977.

60. Howard, J. W., and M. Rothbart. 1980. "Social Categorization and Memory for In-Group and Out-Group Behavior." *Journal of Personality and Social Psychology*, 38: 301–310.

61. Williams, Katherine, and Charles O'Reilly. 1998. "Demography and Diversity in Organizations: A Review of 40 Years of Research." *Research in Organizational Behavior*, 20: 77–140; citing Brewer, M. 1979. "In-Group Bias in the Minimal Intergroup Situation: A Cognitive-Motivational Analysis." *Psychological Bulletin*, 86: 307–324; Tajfel, Henri. 1982. *Social Identity and Intergroup Relations*. Cambridge: Cambridge University Press.

62. Judd, Charles M., and B. Park. 1988. "Out-Group Homogeneity: Judgments of Variability at the Individual and Group Levels." *Journal of Personality and Social Psychology*, 54: 778–788.

63. Harquail, Celia. 1996. "When One Speaks for Many: The Influence of Social Identification on Group Advocacy in Organizations." Unpublished Dissertation, University of Michigan.

64. Piliavin, Jane A., John F. Dovidio, Samuel L. Gaertner, and R. D. Clark. 1981. *Emergency Intervention*. San Diego, CA: Academic Press.

65. Brown, L. David. 1984. "Managing Conflict among Groups." In D. A. Kolb, I. M. Rubin, and I. N. McIntyre (eds.). *Organizational Psychology: Readings on Human Behavior in Organizations*. Upper Saddle River, NJ: Prentice Hall.

66. Ibid.

67. Janis, Irving. 1971. "Groupthink." *Psychology Today*. November: 43–44, 46, 74–76.

68. Marx, Robert, Charles Stubbart, V. Traub, and Michael Cavanaugh. 1987. "The NASA Space Shuttle Disaster: A Case Study." *Journal of Management Case Studies*. Winter: 300–318.

69. 2003. "Report on Columbia Disaster Faults NASA Management." *Wall Street Journal* August 27.

70. Ibid.

71. Kiechel, Walter. 1990. "How to Escape the Echo Chamber." *Fortune*. June 18: 129–130.

72. Janis, Irving. 1982. *Groupthink*. 2nd ed. Boston: Houghton Mifflin.

73. Perdue, Charles, Michael Gurtman, John Dovidio, and Richard Tyler. 1990. "Us and Them: Social Categorization and the Process of Intergroup Bias." *Journal of Personality and Social Psychology*, 59(3): 475–486.

74. Ancona, Deborah, and David Caldwell. 1992. "Bridging the Boundary: External Process and Performance in Organizational Teams." *Administrative Science Quarterly*, 37(4): 634–666.

75. Ancona, Deborah, and Henrik Bresman. 2007. *XTeams: How to Build Teams That Lead, Innovate and Succeed*. Watertown, MA: Harvard Business School Press; Dougherty, Deborah. 1992. "Interpretive Barriers to Successful Product Innovation in Large Firms." *Organization Science*, 3(2): 179–202.

76. Majchrzak, Ann, and Qianwei Wang. 1996. "Breaking the Functional Mindset in Process Organizations." *Harvard Business Review*, 74(5): 92–99.

77. Stewart, Greg, Charles Manz, and Henry Sims. 1999. *Team Work and Group Dynamics*. New York: John Wiley and Sons.

78. Dovidio, John, Ana Validzic, and Samuel Gaertner. 1998. "Intergroup Bias: Status, Differentiation, and a Common In-Group Identity." *Journal of Personality and Social Psychology*, 75(1): 109–120.

79. Majchrzak, Ann, and Qianwei Wang. 1996. "Breaking the Functional Mindset in Process Organizations." *Harvard Business Review*, 74(5): 92–99.

80. Dovidio, John, Ana Validzic, and Samuel Gaertner. 1998. "Intergroup Bias: Status, Differentiation and a Common In-Group Identity." *Journal of Personality and Social Psychology*, 75(1): 109–120.

81. Katz, R., and Tushman, M. L. 1981. "An Investigation into the Managerial Roles and Career Paths of Gatekeepers and Project Supervisors in a Major R&D Facility." *R&D Management*, 11: 103–110.

82. Brown, Shona, and Kathleen M. Eisenhardt. 1995. "Product Development: Past Research, Present Findings, and Future Directions." *Academy of Management Review*, 20(2): 343–378.

83. Ancona, Deborah, and David Caldwell. 1992. "Bridging the Boundary: External Process and

Performance in Organizational Teams." *Administrative Science Quarterly*, 35: 634–665.

84. Gersick, Connie, and Mary Lou Davis. 1990. "Summary: Task Forces." In Hackman, J. Richard (ed.). *Groups That Work (and Those That Don't): Creating Conditions for Effective Teamwork*. San Francisco, CA: Jossey-Bass; Bennis, Warren, and Herbert Shepard. 1956. "A Theory of Group Development." *Human Relations*, 9(4): 415–457; Tuckman, Barry W., and Mary Ann Jensen. 1975. "Stages of Small Group Development Revisited." *Group and Organizational Studies*, 2(4): 419–427.

85. Lipnack, Jessica, and Jeffrey Stamps. 1997. *Virtual Teams: Reaching across Space, Time, and Organizations with Technology*. New York: John Wiley.

86. Tuckman, Barry W., and Mary Ann Jensen. 1975. "Stages of Small Group Development Revisited." *Group and Organizational Studies*, 2(4): 419–427.

87. Hackman, J. Richard. 2002. "New Rules for Team Building." *Optimize Magazine*. July: 50–62.

88. Lester, Scott, Bruce Meglino, and M. Audrey Koorsgaard. 2002. "The Antecedents and Consequences of Group Potency: A Longitudinal Investigation of Newly Formed Work Groups." *Academy of Management Journal*, 45(2): 352–368.

89. Katzenback, Jon, and Douglas K. Smith. 1993. *The Wisdom of Teams: Creating the High-Performance Organization*. New York: HarperBusiness.

90. Hackman, J. Richard. 1990. *Groups That Work (and Those That Don't): Creating Conditions for Effective Teamwork*. San Francisco, CA: Jossey-Bass.

91. Gersick, Connie, and Mary Lou Davis. 1990. "Summary: Task Forces." In Hackman, J. Richard (ed.). *Groups That Work (and Those That Don't): Creating Conditions for Effective Teamwork*. San Francisco, CA: Jossey-Bass.

92. Janis, Irving. 1993. *Groupthink in Small Groups and Social Interaction*. Vol. 2. New York: John Wiley & Sons.

93. Katzenback, Jon, and Douglas K. Smith. 1993. *The Wisdom of Teams: Creating the High-Performance Organization*. New York: HarperBusiness.

94. Gersick, Connie. 1988. "Time and Transition in Work Teams: Toward a New Model of Group Development." *Academy of Management Journal*, 31: 9–41.

95. Hackman, J. Richard. 1990. *Groups That Work (and Those That Don't): Creating Conditions for Effective Teamwork*. San Francisco, CA: Jossey-Bass.

96. Hackman, J. Richard, and Ruth Wageman. 2007. "Asking the Right Questions about Leadership." *American Psychologist*, 62(1): 43–47.

9

■ ■ ■

Diverse Teams and Virtual Teams: Managing Differences and Distances

This chapter will help you:

- Understand the advantages and risks of diverse and virtual teams.
- Learn techniques for effectively managing diverse and virtual teams.
- Understand why managing the relationship dynamics is as important as managing the task and technical aspects of diverse and virtual teams.
- Become a better leader and member of diverse and virtual teams.

Imagine a typical management team in the 1960s in Dallas. The marketing manager is meeting with his new product development team that convenes weekly in the second floor conference room of his company's new high-rise building. The team's task is to develop a strategy to introduce a new product to the U.S. market within the next year. The team is made up of four North American college-educated men of Western European descent, ranging from 32 to 38 years of age. They enjoy their jobs and expect to stay with the company until they retire at age 65. They are all married fathers and sole breadwinners for their families. When they arrive at their homes tonight, each man's wife and children will be waiting for him. Dinner will be on the table.

Fast-forward into the twenty-first century in the United States and it's easier to imagine yourself on the following team. You live in New York and are a marketing manager who is in the middle of a conference call with your transnational team members. Your team's task is to develop a strategy to coordinate the introduction of a new product to five countries simultaneously within the next three months. In addition to yourself, your team is made up of a 55-year-old Chinese man stationed in New York, a 29-year-old North American woman stationed in Tokyo, a 32-year-old Brazilian woman stationed in Mexico City, a 35-year-old Nigerian man stationed in Chicago, a 25-year-old Italian woman stationed in Milan, a 28-year-old North American man stationed in Mumbai, a 40-year-old Australian man stationed in Stockholm, and a 28-year-old man from India stationed in Detroit.

Team members' educational backgrounds include a two-year community college degree, an undergraduate degree in art history, an undergraduate degree in marketing, an undergraduate degree in public policy, two masters degrees in business administration, and two Ph.Ds in engineering. Their tenure with the company ranges from eight months to 25 years. One team member has no college education and has 20 years of experience successfully supervising the most well-run and productive plants in two of the countries in which you want to manufacture the product. In addition to these differences in age, gender, experience, nationality, and geographic location, team members differ in race and religious orientations as well. You began working as a team five months ago, shortly after your company merged with a former competitor.

The conference call has been timed carefully so that all team members can be at the meeting. It's approximately 10:30 A.M. in Chicago and Mexico City, 11:30 A.M. in Detroit and New York, 5:30 P.M. in Milan and Stockholm, 9:00 P.M. in Mumbai, and 12:30 A.M. in Tokyo. You have never met four of the team members in person. All of your interactions with them have been through the telephone, e-mail, and videoconferences.

You enjoy your job, work two days a week out of your home office (and sometimes from a local coffee shop), and spend approximately six days each month traveling on business. You are in a dual-career relationship with the love of your life and have two young children. Before you leave work tonight, you will check your phone and e-mail messages to see if the headhunter who asked you to consider a position as marketing director for a new line of smart phones returned your message. You will then go online to see how well your retirement portfolio has performed today. You plan to retire at age 50, so you are managing your retirement portfolio carefully. When you arrive home tonight after picking your children up from day care, you'll realize that both you and the love of your life forgot to order dinner. At 10:00 P.M. you notice that 45 new e-mails arrived since you left the office at 6:00 P.M.

These two scenarios reflect how shifts in demographics, social norms, work expectations, and new technologies are dramatically transforming the nature of teamwork. Team members are becoming more culturally diverse and geographically dispersed. Work tasks are becoming increasingly complex, and the processes by which team members do their work are being significantly altered by technological advancements, globalization, and increased competition.[1] Yet few people take the time to understand how to systematically manage diverse and virtual teams, despite the increasing amount of research that provides insight into best practices for leading these teams. Consequently, they face the challenges of managing diverse and virtual teams with little knowledge and preparation and miss opportunities for leveraging the benefits of these more complex—yet increasingly common—forms of teams.

As a result of the changes brought about by technology, a typical executive today has to deal with thousands of interdependent relationships. . . . And the diversity of goals, opinions, and beliefs among these players is typically enormous.
—JOHN KOTTER,
Leadership scholar

Certainly, relatively homogeneous teams in which team members primarily meet face-to-face (or, as Leopoldina Fortunati calls it, "body-to-body", reflecting the critical role body language plays in team communication and coordination)[2] in the same place are still common in many organizations. However, diverse teams and virtual teams are becoming increasingly commonplace and taken for granted, providing new opportunities for team members to enhance their team's productivity, their organization's competitiveness, and their own competence in navigating an increasingly diverse, global, and technologically sophisticated work environment.

Many of the skills that we learned for managing relatively homogeneous, co-located teams are necessary yet insufficient for effectively managing diverse and virtual teams. For example, providing clear goals, an enabling design, effective coaching, and connections to external people and groups is critical to all teams, regardless of whether they are relatively homogenous or diverse and whether they meet face-to-face or virtually. However, leading diverse and virtual teams requires an even more sophisticated understanding of team dynamics, as well as a broader set of leadership skills. Therefore, in this chapter, I discuss the characteristics of diverse teams and virtual teams. I focus particularly on the ways in which they differ from relatively homogeneous teams that primarily meet face-to-face. I also discuss team leadership skills that will help you leverage the opportunities and minimize the risks that diverse and virtual teams offer.

PART 1: DIVERSE TEAMS

In their *Training and Development* magazine article, "Diverse Teams: Breakdown or Breakthrough?" Lewis Griggs and Lente-Louise Louw point out:

> Forming a cohesive team from relatively similar individuals is hard enough. The difficulties are multiplied when team members come from different ethnic or national cultures. They not only come to the group with their own individual ways of being, but they also bring cultural or national dictates about the proper ways to do things. As a consequence, diverse teams require more skill facilitation than homogeneous groups, especially in the early stages.[3]

Team diversity, of course, goes beyond ethnic and national culture. Researcher Daan van Knippenerg and colleagues explain that "diversity refers to differences between individuals on any attribute that may lead to the perception that another person is different from self."[4] In the context of work teams, diversity refers to "differences among members of an interdependent work group with respect to a specific personal attribute."[5] Today's team members are likely to differ from each other on relatively observable social categories such as race, gender, nationality, and age, as well as job-related characteristics such as professional affiliation, functional department, hierarchical level, organizational membership, education, and tenure in the organization. Team members are also likely to differ significantly from each other on less visible characteristics such as cognitive styles, values, experience, and skills, as well as more private and often invisible characteristics such as religion, sexual orientation, and health challenges.[6]

After more than 40 years of research on diversity, most researchers agree that differences among team members matter. Specifically, diversity among team members affects:

- the variety of cognitive resources and behavioral styles team members bring to the team;
- the interaction processes by which team members work together, including both task and relationship processes; and
- the team's ability to be a high-performing team; in particular, the team's ability to make effective decisions, promote the development and well-being of all team members, and enhance the team's performance over time.

Although diverse groups offer the potential for achieving better results than relatively homogenous groups in many circumstances, researchers have found inconsistent results for the performance of diverse groups. Some studies have led to the conclusion that diverse groups tend to outperform relatively homogenous groups. Other studies found that diverse groups tend to perform worse than relatively homogenous groups. And other studies have found that diversity has little or no impact on performance.[7] So, it's not very useful to ask whether diverse teams perform better or worse than relatively homogenous teams. Rather, the questions should be: "In what ways do diverse teams differ from relatively homogenous teams?" "Under what conditions do diverse teams outperform relatively homogenous teams?" and "What can I do to help diverse teams achieve their potential?" These questions are addressed in the following sections.

The Diversity Dilemma

Researchers also agree that diversity in teams is a "double-edged sword."[8] Members of diverse teams, when contrasted to relatively homogeneous teams, tend to bring a greater variety of perspectives, information, skills, relationship networks, and behavioral styles to their teams. This greater range of resources can enhance a team's decision-making processes through the generation of more alternatives, increased creativity, better error detection, more critical thinking, more effective prediction of environmental changes, and more constructive task-related conflict. The advantages can result in higher quality decisions and enhanced performance.[9] These advantages are more likely to emerge when the team's resources (e.g., all team members' unique perspectives, experience, skills, networks) are relevant to the team's task (e.g., when breadth of ideas or information about particular markets is important), when these relevant resources are integrated into the group's decision-making processes, when differences among team members are well managed, and when team members put time and effort into learning how to work together productively.[10]

Diversity in teams can also lead to dysfunctional dynamics that compromise the team's ability to leverage team members' resources. These dynamics include cultural ignorance and bias, marginalization of team members, and an inability of team members to identify with the team. These can lead to greater psychological detachment, less cohesion among team members, more communication problems, unproductive social conflict, slower and poorer decision-making, difficulties in coordination, and increased absenteeism and turnover.[11]

Researchers explain the roots of these potential problems in diverse groups through two perspectives: similarity-attraction and structural barriers.

- *The similarity-attraction perspective.* This perspective assumes that people categorize themselves and others into social categories that they believe are relevant (e.g., race, gender, hierarchical level, and functional area); people who share the same social categories tend to see each other as more similar and indeed may be more similar in many ways because they are more likely to share similar life and work experiences; consequently, they may find interacting with each other "easier, positively reinforcing, and more desirable"[12] and may find interactions with people that they perceive as different from themselves as less predictable, more difficult to understand, more stressful, and less desirable.
- *The structural barrier perspective.* This perspective refers to the social barriers that prevent the full participation of all team members. This perspective assumes that the dynamics in diverse teams reflect those of the larger society in which the team and organization are embedded. Consequently, if there is bias, misunderstanding, marginalization, and lack of cohesion among diverse groups in the larger society, then these social dynamics are likely to be replicated to some degree in the team in ways that inhibit maximum contribution of all team members.[13] For example, most societies and organizations promote beliefs about who has the "right stuff" to succeed in particular roles (e.g., manager, engineer, team leader) and may create explicit policies or informal norms that exclude members of some cultural groups from equal participation in these roles regardless of their competence. Even when equal opportunity is promoted and teams are indeed diverse, the teams may not leverage that diversity because the perspectives, decision-making processes, and participation norms reflect those of the dominant cultural group(s). Consequently, the resources that minority teams members bring to the team may not be utilized, and minority team members may feel marginalized.[14]

In short, the diversity dilemma is this: Although diverse team members are more likely to bring a broader range of resources to the team, they also may tend to engage in dysfunctional dynamics that can hinder the team's ability to use those resources effectively. Consequently, we should not focus on whether diverse teams are inherently better or worse than relatively homogeneous teams. Rather, we should focus on how organizational leaders and managers create a work context and culture that leverages the benefits and minimizes the risks.[15] The potential benefits and risks of diverse teams are discussed in more detail in the following sections and are summarized in Figure 9-1.

Potential Benefits and Risks of Diverse Teams

The research on diverse teams provides useful insights into how diversity in teams may affect team process and performance in both positive and negative ways. On the positive side, compared with homogeneous teams, diverse teams (when well managed) tend to have the following advantages:

ENHANCED EFFECTIVENESS ON INTELLECTIVE TASKS   Intellective tasks are defined as those that have objectively correct answers.[16] Research suggests that diverse teams may be more likely to "hit" upon the right answers, particularly if the team has a greater variety of task-relevant knowledge and skill among team members.[17]

ENHANCED EFFECTIVENESS ON CREATIVE AND JUDGMENTAL DECISION-MAKING TASKS
Many problems require using creativity and judgment to interpret a complex environment and come to a consensus on the "best" solution. Substantial research suggests that diverse teams tend to have a wider range of information, skills, and experiences that can increase the breadth of ideas available to the group, help the group detect errors, process information, and solve problems.[18] In contrast, relatively homogeneous teams may miss or misinterpret important data and trends. This was illustrated when Jim Preston was CEO of Avon. *Fortune* magazine described how Preston recognized that Avon was becoming "your grandmother's beauty company," saying "[T]he thing that really gave him religion on women's issues was watching Avon practically destroy itself because the men at the top made a big miscalculation about women. They refused to believe the company's own market research, which even in the early 1970s pointed out that women were entering the labor force and would likely stay there." As a consequence, fewer women were choosing to become Avon ladies" because they were choosing other jobs, and fewer women were home to answer the door when the "Avon ladies" came calling. Yet Avon resisted changing its historically successful strategy of having "Avon ladies" go door-to-door selling Avon products to women at home. In a *Fortune* magazine article, Preston noted that if Avon had women executives at the top when the demographic trends showed that more women were entering the workforce, "they would have acknowledged that women were headed to work, embraced the trend, and said, 'You're damned right this will continue. We'd better change.'"[19]

MORE ATTENTION TO TEAM PROCESS   Because members of diverse teams are more likely to notice differences among each other and be concerned about their ability to work together, they may also pay more attention to the group process.[20] Consequently, they may be particularly thoughtful and systematic about setting explicit norms that enhance the decision-making processes (e.g., "Make sure we consider the benefits and risk of these options from different perspectives" and "Make sure everyone's opinion is given a fair hearing."). Although explicit norms

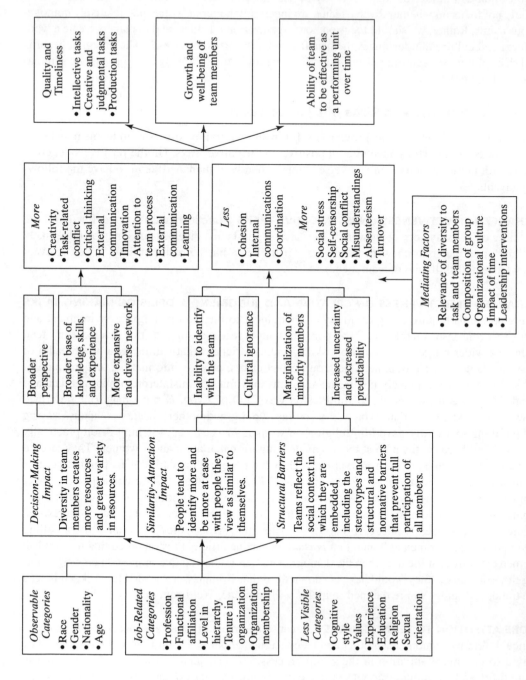

FIGURE 9-1 Effects of Diversity on Team Process and Performance

are beneficial to relatively homogeneous teams as well, members of homogeneous teams may take their relationships for granted, pay less attention to the quality of their interactions, and thus may miss opportunities to enhance their teams' process and productivity.

BROADER AND MORE DIVERSE EXTERNAL NETWORKS   Members of diverse teams tend to have access to a more diverse network outside the team. Access to these external networks can increase the information, resources, and support available to the team, which can enhance the team's performance if it is relevant to the team task and made accessible to the team.[21]

ENHANCED LEARNING   In some cases, teams that have members with different levels of ability (e.g., some members are more proficient than others) may outperform groups whose members have similar ability levels. This suggests that both high- and low-ability members learn from interacting with each other. Certainly, members with lower ability levels can learn from those with higher ability levels. But, says researcher Susan Jackson, higher ability members also may "learn during their interactions with others of lower ability because they take on the role of teacher. Playing the teacher role may lead high-ability members to sharpen their own thinking. Another possibility is that the questions and inputs of more naïve members encourage the more expert members to unbundle the assumptions and rules they automatically use when dealing with issues and problems in which they are experts (Simon 1979). This unbundling may increase the probability of discovering assumptions that warrant scrutiny and decisions rules for which exceptions may be needed."[22]

> Technology can help put us in contact with each other—over oceans and over cultures—but it cannot make us understand one another. For that we must still depend on the oldest systems of all: human imagination, tolerance, determination, and the will to learn continuously.
> —MARY O'HARA-DEVEREAUX AND ROBERT JOHANSEN

CONTINUOUS IMPROVEMENT   Some studies suggest that diverse teams tend to show a "more consistent pattern of improvement over time" than do homogeneous teams.[23] And when diverse teams outperform homogeneous teams, their advantage seems to increase over time.[24] These advantages, however, are more likely to occur when a diverse team is well managed.

Now the Hurdles

Compared with homogeneous teams, diverse teams are more likely to face the following risks:

MORE STRESS   Members of diverse teams are more likely to find the team experience stressful for several reasons. Some team members may engage in negative stereotyping and biases that can result in more negative emotions in the people who exhibit these attitudes as well as in those who are their targets. Furthermore, diversity increases uncertainty and decreases predictability in social relations.[25] Consequently, team members are more likely to misinterpret each other's intentions and may be unsure about how to interact with each other, which can increase confusion and anxiety. For example, researchers Judith Claire, Joy Beattie, and Tammy MacLean note that there can be considerable stress associated with invisible identities such as sexual orientation or health challenges, regardless of whether one chooses to hide some of one's identities or reveal them.[26] If one tries to "pass," then one must conceal parts of oneself that are important and live with the constant concern that someone might find out. If one decides to reveal one's identity, especially if it carries a social stigma, one must explain one's identity repeatedly (which people who do not have this identity do not need to do—e.g., one doesn't have to explain that one is heterosexual or that one doesn't have a particular chronic illness).[27]

REDUCED GROUP COHESION   Social cohesion refers to the degree to which team members feel psychologically connected to each other. Cohesive groups tend to outperform noncohesive groups (as long as they aren't excessively isolated and self-absorbed), and "members of cohesive groups tend to be more satisfied, absent less, and more likely to remain in the group rather than leave it."[28] If not well-managed, members of diverse teams are more likely to have difficulty finding common ground, have problems communicating with each other, experience more stress, and engage in more social conflict, all of which can decrease group cohesiveness.

> If I can't dance, I don't want to be part of your revolution.
> —EMMA GOLDMAN

MORE PSYCHOLOGICAL AND PHYSICAL DETACHMENT FROM THE TEAM   Diverse teams tend to have greater absenteeism and turnover than homogeneous teams.[29] Some studies have shown that people in the minority in groups are more likely to psychologically and physically withdraw from groups in which they are in a minority when they feel marginalized and when their input isn't encouraged or accepted.[30]

DECREASED AND MORE DISTORTED INTERNAL COMMUNICATION   People who view themselves as similar to each other are more likely to feel more comfortable with each other, which increases their desire to communicate with each other.[31] Conversely, people who view themselves as different from each other tend to communicate less often with each other. Furthermore, people who do not share common social and organizational categories (e.g., race, gender, nationality, profession, department, and hierarchical level) are less likely to share the same values, cultural knowledge, and behaviors. It is well known that the same words can mean different things in different cultures. Even silence can mean different things in different cultures. For some people, silence is interpreted as maturity, thoughtfulness, and being attentive to what others are saying. For others, silence is interpreted as lack of interest, confidence, or ability.[32] Consequently, members of diverse groups are more likely to misinterpret each other's words, behaviors, and intent. The assessment in Box 9-1 can help you identify your own communication style, as well as the communication style of your team members.

MORE DIFFICULTY COORDINATING   Team member similarity may make it easier for team members to communicate with each other, trust each other, and anticipate each other's intentions and behaviors that can make coordination easier and faster. Some research suggests that predictable tasks that have objective standards for performance based on proficiency and productivity (e.g., production tasks) may benefit from team member homogeneity.[33] For example, a study of underground mining crews investigated the impact of homogeneous tenure (i.e., all people started working at the company around the same time) on the crew's performance. The researchers concluded, "Familiarity, which included an assessment of how long the crew had worked together, was positively related to higher levels of productivity and lower accident rates."[34]

MORE PERCEPTUAL BIASES OF LEADERS   Several research studies have concluded that leaders tend to feel more positively toward people they perceive as similar to themselves and rate the performance of those they perceive as similar higher than they rate those they perceive as different.[35] Furthermore, research has also found that direct reports expect different styles from leaders based on stereotypes about the leader's sociocultural group membership (e.g., race, gender, nationality). For example, team leaders in some cultures are expected to have the most technical expertise on the project, whereas this level of expertise may not be expected

BOX 9-1   Assess Team Members' Style Preferences

Please circle the number that best reflects your style in work groups. Remember that no one style is better or worse than the others. Then compare your responses with those of other team members.

Continuous Communication Style: When in a conversation, I tend to begin speaking before other people finish their sentences.	1	2	3	4	5	Discrete Communication Style: When in a conversation, I tend to wait for the other person to finish before I begin speaking.
Talker: I tend to be more of a talker than a listener.	1	2	3	4	5	Listener: I tend to be more of a listener than a talker.
Report Talk: I believe that the main purpose of communication is to share information.	1	2	3	4	5	Rapport Talk: I believe that the main purpose of communication is to build relationships.
I tend to think "out loud" so that the group can hear my line of thinking even before I am clear about my ideas.	1	2	3	4	5	I tend to think quietly before expressing my ideas so that I can be clear when I express them.
Self-Enhancing: I like to promote my contributions and stand out from the group.	1	2	3	4	5	Group-Enhancing: I do not like to promote my personal contributions or stand out from the group.
Equality: I am comfortable challenging authority figures, even in public.	1	2	3	4	5	Hierarchy: I am not comfortable challenging authority figures, particularly in public.

from team leaders in other cultures. These differences in expectations can, in turn, influence the team leader's credibility, confidence, and ability to manage the team effectively.[36]

TEAM MEMBERS' MISPERCEPTIONS ABOUT TEAM PERFORMANCE   Some research suggests that even when diverse teams are performing well, team members may underestimate their team's effectiveness, perhaps because social stress in the team may hinder their ability to see their team's task-related strengths. Consequently, leaders may need to provide more positive feedback to ensure that members of effective diverse teams recognize their strengths and accomplishments.[37]

Additional Factors to Consider

Certainly, all diverse teams do not display the preceding characteristics. Furthermore, even relatively homogeneous teams may have many of the advantages (creativity and attention to team process) and disadvantages (member detachment, communication problems, and lack of cohesion) listed earlier. However, these advantages and disadvantages tend to be more pronounced in diverse teams. Several factors influence whether these advantages and disadvantages will emerge in a diverse team.

- *Relevance of diversity to the task.* One of the advantages of diverse teams is that they have access to a greater variety of resources such as knowledge, skills, experience, and networks. If these resources are not relevant to the task, they may contribute less to the immediate task, although they may still increase the long-term team development by increasing learning and flexibility.[38] Diversity of team members appears to be particular advantage for complex, nonroutine problems that require creativity, judgment, and a broad range of information.[39]

- *Relevance of diversity to team members.* Some kinds of diversity tend to be more relevant to team members and have a greater impact than do other kinds of diversity.[40] For example, more visible differences tend to have more of an impact on team process than do less visible differences, particularly early in the team's life. Furthermore, the less diverse a team is, the more likely a member who is different from the group will stand out.[41]

- *Impact of organizational culture.* Recent research suggests that organizations that promote a collectivist (people look out more for each other and organizational goals) rather than individualistic (people look out more for themselves and their own goals) culture are more likely to benefit from team diversity because team members are more likely to focus on their common goals and shared fate rather than on team member differences.[42]

- *Impact of time.* Although members of homogeneous teams tend to feel more comfortable with each other initially, some research suggests that this advantage of homogeneous teams over diverse teams tends to fade over time.[43] For example, in a study of 43 senior managers enrolled in an executive training program, researchers found that "similarity in demographic characteristics and in behavioral style preferences contributed significantly to the prediction of liking and coworkers preference" early on.[44] However, "three weeks after initial interaction, demographic similarity ceased to contribute significantly to social liking and coworker preference. Only similarity in personal values predicted both liking and preference."[45]

- *Team member characteristics: Need for cognition and openness to experience.* Researchers have found that team members who have characteristics called "need for cognition" and "openness to experience" are more likely to perform well in diverse groups and help diverse teams achieve their goals. Researchers define high "need for cognition" as "an individual's tendency to engage in and enjoy effortful cognitive endeavors."[46] Team members who are high in need for cognition tend to seek out and enjoy opportunities to think broadly and learn new ways of thinking, whereas people low in need for cognition "rely more on simple cues, cognitive heuristics, and stereotypes in interpreting situations and judging people."[47] Team members who are open to experience tend to be "broad minded, like novelty, and are not conservative."[48] Researcher Astrid Homan explains that people who are high on openness to experience "tend to be less dogmatic in their ideas, more willing to consider different opinions, more open to all kinds of situations, and less likely to deny conflicts than people who score low on openness to experience." In one study, Homan and colleagues found that teams in which team members scored high overall on openness to experience performed the highest and teams in which team members scored lowest on openness to experience performed the worst.[49]

Although diversity among team members has both advantages and risks, teams can benefit significantly from team member diversity, particularly under certain conditions. Diverse teams may have an advantage over relatively homogeneous teams when:

- the diversity among team members is relevant to the team's task (e.g., when tasks require creativity and judgment, when breadth of ideas is important, or when information about particular markets is important);
- team members have time to learn how to work together productively; and
- diversity among team members is appreciated and well managed.

Leading Diverse Teams

Given the increasing use of diverse teams, as well as diversity's impact on team performance, team leaders cannot afford to mismanage diverse teams. As with all teams, effective leaders of diverse teams create conditions that help diverse teams leverage rather than squander their collective resources.

Certainly, members of effective diverse teams and homogeneous teams share many of the same qualities. They are committed to the team's purpose; they have a specific expertise to offer the team; they are not advocates of a particular method or function; they have general problem-solving, decision-making, and implementation skills; they have strong relationship skills; they know their own strengths and weaknesses and how these affect team performance; and they are adaptive. However, members of diverse teams must be even more adept at understanding cultural and style differences, attending to group process, anticipating the consequences of their perceptions and behavior on others, and dealing with new and unfamiliar situations. When diverse teams are also global teams, team members must be able to adapt to a variety of organizational structures, policies, and norms.[50] The following strategies will help team leaders bring the best out of their diverse teams.

> Resolving conflicts in a productive way that pulls people together, instead of driving them farther apart, and which produces creative decisions, instead of destructive power struggles, is a high level leadership skill.
> —JOHN KOTTER, *Leadership scholar*

CREATE A COMMON IDENTITY AND COLLECTIVIST CULTURE   Because people tend to be attracted to and be more comfortable with people that they perceive as similar to themselves, it is important for team members to develop a collective identity that overrides other identities.[51] Organizations that promote a collectivist culture (one that promotes shared organizational goals, interdependence, cooperation, and a view of employees as being more similar to rather than different from each other) rather than an individualistic culture (one that promotes the view that employees are unique and encourages employees to differentiate themselves from others) are more likely to develop a common identity among employees and benefit from diversity. Specifically, researcher Jennifer Chatman and her colleagues say:

> Feelings of similarity and a common fate among members cultivated in collectivist cultures lead members to consider more of their coworkers to be part of their in-group. Because in-group members seek out and prefer to interact with one another, members of organizations emphasizing collectivist values should interact with one another and participate in joint efforts to solve organizational problems more frequently than would members of individualistic cultures.[52]

Indeed, in their study of organizations with collectivist versus individualistic cultures, they concluded, "Dissimilar people in collective cultures had the highest creative output, both in terms of their own perceptions of creativity and the ratings of their creativity by experts."[53]

CREATE A "VALUE-IN-DIVERSITY" PERSPECTIVE IN THE WORK TEAM   Teams in which team members are encouraged to have a value-in-diversity perspective tend to perform better because they are more likely to seek out, integrate, and make better use of diverse information. Effective leaders of diverse teams encourage the teams to use differences among team members in ways that help them rethink how they do their work, how they define their markets, how they solve problems, and how they conduct business on a day-to-day basis.[54]

> Cultural beliefs separate, through superficial differences, groups that reasonably should be united.
> —JENNIFER JAMES, *Thinking in the Future Tense*

RECRUIT TEAM MEMBERS WHO ARE HIGH ON NEED FOR COGNITION AND OPENNESS TO EXPERIENCE If possible, recruit and reward team members who have characteristics that help the team make the most of the different resources that a diverse team offers. If it is not possible to select team members who have these characteristics, then offer training that explains how these characteristics, as well as a value-in-diversity perspective, can help teams succeed.[55]

PAY PARTICULAR ATTENTION TO FIRST MEETINGS As with all teams, what happens at the beginning of a team's life sets the tone for future interactions among team members. At early stages, team members learn about each other and negotiate their relationships. However, members of diverse groups tend to have more hurdles to overcome than do relatively homogeneous teams, including more stereotyping, bias, and social conflict. Some research suggests that training team members in each other's point of view can improve the team's ability to work together productively.[56] Team leaders can have team members discuss questions such as the following at first meetings:

- What are my preferred ways of relating to other people (communication, level of formality, addressing conflict/avoiding conflict, and dealing with authority)?
- What are my work-related values (time management, problem-solving methods, and definitions of effectiveness)?
- What do I expect from the team leader?

On the basis of team members' individual responses to the preceding questions, the team can consider the following questions collectively:

- In what ways are we similar to and different from each other?
- Which of our differences are relevant to team performance, and which are not?
- What are our collective strengths that can help team performance?
- What are some potential dysfunctional dynamics that may hinder our ability to work together?
- How can we work together in ways that leverage our differences?

PAY EXTRA ATTENTION TO TEAM NORMS AND WORK PROCESSES Developing explicit norms and work processes are particularly important in diverse teams because team members may have more difficulty with cohesion, communication, and coordination. Norms increase predictability, decrease misunderstandings, and reduce stress. Norms related to communication are particular important in diverse teams. For example, team members should be sure to actively request information from all team members and make sure that it is taken seriously. If team members speak different languages, they should speak slowly and clearly, confirm mutual understanding, and avoid using language and mannerisms that may be considered offensive to other cultures. People from different cultural groups tend to have different networks outside the team, so team members should encourage communication with external people and groups who can offer information and support to the team.

PROVIDE EARLY OPPORTUNITIES TO SUCCEED, CLEAR PERFORMANCE MEASURES, AND ONGOING POSITIVE FEEDBACK It may be more important for diverse teams to experience small wins early in their team's life because they may be less optimistic about the team's ability to work together productively. Early visible success can increase team members' trust in each other and confidence in the team, reduce concerns about the team's ability to work together, and increase team members' attractiveness to each other. Furthermore, because members of diverse teams may underestimate their team's effectiveness relative to homogeneous teams (even when they are outperforming homogeneous teams), it is particularly important for team leaders to provide clear and measurable performance measures, as well as ongoing feedback so that team members can see their progress. It is also important for leaders of diverse teams to provide more positive feedback to diverse teams because members of diverse teams may be less likely to recognize the extent of their collective successes.

ROLE-MODEL THE BEHAVIOR THAT YOU WANT TO SEE IN TEAM MEMBERS As always, the leader's behavior sends clear signals to team members about what attitudes, language, and behaviors are appropriate. Effective leaders of diverse teams manage their own stereotypes and biases, actively seek out diversity on the team, and show through their everyday interactions that they respect diversity and believe it benefits the team and organization. Simple things make a difference. For example, one leader of a cross-national management team made several interventions.

> His company badge listed his name in Latin, Cantonese, and Japanese characters. He coached his managers to watch for and address possible culturally based misunderstandings during their meetings. He would interrupt staff that were discussing an issue to see if one was not fully understanding the other. He encouraged his managers to do the same. He would also meet with his managers privately, like a diplomat, to bring up more sensitive issues, such as the possibility that one manager's style might be offensive to another.[57]

PAY ATTENTION TO THE CONTEXT IN WHICH THE TEAM WORKS Teams don't work in isolation from their context, so they are likely to exhibit the biases, norms, and dynamics of the organizations and societies in which they are embedded.[58] Consequently, the context in which a diverse team works can either create opportunities (e.g., the use of all team members' resources) that enable the team to use the team's diversity to enhance its performance or create hurdles (e.g., stereotyping and marginalizing some team members) that inhibit the team from achieving its potential. Researchers Aparna Joshi and Hyuntak Roh explain that "when a single demographic group dominates an occupation, negative stereotype-based categorization process against underrepresented groups are likely" and these stereotypes can hinder the team's ability to see beyond negative stereotypes in ways that enable the team members to make the best use of their diverse team.[59] For example, Caucasian men tend to be the dominant group in engineering and information technology professions in the United States and women tend to be the dominant group in the nursing and teaching professions. Team leaders need to be aware of the potential for dysfunctional dynamics such as stereotyping that can occur in these teams when people from outside the dominant group become team members—and take actions to minimize potential dysfunctional dynamics so that the teams can leverage all of their resources.

Conclusion

Team leaders are responsible for taking actions that enable diverse teams to make the most of their collective resources and avoid dysfunctional dynamics that can hinder their performance. All team members benefit from the competitive advantages gained from valuing and leveraging team diversity, and all team members lose when the unique opportunities available in a diverse team are lost due to dysfunctional team dynamics. Undoubtedly, diverse teams will continue to enrich and challenge the organizations in which we work, and they will have an increasingly powerful impact on our daily lives. They will design and manufacture the products that we use, find cures for the diseases that plague us, perform complex surgeries on our bodies, and take care of our precious children at school. The quality of our lives depends not only on the individual competence of team members but also on their ability to leverage their diversity and work together as a cohesive and effective team.

PART II: VIRTUAL TEAMS: WORKING TOGETHER APART[60]

Increasingly, virtual teams (also called "distributed" teams) are becoming commonplace in organizations. Similar to teams that meet primarily face-to-face (also called "co-located" teams), virtual teams are made up of individuals interacting interdependently on collective tasks to achieve common organizational goals. However, virtual teams differ in significant ways from teams that meet primarily face-to-face:[61]

> Until recently, when you said that you worked with someone, you meant by implication that you worked in the same place for the same organization. Suddenly, in the blink of an evolutionary eye, people no longer must be in the same place—co-located—in order to work together. Now many people work in virtual teams that transcend distance, time zones, and organizational boundaries.[141]
> —JESSICA LIPNACK AND JEFFREY STAMPS, *Virtual Teams: Reaching Across Time, Space, and Technology*

- *Communication is primarily through computer mediated information and communication technologies.* Members of virtual teams use computer-mediated technologies to a much greater degree than do teams that meet primarily face-to-face. These technologies enable team members to communicate, hold meetings, make decisions, create and manage documents, manage projects, serve customers, and conduct their other collective tasks without ever meeting face-to-face if necessary.
- *Flexibility.* Virtual teams tend to be more flexible because schedules can be set "by due dates and milestones, not by the availability of team members."[62]
- *Fluid team membership.* Membership in virtual teams tends to be more fluid, with team membership changing more often whenever different types of expertise and perspectives are needed at different stages of the team's project.
- *Diversity.* Members of virtual teams tend to be more diverse than are those in teams that meet primarily face-to-face because virtual teams are more likely to include people from different departments, regions, nations, and organizations, as well as customers, temporary workers, consultants, and other constituents. Team members also may be diverse in terms of their level of access, familiarity, and skill level with information and communication technologies (e.g., using social networking sites, searching for and evaluating information, intuitively figuring out how to use new tools), and these differences tend to be related to age, class, education, and nationality.[63] Box 9.2 summarizes demographic trends in Internet use.

Note that teams—even when they consider themselves virtual—don't all share the same degree of "virtuality," so it makes more sense to speak of teams in general as being on a continuum of virtuality rather than being either co-located or virtual. For example, although most virtual teams have geographic diversity, in some virtual teams all team members share the same nationality. Other virtual teams have members representing multiple nationalities and face the challenges of language, cultural norms, work routines, and significant time zone differences. Some virtual teams work primarily through e-mail and conference calls, whereas other virtual teams use a broader variety of communication technologies to achieve their collective goals.[64]

All teams, whether they meet face-to-face or virtually, need to effectively manage both their task and relationship processes to achieve their collective goals. They need to be able to build cohesion among team members, communicate effectively internally and externally, obtain the resources (e.g., information, materials, contacts) they need to succeed, and coordinate their efforts so that

BOX 9.2 Demographics for Internet Use and Access

The following statistics are from 2009. These percentages will, of course, change over time. However, the general patterns, if not the exact percentages, are likely to continue (and have been similar since 2000). A recent survey of Internet use in the United States by the Pew Internet & American Life Project found that:

- 93% of 18–29 year olds, 81% of 30–49 year olds, 70% of 50–64 year olds, and 38% of those 65+ used the Internet.
- 76% of 18–29 year olds, 67% of 30–49 year olds, 56% of 50–64 year olds, and 26% of 65+ had broadband Internet access from home.
- 81% of men and 77% of women used the Internet.
- 59% of men and 51% of women used wireless Internet access, as did 80% of 18–29 year olds, 66% of 30–49 year olds, 42% of 50–64 year olds, and 16% of those 65+.
- 76% of the white, non-Hispanic population, 70% of black, non-Hispanic population, and 64% of Hispanic population (English-and Spanish-speaking) used the Internet.
- 94% of households earning $75,000, 83% of households earning $50,000–$74,999, 76% of households earning $30,000–$49,999, and 60% of households earning less than $30,000 year used the Internet.
- 94% of people who graduated from college, 87% of people who had some college, 63% of people who graduated from high school, and 39% of those who had less than a high school education used the Internet.

A recent survey of Internet use worldwide by the Miniwatt Marketing Group found that:

- Less than 27% of the world's population use the Internet.
- 76.2% of people in North American, 68.8% in Oceania/Australia; 53.01% in Europe, 31.9% in Latin America/Caribbean countries, 28.8 in the Middle East, 20.1% in Asia, and 8.7% in Africa use the Internet.
- The percentage of Internet use by world region is: 42.4 % Asia, 23.6% Europe, 14.4% North America, 10.4% Latin America/Caribbean, 4.8% Africa, 3.2% Middle East, and 1.2% Oceania/Australia.

Source: Internet, broadband and cell phone statistics; 2009. http://www.pewinternet.org/Reports/2010/Internet-broadband-and-cell-phone-statistics.aspx?r=1; The Miniwatt Marketing Group, Internet World Statistics for 2009/10, http://www.internetworldstats.com/stats.htm

they can achieve their goals quickly with high quality. However, virtual teams face more challenges than do face-to-face teams. The following sections of this chapter discuss the benefits of virtual teams, the challenges of virtual teams, and best practices for managing virtual teams.

Benefits of Virtual Teams

Several technical, social, and economic trends make virtual teams not only possible but often preferable to co-located teams.

- Electronic and computer-based information and communication technologies are becoming increasingly affordable and available, and new technologies that enable teams to be more efficient and effective continue to emerge.
- Global expansion, mergers, alliances, and acquisitions are creating organizational relationships that cross regional and national boundaries, making it more difficult for organizational members to meet face-to-face.

- A shift from production to knowledge work makes it unnecessary for team members to be in the same place in order to work together.
- Many teams depend on external consultants and experts who may not be able to attend face-to-face meetings on a regular basis.
- E-commerce is creating organizational–customer relationships that are conducted primarily, sometimes solely, through social networking. With e-commerce, customer service can be available 24 hours a day, can offer immediate service, and can always be, at least in spirit, close to the customer.
- Organizations that want to recruit and retain the most talented employees are offering alternative work arrangements, including telecommuting, that are supported by information and communication technologies. Many talented employees are becoming less interested in having grueling travel schedules that affect their health and interfere with their family time and instead look for work opportunities that enable them to telecommute and connect virtually rather than travel extensively.
- Organizations that want to make the best use of limited office space are increasingly using "hot desks" to reduce the number of private office spaces required. Hot desks are office spaces that include desks, computers, telephones, and storage areas that are shared by many people who spend little time in the office (e.g., part-time consultants and employees who spend much of their time working out of the office).[65]
- Because of their ability to free team members from some of the constraints of time and place, information and communication technologies can help teams be faster and more flexible—distinct advantages in today's competitive economic environment.

Increased use of virtual teams may also have environmental benefits because of the reduced need for travel and facility costs. One U.S. government study concluded that "if 20,000 federal employees could telecommute one day per week they would save over two million commuting miles, 102 gallons of gasoline and 81,600 pounds of carbon dioxide emissions each week."[66]

We're only at the start of the dotcom learning curve. As the road gets steeper and you don't drive at Internet speed, you'd better keep an eye out for the tire marks on your back.
—SCOTT MCNEALY,
Co-founder, Sun Microsystems

Certainly, the availability of communication and information technologies will not guarantee that a team will be faster, more flexible, more cost effective, or more productive. To achieve these outcomes, all teams—whether they meet virtually or face-to-face—must have a clear and engaging purpose, clear performance standards and accountability processes, effective work processes for communication and coordination, highly skilled people on the team who focus on both the task and relationships, and opportunities to practice and learn from their collective successes and failures. However, members of virtual teams also must learn how to overcome the challenges associated with communicating and coordinating primarily through computer-mediated information and communication technologies, especially when team members are separated by geographic distance, cultural differences, time zones, and different levels of access and expertise with communication technologies. Consequently, effective leaders of virtual teams understand that they need to work harder to ensure that everyone on the virtual team understands the goals and follows the same work because the team members are less likely to share similar values, priorities, perspectives, and taken-for-granted work routines. In one study, researchers found that unclear goals, inefficient information sharing, and unclear guidelines for accountability were common contributors to poor performance in virtual teams.[67]

If there's a secret to the success of high-performing virtual teams, it's that their team members and leaders realize that managing the virtual teams' relationships within and outside the team is as important as managing the technology and task processes. Bernie DeKoven, director of the Institute for Better Meetings in California, describes effective virtual teams this way:

> When I think of virtual teams in the best light, I think of teams of people who are as comfortable with each other as they are with a wide variety of communication and computing technologies. When they meet "virtually," they take advantage of all their technical know-how to continue their work; and, when they meet face-to-face, they use the same technology to develop, organize, and refine their understanding. They have an emotional bandwidth that is as broad as their communication bandwidth, so that no matter how or where they meet they relate to each other with humor, understanding, and respect.[68]

CHALLENGES OF VIRTUAL TEAMS

Research on distributed teams suggests that the team dynamics in virtual teams differ in many ways from their face-to-face counterparts.[69] For example, many researchers argue that electronic and computer-mediated meetings differ in significant ways from face-to-face meetings. Lee Sproull and Sara Kiesler describe face-to-face meetings this way:

If I could live anywhere, it would be in cyberia.
—GABE DOPPELT,
Editor of Mademoiselle

> Most meetings follow a predictable course. Participation is unequal; one person or a minority clique dominates the floor. Member status predicts who will dominate. Managers speak more than subordinates; men speak more than women; the person at the front of the room speaks more than those at the back. People are polite and considerate, and they avoid controversy. If a decision is necessary, the group converges on a decision over time by narrowing and discarding options through discussion. People prefer options that have obvious popularity. Often we can predict the decision by knowing who dominates the discussion.[70]

Research suggests that when compared with their face-to-face counterparts, teams that meet through electronic and computer-mediated technologies tend to:

- Be somewhat less influenced by the comments of people who have higher status or better social and communication skills.
- Consult more people who have different yet complementary knowledge, which can increase the number of alternatives considered. Teams that meet face-to-face are more likely to have redundant knowledge available to them because they tend to have less diversity in perspectives, knowledge, and experience.
- Have more task-related conflict, perhaps because status effects and politeness norms (e.g., taking turns or appearing to listen attentively) are more relaxed than in face-to-face meetings.[71]

Furthermore, members of teams that use electronic and computer-based information and communication technologies can have immediate access to more information and can communicate with more people more quickly than can members of co-located teams.[72] However, communication and coordination can be more complex. Consider the following description of the problems one virtual team experienced:

> Communications were often fragmented, with gaps and misunderstanding among distant group members. There was confusion in telephone conferences, with

people on different pages of documents. Group members failed to return telephone calls or respond to inquiries from distant members. Key group members at remote sites were left off e-mail distribution lists. Distant members were not informed of key decisions or information. Misunderstandings developed on the basis of different assumptions about the tasks and assignments. Messages were interpreted differently in different places, sometimes fueling ongoing conflicts among office sites.[73]

The first rule of any technology used in a business is that automation applied to an efficient operation will magnify the efficiency. The second is that automation applied to an inefficient operation will magnify the inefficiency.
—BILL GATES,
Co-founder, Microsoft

The preceding scenario illustrates how members of virtual teams, like their face-to-face counterparts, must develop work processes that create cohesion, promote a shared understanding of the task, and develop work processes that enable team members to effectively communicate and coordinate their efforts. When virtual teams lack these processes, "confusion, insecurities, and resentment" can result.[74] The preceding scenario also illustrates how many of the communication and coordination challenges in virtual teams result from the mismanagement of social dynamics rather than the technology. The following section presents the challenges associated with the social dynamics in virtual teams.

Managing Social Dynamics in Virtual Teams

Two social processes that are particularly challenging in virtual teams include team members' ability to (1) develop feelings of cohesion that inspire commitment to each other and the team's goals and (2) communicate effectively with each other and to people/groups outside the team in ways that help them coordinate fluidly with each other.

DEVELOPING COHESION AND COMMITMENT   Human beings are social animals. We have a basic need to belong to a community, interact with others, and depend on others. High-quality relationships at work and in our teams give us a sense of identity, provide us with predictable rules for speaking and behaving in ways that help us coordinate with others, and enhance our physical and psychological health.[75] Consider the following:

- We treat people with whom we have positive relationships differently than we treat people we don't know very well and are more likely to be open to influence from people we know well.[76] In her book, *Managing Virtual Teams*, Martha Haywood explained: "It's a lot harder to ignore someone who has personified themselves to us, somebody who has thoughts, needs, feelings and a boss that might get mad at them if they don't get their work done. I know I'm more likely to respond to an e-mail I receive from my friend John than I am to respond to an e-mail from stranger@obscure.com."[77]
- Teams that develop their social capital, that is, their internal and external networks of relationships, get better results than those that don't develop these networks. Furthermore, the leaders of teams that are externally connected are more likely to get promoted because they achieve better results and have more visibility.[78]
- Teams that have more positive interactions among team members are more likely to get achieve better results because they tend to have more active participation from all team members. They are also likely to be open to ideas and behave more flexibly.[79]
- When people are engaged in high-quality connections—short-term personal connections that create mutual positive energy and positive regard (e.g., brief meetings at the water cooler, informal interactions before or after meetings)—they tend to be more open to ideas,

have better recall, learn better, have more resilience, feel more psychologically safe, and experience immediate positive health effects (e.g., cardiovascular and immune system). Teams and organizations that promote high-quality connections are more likely to inspire more effective communication, cooperation, learning, risk-taking, and change.[80]

Despite the important ways that high-quality relationships contribute to team effectiveness, many researchers and practitioners are concerned that high-quality relationships may be particularly difficult to achieve in virtual teams because team members (1) have fewer opportunities to engage in activities that help them build familiarity, predictability, trust, and mutual regard and (2) are less able to hear and see the social cues that one sees in face-to-face encounters (e.g., tone of voice and body language) that help them understand the meaning of the spoken word more accurately. Co-located employees are more likely to participate in impromptu conversations in the hallway, take breaks together, share meals, see photos of colleagues' families on their desks, and participate in social events sponsored by the organization. Such face-to-face interactions contribute to work outcomes even though they are not directly related to the task because they humanize us to each other; help us develop a shared understanding of the organization and its goals and values; and increase our mutual trust, respect, commitment, and goodwill.[81] Some of our best ideas and opportunities are the result of chance face-to-face encounters and informal discussions.

Psychoanalyst Edward Hallowell refers to these face-to-face encounters as "the human moment." He describes the human moment as "an authentic psychological encounter that can happen only when two people share the same physical space." He explains:

> I have given the human moment a name because I believe that it has started to disappear from modern life. . . . The human moment has two prerequisites: people's physical presence and their emotional and intellectual attention.[82]

John Lock, author of *The De-Voicing of Society: Why We Don't Talk to Each Other Anymore,* poignantly echoes Hallowell's concerns about the impact of technology on human relationships: "Now when the [answering] machine kicks in, we can do something that previously would have been unthinkable as well as socially suicidal: decide whether to respond to the voice of our closest friends."[83]

Technology . . . the knack of arranging the world so that we don't have to deal with it.
—MAX FRISCH,
Swiss author

Most Internet experts are optimistic about technology's impact on human relationships. In a recent study by the Pew Organization, 895 Internet experts worldwide were surveyed about their beliefs about the impact of the Internet on relationships in society.[84] From the survey responses, the researchers concluded, "The social benefits of Internet use will far outweigh the negatives . . . because e-mail, social networks, and other online tools offer . . . opportunities to create, enhance, and rediscover social ties that make a difference in people's lives. The Internet lowers traditional communication's constraints of cost, geography, and time; and it supports the type of open information sharing that brings people together." Specifically, 85% of those surveyed agreed with the statement: "In 2020, when I look at the big picture and consider my personal friendships, marriage and other relationships, I see that the Internet has mostly been a positive force on my social world. And this will only grow more true in the future." One survey respondent explained:

> The enemies of social connectivity are silence, disengagement, distance, and abandonment. In the past, how many individuals and families have suffered from these degenerative influences? Now we have the Internet. High school sweethearts are reunited. Strangers meet and form personal unions. Families are brought together. Adoptees find reunion, too. Interest groups thrive. Businesses leap borders. Genealogies are learned,

and one person in his lifetime can place himself into history, and comprehend his place in the span of time. On the Internet, social alienation remains a factual force. But never before has a person had more opportunity for social integration. More than ever, being inside or outside now is a matter of personal choice.

In contrast, 15% of the survey respondents agreed with the statement: "In 2020, when I look at the big picture and consider my personal friendships, marriage and other relationships, I see that the Internet has mostly been a negative force on my social world. And this will only grow more true in the future." These survey respondents expressed concerns about the negative impact of the Internet on social relationships, including shallower relationships, children who grow up lacking face-to-face social skills, reinforcing social alienation by providing already alienated people who develop a "false sense of connectedness" through the Internet, new outlets for dysfunctional behaviors such as online bullying and other forms of harassment, and a tendency to find and spend online time with people who share similar views, which can lead to narrower and more extreme world views.

Many researchers are optimistic about technology's impact on human relationships at work and argue that psychological closeness is as important as physical closeness. Researchers David Armstrong and Paul Cole conclude that psychological closeness is the result of several conditions, including "the degree of identification with group membership; the similarity of work goals, norms, role and procedure expectations (task cohesion); the accuracy of mutual comprehension; the degree of motivation toward shared goals; the amount of interdependency and mutual trust; and the frequency of communication among members."[85] All of these characteristics can be achieved virtually as well as face-to-face.

> **The most exciting breakthroughs of the 21st century will not occur because of technology but because of an expanding concept of what it means to be human.**
> —JOHN NAISBITT,
> *Author of Megatrends*

Indeed, when well managed, electronic and computer-mediated technologies can help us overcome hurdles that may inhibit psychological closeness in virtual teams. For example, we may find it easier to see ourselves as similar to each other when we don't have visual cues that highlight our differences. We may find it easier to cross traditional professional, functional, and hierarchical barriers in a virtual environment because we remove some of the visual physical reminders of these barriers. Many of us find electronic communication to be easier, more enjoyable, and more effective than face-to-face communication because we can take time to carefully organize and articulate our thoughts, avoid awkwardness and stage fright associated with speaking publicly, and possibly minimize some of the status effects in groups that affect our ability to speak candidly or be taken seriously.

Remember that not everyone wants intimacy at work. Martha Haywood quoted one manager as saying, "I don't care about this guy's inner feelings. I want to know when he's going to call me back."[86] Researcher Lee Sproull, who has been studying trust and relationships in online environments for many years, explains, "If I see this person is going to do a first-rate job with the information I provide, that he [sic] won't undercut it, won't embarrass me, then I'm more likely to trust [that person]."[87]

Indeed, trust is more important than intimacy in virtual work relationships. Teams tend to produce better results when team members trust each other.[88] Trust refers to one's willingness to be vulnerable to another person under the assumption that the other person will have his or her best interests in mind and follow through on promised actions that are important to them even though they may not have the ability to control the other person's actions.[89] Yet it's more challenging to create trust in virtual teams. One reason is that virtual teams make it more difficult to control team members' behavior. For example, you have to trust that team members are listening to each other on conference calls rather than checking their e-mails or cleaning their offices while "attending" the virtual meeting. Cultural differences in assumptions, priorities, and work practices make it more difficult for team members to build trust because we tend to trust people whose behavior we can predict, and it's more difficult to predict behavior when people are from different cultures and when we are unable to see the taken-for-granted social cues that help us make sense of others' words.[90] And it's more difficult for leaders of virtual teams to control team members' behavior when they are scattered around the nation or world. As a virtual team leader, it's often unlikely that you'd be able to answer the question, "Do you know where your employees are?"[91] Despite the challenges in building trust, virtual teams often must develop trust quickly because they often must begin their collective work on projects immediately with little knowledge of each other.

What creates trust in virtual teams? Trust in virtual teams is built on the same qualities that build trust in any kind of relationship: goodwill, responsiveness, ability, predictability, and integrity, and is most likely to be created or lost during initial team interactions. Therefore, the time and planning that virtual team leaders invest up front and throughout the team's life are likely to pay off in the long run. Early leadership behaviors that create trust in virtual teams include articulating a clear task to minimize confusion, showing optimism and enthusiasm about the task to build commitment, making sure team members get to know each other and the valuable skills and perspectives that each person brings to the team, creating shared positive social experiences to build goodwill, developing shared norms for communication and coordination to build predictability, articulating shared norms for accountability to ensure quality, and providing a well-managed technical environment to ensure that all team members have appropriate technology and knowledge of how to use it.[92]

> The U.S. Bill of Rights is just a local ordinance in cyberspace.
> —MARY O'HARA-DEVEREAUX AND ROBERT JOHANSEN, *citing John Perry Barlow*

Managing Communication in Virtual Teams

Effective communication is central to productivity in virtual teams. It is the means by which "all speakers and hearers attempt to construct a shared communication context in which their messages can be produced and understood. . . . [P]articipants in a conversation strive for a shared understanding of the situation, of the task, and of one another's background knowledge, expectations, beliefs, and attitudes."[93] However, constructing a shared reality about work goals and the process for achieving those goals through electronic and computer-mediated technologies can be particularly difficult. This section focuses on three social dynamics that affect the quality of communication in virtual teams: (1) the lack of social cues, (2) the need for a psychologically safe environment that fosters honest communication, and (3) status and power dynamics.

> Science and technology multiply around us. To an increasing extent they dictate the languages in which we speak and think. Either we use those languages, or we remain mute.
> —J. G. BALLARD, *English novelist*

THE LACK OF SOCIAL CUES Researchers agree that one of the most important differences between face-to-face and electronic and computer-mediated communication is that the latter removes or minimizes many of the taken-for-granted social cues that we use to make sense of what people are saying and feeling when they speak.[94] There are three types of social cues that tend to be missing or minimized when communicating through technology: static cues, dynamic cues, and situational cues.

Static cues refer to fixed markers such as titles (doctor or nurse, manager or secretary), appearance (style of dress or demographic group membership such as race, ethnicity, and gender), and seating arrangements (who is sitting at the head of the table). On the basis of these cues, we make

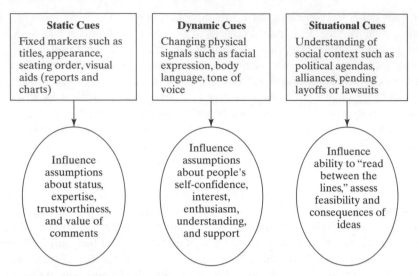

FIGURE 9-2 The Importance of Social Cues

assumptions about the status, expertise, and credibility of the persons with whom we interact, which in turn influence how we interpret the content and value of their comments. Static cues also refer to visual aids such as reports, diagrams, and charts that help us "get on the same page" during meetings.

Dynamic cues refer to changing physical signals such as facial expressions (smiling or frowning), body language (nodding or hand gestures), pace (interrupting or hesitating before replying), and tone of voice (soft-spoken or loud). With these nonverbal cues, we make assumptions about people's self-confidence, enthusiasm, understanding, and support or resistance to our comments.[95]

Situational cues refer to our understanding of the social context in which communication occurs.[96] This social context includes local knowledge of people, relationships, issues, and events in the organization and community (e.g., religious holidays, organizational routines, political agendas and alliances, pending layoffs, and recent or potential lawsuits). Understanding the organizational and cultural context at different locations enables us to "read between the lines" of comments that are made. When making decisions, this reading of the situation helps us understand what alternatives can be realistically considered, as well as the potential intended and unintended consequences that might arise from any decision. However, this "situated knowledge" is more difficult to understand in virtual teams, especially when the teams are nationally diverse and geographically distributed.[97]

Sending e-mail to co-workers instead of walking to deliver messages can contribute to a weight gain over time . . . Over 10 years, that could increase a person's weight by 11 pounds.
—HAIDEE ALLERTON,
citing a study in Training and Development

A study by researchers Ray Friedman and Steven Currall illustrates how the lack of social cues can create problems with distance communication. They found that conflict is more likely to occur when using e-mail than when using face-to-face communication. They also found that using e-mail to resolve existing conflicts can actually escalate the conflicts. They argue that in face-to-face situations, including conflicts, people are better able to develop a shared understanding of the situation—what is often called "common ground"; can read body language and hear vocal tones to make assumptions about how the other person is responding to one's message; and are more likely to engage in shorter and more frequent communication, including turn-taking, which leaves less time for misunderstandings to occur and escalate. In contrast, when communicating through e-mail, people can't read body language or hear vocal tones to help them interpret comments—even well-intended comments can be easily misinterpreted; have more time between responses, which leaves time for misunderstandings and resentment to escalate; tend to write longer responses and bundle ideas together, so they may not get responses to all of their concerns and thus feel resentful; and may spend more time crafting the written response, which may lead the writer to become more committed to his or her position.[98]

In short, social cues help us make assumptions about the person who is speaking—their status, credibility, and trustworthiness; how others react to us and our ideas; and the larger context in which our communication takes place. Consequently, leaders of virtual teams need to (1) understand how the lack of cues can distort communication in ways that affect cohesion and coordination and (2) design team processes that promote effective communication despite the lack of social cues. Figure 9-2 describes the role of social cues in developing shared understanding in teams.

THE NEED FOR A PSYCHOLOGICALLY SAFE ENVIRONMENT   Psychological safety refers to an employee's "sense of being able to show and employ one's self without negative consequences to self-image, status or career."[99] Researcher Amy Edmondson defines team psychological safety as a "shared belief in a team that it is safe to take interpersonal risks."[100] Psychological safety is central to team learning, which Edmondson describes as "the activities carried out by team members through which a team obtains and processes data that allow it to adapt and improve."[101]

Researchers have found that team members who feel psychologically safe tend to communicate more often and more effectively inside and outside the team. Specifically, they tend to be less self-conscious; trust each other more; speak up more; share information more often across hierarchical and functional boundaries; support each other more; value all team members' diverse perspectives and talents; avoid negative stereotypes; reduce ingroup/outgroup conflict; ask for help when needed; admit error; raise difficult issues; engage in quick, informal, and spontaneous face-to-face and e-mail communication; request feedback; take more initiative; challenge current taken-for-granted practices; be more creative; take more risks; and experiment more.[102] Researchers Cristina Gibson and Jennifer Gibbs found that a psychologically safe environment in virtual teams promoted innovation because "it helped to raise and clarify contextual differences, helping teams coordinate and garner resources for innovation across contexts" and "helped raise and clarify cultural differences in national orientations and norms, resolve conflict, and foster an open environment in which team members felt comfortable to ask questions, admit to a lack of understanding, and voice opinions."[103] Not surprisingly, teams that provide a psychologically safe environment tend to get better results because they are able to be more proactive, access the resources inside and outside their teams, learn more from their experiences, adapt more quickly, and make more thoughtful decisions.

It is more challenging to build a psychologically safe environment in virtual teams because of the increased uncertainty and unpredictability in virtual teams, as well as the increased difficulty in building mutually supportive relationships. To build psychological safety in virtual teams, team leaders must take systematic steps to reduce this uncertainty and enhance the quality of the relationships among team members, as well as with the people and groups with whom the team must interact to achieve their goals. These steps include highlighting the value of each team member's unique perspectives and talents early in the team's life, encouraging participation and active listening from all team members/encouraging and rewarding risk-taking, and helping team members build high-quality relationships with relevant people and groups outside the team.

BOX 9-3   Best Practices in Managing Global Distributed Teams

To promote strong group cohesion among site managers around the globe, the leader of a newly desig-nated organization committed his management staff to meeting face-to-face every six to eight weeks. They rotated the location of each meeting around the globe so that they visited each other's country sev-eral times. Telephone conferences were held every three weeks between face-to-face meetings. During their first round of visits to each other's sites, the assembled management team also met face-to-face with each site's staff in discussions facilitated by a consultant. The group even developed shared humor and jokes, such as requiring each site manager to sing a song in his or her native tongue to the assembled management team at his or her first meeting. This became an entry ritual for new managers as member-ship turned over.

Source: From Armstrong, David, and Paul Cole. 1994. *Culture and Social Behavior*. New York: McGraw-Hill.

UNDERSTANDING STATUS AND POWER DYNAMICS IN VIRTUAL TEAMS   Status and power dynamics are a taken-for-granted part of everyday life in organizations. A consistent finding in group research is that "in mixed-status groups, high-status people talk more, speak more frankly, have more control over the agenda, and through their dominance have more influence."[104] One of the most interesting debates among researchers of distributed teams is whether electronic and computer-mediated communication reduces status effects. Many re-searchers argue that the use of electronic and computer-mediated communication technologies can reduce some status effects that are common in face-to-face groups. Researchers Lee Sproull and Sarah Kiesler explain:

> Because it is harder to read status cues in electronic messages than it is in other forms of communication, high-status people do not dominate the discussion in elec-tronic groups as much as they do in face-to-face groups. For instance, when groups of executives met face-to-face, the men in the groups were five times as likely as the women to make the first decision proposal. When those same groups met via com-puter, the women made the first proposal as often as the men did. When pairs of graduate students and undergraduates met face-to-face to decide their joint project, the pairs were likely to choose the topic preferred by the graduate student. When equivalent pairs of students discussed and decided electronically, they were equally likely to choose the topic initially preferred by the undergraduate.[105]

In addition, there is some evidence that e-mail may increase communication across hierarchi-cal boundaries, and employees may be more likely to send bad news to their bosses through e-mail.[106]

However, some researchers argue, quite convincingly, that the "equalization phenome-non" (the reduction of status effects) associated with computer-mediated communication (CMC) is overstated.[107] Researcher Guiseppe Montovani, for example, argues that "CMC is ef-fective in overcoming physical barriers, but not, or at least not necessarily, social barriers."[108] He argues further: "Electronic links primarily enhance existing interaction patterns rather than creating new ones. . . . CMC usually operates by supplementing established preferences, re-specting status barriers and already-developed communication clusters."[109] In other words, if a person is not taken seriously at face-to-face meetings, there is no reason that his or her e-mail will be taken seriously either.

Furthermore, electronic and computer-mediated communication technologies increase the ways that employers can monitor and control employee behavior. Using these technologies, employers can monitor employees' telephone calls, e-mail messages, and Internet use; count keystrokes that record the speed at which employees work; monitor how much time the employee spends on the keyboardand increase the expectation that people will check their electronic and voice mail regularly, even on evenings, weekends, and vacations. A recent study by the American Management Association and the ePolicy Institute concluded that organizations have been increasing electronic monitoring of employees. Of the 526 U.S. companies surveyed, 76% have monitored the Web sites their employees' visited, and approximately "25 percent of employers have fired workers for misusing the Internet; another 25 percent have terminated employees for inappropriate e-mail use."[110]

If there is technological advance without social advance, there is, almost automatically, an increase in human misery, in impoverishment.
—MICHAEL HARRINGTON, *U.S. social scientist*

As with status dynamics, gender dynamics in societies also play out in the world of technology. Researcher Jane Fountain argues that "women are the predominant users of information technology in the workplace." However, she also argues that "women are poorly represented in the sector that constitutes the growth engine of the U.S. economy and that bears primary responsibility for the scientific and technological development of an Information society."[111] Researcher Catherine Ashcrafts who conducted a study for the National Center for Women and Information Technology found that 36% of the IT-related jobs were held by women in 1991, but only 25% of IT-related jobs were held by women in 2008—even though technology jobs make up one of the fastest growing job categories.[112]

In short, as long as there are social and organizational hierarchies, status and power dynamics will be a fact of everyday life in work teams and organizations, regardless of whether people are working face-to-face or virtually. Carly Fiorina, former CEO of Hewlett Packard, exlains: "Many people see technology as the problem behind the so-called digital divide. Others see it as the solution. Technology is neither. It must operate in conjunction with the business, economic, political, and social systems." Team leaders who understand this are more likely to take personal responsibility for and explicit steps towards minimizing dysfunctional power dynamics in virtual teams. These can include employees' feelings of inclusion or exclusion, employees' willingness to speak up and express themselves honestly, employees' feelings of personal security and control, feelings of commitment to their teams and organizations, and unequal access to opportunities technological advances offer.

MANAGING DISTRIBUTED TEAMS

Undoubtedly, distributed teams that effectively use electronic and computer-based information and communication technologies are often able to work faster and more flexibly than their face-to-face counterparts, create productive relationships that span organizational and geographic boundaries, and develop new and improved ways of working together and serving their customers. But, as researcher Mary Munter puts it, "the latest technological changes are only as effective as the people using them."[113]

Information Technology is no longer a business resource. It is the business environment.
—JOHN BROWNING, *The Economist*

This section provides general guidelines for using information and communication technologies in teams. These guidelines are based on three broad recommendations:

- Determine the appropriate level of technology for the team task.
- Manage the technological environment.
- Develop work processes that enhance team performance.

Determine the Appropriate Level of Technology for the Team Task

When used appropriately, these technologies can help team members make and implement decisions faster, overcome the hurdles of time and distance, and use their resources more effectively. Therefore, effective team members and leaders know when it is best to meet face-to-face and when it is best to meet virtually. When misused, electronic and computer-based information and communication technologies can lead to misunderstandings, slow a team down, result in lower-quality decisions, waste opportunities to build high-quality relationships, and squander organizational resources.

Everybody gets so much information all day long that they lose their common sense.
—GERTRUDE STEIN, *American Writer*

DETERMINE WHEN IT'S BEST TO MEET FACE-TO-FACE OR VIRTUALLY When possible, face-to-face meetings are preferable in situations in which human contact is particularly important,[114] when visual cues enhance communication, or when the purpose of the meeting is highly symbolic. These situations include the following:

- First meetings when team members must create a common identity; define problems; develop shared work processes; and gain commitment to the goals, tasks, and each other
- When the team has significant turnover and must re-create a common identity
- When there are "higher levels of complexity and ambiguity in the messages"[115]
- When the goal of the meeting is to persuade team members to commit to a particular belief or course of action[116]
- When the team must deal with sensitive issues (e.g., hiring, promotion, discipline, and termination decisions)[117]
- During complex and delicate negotiations[118]
- When conflicts must be resolved[119]
- When acknowledging important milestones and celebrating successes
- When privacy and confidentiality must be maintained—electronic communications are more accessible and less private than face-to-face conversations or hard copy of documents[120]

Electronic and computer-mediated communication technologies are most useful for "routine tasks done by a defined group with established roles and motives"[121] and situations in which human contact isn't critical. These situations include the following:

- "Fact-finding problems" or "problems that have one right answer"[122]
- Gathering preliminary information and opinions prior to a face-to-face meeting
- Keeping team members informed between meetings
- Working together on tasks that were assigned during face-to-face meetings
- Reducing some dysfunctional dynamics such as status effects or one person dominating conversations (Remember, however, that "technology use will not resolve basic problems in group process.")[123]
- Experimenting with new technologies or new ways of working together that may increase productivity, learning, flexibility, or speed
- When team members cannot meet face-to-face
- When saving money in travel expenses outweighs the benefits of a face-to-face meeting
- When productivity can be increased by managing communication and workflow across time zones, particularly when teams direct their workflow from east to west. Martha Haywood explained: "Consider a hypothetical team where the software-engineering department is in Boston and the testing engineer department is in San Jose. If the software-engineering department arrives in the morning and creates a release for testing, they will be

ready to transfer it to the test department in San Jose at about noon, Boston time. For the engineers in California, it's only 9:00 A.M. The team has gained three working hours."

In addition to considering the task requirements, teams should consider the organizational culture when determining the degree of technology to use in their interactions with each other. Some organizational cultures promote the use of computer-mediated communication, whereas other organizational cultures promote face-to-face communication whenever possible.[124]

I'm skeptical of these devices that find each other and then start doing things among themselves.
—HANDSPRING COFOUNDER
JEFF HAWKINS,
eWeek.com

Manage the Technological Environment

Members of effective virtual teams are flexible enough to adapt to changing technologies, savvy enough to avoid computer viruses that can wreak havoc on a team's information and communication base, and resilient enough to handle hardware or software crashes that can bring a less savvy team's work to a standstill. Team members are likely to resist using electronic and computer-based information and communication technologies when they don't trust them (i.e., when they don't believe that these technologies will make a difference, don't understand how to use them, or are suspicious of them). They wonder, often with good reason: Will the technology break down in the middle of an important discussion or presentation? Will data be safe from being lost and from breaches in confidentiality? Will the technology be used to monitor, control, or evaluate my work behavior? Will the availability of communication technologies mean that I must always be available to the team—anywhere and any time of the day? There are several things that team leaders can do to manage the technological environment.

- Make sure that all team members have compatible information and communication technologies.
- Model and support the professional use of technology when managing both the task and social environment.
- Give team members a realistic picture of what technology can and cannot do for the team. Give specific examples of how it can improve team performance, such as ways that it can help the team manage information better, communicate more quickly, increase flexibility, complete projects faster, and save money.
- Train all team members how to use the various technologies and ensure that all are comfortable using these technologies. Remember to train new team members in the team's technologies when they join the team.
- Provide ongoing organizational support for troubleshooting.
- Provide trained facilitators for meetings that use sophisticated technologies such as videoconferencing and groupware.
- Set up early small wins. Team members who experience early successes with technology will be motivated to continue using the technology.
- Develop and adhere to clear policies regarding privacy, access to information, monitoring of electronic communications, and expectations regarding availability both on and off work time.[125]
- Have contingency plans in place to deal with hardware and software crashes so that the team isn't completely dependent on the technologies and can rebound quickly from technical failures.
- Make sure that all team members have the training and software that helps them avoid computer viruses.

Develop Work Processes That Enhance Cohesion, Communication, and Coordination

Members and leaders of effective virtual teams must pay particular attention to processes that enhance team cohesion, communication, and coordination.

The less often that team members meet face-to-face, the more diversity in the team, and the more the team uses information and communication technologies to organize their work, the more attention team leaders need to pay to building team relationships and designing a clear team process because (1) it is more difficult for virtual team leaders to control team behavior from a distance and (2) virtual teams often need to be more adaptable so that they need to be very clear about the boundaries in which they must work (e.g., their goals, performance standards, and accountability methods).[126]

COHESION   One of the challenges of distributed teams is developing a cohesive group with team members who rarely, if ever, meet each other face-to-face. Jessica Lipnack and Jeffrey Stamps explain, "To work with people you rarely or never meet, you need some basis to believe in their expertise and trustworthiness."[127] As mentioned earlier in this chapter, cohesiveness is built on trust. Trust is built on goodwill, competence, responsiveness, and predictability—all of which can be developed and reinforced by using electronic and computer-mediated communication technologies. To build team cohesiveness:

- *Build team identity.* Give the team a name to help create a common identity.
- *Help team members get to know each other so that they're more than names and titles to each other.* Have team members create personal Web pages about themselves. One team leader created a Web site that encouraged team members to take time to get to learn about each other. Each time a member of the team "logged onto the department Web page, the image of a different remote team member appears behind the picture of a reception desk." When team members clicked on the person's image, they could read information about that team member.[128]
- *Remind the team that the quality of their work relationships matter to team performance.* Remind team members that every interaction—whether virtual or face-to-face—is an opportunity to enhance a relationship.
- *Help the team develop a shared history.* Encourage teams to develop shared language, stories, symbols (e.g., logos or coffee cups), and rituals.
- *Encourage building mutually supportive relationships with people and groups outside the team.* One team had a surprise pizza dinner delivered to their distant colleagues during a videoconference so that they could share a meal together.[129]
- *Respect cultural differences.* Encourage team members to acknowledge and respect cultural values, traditions, and business practices because virtual teams are more likely to have team members from different cultures.
- *Develop norms for integrating new members into the team.* Virtual teams tend to have more fluid membership so it is important to have systematic ways of socializing new team members into the team.
- *Create work policies and norms that enhance predictability.* Trust is based, in part, on having predictable routines and being able to anticipate another's behavior. PricewaterhouseCoopers, for example, has 163,000 employees in more than 150 countries. Sheldon Laube, formerly the National Director of Information and Technology and

now the Chief Innovation Officer, says that "it would be unrealistic to put everyone on a plane for a get-together when all the necessary information can be coalesced quickly on networked computers." The company rarely gets people together in person before they begin working together as a team. Instead, the "company's set methodology and common language for conducting audits eases collaboration."[130]

COMMUNICATION   Although one of the benefits of electronic and computer-based information and communication technologies is the ability to retrieve, store, and analyze large amounts of information quickly, more information is not necessarily better. A survey of more than 1,000 British e-mail users found that "over 90 percent wasted up to an hour per day reading, responding to, and deleting irrelevant messages."[131] Martha Haywood explained, "Poorly trained distributed teams live in a state of unprioritized broadcast information overload."[132] Effective communication and information management occurs when information is well managed (the right information gets to the right people in the right format); the receiver of the message understands what the sender means; and relationships are enhanced, rather than harmed, by the communication. To achieve these ends, effective team members and leaders:

- *Create a repository for storing and using information.* Create a central online location that all team members can go to for obtaining and posting useful information throughout the team's life. Determine what information should be stored where and for what purposes, as well as how information should be maintained (updated and purged). Determine who will be in charge of posting the information, making sure that all documents posted are clearly labeled and up to date (and old documents are removed), and ensuring team members know when new information has been posted.
- *Provide contact information.* Post contact information for all team members (as well as useful information about each team member) in a central online location. In addition, post all routine information such as meeting dates, times, locations, and call in numbers so that all team members can find this information at any time during the team's life.
- *Create norms for sending messages and information.* Determine which kind of communication methods should be used for what purposes (e.g., face-to-face, telephone, e-mail, electronic bulletin boards, Web pages). Determine which messages should be sent to all members and which can be sent to individuals or subgroups. Agree upon common formats for organizing messages (e.g., clear e-mail headings, signaling priorities, brevity of content, type of responses expected). Team members should take care to write clearly and concisely, and consider that people on the team may speak different languages, infer different meanings to words and phrases, and be unfamiliar with slang and acronyms. How will the team confirm that messages are understood as intended?
- *Discuss cultural differences.* Take time to learn about cultural and location differences such as availability and quality of technology and key issues currently facing the organization or local area.[133]
- *Be clear when using documentation.* Refer to page numbers, paragraph numbers, and designators for diagrams when referring to documents (e.g., "Turn to Figure 1 on page 10 of the document titled 'New Products.'"). One study found that teams with poorly annotated documents take up to three times longer to complete a given exercise.[134]
- *Pay attention to the design of video conferences.* Position the angel of cameras when using video so that facial expressions and bodily mannerisms can be easily seen and interpreted.

COORDINATION   Because it is more difficult to monitor team member behavior in virtual teams, leaders of virtual teams need to ensure that all team members understand the goals, quality standards, and work processes (including timeliness) in the same way; inform all team members about important issues and events at the different locations; and provide ongoing feedback about how the team is performing against the clear standards. Your goals in designing the team process are to ensure that all team members are working together proactively to achieve team goals, to help the team develop predictability in how they work together, and to give the team the freedom to be adapt their collective work as needed throughout the team's project. To enhance coordination in virtual teams:

- *Set clear expectations that you are counting on a high level of participation and coordination from all team members.*   This can be challenging when team members have different levels of participation, with some team members participating full time in the team's work, while other team members are participating part time. Each team member needs to know what high performance means for their part of the team's work.
- *Be clear about task ownership.*   The team needs to know who owns each task and how each person and the team will be held accountable for the work. This is particularly important for tasks that must connect across team boundaries (e.g., obtain and deliver work across teams) because this intersection is where misunderstandings are most likely to occur).[135]
- *Develop predictable reporting systems.*   Routine status reports (e.g., weekly) that are e-mailed or posted online help keep track of key deliverables, milestones, and other useful information are very useful for keeping all parties informed about how the team is doing at any point in time.[136]
- *Have regular, well-managed meetings.*   Regularly scheduled meetings (e.g., once weekly, biweekly, or monthly) keep all team members connected to each other and provide a format for discussions that help with creativity, problem solving, and implementation. To make the best use of all team members' time (and not waste anyone's time), it sometimes makes sense to have team members meet in subgroups when there are topics that are not immediately relevant to all team members. To make the best use of meeting times, have a predictable meeting format for managing task and relationship processes in meetings, including having an agenda; systematic decision-making process; ways of ensuring that all team members come to the meeting prepared (e.g., sending out agenda, discussion topics, and relevant reading in advance); ways of ensuring that all team members participate as appropriate, feel able to raise controversial issues and disagree, and feel valued; ways of assigning accountability after the meeting; and ways of following up after the meeting (e.g., posting promised documents and minutes of the meeting if they are useful).
- *Agree on appropriate team-member availability.*   Agree upon how often team members should check their telephone messages, e-mail, and other communications; how they should acknowledge receiving messages, how quickly they should return messages and respond to requests; and whether they should let each other know when they will be out of the office and, if so, how they should do so.[137]
- *Coach team member and the team as a whole as appropriate.*   Once the systems for communicating and coordinating as a virtual team are in place, provide coaching as needed to individual team members and the team as a whole to get to know what they need and how you can help them do their best work. Effective team coaching includes motivating

the team, educating the team, and facilitating the team's efforts to coordinate with each other and parties outside the team. As with teams that meet face-to-face, leaders of virtual teams need to determine when to actively participate in the team and when to stay out of the team's way.

Box 9-4 provides tips for creating successful teleconference and videoconference meetings.

CONCLUSION

Effective members and leaders of distributed teams know that electronic and computer-based information and communication technologies enable organizations to achieve results and a competitive advantage over teams that only meet face-to-face. They also know that virtual teams can perform below their potential when they are not carefully managed. The most effective leaders of virtual teams know that they must create a work context that brings out the best in these teams. They understand that their most important job is to help their virtual teams create effective and predictable task and relationship processes for working together that helps them overcome the ambiguity associated with working through technology and across cultural and time differences.

BOX 9-4   Tips for Successful Teleconference and Videoconference Meetings

Plan in Advance

- ✔ Determine the date, starting and ending times, and number of participants. Be aware of time differences.
- ✔ Determine equipment needs and familiarize yourself with the equipment before the meeting.
- ✔ Prepare the participants:
  - Notify them of the meeting date, how to access the conference, the moderator's name, and start and end times.
  - If the participants have not met, send out an attendance list, as well as a short background of each attendee. Don't just list the names and titles. Where are they from? What do they do? Why are they invited to the meeting? Remember that you're trying to build relationships.
  - Provide an agenda, limited to three to five topics, and let participants know how much time you intend to spend on each topic.
  - Send out supporting documents. Remember to number pages (and paragraphs, if possible) and label diagrams. Let participants know whether they need to have the documents with them at the meeting.
  - Let participants know whether they must prepare anything in advance.
  - Let participants know how absences will be handled (how they should notify the appropriate parties, whether someone will take their place, how they should follow up).
- ✔ Develop an outline or script that includes opening comments, important announcements, agenda items (including the order and amount of time for each item), questions to stimulate discussion, and closing remarks.
- ✔ Be sure that you can pronounce all participants' names prior to the meeting so that you can call them by name. Write the phonetic pronunciation of their names and plan to keep this list in front of you during the meeting.
- ✔ Have a computer (or other system) at each site in case documents need to be sent to participants during the meeting.

(continued)

BOX 9-4 *Continued*

✔ Particularly for videoconferences, consider scheduling a trained facilitator who can manage the technological environment and facilitate the meeting.

✔ Plan to have technical support available in case there are problems with the technology.

✔ If you are leasing equipment, room, and time, make sure that you lease for more time than you need so that you don't get cut off in the middle of a meeting.

✔ Have a contingency plan in place, as well as a way of notifying participants of changes, in case there are problems with technology. Notify participants in advance of this contingency plan.

Manage the Meeting

✔ Make sure that the area is quiet and free of distractions. Ask not to be disturbed during the conference.

✔ Start on time and stick to the schedule.

✔ Project your enthusiasm and interest from the moment you begin the teleconference.

✔ Welcome participants to the conference by:
  • Summarizing key events that led up to the meeting.
  • Taking a roll call. If people have not met, ask them to say something as a warm-up to get to know each other better.
  • Reviewing the agenda and asking whether anyone needs clarification or wants to add or change anything.
  • Identifying the objectives you'd like to achieve by the end of the meeting.

✔ Remind participants of the ground rules for the meeting:
  • State name before speaking.
  • Speak clearly and concisely and keep comments focused on the topic.
  • Be specific when referring to documents (e.g., "Please turn to Figure 4 on page 3 of the document titled 'New Products' that was sent to you prior to the meeting.").
  • Use the mute button when not speaking.
  • Keep background noise to a minimum. For videoconferences, discourage the use of cordless or cellular phones because they may cause static or other interference.

✔ Restate participants' comments to confirm understanding.

✔ Call on people by name and location (e.g., "Let's hear from Maria at McKinsey in Australia about what she believes is the most important problem we face.").

✔ Make sure that you have a process for managing turn-taking. To manage turn-taking, have participants identify themselves because it's difficult to recognize voices when people aren't speaking face-to-face. For example, participants should introduce their comments with, "This is Lee from Sales in the U.K. I have some useful global data."

✔ Rotate the order in which you call on participants.

✔ Keep track of the people and sites that participate, as well as those you haven't heard from. Check in on those who haven't participated to get their input and maintain a balanced discussion.

✔ Ask questions to encourage participation and pause long enough for answers.

✔ Record key comments and decisions for each agenda item. Share your written summary with participants to check for agreement before moving to the next item.

✔ Be aware of cultural differences. These will influence participants' language, turn-taking, and responses to other participants and authority figures.

✔ For videoconferences:
  • Be aware that there is often a slight delay in the transfer of images. Even the laughter that follows a joke may be delayed (which can be discomforting if you are not prepared for the delay).

BOX 9-4 *Continued*

- Be aware of the location of the camera(s). If you want to have eye contact, look into the camera rather than the screen when you are speaking.
- Be yourself; speak naturally (yet slowly) as if you were all in a room together.
- Tell people when you will be using a graphic, and use simple, large-print graphics.
- Wear appropriate clothing. Solid colors (particularly blue and warm gray) are best. White, red, plaids, and prints (particularly bold patterns) may distort the picture. These rules also apply to the backgrounds at each site.

✔ Pay attention to the visual field and camera angle. The optimal visual field is from the top of the head to the bottom of the elbow to capture expressions, hand signals, and so forth. It's best to maintain a horizontal and vertical angle of less than 8 degrees. Otherwise, it will be difficult to "read" people's expressions. For example, if the camera angle isn't right, people may look disinterested or resistant when, in fact, they are engaged and supportive.

Close the Meeting

✔ Ask participants for summary statements.

✔ Summarize decisions and action items, as well as who is responsible for each action and how completion will be communicated to the group.

✔ Thank everyone for participating.

✔ Set a time for the next conference.

✔ End with a process check of meeting effectiveness and determine whether anything should be done to make the next meeting more effective.

✔ Post online or send communication such as a summary of meeting and expected deliverables, as well as who is accountable for these deliverables, as soon after a meeting as possible, preferably within one day. Use all team members' names and locations in the communication.

✔ When there have been technical problems at the meeting, send a follow-up message to explain the technical details.

Chapter Summary

Shifts in demographics, social norms, work expectations, and new technologies are dramatically transforming the nature of teamwork. Team members are becoming more culturally diverse and geographically dispersed. Work tasks are becoming more complex. The processes by which team members work are being significantly altered by technological advancements. Many of the skills we learned for managing relatively homogeneous, co-located teams are insufficient for effectively managing diverse and distributed teams. Team leaders and members who understand how to leverage team diversity and communication and information technologies will have a competitive advantage over those who don't.

DIVERSE TEAMS

Researcher Daan van Knippenberg and colleagues explain that "*Diversity* refers to differences between individuals on any attribute that may lead to the perception that another person is different from self."[138] In the context of work teams, diversity refers to "differences among members of an interdependent work group with respect to a specific personal attribute."[139]

Today's team members are likely to differ from each other on relatively observable social categories such as race, gender, nationality, and age, as well as job-related characteristics such as professional affiliation, functional department, hierarchical level, organizational membership, education, and tenure in the organization. Team members are also likely to differ significantly from each other on less visible characteristics such as cognitive styles, values, experience, and skills, as well as more private and often invisible characteristics such as religion, sexual orientation, and health challenges. These differences among team members influence

- the variety of cognitive resources and behavioral styles team members bring to the team;
- the interaction processes by which team members work together, including both task and relationship processes; and
- the team's ability to become a high performing team; in particular, the team's ability to make effective decisions, promote the well-being of team members, and enhance the team's ability to perform as an effective unit over time.

Teams can benefit significantly from diversity, particularly under certain conditions. Diverse teams may have an advantage over relatively homogeneous teams when

- the diversity among team members is relevant to the team's task (e.g., when tasks require creativity and judgment, when breadth of ideas is important, or when information about particular markets is important);
- when team members have time to learn how to work together productively; and
- when diversity among team members is well managed.

Potential advantages of diverse teams include enhanced effectiveness on intellective tasks, enhanced effectiveness on creative and judgmental decision-making tasks, more attention to team process, broader and more diverse external networks, enhanced learning, and continuous improvement.

Although diverse team members are more likely to have a greater variety of resources to bring to the team's task that can enhance team performance, they also are more likely to engage particular dysfunctional dynamics that can undermine the team's ability to use these resources wisely. These dysfunctional dynamics include more stress, more detachment from the team, reduced cohesion, decreased and more distorted internal communication, more difficulty coordinating, more perceptual biases (including those of team leaders), team members underestimating the team's successes. Two perspectives are used to explain dysfunctional dynamics in teams:

- The similarity-attraction perspective assumes that people tend to prefer to be with and understand people they perceive as similar to themselves. Therefore, they are more likely to find it easier to interact with and understand team members who they see as similar.
- The structural barriers perspective assumes that dynamics in diverse teams reflect those in the larger society in which the organization and team is embedded. Therefore, if there is bias, misunderstanding, and lack of cohesion among diverse groups in the society, the team is at risk for having the same problems.

Factors that influence whether diverse teams will exhibit the potential advantages or disadvantages of diverse teams include the relevance of the team's diversity to the task, the relevance of team member's diversity, the impact of team culture, the impact of time, and whether team members have a high (or low) need for cognition and how open they are to experience.

Team leaders can ensure that they create a context for high-performing diverse teams by paying extra attention to first meetings; training team members in understanding each other's differences and the impact of these on team process and performance; creating a common identity and collectivist culture; paying extra attention to team norms; trying to recruit team members who are high on need for cognition and openness to experience; providing early opportunities to succeed, clear performance measures, and ongoing positive feedback because diverse teams may underestimate their own performance; role-modeling the behavior they want in team members; and paying attention to the context in which the team works because teams tend to display the characteristics (both effective and ineffective) of the organization and cultures in which they are embedded.

VIRTUAL TEAMS

A virtual team, also called a distributed team, is made up of individuals interacting interdependently on collective tasks to achieve shared organizational goals. However, in contrast to co-located teams, virtual teams tend to be geographically dispersed, rarely meet face-to-face, and primarily depend on electronic and computer-based information and communication technologies (e.g., voice mail, conference calls, videoconferences, e-mail, and Web pages) to work together.

In contrast to co-located teams, virtual teams are more likely to bridge organizational and geographical boundaries; are likely to have more diverse team members; can be more flexible because team members aren't limited by availability of team members; and may have different social dynamics.

Benefits of virtual teams include opportunities for global expansion, mergers, alliances, and acquisitions; less need for team members to be in the same place in order to work together; more availability of experts who may not be able to meet face-to-face with the team; more opportunities for e-commerce; more efficient use of office space; the ability to recruit the best talent anywhere; increased flexibility; and increased benefits for the environment because of reduced need for travel and facilities.

The social dynamics in distributed teams may differ from those in co-located teams. For example, members of distributed teams may be somewhat less influenced by status effects, although some researchers argue that technology can increase status effects by enabling higher status employees to exert even more control over employees; may consult more people before making decisions; may have more task-related conflict; may take longer to make complex decisions; may make more extreme and unconventional decisions; may have more difficulty developing feelings of belonging and cohesion; may be more willing to express minority opinions if the opinions are anonymous, but may be less likely to take such opinions seriously; may have more problems coordinating; and may have problems communicating clearly.

Use of technology in teams and organizations can enhance or minimize the status and hierarchy effects, including inequalities, that exit in the broader society. If team leaders want to minimize these effectives, they need to be aware of these dynamics, understand how they play out in virtual teams, and take actions that enhance all team mem-

bers ability to leverage these technologies and do their best work.

Virtual teams have more challenges related to cohesion, communication, and coordination because team members do not have as much access to social cues as they do in face-to-face teams. However, many researchers and practitioners are concerned that high-quality relationships may be particularly difficult to achieve in virtual teams because team members have fewer opportunities to engage in activities that help them build familiarity, liking, predictability, and trust. There are also fewer opportunities to see and correctly interpret the social cues (static cues, dynamic cues, and situational cues) that one can see that help us understand what another person is thinking and feeling, which in turn helps us make better decisions. Other researchers have found that social networking technologies help promote social connections that would not be possible without the use of these technologies.

The quality of relationships among team members and across virtual teams significant influences team effectiveness. Team leaders must remember that psychological closeness is as important as physical closeness. Trust, the foundation of physical closeness, is built on goodwill, responsiveness, ability, predictability, and integrity—all of which can be developed through electronic and computer-mediated communication technologies. The following initiatives can help leaders increase the success of virtual teams by:

- *Determining the appropriate level of technology for the task.* Face-to-face meetings are preferable in situations in which human contact is particularly important, when visual cues enhance understanding, or when the purpose of the meeting is highly symbolic. Virtual meetings are most useful for routine tasks, when human contact isn't critical, and when meeting face-to-face isn't possible.
- *Managing the technological environment.* Team members must have access to compatible technologies, be willing and able to use them, and have ongoing training and technical support.
- *Managing the task and relationships.* Develop work processes that enhance cohesion, communication, and coordination.

Food for Thought

1. What is the most useful thing you learned in this chapter, and why?
2. Based on the strategies for managing diverse teams described in this chapter, what are the three most important things you can do to increase your effectiveness as a leader or member of diverse teams? How will you implement these changes, and how will you measure the outcomes of these changes?
3. Based on the strategies for managing virtual teams described in this chapter, what are the three most important things you can do to increase your effectiveness as a lead member of virtual teams? How will you implement these changes, and how will you measure the outcomes of these changes?
4. Think of a time when you felt like a minority in a work group or team. What did it feel like to be a member of that work group or team? How do you feel you were treated? What were the advantages? What were the disadvantages? Were you able to contribute to your fullest potential? Why or why not? What could you have done differently to be a more effective contributor to the team? What could the team have done differently to help you be a more effective contributor?
5. Observe a diverse team at a meeting. What are the various kinds of diversity represented on the team? What are some of the advantages this team may have (if managed well)? What are some of the dysfunctional dynamics that may occur (if not managed well)? What dynamics, both positive and negative, do you see? If you were a consultant to this group, what three changes would you recommend that the team make to better leverage the team's diversity?
6. Answer the questions in Box 9-1, "Assess Team Members' Style Preferences." Then, work with at least one other person and compare your answers. In what ways are you similar? In what ways are you different?

If you were part of a work team, how might these similarities and differences influence your team process and performance?
7. Attend a meeting or a class and pay attention to the social cues during the meeting. Describe the static, dynamic, and situational cues. How does each of the cues that you describe enhance understanding? How might each of the cues lead to misunderstandings? If these cues were missing in a virtual team or classroom, what might the consequences be?
8. Imagine you were the team leader of the following virtual team. What are the key problems? What steps would you take to improve the team's process and performance? What steps could you take with future virtual teams to prevent these dynamics from happening in the first place?

> Communications were often fragmented, with gaps and misunderstanding among distant group members. There was confusion in telephone conferences, with people on different pages of documents. Group members failed to return telephone calls or respond to inquiries from distant members. Key group members at remote sites were left off e-mail distribution lists. Distant members were not informed of key decisions or information. Misunderstandings developed on the basis of different assumptions about the tasks and assignments. Messages were interpreted differently in different places, sometimes fueling ongoing conflicts among office sites.[140]

9. Imagine you are the team leader of the global, distributed team described at the beginning of this chapter. Describe at least three things the team leader or team members could do to help the team communicate and coordinate more effectively.

Endnotes

1. Nydegger, Rudy, and Liesel Nydegger. 2010. "Challenges in Managing Virtual Teams." *Journal of Business and Economics Research*, 8(3): 69–82; Kearney, Eric, Diether Gebert, and Sven Voelpel. 2009. "When and How Diversity Benefits Teams: The Importance of Team Members' Need for Cognition." *Academy of Management Journal*, 52(3): 581–598; Homan, Astrid, John Hollenbeck, Stephen Humphrey, Daan Van Knippenberg, Daniel Ilgen, and Gerben Van Kleef. 2008. "Facing Differences with an Open Mind: Openness to Experience, Salience of Intragroup Differences, and Performance of Diverse Teams." *Academy of Management Journal*, 51(6): 1204–1222; Gibson, Cristina, and Jennifer L. Gibbs. 2006. "Unpacking the Concept of Virtuality: The Effects of Geographic

Dispersion, Electronic Dependence, Dynamic Structure, and National Diversity on Team Innovation." *Administrative Science Quarterly*, 51: 451–495.

2. Fortunati, Leopoldina. 2005. "Is Body-to-Body Communication Still the Prototype?" *The Information Society*, 21(1).

3. Griggs, Lewis Brown, and Lente-Louise Louw. 1995. "Diverse Teams: Breakdown or Breakthrough." *Training and Development,* October: 22–29.

4. Van Knippenberg, Dann, C. K. De Dreu, and Astrid C. Homan. 2004. "Work Group Diversity and Group Performance: An Integrative Model and Research Agenda." *Journal of Applied Psychology*, 89(6): 1008–1022.

5. Joshi, Aparna, and Hyuntak Roh. 2009. "The Role of Context in Work Team Diversity Research: A Meta-Analytic Review." *Academy of Management Journal*, 52(3): 599–627; Jackson, S., and Aparna Joshi. 2003. "Diversity in Social Context: A Multi-Attribute, Multi-Level Analysis of Team Diversity and Sales Performance." *Journal of Organizational Behavior*, 25: 675–702.

6. Beatty, Joy. 2006. "An Overlooked Dimension of Diversity: The Career Effects of Chronic Illness." *Organizational Dynamics*, 35(2): 182–195; Beatty, Joy, and S. Kirby. 2006. "Beyond the Legal Environment: How Stigma Influences Invisible Identity Groups in the Workplace." *Employee Responsibilities and Rights Journal*, 18(1): 29–44; Clair, Judith, Joy Beatty, and Tammy MacLean. 2003. "Out of Sight but Not Out of Mind, Managing Invisible Social Identities in the Workplace." *Academy of Management Review.* August. 2003

7. Joshi, Aparna, and Hyuntak Roh. 2009. "The Role of Context in Work Team Diversity Research: A Meta-Analytic Review." *Academy of Management Journal,* 52(3): 599–627; Cannela, Albert A., Jong-Hun Park, and Ho-Uk Lee. 2008. "Top Management Team Functional Background Diversity and Firm Performance: Examining the Roles of Team Member Colocation and Environmental Uncertainty." *Academy of Management Journal,* 51(4): 768–784.

8. Chi, Nai-Wen, Yin-Mei Huang, and Shu-Chi Lin. 2009. "A Double-Edged Sword? Exploring the Curvilinear Relationship between Organizational Tenure Diversity and Team Innovation: The Moderating Role of Team-Oriented HR Practices." *Group and Organization Management*, 34(6): 698–726; Milliken, Francis, and Luis Martins. 1996. "Searching for Common Threads: Understanding the Multiple Effects of Diversity in Organizational Groups." *Academy of Management Review,* 21: 402–433.

9. Kearney, Eric, Diether Gebert, and Sven Voelpel. 2009. "When and How Diversity Benefits Teams: The Importance of Team Members' Need for Cognition." *Academy of Management Journal*, 52(3): 581–598; Cannella, Albert, Jong-Hun Park, and Ho-Uk Lee. 2008. "Top Management Team Functional Background Diversity and Firm Performance: Examining the Roles of Team Member Colocation and Environmental Uncertainty." *Academy of Management Journal,* 51(4): 768–784; Homan, Astrid, John Hollenbeck, Stephen Humphrey, Daan Van Knippenberg, Daniel Ilgen, and Gerben Van Kleef. 2008. "Facing Differences with an Open Mind: Openness to Experience, Salience of Intragroup Differences, and Performance of Diverse Teams." *Academy of Management Journal*, 51(6): 1204–1222; Horwitz, S., and Horwitz., I. 2007. "A Meta-Analytic Review of Team Demography." *Journal of Management*, 33: 967–1015; Cannella, Albert, Jong-Hun Park and Ho-Uk Lee. 2008. "Top Management Team Functional Background Diversity and Firm Performance: Examining the Roles of Team Member Colocaiton and Environmental Uncertainty." *Academy of Management Journal*, 51(4): 768–784. Cox, Taylor, Sharon Lobel, and Poppy McLeod. 1991. "Effects of Ethnic Group Cultural Differences on Cooperative and Competitive Behavior on a Group Task." *Academy of Management Journal,* 34: 827–847; Jackson, Susan. 1991. "Team Composition in Organizational Settings: Issues in Managing an Increasingly Diverse Workforce." In S. Worchel, W. Wood, and J. Simpson (eds.). *Group Process and Productivity.* Beverly Hills, CA: Sage; Watson, Warren, Kamalesh Kumar, and Larry Michaelsen. 1993. "Cultural Diversity's Impact on Interaction Process and Performance: Comparing Homogeneous and Diverse Task Groups." *Academy of Management Journal,* 36: 590–602; Williams, Kathleen, and Charles O'Reilly. 1998. "Forty Years of Diversity Research: A Review." In Barry Staw and Larry Cummings (eds.). *Research in Organizational Behavior,* 20: 77–140.

10. Williams, Kathleen, and Charles O'Reilly. 1998. "Forty Years of Diversity Research: A Review." In Barry Staw and Larry Cummings (eds.). *Research in Organizational Behavior,* 20: 77–140.

11. Ibid.

12. Williams, Katherine, and Charles O'Reilly. 1998. "Demography and Diversity in Organizations: A Review of 40 Years of Research." In Barry Staw and Larry Cummings (eds.). *Research in Organizational Behavior,* 20: 77–140; citing Byrne, D. 1971. *The Attraction Paradigm.* New York: Academic Press; Byrne, D., G. Clore, and P. Worchel. 1996. "The Effect of Economic Similarity-Dissimilarity as Determinants of Attraction." *Journal of Personality and Social Psychology,* 4: 220–224.

13. Brief, Arthur, Elizabeth Umphress, Joerg Dietz, John Burrows, Rebecca Butz, and Lotte Scholten. 2005. "Community Matters: Realistic Group Conflict Theory and the Impact of Diversity." *Academy of Management Journal,* 48(5): 830–844.

14. Gutek, Barbara. 1985. *Sex and the Workplace.* San Francisco, CA: Jossey-Bass; Kanter, Rosabeth Moss. 1977. *Men and Women of the Corporation.* New York: Basic Books; Pettigrew, Thomas, and Joanne Martin. 1987. "Shaping the Organizational Context for Black American Inclusion." *Journal of Social Issues,* 43: 41–78; cited in Elsass, Priscilla, and Laura Graves. 1997. "Demographic Diversity in Decision-Making Groups: The Experiences of Women and People of Color." *Academy of Management Review,* 22(4): 946–973.

15. Ely, Robin, and David A. Thomas. 2001. "Cultural Diversity at Work: The Effects of Diversity Perspectives on Work Group Processes and Outcomes." *Administrative Science Quarterly,* 46: 229–273; Kochan, Thomas, Katerina Bezrukova, Roby Ely, Susan Jackson, Aparna Joshi, Karen Jehn, Jonathan Leonard, David Levine, and David Thomas. 2003. "The Effects of Diversity on Business Performance: Report of the Diversity Research Network." *Human Resource Management.* Spring: 3–21.

16. Jackson, Susan 1991. "Team Composition in Organizational Settings: Issues in Managing an Increasingly Diverse Workforce." In S. Worchel, W. Wood, and J. Simpson (eds.). *Group Process and Productivity.* Beverly Hills, CA: Sage.

17. Triandis, Harry, Eleanor Hall, and Robert Ewen. 1965. "Member Heterogeneity and Dyadic Creativity." *Human Relations,* 18: 33–55; Thomas, David, Elizabeth Ravlin, and Alan Wallace. 1991. "Effect of Cultural Diversity in Work Groups." *Research in the Sociology of Organizations,* 14: 1–33.

18. Homan, Astrid, John Hollenbeck, Stephen Humphrey, Daan Van Knippenberg, Daniel Ilgen, and Gerben A. Van Kleef. 2008. "Facing Differences with an Open Mind: Openness to Experience, Salience of Intragroup Differences, and Performance of Diverse Work Groups." *Academy of Management Journal,* 51(6): 1204–1222.

19. Morris, Betsy. 1997. "If Women Ran the World It Would Look a Lot like Avon." *Fortune.* July 21: 74–79.

20. Nemeth, C., and J. Kwan. 1992. "Minority Dissent as a Stimulant to Group Performance." In S. Worchel, W. Wood, and J. A. Simpson (eds.). *Group Process and Productivity.* Newbury Park, CA: Sage; cited in Thomas, David, Elizabeth Ravlin, and Alan Wallace. "Effect of Cultural Diversity in Work Groups." *Research in the Sociology of Organizations,* 14: 1–33.

21. Ancona, Deborah, and David Caldwell. 1990. "Beyond Boundary Spanning: Managing External Dependence in Product Development Teams." *Journal of High-Technology Management Research,* 1: 119–135.

22. Jackson, Susan. 1991. "Team Composition in Organizational Settings: Issues in Managing an Increasingly Diverse Workforce." In Stephen Worchel, Wendy Wood, and Jeffrey Simpson (eds.). *Group Process and Productivity.* Beverly Hills, CA: Sage; citing Simon Herbert. 1979. *The Science of the Artificial.* 2nd ed. Cambridge, MA: MIT Press.

23. Thomas, David, Elizabeth Ravlin, and Alan Wallace. 1996. "Effect of Cultural Diversity in Work Groups." *Research in the Sociology of Organizations,* 14: 1–33.

24. Watson, Warren E., Kamalesh Kumar, and Larry Michaelsen. 1993. "Cultural Diversity's Impact on Interaction Process and Performance: Comparing Homogeneous and Diverse Task Groups." *Academy of Management Journal,* 36: 590–602.

25. Andre, Rae. 1995. "Diversity Stress as Moral Stress." *Journal of Business Ethics* 14: 489–496.

26. Clair, Judith, Joy Beatty, and Tammy MacLean, 2005. "Out of Sight but Not Out of Mind, Managing Invisible Social Identities in the Workplace." *Academy of Management Review.* .90(1): 79–95.

27. Beatty, Joy. 2006. "An Overlooked Dimension of Diversity: The Career Effects of Chronic Illness." *Organizational Dynamics,* 35(2): 182–195; Beatty, Joy, and S. Kirby. 2006. "Beyond the Legal Environment: How Stigma Influences Invisible Identity Groups in the Workplace." *Employee Responsibilities and Rights Journal,* 18:1: 29–44.

28. Jackson, Susan E. 1991. "Team Composition in Organizational Settings: Issues in Managing an

Increasingly Diverse Workforce." In Stephen Worchel, Wendy Wood, and Jeffrey Simpson (eds.). *Group Process and Productivity*. Beverly Hills, CA: Sage.

29. McCain, B., C. O'Reilly, and Jeffrey Pfeffer. 1983. "The Effects of Departmental Demography on Turnover." *Academy of Management Journal,* 26: 626–641; O'Reilly, Charles, David Caldwell, and William Barnett. 1989. "Work Group Demography, Social Integration, and Turnover." *Administrative Science Quarterly,* 34: 21–37.

30. Hood, Jacqueline N., and Christine S. Koberg. 1994. "Patterns of Differential Assimilation and Acculturation for Women in Business Organizations." *Human Relations,* 47: 159–181; Elsass, Priscilla, and Laura M. Graves. 1997. "Demographic Diversity in Decision-Making Groups: The Experiences of Women and People of Color." *Academy of Management Review,* 22(4): 946–973.

31. Zenger, Todd R., and Barbara Lawrence. 1989. "Organizational Demography: The Differential Effects of Age and Tenure on Technical Communication." *Academy of Management Journal,* 32: 353–376.

32. Kim, Heejung. 2002. "We Talk, Therefore We Think? A Cultural Analysis of the Effect of Talking on Thinking." *Journal of Personality and Social Psychology,* 83(4): 824–842; Barnlund, D., and C. Harland. 1963. "Propinquity and Prestige as Determinants of Communications Networks." *Sociometry,* 26: 467–479; Triandis, Harry. 1960. "Cognitive Similarity and Communication in a Dyad." *Human Relations,* 13: 279–287.

33. Jackson, Susan E. 1991. "Team Composition in Organizational Settings: Issues in Managing an Increasingly Diverse Workforce." In S. Worchel, W. Wood, and J. Simpson (eds.). *Group Process and Productivity*. Beverly Hills, CA: Sage.

34. Goodman, P., E. Ravlin, and M. Schminke. 1987. "Understanding Groups in Organizations." In Larry Cummings and Barry Staw (eds.). *Research in Organizational Behavior.* Vol. 9. Greenwich, CT: JAI Press.

35. Cummings, A., J. Zhou, and Gary Oldham. 1993. "Demographic Differences and Employee Work Outcomes: Effects of Multiple Comparison Groups." Paper Presented at the Annual Meeting of the Academy of Management, Atlanta, GA; Judge, Timothy, and Gerald Ferris. 1993. "Social Context of Performance Evaluation Decisions." *Academy of*

Management Journal, 36: 80–105; cited in Williams, Katherine, and Charles O'Reilly. 1998. "Demography and Diversity in Organizations: A Review of 40 Years of Research." *Research in Organizational Behavior,* 20: 77–140.

36. Chemers, Martin, and Susan Jackson. 1995. "Leadership and Diversity in Groups and Organizations." In Chemers, Mark, Stuart Oskamp, and Mark Constanzo (eds.). *Diversity in Organizations: New Perspectives for a Changing Workplace*. Thousand Oaks, CA: Sage.

37. Thomas, David, Elizabeth Ravlin, and Alan Wallace. 1996. "Effect of Cultural Diversity in Work Groups." *Research in the Sociology of Organizations,* 14: 1–33.

38. Jackson, Susan E. 1992. "Team Composition in Organizational Settings: Issues in Managing an Increasingly Diverse Workforce." In Stephen Worchel, Wendy Wood, and Jeffrey A. Simpson (eds.). *Group Process and Productivity*. Newbury Park, CA: Sage; Thomas, David, Elizabeth Ravlin, and Alan Wallace. 1996. "Effect of Cultural Diversity in Work Groups." *Research in the Sociology of Organizations,* 14: 1–33.

39. Shaw, M. E. 1976. *Group Dynamics: The Psychology of Small Group Behavior*. New York: McGraw-Hill; cited in Jackson, Susan E. 1992. "Team Composition in Organizational Settings: Issues in Managing an Increasingly Diverse Workforce." In Stephen Worchel, Wendy Wood, and Jeffrey A. Simpson (eds.). *Group Process and Productivity*. Newbury Park, CA: Sage.

40. Cummings, A., J. Zhou, and Gary Oldham. 1993. "Demographic Differences and Employee Work Outcomes: Effects of Multiple Comparison Groups." Paper Presented at the Annual Academy Meeting of the Academy of Management, Atlanta, GA; Stangor, Charles, Laure Lynch, and B. Glass. 1992. "Categorization of Individuals on the Basis of Multiple Social Features." *Journal of Personality and Social Psychology,* 62: 207–218.

41. Kanter, Rosabeth Moss. 1977. *Men and Women of the Corporation*. New York: Basic Books.

42. Chatman, Jennifer, Jeffrey Polzer, and Margaret Neale. 1998. "Being Different Yet Feeling Similar: The Influence of Demographic Composition and Organizational Culture on Work Processes and Outcomes." *Administrative Science Quarterly,* 43: 749–780.

43. Stewart, Greg, Charles Manz, and Henry Sims. 1999. *Teamwork and Group Dynamics*. New York:

John Wiley and Sons; citing Watson, W. E., K. Kumar, and L. K. Michaelsen. 1993. "Cultural Diversity's Impact on Interaction Process and Performance: Comparing Homogeneous and Diverse Task Groups." *Academy of Management Journal,* 36: 590–602.

44. Glaman, Joan, Allan P. Jones, and Richard M. Rozelle. 1996. "The Effects of Coworker Similarity on the Emergence of Affect in Work Teams." *Group and Organizational Management,* 21(2): 192–215.

45. Ibid.

46. Kearney, Eric, Gebert Diether, and Sven Voelpel. 2009. "When and How Diversity Benefits Teams: The Importance of Team Members' Need for Cognition." *Academy of Management Journal*, 52(3): 581–598; Cacioppo, J., R. E. Petty, J. Feinstein, and W. Jarvis. 1996. "Dispositional Differences in Cognitive Motivation: The Life and Times of Individuals Varying in Need for Cognition." *Psychological Bulletin*, 119: 197–253.

47. Kearney, Eric, Gebert Diether, and Sven Voelpel. 2009. "When and How Diversity Benefits Teams: The Importance of Team Members' Need for Cognition." *Academy of Management Journal*, 52(3): 581–598; Petty, R., P. Brinol, C. Loersch, and M. McCaslin. 2009. "The Need for Cognition." In Leaery, M. R., and R.H. Hoyle (eds.), *Handbook of Individual Differences in Social Behavior*: 318–329. New York: Guilford Press.

48. Homan, Astrid, John Hollenbeck, Stephen Humphrey, Daan Van Knippenberg, Daniel Ilgen, and Gerben A. Van Kleef. 2008. "Facing Differences with an Open Mind: Openness to Experience, Salience of Intragroup Differences, and Performance of Diverse Work Groups." *Academy of Management Journal,* 51(6): 1204–1222; Flynn, F. J. 2005. "Having an Open Mind: The Impact of Openness to Experience on Interracial Attitudes and Impression Formation." *Journal of Personality and Social Psychology*, 88: 816–826; McCrae, R., and P. Costa. 1987. "Validation of the Five Factor Model of Personality Across Instruments and Observers." *Journal of Personality and Social Psychology*, 37: 303–324.

49. Homan, Astrid, John Hollenbeck, Stephen Humphrey, Daan Van Knippenberg, Daniel Ilgen, and Gerben A. Van Kleef. 2008. "Facing Differences with an Open Mind: Openness to Experience, Salience of Intragroup Differences, and Performance of Diverse Work Groups." *Academy of Management Journal*, 51(6): 1204–1222.

50. Harris, Philip, and Robert Moran. 1996. *Managing Cultural Differences: Leadership Strategies for a New World of* Business. 4th ed. Houston, TX: Gulf Publishing.

51. Van der Vegt, G. S., and Bunderson, J.S. 2005. "Learning and Performance in Multidisciplinary Teams: The Importance of Collective Team Identification." *Academy of Management Journal,* 48: 523–547.

52. Chatman, Jennifer, Jeffrey Polzer, and Margaret Neale. 1998. "Being Different Yet Feeling Similar: The Influence of Demographic Composition and Organizational Culture on Work Processes and Outcomes." *Administrative Science Quarterly,* 43: 749–780.

53. Ibid.

54. Homan, A., van Knippenberg, D., Van Kleef, G., and De Dreu, C. 2007a. "Bridging Faultlines by Valuing Diversity: The Effects of Diversity Beliefs on Information Elaboration and Performance in Diverse Groups." *Journal of Applied Psychology*, 92: 1189–1199; van Kippenberg, D., S. A. Haslam, and M. J. Platow. 2007. "Unity through Diversity: Value-in-Diversity Beliefs as Moderator of the Relationship between Work Group Diversity and Group Identification." *Group Dynamics: Theory, Research, and Practice*, 11: 207–222; Ely, Robin, and David A. Thomas, 2001. "Cultural Diversity at Work: The Effects of Diversity Perspectives on Work Group Processes and Outcomes." *Administrative Science Quarterly*, 46: 229–273.

55. Kearney, E., D. Gerbert, and S. Voelpel. 2009. "When and How Diversity Benefits Teams: The Importance of Team Members' Need for Cognition." *Academy of Management Journal*, 52: 581–598; Homan, A., van Knippenberg, D., Van Kleef, G., and De Dreu, C. 2007a. "Bridging Faultlines by Valuing Diversity: The Effects of Diversity Beliefs on Information Elaboration and Performance in Diverse Groups." *Journal of Applied Psychology*, 92: 1189–1199; van Kippenberg, D., S. A. Haslam, and M. J. Platow. 2007. "Unity through Diversity: Value-in-Diversity Beliefs as Moderator of the Relationship between Work Group Diversity and Group Identification." *Group Dynamics: Theory, Research, and Practice*, 11: 207–222.

56. Triandis, Harry, Eleanor Hall, and Robert Ewen. 1965. "Member Heterogeneity and Dyadic Creativity." *Human Relations,* 18: 33–55; Finley, Joycelyn. 1996. "Communication Double Binds: The Catch-22 of Conversations about Racial Issues

in Work Groups." Dissertation Submitted to the University of Michigan.

57. Armstrong, Robert, and Paul Cole. 1994. *Culture and Social Behavior*. New York: McGraw-Hill.

58. Brief, Arthur, Elizabeth Umphress, Joerg Dietz, John Burrows, Rebecca Butz, and Lotte Scholten. 2005. "Community Matters: Realistic Group Conflict Theory and the Impact of Diversity." *Academy of Management Journal*, 48(5): 830–844; Berger, J., C. Ridgeway, and M. Zelditch. 2002. "The Construction of Status and Referential Structures." *Sociological Theory*, 20: 157–179.

59. Joshi, Aparna, and Hyuntak Roh. 2009. "The Role of Context in Work Team Diversity Research: A Meta-Analytic Review." *Academy of Management Journal*, 52(3): 599–627.

60. Lipnack, Jessica, and Jeffrey Stamps. 1997. *Virtual Teams: Reaching across Time, Space, and Technology*. New York: John Wiley.

61. Nydegger, Rudy, and Liesl Nydegger. March 2010. "Challenges in Managing Virtual Teams." *Journal of Business and Economics Research*, 8(3): 69–82; Gibson, Cristina, and Jennifer L. Gibbs. 2006. "Unpacking the Concept of Virtuality: The Effects of Geographic Dispersion, Electronic Dependence, Dynamic Structure, and National Diversity on Team Innovation." *Administrative Science Quarterly*, 51: 451–495.

62. Townsend, Anthony, Samuel DeMarie, and Anthony Hendrickson. 1998. "Virtual Teams: Technology and the Workplace of the Future." *Academy of Management Executive*, 12(3): 17–29.

63. Baym, Nancy K. 2010. *Personal Connections in the Digital Age*. Malden, MA: Polity Press.

64. Nydegger Rudy, and Liesl Nydegger. 2010. "Challenges in Managing Virtual Teams." *Journal of Business and Economics Research*, 8(3): 69–82; Gibson, Christina, and Jennifer L. Gibbs. 2006. "Unpacking the Concept of Virtuality: The Effects of Geographic Dispersion, Electronic Dependence, Dynamic Structure, and National Diversity on Team Innovation." *Administrative Science Quarterly*, 51: 451–495; Griffith, Terri, John Sawyer, and Margaret Neale. June 2003. "Virtualness and Knowledge in Teams: Managing the Love Triangle of Organizations, Individuals, and Information Technology." *MIS Quarterly*, 51(3): 451–459.

65. Townsend, Anthony, Samuel DeMarie, and Anthony Hendrickson. 1996. "Are You Ready for Virtual Teams?" *HR Magazine*. September: 122–226.

66. Nydegger, Rudy, and Liesl Nydegger. 2010. "Challenges in Managing Virtual Teams. *Journal of Business and Economics Research*, 8(3): 69–82; citing Cascio, W. F. 1999. "Virtual Workplaces: Implications for Organizational Behavior." In C. L. Cooper and D. M. Rousseau (eds.). *Trends in Organizational Behavior, Vol 6: The Virtual Organization*. New York: John Wiley & Sons, Ltd, 1–14.

67. Boiney, L. G. 2001. Gender Impacts Virtual Work Teams. *Graziado Business Report*, 4(4): 5.

68. Smith, N., E. Bizot, and T. Hill. 1988. *Use of E-Mail in a Research and Development Organization*. Tulsa, OK: University of Tulsa; Bikson, T. K. 1987. "Understanding the Implementation of Office Technology." In R. Kraut (ed.). *Technology and the Transformation of White Collar Work*. Hillsdale, NJ: Erlbaum.

69. Lipnack, Jessica, and Jeffrey Stamps. 1997. *Virtual Teams: Reaching across Time, Space, and Technology*. New York: John Wiley; citing Bernie DeKoven. 1990. *Connected Executives: A Strategic Communications Plan*. Palo Alto, CA: Institute for Better Meetings.

70. Nydegger, Rudy, and Liesl Nydegger. 2010. "Challenges in Managing Virtual Teams." *Journal of Business and Economics Research*, 8(3): 69–82; Gibson, Christina, and Jennifer L. Gibbs. 2006. "Unpacking the Concept of Virtuality: The Effects of Geographic Dispersion, Electronic Dependence, Dynamic Structure, and National Diversity on Team Innovation." *Administrative Science Quarterly*, 51: 451–495.

71. Sproull, Lee, and Sara Kiesler. 1993. *Connections: New Ways of Working in the Networked Organization*. Cambridge, MA: MIT Press.

72. Ibid.

73. Finholt, Tom, and Lee Sproull. 1990. "Electronic Groups at Work." *Organizational Science*, (1): 41–64.

74. Ibid.

75. Friedman, Raymond, and Steven Currall. 2002. "E-Mail Escalation: Dispute Exacerbating Elements of Electronic Communication." *Sloan Management Review*, 44(1): 14–15.

76. Cialdini, Robert. 2008. *Influence: Science and Practice*. 5th ed. Upper Saddle River, NJ: Prentice Hall.

77. Baumeister, R., and M. Leary. 1995. "The Need to Belong: Desire for interpersonal Attachments as a Fundamental Human Motivation." *Psychological Bulletin*, 117: 497–529.

78. Haywood, Martha. 1998. *Managing Virtual Teams: Practical Techniques for High-Technology Managers.* Boston, MA: Artech House.

79. Losada, Marcial, and Emily Heaphy. 2004. "The Role of Positivity and Connectivity in the Performance of Business Teams: A Nonlinear Dynamics Model. *American Behavioral Scientist,* 47(6): 740–765.

80. Stephens, J. P., E. Heaphy, and J. Dutton. "High Quality Connections." To appear in Cameron, K., and G. Spreitzer. 2011. *The Oxford Handbook of Positive Organizational Scholarship.* 2011.

81. Ancona, Deborah, and Henrick Bresman. 2007. *X-Teams: How to Build Teams that Lead, Innovate, and Succeed.* Cambridge, MA: Harvard Business School Press.

82. Ibid.

83. Hallowell, Edward M. 1999. "The Human Moment at Work." *Harvard Business Review.* January/February: 58–66.

84. Anderson, Janna, and Lee Rainie. July 2, 2010. *The Future of Social Relations.* Pew Research Center's Internet and American Life Project. http://www.pewinternet.org/Reports/2010/The-future-of-social-relations.aspx

85. Locke, John L. 1998. *The De-Voicing of Society: Why We Don't Talk to Each Other Anymore.* New York: Simon & Schuster; cited in 1999. "The Decline of Conversation." *The Futurist.* February: 18–19.

86. Armstrong, David, and Paul Cole. 1995. "Managing Distances and Differences in Geographically Distributed Work Groups." In Jackson, Susan, and Marian Ruderman (eds.). *Diversity in Work Teams.* Washington, DC: American Psychological Association.

87. Haywood, Martha. 1998. *Managing Virtual Teams: Practical Techniques for High-Technology Managers.* Boston, MA: Artech House.

88. Cascio, W. F. 1999. "Virtual Workplaces: Implications for Organizational Behavior." In Cooper, C. L., and D. M. Rousseau (eds.). *Trends in Organizational Behavior, Vol. 6: The Virtual Organization.* New York: John Wiley & Sons, 1–14.

89. Mayer, R., J. Davis, and F. Schoorman. 1995. "An Integrative Model of Organizational Trust." *Academy of Management Review,* 20(3): 709–734, pg. 712.

90. Mitchell, Alanah, and Ilze Zigurs. 2009. "Trust in Virtual Teams: Solved or Still a Mystery?" *The Data Base for Advances in Information Systems,* 40(3): 61–83.

91. Cascio, Wayne, and Stan Shurygailo. 2003. "E-Leadership and Virtual Teams." *Organizational Dynamics,* 31(4): 362–376. Pg. 362.

92. Ibid.; Geber, Beverly. 1995. "Virtual Teams." *Training.* April: 36–40.

93. Hallowell, Edward M. 1999. "The Human Moment at Work." *Harvard Business Review.* January/February: 58–66.

94. Gibson, Cristina, and Jennifer L. Gibbs. 2006. "Unpacking the Concept of Virtuality: The Effects of Geographic Dispersion, Electronic Dependence, Dynamic Structure, and National Diversity on Team Innovation." *Administrative Science Quarterly,* 51: 451–495; Fussell and Benimoff. 1995. "Social and Cognitive Processes in Interpersonal Communication: Implications for Advanced Telecommunications Technologies." *Journal of Human Factors and Ergonomics.* June: 229; cited in Haywood, Martha. 1998. *Managing Virtual Teams: Practical Techniques for High-Technology Managers.* Boston, MA: Artech House.

95. Gibson, Christina, and Jennifer L. Gibbs. 2006. "Unpacking the Concept of Virtuality: The Effects of Geographic Dispersion, Electronic Dependence, Dynamic Structure, and National Diversity on Team Innovation." *Administrative Science Quarterly,* 51: 451–495; Dubrovsky, Vitaly, Sara Kiesler, and Beheruz Sethna. 1991. "The Equalization Phenomenon: Status Effects in Computer-Mediated and Face-to-Face Decision-Making Groups." *Human-Computer Interaction,* 6: 119–146.

96. Ibid.

97. Sole, Deborah, and Amy Edmonson. 2002. "Situated Knowledge and Learning in Dispersed Teams." *British Journal of Management,* 13: 517–534; Cramton, Catherine. 2001. "The Mutual Knowledge Problem and Its Consequences for Dispersed Collaboration." *Organization Science,* 12: 346–371.

98. Haywood, Martha. 1998. *Managing Virtual Teams: Practical Techniques for High-Technology Managers.* Boston, MA: Artech House.

99. Kahn, William. 1990. "Psychological Conditions of Personal Engagement and Disengagement at Work." *Academy of Management Journal,* 33: 692–724; cited in Baer, Markus, and Michael Frese. 2003. "Innovation Is Not Enough: Climates for Initiative and Psychological Safety, Process Improvements, and Firm Performance." *Journal of Organizational Behavior,* 24: 45–68: p. 45.

100. Edmondson, Amy. 1999. "Psychological Safety and Learning Behavior in Work Teams. *Administrative Science Quarterly*, 44: 350–383.

101. Ibid., p. 352.

102. Edmondson, Amy. 1999. "Psychological Safety and Learning Behavior in Work Teams." *Administrative Science Quarterly*, 44: 350–383; Gibson, Christina, and Jennifer L. Gibbs. 2006. "Unpacking the Concept of Virtuality: The Effects of Geographic Dispersion, Electronic Dependence, Dynamic Structure, and National Diversity on Team Innovation." *Administrative Science Quarterly*, 51: 451–495; Jeroen Schepers, Ad de Jong, Martin Wetzels, and Ko de Ruyter. 2008. "Psychological Safety and Social Support in Groupware Adoption: A Multi-Level Assessment in Education." *Computers and Education*, 51(2): 757–775.

103. Gibson, Christina, and Jennifer L. Gibbs. 2006. "Unpacking the Concept of Virtuality: The Effects of Geographic Dispersion, Electronic Dependence, Dynamic Structure, and National Diversity on Team Innovation." *Administrative Science Quarterly*, 51: 451–495, pp. 484–485.

104. Dubrovsky, Vitaly, Sara Kiesler, and Beheruz Sethna. 1991. "The Equalization Phenomenon: Status Effects in Computer-Mediated and Face-to-Face Decision-Making Groups." *Human Computer Interaction*, 6: 119–146.

105. Ibid.

106. Sproull, Lee, and Sara Kiesler. 1993. *Connections: New Ways of Working in the Networked Organizations*. Cambridge, MA: MIT Press.

107. Munter, Mary. 1998. "Meeting Technology: From Low-Tech to High-Tech." *Business Communication Quarterly,* 61(2): 80–87.

108. Mantovani, Giuseppe. 1994. "Is Computer-Mediated Communication Intrinsically Apt to Enhance Democracy in Organizations?" *Human Relations,* 47(1): 45–62.

109. Ibid.

110. Heydary, Javad. 2005. "Companies Step Up Electronic Monitoring of Employees." http://www.ecommercetimes.com/story/44850.html?wlc=1278035677

111. Fountain, Jane. 2000. "Constructing the Information Society: Women, Information Technology, and Design." *Technology in Society*, 22: 45–62.

112. Walton, Marsha. June 4, 2010. "IT Jobs Offer Growth, but Women Are Bailing Out." *Women in Science*. http://womensenews.org/story/women-in-science/100623/it-jobs-offer-growth-women-are-bailing-out

113. Ibid.

114. Mercer, Graham, and Matthew Barritt. 1998. "An Integrated Approach to Business Education." Working Paper. November; 1999. University of Michigan Business School, Global Learning Center Working Paper, p. 1.

115. McLeod, Poppy, Robert Baron, Mollie Marti, and Kuh Yoon. 1997. "The Eyes Have It: Minority Influence in Face-to-Face and Computer-Mediated Group Discussion." *Journal of Applied Psychology,* 82(5): 706–718; Munter, Mary. 1998. "Meeting Technology: From Low-Tech to High-Tech." *Business Communication Quarterly,* 61(2): 80–87.

116. Nohria, Nitin and Robert Eccles. 1992. "Face-to-Face: Making Networking Organizations Work." In Nohria, N., and R. Eccles (eds.). *Networks and Organizations: Structure, Form, and Action*. Boston, MA: Harvard Business School Press.

117. Munter, Mary. 1998. "Meeting Technology: From Low-Tech to High-Tech." *Business Communication Quarterly,* 61(2): 80–87.

118. Ibid.

119. Haywood, Martha. 1998. *Managing Virtual Teams: Practical Techniques for High-Technology Managers*. Boston, MA: Artech House.

120. Sproull, Lee, and Sara Kiesler. 1993. *Connections: New Ways of Working in the Networked Organization*. Cambridge, MA: MIT Press.

121. Munter, Mary. 1998. "Meeting Technology: From Low-Tech to High-Tech." *Business Communication Quarterly,* 61(2): 80–87.

122. Mcgrath, J., and A. Hollinshead. 1994. Groups Interacting with Technology. Newbury Park, CA: Sage.

123. McLeod, Poppy. 1999. "A Literary Examination of Electronic Meeting System Use in Everyday Organizational Life." *Journal of Applied Behavioral Science,* 34(2): 188–206.

124. Ibid.

125. Munter, Mary. 1998. "Meeting Technology: From Low-Tech to High-Tech." *Business Communication Quarterly,* 61(2): 80–87.

126. Kirkman, Bradley, Benson Rosen, Paul Tesluk, and Cristina Gibson. 2004. "The Impact of Team Empowerment on Virtual Team Performance: The Moderating Role of Face-to-Face Interaction. *Academy of Management Journal,* 47(2): 175–192.

127. Townsend, Anthony, Samuel DeMarie, and Anthony Hendrickson. 1998. "Virtual Teams: Technology and the Workplace of the Future." *Academy of Management Executive,* 12(3): 17–29.

128. Lipnack, Jessica, and Jeffrey Stamps. 1997. *Virtual Teams: Reaching across Time, Space, and Technology*. New York: John Wiley; citing Bernie DeKoven. 1990. *Connected Executives: A Strategic Communications Plan*. Palo Alto, CA: Institute for Better Meetings.

129. Haywood, Martha. 1998. *Managing Virtual Teams: Practical Techniques for High-Technology Managers*. Boston, MA: Artech House.

130. Ibid.

131. Hallowell, Edward M. 1999. "The Human Moment at Work." *Harvard Business Review*. January/February: 58–66.

132. Gladstone, Bryan. 1998. "The Medium Is the Message: When Old Paradigms Meet New Technology." *Journal of General Management,* 24(2): 51–68; citing Lewis, David. 1997. *Shaming, Blaming, and Flaming: Corporate Miscommunication in the Information Age*. Bracknell, England: Novell.

133. Christina Gibson, and Susan Cohen (eds.). 2003. *Virtual Teams That Work: Creating Conditions for Virtual Team Effectiveness*. San Francisco, CA: Jossey Bass.

134. Ibid.

135. Cascio, Wayne, and Stan Shurygailo. 2003. "E-Leadership and Virtual Teams." *Organization Dynamics*, 31(4): 362–376.

136. Ibid.

137. Haywood, Martha. 1998. *Managing Virtual Teams: Practical Techniques for High-Technology Managers*. Boston, MA: Artech House.

138. Van Knippenberg, Dann, C. K. De Dreu, and Astrid C. Homan. 2004. "Work Group Diversity and Group Performance: An Integrative Model and Research Agenda." *Journal of Applied Psychology*, 89(6): 1008–1022, pg. 1008.

139. Joshi, Aparna, and Hyuntak Roh. 2009. "The Role of Context in Work Team Diversity Research: A Meta-Analytic Review." *Academy of Management Journal*, 52(3): 599–627; Jackson, S., and Aparna Joshi. 2003. "Diversity in Social Context: A Multi-Attribute, Multi-Level Analysis of team Diversity and Sales Performance." *Journal of Organizational Behavior*, 25: 675–702.

140. Lipnack, Jessica, and Jeffrey Stamps. 1997. *Virtual Teams: Reaching across Time, Space, and Technology*. New York: John Wiley; citing Bernie DeKoven. 1990. *Connected Executives: A Strategic Communications Plan*. Palo Alto, CA: Institute for Better Meetings.

141. Ibid.

10

■ ■ ■

Crafting a Life: Your Guide to the Good Life

This chapter will help you:

■ Learn what does and doesn't predict happiness.

■ Learn why "flow" is important at work and how to create it.

■ Understand how optimism, perfectionism, and Type A behaviors may influence productivity, health, and psychological well-being.

■ Understand when negative emotions, including defensive pessimism, can be helpful.

■ Understand how the design of your job can affect your health.

■ Learn what many working parents want to know: How does day care affect children's well-being?

> *I have realized life is definitely not a straight line getting
> from point A to B but a series of detours; what you make
> of these detours defines your destiny.*
>
> —RAMKUMAR KRISHNAN, *Acts of Faith*

I began this book by discussing the risks of professional derailment. Equally troubling are people who succeed in their professional lives in terms of their effectiveness, career progression, and salary, but who derail in their personal lives. These are people who achieve the external markers of professional success (e.g., status, money, and material possessions), but they do so at the expense of their happiness, health, and relationships. They learn too late that professional success does not, by itself, lead to a fulfilling life. This chapter describes what researchers have found does—and doesn't—lead to a good life. My goal in this chapter is to provide you with information and advice that can help you craft a life that is personally fulfilling as well as professionally rewarding.

What is the good life? As human beings, we all share many of the same needs and goals regardless of our age, race, gender, class, nationality, and life circumstances. These include a need to find meaning in our lives, to feel the love and affection that comes from connecting with others, to experience the challenge of mastering new skills, and to feel a sense of control and consistency in our lives. We experience our lives as pleasurable and worthwhile when these needs are fulfilled. Of course, all human beings have their share of life's joys and heartbreak, opportunities and hurdles, and good moods and bad moods. However, people who experience their lives as pleasurable overall—who feel they are living a good life—are able to bounce back and flourish not only despite the challenges they face, but sometimes because of these challenges.

> How we spend our days is, of course, how we spend our lives.
> —ANN DILLARD,
> *The Writing Life*

Note that I don't say that this chapter will help you achieve "work–life balance." This is because I don't believe that work–life balance is a possible or even desirable goal. If you focus primarily on achieving an "ideal" of work–life balance, you are likely to become increasingly frustrated because that ideal will elude you throughout much of your life. After all, life's joys, opportunities, challenges, and tragedies don't come in neat and perfectly timed packages—and they often arrive when least expected and when you're least prepared. Furthermore, having work–life balance is no guarantee of long-term happiness. How often have you heard of people who seem to "have it all," only to find out that they were crumbling behind the façade of balance or they were unable to adapt when their lives were thrown out of balance by an unexpected turn of events? But take heart, for as the old saying goes, "the situation [in this case, finding balance] is hopeless but not serious." Although few of us are likely to achieve work–life balance for any sustainable length of time, we can all craft meaningful, engaged, and fulfilling lives that give us pride and joy and that contribute to the people, organizations, and communities who depend on us.

I begin this chapter by describing how researchers define happiness and what researchers have found does and doesn't contribute to happiness. On the basis of this research, I offer specific steps you can take to increase your happiness. I then describe what "flow" is, why it is important (including at work), and how you can create conditions that will help you and others experience feelings of flow. Next, I look at how characteristics such as optimism, perfectionism, and Type A behavior can affect your productivity, health, and psychological well-being. I also present research that provides insight into when positive emotions (e.g., optimism, good moods) can lead us astray and so-called negative emotions (e.g., pessimism, bad moods) can be useful. Finally, I discuss the impact of day care on children's well being because working parents make up a significant part of the workforce. Not surprisingly, decisions that involve managing both work and family are some of the most challenging decisions many people face in life.

HAPPINESS

What is happiness? Researchers dryly call happiness "subjective well-being" or, even more dryly, "SWB."[1] They believe that subjectivity is central to definitions of happiness. After all, you're the only one who truly knows if you're happy. For example, you may feel happy even though others say they wouldn't be happy if they were in your situation. Or you may feel unhappy even though others say they would be delighted to have what you have in your life.

> May your every wish be granted.
> —ANCIENT CHINESE CURSE

Researchers David Myers and Ed Diener explain that "high subjective well-being reflects a preponderance of positive thoughts and feelings about one's life." Simply stated, people who are happy are generally and genuinely pleased with themselves and their lives.[2] They believe that their lives are meaningful and feel positive emotions much of the time.[3] In contrast, people with low SWB are generally dissatisfied with their lives and feel more negative emotions, including fear, anger, envy, and depression.[4]

What Doesn't Predict Happiness? Miswanting

Let's begin by discussing what doesn't predict happiness. In general, researchers agree that money has a small impact on one's level of happiness, and that income buys between only 2% and 5% of one's happiness.[5] Money has a greater impact on happiness for the very poor because it can significantly enhance their quality of life by providing access to basic needs such as food, shelter, and health care. But once someone has enough money to buy the basic necessities of life, income is a poor predictor of happiness. People who make a lot of money are slightly more likely to be happy than people with moderate incomes, perhaps because they can pay others to do routine chores such as housecleaning, laundry, and cooking. This leaves them with more time to do things that may give them more pleasure. Keep in mind that expensive leisure activities typically don't tend to make people happy. Indeed, one study concluded, "People engaged in expensive leisure activities were significantly less happy than people engaged in inexpensive activities."[6]

Materialism (a focus on having more money and things) tends to decrease happiness, particularly for people who believe that having more money will make them happier. Researchers Aaron Ahuvia and Douglas Friedman explain, "Having more money doesn't necessarily lead to lower SWB, but wanting more money is likely to. Satisfaction with one's income is more important than the level of income itself."[7]

> You can't have everything. Where would you put it?
> —STEPHEN WRIGHT, *Comedian*

Research by Abhishek Srivastava and colleagues found that "it's not the money, it's the motives" that predict whether money will have a positive or negative impact on a person's happiness. In their study of MBAs and entrepreneurs, they found that people whose drive for money is motivated by "social comparison, seeking power, showing off, and overcoming self-doubt" tend to rate themselves lower on happiness than do those who earn money doing things that are meaningful to them personally.[8]

Researcher Sonja Lyubomirsky illustrates the gap between the acquisition of material goods and happiness. She compares life in the United States in the 1940s with life today, saying:

> Approximately one-third of all homes in 1940 did not have running water, indoor toilets, or bathtubs/showers, and more than half had no central heating. If you were twenty-five years or older in 1940, you would have stood only a 40 percent chance of having completed the eighth grade, a 25 percent chance of having graduated from high school, and only a 5 percent chance of having finished college. When asked to rate their overall satisfaction with life, Americans in 1940 reported being "very happy," with an average score of 7.5 out of 10. However, times have changed. The typical house today not only has running water, two or more baths, and central heating but is twice the size with an average of two rooms per person, not to mention being equipped with microwave ovens, dishwashers, color TVs, DVD players, iPods, and personal computers. And real monthly personal income has more than doubled. So what is the average score for Americans today? It's 7.2.[9]

> It has long been my conviction that we learn far more about the conditions, and values, of a society by contemplating how it chooses to play, to use its free time, to take its leisure, than by examining how it goes about its work.
> —A. BARTLETT GIAMATTI, *Scholar, Former President of Yale University and Former Commissioner of Baseball*

Summarizing several research studies, Ahuvia and Friedman conclude, "Achieving one's intrinsic goals for personal growth, close personal relationships, making a social contribution, and maintaining one's health were generally associated with higher levels of SWB. By contrast, achieving one's extrinsic goals for financial success, social recognition, and having an appealing appearance did not produce similar positive results."[10]

Unfortunately, it turns out that human beings tend to be poor predictors of what will make them happy (e.g., getting a new addition on the house, earning the promotion). People often pursue money, status, and material possessions with the hope that achieving these goals will make them happy. Achieving these goals does tend to make people happy for a little while. However, these don't contribute to long-term happiness because once we acquire these goods and achieve goals related to status, we quickly take them for granted, and we then need more and more of these kinds of goods and goals (e.g., more stuff, more promotions, more salary raises) to feel happy. So, we start looking for the next big things that will make us happy (which will never be enough), and we tend to look in the wrong places.

Researchers Daniel Gilbert and Timothy Wilson label the common belief that money and material possessions will make us happy as "miswanting." They explain that human beings tend to overestimate how much happiness these things will bring because we assume that the momentary pleasure will lead to lasting pleasure. Gilbert and Wilson also found that human beings tend to overestimate how much unhappiness one-time negative events (e.g., losing a job, reductions in salary) will bring because most of us tend to adjust to these losses in a relatively short time, and adapt our lives to accommodate them. The lesson to take from their research is this: If we are aware that we tend to overestimate the impact of both positive and negative events on our long-term happiness, we can make better decisions in how we spend our time, energy, and money in our day-to-day lives (for both short- and long-term planning).[11]

What Predicts Happiness? Adapting Your Beliefs and Activities

Now, back to the question, "What makes people happy?" Many researchers believe that we all have a personal happiness "set point." In other words, they believe that people's genetic makeup might account for up to 50% of the variation in happiness levels across individuals. This belief is based on studies that compare the happiness levels of identical and fraternal twins. On average, identical twins (twins who have identical genes) share more personality traits (e.g., predispositions toward happiness) even when they are each raised in different environments than do fraternal twins (twins who don't have identical genes).[12]

Yet, even if each of us has a happiness "set point," researchers also have found that much of our happiness and unhappiness is in our control.[13] In particular, we can increase our happiness levels by consciously and proactively developing belief systems and taking part in activities that are likely to increase our happiness. In the following sections, I discuss the kinds of beliefs and behaviors that can increase your happiness and that are, to a significant degree, within your control.

BELIEFS THAT CAN MAKE PEOPLE HAPPY

- *Feeling good about oneself.* Say Myers and Diener, "Happy people like themselves." Indeed, happy people tend to have a self-enhancing bias and overestimate their capabilities (such as intelligence, competence, appearance, and taste).[14] Researchers Timothy Judge and Charlice Hurst research has found that people who have "positive core self-evaluations" (high self-esteem, a belief they can achieve goals that are important to them, emotional stability, and a sense of personal control over their environment) tend to have higher life satisfaction, as well as higher job satisfaction and income.[15]
- *Being a "satisficer" rather than "maximizer."* A satisficer is someone who is happy with decisions that "cross the threshold of acceptability—something that is good enough," especially when a perfect decision isn't possible or necessary. A maximizer is someone who habitually wants to make the best possible decision, even when it is impossible or unnecessary. The problem for maximizers is that as options increase, their chances for making the best decision become more difficult. For example, if maximizers try to purchase the "best

car," there are a seemingly infinite number of criteria they can use and there are hundreds of choices in cars. So, they are likely to get frustrated with the arduous process of maximizing their car-buying decision, as well as with their final decision because it will rarely seem good enough. Furthermore, even if they believe their final decision is perfect at the time they make that decision, the situation is likely to soon change in a way that makes the decision seem less optimal (and quite frustrating) to the maximizer. For example, the day after the maximizer purchases the car, it could get recalled, a new model with better options could come out, or the neighbors may buy a car that looks even more appealing. Researcher Barry Schwartz and colleagues explain: "Although maximizers may in general achieve better objective outcomes than satisficers (as a result of their high standards and exhaustive search and decision procedures), they are likely to experience these outcomes as worse subjectively." Because there is often no perfect decision, maximizers experience more feelings of regret, depression, and dissatisfaction with what they have, and these feelings can reduce their feelings of happiness.[16]

- *Savoring experiences.* Savoring means fully experiencing and appreciating the special moments in life. Savoring increases happiness because it creates pleasant feelings and it provides timeless positive experiences. We can savor a memory (e.g., remembering how you met the person you now love), savor the moment (e.g., enjoying the moment when you graduate and share your pride with your family), and savor an upcoming event (e.g., anticipating the arrival of a new baby, imagining what it will feel like to graduate from school and have time again to enjoy other things in life).[17] To illustrate the power of savoring, *New Yorker* magazine recently had an article about the restaurant Civa Sofrasi, located 20 minutes from Istanbul, that specializes in home style foods (stews, pilafs, and dolmas) based on hard-to-find family recipes that are carefully prepared with local ingredients in ways that are true to the foods' local origins. Customers look forward to eating at the restaurant because the food often reminds them of the foods their mothers and grandmothers prepared for them when they were children, and these memories evoke a powerful emotional experience. Says owner and chef Musa Dagdeviren, "Sometimes, one of them [a customer] will start crying and it spreads to other tables."[18]

- *Participating in your faith.* Actively religious people tend to be happier, healthier, and longer-lived than people who are not. They also tend to be more resilient in overcoming traumas, and they report lower levels of depression.[19] Actively participating in a religious community can provide a network of supportive social relationships that enhance well-being, particularly during difficult times. Most religions also have rules that encourage healthy living, moderation in life in general, and commitment to one's family. Furthermore, faith can contribute to happiness because it helps us find meaning and hope throughout life's ups and downs.

- *Having a sense of control.* People who feel that they have a sense of control over parts of their lives that are important to them tend to be more satisfied in general.[20] In fact, having a sense of control over parts of one's life that one believes are important is one of the most significant predictors of well-being in old age.[21]

- *Experiencing positive emotions: Optimism, hope, and gratitude.* People who are optimistic think that life, in general, will turn out well for them.[22] Myers and Diener illustrate happy people's bias toward optimism with Sigmund Freud's joke about the man who told his wife, "If one of us should die, I think I would go live in Paris."[23] Notably, it's the optimists' belief in themselves and their ability to control their environment, not the objective truth of these beliefs, that leads

> Happiness is not something you get, but something you do.
> —MARCELENE COX, *Author*

to optimism. People who are hopeful believe that they can make outcomes that are important to them happen, so they design and implement action plans to make these outcomes happen. They also are willing to persist in the face of obstacles and make sacrifices in order to make their dreams come true. Their vision, planning, and willpower increase the possibility that their hopes will be fulfilled.[24] People who regularly feel grateful toward others and for what they have tend to be happier, feel they have more control over their lives, are able to cope better with adversity, are more generous toward others, have less stress, and experience less depression.[25]

The point of this section so far is this: Your happiness is based, in large part, on your beliefs about yourself (e.g., feeling good about yourself); your beliefs about the value of your possessions (e.g., appreciating what you have rather than wanting what you don't have, satisficing rather than maximizing); your beliefs about the quality of your experiences (e.g., savoring the present, past, and future); your beliefs about the quality of your relationships (e.g., being grateful for the people in your life, seeing the good in others); and your beliefs about the possibilities that lie before you (e.g., believing you have control over outcomes that are important to you). Although there are objective realities in life, it's how you make sense of these realities that predicts your happiness. In the next section, I discuss how you can increase your happiness by choosing activities that increase your well-being.

ACTIVITIES THAT MAKE PEOPLE HAPPY

- *Having goals that you enjoy and that are congruent with each other.* People who are committed to goals that are meaningful to them, aligned with their interests, and draw on their strengths tend to be happy. Researcher Sonja Lyubomirsky explains that it's the process of moving toward our goals, not only achieving our goals, that contribute to happiness because the pursuit of important goals provides meaning, feelings of control, opportunities to interact with others, and structure to our lives (e.g., through planning, prioritization, milestones, and feedback). Achieving small successes as we work toward our goals makes us feel good and motivates us to keep moving forward. Overcoming challenges along the way enhances our competence and belief in our ability to achieve our goals. Says Lyubomirsky, "Find a happy person, and you will find a project."[26]

- *Balancing current and future pleasure.* People who are happy throughout their lives (rather than for a short period of time only) tend to balance time spent doing things that provide immediate pleasure (e.g., spending money on a family vacation, going to a party) and time spent doing things that are likely to bring them future pleasure (e.g., living under their means and saving for the future, forgoing a party to study for an important exam). Says researcher Tal Ben-Shahar, "Happy people live secure in the knowledge that the activities that bring them enjoyment in the present will also lead to a fulfilling future."[27]

Enjoy present pleasures in such a way as not to injure future ones.
—SENECA,
Roman Stoic philosopher

- *Spending time with others.* People with close relationships tend to be happier, healthier, and longer-lived than people without these relationships. In addition, people who choose to be around happy people tend to be happier. Interestingly, recent research suggests that your happiness is affected by how happy your friends' friends are. The closer these happy people are to you geographically (e.g., happy neighbors, happy family members who live a few miles away), the happier you are likely to be.[28]

- *Doing good for others.* People who volunteer, give to charity, and provide support to others tend to rate themselves as happier than those who don't. They also tend to have better mental health and less depression. The reason for the link between giving to others and

BOX 10-1   A Little Advice about Wealth

The media often promotes the image of the wealthy person as having high status and an abundance of material possessions. Yet many people who exhibit a high-status image and collect material possessions aren't financially wealthy. Simply stated, if a person spends all of his or her high salary and bonuses on things that are not financial investments (e.g., expensive cars, dinners out, electronic toys, high-end vacations, etc.), then he or she may not be as wealthy as the person who earns much less money yet saves a significant portion of his or her salary.

In studies of people who become wealthy through their own efforts (not through their parents' substantial financial gifts or inheritances), a few patterns stand out. Many people who are millionaires in the United States don't look like millionaires (and those who do look like millionaires are often worth significantly less). Instead, the millionaires are the people who save, rather than spend, a large percentage of their income. Rather than accumulating material goods or worrying about status, they get pleasure out of watching their investments grow. They tend to live below their means, invest their money wisely, are skilled at finding good opportunities, and regularly spend their time doing financial planning. They tend to be at least moderate risk takers and are less drawn to immediate gratification. They do not dole out a lot of money to their children, except through their support of high-quality education.

In short, your attention to savings, investments, and finding good opportunities—not your salary or attention to appearances—determine your wealth.

Source: Stanley, Thomas, and William Danko. 1996. *The Millionaire Next Door: The Surprising Secrets of America's Wealthy.* New York: Pocketbooks; Kiyosaki, Robert, and Sharon Lechter. 1997. *Rich Dad, Poor Dad.* New York: Warner Books.

mental health may be that thinking of others helps people find greater meaning in life and takes people's minds off themselves and material possessions.
- *Using effective coping strategies.* Researcher C. R. Snyder defines coping as "a response aimed at diminishing the physical, emotional, and psychological burden that is linked to stressful life events and daily hassles."[29] People who cope well with adversity tend to develop perspectives on stressful events that make these events more tolerable, even meaningful. (e.g., "Although I hate it that I lost my job, I can look for work I truly enjoy."). They also use coping strategies that help them get back on track (e.g., getting support from other people, taking courses to develop new skills, taking care of their health, vigorously pursuing new jobs).

The most important thing to take away from this section is this: People who are happy in the long run don't have easier lives or better luck than other people. Rather, they spend time doing activities that are meaningful to them and that contribute to both short-term and long-term pleasure, they invest in their relationships, they give to others, and they use coping strategies that help them overcome the hardships that are an inevitable part of life. In short, happy people make happiness happen through purposeful everyday actions. In the next section, I discuss how people create work environments that make them happy.

HAPPINESS, WORK, AND FLOW

Work, it seems, makes most of us happy. When professor Robert Weiss surveyed people about whether they'd continue to work "if they had inherited enough to live comfortably, roughly 8 out of 10 people said yes."[30] Steve Jobs once had this to say about his work: "If I didn't enjoy it, I'd be on a beach somewhere. . . . Why bother, when running Apple and Pixar is so much fun?"[31] And Time

Warner's former vice chairman, Ted Turner, had this to say about his feelings when he signed a $165-billion deal with America Online: "I did it with as much excitement as I felt the first time I made love some 42 years ago."[32]

> Choose a job you
> love, and you will
> never work a day in
> your life.
> —CONFUCIUS,
> *Chinese Philosopher*

Without dwelling on the comparative pleasures of relaxing on a beach, making love, or working, the important point to be made here is this: When we are engaged in work that we enjoy—whether paid or unpaid, climbing the organizational ladder or caring for a home and family—we feel happy. What is it about work that so powerfully influences our sense of well-being?

Our work helps us define who we are and our place in the world ("I am a good manager," "I am a loving parent," "I am a creative artist," "I am the best deal-maker in my industry."). When our work involves being with others on a regular basis, it helps us fulfill our needs for belonging and social interaction. When our work challenges us, it helps us fulfill our needs for competence and growth. When our work involves familiar routines (e.g., getting children off to school, going to the office, or checking our e-mail in the morning), it helps us fulfill our needs for control and consistency in our everyday life. And, says Brian Dumaine of *Fortune* magazine, "In a time of uncertainty and upheaval, whether in the family or society, work also provides perhaps your best chance to create a world exactly as you want it to be."[33] To make this point, Dumaine quotes Debra Sandler, former marketing director at Pepsi's $8-billion soft drink division and now worldwide group vice president of marketing and strategic ingredient technology at McNeil Nutritional:

> I see myself as an agent of change. There are not many women of color in corporate America, and I place a heavy burden on myself to show that we can do it. And that we do it pretty darn well. And that I'm not here simply because someone said, "Let's pad the affirmative action numbers."[34]

> To deprive a person of work
> is to negate a portion of
> his/her humanity.
> —JOHN CONVERS,
> *The Politics of Unemployment*

Certainly, not all work contributes to our well-being. Most readers of this book can think of work situations that are boring, unfulfilling, and unhealthy. For work to enhance our feelings of well-being—not just to put money on the table—it must be both meaningful and well designed.[35] Psychologist Mihaly Csikszentmihalyi explains that such work provides us with an opportunity to feel "flow," also known as "peak experience" or "optimal experience." We feel flow when we are fully immersed in an activity that is important to us—teaching, gardening, writing, creating a new product, or reading to a child. Csikszentmihalyi explains that we are most likely to feel flow in situations that have the following characteristics:[36]

- *Worthwhile goals.* We are more likely to be committed to and excited by a task if we believe that the work is worth doing.
- *Challenge.* We are more likely to feel engaged in a task if it requires skills that stretch our abilities yet are still within our reach.
- *Clear goals, rules, and feedback.* We are more likely to feel flow if we have clear boundaries, such as goals, rules, and deadlines, which help us focus our attention without being sidetracked by irrelevant concerns. Csikszentmihalyi explains, "It is easy to enter flow in games such as chess, tennis, or poker because they have goals and rules that make it possible for the player to act without questioning what should be done and how."[37]
- *Periods of concentrated attention.* We are more likely to feel flow when we are able to concentrate without distractions for extended periods of time. When we emerge from a concentrated period of flow, we realize that hours have gone by in what seems like minutes. A study of engineers by researcher Leslie Perlow supports Csikszentmihalyi's conclusions.

When she began her study, she found that "on average, only 36 percent of the engineers' time occurs in uninterrupted blocks over one hour long. . . . Moreover, engineers have little control over the fragmentation of their schedules."[38] After Perlow helped the engineers design their jobs so that they would have "uninterrupted blocks of "quiet time' during the day . . . no one found that the imposed structure hurt their productivity, and 65 percent felt that it had enhanced their productivity."[39]

- *Feelings of control.* We are more likely to feel flow if we feel as though we have some control over how to do the task. Notably, we're unlikely to feel flow if the outcome is too easy to achieve. Says Csikszentmihalyi, "What people enjoy is not the sense of being in control, but the sense of exercising control in difficult situations. It is not possible to experience a sense of control unless one is willing to give up the safety of protective routines. Only when a doubtful outcome is at stake, and one is able to influence that outcome, can a person really know whether she [or he] is in control."[40]

In short, Csikszentmihalyi explains, "The best moments usually occur when a person's body or mind is stretched to its limits in a voluntary effort to accomplish something difficult and worthwhile. Optimal experience is something that we make happen."[41] It is not surprising that we're unlikely to feel flow when we're engaging in passive leisure activities such as watching television (although we may have other good feelings such as relaxation and rejuvenation). Activities that inspire flow may not always feel pleasant. Indeed, developing a new product, writing a book, or climbing a mountain can be painful, particularly during those periods in which the challenge of the activity temporarily exceeds our ability. But if we believe that the task is worthwhile, are able to focus on the task without distractions for extended periods of time, and have (or can learn) the required skills to accomplish the task, we are likely to persevere and experience flow.

The human need for challenge begins early in life. Recently, I went on vacation to the beach with my children, a friend, and my friend's children. I was fascinated with the fact that every time we went to the beach, the children's immediate reaction was to pick up their shovels and buckets and get to work digging deep holes that would become their temporary houses and building elaborate sand castles with water-filled moats. The children worked creatively and strenuously for hours. They didn't speak much to each other, except to coordinate their efforts and argue over a shovel now and then. Their bodies and minds were fully engaged in creating and working. It didn't matter to the children that their houses, castles, and moats would be washed away later that day. The children would simply return to the beach the next day to start building again, this time with lessons learned and ideas gained from the day before. This experience, more than any I've recently seen, seemed to most purely reflect our very human need to experience flow.

When we feel flow, we reap many rewards. The process of doing the work often feels good. When we finish the task, we feel a strong sense of accomplishment from a job well done. We gain new skills in the process that make us feel more competent and ready to take on more challenging tasks. And feeling flow is highly motivating. Says Csikszentmihalyi, "Once we have tasted this joy, we will redouble our efforts to taste it again."[42] Another important benefit, says Csikszentmihalyi, is that, "The self becomes more differentiated as a result of flow because overcoming a challenge inevitably leaves a person feeling more capable, more skilled. . . . Our identity becomes more complex. . . . [While we are engaged in flow] our concern for self disappears, yet paradoxically, the sense of self emerges stronger after the flow experience is over."[43]

> Don't aim at success—the more you aim at it and make it a target, the more you are going to miss it. For success, like happiness, cannot be pursued; it must ensue, and it only does so as the unintended side effect of one's personal dedication to a cause greater than oneself or as the by-product of one's surrender to a person other than oneself.
> —VIKTOR FRANKL, *Man's Search for Meaning*

BOX 10-2 Rate Your Work's Potential for "Flow"

Task or Job Being Assessed: _____

  1. Never
  2. Rarely
  3. Sometimes
  4. Often
  5. Always

1. Does the work feel worthwhile to me?	1	2	3	4	5
2. Are the goals clear?	1	2	3	4	5
3. Are the goals achievable?	1	2	3	4	5
4. Are there clear rules for accomplishing the work?	1	2	3	4	5
5. Does the work provide regular feedback so that I know how I'm doing?	1	2	3	4	5
6. Do I have the skills I need to do my work?	1	2	3	4	5
7. Is the work challenging (does it stretch my skills?)?	1	2	3	4	5
8. Am I able to concentrate on my work without distractions?	1	2	3	4	5
9. Does the work enable me to rise above worries and self-consciousness?	1	2	3	4	5
10. Do I feel like I have some control over the work?	1	2	3	4	5

Source: Based on Csikszentmihalyi, Mihaly. 1990. *Flow: The Psychology of Optimal Experience.* New York: HarperPerennial; Csikszentmihalyi, Mihaly. 2003. *Good Business Leadership, Flow, and the Making of Meaning.* New York: Penguin Books.

> If I could build one building in my life, I want to build a building that people feel in the stomach—you can call it comfort, beauty, excitement, guts, tears. . . . There are many ways to describe the reaction to architecture, but tears are as good as any.
> —PHILIP JOHNSON, *age 92, Architect*

Although most of us tend to enjoy working, it seems that many of us don't feel very positively about the organizations in which we do our work. In a study of 30,000 U.S. workers, the consulting firm Opinion Research "found that though most people generally feel positive about working, 47 percent now say they either dislike or are ambivalent about the company they work for."[44] The research on flow suggests why some people don't have strong positive feelings toward their organizations: meaningless work, excessive ambiguity, not having the skills to accomplish the task, not having the opportunity to learn new skills, not feeling in control of one's work, lack of trust, self-consciousness, and excessive distractions. To see if your job is likely to foster feelings of flow, complete the assessment in Box 10.2. The higher the score, the more likely the job is to inspire flow. If you are curious about whether you are creating conditions that inspire flow for the people who work for you, have them complete the assessment as well.

OPTIMISM AND SUCCESS

After decades of studies, researchers are concluding that optimism—in most cases—provides many benefits, including greater achievement, psychological well-being, and better health. Indeed, research by Becca Levy and colleagues found that "older individuals with more positive self-perceptions of aging, measured up to 23 years earlier, lived 7.5 years longer than those with less positive perceptions of aging. This advantage remained after age, gender, socioeconomic status, loneliness, and functional health were included as covariates."[45]

What are the characteristics of optimists? Research by social psychologist Shelly Taylor and others provides ample evidence that happy and effective people tend to be somewhat out of touch with reality. Specifically, they tend to interpret themselves and the world around them with a positive bias. They see themselves as more talented than they are, the environment as more controllable than it is, and the world as a considerably more positive place than watching the nightly news would suggest. They also see the future as holding "an unrealistically bountiful set of opportunities." Taylor calls these generous interpretations of reality "creative self-deceptions" or "positive illusions," and makes a strong case that they are foundations of personal effectiveness and well-being.[46]

> There are two ways to live your life. One is as though nothing is a miracle. The other is as though everything is a miracle.
> —ALBERT EINSTEIN

Taylor notes that although most optimists tend to have unrealistic interpretations of themselves and the world around them, they are not unreasonably optimistic. In other words, they don't deny bad news. Rather, they incorporate it into their lives with a positive bias. For example, an optimistic manager who receives negative feedback may say, "It's a good thing that I got the news now rather than later in my career so that I have time to develop the skills I need." Furthermore, realistic optimists focus their optimism on events over which they have some control. Taylor explains, "These qualities distinguish illusion from delusion. Delusions are false beliefs that persist despite the facts. Illusions accommodate them, though perhaps reluctantly."[47]

> Dreams, if they are any good, are always a little crazy.
> —RAY CHARLES, *Musician*

Taylor suggests that optimism can enhance productivity, health, and psychological well-being because it is likely to lead to self-fulfilling prophecies. Optimists are more likely than others to do the following:[48]

- *Set high goals and standards.* People who tend to judge themselves as more competent than average are likely to set high goals and standards.
- *Be highly motivated.* People who attribute success to themselves rather than to external factors tend to be self-motivated.
- *Work hard and persevere.* People who have positive feelings toward themselves tend to work hard and long on tasks because they believe that they can accomplish them. They tend to persevere to overcome hurdles. This perseverance increases the likelihood that they will reach their goals.
- *Seek out feedback.* Optimists tend to look for feedback so that they can assess whether they are on the right track toward achieving their goals.
- *Increase problem-solving capacity and speed.* A good mood increases the likelihood that a person will use rapid and efficient problem-solving strategies.
- *Take risks.* Optimists tend to take risks perhaps because they don't dwell on what can go wrong or because they assume that they can control the outcome.
- *Postpone gratification.* People who believe that they will succeed tend to stick with their goals even when achieving these goals may take a long time because they can envision a positive outcome.
- *Reward themselves.* People who feel good about themselves tend to reward themselves for their efforts.
- *Gain social support.* People who focus on the positive things in life are typically pleasant to be around and are more likely to get help from others.
- *Effectively manage stress.* Optimists tend to cope well with stress because they believe that things will eventually get better, are able to draw on social support to help them deal with stressful situations, are proactive in taking actions to alleviate the stress, and see the advantages of difficult periods ("I learned a lot from it." or "What doesn't kill me makes me stronger.").

> A fundamental shortcoming in much of business today is that the leadership lacks vision and passion—the two most important ingredients to inspire and motivate. In the Body Shop we have both in abundance and we possess, in addition, a further secret ingredient: an extraordinary level of optimism, almost amounting to euphoria, that permeates the whole company. We are incurable optimists—and incurable optimists believe they can do anything.
> —ANITA RODDICK, *Founder of the Body Shop International*

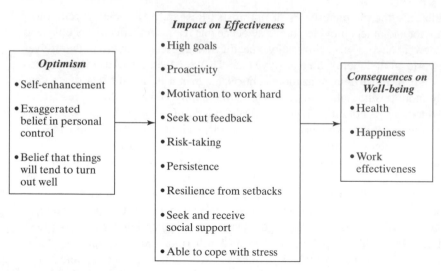

FIGURE 10-1 Relationship between Optimism, Effectiveness, and Well-Being: How Optimism Leads to Self-Fulfilling Prophecies

See Figure 10-1 for a summary of the impact of optimism on health, happiness, and effectiveness. Optimism may be particularly important for leaders. James Kouzes and Barry Posner, authors of the book *Credibility*, explain:

> Constituents look for leaders who demonstrate an enthusiastic and genuine belief in the capacity of others, who strengthen people's will, who supply the means to achieve, and who express optimism for the future. Constituents want leaders who remain passionate despite obstacles and setbacks. In today's uncertain times, leaders with a positive, confident, can-do approach to life and business are desperately needed. . . . Credible leaders sustain hope by painting positive images of the future. They arouse optimistic feelings and enable their constituents to hold positive thoughts about the possibilities of success.[49]

In short, optimism enhances success and well-being because, as Taylor says, a moderate detachment from reality—"an ability to see things not for what they are but what you wish they could be—is an effective offense mechanism, particularly when not taken to extremes and when tempered with the ability to incorporate negative information."[50]

The Role of Explanations in Optimism

Psychologist Martin Seligman argues that the difference between an optimistic and pessimistic view of the world is rooted in the explanations we use to explain the good and bad events in our lives.[51] He says that we use three types of explanatory styles:

- *Permanence (Do you see the cause of good and bad events as permanent or temporary?).* Optimists tend to see the causes of good events as permanent and the causes of bad events as temporary. In contrast, pessimists tend to see the causes of good events as temporary and the causes of bad events as permanent. For example, when an optimist receives a poor performance review, he or she is likely to believe that the poor performance was a temporary setback, whereas a pessimist is likely to believe that the review may reflect his or her future ability to perform well.

- *Pervasiveness (Do you see the causes of good and bad events as specific or global?).* Optimists tend to see the causes of good events as carrying over to several aspects of their lives and the causes of bad events as specific to only one aspect of their lives. In contrast, pessimists tend to see the causes of good events as specific to one aspect of their lives and the causes of bad events as carrying over to several aspects of their lives. For example, when an optimist gives a presentation that receives positive reactions, he or she is likely to think, "I'm very good at my job," whereas the pessimist is likely to think, "I'm good at giving presentations."

- *Personalization (Do you attribute the causes of good and bad events to yourself or to external causes?).* Optimists tend to give credit to themselves for good events and blame others or external causes for bad events. In contrast, pessimists tend to give credit to others or external causes for good events and blame themselves for bad events. For example, when an optimist does well on an exam, he or she is likely to think, "I studied hard" or "I'm smart," whereas the pessimist is likely to think, "It was an easy exam" or "The professor did a good job teaching the material."

Note that the relationship between self-enhancing biases and optimism may be more likely to exist for people from individualistic cultures (self-focused) than for people from collectivist cultures (relationship-focused). This pattern arises because individualistic cultures tend to promote a self-enhancing bias, whereas collectivist cultures tend to promote a self-critical bias.[52] Note also that self-enhancing biases can have negative consequences. For example, people who attribute problems to external causes alone and don't take responsibility for their actions may be overconfident, deny personal responsibility for failure, and avoid self-development.

> Our ability to delude ourselves may be an important survival tool.
> —JANE WAGNER,
> *The Search for Signs of Intelligent Life in the Universe*

Seligman argues that we can learn to be more optimistic by changing the way that we interpret the causes of good and bad events in our lives. He successfully teaches children and adults to become optimists by using what he calls the ABC method.[53] This method involves keeping a record of adverse events and how you react to them. "A" refers to the adversity that occurs ("I forgot to mail the Federal Express package and the package arrived late."). "B" refers to the belief that you have about the causes of that adversity ("I was busy yesterday." or "I'm stupid."). "C" refers to the consequences of your beliefs ("I'll write a list of what I need to accomplish each day and keep it on my desk to refer to throughout the day." or "I can't do much to improve my memory because I'm incompetent." or "There's always too much work to do around here and I'll never be able to get it all done correctly, so I'll just do what I can."). By recording the ways that you interpret adverse situations, you can identify the kinds of explanations that you use, determine how they affect your attitudes and behaviors (e.g., are they likely to make you proactive or reactive), and then reframe negative interpretations into positive ones.

> I am happy and content because I think I am.
> —ALAIN-RENE LESAGE,
> *French Novelist and Playwright*

When Optimism Is Overrated

It's wise to keep in mind that optimism isn't right for all people and all situations. For example, for decades many researchers and other well-intentioned people have been advising people who are ill with serious diseases to be optimistic and to think positively because doing so would enhance their quality of life and perhaps even their longevity. However, some research suggests that such claims may be doing some people a disservice (e.g., the "tyranny of positive thinking."). For some people with serious diseases, being asked to be optimistic may be perceived as an additional burden to carry (e.g., "I'm really sick and now you want me to see the bright side?"). Instead of recommending positive thinking, it is often more helpful to encourage the person who is sick to cope in familiar ways that have worked for the person in the past. To make this point, the *Wall Street Journal* quotes Dr. Jimmie Holland, chair of Psychiatric Oncology at Memorial Sloan-Kettering Hospital in New York: "You can be as curmudgeonly or angry or whiny as you want and still survive cancer, as long as it doesn't cause your doctor to throw you out of the office." Note, however, that having a positive attitude does seem to motivate people who are ill to seek out help, eat the right foods, exercise, and follow their doctors' orders.[54]

Researchers have also found that negative moods, as well as positive moods, can help us make better decisions, depending on the type of problem we are facing. Researchers agree that the way we feel affects the way we think (e.g., how we process the world around us and what we pay attention to), our memory (e.g., "Did the person who stole the purse have dark hair or light hair?"), our judgments (e.g., "Is this job candidate a good fit?"), and our actions (e.g., "Should we hire this job candidate or not?"). They also agree that we make decisions differently depending on whether we're in a good mood or bad mood—even when we're faced with objective facts. Researcher Joseph Forgas agrees that positive emotions help people think more creatively, broadly, and cooperatively, and can help people make better decisions under some circumstances. But he also found that certain types of negative moods also can help people make better decisions. People who are in "mild bad moods" tend to be more attentive to their surroundings, are better able to remember the details of what they see, are less gullible, are less likely to make "snap decisions" (including those based on prejudices), and are better able to identify lying. In short, although good moods undoubtedly provide significant benefits in many aspects of life, including in decision-making, bad moods also play a positive and adaptive function by helping us be more attentive and careful when making decisions.[55]

Researcher Julie Norem found that some people—particularly those who have an anxious temperament—tend to perform better when they have a characteristic she calls "defensive pessimism".[56] Describing her early research, Norem says:

> I found myself surrounded by people who were notably successful, by virtually any definition, and not notably optimistic. According to the research on optimism, this shouldn't be. Pessimism should produce negative results. When we set low expectations, we initiate a self-fulfilling prophecy. . . . There was plenty of research that indicated that people like them should be depressed, sickly, unmotivated, helpless, and hopeless—yet they certainly didn't seem that way to me . . . I asked how these people were able to do so well *despite* their pessimism—and that's when things got really interesting.[57]

Norem found that many people who would be described as pessimists often do well *because* of their pessimism. They assume that anything that can go wrong will go wrong so they overprepare, make back-up plans, take care of all the details, and check their work over and over again. These actions turn out to be effective coping mechanisms that help them harness their anxiety in ways that help them achieve the high-quality results they desire. Norem notes that telling defensive pessimists to relax and not worry can actually decrease their performance. She also notes that defensive pessimists whose anxiety moves them to take results-oriented action are not the same as pessimists whose attitudes paralyze them into inaction. Defensive pessimists are simply *very* careful.

Most of us would agree that the 2010 BP oil spill disaster in the Gulf of Mexico might have been prevented if there were more defensive pessimists on the leadership teams that made decisions about safety and reliability on their oil rigs. Sweating the details pays off in more mundane day-to-day situations as well. Take for example, a team of fishermen who entered the 52nd annual Big Rock Blue Marlin fishing tournament in the summer of 2010. They caught an 883-pound marlin that was the biggest fish caught during that tournament, as well as the biggest fish ever caught in the tournament. After they were declared the winners of the $1-million prize, officials learned that the winning team never applied for a fishing license (a small, yet critical, detail that would have cost the team under $25), so they had to forfeit the prize money. The winning title and prize money instead went to the team that caught the next biggest fish, a 528.3 pound marlin. As defensive pessimists know, details matter—sometimes a lot.[58]

Defensive pessimists should keep in mind that although their anxious behaviors (e.g., worrying, overplanning, and "sweating the small stuff") often help them perform at their best and add value to their teams, customers, and organizations, the same behaviors can lead to problems. One potential problem is that defensive pessimists may micromanage others if they don't learn to delegate and let employees make some mistakes and learn from these mistakes. Another potential problem is that the behaviors associated with defensive pessimism (e.g., worrying and repeatedly checking one's own work) may be perceived as signs of incompetence or lack of confidence by others (even if this is not true). Therefore, the defensive pessimist needs to manage these perceptions, perhaps by fretting in private rather than in public. An engineer and MBA student in one of my classes described how he manages his defensive pessimism. He explained that "being a duck' means that I give the outward appearance that everything is smooth and going well even when I am working on a challenging assignment. Ducks look like they are gliding smoothly on top of the water when they are peddling hard below the water and out of sight of onlookers."

Defensive pessimists also need to manage the stress associated with excessive worrying and the risk of missing meaningful opportunities while focusing on what can wrong. A public policy professional who described herself as a defensive pessimist explained that she performs very well on the job and rarely procrastinates. She also noted that she often "fails to appreciate the present," can "dread an event that is supposed to be joyful for fear of the complicated planning that leads up to it," becomes sick with worry because of the stress," and avoids "spontaneous or risky situations because of the stress of the unknown."

The point is that defensive pessimism can certainly pay off for yourself, your teams, and your organizations if you manage the potential risks. You can complete the assessment in Box 10.3 to determine whether you have tendencies toward defensive pessimism.

WORK AND HEALTH

Your job can be helpful or hazardous to your psychological and physical health.[59] For example, in a study that focused on employees' relationships with their supervisors, researchers concluded that "individuals who perceived supervisory support as being low reported significantly higher physiological and social dysfunction symptoms." Other research has concluded that people are more likely to experience unhealthy stress when the demands of their jobs are high, but they have little control over how they meet those demands. However, when job demands are high and people have control over how they address those demands, they are likely to experience increased motivation.[60]

> Not everybody's life is what they make it. Some people's life is what other people make it.
> —ALICE WALKER,
> *Author*

In a recent study, researchers found that participants who worked three hours or more overtime were more likely to have heart disease. The authors of the study speculate that the type of people who regularly work long hours may also have other risks factors associated with consistently working overtime. For example, they may experience ongoing stress related to constantly

BOX 10-3 Defensive Pessimism Questionnaire

Think of a situation where you want to do your best. It may be related to work, to your social life, or to any of your goals. When you answer the following questions, please think about how you prepare for that kind of situation. Rate how true each statement is for you.

Not at all true of me 1 2 3 4 5 6 7 Very true of me

_____ I often start out expecting the worst, even though I will probably do OK.

_____ I worry about how things will turn out.

_____ I carefully consider all possible outcomes.

_____ I often worry that I won't be able to carry through my intentions.

_____ I spend lots of time imagining what could go wrong.

_____ I imagine how I would feel if things went badly.

_____ I try to picture how I could fix things if something went wrong.

_____ I'm careful not to become overconfident in these situations.

_____ I spend a lot of time planning when one of these situations is coming up.

_____ I imagine how I would feel if things went well.

_____ In these situations, sometimes I worry more about looking like a fool than doing really well.

_____ Considering what can go wrong helps me to prepare.

To figure out where you stand, add your scores for all the questions. Possible scores range from 12 to 84, and higher scores indicate a stronger tendency to use defensive pessimism. If you score above 50, you would qualify as a defensive pessimist in Norem's studies. If you score below 30, you would qualify as a strategic optimist. If you score between 30 and 50, you may use both strategies. How you score will be influenced by the kind of situation you were thinking about when you answered the questions because you may use different strategies in different situations.

Source: Julie Norem. 2002. *The Positive Power of Negative Thinking.* New York: Basic Books
Used with permission.

feeling behind in their work. They also may not take the time to sleep well at night or to seek out medical health when they experience signs of a potential medical problem.[61]

Notably, people at lower levels of the hierarchy are more likely to have heart disease, in part because they are more likely to engage in higher risk activities such as smoking and have a higher incidence of obesity. However, even when controlling for these factors, people at lower levels of organizational hierarchies are still more likely to have heart disease. On the basis of their studies, researchers attribute this higher incidence of heart disease among people at lower levels of organizational hierarchies to feelings of lack of control over their work (especially the pace and demands of the work), lack of predictability, and feelings of unfairness at work. These feelings may lead to chronic stress, which can in turn lead to increases in cortisone, a stress hormone that can suppress the strength of the immune system. The researchers conclude: "The way work is organized" and "the work climate" can influence one's health.[62]

Your relationship with your supervisor, the amount of control you have over the demands of your job, the amount of overtime you work, and your level in the organizational hierarchy aren't the only predictors of your health and well-being. Your attitude toward your work—particularly your tendencies toward perfectionism and Type A behavior—can influence your psychological and physical health, as well as your job effectiveness.

Perfectionism

Up to a point, perfectionism can be an admirable personal quality.[63] Indeed, when not taken to the extreme, some characteristics associated with perfectionism can contribute to high performance and career success. These characteristics include orderliness, setting high standards, and the pursuit of excellence.[64] However, research suggests that excessive perfectionism can interfere with your judgment, damage your interpersonal relationships, decrease your productivity, and harm your health.[65]

Researcher Robert Slaney and his colleagues explain that people who are excessively perfectionistic "have extremely high, perhaps unattainable, standards for their own performance" and "tend to see anything short of perfection as unacceptable."[66] Although effective perfectionists enjoy what they do and are able to turn their perfectionism on and off as appropriate, extreme perfectionists are prisoners of their perfection. Psychologist Asher Pacht describes the self-defeating bind perfectionists put themselves in:

> Their goals are so unrealistically high that they cannot possibly succeed. They are constantly frustrated by their need to achieve and their failure to do so. . . . For them, being perfect is the magic formula for success. Even when perfectionists do something successfully, they are seldom able to savor the fruits of their accomplishments. . . . The real tragedy lies in the fact that, for the perfectionist, achieving 95 percent or even 99 percent of the goal is usually seen as a failure because it is not perfect.[67]

Effective perfectionists know that perfectionism is critical when designing airbags for automobiles, yet less important when choosing the font for a PowerPoint presentation, and even less important when choosing the dessert for an informal dinner party. Extreme perfectionists, however, see most situations as needing the same level of effort because the perfectionism is tied to their self-worth rather than to the demands of the situation. In short, extreme perfectionists have a distorted view of what is possible and desirable. Specifically, perfectionism becomes a problem when any of the following occurs:

- It is excessive and uncontrollable.[68]
- It is rooted in an obsessive desire to be perfect to fulfill one's own needs (self-worth or fear of failure) rather than the demands of the situation.[69]
- It involves excessive rumination about failures to meet personal or social standards (perfectionists can't stop thinking about their performance because they feel it is never good enough).[70]
- It results in "all or none" thinking (perfectionists tend to see performance as "perfect" or "bad" with nothing in between).[71]

Extreme perfectionism creates several problems. It can result in anxiety, depression, and life dissatisfaction.[72] It can harm relationships because extreme perfectionists tend to set unrealistically high standards for others and can be excessively critical when others don't meet their relentless and impossible standards. It can harm work performance because perfectionists may be more likely to micromanage their employees, less likely to delegate, and have a difficult time finishing projects because they are unable to complete assignments to their own satisfaction.[73] Perfectionists may be less likely to admit failure and take risks because their self-worth is tied to their desire to be perfect.[74] Notably, extreme perfectionists tend to become even more perfectionistic in ambiguous situations in which performance is hard to measure because they have difficulty judging when good is good enough.[75]

> **True perfection exists only in obituaries and eulogies.**
> —ASHER PACHT,
> *Psychologist*

Unfortunately, the perfectionists' unrealistic standards for themselves and others can undermine the success that they hope to achieve.[76]

Fortunately, these tendencies can be tempered. Indeed, psychologist Pacht argues that "the very nature of the problem makes perfectionists good patients once the intellectual defenses are breached." Furthermore, Pacht argues, "For the vast majority of patients, 20 to 30 degrees of change is far more than enough."[77] To temper tendencies toward perfectionism, Pacht offers the following advice:[78]

- Do not attach all of your self-worth to your performance.
- Give yourself permission to be imperfect.
- Set reasonable, achievable goals.
- Be more discriminating about when orderliness and high standards are critical and when they are not.
- Choose some activities that you can do without aiming for perfection.

Finally, remember that our imperfections make us human. Says Pacht, "To be perfect would require an individual to be an automaton without charm. . . . The human quality in each of us comes from our imperfections, from all those 'defects' that give us our unique personalities and makes us real people."[79]

Type A Behavior

Type A behavior refers to a tendency toward extreme ambitiousness, achievement-striving, high-performance standards, competitiveness, impatience/irritability, anger/hostility, speed in speech and behavior, and desire to do multiple tasks simultaneously.[80] Researchers have concluded that some of these characteristics—ambitiousness, high achievement-striving, and high-performance standards—are associated with higher performance in a variety of settings: college students' grades in schools as well as their tendency to finish college; insurance agents' number of policies sold; academics' research productivity in terms of quality and quantity of publications; and employees' job performance, career success, and job satisfaction.

Although Type A behavior can be problematic, many people with Type A characteristics are happy peak performers. Says psychology professor Charles Garfield:

> Although peak performers may work very long hours, they experience their work as replenishing and nourishing rather than toxic; . . . They know how to use time wisely and, unlike workaholics, they tolerate chaos and ambiguity and aren't paralyzed by perfectionism. . . . [Poor performers] often end up managing details and are powerfully addicted to busyness. . . . Although peak performers are motivated by a commitment to their work, workaholics are motivated by a fear of failure.[81]

Researcher Cynthia Lee and her colleagues studied the relationship between achievement orientation and optimism. They concluded that when achievement-oriented people are also optimistic (i.e., they believe that they can make things go their way and that things will turn out well), they are likely to be more productive than others because they will continue to "strive, work hard, persist when faced with obstacles, and cope actively with problems they encounter, whereas pessimists would give up and turn away."[82]

Lee and her colleagues also found that the optimistic achievement-oriented people in their study reported less anxiety and fewer health problems, perhaps because they tend to deal with "stressful encounters by using problem-focused strategies such as formulating action plans, keeping their minds on the task at hand, and not thinking about the negative emotions with which the stress was associated. Pessimism was associated with emotion-focused coping strategies of denial and distancing, focusing on stressful feelings, and avoidance or disengaging from the goal with which the stressor was interfering."[83]

Some Type A characteristics—particularly impatience, irritability, and hostility—do not predict productivity and are associated with health problems such as loss of appetite, depression, headaches, and heart disease.[84] Research suggests that anger and hostility are the "most toxic" and are most closely associated with coronary heart disease.[85] In a recent study of 13,000 people published in the British journal *Lancet*, the researchers concluded that anger-prone people are three times as likely to have heart attacks than those who are not.[86] And it appears that the link between anger and heart attacks exists for both men and women.

The bottom line on Type A behavior is this: When focused on achievement-striving, not taken to extremes, and coupled with optimism, Type A behavior can be good for the individual and the organization. But if the Type A behavior is driven by hostility, fear of failure, or an excessive need for control, it can be hazardous to your health and is of little benefit, if any, to your productivity.

> It's true that hard work never killed anybody, but I figure, why take the chance.
> —RONALD REAGAN,
> *Former U.S. president*

What Are the Organizational Consequences of Perfectionism and Type A Behavior?

On the surface, it may seem that people who are obsessed with perfection or achievement may be an asset to their organizations because of the extreme focus, energy, and time they are willing to commit to their work. Certainly, many organizations reward such behaviors even when they come at the expense of employees' health and personal commitments. However, Center for Creative Leadership researcher Joan Kofodimos makes a compelling case that managers who exhibit these behaviors may in fact be detrimental to their organizations.[87]

Kofodimos cautions that these managers are often unconscious of what drives them to invest primarily in their work—which is often a desire to avoid intimacy—and thus are "likely to make decisions, take actions, and approach problems in ways intended to serve [their] inner needs." For example, rather than focus on the needs of the organization, colleagues, direct reports, and customers, they may make decisions and take actions designed to fulfill their ego needs, prove themselves, gain recognition, and avoid failure. They may also be "insensitive to the emotional life of coworkers—their needs, their feelings, and the things that motivate them" because they are insensitive to their own emotional needs. Unable to provide empathy, support, and compassion, such managers are unlikely to receive "wholehearted support and commitment" from their employees.[88] Notably, perfectionism and Type A behaviors tend to escalate in stressful and ambiguous situations, precisely when clear thinking, strong relationships, and organizational focus are critical.

The assessment in Box 10.4 can help you determine whether your work behaviors might be undermining your effectiveness, as well as your psychological and physical health.

INTEGRATING WORK AND FAMILY

For many managers today, one of their most pressing challenges is combining their responsibilities toward work and family in ways that enable them to contribute responsibly and wholeheartedly to both.[89] As many readers of this book know, this can be tricky to achieve. The difficulty is fueled by scary headlines such as "The Workaholic Generation,"[90] "Why Grade "A" Executives Get an "F" As

BOX 10-4   Ten Signs That Your Work Behaviors May Be Having a Negative Impact on Your Effectiveness as well as Psychological and Physical Health

1. Do you enjoy your work more than spending time with your family, friends, and loved ones?
2. Do you take your work with you on every vacation?
3. Do you check your work e-mail every day, including weekends and vacations?
4. Are you able to distinguish between critical tasks that demand perfection and those for which perfection isn't important?
5. Do you worry about the future, even when everything seems to be going well?
6. Do you think about your work when others are talking to you about nonwork topics?
7. Do you assume that people who have other commitments besides work are less effective than those who don't?
8. Do you judge your own and other's work performance by face-time rather than results?
9. Is your commitment to your work hurting your personal relationships?
10. Do you often feel irritable and hostile at work or at home?

Parents,"[91] "Can Your Career Hurt Your Kids?"[92] "Is Your Family Wrecking Your Career (and vice versa)?"[93] and "Why on Earth Should I Promote a Pregnant Woman?"[94] Although these headlines sell magazines and newspapers, they also contribute to many myths about working parents and make it difficult for parents to make thoughtful choices about how to live their lives.

As healthcare gets better and expected life spans get longer, more employees are taking care of elderly relatives—and many are taking care of children and elderly relatives at the same time. My goal in this section is to provide you with data and insights from research that can help you make thoughtful choices as you take on different caretaking roles throughout your life.

Ever since mothers began to join the paid workforce in droves, the academic and popular press have framed working parents (particularly working mothers) as an organizational and social problem: Can employees with responsibilities at home also fulfill their responsibilities at work? If both men and women are working, who is looking after children, aging parents, and the community? How do working parents manage the stress of combining work and family?

From an organization's perspective, supporting employee's family responsibilities is likely to be a good thing. A recent study by Center for Creative Leadership researcher Marian Ruderman and colleagues found that managers in their study who were parents and who were committed to raising a family tended to get higher ratings in surveys from their bosses, peers, direct reports, and others.[95] The researchers speculate that there could be several reasons for this. It could be that people who are very committed to raising their families also show the same level of commitment to other parts of their lives, including their work and the people who depend on them at work. It could also be that committed parents learn skills at home that help them be better managers. These skills include seeing the world through the perspectives of others, empathizing, negotiating, organizing, managing time, prioritizing, and multitasking. Furthermore, parenting may even have a "buffering" effect on the stress of managerial work because the skills they learn for managing stress at home are useful for work as well.

Researchers are finding that organizations that implement and announce work-family initiatives reap rewards in terms of shareholder returns. In one study of *Fortune* 500 firms, "the share price reaction to the announcement of a work-family initiative over a three-day window [was] .39 percent. The average share price reaction occurring after legitimation of work-family initiatives was slightly higher at .48 percent. . . . The average dollar value of the change in share price associated with a work-family initiative is approximately 60 million dollars per firm." The results were particularly strong in high-tech industries and industries that employ a high proportion of women.[96] Another study found that the average increase in share price for firms named "The Best Companies for Working Mothers" was .69 percent.[97] Yet another study of 527 U.S. firms found that organizations with extensive work-family policies "have higher levels of organizational performance, market performance, and profit-sales growth," especially in older firms and those that employ larger proportions of women.[98]

A growing number of researchers are finding that integrating work and family has positive outcomes for many employees as well.[99] Say researchers Samuel Aryee and Vivienne Luk, "The expanded meaning of a successful life . . . suggests that the work-family interaction be conceptualized not as a social problem but instead as a source of meaning and identity to which adults balance commitment."[100] As many working parents have learned, both work and family can be a "major source of gratification."[101]

Indeed, having multiple roles—parent, caregiver, and employee—can be an effective coping mechanism.[102] For example, after a bad day at work, it can be a relief to come home to your family. After a frenetic morning getting children off to school, it can be relaxing to quietly read your e-mail at the office. If you stumble in one part of your life, there is another in which to find comfort. For example, several years ago I told my daughter Julia, then five years old, that I had been fired as a waitress when I was a teenager. She sweetly replied, "You may not be a good waitress, but you're a really good mother."

> In the midst of a turbulent week, I enjoy nothing more than spending a few private moments with my family, especially my three grandkids. They are the perfect reminder of why I take my work so seriously.
> —PAUL WELLSTONE,
> *Former U.S. senator*

Many questions come to mind regarding working parents. Who is happier, working mothers or stay-at-home mothers? Research suggests that it's not whether a woman stays at home or goes to work that determines her satisfaction, but whether the choice to stay home or work outside the home was her own.[103] What about the consequences of day care on children's well-being? As you will read later in this section, research suggests that high-quality day care can benefit parents and children, but poor-quality day care can adversely affect children's cognitive and social development. Barring abuse or neglect at day care, the most important influence on young children is their parents.[104]

In the next section, I provide information about the changing demographics and trends in caretaking. Then, I provide insights from research that can help you make informed choices about integrating your own work-family responsibilities—now or in the future—and help you enable your employees do the same. I also discuss the impact of working parents on organizations, particularly how work-family benefits such as flextime, condensed work weeks, and on-site day care centers influence organizations and how having children affects parents' career advancement. I next present conclusions from the National Institute of Child Health and Development's study of more than 1,300 children on the impact of day care on children's development.

Demographics and Trends in Caretaking

Women at all income levels increasingly are a significant part of the workforce and contributors to family income. They are now approximately 50% of all workers in the United States, and 40% of mothers are completely financially responsible for their families or bringing in at least as much as their spouse (compared with the 1960s when only 25% of women had these financial responsibilities in their families). The majority of low-income women are the sole breadwinners in their families. Women now hold at least 50% of managerial and professional positions in the

United States.[105] As the population around the world ages, both men and women are spending more time taking care of ill and aging relatives, often while they are also taking care of children at home. Because of these changes in the family, employment, and income patterns of both men and women, the husband's career is less likely to take precedent over the wife's career today than in the past.[106] Consequently, power dynamics in families are shifting, as are purchasing patterns (particularly those related to clothing, food away from home, and day care) and the career and social expectations of boys and girls.[107] Research suggests that women still spend more time on family care such as child care, elder care, housework, and shopping. However, men are spending more time on these activities today than men did in the past, and women are spending less time on these activities today than women did in the past.[108]

Legislation in the United States suggests that the model of a "good mother" may be changing as well. Researchers Phillip Cohen and Suzanne Bianchi explain:

> Originally, mothers who had lost the wage support of the father of their young children because of his early death (or who were indigent because the child's father deserted the family or was unwilling or unable to financially support his children) were supported, at least at some minimal level, so that they could remain out of the labor force to nurture and raise their children. The Personal Responsibility and Work Opportunity Reconciliation Act is based on a quite different model of motherhood: A "good mother" locates child care for her young children and finds a job, perhaps after some additional job training, by means of which she can financially support herself and her children.[109]

Given these changes in demographics and perceptions of men's and women's responsibilities for caretaking, as well as their family's financial security, it's no surprise that decisions regarding how to manage both the caretaking and financial responsibilities in a family are becoming increasingly complex. The following sections are designed to give you information that can help you make wise decisions as you decide what is best for yourself, your family, and your organizations.

What Is the Impact of Working Parents on Organizations?

In response to these trends, many organizations are offering employees options such as flextime, condensed workweeks, telecommuting, and on-site day-care centers. Some companies, such as Baxter International, base managers' pay, in part, on how well they "provide a supportive work–life environment."[110] Firms that promote supportive work–life programs believe that doing so helps them recruit and retain high-quality employees, encourage more efficient ways of working, and enhance their public image as family-friendly social citizens. Supportive work–life benefits may be particularly important to organizations wanting to recruit and retain high-potential employees in tight labor markets.

Researcher Ellen Kossek and her colleagues, in their extensive reviews of the research on corporate work–life programs, conclude that supportive work–life programs indeed tend to enhance employee recruitment, retention, and job satisfaction. This is illustrated in the following story from *Forbes* magazine:

> Wilfredo Tejada, a 34-year-old former marketing vice president at Cupertino, California-based Net-Manage, calls it "psychological warfare." One day every other week he got to work at 10:00 A.M. because he sat in on his daughter's first-grade

class. "The whole time I was there I was thinking I just can't wait to be done because I need to be back at the office," he says. And why was that? Because the boss arrived at 6:30 A.M. and sat in a glass office where he could monitor everyone's comings and goings. Tejada left three years ago to co-found an Internet company, Aeneid Corp., where he vows to let his employees come and go as they please, as long as they get their work done.[111]

Tejada, like many managers today, believes productivity is best measured through bottom-line results, not through face-time at the office. His view is shared by many others. Say James Levine and Todd Pittinsky, both of the Fatherhood Project at the Families and Work Institute, "When IBM asked a group of employees to assess the factors that influenced their decision to stay with the company, work-family benefits ranked five overall, and second among the company's top performers."[112]

> Our society has become schizophrenic. We praise people who want balance in their lives, but reward those who work themselves to death.
> —ROY NEEL,
> *President Clinton's former Deputy Chief of Staff*

Notably, unlike the studies cited earlier, Kossek and her colleagues found no consistent pattern of relationship between work–life benefits and employee productivity. This suggests that although these benefits are increasingly important for recruitment and retention, other factors such as job design and managerial support that enable work–life integration may be more likely to influence employee productivity.

What Is the Impact of Working Parents on Their Children's Well-Being?

Single-mother Allison Anders, director of the films *Gas Food Lodging* and *Mi Vida Loca*, wanted to add the names of the nannies who took care of Ruben, her seven-year-old son, to the credits of her film *Grace of My Heart*. Initially, Universal Pictures resisted, saying "there was no precedent for it." But Anders convinced them by explaining, "I was flying back and forth between Los Angeles and New York; I couldn't have made the film without them." The studio finally agreed, and "Ruben's nannies got on-screen credit for their indispensable—if invisible—roles."[113]

Anders' story illustrates the gratitude that many working parents feel toward the people who help them care for their loved ones. For many men and women, deciding the best way to integrate work and family—indeed, whether to attempt to do so at all—is a difficult and often gut-wrenching decision. Access to thoughtful information can make that decision a bit easier. As *Wall Street Journal* columnist and parent Sue Shellenbarger says, this is "high time for an era of empowered child-care consumerism."[114]

The information presented in this section is primarily based on conclusions from the National Institute of Child Health and Human Development's (NICHD) study of a diverse group of more than 1,300 children. Begun in 1991, this project is headed by Dr. Sarah L. Friedman and represents the largest and most comprehensive study done on the impact of child care on children in the United States. The children,

> In the small matters, trust the mind; in the large ones, the heart.
> —SIGMUND FREUD,
> *Father of Psychoanalysis*

who were less than one month old at the beginning of the research, come from all across the nation and from different income levels.

Researchers from 14 universities are participating in the study. They are focusing on the impact of child care on the children's cognitive development (ability to perform at appropriate levels of intellectual development), social development (ability to get along with others), and attachment to their mothers. Researchers believe that children's early attachment to their mothers is important because infants who have secure attachments to their mothers are more likely to have positive outcomes as toddlers and in the preschool years (e.g., problem solving, willingness to explore and be independent, social skills with other children, and cooperation with adults).

COGNITIVE DEVELOPMENT   Children in high-quality day care tended to score higher on tests of school readiness and language comprehension than did those in low-quality day care. High-quality day care is characterized by caregivers who spend ample time interacting with the children, who demonstrate warmth and support, and who provide cognitive stimulation. The slight academic benefit of high quality day care in early childhood lasted at least until the children were 15 years old.[115] Indeed, on average, children in day care settings that met all the standards developed by the American Public Health Association and the American Academy of Pediatrics performed at above-average levels. On average, the children in day care settings that did not meet those standards performed at below-average levels. The acceptable standards include "child/staff ratios (3:1 for infants, 4:1 for 2-year-olds, 7:1 for three-year-olds); group sizes (six infants, or eight two-year-olds, or 14 three-year-olds); and teacher training (some post-secondary training in child development and early childhood education or a related field)."[116]

SOCIAL BEHAVIOR   "Children's social behavior is influenced by the quality of the day care, the number of children in the day care, the consistency of the day care, and the mother's psychological well-being and behavior toward the child."[117] Specifically, children who were in high-quality day care (those that met the guidelines described earlier) and in day care with at least three other children were more socially competent and had fewer behavioral problems at ages two and three than those who weren't. "At age two, children who had been in a number of different day care arrangements showed more problem behavior than did children who had been in fewer day care arrangements." Furthermore, although children who spent moderate hours in day care in the first four years of their lives tended to have fewer behavior problems as adolescents, children who spent the most hours in day care showed slightly greater aggressiveness and impulsiveness at age 15.[118] The mothers' attitudes and behaviors toward their children appear to have a greater influence on children's social competence than does the children's day care arrangement.

ATTACHMENT   "Child-care experience has no discernible influence on the security of children's attachments to their mothers by age three. Earlier reported findings from the study indicated that more experience with child care and lower quality child care in infancy were only related to secure infants' attachments to their mothers when mothers were relatively insensitive to their infants. In general, the education of the mothers was more strongly related to positive qualities of maternal care than was the amount or quality of child care. However, mothers were slightly more positive and supportive with their children when less child care was used or when child-care quality was higher."[119]

In another study of the impact of day care on children, researcher Megan Gunnar and colleagues found that the behavior of child care providers had a significant impact. Children who had intrusive and controlling caregivers were more likely to have higher levels of the stress hormone cortisone. In these settings, the children participated in too many structured activities, activities that required rote learning, spent little time in free play, and were required to move frequently between activities. Girls who had increased levels of cortisone were more likely to experience anxiety, whereas boys who had increased levels of cortisone were more likely to be angry and aggressive.[120]

Some researchers remain skeptical of the positive effects of day care on children, particularly when it is used when children are less than one year old and when it is used extensively (more than 30 hours a week). Researcher Jay Belsky, who has conducted many studies on the impact of day care on children, argues that the less time a mother spends with her child in the first year of life, the less time she has to "learn the baby's signaling patterns and rhythms" and the less able she is to respond to the child appropriately and with sensitivity.[121]

Belsky cites studies, including his own, that suggest that children who were in early and extensive child care tended to be slightly more aggressive and disobedient than those who did not. However, he notes that these effects are small, that these studies typically did not consider the quality of the day care arrangements, and that most of these studies had fewer and less diverse families involved in the study than did the NICHD research (The NICHD also found a small but significant positive relationship between hours in day care and aggressiveness in young children and a lower tendency for teens who had higher quality day care to be impulsive as teens.). Although Belsky remains reasonably cautious about the use of early and extensive day care, he concludes:

> Nobody has ever before asked the nuclear family to live all by itself in a box the way we do. With no relatives, no support, we've put it in an impossible situation.
> —MARGARET MEAD, *Anthropologist*

> At the same time, however, my reading of the evidence does not lead me to conclude that day care, even when provided to our youngest citizens, is inherently bad. Too much evidence indicates just the opposite when children experience good-quality care. Day care works when children receive care from individuals who will remain with them for a relatively long period of time (low staff turnover), who are knowledgeable about child development, and who provide care that is sensitive and responsive to their individualized needs.[122]

In general, researchers agree that day care can have a positive or negative effect on children's well-being and that the decision to use day care should be made thoughtfully. Furthermore, they believe that many factors influence the well-being of children of working parents, including the following:

Quality of Day Care.   One of the most important conclusions of the NICHD study is that high-quality day care can provide benefits to children, and low-quality day care can harm children's cognitive and social development. Say the researchers, "When child-care providers talk to children, encourage them to ask questions, respond to children's questions, read to them, challenge them to attend to others' feelings, and to develop different ways of thinking—children's language abilities and thinking skills are better than under conditions that are less enriched."[123]

> If our American way of life fails the child, it fails us all.
> —PEARL S. BUCK, *Author*

Unfortunately, the researchers in the NICHD study concluded that only about 10% of the infant day care settings of children in the study met standards set by the American Public Health Association and the American Academy of Pediatrics, and 34% of the day care settings for three-year-olds met these standards. Furthermore, only three of the 50 states have child care regulations that meet the APHA/AAP standards for child/staff ratios for toddlers, and only nine states have regulations that meet the recommended standards for teaching training for infants.[124]

In general, researchers who study the impact of child care on children's well-being argue for increasing the quality of day care available to parents in the United States (by promoting high wages for day care employees, setting and enforcing high standards for day care, and providing family leave for mothers and fathers so that they have more choices in how they manage the early months of a child's life). Says Ellen Galinsky, president of the Families and Work Institute in New York, "We know how to provide quality child care. We fail not because of a lack of knowledge but because of a lack of will."[125]

Parents' Personality, Self-Esteem, Education, and Income.   Parents have a critical influence on their children's development, regardless of the quality of day care or the amount of hours the children spend in day care. For example, research suggests that working parents' self-esteem, education, and income influence the quality of care that they provide for their children. Education and income may be important because they enable parents to find and afford higher quality day care.

Marital/Relationship Quality.   Parents who are supportive toward each other and who work well together as co-parents are more likely to provide high-quality care for their children.[126]

Try this bracelet: If it fits
you, wear it; but if it hurts
you, throw it away no
matter how shiny.
—KENYAN PROVERB

Choice.   Research suggests that whether a mother *chooses* to work outside the home or stay at home to care for the children influences her emotional well-being, which in turn influences her child-rearing practices and the children's well-being.[127] In other words, it's not whether mothers work that makes them happy, but whether the choice to work or stay home was their own.

Parents' Work Experiences.   For fathers and mothers, the quality of their work—such as supervisor sensitivity, interesting work, job autonomy, and schedule flexibility—affects their ability to be responsive and nurturing toward their children. This, in turn, can affect their children's cognitive skills and social behavior.[128] For example, in a study on the effects of fathers' employment on child development, researchers Wendy Stewart and Julian Barling concluded that a father's job decision latitude (e.g., "On my job, I am given a lot of freedom to decide how I do my work."), job demands (e.g., "My job requires working very fast."), job insecurity (e.g., "I can be sure of my present job as long as I do good work."), and interrole conflict (e.g., "My job takes up time I'd like to spend with my family.") can influence child outcomes such as "school-related competence" and social behavior.[129]

Researchers Toby Parcel and Elizabeth Menaghan concluded that children whose mothers have "more complex, responsible jobs have better home environments and in turn behave better and perform better over time on verbal, math and reading tests, after controlling for mothers' own education and mental skills."[130] The University of California Irvine researcher Ellen Greenberger and others have concluded, "Parents with more stimulating, challenging jobs are warmer, less harsh and more responsive in their parenting."[131] Researcher Stewart Friedman and his colleagues concluded that children whose mothers have more control over their day-to-day work tend to have fewer behavior problems.[132]

As you probably noticed in the previous section, researchers have paid more attention to the impact of working mothers on their children than to the impact of working fathers on their children. This is a problem because fathers increasingly are participating in the day-to-day care of their children and feel the pleasures and stresses of managing their dual roles as fathers and employees, and it encourages organizations to focus on working mothers' needs more so than those of working fathers.[133]

DAY CARE'S BENEFITS FOR PARENTS   In addition to providing parents with help in raising their children and enabling parents to go to work, recent research has found that day care provides another benefit to parents. In a study of 300 New York day care centers, University of Chicago researcher Mario Small found that day care centers provide parents with social connections that help them get support and useful child care advice (e.g., information about health care) from the other parents and day care providers. Says Small, "Parents come to school to find someone to take care for their children, and they end up learning ways of taking care of each other. . . . When you are a parent, particularly a first-time parent, the best resource you have is another parent." Small found that taken-for-granted and seemingly trivial organizational practices that involve parents—social events, fund raising efforts, and field trips—provide significant gains to the parents' social capital—the resources they gain through their connections with other parents. Day care centers that offer parents opportunities to get to know each other help parents develop their parenting networks. Interestingly, day cares that have strict drop-off and pick-up times (e.g., all parents must pick up their children by 5:30 P.M.) tend to offer more networking opportunities for parents because more parents gather at the day care during the same time during the day. Notably, low-income parents as well as non-low-income parents benefit from the connections they make at day care centers. Low-income parents who had children in day care were less likely to become homeless. Fewer non-low-income parents who made friends at their child's day care they were likely to become depressed.[134]

What Do Children Say about Their Working Parents?

In a landmark study, Ellen Galinsky, president of the Families and Work Institute, asked more than 1,000 children between the third and twelfth grade what they think about their working parents. The results: "Having a working mother is never once predictive of how children assess their mother's parenting skills on a series of 12 items that are strongly linked to children's healthy development, school readiness, and school success."[135] Galinsky also noted, "Children with employed mothers and those with mothers at home do not differ on whether they feel they have too little time with Mom."[136] This is supported by research by Sandra Hofferth at the University of Michigan Institute for Social Research, who concludes that working parents spend approximately 19 hours per week engaged with their children compared with 22 hours a week for families with stay-at-home mothers.[137]

> There is always one moment in childhood when the door opens and lets the future in.
> —GRAHAM GREENE, *Novelist*

Although 56% of the parents thought that their children would benefit from spending more time together, 67% of the children said that they spent enough time with their mothers, and 60% said they spent enough time with their fathers. The number of hours that parents spend with their children (within reason—remember that 33% of the children didn't feel they spent enough time with their mothers, and 40% felt the same about their time with their fathers) seems less important to children than the parents' attitudes and behavior during that time. For example, more than 44.5% of the children felt that their time with their mother is rushed, and 37% felt the same about the time with their father.[138]

Galsinky concluded, "Although the amount of time children and parents spend together is very important, most children don't want more time with their parents. Instead, they give their mothers and fathers higher grades if the time they do spend together is not rushed but focused and rich in shared activities."[139] And, it's the simple things—not expensive vacations or elaborate hobbies—that seem to matter most. The children's responses suggest that eating meals together is particularly important, as are activities such as playing games or sports, doing homework, and watching television with parents. Children whose parents participate in these activities with them are more likely to see their parents as "putting families first" and being able to effectively manage both work and family.

> It doesn't matter who my father was; it matters who I remember he was.
> —ANNE SEXTON, *Writer*

Less than 43% of the children in Galinsky's study "think their parents like their work a lot, compared with 62.5% of parents who say they do."[140] It is not surprising that the children who hear good things about work from their parents are more likely to want to manage work and family like their parents do. In addition, the children said that they learn more about their mothers' work than their fathers' work. Many parents, it seems, are less than inspiring when it comes to setting positive examples for the next generation of workers. When parents don't talk about their work, complain about their work, or say things like "I wish I didn't have to go to work today" (perhaps because they feel guilty about leaving the children), they may be intentionally or unintentionally giving children a negative impression of work.

The next generation of workers will be an interesting one, and their choices will be based, in part, on our work/life choices and the way that we talk about our choices. Galinsky notes, "Few children want to work harder than their employed mothers and fathers. Only 11 percent of children want to work more than their fathers do. Children whose fathers work the longest and hardest are the most likely to want to work less than their fathers. Only 25 percent of children want to work more than their mothers do now."[141]

> Each child is an adventure into a better life—an opportunity to change the old pattern and make it new.
> —HUBERT H. HUMPHREY,
> *Former U.S. vice president*

Boys are more likely than girls to favor the father-as-breadwinner and mother-at-home lifestyle. Says Galinsky, "Almost twice as many boys as girls strongly agree with the idea that men should earn the money, and women should take care of the home and children. Forty-two percent of girls in the seventh through twelfth grades agree that children do just as well if mothers have the primary responsibility for earning the money, and fathers have the primary responsibility for caring for the children. Only 25 percent of boys agreed with that statement."[142] Because of these differences in expectations, these are going to be very interesting relationships when these children grow up.

In short, it seems that the issue isn't whether parents work or stay home with their children, but rather how parents feel about their work, how they talk with their children about their work, and how they use the time that they have with their children. Parenting skills seem to matter most of all. Galinsky identified eight critical parenting skills from her research:[143]

- *Make the child feel important and loved.* To reinforce this point, Galinsky quotes developmental psychologist Urie Bronfenner, "In order to thrive, every child needs someone who is crazy about him or her."[144]
- *Respond to the child's cues.* This means being emotionally and intellectually responsive to the child. Children who feel listened and responded to are better able to cope with stress.
- *Accept the child for who he or she is, but expect success.* Children see themselves as others see them, so the more you believe in a child, the more that child will believe in himself or herself.
- *Promote strong values.* This means talking and living the values that are important to the family.
- *Use constructive discipline.* Such discipline is designed to "teach children to internalize limits rather than to humiliate, hurt, or demean them."
- *Provide routines and rituals.* Routines associated with daily activities such as waking up, eating, playing, and bedtimes help children feel that their world is orderly, consistent, and predictable. Engaging in family rituals such as singing special songs, reading favorite books, watching television shows together, and participating in birthday and holiday traditions help children develop memories and a family identity. Many parents say that the time they spend in the car driving their children to school and other events can be precious time to catch up away from the other distractions of everyday life.

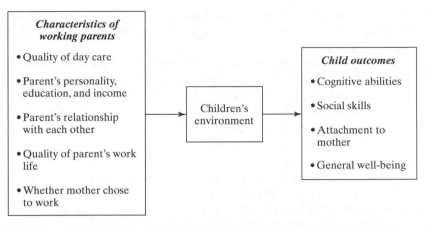

FIGURE 10-2   Factors That Influence the Well-Being of Children of Working Parents

- *Be involved in the child's education.* Children's academic achievement is higher when parents participate in their education, both at the school and at home.
- *Be there for the child.* Children want to know that they can count on their parents to be there for them when they need them, particularly when they are sick or for important events.

My conclusion from the research on working parents is this: Sure, your career can hurt your kids if you place them in low-quality child care or if you have a nasty job that makes you tired, cranky, or distant from your children when you come home. Your career can also hurt your kids if you're a high-achieving perfectionist that treats your home like an office and your children like underachieving mini-employees. But if you are a loving and well-meaning parent who understands what children need to be happy and develop into loving and responsible adults, are emotionally and physically accessible to your children, have a job that you willingly chose and enjoy, have a supportive partner, and have high-quality day care for your children, research suggests that you can relax, knowing that you can make a contribution to your work and be a loving and competent parent as well. For a summary of the research on the impact of working parents on children's well-being, see Figure 10-2.

If you want to make integrating work and family easier for all working parents, be a supportive boss and coworker and support policies that promote high-quality day care (e.g., higher wages for day care employees and enforced standards for teacher/child ratios, group size, and teacher training). The next generation (who will take care of you in your old age and shape future policies on elder care) will thank you for it.

CONCLUSION

Crafting a life at the beginning of the twenty-first century requires that we let go of many old assumptions about success (e.g., the belief that money will make us happy), productivity (e.g., the belief that face-time at the office equals bottom-line results), happy families (the dad-at-work and mom-at-home model), and work–life balance (the belief that work–life balance is a desirable and achievable goal).

Our organizational and social worlds are not the same as those of our parents' generation. For that matter, our organizational and social worlds have changed

> Today, the materials and skills from which a life is composed are no longer clear. It is no longer possible to follow the paths of previous generations. . . . Many of the most basic concepts we use to construct a sense of self or the design of a life have changed their meanings.
> —MARY CATHERINE BATESON,
> *Composing a Life*

considerably in just the last decade and no doubt will change considerably in the next. Consequently, many of the assumptions and strategies that people used to craft a life in the past are less useful today.

No matter how long you've gone on a wrong road, turn back.
—Turkish Proverb

Furthermore, we have more choices today in terms of the kinds of lives we can live. We can work from the office, the home, or the beach. We can meet with colleagues and customers face-to-face or conduct our business through the Internet. We can be full-fledged employees or offer our services as contractors, working on our own time and terms. We can be working parents or stay-at-home parents (or working-stay-at-home parents). And because we're more likely to live longer than our counterparts in the past, we will have many opportunities to change our minds and make new choices about how to live our lives. At least one thing won't change: No matter how long we live, life will still be short enough to inspire us to make thoughtful choices.

There is no one formula for a good life. What works for one person may not work for another, and what works at one stage of one's life may not work at another stage. The late psychologist Viktor Frankl explained:

> What matters, therefore, is not the meaning of life in general but rather the specific meaning of a person's life at a given moment. To put the question in general terms would be comparable to the question posed to a chess champion, "Tell me, Master, what is the best move in the world?" There simply is no such thing as the best or even a good move apart from a particular situation in a game and the particular personality of one's opponent.[145]

More recently, researcher Julie Norem explains, "We can't casually adopt another person's strategy and expect it to work for us, any more than we can put their shoes on and expect to be comfortable. . . . Indeed, we may find blisters instead of bliss if we aren't careful to equip ourselves properly."[146]

All growth is a leap in the dark, a spontaneous unpremeditated act without benefit of experience.
—Henry Miller, *Author*

As I noted in the first chapter of this book, successful careers are built on several characteristics, including an expertise that matters to us and others, a fluid rather than concrete view of intelligence and personality, conscientiousness, proactivity, a learning orientation, creativity and a willingness to improvise, practical skills, self-awareness, social skills, emotional intelligence, positive emotions, and hardiness. These characteristics are even more important when crafting a life because the events we face in life can be even more rewarding and challenging than those we face at work. Furthermore, our life goals are often less clear than our day-to-day work goals, and we often don't get feedback from our life decisions until years after we make them. For example, we don't know if the choices we make about our careers or raising our children will pay off until years after we make our initial choices. All we can do is try to be thoughtful, consider the consequences of our decisions, and be willing to adapt as we learn from our experience and as we face the inevitable and unpredictable twists and turns of our life.

I'd like to end this book with one final piece of advice. Several years ago, I was helping out in my spunky daughter Leah's kindergarten classroom, and I heard a little girl ask the teacher, "Mrs. Weinmann, do dreams come true?" Without skipping a beat, the teacher replied, "Well, a dream can become a wish, and a wish can become a plan, and a plan can come true." The teacher responded so quickly and with such caring certainty that I felt as though she had heard and answered this question for kindergartners many times. And I thought her words would be a fine way to end this book because I hope this book has given you many ideas that can help you make your dreams come true.

Chapter Summary

People who are happy are generally and genuinely pleased with their lives. Research suggests that money predicts only about 2% to 5% of one's happiness. Gender, race, and age are also poor predictors of happiness, as are significant life events such as winning the lottery and handicapping accidents. Predictors of happiness include our beliefs (having a positive self-concept; being a satisficer rather than a maximizer; temperament; savoring experiences; actively participating in a faith; and experiencing positive emotions such as optimism, hope, and gratitude), as well as the actions we choose to take (e.g., having goals that one enjoys, balancing current and future pleasure, having relationships, and having effective coping strategies).

Most people enjoy working because it fulfills basic human needs for identity ("I am a manager"), belonging (we tend to work with others), competence (we tend to learn and stretch our skills when we work), consistency and control (we tend to have routines at work), and making a difference (sometimes we can use our work to make an impact on the world).

We feel flow (optimal experience or peak performance) when we are fully engaged in doing something that we believe is important; when we have clear goals, rules, and feedback; when we can concentrate on the task without distraction; when we have the skills to do the job yet feel challenged to learn new skills; and when we have control over how we do the task.

People who are optimistic have a positive bias toward themselves and the world. They see themselves as more competent than they are and the world as a more positive place than data would suggest. Research suggests that optimists tend to be happier, healthier, and more effective because they are likely to set higher goals for themselves, be persistent, take risks, reward themselves, and cope better with stress. Optimism can be learned by paying attention to the ways that we interpret the positive and negative events in our lives. However, optimism can sometimes be overrated. Recent research has shown that some people—defensive pessimists—tend to assume the worst and then plan to avoid the worst outcome, and thus enhance their performance through

their excessive planning. Furthermore, it's unclear whether encouraging people to "think positive" when they are ill is always helpful, especially if they tend to have a history of success with other types of coping mechanisms.

Although there are many benefits to positive moods, negative moods can sometimes make us better decision makers because people who are in "mild bad moods" are less gullible, pay more attention to what's going on around them, remember events more accurately, are less likely to make "snap decisions" (including those made on the basis of prejudices), pay more attention to details, and are better able to identify lying.

Your job can affect your health. A poor relationship with a supervisor can increase your stress. Other health risks at work include a lack of control over your work, feelings of unfairness at work, excessive overtime, and lack of predictability. People at lower levels of the organizational hierarchy are more likely to experience low control, unpredictability, and unfairness and are likely to have a higher incidence of coronary disease (after controlling for other risk factors such as smoking and being overweight).

Both perfectionism and Type A behavior can positively influence your effectiveness and career when they are not extreme. However, extreme perfectionism and Type A behavior (particularly the hostility component of Type A behavior) can negatively influence your effectiveness, psychological well-being, and physical health. Notably, perfectionism and Type A behavior can become more extreme in ambiguous and high-pressured situations, precisely when they can be most damaging.

Data from the U.S. Department of Labor suggest that the work patterns of the U.S. workforce have changed dramatically in the past 40 years. Women at all income levels are working more than in the past. The father-at-work and mother-at-home family is on the decline. There are more dual-career couples, single-parent families, women as primary breadwinners in families, and women with young children working full-time. Many working women earn more than their husbands. An increasing number of women and men are taking care of ill and aging adults.

Many working parents must rely on day care to help take care of their children's needs while they are working. Research suggests that high-quality day care can benefit children's intellectual and behavioral development and interferes little, if at all, with children's feelings of attachment to their mothers. However, poor-quality day care can harm children's intellectual and behavioral development.

Working parents' attitudes and behaviors influence their children's development more than day care does (unless day care is of very poor quality). Several factors influence parents' ability to positively influence their children: parents' self-esteem, income, and education; job quality; marital relationship quality; and whether the mother made her own decision about whether to work or not.

Parents who have children in day care tend to enjoy the benefits of the social capital they gain from interacting with other parents and the staff at day care centers.

Food for Thought

1. What is the most useful thing you learned in this chapter, and why?

2. On the basis of the personal strategies described in this chapter, what can you do to enhance the quality of your life (e.g., happiness, health, and longevity)? Make at least one of these changes, and note any benefits and progress you make.

3. Imagine you had all the money you needed to live comfortably and to ensure that your children and grandchildren had enough money to get a good education and that your parents would be well-taken care of as they age. What would you do with your life? Why?

4. If you knew you only had five more years to live and you would be healthy up to your very last day, what would you do with your life? Why? If you knew you had only one more year to live and you would be healthy up until your last day, what would you do with your life? Why?

5. Using the assessment in Box 10.2, assess your day-to-day work (your job, classes, family caretaking). Is your day-to-day work high, medium, or low on flow? What parts of your work did you rate highest and lowest? Why? What can you do to increase flow in your day-to-day life? If you are responsible for others, what can you do to increase flow in their day-to-day life?

6. Tom and Kate Chappell founded Tom's of Maine, which produces organic toothpaste and other personal care products because they wanted to give people organic personal care options. John Scully left his job as president of Pepsi-Cola to become CEO of Apple Computer because he felt that "personal computers could change the way we live and learn."[147] What makes your day-to-day work—at the workplace, at school, or at home—meaningful?

7. If you could hire a perfectionist or someone with Type A personality characteristics, would you want to? Why or why not? Would you want to work for a perfectionist? Why or why not?

8. Take the assessment in Box 10.3 to identify whether you tend to be more like a strategic optimist or defensive pessimist. Under what conditions does your general strategy work for you? Under what conditions is it a problem?

9. Take the assessment in Box 10.7, "The Polychronicity Scale: How Many Things Do You Like to Do at Once?" Are you more monochronic (lower scores) or polychronic (higher scores) in your use of time? In what situations is your style helpful in managing your life? Not helpful?

10. Assume that you are managing a high-performing working parent. The employee missed a key deadline recently and seemed unprepared for a presentation yesterday. Otherwise, the employee's work continues to be among the best in the department. You've heard that the employee recently started caring for an elderly and ailing parent at home. You are about to meet with the employee for a performance review. What will you say? Why? What kind of support can you offer the employee if needed?

11. If you want to increase your chances of living a long and healthy life, what changes do you need to make in your everyday life? What one change will you make immediately and why? How will you ensure that you maintain this change? Take either the www.realage.com or www.livingto100.com assessment to identify key areas that you can attend to that are likely to enhance your health and longevity.

BOX 10-5   A Note on Sleep Deprivation

Many people work long hours because of the demands of the job. Others do so because organizations reward face-time at the office. And others do so because of professional norms, as is the case with physicians and pilots. Regardless of the reasons that people find themselves working with too little sleep, research suggests that sleep deprivation can result in decreased alertness, slowed thinking, lapses in attention, and decreased motivation. Researcher Gregory Belenky and his colleagues who study performance of military personnel during combat operations concluded, "Sleep deprivation impairs alertness, cognitive performance, and mood. The ability to do useful mental work declines 25 percent for every successive 24 hours that an individual is awake. . . . Sleep deprivation degrades the most complex useful functions, including the ability to understand, adapt, and plan under rapidly changing situations."[148]

Sleep deprivation and disruption can result in what researchers call the "speed-accuracy trade-off."[149] This means that in tasks involving attention, reasoning abilities, and reaction time, a tired person is likely to be accurate or fast, but is unlikely to be both. The risks of sleep deprivation increase in non-routine situations.

Source: Belenky, Gregory et al. 1994. "The Effects of Sleep Deprivation on Performance during Continuous Combat Operations." In Bernadette M. Marriott (ed.). *Food Components to Enhance Performance*. Washington, DC: National Academy Press.

BOX 10-6   Steps to a Long Life: Lessons from Centenarian Studies

Thomas Perls, MD, and lead researcher on the New England Centenarian Studies, says that extreme longevity—living for a century or more—is rare and that most people who live this long probably have "genetic rocket boosters" that enable them to avoid age-related diseases such as diabetes, Alzheimer's, and cardiovascular disease. About 85% of the centenarians are women and 15% are men, but the men who reach extreme old age tend to function better than the women do. But Perls believes that most of us have the genetic makeup that would enable us to live to at least 85 years old in good health. Whether we reach or exceed this age depends, in large part, on how we spend our everyday lives. The following advice is based in large part on what researchers have learned in the New England Centenarian Studies, the Georgia Centenarian Study, and the Okinawa Centenarian Study.

- *Have good eating habits. Eat lots of colorful fruits and vegetables.* Cut down on fatty and salty foods. Eat lean meats, poultry, and fish. Eat whole grains. And eat less. In the study of Okinawan centenarians, the centenarians tended to eat about 500 fewer calories less than most people.
- *Have good health care habits.* See your physician regularly to identify and treat any problems that may exist. Be sure you get your vaccinations. Although it may seem trite, evidence is growing that flossing your teeth may increase your longevity because flossing may be related to better cardiovascular health.
- *Stay physically active and engaged.* People's bodies and minds have more problems as they age in part because of lack of exercise.
- *Cope well with stress.* Although the centenarians studied didn't have fewer stressful events in life (some had very traumatic experiences), they did cope more effectively with these events. They faced their problems, grieved, accepted their losses, forgave themselves and others, made adjustments, moved on, and didn't dwell on the past. Meditation also helps to reduce stress.
- *Stay intellectually engaged.* Taking on new challenges that stretch the brain helps it stay nimble.

(continued)

BOX 10-6 *Continued*

- *Have an optimistic attitude, especially toward aging.* In one study, people who had an optimistic attitude toward aging lived 7.1 years longer than those who did not.
- *Socialize with a supportive network of family and friends.* Social connections help fight depression and may enhance the body's immune system.

Which parts of the world have the longest and healthiest average life expectancy? The World Health Organization now ranks countries not by life expectancy only but by healthy life expectancy. The most recent ratings reflect "the expected number of years to be lived in what might be termed the equivalent of full health. The top countries are Japan (74.5), Australia (73.2), France (73.1), Sweden (73.0), Spain (72.8), Italy (72.7), Greece (72.5), Switzerland (72.5), Monaco (72.4), and Andorra (72.3). Women's healthy life expectancy is approximately four–seven years longer than men's. The United States ranks 24, which is low among wealthy nations due to several factors: many people living in conditions that are equivalent to those "more characteristic of a poor developing country rather than a rich industrialized one," the HIV epidemic, cancers related to tobacco, a high coronary disease rate, and fairly high levels of violence. You can find the full rankings at the World Health Organization Web site.

Two useful Web sites that have free on-line assessments that will help you identify whether your everyday attitudes and behaviors are increasing or decreasing your chances of living a long and healthy life are: www.realage.com and www.livingto100.com.

BOX 10-7   The Polychronicity Scale: How Many Things Do You Like to Do at Once?

Please use the following scale to indicate the extent to which you agree or disagree with each of the 10 statements by circling the appropriate number for each statement.

I like to juggle several activities at the same time.

Strongly Disagree	Somewhat Disagree	Slightly Disagree	Neutral	Slightly Agree	Somewhat Agree	Strongly Agree
1 pt	2 pts	3 pts	4 pts	5 pts	6 pts	7 pts

I would rather complete an entire project every day than complete parts of several projects.

Strongly Disagree	Somewhat Disagree	Slightly Disagree	Neutral	Slightly Agree	Somewhat Agree	Strongly Agree
7 pts	6 pts	5 pts	4 pts	3 pts	2 pts	1 pt

I believe people should try to do many things at once.

Strongly Disagree	Somewhat Disagree	Slightly Disagree	Neutral	Slightly Agree	Somewhat Agree	Strongly Agree
1 pt	2 pts	3 pts	4 pts	5 pts	6 pts	7 pts

When I work by myself, I usually work on one project at a time.

Strongly Disagree	Somewhat Disagree	Slightly Disagree	Neutral	Slightly Agree	Somewhat Agree	Strongly Agree
7 pts	6 pts	5 pts	4 pts	3 pts	2 pts	1 pt

I prefer to do one thing at a time.

Strongly Disagree	Somewhat Disagree	Slightly Disagree	Neutral	Slightly Agree	Somewhat Agree	Strongly Agree
7 pts	6 pts	5 pts	4 pts	3 pts	2 pts	1 pt

BOX 10-7   *Continued*

I believe people do their best work when they have many tasks to complete.

Strongly Disagree	Somewhat Disagree	Slightly Disagree	Neutral	Slightly Agree	Somewhat Agree	Strongly Agree
1 pt	2 pts	3 pts	4 pts	5 pts	6 pts	7 pts

I believe it is best to complete one task before beginning another.

Strongly Disagree	Somewhat Disagree	Slightly Disagree	Neutral	Slightly Agree	Somewhat Agree	Strongly Agree
7 pts	6 pts	5 pts	4 pts	3 pts	2 pts	1 pt

I believe it is best for people to be given several tasks and assignments to perform.

Strongly Disagree	Somewhat Disagree	Slightly Disagree	Neutral	Slightly Agree	Somewhat Agree	Strongly Agree
1 pt	2 pts	3 pts	4 pts	5 pts	6 pts	7 pts

I seldom like to work on more than a single task or assignment at the same time.

Strongly Disagree	Somewhat Disagree	Slightly Disagree	Neutral	Slightly Agree	Somewhat Agree	Strongly Agree
7 pts	6 pts	5 pts	4 pts	3 pts	2 pts	1 pt

I would rather complete parts of several projects every day than complete an entire project.

Strongly Disagree	Somewhat Disagree	Slightly Disagree	Neutral	Slightly Agree	Somewhat Agree	Strongly Agree
1 pt	2 pts	3 pts	4 pts	5 pts	6 pts	7 pts

Now add your points and divide the total by 10. Then plot your score on the scale below.

1.0	2.0	3.0	4.0	5.0	6.0	7.0

You can compare your score with the mean score of 3.720, marked on the scale with an H (standard deviation = 1.06) from 1,190 respondents in a study of a St. Louis area hospital system.

Source: Allen C. Bluedorn, Thomas J. Kallath, Michael J. Strube, and Gregg D. Martin. 1998. "Polychronicity and the Inventory of Polychronic Values (IPV). The Development of an Instrument to Measure a Fundamental Dimension of Organizational Culture." *Journal of Managerial Psychology*, 14(3): 205–230. Reprinted with permission of MCB University Press.

Endnotes

1. Diener, Ed, Richard Lucas, and Shigehiro Oishi. 2002. "Subjective Well-Being." In C. R. Snyder and Shane Lopez (eds.). *Handbook of Positive Psychology*. Oxford: Oxford University Press, 63–73.

2. Myers, David, and Ed Diener. 1995. "Who Is Happy?" *Psychological Science*, 6(1): 10–19.

3. Ben-Shahar, Tal. 2007. *Happier*. New York: McGraw Hill.

4. Myers, David, and Ed Diener. 1995. "Who Is Happy?" *Psychological Science*, 6(1): 10–19.

5. Ahuvia, Aaron C., and Douglas Friedman. 1998. "Income, Consumption, and Subjective Well-Being: Toward a Composite Macromarketing Model." *Journal of Macromarketing*. Fall: 153–168.

6. Graef, R., Gianinno McManama, and Mihaly Csikszentmihalyi. 1981. "Energy Consumption in Leisure and Perceived Happiness." In J. D. Clayton and others (eds.). *Consumers and Energy Conservation*. New York: Praeger; cited in Ahuvia, Aaron, and Douglas Friedman. 1998. "Income, Consumption, and Subjective Well-Being: Toward a Composite Macromarketing Model." *Journal of Macromarketing*. Fall: 153–168.

7. Ahuvia, Aaron C., and Douglas Friedman. 1998. Income, Consumption, and Subjective Well-Being: Toward a Composite Macromarketing Model. *Journal of Macromarketing*. Fall: 153–168.

8. Srivastava, Abhishek, Edwin Locke, and Kathryn Bartol. 2001. "Money and Subjective Well-Being: It's Not the Money, It's the Motives." *Journal of Personality and Social Psychology*, 80(6): 959–971.

9. Lyubomirsky, Sonja. 2007. *The How of Happiness: A Scientific Approach to Getting the Life You Want*. New York: Penguin Press.

10. Ahuvia, Aaron C., and Douglas Friedman. 1998. "Income, Consumption, and Subjective Well-Being: Toward a Composite Macromarketing Model." *Journal of Macromarketing*. Fall: 153–168; citing Kasser, T., and R. Ryan. "Be Careful of What You Wish for: Optimal Functioning and the Relative Attainment of Intrinsic and Extrinsic Goals." In P. Schmuck, and K. M. Sheldon (Eds.). *Life Goals and Well-Being*. Lengerich, Germany: Pabst Science Publishers.

11. Gilbert, Daniel, and Timothy Wilson. 2000. "Miswanting: Some Problems in the Forecasting of Future Affective States." In Forgas, J. P. (ed.). *Feeling and Thinking: The Role of Affect in Social Cognition*. New York: Cambridge University Press, 178–200.

12. Weiss, Alexander, Timothy Bates, and Michelle Luciano. 2008. "Happiness Is a Personal(ity) Thing: The Genetics of Personality and Well-Being in a Representative Sample." *Psychological Science*, 19: 205–210.

13. Lyubomirsky, Sonja. 2007. *The How of Happiness: A Scientific Approach to Getting the Life You Want*. New York: Penguin Press.

14. Myers, David, and Ed Diener. 1995. "Who Is Happy?" *Psychological Science*, 6(1): 10–19.

15. Judge, Timothy, and Charlice Hurst. 2007. "Capitalizing on One's Advantages: Role of Core Self-Evaluation." *Journal of Applied Psychology*, 92(5): 1212–1227.

16. Schwartz, Barry, Andrew Ward, Sonja Lyubomirsky, John Monterosso, Katherine White, and Darrin Lehman. 2002. "Maximizing Versus Satisficing: Happiness Is a Matter of Choice." *Journal of Personality and Social Psychology*, 83(5): 1178–1197.

17. Bryant, Frank, and J. Veroff. 2006. *Savoring: A New Model of Positive Experience*. Mahwah, NJ: Erlbaum; Bryant, Fred. 1989. "A Four-Factor Model of Perceived Control: Avoiding, Coping, Obtaining, and Savoring." *Journal of Personality*, 57: 773–97; Bryant, Fred. 2003. "Savoring Beliefs Inventory (SBI): A Scale for Measuring Beliefs about Savoring." *Journal of Mental Health*, 12: 175–96.

18. Ibid.

19. Lyubomirsky, Sonja. 2007. *The How of Happiness: A Scientific Approach to Getting the Life You Want*. New York: Penguin Press; Ellison, C. G., and Levin, J. S. 1998. "The Religion-Health Connection: Evidence, Theory and Future Directions." *Health Education and Behavior*. 25: 700–720; Myers, David. 2008. "Religion and Human Flourishing." In Eid, M. and R. Larsen (eds.) *The Science of Subjective Well-Being*. New York: Guilford, 323–343

20. Staudinger, Ursula, William Fleeson, and Paul Baltes. 1999. "Predictors of Subjective Physical Health and Global Well Being: Similarities and Differences Between the United States and Germany." *Journal of Personality and Social Psychology*, 76(2): 305–319.

21. Diener, Ed, Richard Lucas, and Shigehiro Oishi. 2002. "Subjective Well-Being." In C. R. Snyder, and Shane Lopez (eds.). *Handbook of Positive Psychology*. Oxford: Oxford University Press, 63–73.

22. Peterson, Christopher, and Edward Chang. 2003. Optimism and Flourishing. In Keys, Corey, and Jonathan Haidt (eds.). *Flourishing: Positive Psychology and the Life Well-Lived*. Washington, DC: American Psychological Association.

23. Myers, David, and Ed Diener. 1995. "Who Is Happy?" *Psychological Science*, 6(1): 10–19, page 14.

24. Snyder, C. R. 2003. *Psychology of Hope: You Can Get There From Here*. New York: The Free Press; Snyder, C. R, Susie Sympson, Florence Ybasco, Tyrone Borders, Michael Babyak, and Raymond Higgens. 1996. "Development and Validation of the State Hope Scale." *Journal of Personality and Social Psychology*, 70(2): 321–335.

25. DeSteno, David, Monica Bartlett, Jolie Baumann, Lisa Williams, and Leah Dickens. 2010. "Gratitude as a Moral Sentiment: Emotion Guided Cooperation in Economic Exchange." *Emotion*, 10(2): 289–293; Wood, Alex , Stephen Joseph, and John Maltby. 2009. "Gratitude Predicts Psychological Well-Being Above the Big Five Facets." *Personality and Individual Differences*, 46: 443–447; Watkins, P.C., K. Woodward, T. Stone, and R. Kolts. 2003. "Gratitude and Happiness: Development of a Measure of Gratitude, and Relationships with Subjective Well-Being." *Social Behavior and Personality*, 31: 431–451; McCollough, M. E., R. A. Emmons, and J. Tsang. 2002. "The Grateful Disposition: A Conceptual and Empirical Topography." *Journal of Personality and Social Psychology*, 82: 112–127.

26. Lyubomirsky, Sonja. 2007. *The How of Happiness: A Scientific Approach to Getting the Life You Want*. New York: Penguin Press, 205; Richardson, John. 2002. "Wheee!: A Special Report from the Happiness Project." *Esquire*. June: 83–130.

27. Ben-Shahar, Tal. 2007. *Happier*. New York: McGraw Hill, 15.

28. Fowler, James, and Nicholas Christakis. 2008. "Dynamic Spread of Happiness in a Large Social Network: Longitudinal Analysis Over 20 Years in the Framingham Heart Study." *British Medical Journal*, 3307(a2338): 1–9.

29. Snyder, C. R. 1999. *Coping: The Psychology of What Works*. New York: Oxford University Press, 5.

30. Dumaine, Brian. 1994. "Why Do We Work?" *Fortune*. December 26: 196–204.

31. 2000. "Job's Juggling Act." *Business Week*. January 10: 69.

32. 2000. "Perspectives." *Newsweek*. January 24: 17.

33. Dumaine, Brian. 1994. "Why Do We Work?" *Fortune*. December 26: 196–204.

34. Ibid.

35. Csikszentmihalyi, Mihaly. 1990. *Flow: The Psychology of Optimal Experience*. New York: HarperPerennial.

36. Csikszentmihalyi, Mihaly. 2003. *Good Business Leadership, Flow, and the Making of Meaning*. New York: Penguin Books; Csikszentmihalyi, Mihaly. 2000. *Beyond Boredom and Anxiety: Experiencing Flow in Work and Play*. San Francisco, CA: Jossey-Bass. Csikszentmihalyi, Mihaly. 1990. *Flow: The Psychology of Optimal Experience*. New York: HarperPerennial.

37. Csikszentmihalyi, Mihaly. 1997. "Finding Flow." *Psychology Today*, 30(4): 47–71.

38. Perlow, Leslie. 1997. *Finding Time: How Corporations, Individuals, and Families can Benefit from New Work Practices*. Ithaca: Cornell University Press, 77.

39. Ibid., pp. 116–122.

40. Csikszentmihalyi, Mihaly. 1990. *Flow: The Psychology of Optimal Experience*. New York: HarperPerennial, 61.

41. Ibid., p. 3.

42. Ibid., p. 42.

43. Ibid., pp. 41–49.

44. Dumaine, Brian. 1994. "Why do we work?" *Fortune*. December 26: 196–204.

45. Levy, Becca, Martin Slade, Suzanne Kunkel, and Stanislav Kasi. 2002. "Longevity Increased by Positive Self-Perceptions of Aging." *Journal of Personality and Social Psychology*, 83(2): 261–270.

46. Taylor, Shelley. 1989. *Positive Illusions: Creative Self-Deception and the Healthy Mind*. New York: Basic Books.

47. Ibid.

48. Ibid.

49. Kouzes, James, and Barry Posner. 1995. *Credibility: How People Gain and Lose It, Why People Demand It*. San Francisco, CA: Jossey-Bass.

50. Taylor, Shelley. 1989. *Positive Illusions: Creative Self-Deception and the Healthy Mind*. New York: Basic Books.

51. Seligman, Martin. 1978. *Learned Optimism: How to Change Your Mind and Your Life*. New York: Pocket Books.

52. Shinobu Kitayama, Hisaya Matsumoto, Hazel Rose Markus, and Vinai Norasakkunkit. 1997. "Individual and Collective Processes in the

Construction of the Self: Self-Enhancement in the United States and Self-Criticism in Japan." *Journal of Personality and Social Psychology*, 72(6): 1245–1267.

53. Tennen, Howard, and Glenn Affleck. 2006. "The Costs and Benefits of Optimistic Explanations and Dispositional Optimism." *Journal of Personality*, 66(2): 377–382; Seligman, Martin. 1990. *Learned Optimism: How to Change Your Mind and Your Life.* New York: Pocket Books.

54. Dockster Marcus, Amy. 2004."Fighting Cancer With a Frown." *Wall Street Journal.* April 6: D1 and D5.

55. Forgas, Joseph. 2007. "When Sad Is Better than Happy: Negative Affect Can Improve the Quality and Effectiveness of Persuasive Messages and Social Influence Strategies." *Journal of Experimental Social Psychology*, 43: 513–528.

56. Norem, Julie. 2001. *The Positive Power of Negative Thinking: Using Defensive Pessimism to Harness Anxiety and Perform at Your Best.* New York: Perseus Books.

57. Ibid., pp. 4–5.

58. Thomas, Pete. "For this Fishing Team, $1-Million Prize Is the One that Got Away." *The GrindTV Blog.* June 22, 2010. http://www.grindtv.com/outdoor/blog/ 18199/angler+makes+1-million+mistake+in+north+ carolina+marlin+tournament/

59. Barnett, Rosalind, Nancy Marshall, Stephen Raudenbush, and Robert Brennan. 1993. "Gender and the Relationship between Job Experiences and Psychological Distress: A Study of Dual-Earner Couples." *Journal of Personality and Social Psychology*, 6(5): 794–806.

60. Daniels, Kevin, and Andrew Guppy. 1994. "Occupational Stress, Social Support, Job Control and Psychological Well-Being." *Human Relations*, 47(12): 1433–1592.

61. Virtanen, Marianna, Jane Ferrie, Archana Singh-Manoux, Martin Shipley, Jussi Vahtera, Michael Marmot, and Mika Kivimaki. 2010. "Overtime Work and Incident Coronary Heart Disease: The Whitehall II Prospective Cohort Study. *European Heart Journal,* 29: 640–648.

62. Marmot, M., G. Rose, M. Shipley, and P. Hamilton. 1978. "Employment Grade and Coronary Heart Disease in British Civil Servants." *Journal of Epidemiology and Community Health*, 32: 244–249; De Vogli, Robert, Jane Ferrie, Tarani Chandola, Mika Kivimaki, and Michael Marmot. 2007. "Unfairness and Health: Evidence from the Whitehall II Study." *Community Health,* 61(6).

(http://jech.bmj.com/content/61/6/513.full); Marmot, M., Davey Smith, S. Stansfield, C Patel. F. North, J. Head, I. White, E. Brunner, and A. Feeney. 1991. "Health Inqualities among British Civil Servants: The Whitehall II Study." *Lancet,* 337: 1387–1393; Vaananen, A., A. Koshkinen, M. Joensuu, et al. 2008. "Lack of predictability at Work and Risk of Acute Myocardial Infarction: An 18 Year Prospective Study of Industrial Employees." *American Journal of Public Health*, 98: 2264–2271; Ferrie, J. E., M. Shipley, G. Davey Smith, S. Stanfeld, and M. Marmot. 2002. "Change in Health Inequalities Among British Civil Servants: The Whitehall II Study." *Journal of Epidemial Community Health.* 56: 922–926, page 922.

63. Frost, R., P. Marten, C. Hart, and R. Rosenblate. 1990. "The Dimensions of Perfectionism." *Cognitive Therapy and Research*, 14: 449–468.

64. Slaney, Robert, and Jeffrey Ashby. 1996. "Perfectionists: A Study of a Criterion Group." *Journal of Counseling and Development*, 74 (March/April): 393–398.

65. Burns, D. D. 1980. "The Perfectionist's Script for Self-Defeat." *Psychology Today.* November: 34–52.

66. Slaney, Robert, Jeffrey Ashby, and Joseph Trippi. 1995. "Perfectionism: Its Measurement and Career Relevance." *Journal of Career Advancement*, 3(3): 279–297.

67. Pacht, Asher. 1984. "Reflections on Perfection." *American Psychologist.* April: 386–390.

68. Flett, Gordon, Paul Hewitt, Kirk Blank-stein, and Lisa Gray. 1988. "Psychological Distress and the Frequency of Perfectionistic Thinking." *Journal of Personality and Social Psychology*, 75: 1363–1381.

69. Pacht, Asher. 1984. "Reflections on Perfection." *American Psychologist.* April: 386–390.

70. Flett, Gordon, Paul Hewitt, Kirk Blank-stein, and Lisa Gray. 1998. "Psychological Distress and the Frequency of Perfectionistic Thinking." *Journal of Personality and Social Psychology*, 75: 1363–1381.

71. Slaney, Robert, and Ashby Jeffrey. 1996. "Perfectionists: A Study of a Criterion Group." *Journal of Counseling and Development*, 74 (March / April): 393–398.

72. Ibid.

73. Slaney, Robert, Jeffrey Ashby, and Joseph Trippi. 1995. "Perfectionism: Its Measurement and Career Relevance." *Journal of Career Advancement*, 3(3): 279–297.

74. Kofodimos, Joan. 1990. "Why Executives Lose Their Balance." *Organization Science* 58–73.

75. Slaney, Robert, and Jeffrey Ashby. 1996. "Perfectionists: A Study of a Criterion Group." *Journal of Counseling and Development*, 74 March/April.

76. Kofodimos, Joan. 1990. "Why Executives Lose Their Balance." *Organization Science* 58–73.

77. Pacht, Asher. 1984. "Reflections on Perfection." *American Psychologist*. April: 386–390.

78. Ibid.

79. Ibid.

80. Fleet, Gordon, Paul Hewitt, Kirk Blank-stein, and Cyrill Dyninl. 1994. "Dimensions of Perfectionism and Type A Behavior." *Personality and Individual Differences*, 16(3): 447–485; Friedman, M., and R. H. Rosenman. 1974. *Type A Behavior and Your Heart*. New York: Knopf; Glass, D. C. *Behavior Patterns, Stress, and Coronary Disease*. Hillsdale, NJ: Erlbaum; Scherwitz, K., K. Bertonk, and H. Levanthal. 1978. "Type A Behavior, Self-Involvement, and Cardiovascular Response." *Psychosomatic Medicine* 1978. 593–609; Lee, Cynthia, Susan Ashford, and Linda Jameson. 1993. "The Effects of Type A Behavior Dimensions and Optimism on Coping Strategy, Health, and Performance." *Journal of Organizational Behavior*, 14: 143–157.

81. Glicken, Morley. 1997. "When It's OK to Be a Workaholic." http://public.wsj.com/ careers/resources/documents/19971231glicken.html.

82. Lee, Cynthia, Susan J. Ashford, and Linda F. Jameson 1993. "The Effects of Type A Behavior Dimensions and Optimism on Coping Strategy, Health, and Performance." *Journal of Organizational Behavior*, 14: 143–157.

83. Scheier, Michael, F. Weintraub, Jagdish Kumari, and Charles S. Carver. 1986. "Coping with Stress: Divergent Strategies of Optimists and Pessimists." *Journal of Personality and Social Psychology*, 51(6); cited in Lee, Cynthia, Susan J. Ashford, and Linda F. Jamieson. 1993. "The Effects of Type A Behavior Dimensions and Optimism on Coping Strategy, Health, and Performance." *Journal of Organizational Behavior*, 14: 143–157.

84. Iribarren, Carlos, Stephen Sidney, Diane Bild, and Kiang Liu. 2000. "Association of Hostility with Coronary Artery Calcification in Young Adults: The CARDIA Study." *Journal of the American Medical Association*, 283(19): 246–2551; Barling, Julian, and Danielle Charbonneau. 1992. "Disentangling the Relationship between the Achievement-Striving and Impatience-Irritability Dimensions of Type A Behavior, Performance and Health." *Journal of Organizational Behavior*, 13: 369–377; Spence, Janet T., Robert Helmreich, and Robert Pred. 1987. "Impatience versus Achievement Strivings in the Type A Pattern." *Journal of Applied Psychology*, 72(4): 522–529.

85. Barefoot, J. C., G. Dallstrom, and R. B. Williams. 1983. "Hostility, CHD Incidence, and Total Mortality: A 25-Year Follow-Up Study of 255 Physicians." *Psychosomatic Medicine*, 45: 59–63; Booth-Kewley, Stephanie, and Howard Friedman. 1987. "Psychological Predictors of Heart Disease: A Quantitative Review." *Psychological Bulletin*, 101: 343–362; Williams, R. B., J. C. Barefoot, and R. B. Shekelle. 1985. "The Health Consequences of Hostility." In Chesney, M. A., and R. G. H. Rosenman (eds.). *Anger, Hostility, and Behavioral Medicine*. New York: Hemisphere/McGraw-Hill.

86. Williams, Stephen. 2000. "That Gnawing Anger." *Newsweek*. May 22: 81.

87. Kofodimos, Joan. 1990. "Why Executives Lose Their Balance." *Organization Science*. Summer: 58–73.

88. Ibid.

89. Glicken, Morley. 1997. "When It's OK to Be a Workaholic." http://public.wsj.com/careers/resources/documents/19971231glicken.html.

90. Kiechel, Walter. 1989. "The Workaholic Generation." *Fortune*. April 10: 50–62.

91. Labich, Kenneth. 1991. "Why Grade A Executives Get an F as Parents." *Fortune*. May 20: 38–56.

92. O'Reilly, Brian. 1990. "Can Your Career Hurt Your Kids?" *Fortune*. January 1: 36–46.

93. Morris, Betsy. 1997. "Is Your Family Wrecking Your Career (and vice versa)?" *Fortune*. March 17: 70–73.

94. Schwartz, Felice. 1992. "Why on Earth Should I Promote a Pregnant Woman?" *Executive Female*. July/August: 38–41.

95. Ruderman, M., L. Graves, and P. Ohlott. 2007. "Commitment to Family Roles: Effects on Managers' Attitudes and Performance." *Journal of Applied Psychology,* 92: 44–56.

96. Arthur, Michelle. 2003. "Share Price Reactions to Work-Family Initiatives: An Institutional Perspective." *Academy of Management Journal*, 46(4): 497–505.

97. Hannon, John and George Milkovich. 1996. "The Effect of Human Resource Reputation Signals on Share Prices: An Event Study." *Human Resource Management*, 35(3): 405–424.

98. Perry-Smith, Jill, and Terry Blum. 2000. "Work-Family Human Resource Bundles and Perceived Organizational Performance." *Academy of Management Journal*, 23(6): 1107–1117.

99. Beyer, Janice, and David R. Hannah. 2002. "Building on the Past: Enacting Established Personal Identities in a New Work Setting." *Organization Science*, 13(6): 636–652; Ruderman, Marian, Patricia Ohlott, Kate Panzer, Sara King. 2002. "Benefits of Multiple Roles for Managerial Women." *Academy of Management Journal*, 45(2): 369–386; Settles, Iris, Robert Sellers, and Alphonse Damas, Jr. 2002. "One Role or Two? The Function of Psychological Separation in Role Conflict." *Journal of Applied Psychology*, 87(3) 574–582; Rothbard, Nancy. 2001. "Enriching or Depleting? The Dynamics of Engagement in Work and Family Roles." *Administrative Science Quarterly*, 46(4): 655–685; Ibarra, Herminia. 2003. *Working Identity: Unconventional Strategies for Reinventing Your Career*. Boston, MA: Harvard Business School Press, 33; Moen, Phyllis, Donna Dempster-McClain, and Robin M. Williams Jr., 1992. "Successful Aging: A Life Course Perspective on Women's Multiple Roles and Health." *American Journal of Sociology*, 97(6): 1612–1638.

100. Aryee, Samuel, and Vivienne Luk. 1996. "Balancing Two Major Parts of Adult Life Experience: Work and Family Identity among Dual-Earner Couples." *Human Relations*, 49(4): 465–479.

101. Higgens, Christopher, and Linda Duxbury. 1992. "Work-Family Conflict: A Comparison of Dual-Career and Traditional Career Men." *Journal of Organizational Behavior*, 13: 389–411.

102. Ibid.

103. Gilligan, Carol. 1993. *A Different Voice: Psychological Theory and Women's Development*. Cambridge, MA: Harvard University Press.

104. 1999. "Only Small Link Found between Hours in Child Care and Mother-Child Interaction." *NIH News Alert*. http://www. nichd.nih.gov/new/releases/timeinchild care.html, November 7.

105. Boushey, Heather, and Ann O'Leary. March 2010. "Our Working Nation: How Working Women Are Reshaping America's Families and Economy and What It Means for Policymakers." Center for American Progress. http://www.americanprogress.org/issues/2010/03/our_working_nation.html

106. Winkler, Anne E. 1998. "Earnings of Husbands and Wives in Dual-Earner Families." *Monthly Labor Review*, 121(4): 42–48.

107. Jacobs, Eva, Stephanie Shipp, and Gregory Brown. 1989. "Families of Working Wives Spending More on Services and Nondurables." *Monthly Labor Review*, 112(2): 15–23.

108. Robinson, John P., and Geoffrey Godbey. 1997. *Time for Life: The Surprising Ways Americans Use Their Time*. University Park, PA: The Pennsylvania State University Press.

109. Cohen, Phillip, and Suzanne Bianchi. 1999. "Marriage, Children, and Women's Employment: What Do We Know?" *Monthly Labor Review*. December: 22–31.

110. Lublin, Joan. 2000. "Working Dads Find Family Involvement Can Help Out Careers." *Wall Street Journal*. May 30: B1.

111. Grover, Mary Beth. 1999. "Daddy Stress." *Forbes*. September 6: 203.

112. Levine, James, and Todd Pittinsky. 1997. *Working Fathers: New Strategies for Balancing Work and Family*. Reading, MA: Addison-Wesley.

113. 1997. *Family Circle*. May 13: 15.

114. Shellenbarger, Sue. 1997. "Good, Early Day Care Has a Huge Impact on Kids, Studies Say." *Wall Street Journal*. April 9: B1.

115. Griffin, James. May 14, 2010. "Transcript: Link Between Child care and Academic Achievement and Behavior Persists Into Adolescence." National Institute of Child Health and Human Development. http://www.nichd.nih.gov/news/resources/links/transcript051410.cfm

116. Children Score Higher on Tests When Childcare Meets Professional Standards. *NIH News Alert*. http://nichd.nih.gov/news/releases/daycr992.cfm, July 1, 1999.

117. Children Score Higher on Tests When Childcare Meets Professional Standards. *NIH News Alert* http://nichd.nih.gov/news/releases/daycr992.cfm, July 1, 1999.

118. Griffin, James. May 14, 2010. "Transcript: Link Between Child care and Academic Achievement and Behavior Persists Into Adolescence." National Institute of Child Health and Human Development. http://www.nichd.nih.gov/news/resources/links/transcript051410.cfm

119. Children Score Higher on Tests When Childcare Meets Professional Standards. *NIH News Alert*, http://www.nichd.nih.gov/new/releases.DAYCR999.htm, July 1, 1999.

120. Gunnar, Meegan, Mark Van Ryzin, and Deborah Phillips. 2010. "The Rise in Cortisol in Family Day Care: Associations with Aspects of Care Quality,

Child Behavior, and Child Sex." *Child Development*, 81(3): 851–869.

121. Belsky, Jay. 1999. "Quantity of Nonmaternal Care and Boys' Problem Behavior/ Adjustment at Ages 3 and 5: Exploring the Mediating Role of Parenting." *Psychiatry*, 62(1): 1–20.

122. Belsky, Jay. 1995. "A Nation (Still) at Risk?" *National Forum*, 75(3): 36.

123. Only Small Link Found between Hours in Childcare and Mother-Child Interaction. *NIH News Alert*. http://www.nichd.nih.gov/ new/releases/timeinchildcare.htm.

124. Children Score Higher on Tests When Child Care Meets Professional Standards. 1999. *NIH News Alert*. www.nichd.nih.gov/ new/releases/DAYCAR99.htm, July 1.

125. Galinsky, Ellen. 1993. "Infant Morality." *People Weekly*, 39(6): February 15: 103.

126. Gable, Sara, Jay Belsky, and Keith Crnic. 1995. "Co-Parenting During the Child's 2nd Year: A Descriptive Account." *Journal of Marriage and the Family,* 57(3): 609.

127. DeMeis, D. K., E. Hock, and S. L. McBride. 1986. "The Balance of Employment and Motherhood: Longitudinal Study of Mothers' Feelings about Separation from their First-Born Infant." *Developmental Psychology*, 22: 627–632; Hock, E., 1978. "Working and Nonworking Mothers with Infants: Perceptions of Their Careers, Their Infants' Needs, and Satisfaction with Mothering." *Developmental Psychology*, 14: 37–43; Volling, Brenda, and Jay Belsky. 1993. "Parent, Infant, and Contextual Characteristics Related to Maternal Employment Decisions in the First Year of Infancy. *Family Relations*, 42: 4–12; Volling, Brenda, and Jay Belsky. 1991. "Multiple Determinants of Father Involvement during Infancy in Dual-Earner and Single-Earner Families." *Journal of Marriage and the Family*, May: 461–474.

128. Piotrkowski, C. S., and Crits-Christoph, P. 1982. "Women's Jobs and Family Adjustment." In J. Aldous (ed.). *Two Paychecks: Life in Dual-Earner Families*. Beverly Hills, CA: Sage, 105–127; MacEwen, K., and Julian Barling. 1982. "Effects of Maternal Employment Experiences on Children's Behavior via Mood, Cognitive Difficulties and Parenting Behavior." *Journal of Marriage and the Family*, 53: 635–644; Stewart, Wendy, and Julian Barling. 1996. "Fathers' Work Experiences Affect Children's Behaviors via Job-Related Affect and Parenting Behaviors." *Journal of Organizational Behavior*, 17: 221–232.

129. Stewart, Wendy, and Julian Barling, 1996. "Fathers' Work Experiences Affect Children's Behaviors via Job-Related Affect and Parenting Behaviors." *Journal of Organizational Behavior*, 17: 221–232.

130. Shellenbarger, Sue. 1996. "Work and Family: It's the Type of Job You Have that Affects the Kids, Studies Say." *Wall Street Journal*. July 31: B1.

131. Ibid.

132. Ibid.

133. Levine, James, and Todd Pettinsky. 1997. *Working Fathers: New Strategies for Balancing Work and Family*. Reading, MA: Addison-Wesley.

134. Small, Mario. 2009. *Unanticipated Gains: Origins of Network Inequality in Everyday Life*. New York: Oxford University Press; University of Chicago News. August 25, 2009. "Child Care Pays Unexpected Dividends to Parents." http://news.uchicago.edu/news.php?asset_id=1694

135. Galinsky, Ellen. 1999. *Ask the Children: What America's Children Really Think About Working Parents*. New York: William Morrow and Company.

136. Galinsky, Ellen. 1999. "Do Working Parents Make the Grade?" *Newsweek*. August 30: 52–55.

137. 1999. "Less Guilt for Working Mothers." *Good Housekeeping*. April: 83; citing Sandra Hofferth, Sr. research scientist, University of Michigan's Institute for Social Research.

138. Galinsky, Ellen. 1999. "Do Working Parents Make the Grade?" *Newsweek*. August 30: 52–55.

139. Ibid.

140. Gallinsky, Ellen. 1999. "Today's Kids, Tomorrow's Employees: What Children Are Learning about Work." *HR Magazine*, 44(11): 74–84.

141. Ibid.

142. Ibid.

143. Galinsky, Ellen. 1999. *Ask the Children: What America's Children Really Think about Working Parents*. New York: William Morrow and Company.

144. Ibid.

145. Frankl, Viktor. 1984. *Man's Search for Meaning*. Revised edition. New York: Simon & Schuster; originally published in 1959.

146. Norem, Julie. 2001. *The Positive Power of Negative Thinking: Using Defensive Pessimism to Harness Anxiety and Perform at Your Best*, New York: Perseus Books.

147. Dumaine, Brian. 1994. "Why Do We Work?" *Fortune*. December 26: 196–204.

148. Belenky, Gregory, David Penetar, David Thorne, Katheryn Popp, John Leu, Maria Thomas, Helen Sing, Thomas Balkin, Nancy Wesensten, and Daniel

Redmond. 1994. "The Effects of Sleep Deprivation on Performance during Continuous Combat Operations." In Bernadette M. Marriott (ed.). *Food Components to Enhance Performance*. Washington, DC: National Academy Press.

149. Penetar, David, Una McCann, David Thorne, Aline Schelling, Cynthia Galinski, Helen Sing, Maria Thomas, and Gregory Belenky. 1994. "The Effects of Caffeine on Cognitive Performance, Mood, and Alertness in Sleep-Deprived Human Beings." In Bernadette M. Marriott (ed.). *Food Components to Enhance Performance*. Washington, DC: National Academy Press.

INDEX

Page numbers followed by *f* indicate figures; page numbers followed by *t* indicate tables; page numbers followed by *b* indicate boxes.